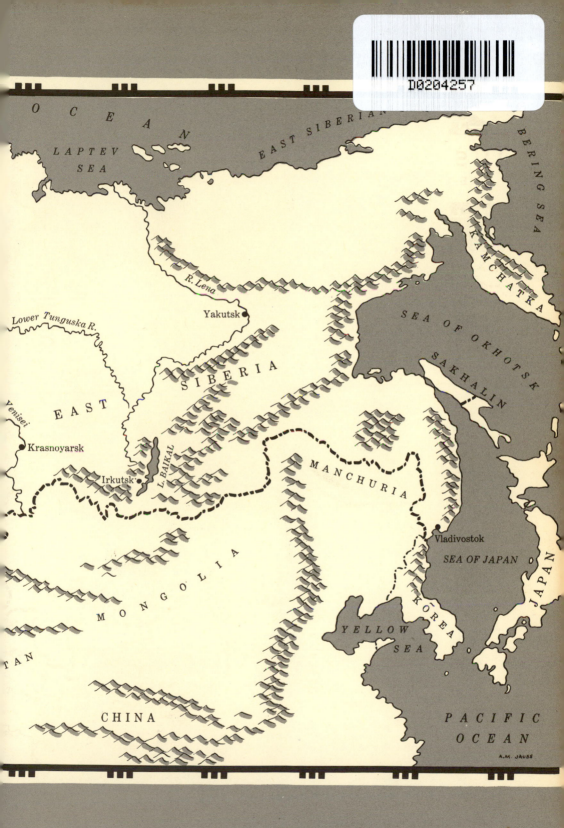

O C E A N

LAPTEV
SEA

EAST SIBERIAN

BERING SEA

KAMCHATKA

R. Lena

Yakutsk

SEA OF OKHOTSK

Lower Tunguska R.

SIBERIA

SAKHALIN

Yenisei

EAST

Krasnoyarsk

L. BAIKAL

Irkutsk

MANCHURIA

Vladivostok

SEA OF JAPAN

JAPAN

KOREA

MONGOLIA

YELLOW
SEA

TAN

CHINA

PACIFIC
OCEAN

A.M. JAUSS

WHITE
AGAINST
RED

Dimitry V. Lehovich

WHITE AGAINST RED

The Life of
General Anton Denikin

W · W · NORTON & COMPANY · INC ·

NEW YORK

This book was designed by Margaret F. Plympton.
Typefaces used are Times Roman and Baskerville,
set by Spartan Typographers.
Printing and binding were done by Vail-Ballou Press, Inc.

Library of Congress Cataloging in Publication Data
Lehovich, Dimitry V
    White against Red; a biography of General Anton
Denikin.

    Bibliography: p.
    1. Denikin, Anton Ivanovich, 1872–1947.
2. Russia—History—Revolution, 1917–1921.   I. Title.
DK254.D45L44   1974   947.084′092′4   [B]   74–4075
ISBN 0 393 07485 4

PRINTED IN THE UNITED STATES OF AMERICA

1   2   3   4   5   6   7   8   9   0

To *My Wife*

CONTENTS

ILLUSTRATIONS

MAPS

INTRODUCTION

The Russian civil war, which lasted from December, 1917, to November, 1920, was the first in a series of civil conflicts provoked by the rise of Communism. Eventually they swept through Spain, Yugoslavia, Greece, Korea, and Indochina.

One of the leaders in the creation of the anti-Communist, or "White," movement in Russia was General Anton Denikin, whose armies in their spectacular advance on Moscow from south Russia in 1919 occupied an area of approximately 820,000 square kilometers, with a population of over 42 million people.

The White movement failed, and the tremendous upheavals of the last fifty years, with World War II and its consequences, relegated to a dim historical past the name of a man whose successes in 1919 were carefully watched throughout the world, with hope by some and with undisguised hatred by others.

I volunteered into General Denikin's army at seventeen and took part in the big offensive of his troops from south Russia aimed at the capture of Moscow; I participated in the retreat of his army from the center of Russia, and in its catastrophic debacle on the Black Sea coast, was wounded, frostbitten, temporarily incapacitated by typhus. In other words, I went through all the stages so familiar to those who took part in the Russian civil war. Obviously, my field of vision was limited; I saw the events of the struggle from below, from the angle of a simple soldier. But I saw enough to remember, for the rest of my life, the climate of the times, its fluctuations from hope to despair depending on the successes or reverses of the White movement. I vividly remember the behavior of the troops, the attitude of the population toward them, some examples of great chivalry and others of hideous conduct.

Later, for several years, I was oppressed by the memories of that struggle; but then came an urge to understand the events of the Russian turmoil; and the more I absorbed books, articles, memoirs, and documents, published both in the Soviet Union and in the Western world, the more I became interested in the personality and life of General Denikin. My opportunity to meet the General came rather late. I got to know him well only during the last two years of his life, when, after the end of World War II, he left France and moved with his wife to the United States. My conversations with Anton Ivanovich Denikin disclosed episodes of his life of which I had had no inkling; and when, after his death, Xenia Vasilievna, his widow, gave me permission to study the contents of the General's archive, I became convinced that the biography of General Denikin deserved very serious attention and careful treatment.

After General Denikin's death, all these papers and documents were given by his widow to the Columbia University Russian Archive with the proviso that the Denikin collection, in its entirety, would not be made available to researchers until January, 1980, unless specifically authorized by designated heirs of the General. I am deeply grateful to Xenia Vasilievna (who died in March, 1973) for the exception she made in my case by allowing me at this time to quote at will from the documents and papers in her husband's collection, and to utilize for my work the materials in her personal archive, including her own journals, the General's letters to her and to various friends, and a number of unpublished notes and essays written by him.

Among the personal papers of General Denikin's widow is a letter from William Henry Chamberlin. Once an enthusiastic advocate of the Soviet regime, he spent twelve years in Russia as the Moscow correspondent of the *Christian Science Monitor*. Having observed at close range how the theories of Karl Marx were implemented in the USSR, Chamberlin changed his attitude toward Communism. His two-volume history, *The Russian Revolution 1917–1921* (1954), was one of the first serious attempts to present a carefully balanced analysis of that complex and intricate period.

Many years later, in March, 1965, he wrote Mrs. Denikin:

"From your husband's work, *Ocherki Russkoi Smuty,* and from other sources I conceived a great admiration for General Denikin and his gallant effort to vindicate the true values of civilization against Communism. This is reflected in the second volume of my history.

"It has always been a matter of deep regret that I never met General Denikin in life. Coming across your name in a telephone book, I felt impelled to pay my respects to you, and to express to you my admiration for your husband as a fine Russian patriot, and my regret, even at this late date, that the drive of the Volunteer Army stopped after Orel. The history of Russia and of Europe would have been much happier, I am sure, if your husband had succeeded as General Franco did in Spain."

There is no doubt that, had General Denikin succeeded in crushing the breeding ground of Communism in 1919, the subsequent history of the world would have taken an entirely different course. It is also true that both Denikin and Franco were fighting against what they considered to be evil and destructive forces. This, however, is as far as a parallel between the two generals can be drawn. After his victory, Franco retained dictatorial powers for the rest of his life. Denikin, however, was an enemy of autocracy and a firm supporter of a constitutional form of government; he did not seek supreme power, but accepted as a duty the heavy burden imposed on him by fate. He regarded his "dictatorship" of the civil-war period as a purely temporary, transitional phase leading to the establishment in Russia of the truly democratic form of government in which he sincerely believed.

What follows is an attempt to restore to memory and to a proper historical perspective the personality and role of General Denikin in an absorbing chapter of world history whose impact on our present and future is only beginning to be understood.

ACKNOWLEDGMENTS

First among the many people to whom I owe a debt of gratitude for their assistance to me in writing this book are General Denikin's widow, the late Mrs. Xenia Vasilievna Denikin, whose invaluable contribution I have further acknowledged in the Introduction, and the late Professor Philip E. Mosely, who gave me unrestricted permission to study the material at the Columbia University Archive of Russian and East European History and Culture, and encouraged me in my research. I wish also to thank General Denikin's daughter, Mme. Marina Chiappe, for sharing with me the recollections of her childhood and youth with her father.

I am deeply grateful to Alexander I. Nazaroff, who read the whole manuscript; to Robert K. Massie, who read the major part of it and suggested its title—*White against Red;* and to Lincoln Kirstein and Mrs. Henry T. Curtiss for their interest and advice. I wish to express my heartfelt thanks to the trustees of the Chapelbrook Foundation, whose generous grant enabled me to devote my full time to General Denikin's biography.

I have received valuable and exclusive historical material through the kind offices of many persons, to all of whom I am greatly indebted: the late Colonels Nicholas P. Ukraintsev, Dimitry N. Tikhobrazov, and Vladimir S. Khitrovo for unpublished material on the Kornilov affair, on conditions at the Russian Supreme Headquarters before and after the abdication of Nicholas II, and on General Romanovsky's assassination; B. S. Kutsevalov for his personal statement concerning this crime; the late Colonel B. A. Lagodovsky for generously allowing me to quote the description of the evacuation of Denikin's army from Novorossiisk contained in his unpublished memoirs; Princess Marie S. Troubetzkoy for letting me read her unpublished diary of the Russian civil-war period; Mrs. Alexandra I. Sannikov for lending me the unpublished memoirs of her husband, General Sannikov, dealing with the French occupation of Odessa; V. N. Podlesski for a snapshot of General Denikin at the front; and A. B. Tatistcheff for a rare brochure published by General Denikin's headquarters in 1919.

I wish to thank L. F. Magerovsky, curator of the Columbia University Russian Archive, Dr. Vitold Sworakowski, Mrs. Marina B. Tinkoff, and Mrs. Anna M. Bourguina of the Hoover Institution for their many courtesies; Jacques Kayaloff for the use of his extensive reference library; and the late J. W. Auburn and Peter Clarke of London for providing me with data from British newspapers concerning Denikin's stay in England in 1920.

In preparing this book for publication, several people were helpful. I am grateful to Starling Lawrence, my editor at W. W. Norton & Company, for his aid and guidance; to Mrs. Esther Jacobson, copy editor, for her careful review of my manuscript; and to Mrs. Sophie Nabokov not only for her typing of my manuscript, but for the excellent suggestions that went with it.

I owe special gratitude to my children—Olga and Vladimir. They have never failed in giving me encouragement and moral support, and have always helped with their suggestions and constructive criticism.

General Denikin's widow never interfered with my selection from the unpublished documents she had placed at my disposal. There was only one condition on which she insisted—that her husband's biography be written not only in English but also in Russian, in order to acquaint Russian readers with the man whose character had been greatly misrepresented following the failure of the White movement which he headed.

Conforming to her wishes, I began to write my book in Russian, with the intention of promptly translating the Russian chapters into English. But it soon became evident that this double task would postpone completion of the work for an indefinite period. The problem was resolved by my wife, Evgenia Ouroussow Lehovich, who undertook to translate the Russian text as well as all excerpts from Denikin's writings and other Russian sources into English. For this, and for the unfailing encouragement she gave me, I dedicate this book to her with profound gratitude and fondest love.

DIMITRY V. LEHOVICH

WHITE
AGAINST
RED

During the 1917–1920 period in Russia, two different systems of dating were employed simultaneously.

The official calendar of the Russian Empire was the Julian, which in the twentieth century is thirteen days behind the Gregorian, used in the West. Although the Soviet regime adopted the Gregorian calendar in 1918, the anti-Bolshevik forces during the Russian civil war continued to adhere to the old calendar.

In this book, the dates of all events are given as they appear in documents relating to the events; therefore, occurrences in prerevolutionary Russia and activities involving the anti-Bolshevik forces during the Russian civil war are dated according to the Old Style, or Julian, calendar, while quotations from Soviet and Western documents of the period and documents subsequently published in the Soviet Union are dated according to the Gregorian calendar. Where there is any possibility of misunderstanding, the calendar in use has been specified. This procedure has been adopted to enable students of the period to refer to the proper source material.

From the moment of General Denikin's arrival in England in April, 1920, all dates are given according to the Gregorian calendar.

I

THE DISTANT PAST

"I certify by these presents, with the church seal affixed, that in the Register of Births of the Lowicz parish church of the Precursor for the year 1872, the act of baptism of the infant Anton, son of Major Ivan Efimov Denikin, retired, of the Orthodox faith, and of his legal spouse Elizaveta Fedorovna of the Roman Catholic faith, is recorded as follows:

"In the order of male births No. 33. Date of birth: the fourth day of December of the year one thousand eight hundred seventy-second—Date of baptism: the twenty-fifth day of December of the same year.

"[Signed by] the Rector of the Lowicz parish church of the Precursor the priest Veniamin Skvortzov." [1]

Thus was recorded in the formal language of a church register the arrival in this world and the Russian Orthodox baptism of the future Commander in Chief of the Armed Forces of South Russia.

Anton Denikin was born in Wloclawek. In 1872 it was a quiet out-of-the-way place with a Polish and Jewish population of under twenty thousand. It was in the district of Warsaw, which was then a part of the Russian Empire. There was no cultural or social life in Wloclawek, not even a public library. There was, however, a secondary school, which young Anton later attended. The Russian population of Wloclawek consisted of a small number of military and civilian government employees and of the military units stationed in the district.

The Denikins were desperately poor. Anton's father, Ivan Efimovich Denikin, came from a family of peasant serfs in the province of Saratov. He was born in 1807, five years before Napoleon's invasion of Russia, and at the age of twenty-seven was enrolled in the army at his landowner's behest. It was customary then for the landowner to choose among his serfs the young men he was required to furnish to the army, and Ivan Denikin was among those selected in his village.

During the harsh reign of Nicholas I, a soldier was committed to the

army for twenty-five years. In the course of that long term, Ivan Efimovich
changed regiments and locations a good many times and eventually lost
touch with his family and his native village. His parents died. There remained his wife and a brother and sister, but he lost track of them too.
Only once, while still a private, Ivan Denikin found himself in a town
where his brother was living. He joyously went to look him up, but his visit
culminated in a terrible disappointment. His brother, who had risen in the
world in the intervening years, was giving a dinner party that evening and
did not invite Ivan Efimovich to his table. Instead, his wife served her
brother-in-law in the kitchen but did not allow him to enter the rest of the
apartment. Ivan Efimovich left his brother's inhospitable home without a
parting word. He never saw him again.

Ivan Efimovich, who knew only how to read and write when he joined
the army, was able to broaden his knowledge and experience in the course
of his military career. He took part in the Hungarian campaign (1849),
and in the Crimean War (1854–55). He was promoted from master ser-
geant to ensign in 1856 and assigned to a brigade of frontier guards on the
Prussian border. In 1863, he participated with his unit in the suppression
of the Polish insurrection. Ivan Efimovich was pensioned off in 1869 with
the rank of major, and two years later, at the age of sixty-four, married his
second wife, the Polish Catholic Elizaveta Fedorovna Vrjesinski. A son,
Anton, was born in 1872.[2]

Elizaveta Fedorovna came from a family of impoverished small landowners. At the time of her first meeting with Ivan Efimovich, her only
source of income was sewing, and she had to support both herself and her
old father by her meager earnings.

"I remember our squalid apartment in a courtyard of Pekarski Street in
Wloclawek," wrote Denikin in later years: "two rooms, a windowless
storeroom and a kitchen. One room was used as the 'parlor' for receiving
guests; it was also our dining room, workroom, etc. A second, darker room
served as bedroom for my father, my mother, and myself; grandfather
slept in the storeroom and our nurse in the kitchen." [3]

The Denikin family, which with the grandfather and the nurse consisted
of five people, lived on Ivan Efimovich's pension of thirty-six rubles (approximately eighteen dollars) a month. Although the amount was insufficient even for them, "on the day the pension came, Father managed to
distribute some trifling sums to people who were in even greater need than
ourselves, ostensibly as loans but without much hope of repayment. . . .
This irritated my mother who was trying to protect her precarious nest
from utter ruin—'Have a heart, Efimovich,' she reproached him, 'you
know that we have nothing to eat ourselves.'" [4]

After reading these lines from Denikin's unfinished autobiography, one
is shocked to discover that in 1966 the Moscow University Press approved
the issue of a book, *Krakh Denikinshchiny* (*The Collapse of the Denikin*

Movement), whose author, A. P. Aleksashenko affirms that Denikin was "born of a family of landowners in the province of Kursk." The surprising truth is that General Denikin, a leader of the Russian anti-Communist movement, was unquestionably more of a "proletarian" by birth than his future opponents, Lenin, Trotsky, and a large number of other Bolshevik leaders.

Despite the strained Russo-Polish relations of the period, the Denikin family life was peaceful and united. As a matter of course, Anton's father always spoke Russian at home, while his mother talked in her native Polish. There was no religious friction—Anton's father attended the Orthodox Church and his mother, the Roman Catholic Church, or *Kosciel*. The boy was brought up with the respect of Russia and Orthodoxy by his father, a deeply religious man who faithfully attended church services and always took his son with him. Anton served as an altar boy from early childhood, learned to sing in the choir and to ring the church bells, and later, to read aloud to the congregation the Hexapsalmos and the writings of the Apostles. But, sometimes, in order to please his mother, he chose to accompany her to the *Kosciel*.

He absorbed the Orthodox liturgy at the modest regimental church he attended as "my own, native, profoundly congenial," whereas the Roman Catholic rite at the *Kosciel* remained in his memory merely as an interesting spectacle.

In a few instances, however, the Russo-Polish conflict penetrated even the Denikins' quiet family life. One episode in particular made a lasting impression on the nine-year-old Anton: His mother had returned from the *Kosciel* red-eyed and very upset; she finally admitted, at her husband's insistent questioning, that the Catholic priest, or *Ksiadz*, had refused to give her Communion and had ordered her forthwith to bring up her son secretly as a Catholic and a Pole. Upon hearing this, Anton's father, always outspoken and hot-tempered, swore roundly and went off to see the *Ksiadz*. There followed a tempestuous interview at the end of which the frightened priest begged Anton's father not to bring ruin on him. The affair, of course, ended there. Had it not, the "attempt at religious seduction" might have had serious consequences for the priest, as at that time, the Russian authorities dealt roughly with such offenses.

"I don't know how my mother proceeded with her devotions after that day," wrote Anton Ivanovich in later years, "for my parents never mentioned the subject again—but by some inner instinct I gave up my visits to the *Kosciel*." [5]

Anton's mother often complained about their fate, their hopeless poverty; his father never did. In a trunk, sprinkled with snuff to protect it from moths, lay his last military uniform. He guarded it scrupulously in order that "in the event of an honorable death, he could at least be laid to rest as befits a soldier."

Denikin also recorded another very revealing story about his father:

When the Russo-Turkish War broke out [1877], Father was already in his seventieth year. He became noticeably despondent, increasingly silent and gloomy. He simply didn't know what to do with himself. Finally, without his wife's knowledge, he sent in an application to reenter active military service. . . . We learned about this a good deal later when a notice arrived ordering Major Ivan Denikin to Fort Novogeorgievsk for the purpose of assembling a reserve battalion with which he was later to join the theater of operations.

Tears and reproaches from Mother: "How could you, Efimovich—without a word to me? In God's name where do you think you're going at your age?"— I cried, too, although deep down I was secretly proud that my father was going to war.

But he did not go, as the war ended shortly after, and the formation of new army units was discontinued.[6]

Antos, as young Denikin was called at home, could read Russian by the time he was four. In 1882, at the age of nine, he passed the entrance examinations and was admitted to the first grade of the Wloclawek *Realschule.* This was an important family event and a great joy to his parents. To celebrate it, they took the boy for the first time in his life to a confectioner's and treated him to hot chocolate and pastries.

Realschulen, which had existed in Germany since the eighteenth century, had been adopted by the Russian educational system in the late 1830's. In contrast to the classical *Gymnasiums,* the aim of these secondary schools was to provide a practical contemporary education. In the *Realschulen,* emphasis was shifted from the humanities, with their study of ancient languages and Latin and Greek classics, to mathematics, physics, chemistry, cosmography, natural science, drawing, and draftsmanship. The program constituted an excellent preparation for specialization in engineering and the sciences at the university level.

Toward the end of his life, Ivan Efimovich, who had always enjoyed excellent health, began to suffer from intestinal pains which were found to be the symptoms of cancer. By the spring of 1885 he could no longer leave his bed. "Lord, grant me to die on the same day as Thyself," he prayed aloud in the last days of Lent; he died on Good Friday and was buried on the third day of Easter. His colleagues had the following epitaph carved on his tombstone: "In the simplicity of his soul, he feared God, loved his fellowmen, and remembered not evil."

As soon as the father died, his pension was curtailed, leaving only twenty rubles a month for his widow. Anton, then a thirteen-year-old *Realschule* student, had to start earning some extra money by coaching younger pupils of his school.

In less than two years, the Denikins' financial situation became critical. At a "family council" consisting of Anton, his mother, and his old nurse, it was decided to petition the director of the *Realschule* for permission to establish a boarding house for its students. To the Denikins' great joy, they were authorized to operate a dormitory-apartment for eight students, each of whom was to pay them twenty rubles a month. Young Denikin, who was fifteen by that time and had an excellent standing at school, was appointed monitor. A new apartment was found and for the first time a glimmer of hope penetrated the destitute household.

One incident from this period is particularly interesting in the light of later charges (repeated many times by erring historians) that Denikin was anti-Polish.

Being the son of Russo-Polish parents, Anton soon realized the absurdity of the "unrealistic, harsh and offending russification program" which the Russian government was enforcing in the Territory of the Vistula. For example, speaking Polish was strictly forbidden, not only at school but even in student apartments such as the one operated by the Denikins. Students who broke the rule were severely punished. In spite of this, Anton spoke with his Polish and Russian schoolmates in their respective languages. As monitor of a students' residence, he had to file a monthly report, one of whose columns was entitled "Convicted of Speaking Polish."

"This was painful," wrote Denikin in his memoirs, "as it was simply an order to inform. At the risk of losing my position, which could seriously undermine our budget, I always wrote 'nothing to report' in this particular column." And even when summoned to the director's office, Anton met with silence the reproach that he was not telling the truth.

In these far-off days, when Russian youth was often alienated from the Church, Anton went through a period of spiritual distress. He was concerned not with the differences among religious denominations, but with the main problem—that of the existence of God. He lived through every stage of hesitation and doubt, through sleepless nights, reading the Bible alongside Renan and "other 'godless' literature," until, when he was a junior, "literally in one night," wrote Denikin in the last years of his life, "I came to the final and irrevocable conclusion: Man is a three-dimensional creature incapable of apprehending the highest laws of existence and creation. I reject the savage psychology of the Old Testament but accept wholeheartedly Christianity and the Orthodox faith. Thus have I lived ever since and thus do I intend to live the remainder of my days." [7]

Although the *Realschule* diploma, which he obtained in 1889, opened the way to a variety of careers, Denikin's choice was predetermined by his environment. His father's influence and war stories had disposed him from early childhood toward a military career; the continuous presence in Wloclawek of military units also added to the attraction of army life. Anton liked to ride with the local uhlans to water and bathe their horses and to go to the shooting range with the rifle brigades. If a few kopecks came his way, he would buy cartridges from the soldiers, unload them himself, and explode self-made land mines. The military life soon became his dream. He also grew to be a good athlete and an excellent swimmer.

Having first enlisted as a private in one of the infantry riflemen regiments, Anton Denikin applied for admission to the recently opened Kiev officer candidate school in the fall of 1890.

Life at the school was fairly grim—a soldier's diet, clothing, and underwear, and to top it all, a private's salary of 22½ kopecks a month! This pittance sufficed for the bare necessities of life, but did not allow for such luxuries as tobacco. Denikin's mother sent him five rubles a month out of her meager earnings from fine embroidery work.

Upon completing the two-year course at the school, Denikin received his commission and was assigned as a second lieutenant to the Second Field Artillery Brigade, stationed in the town of Biala in the province of Siedlce, 159 kilometers from Warsaw.

The tradition of limiting the rank of officer to members of the nobility and gentry persisted solely in the regiments of the imperial guard. It was disappearing in the regular army, in which the democratic process was gaining momentum.

"A new generation came into being," wrote Denikin, "less glamorous in appearance and more modest in life, but competent and hardworking, with the same qualities and defects as the Russian intellectuals." [8]

Denikin undoubtedly included himself in that category.

People who are not familiar with Russian military history may find it hard to believe that at the start of World War I, 60 percent of the officers in the old imperial army were *raznochintsi,* people not belonging to the nobility or gentry.[9]

It is significant that at a time when *raznochintsi* in other walks of life, and particularly in literature, were generally bitter about the existing regime, the majority of *raznochintsi* who became part of the officer corps were staunch supporters of the Russian state. *Raznochintsi* generals Alekseev, Kornilov, and Denikin were the first to rise in arms against the seizure of power by the Bolsheviks.

The town of Biala, where Denikin found himself, was no improvement on Wloclawek from a social and cultural point of view.

He described it as a typical army station serving as headquarters for the military units relegated to the remote regions of the Warsaw, Vilna, and part of the Kiev military districts.

In those days, most of the city commerce in the western and southwestern provinces of Russia was the domain of the Jewish population. Suppliers, contractors, and middlemen ("factors"), were all Jewish. "One couldn't take a step without a factor," wrote Denikin. "They really made our material life easy by being able to secure anything, from anywhere at any time. They could get you furniture and clothing on long-term credit, and would even lend money on a promissory note when an officer's budget refused to balance. For our budget was modest indeed—my monthly salary, for example, was fifty-one rubles. . . . Although the Russian servicemen were tied to the Jewish population in all matters of economy, they had no contact with it in any other aspects of their life." [10]

The Polish community kept to itself and remained aloof from the Russians. The Russian intelligentsia of Biala consisted exclusively of military and civilian government employees. "Our entire social life," wrote Denikin, "was limited to that circle. In it we 'visited,' quarreled, made up, established and lost friendships, courted and married.

"Nothing, nothing varied from year to year. Neither the conversations nor the jokes. . . . Not a single lecturer or touring company ventured into our backwoods. In a word, our life was drab and our interests as trivial as those in a Chekhov play."

It took great strength of character to resist being bogged down in this morass and to keep alive one's spiritual and cultural interests. Denikin read a great deal and diligently prepared himself for the entrance examinations of the Academy of the General Staff. At the same time he gave himself wholeheartedly to his artillery service.

Denikin's education and intellectual interests set him apart from the average officer. This may have been the reason for his reticence with his colleagues in the regiment, who nevertheless respected him and deferred to his authority. His opinions were valued, as was his presence at any gathering: "Drop in tonight for a good talk—Denikin will be there." We have many testimonies to this effect from people who knew him then.[11]

He was an unusually good speaker. At the time, this particular talent expressed itself only in after-dinner addresses, at farewell or welcoming parties, and sometimes in the talks he gave on current military topics. After the 1917 revolution, Denikin became known throughout Russia as an exceptional orator. His deep voice carried far without the help of loudspeakers. He was below average height, solid and stocky, with a tendency to stoutness. He had an open face with intelligent, piercing eyes under low beetling eyebrows, a long moustache, and a short triangular beard. Later, when he grew bald, Denikin began to shave his head completely.

In the autumn of 1895, after several years of preparation, Lieutenant Denikin passed the competitive examinations for admission to the Academy of the General Staff. To an able and successful officer, graduation from the Academy could be the gateway to an important military career.

His arrival in St. Petersburg, after the remote provincialism of his childhood and youth, opened up for Denikin a whole new world of events and impressions. He saw Tsar Nicholas II for the first time and attended his first court ball at the Winter Palace, having received one of the twenty invitations issued to the Academy of the General Staff. Denikin and two of his friends kept together. Here is how he describes their impressions: "Our provincial eyes were dazzled by the whole fairyland spectacle of the ball, the grandiose dimensions and decorations of the palace halls, the brilliance of military and court uniforms, by the attire of the ladies and by the whole distinctive ritual of the court. Yet, in spite of all this, there was somehow no feeling of constraint in this assembly, including ourselves, either from the ritual or from the irregularity of the guests' social positions." [12]

It was also in St. Petersburg that Denikin became acquainted for the first time with the various trends of thought and other aspects of the Russian intelligentsia. He met university students and girls attending the university courses for women who were active in the political underground, and read the illegal literature published abroad and smuggled into Russia by leftist political émigrés. All this was new and interesting and further stimulated his personal independent approach to these questions.

To combine all these new impressions and activities with his studies at the Academy was no easy task for young Denikin. One of his fellow officers at the Academy, who had known him since his first promotion to officer's rank, wrote that Anton Ivanovich was a poor student and graduated last among those who rated an appointment to the General Staff. This, however, was not due to any difficulty on his part in assimilating the Academy's program of courses. Denikin simply could not resist spending some of his time in extracurricular activities, to the detriment of his studies. "If he succeeded in graduating from the Academy," wrote Denikin's friend, "it was solely thanks to his innate ability." [13]

Although he was fully entitled to do so, Denikin was not destined to join the General Staff immediately. He and three other officers who were among those with the lowest passing marks were removed from the list of candidates for the General Staff.

This episode played such an important part in Denikin's life that it deserves to be examined in detail.

At the time of Denikin's graduation, the Academy of the General Staff was undergoing a drastic transformation. Its chief, General Leër, who was well known in European military circles as an outstanding authority on military strategy and philosophy, was removed from his position and replaced by General Soukhotin. The latter was a coarse, authoritarian, and erratic man, but one who enjoyed the Minister of War's friendship. Soukhotin openly criticized his predecessor's methods and system of instruction, which he immediately proceeded to break up. Soukhotin also arbitrarily altered the list of officers to be appointed to the General Staff four times. Denikin's name figured in the first two lists, but was deleted in the last two.

This was contrary to all existing rules. It soon transpired that Soukhotin was using his close relationship with the Minister of War, General Kouropatkin, to bypass the Academy's council and his immediate superiors. He took his reports on "academic reforms" directly to Kouropatkin who approved them personally.

Denikin could not accept such injustice. Years of privation and intense effort, the erudition and widened horizons he had acquired, his hopes for the future—all would be wasted through one man's arbitrary decision. He decided to resort to the only legal measure permitted by the disciplinary code—the filing of an official complaint.

"As the law and our rights were infringed by a resolution of the Minister of War," wrote Denikin later, "my complaint against him had to be lodged with his immediate superior, i.e., the Emperor himself. . . . I therefore addressed my complaint to His Imperial Majesty." [14]

"In military life, permeated as it was with the idea of submission, such an appeal to the very apex of the hierarchical scale was unheard of." [15]

Denikin advised his three fellow sufferers to follow his example, but they politely declined.

In bureaucratic St. Petersburg this episode soon became a *cause célèbre*. People talked and argued about it and offered guesses as to how the scandal would end. It seemed incredible that this young man from nowhere, unknown and devoid of connections, should dare to rise against the almighty bureaucracy. A captain second grade—against the Minister of War! The faculty and all Denikin's fellow officers at the Academy were on his side. They realized that a grave injustice had been committed and went out of their way to express their consideration and sympathy for him. General Soukhotin, on the other hand, implied that Denikin's complaint was "seditious." The Academy's council was convened by order of the Minister of War to argue the question. It decided that the actions of the Academy's chief were illegal, but the decision was hushed up. Nevertheless, Denikin and the three other luckless candidates were summoned to the Academy and "congratulated" upon their appointment to the General Staff. But Denikin was advised at the same time that his appointment would go through on condition that he withdrew his complaint and filed a statement to the effect that, though not entitled to this promotion, "he begs his superiors' favor in consideration of his years of study and hard work. . . ." [16]

In making this shameless proposal, the Academy's administration overlooked one factor—Denikin's character. His response was to lose his temper and indignantly counter, "I am not asking for favors, but only claiming that which is due me by right."

By this time, however, too much bureaucratic dignity was at stake. Denikin was not appointed to the General Staff *on account of his disposition*. A short time later, a reply to Denikin's complaint was received from the "Chancellery of requests addressed to His Imperial Majesty." The Chancellery's decision had been to take no action.

Thus, the whole affair had benefited Denikin's three companions who had refused to file a complaint, while he remained the only loser.

"Young Captain Denikin took this injustice very hard" observed a man who knew him intimately at the time. "Traces of indignation provoked by this incident remained in old General Denikin to the end of his life. His resentment of the people directly implicated in the affair was extended by him with undue harshness to the regime and government structure as a whole up to its highest point of authority." [17]

This may be an exaggeration. Nevertheless, the fact remains that this episode left its mark on Denikin and shook his faith in "the rectitude of sovereign justice." "What dense thickets have overgrown the path of truth" he commented bitterly.[18]

There was no further hope of doing anything about the case. In the spring of 1900, Denikin rejoined his old artillery brigade in Biala, and his painfully humdrum provincial existence began anew.

Two years later, when passions had subsided, he wrote a personal letter to the Minister of War, General Kouropatkin, in which he calmly set forth the entire truth of the matter.

This time Kouropatkin, who had formerly seen the occurrence solely through Soukhotin's eyes, personally checked all the facts and realized that he had been wrong. It is to his credit that, at his next audience with the Tsar, he expressed regret at having acted unjustly and requested permission for Denikin's appointment to the General Staff.

The two additional years which Denikin spent in Biala were not entirely wasted, as it is then that he began his career as a writer. His tales of military life and his articles on political and military subjects were published over a period of several years preceding World War I. They came out under the pen name of I. Nochin in the military periodical *The Scout,* and until 1904, in the *Warsaw Journal.* In his *Armeiskia Zametki (Army Sketches)* Denikin managed, without infringing army discipline, to give a biting portrayal of the negative aspects of army life and of the lack of progressiveness in the officer corps.

At that time there lived in Biala a certain Vasili Ivanovich Chizh, a former artillery officer who occupied the post of local tax inspector. He and his wife became warm friends of Denikin's. In the year of the latter's promotion to officer's rank, a daughter, Assia, was born to the Chizhes. When she was three years old, Denikin gave her for Christmas a doll which could open and close her eyes. The little girl would never forget that present: In January, 1918, in Novocherkassk, just before the Volunteer Army set out on its famous first campaign, she became General Denikin's wife.

In the summer of 1902, after two uneventful years in Biala, Denikin was finally transferred to the General Staff, thanks to Kouropatkin's change of heart. He was first attached to headquarters of the Second Infantry Division in Brest-Litovsk; then, to obtain required experience, commanded a squad of the 183rd Infantry Poltusski regiment stationed in Warsaw, and finally, in the fall of 1903, was appointed as an officer of the General Staff to headquarters of the Second Cavalry Corps, also located in Warsaw. He was serving there with the rank of captain at the outbreak of the Russo-Japanese War.

The Russian expansionist policy in the Far East clashed with a similar policy of the Japanese. Japan was ready for war, and knew that Russia was totally unprepared to face an armed conflict thousands of miles away from the center of the country. Without declaring war, Japan attacked the Russian fleet in Port Arthur on the night of February 9, 1904, disabling the battleship *Retvisan* and *Tsesarevich* and the cruiser *Pollada*. This act of piracy gave the upper hand to the Japanese navy and allowed it to transport Japan's army to the continent without danger of interference.

The war with Japan was unpopular in Russia. "This is why," commented Denikin, "for a great many people at the beginning of this war, the only stimulus which revived their feelings of patriotism and wounded national pride was the treacherous attack on Port Arthur made with no declaration of war." [19]

Denikin himself felt the blow of this attack very sharply and considered it his duty to go to the battlefront as soon as possible.

The troops of the Warsaw military district in which he was serving were not being sent to the Far East, but were left to guard Russia's frontier with Germany and Austria-Hungary. Although he was disabled at the time by a torn ligament, Denikin immediately filed a request for his transfer to the theater of operations. At first he was refused, then, asked if he knew English, Denikin replied that he did not know English, but would fight as well as anyone who did. He was nervous and restless, but finally got his way. At the end of February, 1904, he started out across all of European and Asiatic Russia toward the theater of operations.

While the Russian army in the Far East fought valiantly, the High Command proved to be incompetent, and defeat followed defeat.

Denikin entered the war with the rank of captain. Active duty at the front soon placed him among the promising officers of the General Staff, and he began to attract attention. He acquired a reputation for personal bravery and for ability to make a quick assessment of combat situations. Having first been appointed chief of staff of one of the border-guard brigades of the Trans-Amur district, Denikin next served in the same capacity with the Transbaikal Cossack division commanded by General Rennenkampf. Toward the end of the war, he became chief of staff of the Ural-Transbaikal division in the mounted detachment of the army corps commander General Mistchenko. By nature, Denikin was not overly fond of staff work. He was far more attracted to active command posts in the field of battle and succeeded several times in brilliantly combining this role with his duties as chief of staff.

Denikin's first combat experience occurred in November, 1904, in the battle of Tsinchentchen. At his own request, General Rennenkampf sent him to replace the commanding officer of one of the Cossack regiments in the front lines. Denikin carried out his mission with distinction, repulsing the Japanese attacks with bayonet charges. For distinguished service in the field, Denikin was soon promoted to lieutenant colonel, then to colonel. At that period, promotion to the rank of colonel after thirteen years of service as an officer was quite an achievement in the Russian army. The combined military talents of Mistchenko and Denikin brought considerable renown to the former's mounted detachment, especially after its successful raid on the enemy's rearguard positions in May, 1905. The raid destroyed Japanese depots and transports, played havoc with the enemy's supply routes and telegraph system, and resulted in the capture of a number of prisoners. But its most important effect was to raise the morale of an army which had few successes to its credit. In the history of the Russo-Japanese War the names of several *sopka* (as isolated mountains and high hills are called in Manchuria) are identified with feats of Russian military valor. Among them is the "Denikin *Sopka*" commemorating the bayonet counterattack led by Denikin at the battle of Tsinchentchen.[20]

Each unsuccessful action at the front added to the general irritation in Russia. The resentment, artfully exploited for political purposes by the leftist opposition, engendered riots and culminated in terrorist acts and agrarian uprisings. The peasants settled their scores with their landlords, burning and looting the country estates. Councils, or "soviets," of "workers' deputies," forerunners of the 1917 soviets, were formed in St. Petersburg and other cities, and for the first time, Leon Trotsky made a fleeting appearance on the political stage, as a leading figure in the St. Petersburg soviet. A wave of strikes rolled over Russia; a series of military mutinies flared up, as well as an armed popular uprising in Moscow. Chaos and anarchy gripped the entire nation. It was the beginning of the "first revolution"—the prelude to the catastrophic events of 1917.

The Russian government realized that it could not continue the war under such conditions, and in September, 1905, a peace treaty with Japan was signed in Portsmouth, New Hampshire.

Waves of demobilized reserve soldiers began to flow homeward on the great Trans-Siberian railroad. Denikin, returning from the front, was caught up in that tide. While the Russian field forces had miraculously preserved their discipline, the soldiers of the reserve troops had quickly fallen prey to antigovernment propaganda. They demanded immediate repatriation and rioted along the entire rear guard of the army. The military authorities lost their heads. Without organizing food depots along the Trans-Siberian or establishing guards for its endless stretches, they paid the disbanded reservists their entire travel allowance in a lump sum. They then let them go, unsupervised, on trains which had not been provided with any kind of military or police protection. The results could have been easily foreseen: The demobilized soldiers squandered their money on drink as soon as they received it, and later, their hungry mobs ransacked everything they passed along the Siberian main line.

The stormiest period of the revolution was spent by Denikin in transit on the Trans-Siberian railroad. There were no newspapers, and the wildest rumors circulated. Chaos reigned everywhere. At first Denikin's train, filled with soldiers, officers, and railroad personnel, attempted to follow a certain itinerary and order of precedence. Nothing came of this attempt. They made no more than 150 kilometers a day, and often woke up in the morning to find themselves at the same station where they had fallen asleep, because during the night, the reservists of a passing troop train had detached and appropriated their engine. At last, losing all patience, Denikin and three other colonels organized a small armed unit of officers and men. An engine was requisitioned from one of the rioting troop trains, and the train, with its own armed guard, set off at full speed. Trains of rioting soldiers pursued it from the rear, and others waited in front to block the way. A bloody reprisal could have overtaken its passengers at any time, but the sight of their well-organized armed command forestalled possible attacks. Most of the time the train proceeded without clearance; occasionally orders were telephoned to the stationmasters of forthcoming stops to "clear the tracks."

This fantastic journey ended successfully. Denikin learned an important lesson at that time: In a period of anarchy and government disintegration, even a small fist is to be reckoned with. He reached St. Petersburg at the beginning of January, 1906, after spending two weeks in Harbin and over thirty days in transit.

The pressure of political events had forced the Russian government to agree to a series of compromises. In August, 1905, a manifesto proclaimed the establishment of a State Duma (a national assembly), and on October 30, 1905, a new manifesto promised to grant the Russian people a constitution based on national representation, freedom of conscience and opinion, guarantees for individual liberty. It also promised that no laws would be enacted without the Duma's approval. Thus, the State Duma became the lower house of the new Russian parliament; the Council of the Empire, which had been in existence for over a century, became the upper house, with half of its members elected and the other half appointed by the Tsar. Legislation proposed by the Duma had to receive the approval of the Council, and only then could be submitted to the Tsar for final confirmation. The electoral law definitely favored the more stable and propertied section of the population. Even so, the mere fact that elected representatives of the people were to participate in the government was very significant.

Denikin, who considered that "the autocratic and bureaucratic regime of Russia was anachronistic," welcomed the October manifesto. He believed that, though belated, it was an event of immense historical importance which heralded a new era for the nation. "Despite the imperfection of an electoral system limited to qualified electors," wrote Denikin, "despite the absence of parliamentary privileges of the West European type in the Russian constitution . . . , despite the Duma's limited rights, especially in budgetary matters . . . , the manifesto provided a solid basis for the development of legal justice and political and civic freedom; and made it possible to contend legally for further implementation of true popular rule." [21]

Toward the very end of 1905, the government began to come out of its lethargy and to undertake measures for quelling the prevailing anarchy. It arrested members of the St. Petersburg soviet, suppressed with rigor an armed uprising in Moscow, and by the middle of February, 1906, restored order on the Trans-Siberian railroad.

Disturbances from the left had brought about a rightist reaction. Its activity was directed against the revolutionary intelligentsia, the Jews, and the October "constitution," and resulted in several pogroms.

The revolutionary movement of 1905–6 was led by people whose ultimate political aims varied too much for the movement to be effective. It lacked a recognized popular leader and had no unifying common policy except a general desire to do away with autocracy.

By the end of the nineteenth century and the beginning of the present one, the progressive ideas in Russia had begun to take shape as programs of various political parties. In 1898, the Russian followers of Karl Marx organized the Social Democratic Workers' party.

Russian was the first foreign language into which *Das Kapital* was translated, and the original Russian interpreters of the ideas of Marx insisted that Russia had to pass through the evolutionary stage of capitalism which would develop an industrial proletariat; this, in turn, would help to bring about socialism. In 1903, the party split into Bolsheviks and Mensheviks. The Mensheviks believed that Russia's economic and industrial backwardness and lack of any significant percentage of industrial workers precluded the immediate establishment of a socialist regime. With time, the indispensable growth of capitalism in Russia would, in their opinion, create the necessary conditions for a transition to socialism. They pinned their hopes on industrial workers and attached little importance to the role to be played by the peasants.

Lenin, who represented the Bolsheviks, but was otherwise little known, agreed that a socialist revolution would have to be preceded by a bourgeois-democratic period. Apart from this, he violently disagreed with the Mensheviks in every respect. They were in his view people of words, not deeds. Lenin could wait when necessary, but as a rule, he was all for spontaneous action in accordance with the events of the moment and for the shortest way to any goal. The Mensheviks rejected terrorism, whereas Lenin considered that under certain circumstances it was an indispensable weapon. He believed that his party could be founded only on a small organization of professional revolutionaries held together by an iron discipline and submitting blindly to the will of the Central Committee, i.e., to the will of Lenin himself. Far from depending on a broad basis of support from the masses, this approach made conspiracy mandatory.

The peasant uprisings of 1905–6 proved to Lenin that destitute villagers could become useful allies of the industrial proletariat. From then on, they became an important element in his plans.

Another important factor in the emergence of Russian party politics was the Socialist Revolutionary party (S.R.). While the Marxists (the Social Democrats) concentrated on the workers, the S.R.'s considered themselves primarily champions of the peasantry. Although the party's first congress took place in 1905, its actual origins went back to the Russian populist movement of the 1870's. Its program relating to the agrarian problem was based on confiscating the land from its owners without compensation and transforming it into communal property. The S.R.'s believed that terrorist attempts against individuals were an effective means of creating confusion in government circles and of inciting the inert masses of the population to armed rebellion. Terrorist acts were widely used by them as a political instrument. In 1917, the S.R. party was the largest political alignment in Russia, and it received the majority of the peasant votes during the elections to the ill-fated Constituent Assembly which the Bolsheviks dispersed as soon as it met in January, 1918.

A nonrevolutionary political party of the liberal-minded intelligentsia was founded in October, 1905, when both socialist parties were already in existence. The Constitutional Democratic party, or K.D. party, became popularly known as the Cadet Party, and its members were called Cadets. The party included the flower of Russian cultural life: professors, lawyers, doctors, members of the rural and town local governments, and liberal landowners, all of whom craved the end of autocracy, but were opposed to a social revolution. The aim of the Cadets was to establish in Russia a parliamentary regime similar to that of England or France.

To the left of the Cadets were two moderate socialist political groups: the Laborites (*Trudoviki*) and the People's Socialists (*Narodnyi Sotsialisty*). To the right of the Cadets were the Octobrists, a group which upheld the principles proclaimed in the October, 1905, manifesto. The extreme right was represented by two uncompromisingly reactionary groups: the Russian Monarchists party and the Russian People's Alliance (*Soyuz Russkogo Naroda*).

What were Denikin's political beliefs in those confusing times? He stated them later in one of his books:

My political convictions were formed during my years at the Academy of the General Staff. I never sympathized with the populist movement which was the precursor of the Socialist Revolutionary party, with its terrorist activities and its policy predicated upon the necessity of a peasant uprising; nor with Marxism, in which material values prevail over spiritual ones, and the human individual is negated.

I accepted Russian liberalism in its ideological essence, without any party

dogmatism whatsoever. In general terms, this acceptance led me to the following three propositions: 1. constitutional monarchy, 2. drastic reforms, and
3. regenerating the country by peaceful means. I remained completely faithful
to this ideology until the 1917 revolution, taking no part in politics and devot-
ing all my energy and strength to the army.[22]

For an officer of that period, Denikin had an undeniable leftist orientation. He hoped that the Cadet party, whose ideas closely reflected his own,
would agree to a collaboration with the existing regime, which was seeking
the support of the liberal community. The Cadet party, however, rejected
the advances of the government, and Denikin felt that by their aggressive
opposition to the regime, the Cadets were serving the aims of the socialists,
whose primary purpose was to bring about a socialist revolution.

His feelings on the subject were so strong that a somewhat detailed
explanation of the transitional period between the two revolutions appears
necessary, if we are to see his opinions in their proper historical context.

In 1905, the government proved itself totally incapable of coping with
the political situation. At this time of crisis, the Russian monarchy was
saved mainly by the efforts of two outstanding personalities endowed with
initiative, imagination, and will power: Sergei Iulievich Witte (1849–
1915) and Peter Arkadievich Stolypin (1862–1911). Denikin fully
recognized the great services rendered by Witte to the Russian government, particularly in the economic development of the nation. He welcomed the October manifesto, originated by Witte, as the beginning of
sweeping reforms aimed at establishing a true constitutional regime in
Russia. Yet, in Denikin's memories and feelings, Witte is clearly superseded by Stolypin, who succeeded the former as prime minister three
months after his dismissal, in July, 1906.

Stolypin was a graduate of the physicomathematical faculty of St. Petersburg's university. He was not a member of the capital's bureaucracy, and
had distinguished himself as governor of the province of Saratov before
being summoned to a ministerial post. Though a confirmed monarchist,
he was a staunch supporter of the changes which the October manifesto
brought to the regime. He was thoroughly conversant with the problems
of the Russian peasant, and considered radical agrarian reform affecting
peasant landownership to be of paramount importance.

After the liberation of the serfs in 1861, approximately half of the
nation's agricultural land had been transferred to the peasants. However,
the lands allocated to them did not become their private property, but
were part of the holdings of peasant *obshchinas,* or communes. The
obshchina allocated the land to be cultivated and used by each of its members. Having been liberated from the landlord, the peasant found himself
virtually tied to his commune by a whole complex of obligations, such as
the allocation of taxes, the selection of military recruits, and many others.

Leaving a commune was a slow and complicated process for each individual, and was against the interests of the commune as a whole.

Long before he assumed the post of prime minister, Stolypin had come to the conclusion that the peasant commune destroyed individual initiative, hindered the development of rural economy, and was in some of its aspects a continuation of serfdom. His principal aim, therefore, was to give the peasants the freedom to leave their communes, and the right to dispose of their land as private property. The peasant unrest and uprisings of 1905–6 only strengthened Stolypin's conviction that private ownership would bring out the conservative qualities of the peasants, and encourage them to defend the existing regime against the threat of social revolution.

In 1906 the revolutionaries had not laid down their arms. Terrorist acts accounted for 1,500 dead and wounded government servants. An attempt was made on Stolypin's life in which his son and daughter were gravely injured. In addition to terrorism, Stolypin had to face another problem: A new weapon had recently been added to the revolutionary arsenal. Lenin, whose party needed funds for the continuation of its revolutionary activity, had recourse to certain old, well-tried moneymaking devices, which for the sake of propriety were now being called "expropriations," or "exes." These were robberies of banks, state treasuries, and post offices. Lenin's fellow party members performed them with great success throughout 1906 and the first half of 1907. Lenin's closest associate in these financial operations was Joseph Stalin (Dzhugashvili).

This new Bolshevik activity was soon imitated by the Socialist Revolutionaries, who undertook their own exes to replenish their party coffers. Ordinary thieves also joined in the game, using the party cause as a shield for pursuing their personal gain.[23]

At this point, Stolypin came to a dual decision: to take a firm stand against revolutionary activity and terrorism, and to implement with utmost energy his agrarian reform and a series of other urgent measures.

He had been in favor of the October manifesto and was prepared to cooperate with the Duma. Unfortunately, the Duma did not wish to cooperate with the government, was highly critical of it, and sought its overthrow. Elections to the Duma had given an overwhelming majority to the parties of the opposition, which consistently obstructed the reforms proposed by the government. The relationship between the Duma and the government became inimical and strained to an extent that made collaboration impossible. The first Duma, which opened in April, was dissolved by imperial decree in July, 1906, having been in session less than three months. The second Duma met a similar fate. It had an even larger leftist majority than the preceding one, and having begun to function in February, 1907, was disbanded at the beginning of July of the same year.

The results of the elections to the third Duma could hardly have been expected to be more favorable to the government. Stolypin therefore had recourse to an unconstitutional measure—alteration of the electoral law. The new law, which favored the well-to-do classes, encouraged the election of deputies willing to collaborate with the government and its program. As Stolypin expected, the third Duma, which convened in November, 1907, proved to be more cooperative than its predecessors.

The Basic Laws of the State developed under Witte required the government to submit all new legislation for the approval of the State Duma and the Council of the Empire. They contained, however, a stipulation which Stolypin found extremely useful. Widely known as "Clause 87 of the Basic Laws," this stipulation gave the government the right to enact laws by imperial decree, in case of necessity, when the legislative chambers were not in session. However, such emergency legislation had to be submitted to the chambers for approval when they reconvened.

Since the interruptions of the Duma sessions were numerous and quite long, while conditions in the nation required immediate action, Stolypin began to make full use of the imperial decrees. In August, 1906, he used Clause 87 to create courts-martial to combat terrorism. The courts acted swiftly and carried out their sentences without delay. Although the courts were revoked by the second Duma in the spring of 1907, they had fulfilled Stolypin's expectations; terrorism began to die down.

With the help of the same Clause 87, Stolypin began to carry out his agrarian reform at the end of 1906.

From his retreat in Switzerland, Lenin followed Stolypin's activity with mounting interest and respect for this steadfast representative of the hateful tsarist regime. Although his aims were diametrically opposed to those of Marxism, Stolypin was pursuing them by means whose logic Lenin found admirable.

To begin with, he had dissolved the first and second Dumas and instituted, by decree, a law which precluded the election to the Duma of a majority of "undesirable" deputies.

Second, he had broken the hold of the communal *obshchina* and thus created a new class of small peasant landowners. In time, he expected this class to become the bulwark of the existing government system. Stolypin had given the peasants legal rights equal to those of the rest of the population. They were now free to move where they wished without the consent of the *obshchina*, and to pursue any profession they chose, instead of being limited to agriculture. Laws were passed guaranteeing loans and credit to peasants in connection with agricultural undertakings, and measures were taken to facilitate their migration to the rich, sparsely populated reaches of Siberia. The response to Stolypin's reform by a large percentage of the peasants, who realized its advantages, was quick and businesslike. By 1915, approximately 2,500,000 peasant families had left the *obshchinas* and become private landowners. At the beginning of 1916,

6,000,000 more families applied for withdrawal from the *obshchinas,* and over 3,500,000 peasants moved beyond the Ural Mountains.[24]

Observing from a distance the success of Stolypin's reform, Lenin was arriving at some gloomy conclusions. He feared that in a couple of decades, unless impeded by political unrest, Russian agriculture would acquire a completely bourgeois character and the revolutionary leaders would no longer be able to count on the support of the peasantry.

From his opposite point of view, Denikin welcomed Stolypin's reform and his measures for combating disturbances. He saw their positive aspects and was happy that a true statesman had at last appeared. In addition, Denikin, an excellent speaker himself, admired Stolypin's talent as an orator. In one of his Duma speeches concerning his differences with the revolutionary parties Stolypin said, "They want great upheavals, but we want a great Russia." These words evoked a warm response in Denikin's heart.

Many years later, prominent representatives of the liberal opposition, who had emigrated after the Bolshevik revolution, and who had in their time harassed Stolypin from the tribune of the Duma, recognized, in the press, their mistake in refusing to respond to his bid for their collaboration. With the exception of P. N. Milyukov, most of the former members of the Cadet party came to this conclusion.

Although they continued to criticize many aspects of Stolypin's activity, they admitted in retrospect that he had been an exceptionally gifted statesman and the last hope for constitutional monarchy in Russia.

II

BETWEEN
TWO WARS

———◄ ►———

At the end of the Japanese war, when Denikin was leaving the Far East for St. Petersburg, Army Headquarters in Manchuria sent a telegram to the General Staff in St. Petersburg requesting for him the post of divisional chief of staff. As no such post was vacant at the time, Denikin agreed to accept temporarily the lesser position of staff officer with the Second Cavalry Corps stationed in Warsaw. He had plenty of time on his hands and devoted much of it to lecturing on the Japanese war in the garrisons of the Warsaw district which he visited, and to writing articles on military history and contemporary army life for military periodicals. He hoped by this means to awaken a fresh interest in the science and methods of modern warfare in career officers. During the term of his service in Warsaw, he also took a leave of absence for a trip to Western Europe and visited Austria, Germany, France, Italy, and Switzerland as a tourist. This was his first and only journey abroad until he left Russia as an émigré, and it made a great impression on him.

Denikin's temporary assignment to Warsaw had lasted for almost a year before he decided to remind the General Staff of his existence. The terms of the reminder, as Denikin himself admitted, were somewhat abrupt, and they elicited a harsh response: "Offer Colonel Denikin the position of chief of staff of the Eighth Siberian Division. In case of refusal, he will be crossed off the list of candidates." Nominations to the General Staff had never been compulsory, and Denikin was outraged by the tone of this communication. He answered shortly: "I refuse." [1]

Instead of further annoyances, which he fully expected, Denikin received the offer from St. Petersburg to head the staff of the Fifty-seventh

Reserve Brigade, stationed at Saratov, on the Volga. Since reserve brigades consisted of four regiments, Denikin's position would be equal in importance to that of a divisional chief of staff. At the same time, the location of the brigade was greatly preferable to that of the Siberian division. He accepted the assignment, and remained in Saratov from January, 1907, to June, 1910.

During the time that Denikin spent at Saratov, members of the more enlightened military circles in Russia were urgently and intently examining the reasons for their country's defeat in the Far East.

The reverses of the Japanese war had dealt a painful blow to the national pride of the officer corps. It was evident that the high command functioned in an outdated, traditional way and that radical changes in its approach to contemporary military science and tactics were urgently needed. There began a feverish reorganization of the army, coupled with an intensified program of translating all foreign military literature into Russian. A study of the German military-naval program indicated that a large-scale European war was inevitable. Russian military experts of the period predicted its beginning by 1915. There was no time to lose.

Denikin considered that "never before, in all probability, had military thinking been as intensive as in the years following the Japanese war." [2] Small, semiofficial societies or circles, composed of energetic and educated young officers, were formed in the army and navy. Their aim was the regeneration of the army and the reconstitution of the navy shattered by the Japanese. The members of these circles, which originated in St. Petersburg, were jokingly nicknamed the "young Turks." Their activity found support both in the Ministry of War and the Ministry of the Navy and in the third Duma's Commission of National Defense.

Denikin, who was serving in the provinces, could not participate directly in the activity of the circles, but was in full sympathy with it. He did his best to add to its success by contributing his opinions, frequently based on his experience acquired in the war with Japan, and by his articles in the military press.

The year 1906 saw the beginning of various reforms aimed at rejuvenating and improving military command personnel and at raising their educational level. All senior commanding officers were subject to tests verifying their military competence. According to Denikin, "During 1906 and 1907, from 50 to 80 percent of command personnel, ranging from regimental commander to district army commander, were dismissed and replaced." [3] The roster of senior generals still left much to be desired, but the young cadre of Russian officers on the eve of World War I was of a high caliber. Later, this was recognized by the British and French High Command and even by Soviet military historians, not overly generous as a rule toward the officers of the old Russian army.[4] "One may be certain," wrote Denikin later, "that if it had not learned the hard way in Manchuria, Russia would have been crushed in the first few months of the World War." [5]

In Saratov, as in Warsaw, Denikin's service left him ample time for meditation. He used it to clarify in his own mind many military problems. At the same time, he directed all his energy to promoting the changes that he considered indispensable for the contemporary army.

In June, 1910, Colonel Denikin was given the command of the Seventeenth Infantry Arkhangelgorod regiment, stationed at Zhitomir, in the Kiev military district.

By that time, the conditions of his service in Saratov had palled to such an extent that he accepted his new assignment with pleasure. Moreover, the Arkhangelgorod regiment, founded by Peter the Great, was famous for its war exploits, which included the crossing of the St. Gotthard Pass with Suvórov in 1799, when this greatest of Russia's generals led the Russo-Austrian army against revolutionary France.

Denikin gave himself over with enthusiasm to the work of educating his regiment in the new tactical concepts which he had learned during the Japanese war. Forgetting all about parades and showmanship, he concentrated on training his men in the practical aspects of warfare: marksmanship, maneuvers, forced marches, the crossing of rivers without bridges or pontoons. Such crossings were usually unexpected, and the regiment would therefore be totally unprepared for them. The men had to exercise initiative and ingenuity in utilizing material found on the spot. Denikin's war games involved all of the regiment's men—three thousand, not counting the officers.

Denikin met his fellow officers at mess, but seldom invited them to his home and generally avoided having guests. His mother and his old nurse followed him from post to post. Both of them spoke only Polish, although they understood Russian. His mother was shy of playing hostess to guests with whom she had no common language, and to spare her feelings, her son led an extremely secluded life. He received at home only two or three of his closest friends. The old nurse, Polossia, died in Zhitomir. From then on, Denikin was the only person with whom his mother could speak and share her innermost thoughts.

At the beginning of September, 1911, in Kiev, took place the solemn unveiling of a monument to Alexander II, grandfather of the reigning monarch. Nicholas II and his wife, accompanied by their daughters Olga and Tatiana, arrived from St. Petersburg to attend the celebrations, as did Prime Minister Stolypin, several members of his cabinet, and other prominent public figures.

The festivities accompanying the event included, in addition to concerts and operatic performances, war games in the presence of the Tsar and an army review by the Tsar in the vicinity of Kiev. The regiment commanded by Denikin participated in the latter.

"I was a witness," wrote Denikin later, "of the quasi-mystical enthusiasm which the Tsar's appearance evoked wherever he went. It was evident in the thundering, continuous 'hurrahs,' the feverish glitter of eyes, the tremor of rifles held at attention; and in the inexplicable upsurge of emotion which swept through officers, generals and soldiers—the Russian people in army guise. . . . The same people which a few years later would attack anything connected with the imperial family with indescribable cruelty and would tolerate its inhuman murder." [6]

But at that time, in September, 1911, the Tsar's life was spared and the assassin's victim was Stolypin.

The tragedy occurred in the Kiev theater at a performance of the opera *Tsar Saltan* which followed the war games. During the second intermission, Stolypin was standing near his front-row stall, with his back to the parapet of the orchestra pit. He was rapidly approached from the aisle by a tall individual in formal dress who shot at him twice with a pistol, from a distance of a few feet. One bullet pierced the center of the cross of St. Vladimir hanging from the buttonhole of Stolypin's white uniform tunic, and lodged in the right side of his chest. The other bullet went through his right wrist.

"With slow, measured movements," wrote an eyewitness, "Stolypin placed his visored hat and gloves on the parapet and unbuttoned his coat. Seeing that his waistcoat was drenched with blood, he gestured with his hand as if to say, 'This is the end.' Then he heavily lowered himself in the stall and said clearly and distinctly, in a voice heard by all those who surrounded him, 'I am happy to die for the Tsar.' Having noticed the Emperor coming to the front of his box, Stolypin raised his left arm and gestured to the Tsar to remain in the back. The Tsar would not move away and remained standing; then, Stolypin blessed him in full view of the crowd with a large sign of the cross." [7]

The indignant crowd which filled the theater almost lynched the assassin. He proved to be one Dimitri Bogrov, at one time a Socialist revolutionary and subsequently an anarchist, who was also an agent of the secret police. Ironically, it was the latter which had provided him with a pass to the theater, to guard the security of its distinguished guests. No details were published concerning the assassination plot. Nevertheless, the fact that Bogrov was associated with the secret police, and the laxity of the security measures for Stolypin's protection in Kiev, gave rise to rumors, never confirmed, of police connivance in this crime. [8]

Stolypin died at the age of forty-nine on the fourth day after the shooting.

His death gladdened those who, like Lenin, were dreaming of "great upheavals." It deeply grieved Colonel Denikin, who saw in him a great patriot, an intelligent and strong man who had liquidated the first revolution and restored order in the nation without disrupting the foundations of the state. Stolypin's agrarian reform continued to develop successfully despite his death. Denikin considered that in it lay the hope of solving Russia's most painful and most urgent problem, peasant landownership.

Ironically, Stolypin, who had done so much to strengthen the throne, was at the time of his assassination already in disfavor at court, and his dismissal was imminent.

The peculiarities of the Tsar's character seemed to predispose him against ministers endowed with firmness, clear and independent views and a well-planned program of reforms.

The success of Stolypin's agrarian reform affected the thinking and calculations of the German high command, for in their war preparations, the Germans paid as much attention to Russia's unstable internal situation, on which they were banking, as to the development of their army's strategic plans. To their great displeasure, they had to face the fact that, under Stolypin's regime, a substantial percentage of peasant families had left the communes and become private landowners, thereby strengthening the social basis of the nation. In place of a peasant proletariat, which in the past had always been ready to participate in agrarian uprisings, the peasant-landowners were gradually being transformed into those practical and efficient *kulaks* whom the Communist government was to liquidate in the early 1930's.[9]

Russia's economic and industrial development was progressing with extraordinary rapidity. Although the percentage of illiterates was still considerable, its educational level was also rising very quickly, and in the field of higher education equaled that of Europe and America.

In June, 1914, Denikin was promoted to major general and assigned to the staff of the commander of the Kiev military district. A month later, the general mobilization of Russia's armed forces was ordered.

It was preceded by Tsar Nicholas' desperate but unsuccessful attempts to avert the conflict and to save his country from catastrophe.

Germany declared war on Russia on August 1 (Gregorian calendar) and on France on August 3, having occupied Luxembourg on the preceding day. The Germans next invaded Belgium, and on August 4, Great Britain declared war on Germany.

Thus began World War I, which was to bring about sweeping social, political, and economic changes in Russia.

III

THE FIRST
WORLD WAR

———————◀ ▶———————

The Franco-Russian war plan depended on whether Germany's main forces would attack Russia or France first. Hence, there were two variants of possible joint action, contingent on Germany's initiative. The vastness of Germany's military program worried both Paris and St. Petersburg. The memory of their army's defeat in 1870–71 was still fresh in the minds of the French and heightened their fear of a possible major German blow directed against them. They did everything to extract from Russia the promise of an immediate offensive and demanded that a schedule of military action in case of war be agreed upon beforehand.

Under pressure from the French, the Russian General Staff promised that the Russian offensive against Germany would begin almost at the same time as the French one. The French were to attack on the tenth day, and the Russians on the fifteenth day, following the start of their mobilization.

This promise was completely unrealistic in view of the actual state of affairs. The enormous distances of Russia's vast territory and its inadequate railroad network would not allow it to complete its military preparations, move and concentrate its forces on its western frontiers, and be fully prepared for battle, in less than twenty-nine days after declaring general mobilization. The decision to engage in large-scale military operations on the fifteenth day of mobilization was at best a gamble.[1]

The Russian frontier with Germany and Austria-Hungary—from the Baltic Sea to the Rumanian border—was more than two thousand kilometers long. The vast triangle of Russian Poland was wedged between the Central Powers, with East Prussia to the north, Silesia to the west, and Austrian Galicia to the south. A merging movement of large enemy forces from north to south or vice versa could mean the loss of most of Russian Poland.

The bulk of Germany's forces was initially directed against France, and on August 5 (Gregorian calendar), the latter appealed to Russia to carry out its obligations and relieve it from the pressure of Germany's onslaught by entering the conflict without delay.[2] As a result, the two Russian armies at the northwestern front were thrown into action against East Prussia on the fifteenth day of mobilization.

In the words of the military historian General N. N. Golovin, all these circumstances "forced Russia to enter the fray at a time when only one third of its armed forces could be deployed. This was an enormous strategic mistake, dearly paid for in blood by the army."[3] Golovin pointed out another, equally important mistake in the Russian war plan:

Instead of concentrating all our efforts against one of our enemies in order to disable him, and having done so, using the bulk of our forces to engage and overcome our second enemy, Sukhomlinov [the Minister of War] and his aides decided to launch simultaneous attacks against the Austro-Hungarian armies concentrated in Galicia and the German forces remaining in East Prussia, i.e., along two divergent lines of operation. This dispersion of forces led to catastrophe in East Prussia and diminished the strategic results of our victory in Galicia. . . . Such an overestimation of our resources by the Russian General Staff had one inevitable consequence: Our French allies immediately began to make demands which Russia was completely incapable of fulfilling.[4]

The march on East Prussia ended in the Russian disaster at Tannenberg. But Russia had kept its word, and at a terrible cost to itself, saved the French army. The Germans transferred two army corps from the French to the Russian front, and this lessening of pressure enabled the French to win the victory of the Marne.

Later, General Foch acknowledged this in the following words: *Si la France n'a pas été effacée de la carte de l'Europe, c'est avant tout à la Russie que nous le devons.*[5]

The grandiose scale along which the war developed played havoc with the original strategic plans and calculations of its participants and precluded all hope of a rapid end to the hostilities. It became evident that the indefinite lengthening of the war period would demand a production of war supplies from Russia which the maximum efforts of its industry could not possibly furnish at that time.

While the tragedy in East Prussia was ending in victory for the Germans, the success of the Russian armies on the southwestern front did a great deal to raise Russian morale. Four Austro-Hungarian armies were defeated in Galicia. The Russians occupied Lvov and most of eastern Galicia, and took hundreds of thousands of prisoners and quantities of cannon and war supplies; the routed Austro-Hungarians were retreating rapidly in the direction of Krakow and the Carpathian Mountains. One of the most active of the four Russian armies at the southwestern front was the Eighth Army, commanded by General Brusilov.

Among the officers of the Eighth Army were those around whom the White movement would later be formed: Kaledin, Kornilov, Denikin, Markov.

General Alekseev, whose name is also inseparably linked with the origins of the White Army, was then chief of staff of the southwestern front.

Denikin was Brusilov's deputy chief of staff,* but staff work did not satisfy him and, having learned at the outset of the war that the post of commander of the Fourth Rifle Brigade was vacant, he applied for the position. On September 6, 1914, General Denikin assumed command of this brigade, which formed part of the Eighth Army. As far back as the days of the Russo-Turkish War, it had earned the name of "Iron Brigade."

Under Denikin's leadership the Iron Brigade, which in 1915 was enlarged to a division, became widely known and acclaimed as one of the most valiant units of the Russian army.

"For two years," wrote Denikin, "it marched with me on bloody battlefields, adding many a glorious page to the annals of the great war. Unfortunately, these pages are missing in the official histories: Bolshevik censorship, which had access to all archives and historic materials, has reworked them in its own way, carefully eradicating every episode of the brigade's fighting activity which was linked with my name." [6]

One of the major battles in which Denikin participated in 1914 began on September 6, the day he assumed command of his brigade. At that time, the Austro-Hungarian commander in chief attempted to encircle the Third and Eighth Russian armies near the town of Grodek, in Galicia, with his three armies (one of which had been transferred from the Serbian front). The enemy's main thrust was directed against the Eighth Army, which it almost completely surrounded. One attack followed another, and the situation appeared critical. Two adjacent Russian armies, however, the Fourth and Fifth, came to the rescue. Joining forces with the Eighth Army, they repulsed the Austrians and the enemy began to retreat, closely pursued by the Russians. The retreat soon became a rout. The battle ended as an important Russian victory, in which the Austrians lost 326,000 men and four hundred cannon. Cited for their bravery and initiative in this action were General Kaledin, commander of the Twelfth Cavalry Division (later commander of the Eighth Army, and *Ataman*† of the Don Cossacks after the revolution), General Kornilov, commander of the 48th Infantry Division (later commander in chief and founder of

---

* In the old Russian army as in the German army, the deputies of the chief of staff of an army or of the group of armies in a "front" had the title of "quartermaster general." In this book, the term "deputy chief of staff" has been used instead.

† The *Ataman* was the head of the military and civil administration of a Cossack community, and was elected by the Cossack population of the region.

the White Army), and the commander of the Iron Brigade—General Denikin.

Denikin was awarded the Sword of St. George.[7]

In October, 1914, when the fighting had already lost its mobility and become trench warfare, the Austrian regiments, reorganized and reinforced by fresh units, renewed their offensive. The Russian front in Galicia was overextended, so the Eighth Army had to bring all its reserves into action. Here, again, General Denikin distinguished himself by his initiative. He received the Cross of St. George, Fourth Class, for the daring exploit of his brigade. Here is his description of the action:

> On October 24 I noticed a certain weakening of the enemy line, which was only 500–600 feet away from our trenches. I alerted the brigade and moved it against the enemy trenches without any preliminary shelling. The attack was so unexpected that the Austrians panicked. Having dispatched a short telegram to the headquarters ("beating and routing the Austrians"), I pursued them full speed with my riflemen, overcoming their disorganized resistance and penetrating deep into the enemy rear guard. We took the village of Gorny Lujek, which, as we discovered, housed the headquarters of Archduke Joseph. When I burst into the village with our advance units and reported this fact to the army corps staff, they did not believe me and asked me to check "if there had not been a confusion of names."
>
> Nor could the Archduke immediately believe what was happening. He was so certain of his safety that he rushed off with his staff only when he heard the sound of Russian machine guns in the streets. Having occupied his quarters, we found the table set with the Archduke's monogrammed service and drank some Austrian coffee which was still hot.[8]

During November, 1914, the Eighth Army was continuously engaged in combat. The Russians' aim was to capture the Carpathian mountain passes; the Austrians were anxious to lift the siege of Przemysl, surrounded by Russian troops. General Brusilov ordered two of his army corps to advance and take the Beskid ridge of the Carpathian Mountains between the passes of Lupkov and Rostok. The troops detached for this operation included General Kornilov's division and General Denikin's brigade. The weather was terrible, with hard frost, cold piercing winds, and snowstorms. There were no mountain roads in the sector which the Iron Brigade was to traverse. In order to take some of the pressure off the units adjacent to his, and to give them access to the highway, Denikin decided on a very risky move. Leaving his artillery and transport under cover of a single battalion, he led all the rest of his brigade up the mountainside, along narrow and steep wild-goat tracks slippery with ice. The men were followed by horses laden with bags of ammunition and dried bread. Despite the difficulty and hardships of the expedition, Denikin's brigade crossed the Carpathians and invaded Hungary in the rear of the Austrian army, taking the town of Mezo

Laborcz, 3,730 prisoners, nine cannon, and many firearms and other trophies.

This exploit made a tremendous impression on the army. Denikin was showered with telegrams, greetings, and expressions of gratitude and received messages of congratulation from the Supreme Commander, Grand Duke Nicholas, and from General Brusilov. The latter's telegram read: "I salute the valiant brigade for its dashing action and the brilliant execution of its assignment and thank from the bottom of my heart yourself, your officers, and the heroic riflemen. The hardships and deprivations overcome by the brigade, and its glorious deeds, testify that the old traditions of the Iron Brigade are alive in its heroic regiments and will continue to lead them to victory and fame." [9]

At the beginning of February, 1915, the Iron Brigade was sent to aid the detached force commanded by General Kaledin. The action took place near the village of Lutovisko in the direction of Uzhgorod.

This was one of our hardest battles [recollected General Denikin]. Biting frost; snow up to our chests; Kaledin's last reserve—his dismounted cavalry brigade—already thrown into action.

I shall never forget that eerie battlefield. . . . The whole distance which my riflemen had to cross was marked by motionless human figures jutting out of the snow with their rifles clutched in their hands. They were dead, frozen in the positions in which they had been hit by enemy bullets while making their way across the deep snow. Between them, floundering in the snow among the bodies and using them for cover, the living were winding their way toward death. The brigade was melting away. . . . Next to the Iron Brigade, under devastating fire, I saw the one-armed hero, Colonel Noskov, leading his regiment in an attack directed straight at the sheer icy rocks of Hill 804. . . .

During those same February battles, Kaledin unexpectedly rode up to us. The General scrambled up the cliff and sat down next to me; the spot was under intensive fire. Kaledin calmly conversed with the officers and riflemen, questioning them about their actions and losses. Somehow, this simple appearance of the commanding officer encouraged everybody and awakened a feeling of trust and respect toward him.[10]

For the same reasons and to the same extent as Kaledin, Denikin enjoyed the respect and trust of his officers and men. They knew that their commander was strict, exacting, and stingy of praise. But they also knew that at the moment of danger he was always with them in the line of fire, exposing his head as well as theirs to the enemy bullets.

This confidence, however, had to be earned, for at first, the Iron Brigade's attitude toward its new commander had been somewhat negative. There was some antagonism among combat officers toward their colleagues serving on army staffs, particularly those who were graduates of the Academy of the General Staff. Denikin's predecessor, General Baufal, had spent his whole career in the brigade, which he had joined in his early youth.

His officers and men regarded him as one of their own. When his place was taken by a general from the outside—one of those General Staff officers whom the ranks had sarcastically nicknamed "fleeting moments" —the officers of the brigade decided among themselves that the newcomer would cross their horizon like a meteor. They expected him to stay just long enough to disorganize the brigade and to further his career by grabbing a few decorations at their expense.

The ice began to thaw as soon as the riflemen saw General Denikin in the front lines in their first battles together. When, later, they learned that at the beginning of 1915, Denikin had refused the command of a division in order to stay with the Iron Brigade, in the words of one of its senior officers, "Anton Ivanovich became one of us. Our Iron Rifleman, period." [11]

A curious detail: although Russian officers easily adopted the familiar *Ty* ("thou") in addressing each other, Denikin was on "thee" and "thou" terms only with his childhood friends and the comrades of his youthful years in the second Field Artillery Brigade. He never crossed this invisible barrier between "you" and "thou" at the Academy of the General Staff or at any subsequent time in his career. Later, he kept this surface distance even with such close associates as Generals Markov and Romanovsky, to whom he was deeply attached and who were extremely close to him.

His role in the February battles brought Denikin the Cross of St. George, Third Class.

The events which took place at the Russian front in 1915, affected the life and psychology of the entire country. By the end of 1914, an acute shortage of artillery shells, cartridges, and rifles began to affect the army. The supplies, which had been naïvely expected to suffice for a short war, were spent, and the national industry was incapable of satisfying the enormous, growing needs at the front. The crisis in army materiel was further complicated by Turkey's entrance into the war, which cut off the possibility of foreign arms eventually coming in through the Black Sea. Russia was isolated from its allies. Orders for armament placed abroad took a long time to fill and could be delivered only through Vladivostok, or through Archangel, on the White Sea, which was icebound during the winter. Only much later did some of the war supplies begin to arrive by way of Murmansk, whose railroad connection with St. Petersburg (renamed Petrograd at the beginning of the war), was completed at the end of 1916.

In spite of all this, the morale of the Russian army was still high in the early part of 1915. Przemysl fell in March, and the Russians captured nine generals, 2,500 officers, 120,000 privates, nine hundred guns, and countless other trophies there. It was a great victory; however, the vast expenditure of artillery ammunition during the siege of Przemysl contributed to the approaching crisis. At this point, in the summer of 1915, the German High Command, which was thoroughly informed of the shortages in the Russian army, decided to make an attempt at putting Russia out of action. The center of German operations was transferred from the west to the east. As early as May, General Mackensen's army was sent to the aid of Austrians on the Russian southwestern front. The enemy's technical superiority was overwhelming. Soon, the "great retreat of 1915" was undertaken, in the hope that, by the surrender of territory, the Russian army itself could be saved from encirclement and annihilation. By the end of the summer, enemy forces had occupied all of Russian Poland, Lithuania, Belorussia, and a part of Volynia. The Germans made use of their tremendous superiority in artillery, but avoided involving their infantry in combat. They overcame the Russians by artillery fire alone. As a result, their losses were insignificant, whereas those of the Russians during that summer were immense: almost 1,400,000 men killed and wounded, and 976,000 taken prisoner.[12]

This defeat dealt a stunning blow to Russian morale. It gave rise to rumors of treason and to a search for the guilty parties. In June, the Minister of War, Sukhomlinov, was dismissed. Indignation against him in army circles and among the general public, had reached the boiling point. Among the officers, Denikin's generation, which had put all its soul into a reorganization of the army after the disaster of the Japanese war, was especially bitter. The government responded by instituting a special commission to find and indict the officials guilty of inadequately supplying the army. Public opinion blamed the Russian General Headquarters, or *Stavka,* for the reverses at the front and for exceeding its authority. The excess of authority of the *Stavka* stemmed from the imperial "Statute on the Administration of the Army in the Field in Wartime" of June 29, 1914. According to this statute, the High Command was invested with dictatorial powers over the vast territory adjoining the front. The area of the Russian Empire dominated by the military command included at that time Russian Poland, Finland, the Baltic provinces, with the Caucasus, Archangel, and Vladivostok as ports of access for foreign supplies, and even the capital—Petrograd itself.

In 1915, as the front receded rapidly, the domination of the *Stavka* quickly expanded over large territories in the interior of Russia. All government agencies included in that zone were automatically subject to military jurisdiction. More often than not, the *Stavka* failed to notify the government of its decisions and actions in the realm of civilian administration. The result was utter confusion and arbitrary rule by local military authorities. All this contributed to an increasing loss of prestige for the government.

The High Command was applying a scorched-earth policy in the territories abandoned to the enemy. In this respect, Stalin's actions during the Russian retreat in World War II were nothing new. Fire and destruction had been used in similar situations since ancient times.

Crowds of hungry, ragged, exhausted, and exasperated refugees laden with their chattels, moved eastward, trampling the crops and pastures, exhausting the food supply of both the near and far rear of the army. Part of this migrating mass had left home voluntarily in fear of German atrocities, but most had been forced to leave by the military authorities. Their homes and remaining belongings had been set on fire before their eyes. Among the refugees—Poles, Great Russians, White Russians, Ukrainians—were many Jews. Their fate was particularly hard: At the beginning of the war, the German Zionists had formed (with the approval of the German Ministry of Foreign Affairs) a Committee for Liberating Russian Jews. The German General Staff had at the same time wanted to exploit the Jews for its own aims, notably the provocation of an uprising in the rear of the Russian armies.[13] And although this plan did not succeed—and all that the destitute Jews of Galicia and the southwestern region really wanted was to be left alone and to be involved in the war as little as possible—the poison of doubt sown by the Germans penetrated the minds of the Russian High Command. Quite possibly the entire situation was consciously created by the Germans to provoke a further disruption of Russian conditions near the front; in any event, the Russians took the bait brought to them by their own intelligence service. Their watchfulness alerted, they began to suspect the Jews of aiding the enemy. Here, the military command's patriotic zeal, with an admixture of antisemitism, reached the height of absurdity: It began to transplant to the interior of Russia not only Russian Jews, but Austrian Jews from Galicia as well. Thousands of these unfortunates, moving across an alien country with the wave of refugees, faced the ill will and anger of the local populations. The flow of refugees created a food crisis wherever it went, raised the cost of living, spread contagious diseases, and became the focus of all the discontent that had been building up during the war. Among the refugees themselves, and especially the Jewish masses, resentment against the government and a revolutionary spirit were growing with uncontrollable rapidity.

The human tragedy went hand in hand with economic disaster. What was to be done with those masses? How were they to be fed and relocated?

At a meeting of the Council of Ministers in August, 1915, at which emergency funds for the needs of the refugees were being discussed, the new Minister of War, Polivanov, unctuously declared, "We put our hope in immeasurable distances, in impassable mud, and in the mercy of St. Nicholas patron of holy Russia."[14] Polivanov, it appears, liked flowery phrases, but the situation was truly threatening.

The oratory and caustic remarks directed at the *Stavka* by other members of the government brought results totally unexpected by them. Their criticism contributed to the removal of the popular Grand Duke Nicholas from the post of Supreme Commander in Chief. None of the ministers had sought his discharge.

The only person who desired it, and used her influence to obtain it, was the Tsarina Alexandra Fedorovna. Under the influence of her circle of intimates and particularly of Rasputin, but without the least foundation, she had begun to suspect the Grand Duke of a desire to encroach on the powers of the monarch.

In a series of letters to her husband, she demanded with a passionate, morbid insistence that he dismiss the Grand Duke and assume the High Command of the army himself. In September, 1915, to the surprise of his own government, the Tsar proclaimed himself Supreme Commander in Chief and relegated Grand Duke Nicholas to the role of Viceroy and commander in chief of the Caucasus.

As soon as this development became known, all but two of the Tsar's ministers submitted to him a collective petition begging him to reconsider a step which, in their words, "to the best of our understanding threatens Russia, Yourself, and Your dynasty with grave consequences." [15] An appeal of this kind was unprecedented. It was a gesture of despair.

Although the general public was appalled at the change in the High Command, the army masses, according to Denikin, took it rather philosophically.

This important event [wrote Denikin] did not make a great impression on the army. The generals and officers realized that the Tsar's participation in the High Command would be only nominal and were mainly preoccupied by the question of who would be chief of staff.

The nomination of Alekseev to that post satisfied the officers. As to the soldiers, they were not used to analyzing the technical aspects of army command, and for them the Tsar had always been the supreme head of the army. Only one factor worried them: the ingrained popular belief that the Tsar was unlucky. . . .

To all intents and purposes, the new chief of staff, General Alekseev, assumed the command of Russia's armed forces.[16]

Many years later, Winston Churchill compared Alekseev's strategic talent to that of Foch and Ludendorff.[17] Despite Alekseev's great ability, however, the successful conduct of the war depended most of all on the fighting efficiency of the army. And by the fall of 1915, the army had lost in combat an enormous percentage of its original cadres of officers and men. After one year of war, the Russian army had become a huge mass of uniformed civilians, and was showing the first symptoms of demoralization. The troops were tired of retreating and increasingly indignant at the lack of military supplies. Only a tremendous influx of war materiel and a great victory over the enemy could have imbued the army with a true military spirit.

The military spirit still persisted in the Iron Brigade, despite the fact that it had lost a great number of officers and men. Reorganized into a division in April, 1915, it was constantly moved from one sector to another, being called to the rescue wherever things were going badly, and was nicknamed the "fire brigade" of the Eighth Army. Many of its exploits have become legendary. All of them testify to the extraordinary bravery and endurance of the unit and its commander. But at what cost!

I shall never forget the spring of 1915 [wrote General Denikin]. The great tragedy of the Russian army—the Galician retreat. No cartridges, no shells. Day after day, bloody encounters, exhausting marches, infinite physical and moral weariness; from timid hopes we plunged into unmitigated gloom.

I recall the battle near Przemysl in the middle of May. Eleven days of fierce combat by the Fourth Rifle Division [the Iron Division]. . . . Eleven days of infernal din from the German artillery which literally uprooted whole rows of trenches with their occupants. We scarcely answered them, having nothing to reply with. Our utterly exhausted regiments parried one attack after another with bayonets or point-blank rifle fire; blood flowed, the ranks were thinning and the burial mounds multiplying. . . . Two regiments were almost completely annihilated solely by shellfire. . . . When our only six-inch battery, which had been silent for three days, was supplied with fifty shells, this was announced by telephone to every regiment and company; and all the riflemen heaved a sigh of contentment and relief.[18]

Even in retreat, and with little ammunition, Denikin's division managed to deal some painful blows to the enemy.

In mid-September, 1915, the Russian army, sorely depleted by heavy losses, was outnumbered 3 to 1 by enemy forces along the Lutsk-Rovno line. The Germans were pouring reinforcements into the battle in an attempt to cut off the Eighth Army's right flank. In order to relieve the situation of an adjacent army corps, Brusilov's staff ordered Denikin to divert the enemy fire to his own unit by firing the Iron Division's batteries throughout the night. Denikin was opposed to this decision and annoyed at the waste of precious ammunition it involved. Nevertheless, he obeyed, knowing full well that he was disclosing the disposition of his batteries to the enemy and that by morning the Austrian artillery fire would be concentrated on his troops. To save other units, Denikin was exposing his own division to the full force of the enemy's impact.

During the night, Denikin summoned his regimental commanders and told them to be ready at dawn for the assault of Lutsk. "Our position is desperate," he told them; "the only solution is to attack!"

The onslaught was completely unexpected by the enemy. The Iron Division captured 158 officers and 9,773 soldiers—according to Denikin, as many as there were in his entire division.

"Denikin," wrote General Brusilov in his memoirs, "disregarding all obstacles, threw himself at Lutsk and took it in one thrust. He drove into it by car while the battle was still raging and telegraphed me that the Fourth Rifle Division had taken Lutsk." [19] As a result of this action, Denikin was promoted to lieutenant general.

No less daring an action took place in the middle of October of the same year. The German troops, sent to the Austrians' assistance, occupied the ancient town of Chartoryisk, threatening to cut off the Eighth Army from the rest of the Russian forces at the southwestern front. Brusilov entrusted Denikin with the problem of liberating Chartoryisk. On October 16 the Iron Division was deployed opposite Chartoryisk and Novoselok. On the same night, it crossed the river Styr, and three days later had made a deep breach in the enemy line. The wedge was eighteen kilometers wide and twenty kilometers deep; to hold it meant facing the enemy on three, and sometimes on four sides. Sergei L. Markov, a future hero of the White Army, who was then commanding one of the Iron Division's regiments, found himself and his regiment at the foremost point of the breach. "A very original situation," he reported to Denikin by telephone; "am fighting the enemy in all four directions. It's so difficult that it's even fun!"

Denikin's division took Chartoryisk and captured 8,500 nonwounded prisoners, and many guns, machine guns, and supply trains; it almost completely annihilated the German First Grenadier Crown Prince (*Kronprinz*) regiment, and decimated two Austrian divisions. Then the Iron Division proceeded to clear the enemy from the surrounding villages and farms.

The Austrians awakened to an unpleasant surprise [wrote an eyewitness, Colonel of the General Staff B. N. Sergeevsky]. At the crack of dawn all the woods surrounding them came to life in the strangest, most uncontemporary way.

From the north approached the loud strains of a Russian military band. The blasts of regimental trumpets responded to it from the west and south. By the time that three Russian columns, coming from different directions, emerged at the edge of the wood, the Austrian brigade was lined up in formation, with raised arms, before the farmstead's little wooden houses. The regimental band, still playing, marched past the Austrians and turned eastward, toward Chartoryisk.

Colonel Markov galloped up to the Austrian command, shouting, *"Zeremonialmarsch! Nach Chartoryisk!"* [20]

Here again, General Denikin displayed his understanding of war psychology. Having pierced the Austrian front, he ran the risk of being cut off from the Russians at any moment. Although he was actually behind enemy lines, Denikin chose this moment to strike up the band and regimental trumpets. The rolling of drums and the music encouraged the Russians while it confused and panicked the enemy.

At the beginning of 1916, Denikin's mother, Elizaveta Fedorovna, became gravely ill with pneumonia complicated by pleurisy. She was not to recover from this illness. She spent about eight months in bed, was often unconscious, and died in October, 1916, at the age of seventy-three. Denikin was deeply affected by his mother's illness and death. The front was far away, and he came to see her only twice, having been summoned by telegrams from her physician. During both of these sad furloughs he never left his mother's bedside. In the fall, when he arrived a third time at the doctor's request, he found her already dead. The last link with his childhood and youth, which were precious to him in spite of all their hardship and poverty, had been broken. Elizaveta Fedorovna had been living in her son's Kiev apartment, which he had rented in the spring of 1914. He had brought his mother there from Zhitomir, and surrounded her with everything that could make her approaching old age comfortable. Having had her fill of poverty and grief during her difficult life, she was able to spend her last years in security and comfort.

At the death of his mother, Denikin faced a lonely future. His ripe age —he was almost forty-four—seemed to him a serious obstacle to marriage and a fresh start in life. There seemed to be nothing to look forward to except total solitude.

There was one person in Denikin's life to whom he was strongly attached, but at that time he was afraid to formulate even to himself the hope that their lives could be united. This was Xenia Chizh—Assia—the little girl born in the year of his promotion to the rank of officer, to whom he had once given a doll that could open and close her eyes. Assia was now an attractive young woman. She had graduated from the Institute for Young Ladies in Warsaw a short time before the war, and was in Petrograd attending Professor Platonov's history course for future teachers. She had been engaged to a young hussar officer, but he had been killed in action. Her parents were divorced and had both remarried; Biala, her native town, was in enemy hands. In a way, she was as lonely as Anton Ivanovich. But he realized that before taking a decisive step it was necessary to explore the terrain and to sound out by correspondence the possibility of a favorable reply from the woman who had captured his imagination.

Fortunately, these letters from General Denikin, written at the front and filled with his thoughts and impressions, have been preserved. Ninety-six letters, hitherto unpublished, remained in the possession of the General's widow, Xenia Vasilievna Denikin. They cover the period from October 15, 1915 to the end of August, 1917—the time of Denikin's arrest by the Provisional Government and his incarceration in the Berdichev prison, for allegedly participating in the "Kornilov uprising."

The excerpts presented here, with Mrs. Denikin's permission, shed a new light on the spiritual qualities of a reserved man, unused to admitting anyone into his inner world.[21]

October 15, 1915
I am so filled with impressions that they could last me a lifetime. I am burn-

ing with excitement, without rest or a minute of peace, and alternate between grief and feelings of joy and accomplishment.

The valiant division with which a kind fate has entrusted me for the past fourteen months has earned a unique reputation: it has sustained enormous losses, roamed all over Galicia, reached beyond the Carpathians; it has been decimated and restored anew by replacements; it is anxiously awaited everywhere and fulfills its duty with complete selflessness. . . . My health is better than in peacetime. I feel fine, but my nerves are exhausted. Sometimes, when I spend one of our rare periods of calm in a narrow, dirty hovel of this deserted swampy region, I dream of the happy days which will follow the end of the war (a victorious one, of course), and bring us the moral right to rest. Complete rest, with no trace of a shadow to spoil it: the sea, sunshine, and quiet—what bliss! Will there be happiness? I hardly know what it is and am not sure that it will ever come. But at least I feel entitled to some peace.

November 13, 1915

The pulse of the battle, which we unconsciously register, tells us that the enemy no longer has a trace of the moral strength with which they [the Germans] had started their campaign: Their flight and surrender have become commonplace; their proud bearing has given way to the sloppy appearance and the tired expression of elderly burghers. Their confiscated journals register apathy, weariness, and the desire to end the war. The end is not near yet, but one clearly feels that the Austro-Germans are doomed to be defeated. Then, a new bright era will begin, if only . . . our helmsmen will be able to steer our country away from internal upheavals.

December 16, 1915

It is about four months since I have had any privacy. We are always three or four people to a room. I could, of course, use my commander's privileges to make a better arrangement, but this would be extremely hard on all the others. And so, I want to be alone, but it is impossible. Impossible to concentrate, to think, or simply—not think. . . . I am surrounded by the shouting of the telephone operators; by the noise, laughter and conversation of my gay and lively young staff members. . . .

I am writing very badly. This is because six eyes follow my pen and three heads are ironically thinking: How come our general, who is a master of succinctness, is well into the fourth page of his letter?

February 6, 1916

My mother fell gravely ill with pneumonia on January 10. On the twenty-fourth I was able to tear myself away on furlough. Have remained at her bedside until February 5. Am morally and physically exhausted. The issue is doubtful. Sometimes there is hope, and sometimes none. I am faced with a sinister, empty, and completely solitary future. You know that I have no one except her.

March 4, 1916

Was lightly wounded March 2 by a piece of shrapnel through the left arm; the bone is intact; a blood vessel burst, but (stout fellow) closed of its own accord. Even my temperature doesn't rise beyond 37.4 [99.3F.]. No need to stay in bed. I continue to be in command.

March 27, 1916

It is almost three months now that Mother has been in this hopeless and helpless condition. And in the meantime, life continues to surge all around us, the sun is shining brightly and the joyous Easter feast is drawing near. No lack of faith can diminish the spell of this festival of spring, Resurrection and renewal. We shall celebrate Easter at the front, in a small church hidden in a ravine but quite well known to the Austrians.

My thoughts will be far, far away, divided between two dear ones—the one whose life is waning and the other who has so closely entered my life.

In his letters to the woman who was becoming the center of his thoughts, to whom he wrote most often, and who had "so closely entered" his life, Anton Ivanovich was seeking "answers to unformulated questions and unexpressed thoughts."

"I don't want to invade your inner world unbidden" he wrote her in March. But he knew full well that his veiled declarations, transparent as they were, could not elicit a written answer to the question which obsessed him. He only hoped that some hint of response in her letters would give him the courage to propose to her in writing.

On April 4 he decided to take this step and to formulate "that long-suppressed but imminent question." Two possible obstacles worried him. One was his bachelor past, which he felt obliged to confess, but not on paper. About the other he wrote, "I fear your imagination: What if those kind, tender lines I read are addressed to an ideal person you have created in your mind and not to me whom you haven't seen for six years and whose spiritual and physical appearance has changed in that time? Disappointment? For you it would mean an unpleasant episode. For me—ruin. . . . My letter will reach you by Easter," he concluded, "Christ is arisen! I would like your letter not only to voice the traditional Easter response, but good news for me as well."

One might expect that the lengthy correspondence between Anton Ivanovich and Xenia Vasilievna would have prepared the latter to expect a proposal. Nevertheless, it took her completely by surprise.

She did not say no, but asked for time to get used to the idea of marriage and to learn to know Anton Ivanovich better, before coming to a final decision.

After his months of patience and diplomacy, the General suddenly found this very hard to bear. "I have never spoken to anyone in my life as I have to you in my letter of the fourth," he replied. "You can imagine with what impatience I awaited your answer, even a conditional one; you can't imagine with what emotion I opened your letter. Your letter of the twelfth . . . so careful, so well thought out. This is probably as it should be. As for me, I have rejected my usual reserved, mistrustful, somewhat analytical self, and opened my whole heart to you."

It took several weeks of insistent persuading by correspondence to make Xenia Vasilievna agree to the engagement and to accept the idea of plighting her troth with General Denikin's. Until this decision was reached, the General was "as tense as during a battle whose issue was in doubt." [22]

They decided not to announce their engagement for the time being, but by the summer of 1916, it was already known to Xenia Vasilievna's family. At that time, too, because of Denikin's insistence, they decided to postpone their marriage until the end of the war. This decision was not easy for Anton Ivanovich to make, and was dictated solely by his concern for his fiancée.

From the end of April, 1916, his letters to her were full of hopes for a radiantly happy future. If a momentary doubt sometimes appeared in them, it was quickly dissipated: "Never has life been so full. Now, besides my work, I have a personal life. Sometimes I worry about the unsolved problems of our future relationship (the one remaining problem really) and am tortured by doubt. Always the same one: Is your tenderness really for me, or for an imaginary personality that you have created in your mind?" [23]

"If our future happiness depends mainly on me—then it is almost assured. I have no intention of re-educating or changing you in any way, dear one. Will I be able to draw close to you? I think I will, because . . . because I love you. And in my lonely thoughts, acute and joyful, I picture Assia—my wife and friend. Then my doubts leave me and the future brightens." [24]

The joyousness of most of these letters, written during the spring and summer of 1916, is tempered by Denikin's profound distress at his mother's failing health. He summed up the emotional conflict of these painful months, after his mother's death had resolved it, in a letter dated October 27, 1916. It was written en route to the front from Kiev, after his mother's funeral, at which he had seen Xenia Vasilievna for the first time in six years: "The last few weeks were of immense importance in my life. They sharply divided the past from the future. Grief and joy. Death and life. The end and the beginning. No wonder that I am a little lost and off balance."

The autumn of 1915 brought a lull in war activity on the Russian–Austro-Hungarian front. Both sides dug in for the winter and spent most of it in their trenches. Except for some rare action in December and March, newspaper bulletins from the *Stavka* reported laconically, "exchange of fire and scouting activities." Russia made the most of this period of calm by accumulating war supplies and replacing the preceding summer's terrible losses in manpower with new recruits. Drastic changes took place in the Ministry of War. Unlike Sukhomlinov, its new officials were anxious to collaborate with public organizations such as the Union of *Zemstvos* * and the Union of Towns, in a combined effort to intensify

---

* The *zemstvo* was a provincial or county council, elected by townsfolk and peasants. It supervised such local matters as roads, schools, hospitals, pubilic health, veterinary service, and the like, and exercised the right to impose local taxes.

the production of ammunition and supplies for the army. The collaboration proved fruitful. It put industry on a war footing and was responsible for the formation of the Special Council for National Defense and the War Industries Committee.

The enterprise of a number of energetic private businessmen, assisted by substantial government loans and supported by the Ministry of War, achieved notable results. The manufacture of artillery ordnance and rifle cartridges increased considerably. Allied military and diplomatic representatives in Russia sent their governments jubilant reports on the unexpected and impressive achievements of the Russian armament industry. At the same time, the long-awaited flow of foreign supplies began to reach the country in increasing quantities. The break had come, and with it a renewal of hope.

In the meantime, an inter-Allied conference, held at Chantilly in December, 1915, had decided to initiate an all-out offensive against Germany by the middle of June, 1916, attacking it simultaneously on its western and eastern fronts. The Allies were to strike their main blow in the area of the Somme, but an unexpected turn of events soon obliged them to modify their plans. In February, the Germans launched a violent attack aimed at breaking through the French front at Verdun. Russia, which hoped to receive some help from its allies, was instead urgently called to their assistance. Russia responded immediately, and in March, moved its armies at the northern and western fronts against the Germans, disregarding the bad roads and slush brought on by the melting snow.

Denikin and his division remained at the southwestern front and did not participate in this offensive. He summarized it in one terse sentence: "This operation, hastily organized and badly carried out . . . was literally drowned in mud and ended in complete failure." [25]

Nevertheless, it helped temporarily to stop the attacks against Verdun. The Allies, however, were soon faced with another crisis and renewed their insistent demand for Russian help. This time it was more than a call for assistance—a veritable wail of despair came to Russia from Rome.

Italy had declared war against Austria, its former ally, in May, 1915, and the Austrians thirsted for revenge. In the spring of 1916, they moved a considerable part of their forces from the Russian to the Italian front. They defeated the Italians at Trentino in the middle of May and were advancing in the general direction of Verona. Foreseeing a catastrophe, the Italian High Command, supported by General Joffre, requested, then begged, the *Stavka* to start an immediate offensive against Austria-Hungary, in order to divert its forces from the Italian front.

Once again, as Churchill later wrote, "in that emulation of comradeship which was characteristic of the Czar's armies," the Russians dealt a new, and this time tremendously effective, blow to the Austrians. [26]

"Few episodes of the Great War," said Churchill elsewhere, "are more impressive than the resuscitation, re-equipment and renewed giant effort of Russia in 1916. It was the last glorious exertion of the Czar and the Russian people for victory before both were to sink into the abyss of ruin and horror." [27]

At daybreak on May 22, the entire length of the Russian southwestern front erupted with intensive artillery fire, with no thought of sparing ammunition, which was plentiful. After the initial artillery softening up, the Russian troops began to advance along the entire 350-kilometer front. The enemy was so unprepared for the attack that although its lines had been heavily fortified during the winter months, it was unable to put up any resistance. The Austrians were routed and their front broken.

General Brusilov, recently named to the post of commander in chief of the southwestern front, was responsible for the entire operation, in which four Russian armies (the Eighth, Eleventh, Seventh, and Ninth) were lined up from north to south.[28] The Eighth Army, formerly led by Brusilov, was now under the command of General Kaledin and still included the Iron Division, headed by Denikin. The two generals knew each other well, and there were no doubts in Kaledin's mind concerning the division's staunchness and the reliability of its leader.

In a new strategic approach devised by Brusilov, all four armies attacked simultaneously. By launching his attack along the entire length of the front instead of concentrating it in one area, to which the enemy could move its reserves, Brusilov was able to break the enemy lines in several places at once. "This form of breakthrough," commented one of the Russian participants, "deprived the enemy of the possibility of defining the main area of attack and of moving its reserves accordingly. Thus, the attacking side could benefit fully from surprise, keeping the enemy guessing and its forces tied along the entire front." [29]

The principal blow of this operation was aimed by Kaledin's army, and specifically, by Denikin's division, at the town of Lutsk. Denikin was familiar with the town, having captured it in September, 1915. Since then, Lutsk had been retaken and strongly fortified by the enemy.

Despite the shrapnel wound in his left arm, incurred in March, which had only partly healed, Denikin led the attack and moved with the front lines of his division.

Fifteen years later, he described this experience in an article written for an émigré bimonthly published in Paris:

At 4 A.M. of May 22 all the front-line batteries of the Eighth Army opened fire. The lines of our own trenches and those of the enemy were clearly visible from our observation point. Never had my riflemen heard such a cannonade. At times the thunder of the cannons merged into a deep roar, as if an abyss had broken open and was releasing a chaos of sounds which shook the world. A thousand fountains of black earth rose into the air from the Austrian trenches, throwing up fragments of lumber and tangled masses of barbed wire. . . . In the course of thirty-six hours, on May 22 and 23, the division batteries fired 27,700 shells. This is not a large number compared to the scale of the European front where in the battle of Vimy, for example, in April, 1917, the British concentrated four thousand cannon on a twenty-kilometer front and fired four million shells in the first ten days of the offensive. But for us such saturated firing was a record. For the first time our artillery was able to achieve the goal which previously had to be paid for with blood.

On May 23, General Kaledin issued general instructions to start the breakthrough at 9 A.M. I gave the following brief order of the day: "At 9 o'clock all units of the division are ordered to attack. God be with us."

. . . The spectacle was unprecedented. The battlefield sprang into life. Thousands of men swarmed over the breastwork and rushed forward, scattering over the field and reassembling at the passages cleared through the wire obstacles. . . . And then they vanished from sight. The field was empty once more. An invisible bayonet battle was taking place in two areas, the communication passages and the dugouts of the first line. . . . About two hours went by. Suddenly, far away, beyond the first Austrian defenses, appeared the strung-out lines of our riflemen, so isolated and solitary-looking. . . . They were advancing toward the second line of fortifications under strong artillery fire from the Austrians. At their head was Lieutenant Colonel Timanovsky of the Thirteenth Regiment—the famous "Stepanovich," one of the bravest Iron Riflemen, who later became commander of the Markov division in the civil war. Leaning on a cane, for he never carried arms in an attack, he strode along unhurriedly, stopping occasionally, beckoning someone with his hand. The emergence of this battalion beyond the enemy lines greatly impressed our foreign guests at the observation point. [Allied military attachés had been permitted by the *Stavka* to observe the beginning of the Iron Division's offensive]. They ran up an exposed hill to get a better view, and the most enthusiastic of them, Italy's military attaché, Colonel Marsengo, began to applaud and to shout "Bravo! Bravo!" at the top of his voice.

. . . At 9 A.M. the Sixteenth Regiment, with the division staff, preceded by a motorized machine-gun platoon, entered the town of Lutsk.[30]

It was a characteristic of Denikin never to mention himself in describing one of the outstanding exploits of his division. There are, however, eyewitness reports of his participation in the action. "Denikin," wrote one observer, "joined in the assault of Lutsk's fortified position and was the first to enter the town in his car, overtaking a number of routed Austrians on the way. He was in Lutsk's main square to welcome his riflemen and the companies of an adjoining corps." [31]

In the first three days of the advance, Kaledin's Eighth Army had penetrated the Austro-Hungarian positions by fifty kilometers, on a front eighty kilometers wide.

General Denikin wrote to his fiancée: "I hear my riflemen commented upon from all sides with a feeling of profound satisfaction and joy. A mist of legend already surrounds their exceptional and very real feats. I bless the fate which gave me such troops to lead into battle.

"Our successes at the southwestern front will unquestionably lead to a wider offensive; and will perhaps help to spur on our allies as well." [32]

For his participation in the capture of Lutsk, Denikin received a rare decoration—the Sword of St. George Studded with Diamonds. This was an award given only for feats in which personal valor contributed to important general results.

The Brusilov offensive, known also as the Lutsk breakthrough, lasted nearly four months. "The tactical results of this action were enormous," wrote the historian Golovin. "Our forces captured 8,924 officers, 408,000 soldiers, 581 cannon, 17,795 machine guns, 448 bomb-throwers and mortars. The territory taken away from the enemy exceeded 25,000 square kilometers. None of the offiensives of our allies in 1915, 1916, or 1917 ever achieved similar results." [33]

The consequences of the Brusilov success exceeded all expectations. Italy was saved. The Austro-Hungarian forces were on the verge of disintegration. To save their allies from complete defeat, the Germans transferred eighteen of their divisions from the French to the Russian front. Pressure was also removed from the Allied front at Salonika by the redirection against Russia of 3½ German divisions and two of the more reliable Turkish divisions. Rumania, which had been sitting on the fence, waiting to see in what direction the wind of victory would blow, suddenly decided that Germany was losing the contest, and on August 27, declared war on the Central Powers. This was a serious blow to German morale. The fact that the notoriously calculating Rumanians dared to declare war on Germany showed how low the latter's stock had fallen. An even greater shock was the unexpected military aggressiveness displayed by the Russian army which the German General Staff had considered completely ineffective since the summer of 1915. Someone was obviously guilty of gross miscalculation! The German High Command replaced General von Falkenhayn by Field Marshal von Hindenburg. The latter's chief of staff, Ludendorff, became the actual brain behind Germany's subsequent war strategy.

All these events had a direct bearing on General Denikin's career. At the beginning of September, 1916, he was made commander of the Eighth Army Corps, and shortly after this, dispatched to the rescue of the Rumanian army.

Many Russian military leaders, including General Alekseev and Denikin himself, were opposed to Rumania's involvement in the war on the side of the Allies. Denikin considered that Rumania could be more useful to the Entente as a neutral power than as an ally, and proved to be right. Anxious to teach the Rumanians a good lesson and to show the world that they could still hold the upper hand, the Germans managed to occupy most of Rumania, including Bucharest, by the end of December, 1916. This, in turn, obliged Russia to come to the aid of its new ally by transferring twenty divisions to the Rumanian front.

Despite his promotion, Denikin was deeply grieved at having to leave his beloved Iron Division. For two years his life had been linked with the lives of his riflemen, and his personal destiny was intertwined with theirs. His leadership and victories were all part of their unified war comradeship, deep mutual attachment, and pride in their common achievements. In speaking of his long years of warfare, at the end of an eventful life, Denikin said that the two years with the Iron Division had been the best years of his life.

General Brusilov, who threw in his lot with the Bolsheviks following the October revolution, and was antagonistic to Denikin after that time, nevertheless recognized his valor in the memoirs he wrote in the Soviet Union.

"The Fourth [Iron] Rifle Division," wrote the General, "always came to my rescue at critical moments and I consistently entrusted it with the most difficult tasks, which it carried out unerringly in each instance." [34]

"Denikin, who subsequently played such an important role, was a good, extremely quick-witted and determined fighting general." [35]

But later, in the same book, Brusilov found it necessary to dilute his praise of General Denikin considerably, presumably in order to placate the Soviet government and to reassure it in regard to his own political trustworthiness. Brusilov charged Denikin with being a self-seeking careerist who claimed for himself the military prowess of others. However, we have too much evidence to the contrary to take this allegation seriously.

An Eighth Army officer who knew Denikin particularly well as a result of their frequent collaboration left the following portrait of the General on active duty:

> There was no operation which he did not accomplish brilliantly, nor a single engagement which he did not win. I was at that time deputy chief of General Brusilov's staff. I frequently conferred with Denikin by field telephone on the coordination of his activities with those of adjoining units, especially when his help was needed to rescue them in a tight spot. There never was an instance of Denikin saying that his soldiers were too tired or asking to be assisted by reserve troops.
>
> He was natural and completely untheatrical with his men. His orders were short and matter-of-fact, but forceful and clear. He was always calm in action and always managed to be in the places where his presence was most needed. . . . He did not hesitate to criticize directives which seemed inexpedient to him, but did so with tact, without offending or disparaging anyone. . . . Denikin knew how to appraise a situation soberly, eliminating all unimportant details. He never lost his presence of mind in a difficult moment, but immediately took the necessary measures to offset the impending danger.[36]

The Eighth Army Corps and its newly appointed commander, General Denikin, reached Rumania at a time when it was being segmented by the simultaneous advance from different directions of two German armies, commanded by General Mackensen and General von Falkenhayn.

Denikin, who spent several months in combat near Buzeo, Rymnik, and Fokshan, and at different times had two Rumanian corps under his command, later wrote the following impressions of the Rumanian army:

"The lessons of the World War, which had been taking place under their eyes, were completely ignored by the Rumanian army; its equipment and supplies were criminally inadequate; it had a few good generals, an effeminate officer corps, and excellent soldiers." [37]

Despite all the hardships he had been through in the last two years, conditions at the Rumanian front proved worse than anything Denikin had expected. What was left of Rumania was in a state of total collapse. The transport of supplies and foodstuffs from Russia was disrupted both by the poor condition of Russian railroads and by the chaotic state of all Rumanian means of communication. Horses died of hunger, men froze without boots and warm underwear, and fell ill by the thousand. Small wonder that in this situation Rumania failed to charm the General. "An inhospitable country, unfriendly people, and considerable chaos," he wrote to his fiancée; "the consensus of opinion is that bad as things seemed at home, abroad they proved even worse.[38]

In one of his letters concerning the Russian advance on the south-western front, Denikin had expressed the hope that this success might lead to a wider offensive and possibly "spur on" the Allies.

In the course of the war, Russian public opinion went through several phases in its attitude toward the Allies. At the beginning it was enthusiastic and ready for sacrifice in the pursuit of a common goal. Later, the enthusiasm cooled, but there remained a firm determination to fulfill unreservedly all Russian obligations to the Allies, regardless of the difficulties and risks involved. Finally, as was noted by Golovin, the realization that the Allies were not prepared to reciprocate the Russian army's efforts—by diverting some of Germany's forces in their own direction—gradually gave rise to doubts, which later changed into mistrust.

The Germans had always come to the Austrians' rescue, and the Russians to that of their allies, by drawing off the enemy forces attacking them. Yet, these allies had never displayed a similar initiative when conditions at the Russian front became critical. Their one unsuccessful attempt to land troops at Gallipoli was not taken into consideration. The Russian public accused them of egoism, while more and more soldiers at the front picked up the phrase (possibly dreamed up by German propaganda) that "the Allies had decided to fight to the last drop of Russian blood." This, of course, lowered the fighting spirit of the soldier masses.

It should be noted, however, that although Denikin anxiously desired more active strategic assistance from the Allies, he had never accused them of trying to win the war at Russia's expense.

Even more important than their lack of confidence in the Allies, was the Russians' lack of confidence in their own government.

Ever since the Tsar had left the capital for the *Stavka* in the fall of 1915, the Tsarina had begun to interfere with extraordinary insistence in the affairs of state. She chose the candidates for ministerial posts on the advice of her entourage, and with rare exceptions, got them approved by the Tsar. The nominations of these negative, often unworthy persons, who were totally unprepared for their new responsibilities, were sharply condemned by the public and by the Duma. Starting in the fall of 1916, the latter became the scene of violent protests not only against government executives, but against the person of the Tsarina herself, and of the "dark forces" surrounding the throne. The authority and prestige of the dynasty were deteriorating with extraordinary rapidity. The Progressive Bloc, formed in 1915 by members of the Cadet, Octobrist, and even conservative elements of the Duma and Council of the Empire, demanded the formation of a ministry "enjoying the confidence of the nation," which would collaborate with the legislative branch in implementing a new program of action. The moderately conservative circles and some members of the imperial family were increasingly in favor of such measures. Several of the grand dukes, realizing that both the nation and the dynasty were in danger, frankly and insistently expressed to the Tsar their conviction of the need for drastic changes, but Tsar Nicholas stubbornly resisted all such advice. Rasputin, because of his personality and his influence at court, became an object of hatred, especially on the part of those who wished to preserve the monarchy. From the tribune of the Duma, Milyukov flung at the government and the Tsarina his accusation of "stupidity or treason?" The monarchist member, Purishkevich, demanded the removal of Rasputin. The murder of the latter, in which Grand Duke Dimitri Pavlovich, Prince Yussoupov (married to the Tsar's niece), and Purishkevich himself participated, increased the isolation of the Tsar and his wife. The imperial couple's moral and political solitude became complete.

In the meantime, Guchkov, Prince Lvov, and other representatives of such groups as the Union of *Zemstvos,* the Union of Towns, and the War Industries Committee, which had played an important part in setting Russian war industry on its feet, were insisting on a ministry which would not only enjoy the confidence of the nation, but also be directly responsible to the Duma. Having lost all hope of collaborating with the Tsar, they decided to get rid of him, and made use of their widespread connections in the army and in political circles to spread extensive propaganda against the regime. The Duma's antigovernment pronouncements, though kept out of the newspapers by censorship, were reproduced and circulated by them throughout the country.

Rumors were also circulated concerning the Tsarina, her demands for a separate peace, and the like. After the revolution, a special commission charged by the Provisional Government with investigating the whole matter, found to its disappointment that these rumors had been completely unfounded and wickedly slanderous. The Tsarina, though German by birth, was loyal to Russia and totally opposed to the idea of a separate peace.

The antigovernment speeches circulated by Guchkov and his associates in all parts of Russia and its army, also reached Denikin in far-off Rumania. He noted the fact briefly and without comment in a letter to his fiancée written on December 27, 1916:

"I read the Duma speeches (very aggressive) in lithographic form." On January 12, 1917, he wrote, "Things at home are getting completely out of hand. *They are cutting off the limb on which they have been sitting from times immemorial* [italics added]." And on January 7, 1917, he asked, "What moral forces can the army draw from this collapse? We need inspiration, confidence."

Denikin, who kept out of politics as a matter of principle and had no part in any behind-the-scenes intrigues against the government, was sick at heart at the realization of what was happening to his country. And to his fear of a collapse of the government in the midst of war, was added the premonition of the effect such a collapse would have on the army.

Thus began the year 1917, the fearful year of reckoning for past sins, mistakes, and failures; the year also which elevated Denikin to the role he was to assume in the Russian civil war.

I V

THE YEAR OF

RECKONING

The year 1917 began in an atmosphere of dark premonition, but at that time neither Denikin nor anyone else could foresee the scope and tempo of the events to come.

The impending storm finally broke over Russia. Its thunder struck the capital and resounded throughout the country; a revolution had begun in Petrograd. "Events are moving with unexpected swiftness and threatening force," wrote Denikin to his fiancée on March 4. "May God grant happiness to Russia!"

A page of history has been turned [he continued four days later]. "The first impression is overwhelming in its unexpectedness and tremendous scope. The troops, however, have generally reacted to the events very calmly. They are careful in expressing their opinions, but some currents of thought can be clearly detected in the mood of the masses:

1. There is no turning back.

2. The country will achieve a form of government worthy of a great people: probably a constitutional monarchy.

3. Pro-German influence at court will end and the war will continue to a victorious end.

My constant and sincere hope had been that Russia would reach these goals by evolutionary and not by revolutionary means [italics added]. This hope was not fulfilled. The dark forces which, in their madness, were trying to turn back the clock of history, have only hastened the inevitable outcome.

We must beware of one thing now: the possibility that the scum hiding behind the banners of the liberation movement will try to impede the nation's return to normality. . . . How wonderful for Russia if this historic cycle were to close with the tragic events in the capital and allow the country to enter a new era without further upheavals.

These reflections, expressed by Denikin in a personal letter, show to what extent the command personnel of the army was remote from the capital and unaware of its rapidly changing moods. The sequence of political events in the center of Russia flickered and changed with cinematographic speed. By March 8, when Denikin's letter was written, the political climate in Petrograd had already undergone such changes that the prospect of a constitutional monarchy in Russia had become improbable.

The *Stavka* in Mogilev was doing its best to keep the senior commanders of the army informed about the events in Petrograd. Unfortunately the *Stavka* itself, as will be seen later, was far from being correctly informed at all times. As a result, the most contradictory and fantastic rumors circulated at the front. One distressing aspect of the far-reaching changes occurring in the country was becoming increasingly evident to the officer corps: The morale of the army was deteriorating.

There exists a whole literature concerning the complex history of 1917 in Russia. This book will limit itself to a short chronology of the February events, giving a detailed account only of that phase in their development which directly affected the Russian army and Denikin himself.

As a result of the strikes which flared up in Petrograd after February 20, mobs of workmen invaded the city streets. Crowds of them demonstrated in various parts of the capital, carrying red banners and singing revolutionary songs. Public order in the city was entrusted to the police and to Petrograd's military garrison, which consisted, at that time, of the reserve battalions of several imperial guard regiments. The imperial guard continued to fight valiantly on the southwestern front despite heavy losses at the beginning of the war, but its reserve units, like many army sections stationed at the rear, were becoming demoralized and undisciplined. The fact that the imperial government counted on their firmness in restoring order was an example of the thoughtlessness with which it was sliding toward a revolution.

On February 26, an imperial decree adjourned the session of the State Duma.

On February 27, disturbances in the street became menacing. A series of momentous events took place. The Volynsky regiment rebelled and was soon followed by other units of the Petrograd garrison; some officers were killed. The government and Petrograd's military authorities showed a complete lack of initiative. Mobs stormed the police precincts, ruthlessly murdering the policemen; they emptied the prisons not only of political prisoners but of ordinary criminals as well, and set fire to the Regional Courthouse. Anarchy was rampant.[1] There were no leaders—only a triumphant mob. The soldiers' uprising had touched off a revolution which took everyone by surprise, and no one more so than the professional revolutionaries themselves.

The Duma, aware and fearful of possible reprisals if the government regained the upper hand, nevertheless reacted to the pressure of events by forming a Provisional Committee of the State Duma. The Committee was composed of members of the Progressive Bloc, representing the Cadet and Octobrist parties; it also included the *Trudovik* Kerensky and the *Menshevik* Chkheidze.

The Committee's resolve to create a new government without the authorization of the still-reigning monarch was an act of insubordination. By their participation, the Committee's members had thrown in their lot with the revolutionary movement which many of them had wanted to forestall.

At the same time as the formation of the Provisional Committee of the Duma (and before the formation of the Provisional Government), there came into existence, on February 27, the Soviet of Workers' Deputies, soon to be renamed the Soviet of Workers' and Soldiers' Deputies. It established its quarters in the Tauride Palace, the seat of the State Duma. It was not elected, but came into being as it did in 1905, through the initiative of the socialists, of whom Mensheviks and Socialist Revolutionaries formed a majority. Without mandates or any kind of delegated authority, a group of radically oriented intellectuals, who happened to attend the first meeting of the Soviet, elected its presidium.

Three members of the Duma were among those elected: the Mensheviks Chkheidze and Skobelev, and the *Trudovik* Kerensky. Chkheidze, elected chairman of the Soviet, resigned from his minor role in the Provisional Committee of the Duma. Kerensky, who was voted deputy chairman of the Soviet, retained his Duma functions and became the link between the two organizations.

It was clear from the beginning that the Soviet and the Committee of the Duma, both of which came into being on the same day and at the same place, would not be able to coexist peacefully under one roof. Despite its unofficial status, the Soviet systematically began to usurp the functions of the new government which was formed by the Provisional Committee of the Duma. It consciously followed the turbulent stream of social upheaval, whereas the Provisional Government at that juncture still hoped to remain within the limits of a bourgeois, or liberal, democratic revolution. And while the government tried to speak of obligations, the Soviet clamored for rights. Born in the rebellious underground, the Soviet, by Denikin's definition, was the absolute negation of the old rgime.

Having become a member of the Provisional Government, Kerensky did not give up his position as deputy chairman of the Soviet. Like an acrobat on a tightrope, he tried to juggle and keep his balance in his self-appointed role of intermediary between two widely divergent forces. He soon switched from the *Trudovik* party to the more powerful Socialist Revolutionaries, and as Milyukov sarcastically put it, "prepared himself for the part of revolutionary hostage in the bourgeois camp." The Soviet was opposed to his participation in the government, but Kerensky was determined to obtain

its approval at all costs, and finally succeeded. Again according to Milyukov, who based his information on the memoirs of Sukhanov, Mstislavsky,
and other participants in the Soviet's meetings, Kerensky begged for the
latter's confidence and support "in a tremulous voice, passing from a dying
whisper to a thrilling crescendo. . . . 'I cannot live without the people,'
he intoned; 'at the moment when you begin to doubt me, slay me!' " [2]

This was a time of emotional outpourings. People who had long been
silent began to speak and spoke endlessly . . . and delighted in the sound
of their own voices.

By February 28 most of the Tsar's ministers had already been arrested.
The Tsar, consumed with worry for the Tsarina and his children, decided
to leave the *Stavka* for Tsarskoie Selo, but orders from Petrograd prevented his train from reaching the capital. Instead of returning to the
Stavka, the Tsar went to Pskov, where the headquarters of the northern
front, commanded by General Ruzsky, were located. Ruzsky thereby
became a witness and an active participant in the drama of the last days
of the reign of Nicholas II.

Before leaving the *Stavka,* on February 28, the Tsar had named General
N. I. Ivànov commander in chief of the Petrograd military district and endowed him with "exceptional powers" for quelling the rebellion. Ivànov
left the *Stavka* with a battalion composed of soldiers decorated with the
Order of St. George, who were by that token considered the most reliable
element in the army. In addition, each of the commanders of the northern
and western fronts was to send two cavalry and two infantry regiments to
Ivànov's assistance in Petrograd. On the day after his arrival in Pskov,
however, the Tsar canceled his order for moving these troops to Petrograd.
He also telegraphed Ivànov to withhold any action in the capital pending
his own return to Tsarskoie Selo.

When the news reached Petrograd that the movement of troops designed
to quell the rebellion had been canceled, the revolutionary elements immediately increased their demands. No longer content with asking for a
ministry responsible to the elected chambers and for a cabinet formed by
the President of the Duma, they demanded the abdication of the Tsar in
favor of his son, with the Tsar's brother—Grand Duke Michael—as
regent. At this point, the chief of staff of the High Command, General
Alekseev, under the pressure of events in the capital and at the insistence
of General Ruzsky, assumed the responsibility for an extremely serious
step. He telegraphed the commanders in chief of all the fronts requesting
the opinion of each of them on the existing crisis. The text of his telegram,
dated March 2, follows:

His Majesty is in Pskov, where he has expressed his consent to issue a manifesto complying with the popular desire for the establishment of a ministry
responsibile to the representative chambers and entrusting the President of
the State Duma with the formation of a new cabinet.
Having been advised of this decision by the commander in chief of the

northern front, the President of the State Duma answered by telegram, at three thirty this second of March, that the issuance of such a manifesto would have been timely on February 27; at the present time, however, it is too late for such an act, as one of the great revolutions is already in progress; the passions of the populace are difficult to curb; the troops are demoralized. Although there is still confidence in the President of the State Duma, he fears that it will be impossible to curb the passions of the populace. The dynastic problem is at stake and the war can be continued to a victorious end only by fulfilling the demands concerning the abdication in favor of the son with Michael Aleksandrovich as regent. The situation does not appear to allow for a different solution. . . . It is imperative to save the field forces from disintegration; to continue fighting our external enemies to the end; to save Russia's independence and the fate of the dynasty. This must be our first concern, even at the cost of major concessions. If you share this point of view, will you be kind enough to telegraph very urgently your loyal request to His Majesty through the commander in chief of the northern front, notifying me concurrently.

I repeat that the loss of each minute may be fatal to Russia's existence and that it is imperative to unify the thinking and the aims of the commanders of the field forces and to save the army from wavering and possible failure in the performance of its duty. The army must concentrate all its strength on fighting our external enemies, and a solution of our internal problems should save it from the temptation to participate in an upheaval which can be achieved less painfully with the help of a decision from above.[3]

General Alekseev did not have a clear idea of what was going on in the capital when he dispatched this message, and the commanders in chief who received it were even less well informed. Alekseev's principal source of information was the president of the State Duma M. V. Rodzianko (mainly by way of General Ruzsky, in Pskov, where the Tsar was at that time).

At first, Rodzianko, a former guards officer and a confirmed monarchist, had made sincere efforts to save the throne, but later circumstances involved him against his will in a revolutionary course of action. He felt that he was losing ground to the socialists of the Soviet of Workers' Deputies and realized that he no longer could cope with the problem of guiding the revolutionary movement toward a constitutional monarchy. On the one hand, Rodzianko saw the menace of approaching chaos; on the other, he was afraid that the repression of Petrograd's military uprising by troops dispatched from the front and loyal to the throne would call forth a reaction and repressive measures toward all those who in some measure had joined the insurrection, including the Provisional Committee of the State Duma, with Rodzianko and his associates. Pressed by danger from all sides, he lost his bearings. Yet, in dealing with the *Stavka* whose neutrality was essential to all those who had joined the revolution, Rodzianko drew for Alekseev a consciously distorted picture of the existing political situation. Alekseev was given the impression that the Progressive

Bloc, with Rodzianko at its head, had somehow succeeded in securing the confidence of the popular movement, but that at the moment it was menaced by danger from the left. In order to retain the leadership of the movement in the hands of the moderates, to contain "the passions of the populace," and to pursue the war to a "victorious end," it was therefore necessary to apply a drastic measure: the Tsar's abdication in favor of his son, under the regency of his brother.

It was on the strength of the erroneous conviction that the power of the crumbling regime had fallen into the hands of Rodzianko and the Progressive Bloc, that Alekseev dispatched his telegram to the commanders in chief of the army and that they, in turn, pronounced themselves for the abdication.

General Ruzsky submitted the opinions of the commanders in chief to the Tsar on March 2. Faced with the evidence that even his High Command had lost faith in him, the Tsar ordered the immediate preparation of a manifesto announcing his abdication in favor of the Tsarevich Alexis. However, having found out that two representatives of the Duma's Provisional Committee, Guchkov and Shulgin, were on their way to Pskov, he held up the publication of the manifesto pending an interview with them. And in that interview he declared, quite unexpectedly, that he had thought over his decision to abdicate in favor of the Tsarevich, and realizing that he could not face a separation from his son, had decided to abdicate in his own and in his son's name in favor of his brother.

The effect of this announcement was—stunning. Nevertheless, the Duma representatives, deferring to the Tsar's paternal feelings, accepted the monarch's last decision and returned to Petrograd with the altered and signed manifesto by which the throne passed to Grand Duke Michael Alexandrovich. In order to legalize a *fait accompli* and to satisfy the wishes of the Provisional Committee of the Duma, the Tsar, before signing his act of abdication, issued a decree appointing Prince G. E. Lvov (and not Rodzianko) President of the Council of Ministers (i.e., Prime Minister). Another decree named Grand Duke Nicholas to the post of Supreme Commander in Chief. Both documents were dated March 2.

It never occurred to those present that by the law of succession, the Tsar could renounce his own rights to the throne but could not do so for his son. The abdication document itself was therefore illegal, besides dealing a fatal blow to the dynasty.

The text of the documents was immediately telegraphed by the *Stavka* to the commanders in chief of all the fronts.

In the meantime, General Alekseev was becoming aware that the power which Rodzianko and the moderate liberals of the Duma were hoping to capture, was slipping through their fingers, and that they did not have the strength to oppose the leftist parties of the Soviet of Workers' and Soldiers' Deputies.

Alekseev's worry over the political fluctuations in the capital is clearly evident in his telegram of March 3 to the commanders in chief at the army fronts:

The President of the State Duma communicated to me by telegram that events in Petrograd are far from calm, the situation is precarious and confusing. Therefore, he insistently requests not to circulate the manifesto, which was signed March 2 and already communicated to the commanders in chief, and to withhold its publication. The reason for his insistence is more clearly and precisely stated in the telegram conversation of the President of the Duma with the commander in chief of the northern front [General Ruzsky]; copy of said conversation has just been received by me. Rodzianko says that the regency of the Grand Duke and coming to the throne of the Heir Apparent might have been tolerated, but that the candidacy of the Grand Duke for the role of Emperor is not acceptable to anyone and a civil war is probable.

Alekseev went on to make it clear that on the strength of his communications with the President of the State Duma, he had come to the conclusion that the Provisional Committee of the Duma lacked unity, that the leftist parties of the Soviet of Workers' and Soldiers' Deputies had a strong influence on it and were "putting powerful pressure" on the President of the Duma and its Provisional Committee—Rodzianko—whose own reports "were not frank and sincere." Alekseev concluded that "the withdrawal of a previously announced manifesto could lead to loss of confidence and low morale in fighting the external enemy." [4]

General Alekseev realized that the prestige of his name and position had been used for political purposes to which he was opposed. This became especially clear when he noted to his distress that the Progressive Bloc, with whose views he had sympathized, was beginning to lose ground and to surrender its positions to socialist pressure.

General Lukomsky, Alekseev's closest associate at the *Stavka*, testified later that "General Alekseev, returning to his office after dispatching this telegram, said, 'I shall never forgive myself for having believed in the integrity of certain people, and acting on their advice, having dispatched my telegram to the commanders in chief on the subject of the Tsar's abdication.' " [5]

This was the first evidence of mutual mistrust between the emerging new governing power and the army command. This initial rift was soon to become an unbridgeable gulf.

General Alekseev's decision to send the telegram of March 2 had placed on him the responsibility of mediating between the Tsar and his rebellious capital. He had dictated terms to the monarch without imposing any conditions on the insurgents.

The *Stavka*, whose members had been deeply concerned with the inadequacy of the deposed regime, had no aspirations to restore it. At that moment, however, the High Command had not lost its authority and control over the army in the field, which still retained its discipline. It was, therefore, in a position to dictate its own terms to the revolutionary elements. One of the reasons for Alekseev's failure to do so was his fear of provoking a civil war, thus weakening Russia's resistance at the front. Nevertheless, both of these fears became reality when uncontrollable chaos broke over the country. At the end of 1917, and under much less favorable circumstances, Alekseev was faced with the task of uniting the remnants of the officer corps, military cadets, students and patriotic intellectuals into a Volunteer Army to fight the forces of anarchy. The fact that the High Command had failed to contain the conflict by dealing firmly with the Petrograd Soviet and the city's demoralized garrison, had undermined its authority which, several months later, General Kornilov tried in vain to restore.

In Denikin's opinion, it was at this moment of inertia that "the *Stavka* let the control of the army slip out of its hands." [6]

On March 3, the day that Alekseev telegraphed his doubts and misgivings at the turn of events in Petrograd to the army commanders, the curtain came down on the last act of the reign of the Romanov dynasty: Grand Duke Michael Aleksandrovich declined to accept the throne.

On the same day, he announced to the people that he would agree to become tsar only at the request of a Constituent Assembly, and summoned "all citizens of the Russian state to submit themselves to the Provisional Government." [7]

As early as March 1, twenty-four hours before the abdication of Nicholas II, the Soviet of Workers' and Soldiers' Deputies issued its Order No. 1 (as it came to be known); although nominally addressed to the Petrograd garrison, this order was dispatched to all army units at the front and at the rear "for immediate and exact implementation." [8]

Order No. 1 stipulated that the "lower ranks" of all army and navy units elect their representatives, one for each company, to the Soviet of Workers' and Soldiers' Deputies; that the political activity of all army and navy units be under complete control of the Soviet; that orders issued by the newly created military commission of the State Duma be complied with only in those cases when they did not conflict with orders issued by the Soviet; that arms (rifles, machine guns, armored cars, and so on) be under control of soldiers' committees, and under no circumstances be given to officers; that discipline be maintained while on duty, but that otherwise soldiers were to enjoy all civil rights of private citizens, discontinue saluting officers and standing at attention; that all misunderstandings between officers and men be reported by the latter to the company committees.

This order led, in Denikin's words to the transfer of actual military power to the soldiers' committees and to the election of officers to command posts by the soldiers. It gave the first and major impetus to the disintegration of the army.

Unlike the imperial government, which had not learned from past experience, the Soviet of Workers' and Soldiers' Deputies was fully aware that to a large extent, the revolution of 1905 had failed because the troops remained loyal. Although military insurrections did break out in various parts of Russia at that time, the army as a whole had remained the bulwark of the state.

Realizing this fact, the Soviet proceeded without delay to undermine the authority of the commanders and of the officer corps and to implement the ideas which had long been evolving in Russia's political underground. Shortly after issuing Order No. 1, the Soviet, which feared a possible counterrevolution, sent to the front a whole stream of socialist agitators chosen from among the intellectuals who had avoided active duty. Their mission was to undermine the authority of the officers.

The Petrograd Soviet also forced the Provisional Government to remove Grand Duke Nicholas from the post of Supreme Commander in Chief, although his nomination a few days earlier had been made with the approval of a majority of the Provisional Committee of the Duma.

A representative of the fallen dynasty no longer had a place in the new Russia.

Under pressure from the Soviet, the Provisional Government agreed not to send to the front the reserve units which formed Petrograd's garrison, but to leave them in the capital "to defend the revolution." Besides being of tactical advantage to the Soviet, this decision offered a reward to these disaffected soldiers for their role in the revolutionary movement, i.e., for their participation in a military insurrection in wartime. Later the Petrograd garrison amply repaid their benefactors by siding with the Bolsheviks in the October revolution.

Let us go back to the first days of the revolution, when the demoralizing activity of the Soviet had not yet reached the army. General Denikin has left us a vivid description of the reaction of the army at the front to the fall of the monarchy:

The men were astounded—there is no other word to describe the first impression made on them by the promulgation of the manifesto. They showed neither joy nor sorrow, only quiet, concentrated silence. Thus did the regiments of the Fourteenth and Fifteenth divisions receive the news of their Tsar's abdication. But—occasionally, one of the rifles held at attention wavered and tears coursed down the cheeks of an old soldier. . . .

Many find it surprising and incomprehensible that an army brought up in the traditions of a centuries-old monarchy, not only failed to rise to its defense in a body, but did not even do so in separate instances. In short, that the army did not create its own Vendée.

. . . It would be a mistake to think that the army was fully prepared to accept a temporary "democratic republic" and that it did not contain "loyal units" and "loyal leaders" who were willing to enter the fray. They unquestionably existed, but two factors served to discourage them from action: one was the apparent legality of both abdications, the last of which, moreover, exhorted them to submit to the Provisional Government "invested with full power," and thus reduced the monarchists to helplessness; the second factor was the fear that a civil war would expose the front to the enemy. At that time the army obeyed its leaders, and the latter—General Alekseev and all the commanders in chief—accepted the new government. Grand Duke Nicholas, newly returned to the post of Supreme Commander, wrote in his first order of the day: "The power is vested in our new government. I, as Supreme Commander, have recognized it for the good of our motherland, thus setting the example of our military duty. I order all ranks of our valiant army and navy to submit to the established government unfailingly through their direct superiors. Only then will God grant us victory." [9]

The moods described by General Denikin predominated among the officers and a percentage of the army's old regular soldiers. As regards the soldier masses, Denikin thought them too backward to have a clear conception of the events, too inert to react to them immediately, and not ready, therefore, to form an opinion.

It took but a couple of months, however, for socialist propaganda to prod that inert mass into action.

The letter from Denikin partially quoted at the beginning of this chapter gives us an indication of his personal reaction to the revolution.

He was not an admirer of the old regime, being fully aware of its weaknesses and mistakes. He realized the need, especially in wartime, for a strong national government enjoying the confidence of all classes. He observed with mounting dismay and indignation the unreasonable actions and lack of creative planning of the government, which antagonized even the law-abiding elements of the nation.

"An unrestrained bacchanalia," wrote Denikin, "a kind of sadism of power indulged in by the string of high officials, protégés of Rasputin, led to the absence, in 1917, of a single political party or a single class or estate on which the government could lean for support. Everybody was against it: Purishkevich and Chkheidze, the nobility and gentry as well as the organized workers, the grand dukes and the more literate soldiers." [10]

And yet, to the very last moment, Denikin hoped that the obsolete principles and methods of the old regime could be replaced by evolutionary and not by revolutionary means. He knew Russian history well, and having witnessed the anarchy of 1905, knew that it would not be possible for his backward country to adjust overnight to the most progressive forms of democracy and political freedom. He did not share the illusions of moderate socialists who naïvely believed that the fall of tsarism would give way—almost immediately—to an era of unlimited freedom in a country in which three-quarters of the people were still ignorant and uneducated. Small wonder, then, that his first reaction to the Petrograd uprising was fear that "the scum hiding behind the banners of the liberation movement will try to impede the nation's return to normality." He would have liked Russia to adopt a constitutional monarchy of the British type; but his thinking was not dominated by the form of government that would eventually prevail. His first concern was for his country, threatened with deadly danger by its external foe, German imperialism. He therefore considered it imperative to continue the war. The Provisional Government expressed similar views and Denikin accepted it sincerely and wholeheartedly. Like most of the army's commanding generals, he was at first completely loyal to the new government.

He soon became aware, however, that besides the official government in the capital, there functioned the unofficial but aggressive power of the Soviet of Workers' and Soldiers' Deputies, whose views and aims radically differed from his own. He understood that the Provisional Government was helpless, especially on the local level, without the colossal administrative machinery which the revolution had destroyed, and was aware that in all of Russia's provinces this void was being filled by Soviet sympathizers.

At last, heartsick and indignant at the blow which Order No. 1 and the Soviet's subsequent activity had dealt to the army, Denikin decided to take an open stand against the forces that were seeking to disintegrate it.

He did not reach this decision at once, but with the passage of time, came to realize more and more clearly that Russia was approaching one of those rare crossroads of history at which a country's traditional concepts of morality, law, and order encounter the sweeping onslaught and devastating chaos of new utopian ideas. He also understood that no one would be exempt from the consequences of this fearsome confrontation.

Denikin felt that the February revolution, so proudly surnamed "the great and bloodless," "had engendered a storm and called forth from the abyss all the spirits of evil." [11]

Denikin's nature did not allow for vacillation or opportunism in such matters. He saw only one way to fulfill his civic duty, and having reached a decision, he remained faithful to it until the end.

V

NEW TRENDS

On March 18, sixteen days after the Tsar's abdication, Denikin received a telegram at his Rumanian headquarters requesting his immediate arrival in Petrograd for an interview with the Minister of War of the Provisional Government. The General left for the capital that same night, anxiously wondering about the reason for this unexpected summons. As his train stood in the Kiev station, he heard the shouts of news vendors: "Extra! . . . General Denikin named chief of staff of the Supreme Commander."

Upon his arrival in Petrograd, Denikin immediately reported to the new Minister of War, A. I. Guchkov, whom he had never even met. In the course of their conversation, Guchkov advised him that there had been considerable dissension among the members of the Provisional Government, and the Provisional Committee of the State Duma, concerning the choice of a new Supreme Commander of the armed forces. Some of the members favored General Alekseev; others, and among them Rodzianko, were opposed to his nomination. The question was finally decided in favor of Alekseev, on condition that his "lack of firmness" would be counteracted by the presence of "a combat general in the role of chief of staff." The choice of such a general fell on Denikin.

Although the "news and gossip" column of the Kiev paper had prepared me to a certain extent for such an offer [wrote Denikin], I was, nevertheless, perturbed and even somewhat depressed by the scope of the functions which were so unexpectedly being thrust on me, and by the enormous moral responsibility which they implied. I tried to refuse the offer at length and in all sincerity and gave several sufficiently serious reasons for doing so: I had always served in active army units and their local staffs; I had been division and corps commander during the war and felt a real vocation and attraction to such combat duty in the field. On the other hand, I had no experience whatsoever in matters of politics, defense, and adminstration on such a huge, nationwide scale.[1]

Further in the conversation, Guchkov intimated that he had explained to Alekseev the motives underlying Denikin's nomination and had made it fairly clear to him that he had no choice but to accept it. This placed Denikin in a very delicate position in relation to his future superior, and he therefore reserved the right to withhold his decision prior to an interview with Alekseev. Their meeting took place at the *Stavka* on March 25.

Mikhail Vasilievich Alekseev (1857–1918), who was to have a major influence on Denikin's life, played an extremely important role in the conduct of World War I, in the abdication of the Tsar, and in the creation of the White movement in south Russia. Like Denikin, he was of very modest origins. Both men had grown up in poverty and had achieved success by their own efforts and natural ability. Impressions of Alekseev, jotted down by people who had met him for the first time, show us a man of short stature and compact build, with small eyes and a pronounced squint under his round eyeglasses. There was nothing martial in Alekseev's appearance, and his simple and accessible manner was refreshing. He was modest, very intelligent, and a great specialist in his field.

When the Tsar assumed supreme command of the armed forces, Alekseev, as chief of staff, became his closest assistant. At a time when Denikin was still far from the top of the military ladder in the limited role of a division commander, Alekseev had already become the *de facto* leader of Russia's armed forces. He was constantly involved in problems of national scope and significance, and could no longer avoid participating in the internal politics of the country, which were invading his field of action.

On March 25, when General Alekseev received Denikin as his prospective chief of staff, an undercurrent of strain and resentment could be felt in the conversation. General Denikin repeated all the arguments he had given Guchkov against his nomination, and assured Alekseev that he would consider it impossible to accept Guchkov's offer without Alekseev's wholehearted consent and approval.

Alekseev's reply was dry and evasive: "Well, if these are my orders. . . ." It was not in Denikin's nature to accept such an answer. He told Alekseev that he would not only refuse the nomination, but would make it clear that the entire responsibility for the refusal was his, in order to prevent any further friction between the Supreme Commander and the government. At this point, Alekseev's attitude changed completely, and he sincerely urged Denikin to accept. "Let us work together," he said, "I shall help you. At worst, should your work not satisfy you, nothing can prevent your transferring, a few months later, to the first acceptable vacancy in the army."

Denikin agreed, but for a while a sense of strain remained in the collaboration of the two generals. Alekseev could not help resenting the lack of confidence in him which underlay the government's enforced choice of his assistant. But as he came to know Denikin better, he saw that his new chief of staff did everything in his power to protect him from possible disagreement and trouble with the authorities in Petrograd. "In time," wrote Denikin later, "my relationship with Alekseev acquired an intimate warmth and mutual confidence which lasted until his death." [2]

What were the reasons for Denikin's unexpected rise to one of the top positions in the military hierarchy?

Unquestionably, his brilliant reputation as a combat general played a major part in the decision. The blows dealt to the enemy by Denikin in the course of the retreat of an army deprived of adequate ammunition, had amazed both the Russians and the Austro-Germans, and the dashing episodes of the two victories near Lutsk were common knowledge. As we have already seen, even Brusilov, who disliked Denikin, had to praise him in his memoirs.

Considerations of a purely political nature, however, also played an important part in the choice. The new Minister of War, Guchkov, though not personally acquainted with Denikin, was aware of the latter's reputation as a critic of the army's bureaucracy and outdated methods. Concurrently, the members of the new government, in their desire to conciliate the Soviet of Workers' and Soldiers' Deputies, hoped to find in Denikin an acceptance and even an idealization of the revolution as well as readiness to cooperate in the "democratization of the army." Denikin's peasant antecedents would also be favorably considered by the increasingly powerful Soviet.

They did not know at the time that General Denikin, who was critical of many aspects in the old regime and had accepted the February revolution "wholeheartedly and unreservedly," was at the same time totally opposed to the revolutionizing of the armed forces and considered that their "democratization" would result in disaster. If the government had hoped to exert some kind of control over the *Stavka* with Denikin's help, it was completely disappointed in its expectations.

Alekseev's was a complicated nature. He lacked the singlemindedness which characterized Denikin, and this may explain his hesitancy and occasional lack of firmness. We have already seen how these traits affected the position of the *Stavka* in relation to the Petrograd authorities after the February revolution.

Nevertheless, some of the personal experiences related by Alekseev to Denikin, and written down by the latter, testify that he unquestionably had the courage of his opinions.

Soon after the Tsar assumed the supreme command, the Tsarina Alexandra visited him at the *Stavka*. While walking in the garden with Alekseev, she took his arm and began speaking to him about Rasputin.

With some agitation [related Denikin], the Empress launched into an impassioned argument on Alekseev's mistaken attitude toward Rasputin. She tried to convince him that "the *staretz* was a wonderful and holy man" who was a victim of calumny; that he was devoted to the imperial family and that, most important of all, his visit would bring luck to the *Stavka*. . . . Alekseev replied that, so far as he was concerned, the question had long since been settled and that Rasputin's arrival at the *Stavka* would be immediately followed by his own resignation as chief of staff.

"Is this your final word?"

"Yes, definitely."

The Empress abruptly terminated the conversation and walked off without saying goodbye. According to Mikhail Vasilievich [Alekseev], this incident had an ill effect upon the Emperor's attitude toward him. Popular belief notwithstanding, their relations, which appeared excellent on the surface, held neither intimacy nor friendship, nor even particular confidence.*

Several times, Alekseev, who was distressed by the growing popular resentment against the regime and the throne, tried to go beyond the limits of a formal report and present the facts to the Emperor in their true perspective. At any mention of Rasputin or of the need for a responsible ministry, he would encounter the Emperor's well-known impenetrable glance and hear his impassive and final "I know."

In all military matters, however, the Emperor had complete confidence in Alekseev.[3]

When the Tsar, after his abdication in Pskov, returned for a few days to Mogilev to take leave of the personnel of the *Stavka*, General Alekseev met him with all the homage and deference befitting a monarch. At his orders, the routine of the *Stavka* continued as usual, the former Tsar was still addressed as "Your Majesty," and the portraits of the imperial family remained in their places. No shadow of a desire to curry favor with the new revolutionary power in the capital could be detected in Alekseev's manner, which was full of respectful attention toward the former Tsar.

The Tsar's farewell visit to the *Stavka* was marked by an extraordinary incident, which Denikin recorded after learning about it from General Alekseev:

No one will ever find out what emotional conflict went on in Nicholas II— father, monarch, and ordinary man—at the time of his meeting with Alekseev in Mogilev. Looking at Alekseev with kind, tired eyes, he said with a sort of diffidence, "I have changed my mind. Please send this telegram to Petrograd."

The message written by the Tsar in a clear, legible hand, gave his consent to the acceptance of the throne by his son Alexis. . . .

Alekseev left with the telegram but . . . did not dispatch it. It was too late: two manifestoes had already been made public to the country and to the army.

Alekseev showed the telegram to no one "to avoid instilling doubt," carried it in his wallet, and entrusted it to me when he resigned fom the High Command. This document, of great interest to future biographers of Nicholas II, was subsequently kept in a secret file of the deputy chief of staff's section of the *Stavka*.[4]

---

* Nevertheless, in writing to his wife, Nicholas II referred to Alekseev as "my cross-eyed friend," always spoke of him favorably, and considered his collaboration with him "breathtakingly interesting."

Some Russian émigré historians were surprised to hear of this document. A few of them conjectured that Denikin's testimony stemmed from a misunderstanding or mistake and that the document he saw and about which Alekseev told him may have been the first abdication, signed by the Tsar in favor of the Tsarevich on March 2 in Pskov. This version was never sent to Petrograd and was superseded by the abdication in the name of the Tsar and of his son, in favor of his brother Michael.[5]

Denikin's testimony, however, was later corroborated by a comparative outsider, Colonel D. N. Tikhobrazov, one of the officers attached to the *Stavka,* who happened to witness the entire incident. The unpublished manuscript of Tikhobrazov's memoirs is in the Columbia University Russian Archive. In his memoirs, Tikhobrazov not only relates in detail Nicholas II's conversation with Alekseev, but states that it took place in Mogilev on March 4, i.e. two days after the Tsar's abdication was signed in Pskov.[6]

The text of the last Tsar's unsent telegram was never published. We have no way of telling at present whether it has been lost or destroyed, or whether it is lying in some Soviet archive.

Mogilev, where the *Stavka* was located, was a small, quiet, rather picturesque provincial town, whose two sections faced each other across the Dnieper from the high, hilly sides of the river. According to tradition, its name was derived from the large number of tombs (*mogily*) and barrows which surrounded it and the excavation of which had brought to light some ancient and very rare Arab coins.

Until the revolution, the Tsar's residence at the *Stavka* was in the modest and simply furnished house of Mogilev's provincial governor. After the abdication, this house was occupied by Alekseev, Denikin, their aides, and secretaries. According to Denikin, they all lived there in "patriarchal simplicity" without any ceremonial. The only sign which distinguished the residence of the supreme commander from other houses in the town was the constant presence of two sentries at its entrance.

General Denikin served only two months in Mogilev, but it was in this city that his future role was shaped.

Having assumed his functions, the new chief of staff immersed himself in his complicated and often tedious duties, whose variety and scope he found at first quite overwhelming. He had to acquaint himself with the past and present history of numerous military, political, and economic problems; attend to current business; work out the plans of future military actions; listen to the reports of others and prepare his own; take important decisions; participate in various receptions; receive in his office countless military and civilian visitors—delegates of newly formed revolutionary organizations, petitioners who had been deprived of their positions by the new government, various business operators, in short the extraordinary assortment of people who came to the *Stavka* at that time.

Despite the good rapport established between Alekseev and Denikin, the latter was constantly irritated by one trait of Alekseev's character; he was either unable or unwilling to delegate any of the *Stavka*'s operations planning to his closest associates, but did all of the work himself.

Denikin, who was used to independent work and responsibility, finally brought the question into the open. General Alekseev was sincerely surprised: "Why, Anton Ivanovich, haven't I encouraged your fullest participation in my work?"

In the rest of the conversation summed up by Denikin, both generals "became emotional, remained good friends, but did not solve the problem." [7]

Anton Ivanovich put in seventeen hours a day of nerve-racking, intensive work, with no time for exercise. This is where the good health built up by three years of combat duty in the open air served him well. He had an exceptional capacity for work, and soon learned to cope with his new activity despite all its pressures and tensions. But he could not get used to and accept the so-called "democratization" of the army and instinctively rejected the innumerable "military reforms" that originated in the capital. They were decisions arrived at by the revolutionary government, without the *Stavka*'s advice or consent, with no thought of their consequences and their destructive effect on army discipline.

With the exception of purely strategic decisions, the *Stavka* had lost its power and influence in the first three weeks following the revolution and had become a mere instrument in the hands of the Minister of War.

The new Minister of War, Aleksandr Ivanovich Guchkov (1862–1936) was the first civilian to occupy this post. Guchkov's reputation as an energetic and successful organizer, with wide connections in military circles and a superior knowledge of army needs, seemingly qualified him to head Russia's military establishment and to strengthen its defenses, as did Carnot and his Committee of Public Safety in the French Revolution. Unfortunately, Guchkov's activity as Minister of War proved to be the very opposite of constructive and did not bear out the hopes of his supporters. He showed himself unable to resist the overwhelming pressure from the left, and instead of preserving the discipline of the army, gave up one position after another and ended by drifting with the current and currying the favor of the soldier masses. Having finally realized his total helplessness, tired and broken, he resigned in early May, 1917, leaving behind a bitter memory and the resentment of all the officers of the Russian army.

The "democratization" of the army began with a purge of its command under the slogan, "Make way for talent." Denikin stated that in the first few weeks following the February revolution, over a hundred and fifty generals were removed from active service, including seventy infantry and cavalry division commanders.

In implementing this purge, Guchkov used a list drawn up by a group of his close collaborators. These had paid less attention to the military ability of the generals in question than to personal and political considerations. A number of able and deserving but insufficiently flexible commanders were removed and replaced by political opportunists.

Guchkov founded a special board for passing reforms "conforming with the new regime" in the military establishment and named General Polivanov, the former Minister of War who had replaced Sukhomlinov in the tsarist government, as its president. Polivanov had lost no time in changing his political orientation after the revolution, and ended his career as the Soviet government's military expert at the conclusion of the peace with Poland in Riga in 1920. Denikin's opinion was that Polivanov and his colleagues vied with each other in abjectly currying the favor of their new masters.

For the "democratization" of the army they decreed the election of committees in all army units, created the office of army commissar, and, finally, proclaimed the "Declaration of the Rights of the Soldiers." This gave each serviceman the right to belong to any political organization and to express his political views freely when off duty. It guaranteed the delivery to soldiers of all printed matter without exception, abolished the obligatory saluting of officers, replacing it with "voluntary greetings," deprived the officers of the right to impose disciplinary measures, and gave the soldiers the right to "internal self-government" through elected regimental organizations. The Polivanov board decreed that the duties of soldiers' committees included "taking legal measures against the misuse and exceeding of power by any functionary in their unit." This enabled the soldiers not only to supervise every action of their officers but, sometimes, to interfere in purely strategic decisions.

The Polivanov board also required the soldiers' committees to be in constant communication with all political parties. The latter were to send speakers and party literature to army units in order to explain to the soldiers the programs of the various political parties and to prepare them for the forthcoming elections to the Constituent Assembly.

The result was the release of a flood of Bolshevik propaganda both at the front and in the rear guard of the army.

The Soviet's fear of a counterrevolution and its uncertainty about the political reliability of the army command, gave rise to the institution of commissars attached to the larger military units. Army commissars were chosen by mutual agreement of the government and the Soviet. Though technically responsible to both institutions, the commissars usually catered to the leftist orientation of the Soviet.

"Thus," wrote General Denikin, "the Russian army acquired three heterogeneous, mutually exclusive leaderships: the commander, the committee, and the commissar. The power of all three was illusory. It was overshadowed, morally crushed and weighted down by the sinister pressure of mob rule." [8]

Despite the effects of Order No. 1 and the process of "democratization" fostered by the Petrograd Soviet, the army at the front somehow still held together. Its disintegration gained momentum under the pressure of two forces, one of which was foreign and the other internal.

During the war, the German General Staff had spared no effort or expense to foster the Russian revolution. Ludendorff, whose pet dream it was, wrote in his memoirs that when the revolution finally occurred, "a great weight fell off my shoulders." Other excerpts from Ludendorff's writings all point in the same direction:

"It was necessary to develop through propaganda a spontaneous and pronounced desire for peace in the Russian army."

"Our first objective was to keep track of the process of disintegration in Russia, to assist in it, and to encourage Russia's attempts to find suitable grounds for concluding peace."

"We were convinced beforehand that the revolution would lower the combat effectiveness of the Russian army and our conviction was justified."

"Gradually, animated communications were established between the enemy trenches and our own on the whole enormous extent of the front. We continued to encourage the Russian army's thirst for peace." [9]

From the moment the revolution occurred, the German General Staff had systematically established a policy of fraternization at the Russian front. A whole set of special instructions was issued to commanding officers, and the soldiers sent to the Russian trenches under a flag of truce were politically reliable and conversant with Russian. Their peace propaganda followed a set pattern which included discussions about the meaninglessness of war, and the distribution in the Russian trenches of hundreds of thousands of defeatist pamphlets printed in Germany. The Germans asserted that only the Provisional Government and the generals would profit by the continuation of the war. Therefore, in order to end the war, it was necessary to eliminate both the government and the officer corps. In short, they advocated peace at the front and strife in the interior. At the same time, they carried out a careful study of Russian forces and positions.

The same idea of replacing the war against Russia's external enemies by a class war in her interior, was advocated with extraordinary energy by Lenin, who had arrived from Switzerland, by way of Germany, in a "sealed coach."

"Our government," wrote Ludendorff, "assumed a great responsibility in dispatching Lenin to Russia. It was justified from a military point of view: Russia had to be defeated!" [10]

Before leaving Switzerland, Lenin made a farewell speech in Zurich in which he called Kerensky a traitor to the revolution and denounced Chkheidze, the Menshevik chairman of the Petrograd Soviet, as having also entered the path of treason. Nevertheless, Chkheidze welcomed Lenin in the name of the Soviet upon his arrival at the Finland Station on the night of April 3. A band played the "Marseillaise," an honorary guard stood at attention, and a large crowd of confederates, well-wishers and the curious surrounded the station.

During this honeymoon of Russian emancipation, the Provisional Government raised no objections to the arrival of the man who had come to destroy it.

The next day, April 4, Lenin formulated his famous "April theses." Their content boiled down to the following: The republic which emerged as a result of the February revolution is not our republic; the war is not our war. The aim of the Bolsheviks is to overthrow the imperialist government, engage in a class war, transform the world war into a world revolution, and establish the dictatorship of the proletariat. All private land holdings are to be confiscated, all the land in the country is to be nationalized.

Lenin's oratory not only dumbfounded the moderate socialists, but embarrassed even the members of his own party. His enemies rubbed their hands in glee at what they considered the ravings of a maniac, which were bound to discredit him completely.

The officers were generally indignant at Lenin's arrival, and most of all indignant at the government which had permitted his return to Russia. As to Lenin himself, in those early April days, some officers considered him a paid German agent, others—a lunatic. No one realized how dangerous he really was.

Yet, Lenin's was not the voice of one crying in the wilderness. He proved to be the spokesman and unquestionable leader of a movement whose unrealizable promises stirred credulous people to the very depths of their being.

VI

DISINTEGRATION

Guchkov's resignation was followed a short time later by that of the Minister of Foreign Affairs, P. N. Milyukov, the strongest and most stubborn representative of the Provisional Government's bourgeois section. Milyukov was the leader of the Cadet party and a well-known historian.

Milyukov found it impossible to reconcile the socialist formula of "peace without annexations and indemnities" with his own views on Russia's foreign policy and war aims. This attitude subjected him to systematic persecution by the Soviet and eventually forced him to hand in his resignation.

Prince George Lvov, the former president of the Union of *Zemstvos,* who, like Guchkov, had shown considerable organizing ability during the war, retained for the time being the posts of Prime Minister and Minister of the Interior. However, like Guchkov, he proved incapable of coping with the political situation after the revolution.

In 1920, when the exiled Denikin was spending some months in England, he asked Milyukov, who had played an active role in the formation of the Provisional Government, why the choice for Prime Minister had fallen on the colorless personality of Prince Lvov. Milyukov answered frankly, "We had two candidates [Rodzianko and Prince Lvov]; one was a notorious *zhopa* [Russian vernacular for "rear end"], while the other was still unknown to us." [1]

Professor Milyukov's scarcely polite but picturesque appraisal of the Provisional Government's first Prime Minister highlights a curious aspect of the Progressive Bloc's prerevolutionary activity.

As we know, the February revolution came as a surprise to all political parties. Nevertheless, as far back as the beginning of 1916, Milyukov and other members of the Progressive Bloc had been considering candidates for a ministry that would enjoy the confidence of the nation. This ministry, according to their plan, was to replace the obsolete and worthless government without going through a revolutionary process. On March 1, when the pressure of events called for the immediate formation of a provisional government, the name of Prince Lvov was found at the top of the latest list of candidates. His nomination to the post of Prime Minister was a perfect example of the thoughtlessness and frivolity with which the Russian liberals approached the cardinal question of choosing the nation's leadership.

Professor Pavel Nikolaevich Milyukov (1859–1943), an eminent historian and leader of the Cadet party, was handicapped by a singular lack of political foresight. He did not desire the downfall of the monarchy, but greatly undermined its authority by his Duma speeches of 1916. He was instrumental in selecting for the post of Prime Minister and Minister of the Interior in the Provisional Government Prince G. E. Lvov, whom he hardly knew and whom later he characterized as a man of a Hamlet-like indecision. Despite the Soviet's formula of a future peace without annexations and indemnities, Milyukov insisted on Russia's postwar rights to Constantinople and the Straits; and finally in 1918, shortly before the total collapse of the Central Powers, Milyukov became an advocate of a pro-German orientation.

Small wonder, therefore, that the nearsighted endeavors of Milyukov and his other liberal colleagues ended in the immediate surrender of their positions to the forceful pressure of the Soviet of Workers' and Soldiers' Deputies.

Thinking of the past and evaluating the liberal circles with whose aims he had had so much in common, Anton Denikin gave us a penetrating appraisal of them: "The revolution was expected and fomented, *but not one of the political parties was prepared for it* [italics Denikin's]. It came in the night and surprised them, like the foolish virgins of the Bible, with no oil for their lamps. This cannot be explained or justified solely by the elemental pressure of events. No one had created beforehand a general plan of canals and locks which would prevent the torrent from becoming a flood." [2]

Early in May, after Guchkov's and Milyukov's departure, the government entered into its first coalition with the socialists by including three Socialist Revolutionaries, two Mensheviks, and one People's Socialist in its cabinet.

Alexander Kerensky was the most prominent of the socialist ministers. Having begun his career and acquired a certain notoriety as defense counsel in the political trials resulting from workers' and peasants' disturbances, he was elected delegate to the Duma in 1912 by the *Trudovik* party. He became Minister of Justice in March, 1917, before reaching his thirty-sixth birthday.

Following the February revolution, Kerensky became a member of the Provisional Committee of the Duma, and at the same time, was elected deputy chairman of the Petrograd Soviet of Workers' Deputies. As soon as the Provisional Government was formed, he accepted the post of Minister of Justice. He used his connection with the Soviet very astutely to broaden his influence in the government. This, and the exceptional gift of oratory which soon made him famous throughout Russia, raised him to a dominating position in the government within a few days of the revolution.

Alexander Fedorovich Kerensky had the most superficial knowledge of the army, was totally unfamiliar with its functioning, and had not even seen military service. All of a sudden, after Guchkov's resignation, he found himself in the role of Minister of War and Minister of the Navy. The revolutionary intelligentsia, to which Kerensky belonged, had a negative attitude toward the army; it looked at officers as praetorians and considered the army to be the tool of the bourgeoisie and landowners, supporting a regime which they hated.

It was not surprising, therefore, that when radical intellectuals, whose memories of Cossack reprisals during the riots and demonstrations of 1905 were still fresh, came to power, they saw the specter of counter-revolution in the officer corps and could not restrain their mistrust and suspicion of its members.

Nevertheless, at that time the choice of Kerensky for the post of War Minister was justifiable to a large extent. General Denikin, who followed the events in Petrograd from a distance, noted that the *Stavka* was not inimical to Kerensky's nomination. "Kerensky," wrote Denikin, "has no conception of military matters and life but may be helped by good advisers; what is presently happening in the army is sheer madness, as is quite obvious to any civilian. Guchkov, a representative of the bourgeoisie and a rightist, was not trusted; let us hope that now this socialist minister and minion of democracy will succeed in dispersing the dense fog which has enveloped the consciousness of our soldiers." [3]

Kerensky was convinced of the need for a military offensive. In view of the demoralized condition of the troops, this could only be achieved by stimulating the "revolutionary patriotism" of the soldiers, and Kerensky undertook to carry out this task personally in the disintegrating army. Thus began his series of innumerable visits to the front lines and the immediate rear.

Although Milyukov seldom missed an opportunity to ridicule Kerensky, he left us a faithful portrait of him at the time of his public appearances in the spring and early summer of 1917:

In public buildings and at the front, at the conferences of various organizations and at gala receptions, hundreds of thousands of soldiers saw the slim figure of a young man clad in a rumpled field jacket devoid of insignia and decorations, with his lame arm bent at the elbow and his hand in the breast of his coat, and a pale, sickly face marked by nervousness and extreme fatigue. They heard his fiery speeches, which told in short, clipped phrases of freedom, light, and truth. These were constantly interrupted by wild surges of applause

and enthusiastic promises to believe and obey the socialist-minister and to follow his lead in the defense of the republic and of peace.[4]

The newspapers quoted Kerensky's speeches to the troops: "Comrades,
I perceive in our encounter the great enthusiasm with which our entire
country is filled and I feel the great upsurge which transforms the world
once in a century. There are few miracles such as the Russian revolution,
which has made free people out of slaves. We are fated to reenact the
legend of the French revolution. Let us surge forward to defend the peace
of all the world, with faith in the happiness and greatness of the people."
And again: "If you are destined to die an honorable death with the eyes of
the whole world upon you, call me: I shall lead you with rifle in hand
[thunderous applause]. . . . Forward, to the defense of freedom, not to
a feast but to death do I summon you." [5]

In this torrent of demagogy mixed with patriotism, Kerensky implored
the army to take the offensive, but he did not hesitate, at the same time, to
sign the Declaration of the Rights of the Soldiers. Concurrently, in order
to intimidate the senior officers who disagreed with his actions, he issued
an order forbidding them to resign from their posts.

At the end of April, some time before his resignation, Guchkov had
submitted an outline of the projected Declaration for appraisal by the
Stavka, whose reaction to it was described by Denikin: "In our violent
rejection, the Supreme Commander and I expressed all the moral suffering to which we had been subjected and the grief we felt for the hopeless
future of the army. The Declaration was the last nail in the army's coffin,
such was our definitive conclusion." [6]

The reaction in officer circles was summarized by General Golovin:
"This declaration, which spoke only of the 'rights of the soldier,' was interpreted by the soldier masses as a negation of any kind of 'duties' on
their part. It deprived the officer complement of all disciplinary power,
undermined its military authority, legalized the complete lack of discipline of the reserve troops at the rear, and afforded unlimited possibilities for further revolutionizing the soldier masses at the front." [7]

In this confusing period, Denikin retained his moral equilibrium.
There was no room in his nature for a compromise between thought and
deed and he said exactly what he thought. The letters he wrote to his
fiancée at that time, contain the same thoughts and convictions which he
openly expressed to the new government leaders in Petrograd. Excerpts
from these letters are published here for the first time:

April 5, 1917
    The political situation is unstable. Fate may have strange grimacings in
store for us. Personally, my exceptional "rise to power" does not please my
vanity but apears to me as a hard and extremely responsible duty. All I can
say is that I shall try to preserve the good name which the Iron riflemen have

given me, and will not deviate by one step from my convictions in order to strengthen my position.

Denikin went on to describe the tiring and nerve-racking routine of his life at the *Stavka* and concluded the letter by saying, "All this is unimportant. If only . . . a wave of anarchy does not submerge the army."

May 14, 1917

Disintegration is setting in slowly but surely. I resist it with all my strength. I clearly and unequivocally condemn every measure harmful to the army in my reports as well as in direct communications to the capital. The results are negligible. My only moral satisfaction is that I did not have to compromise with my convictions a single time. This, however, has given me a definite reputation. It is bad for my career (which is essentially of no importance), but leaves my conscience in peace.

Discontent with the new government was growing at the *Stavka*, but had not yet reached the point of desperation which had overwhelmed Guchkov. General Alekseev decided to go to Petrograd, with his commanders in chief, in order to warn the government, arrest the flow of harmful legislation, and prevent the Declaration of the Rights of the Soldiers (then being considered) from being promulgated.

The commanders in chief headed by Alekseev, participated in the May 4 joint session of the Provisional Government and the Executive Committee of the Soviet of Workers' and Soldiers' Deputies. The statements of the generals were countered by a member of the Soviets' Executive Committee, Skobelev, who announced that he and his colleagues "had not come to the meeting to listen to reproaches. . . . I consider it indispensable," he continued, "to clarify the situation which led to the publication of Order No. 1. The officers of the regiments which had toppled the old regime did not join in the insurrection. In order to discredit them, we were obliged to issue Order No. 1. We were secretly worried as to how the army at the front would react to the revolution. . . . We see today that our fears were justified."

Skobelev's statement set the seal of approval of the Petrograd Soviet on the measures aimed at undermining the authority of the army's officers.

Kerensky, who had just assumed the post of Minister of War, did his best to smooth things over. He insisted that no reproaches were intended, that everyone shared the same aims, that the officer corps had borne the brunt of the revolution on its shoulders with the rest of the Russian people.

However, he promptly added to his speech the following significant statement: "The Provisional Government recognizes the outstanding role and organizational work of the Soviet of Workers' and Soldiers' Deputies; otherwise I would not have agreed to become Minister of War. No one can address a reproach to this Soviet." [8]

Kerensky's praise of the Soviet's "outstanding" organizational work did not enhance the generals' confidence in him. On many occasions and

at different times, many members of the Petrograd Soviet, besides Skobelev, had freely expressed their antagonism to the army command. For
example, a certain Joseph Goldenberg openly declared to the French
writer Claude Anet that "Order No. 1 was not a mistake: it was a necessity. On the day that we made the revolution, we realized that it would be
quelled by the old army unless we destroyed it first. We had to choose
between the army and the revolution. We did not hesitate. We chose the
revolution, and if I may say so, launched a series of brilliantly indispensable measures." [9]

The May 4 conference convinced the commanders that any effort to
sway the authorities was a losing proposition. It was obvious that the
activity of the Provisional Government was completely paralyzed by the
power of the Soviet.

General Denikin had already reached this conclusion independently
some time before. When he became convinced that the opinion of the
army command fell on deaf ears and that the decisions of the Minister
of War depended on the political approval of the Soviet, his reports to the
government gradually acquired a harsher tone.

The change was signaled by two speeches Denikin made at the *Stavka,*
on May 7 and 22, to a conference of the Alliance of Army and Navy
Officers. Over three hundred representatives of the Alliance had come to
Mogilev, from the front and the rear. The conference was opened by
General Alekseev.

"For the first time on that day," recollected Denikin, "not in a secret
session or confidential letter, but openly and loudly, the High Command
said: Russia is in mortal danger." [10]

General Alekseev urged the officers first to join in an unanimous effort
to end the discord which had been artificially implanted in the army family from outside, then to inspire the army with the enthusiasm necessary
to lead it to victory.

General Denikin followed Alekseev with a short address:

By the inevitable laws of history, autocracy has fallen and the rule of the
country has passed to the people. We are on the verge of a new life, passionately desired and long awaited, for which many thousands of idealists have
laid down their lives, languished in mines and pined in the Tundra.

But we look at the future in fear and bewilderment. For there is no freedom in revolutionary torture chambers! There is no truth in falsifying the people's voice! No equality in the hounding of classes! And there is no strength
in the mad bacchanalia where everyone grabs what he can at the expense of
his martyred country, where thousands of greedy hands are reaching for power,
weakening its already shaky foundations.[11]

Although Denikin's speech was far more violent than Alekseev's, it did
not bring on him the wrath of the Soviet at that time. The leftist press
led a noisy attack against Alekseev. The Petrograd Soviet of Workers' and
Soldiers' Deputies demanded his immediate resignation. According to

Denikin, the campaign gathered further momentum due to Kerensky's support of the Soviet point of view.

General Alekseev was removed from his post on the last day of the officers' conference in Mogilev. The farewell address at the close of the session, on May 22, was given by General Denikin, as the senior officer present:

> The Supreme Commander, who is leaving his post, has asked me to bring to you, gentlemen, his sincere greetings and to tell you that his old soldier's heart beats in unison with yours, suffers the same pain, and lives by the same hope in the restoration of our long-suffering but great Russian army. May I also add a few words on my own behalf.
>
> You have come here from the blood-sprayed far reaches of our land with your desperate grief, your spiritual bereavement.
>
> You have brought to life before us the appalling facts of the officers' life and work in the turbulent sea of the army.

Denikin's speech did not contain any proposals. Rather, it was a blunt warning to the new rulers of Russia to remember the past sacrifices and service of the officer corps and to treat it accordingly:

> As one who for three years has lived the same life and thought the same thoughts with you, who has shared with you the splendid joy of victory and the burning pain of retreat, I have the right to hurl an answer at the people who have spat into our souls, who from the first days of the revolution have perpetrated the sin of Cain on the officer corps. . . . I have the right to hurl at them: You lie! The Russian officer has never been either a mercenary or a praetorian. . . . May my appeal reach beyond those walls to the builders of our new national life: Cherish your officers! From time immemorial and to this day they have steadfastly guarded Russia's statehood. Only death can relieve them of this task.[12]

Within a few days, Denikin's speech had reached all the literate population of Russia and made a tremendous impression on it. It was read and discussed everywhere. For the first time since February 27, someone had clearly and openly expressed the hidden thoughts and feelings of the officers and the liberal-oriented intelligentsia. Denikin became the mouthpiece through which the Russian officer, stepchild of the revolution, was at last able to vent his pent-up misery.

Alekseev's resignation from the post of Supreme Commander determined General Denikin's future at the *Stavka*. Denikin's obvious disapproval of the "democratization" of the army was viewed unfavorably in Petrograd, and the directness with which he expressed his opinions displeased the leftist circles. His presence at the *Stavka* irritated the Executive Committee of the Soviet of Workers' and Soldiers' Deputies. The appointment of General Brusilov in place of Alekseev brought the issue to a head: Denikin simply did not wish to collaborate with Brusilov. The divergence in their outlook and principles had become too wide.

Like Polivanov, General Alexis Brusilov (1853–1926) was one of the small number of senior commanders who drastically changed their political attitude immediately after the revolution.

A graduate of the *Corps des Pages,* brought up in the traditions of the old imperial army, commander of the Officer Cavalry School, commander of the Guards Second Cavalry division, aide-de-camp of the last Tsar, and a gifted, strict and exacting military leader famous for his successes at the southwestern front, the sixty-four year old Brusilov suddenly decided to pursue a revolutionary career.

Following the February upheaval, Brusilov, unlike most of the commanding officers, accommodated himself to the new system and catered to the soldiers' committees and soviets which were organized throughout the country. There could no longer be a common language between him and General Denikin. The latter looked back at Brusilov's past and his political turnabout in 1917 with considerable distaste: "How can one spend a whole life lying to oneself and to others?" [13]

General Brusilov's nomination [wrote Denikin] symbolized the final depersonalization and change of direction of the *Stavka.* His boundless and inexplicable opportunism and pursuit of a revolutionary's reputation deprived the army command even of that modicum of moral support which it found in the former *Stavka.*

The Supreme Commander's reception at Mogilev was unusually cool and aloof. Instead of the usual enthusiastic ovations, the "revolutionary general," whom the crowd at Kamenets-Podolsk had borne aloft in a red armchair, was greeted in the deserted station by a stricly formal parade, expressionless faces, and conventional phrases. Brusilov's first moves, unimportant but characteristic, deepened our gloom. In reviewing the honor guard of bearers of the Order of St. George, he failed to greet their valiant, heavily wounded commander Colonel Timanovsky [14] and other officers, but fervently shook hands with the privates: an orderly and a messenger. The latter were so surprised and embarrassed that they dropped their rifles held at attention. . . . Brusilov handed me his handwritten greeting to the armies, . . . for submission to Kerensky's preliminary approval. . . .

. . . My line of action at the *Stavka,* like Alekseev's did not coincide with the wishes of the Provisional Government. Besides, my complete divergence of views with Brusilov made my collaboration with him impossible.[15]

As a result of this incompatibility, General Denikin was nominated commander in chief of the western front and replaced at the *Stavka* by General A. S. Lukomsky.

Although the political standing of the unruly general obstinately bucking the current was very insecure, his strategic ability, firmness, and drive made him extremely valuable from a military point of view. In addition, Brusilov (and through him Kerensky, who at that time consulted and valued his opinion) knew that Denikin, despite his complete disapproval of what was going on in the army, was still prepared to start an offensive.

The General realized that the idea of an offensive could not be popular with the army; he was not even sure whether the troops would carry out the order to advance. He realized that the Russian front still held by inertia and could hold a while longer in passive defense. And he feared that an unsuccessful offensive would expose the utter helplessness of the army.

But having examined various alternatives, he concluded that too many arguments were in favor of the offensive. The Central Powers had exhausted their resources in manpower and in material and moral strength.

If in the fall of 1916 [wrote Denikin, describing the gruadual process by which he reached this decision] our offensive which was not a complete strategic success, placed the enemy armies in a critical position, what could happen now, that our strength and technique had developed, their ratio had altered considerably in our favor, and our allies were threatening the enemy with a crushing blow in the spring of 1917.

. . . *We had to take the offensive.* . . . Our decision to the contrary would have become known to the enemy, who would have immediately begun to transfer his forces to the west. This would have been tantamount to a betrayal of the Allied nations. . . .

. . . Finally, the *Stavka* had one more reason for its decision: The Russian army in its present passive condition, without incentive and stimulus for military achievement, would soon become rotten to the core; whereas a successful offensive could raise and improve its morale. . . .

The Supreme Commander [General Alekseev], the deputy chief of staff, and myself were unanimous as to the need of an *offensive*. The senior commanders agreed with us in principle. Their hesitations, which were considerable at some of the fronts, related to the degree of military readiness and moral preparedness of their troops.[16]

Several years later, in reviewing the past and the decision to take the offensive, Denikin wrote, "I affirm with complete conviction that *this decision in itself* [italics Denikin's], regardless of its outcome, unquestionably served the Allied cause by keeping the enemy's forces, equipment, and attention focused on the Russian front. Sphinxlike, this front, though no longer a threatening force, still presented the enemy with an unresolved riddle." [17]

Twelve years later, in *The World Crisis,* Churchill expressed his admiration for Russia's contribution to the Allied cause in World War I, both before and after the fall of the monarchy:

At the beginning of the war France and Britain had counted heavily upon Russia. Certainly the Russian effort had been enormous. Nothing had been stinted; everything had been risked. The forward mobilisation of the Imperial Armies and their headlong onslaught upon Germany and Austria may be held to have played an indispensable part in saving France from destruction in the first two months of the war. Thereafter in spite of disasters and slaughters on an unimaginable scale Russia had remained a faithful and mighty ally. For nearly three years she had held on her fronts considerably more than half of the total number of enemy divisions, and she had lost in this struggle nearly as many men killed as all the other allies put together. The victory of Brusilov in 1916 had been of important service to France and still more to Italy; and even as late as the summer of 1917, *after the fall of the Czar* [italics Churchill's], the Kerensky Government was still attempting offensives in aid of the common cause. The endurance of Russia as a prime factor, until the United States had entered the war, ranked second only to the defeat of the German submarines as a final turning-point of the struggle.[18]

The stand taken by Denikin in favor of the Russian offensive of 1917, which ended in disaster, has earned him considerable criticism.

To the biographer, however, it is Denikin's process of thinking at the time which is of vital importance, as it reveals his sense of duty and honor, which was to govern all of his subsequent actions.

The problem of whether to initiate an offensive or sit it out in the trenches was complicated by another tormenting possibility: the temptation to engage in negotiations with the enemy independently of the Allies, in order to conclude the war as painlessly as possible by a separate peace between Russia and the Central Powers. Although for the time being, only the comparatively small group of Bolsheviks and other parties of the extreme left sponsored the idea of a separate peace, the soldier masses were very receptive to it. On the other hand, the majority of patriotically minded Russians, from the deposed Tsar to the moderate socialists, favored the pursuit of the war to a victorious end.

Yet, many people whose patriotism was above reproach, doubted that any important military operations could be carried out successfully while Russia was struggling with the internal problems posed by the revolution. They were also aware that exhaustion from the war and the desire to terminate it had helped to bring about the revolution.[19]

But for Denikin even the thought of a separate peace was a betrayal. "Such a peace," he said, "would bring temporary relief to our tortured country. But the curse of betrayal precludes happiness. In the end, it points the way to political, moral, and economic enslavement." [20]

"I know," wrote Denikin later, "that some Russian circles criticized this unswerving adherence to moral principles in a political decision. They considered such idealism untimely and harmful and maintained that Russia's interests should be placed over and above any 'conventional political morality.' . . . But a people's history expresses itself in centuries, not in years! . . . And the psychology of Russia's military leaders could not accept such compromises with their conscience. . . . Quixotism? Perhaps. The fact is that a different policy would have to be shaped by different hands . . . less clean ones." [21]

VII

THE BATTLE
AGAINST CHAOS

As soon as Denikin assumed the command of the western front, which he was to prepare for an offensive, he ran into almost unsurmountable difficulties. The committees of the front and of one of the armies, and the Soviet of Workers' and Soldiers' Deputies of the city of Minsk, where Denikin's headquarters was situated, all voted against an offensive. The Minsk Soviet went so far as to express its lack of confidence in the Provisional Government and to define the projected operation as a betrayal of the revolution. Eventually, some of these groups revised their decisions to the point of tolerating the concept of an offensive, but enough harm had already been done to jeopardize its success. With his usual frankness, Denikin declared that any kind of collaboration between him and the committees of the front was out of the question. Relations went from bad to worse. The committees were furious with Denikin and accused him of counterrevolutionary attitudes. In spite of this, he continued to inspect all the sectors of his front, exhorting the soldiers to carry out their duty to their country and meeting with the officers and generals. He was grief-stricken as the demoralization of the troops became increasingly evident to him during those trips. He was willing to order, shame, exhort to patriotism, but he was totally incapable of currying favor with the disgruntled soldiery.

Some of Denikin's experiences during his tours of the front were shocking:

I asked to be shown the worst unit in one of the army corps [wrote the General], and was driven to the 703rd Suramski regiment. We approached an immense crowd of unarmed men who were standing, sitting, or wandering about on a field in back of the village. They were clothed in rags (having sold their uniforms and spent the money on liquor), barefooted, unshaven, unkempt. They seemed to have reached the last stages of physical coarseness. . . . No one ordered "Attention"; none of the soliders rose; the nearest ones approached our cars. My first impulse was to reprimand the regiment and drive away. However, as this could have been attributed to cowardice, I got out of the car and entered the crowd.

I spent about an hour in its midst. Lord, what had befallen these men, the reasonable human beings created by You, the hardworking Russian peasants! They seemed possessed or demented, confused of mind. They argued obstinately, without any logic or common sense, with hysterical shouts, blasphemy, and coarse, vile swearing. . . . I remember that gradually the indignation of an old soldier began to recede in me and give place to infinite pity for these dirty, unenlightened Russian people to whom too little had been given and of whom so little could be asked. I wished that the rulers of our revolutionary democracy had been there, in this field, and witnessed what I had seen and heard. I wanted to say to them: "This is no time to sift the blame. Whether the guilt is ours, yours, the bourgeoisie's, or the monarchy's is immaterial. First, render these people literate and human, then go on to your socializing, nationalizing, and communizing . . . provided that they will still be willing to follow your lead." [1]

Brusilov came to Denikin's front to raise the morale of the troops, but his visit resulted in a rather unfortunate incident. Apparently the soldiers had been told that their visitor would be Comrade Kerensky. They were indignant when Brusilov arrived instead. They affirmed that they were being deceived and that they would not budge from their position until Kerensky in person ordered them to advance. Denikin had no choice but to summon Kerensky.

"Kerensky came unwillingly," he wrote, "already disappointed by an unsuccessful campaign of speeches at the southwestern front. He toured the troops for several days, received ovations, and occasionally, unexpected reprimands. . . . Having completed the circuit of the front and returned to the *Stavka,* he stated emphatically to Brusilov that he 'had no belief whatsoever in the success of the offensive.' " [2]

Kerensky did not mention this phrase in his memoirs, but said on the contrary that his impression of the western front was much better than Denikin's own. He wrote also that he was worried by Denikin's peremptory tone with the members of various committees, whereas seemingly Denikin was shocked by certain expressions he (Kerensky) used and by the "hysterical tone" of his speeches. [3]

There is no doubt that Denikin was shocked by Kerensky's entire personality and career. From the beginning of the February events, he did not rate him highly, and he was of the opinion that Kerensky, a man of mediocre talents, but drunk with his own gift for oratory, had risen to extraordinary heights by a freak of fate. Behind Kerensky's facade of resounding phrases, Denikin perceived an unsubstantial, somewhat unbalanced personality, with a mania for grandeur and a leaning toward hysteria, dangerously inclined to make irresponsible statements, and commit irresponsible acts.

Yet, at the time of their joint tour of the western front, Denikin still hoped to derive some benefit from Kerensky's presence, as witnessed by this passage from a personal letter: "Returned from the front with Kerensky. He had delivered a truly inspired speech to the committees. Its reporting in the newspapers was incorrect and pale. It had unquestionably made an impression." [4]

Several years later, Denikin returned again to his impressions at that time:

> There was, undoubtedly, a short but brilliant period in Kerensky's term as Minister of War. I place it roughly in June, when not only the civilian population, but most of the officers too, fell under the spell of his exalted phrases and hysterical pathos. At that time the Russian officers, already threatened with extermination, forgot and forgave everything and waited breathlessly for him to save the army. Their promise to die in the front ranks was by no means an empty phrase.
> It hurt when many times during my trips with Kerensky, I saw the eyes of these condemned people light up with enthusiasm and sensed the bright hope in their hearts. A hope that would soon be coarsely and pitilessly stamped out. [5]

Shortly after Kerensky's departure, General Denikin received a special invitation to be present at a meeting of delegates of one of his army corps. "The delegates," wrote Denikin later, "discussed the fact that the commander in chief, the army commander, their corps commander, the staff officers, in short all the top brass, were there; this was a good occasion, they argued, to get rid of the whole lot in one stroke, thus putting an end to the offensive." [6]

Denikin no longer believed in the success of his undertaking, barring a miracle. Nevertheless, with the persistence of despair and despite his awareness of impending defeat, he made every effort to detain as many enemy units as possible at his front, thus keeping them away from the southwestern front, where the offensive had already started.

On June 18 he issued an order of the day in which he urged the troops at his front to bend their efforts to a rapid preparation for action in order to assist the offensive at the adjoining southwestern front. Contrary to the rules of secrecy governing military planning, he deliberately released the text of his order to the press.

"I don't know," wrote the General later, "whether those who read this order, which appeared in the papers in flagrant disregard of elementary military secrecy, were fully aware of the internal drama of the Russian army at that time. All its strategy was disrupted. The Russian commander in chief lacked the authority to engage his troops in an offensive in order to draw off some of the pressure from the adjoining front. He hoped that, by divulging his intention to advance, he could at least detain at his own front the German divisions that were being removed from it and directed against the southwestern front and against the Allies." [7]

On July 7, Denikin's artillery began firing in preparation for the attack; the offensive was launched on July 9. "Three days later," he wrote, "I was returning to Minsk from the Tenth Army with despair in my heart, fully conscious that the last spark of hope in a miracle had been extinguished." [8]

General Alekseev, who was sitting in enforced idleness after his removal from the *Stavka,* was intensely interested in the events at Denikin's front. We find the following notation in his diary for July 10: "At the western front, commanded by Denikin, following intensive softening up by our artillery, the first line of enemy fortifications was taken almost without resistance and a thousand prisoners captured. But after this, those good-for-nothing 'comrades' returned to their trenches, refusing the effort of fortifying and securing the new positions." On the same day, Alekseev made another grim notation: "The disintegration of the troops is increasing; we hear that in some units the officers have been exterminated by their own blackguards of soldiers. Today we received the report that a division chief of staff had been killed in his own division." [9]

The February revolution had played havoc with the plans of all military operations. The concerted onslaught of the Russian armies which had been scheduled for May proved impossible to carry out for psychological reasons. The *Stavka* was forced to abandon its initial strategic planning and to let the commanders of the individual fronts act on their own initiative when they considered themselves ready to do so. Essentially, the strategy of the war was reduced to improvisation. The effort of the High Command, still governed by the principle of loyalty to the Allies, was directed at retaining the enemy forces at the various Russian fronts, thus preventing the Germans from gaining the upper hand over the French, British, and Italians, as well as over the Americans, who had recently entered the war.

The Russian summer offensive of 1917 began on June 16 at the southwestern front, on July 7 at the western front, on July 8 at the northern front, and on July 9 at the Rumanian front.

The lapse of time between June 16 and July 7 allowed the Germans to concentrate their forces for a thrust directed at the southwestern front. The impact of that thrust destroyed the last hope of restoring the decaying morale of the army.

The attempted offensives in the summer of 1917 all followed approximately the same pattern at the various fronts: The onslaught was led by officers at the head of small detachments of the more disciplined soldiers. The initial attack was successful, but when it had to be followed up and consolidated by units from the rear, the latter immediately called meetings of soldiers. The meetings resulted in the soldiers' refusal to obey orders and to expose themselves to danger. When the enemy, who had been given time to recover from surprise, countered by a blow at the Russians, the soldiers spontaneously left their positions and trenches with no attempt at defense, and rolled like a tidal wave toward the rear, wreaking havoc along the way.

The southwestern front, where Russian forces dealt the most severe blow to the enemy, also provided the most frightful example of the debacle. The artillery cannonade, on a scale which was unprecedented in Russia, destroyed the enemy fortifications. Shock troops broke through the enemy front, and in two days of combat, captured three hundred Austrian officers, eighteen thousand men, twenty-nine guns, and many other trophies. But the odds were reversed when the Germans came to the rescue of the faltering Austrians. The Russian soldiers, under the influence of Bolshevik propaganda, fled from the trenches along all the roads to the rear, killing their officers, looting the population, and raping the women.

A telegram sent to the Provisional Government on July 9 by the commissars of one of the armies at the southwestern front describes the situation:

The German offensive, started July 6 at the Eleventh Army front, is developing into an indescribable calamity which threatens the possible collapse of revolutionary Russia. . . . Most units are in a state of growing disintegration. Authority and obedience no longer exist, argument and persuasion are ineffective. . . . Lines of deserters along hundreds of versts are moving toward the rear, with and without their rifles, healthy and hale and confident in their impunity. Sometimes whole units leave in this way. . . . The situation demands the most drastic measures. . . . Today the commander in chief, with the consent of the commissars and committees, gave the order to shoot at the deserters. Let the whole country learn the truth, . . . shudder at the danger, and find the determination to prosecute without pity all those whose cowardice is destroying and betraying Russia and the revolution." [10]

This report, coming from a source not connected with the officer corps, made a strong impression on Kerensky.

The catastrophe at the southwestern front was repeated in a slightly milder form at the western, northern, and even the Rumanian fronts. The Russian troops in Rumania held together longer than the others, as they were further removed from the influence of Petrograd, but finally even they succumbed.

By an irony of fate, it was at the moment of its moral disintegration that the Russian army at last had been amply supplied with every kind of ordnance, small arms, and ammunition. This reserve of armament, accumulated with great effort by the Department of Artillery, later fell into the hands of the Soviet government. It amply supplied the Bolshevik army during the three years of the civil war. The replenishments occasionally extracted by the Bolsheviks from the disrupted and disorganized war factories that fell into their hands were totally insignificant by comparison. In their fight against Denikin, Kolchak, Iudenich, Miller, and Wrangel, and later against Poland, the Bolsheviks relied almost exclusively on the military armament stockpiled toward the spring of 1917 for a very different purpose.

On July 16, at Kerensky's initiative, the *Stavka* called the commanders in chief and the ministers of the Provisional Government to a conference in order to determine the state of the front after the rout, and to formulate a new military policy.[11]

The cabinet was represented by two persons only—Kerensky and the Minister of Foreign Affairs, Tereshchenko. The former, however, already carried three ministerial portfolios, having replaced Prince Lvov as Prime Minister and retained the functions of Minister of War and Minister of the Navy. Also present was the commissar of the southwestern front, Boris Savinkov, already chosen by Kerensky to assist him as Acting Minister of War.

The senior commanding generals participating in the conference were Supreme Commander in Chief Brusilov, Commander in Chief of the Western Front Denikin, Commander in Chief of the Northern Front Klembovsky, Generals Alekseev and Ruzsky, both without official functions, and General Lukomsky, who had replaced Denikin at the *Stavka*. General Kornilov, soon to play a part in this narrative, was not present. He could not leave the southwestern front, whose command he had recently assumed after its catastrophic defeat, and sent his written considerations to the *Stavka*.

The conference opened in an atmosphere of nervousness and tension. Denikin was invited to speak first. Disregarding all conventional niceties, he "painted a picture of conditions in the army in all their horrifying nakedness."

"I spoke frankly and openly under the tsarist autocracy and will do the same under a revolutionary autocracy," said Denikin. His report, which described the causes of the army's disintegration, was aimed at the new government and its Prime Minister. Denikin's antagonism toward them, revealed in the address in May to the conference of the Alliance of Army and Navy Officers in Mogilev, became fully evident in his report of July 16 at the *Stavka*. Now it held not only a reproach but a challenge. The General described the preparations for the offensive at his front. The troops which he took over were already completely demoralized. In most regiments the soldiers had installed their own stills. Drunkenness, gambling, violence, theft, occasionally murder, were everyday occurrences. When the time came for them to do their duty and move into position for the offensive, the instinct to save their skin prevailed over all others. As many as ten divisions refused to move to the points from which the attack was to begin. Driven to extreme measures, Denikin had removed to the rear and disbanded an entire army corps plus an additional infantry division. Thus, he was already deprived of thirty thousand bayonets before the operation started. He had moved in their place two infantry divisions, which were considered to be the best at the front, but did not live up to their reputation. One of them, having reached the starting point of the attack, left it of its own accord on the next day. The other, having sent forward a single regiment, decided at a soldiers' meeting "not to advance."

Denikin then went on to the role played by the commissars and committees. He insisted that they had done enormous harm to the army: "As a result of a whole series of legislative measures, discipline and authority have been abolished, the officer corps humiliated by clearly expressed mistrust and disrespect, senior military leaders, including commanders in chief, are being fired like domestics."

Denikin described with bitter regret his technical and numerical advantages over the enemy, advantages he had enjoyed for the first time in the whole course of the war. Along the most important twenty-kilometer section of the front, he had had 184 battalions agains twenty-nine of the enemy's, nine hundred guns against three hundred of the Germans'. In three days his artillery devastated the enemy trenches, inflicting heavy losses on the Germans and clearing the way for his infantry.

"But night fell. . . . Anxious messages from the commanders in the combat zone began coming in, reporting mass defection of the soldiers. . . . Some reports stated that, out of the entire regiment, only its commander with his staff and a handful of soldiers remained in the line of combat."

Denikin's speech became stronger and stronger. It was now addressed personally to Prime Minister and Minister of War Kerensky. The nervous tension of his listeners was mounting. Kerensky could no longer face him. He sat bent over a table, with his head resting on his arms, and remained in this position to the end of Denikin's address. These intense moments have been vividly described by Colonel of the General Staff Tikhobrazov, who had been entrusted with keeping a complete record of the conference and writing up its minutes:

"No wonder that Kerensky's nerves gave out. My own hand shook so much with emotion that I was unable to form a single letter, as if a strong electric current ran through my arm contracting its muscles. Tears coursed down the face of the Minister of Foreign Affairs M. I. Tereshchenko." [12]

The General went on, looking at Kerensky: "Soon after he assumed his new office, the War Minister told me, 'The revolutionizing of the country and the army is completed. We should now proceed only with creative work. . . .' I allowed myself to rejoin, 'Isn't it somewhat late?' "

Denikin recalled with indignation how in one of his speeches to the troops at the western front Kerensky said, "In the tsarist army you were driven into battle by knouts and machine guns. The tsarist leaders led you

to be slaughtered, but now every drop of your blood is precious . . . ,"
and Denikin continued, "I, the commander in chief, stood under the ped-
estal erected for the War Minister and my heart smote me, while my
conscience cried, "This is a lie! My Iron Riflemen . . . had taken over
sixty thousand prisoners, forty-three guns . . . yet I never drove them to
battle with machine guns."

Then, Denikin pointed out to two parallel cases. He related first how
Sokolov, a member of the Petrograd Soviet and coauthor of the famous
Order No. 1, visited one of the most undisciplined regiments at the
western front in the hope of raising its morale. The soldiers, who were
against participating in the offensive, gave Sokolov a merciless beating.
Minister of War Kerensky condemned the cowardly action and sent a
telegram of sympathy to Sokolov.

Denikin then went on to his second case. "I remember a day in January, 1915 [in reality, probably February], near Lutovisco. In bitter
frost, up to his middle in snow, the fearless one-armed hero Colonel
Noskov was leading his regiment to the attack. They were advancing,
next to my Iron Riflemen, to storm the vertical, unscalable heights of
Hill 804. . . . Death spared him on that day. But now, two squads of
soldiers came and asked to see him, killed him, and left.

"I ask his honor the Minister of War: Did he vent all the force of his
fiery oratory, all the force of his anger and powerful authority on the
miserable assassins? Did he send a telegram of condolence to the fallen
hero's family?" Fixing his eyes on Brusilov, Denikin bluntly condemned
the behavior of certain senior commanders "who frantically wave the red
flag and, reverting to a habit acquired under the Tartar yoke, grovel on
their bellies before the new gods of the revolution, as they did before the
tsars."

"The army has gone to pieces," he said. "We need heroic measures
to set it on the right path." At this point he stated the measures which, in
his opinion, would serve as a healthy basis for the future: to revoke the
"Declaration of the Rights of the Soldiers" in its major part, to eliminate
all politics from the army, to reestablish discipline and restore authority
to the commanders, to create hand-picked and law-abiding units in the
rear to cope with possible military uprisings and "the horrors of the eventual demobilization," and to introduce the death penalty in the rear.

Addressing himself with emotion to the Provisional Government in the
person of its two members at the conference, Denikin concluded his
speech with the following appeal: "Direct Russia's life toward truth and
light under the banner of freedom! But give us, too, a real possibility to
defend this freedom by leading our regiments into battle with our
war-scarred banners. . . . It is you who have trampled our banners in
the mud. The time has come for you to raise them up and salute them . . .
if you still have a conscience!"

The address ended. Its listeners had been spellbound by the speaker's profound spiritual distress, by his sincerity and honesty, and the tragic picture he painted for them. The emotional tension had reached a climax and they continued to sit in pertrified silence. Kerensky was the first to recover. He rose and approached Denikin with outstretched hand: "Thank you, General, for your courageous and outspoken statement."

Denikin himself was so shaken that he asked leave to absent himself for fifteen minutes in order to calm down.

"If one may say so, Denikin was the hero of the occasion," noted Alekseev in his diary. He also added the following remark: "At the end of the first half of the meeting . . . Kerensky referred fleetingly to the reproach, so openly flung at him by Denikin: 'It is true that, due to the pressure of affairs, I failed to send a telegram of condolence to General Noskov's family. However, being strictly impartial in relation to the officer corps, I gave orders to assure the financial security of the slain officer's family.' " [13]

Kerensky explained later that he had shaken Denikin's hand to avoid a scandal and to express, at the same time, his respect for any independent opinion, even one which did not coincide with the government's point of view. He also said that "General Denikin was the first to outline a program of retaliation, setting the tune for future military reaction." [14]

In the interests of "military secrecy," Denikin's speech was not released to the papers. Its content, however, could not be suppressed after the extraordinary impact it had made on Denikin's listeners.

It is difficult to deduce any hint of restoration tendencies or "future military reaction" in Denikin's speech. It was, essentially, a protest against the government's failure to counteract the destructive forces of impending anarchy and a formulation of severe measures for restoring the military effectiveness of the army.

Denikin's address was followed by those of Generals Klembovsky, Alekseev and Ruzsky, who spoke along similar lines but in a more restrained manner.

Then the written report of General Kornilov was read to the assembly. It advocated introducing the death penalty in the army rear guard in order to restore discipline. The general lines of Kornilov's program coincided with those advanced by Denikin. It contained, however, two important suggestions which Denikin's program lacked: to broaden the role of the commissars by giving them the authority to confirm sentences passed by military courts-martial, and to purge the army command of undesirable elements.

By submitting this program General Kornilov quite involuntarily gave Kerensky an erroneous idea of his intentions. The latter decided that here, at last, was a general the "broadness" and "depth" of whose views answered to the needs of the moment. Kornilov was not present to explain that the purge he advocated was to be directed against the mercenaries of the revolution, i.e., the opportunists drifting with the current, and not against officers who upheld the old military traditions and whom Kerensky was mistakenly inclined to identify with monarchists and reactionaries.

Kornilov's absence and the lack of precision in the formulation of the intentions of both parties inadvertently led to the misunderstanding which within a month culminated in the fatal break between Kerensky and Kornilov.

The concluding words at the conference were pronounced by Kerensky and were described as follows by Denikin:

> He tried to justify himself by pointing out the inevitability and elemental scope of the army's "democratization", accused us of blaming the July defeat solely on the revolution and its influence on the Russian soldier, fiercely accused the old regime, and in the final analysis, gave us no directives whatsoever for further cooperation with him.
>
> All the participants left the conference depressed by a feeling of mutual misunderstanding. I—not the least of them. Nevertheless, deep down, there remained the feeling—which proved false, alas—that, in spite of everything, our voice had been heard.[15]

On the night of July 16, following the conference at the *Stavka,* Kerensky, who was returning by train from Mogilev to Petrograd, decided to remove Brusilov from the post of Supreme Commander. He was accompanied on the train by Boris Savinkov, the commissar of the southwestern front, already chosen as Acting Minister of War. Savinkov, a former terrorist, had seen Kornilov in action at the front and come to the conclusion that "it was precisely Kornilov, and possibly only Kornilov, who was capable of restoring the fighting efficiency of the army at that time." [16]

VIII

THE STAVKA PLANS COUNTERMEASURES

The conference at the *Stavka* had been preceded by several important events.

Starting in the month of June, the conflict between bourgeois-liberal elements and the Petrograd Soviet of Workers' and Soldiers' Deputies reached such proportions that, as Milyukov observed, it entered a new phase. The growing conflict was between the moderate socialists who headed the Petrograd Soviet, and the numerically insignificant but well-organized Bolshevik party. At the June conference of Soviets, Lenin had already stated that his party was ready to assume power. Lenin had no armed support at that time; it was natural, therefore, that his attention turned to Petrograd's undisciplined garrison and to the capital's workers, who were ready to invade the streets and do away with all bourgeois and moderate elements, and use the occasion for some plundering according to the Bolshevik formula of "loot the looters."

The armed rebellion began on July 3. It seemed to have started spontaneously, with no apparent stimulation from the Bolsheviks. The latter, however, immediately decided to place themselves at its head, assume control, and turn it in the direction they desired. Should the rebellion fail, it would still have served Lenin as a trial balloon, as a means of determining the strength of the forces on which he could count for support in the future.

The key slogan around which the crowd rallied was "All power to the Soviets!" This slogan was misleading, since at the time the majority of the Petrograd Soviet's members were Mensheviks and right-wing Socialist Revolutionaries, inimical to the Bolsheviks; they wanted the uprising to end as soon as possible and had no desire to take power into their hands.

Willing or not, they already held this power. The socialist ministers were, in fact, responsible to the Petrograd Soviet for their actions. The Soviet decided and the socialist government members simply carried out its wishes. The Menshevik members of the Soviet, following the abstract theories of Marxism, still considered that Russia's economic development and backward industry allowed only for a bourgeois revolution and that, in its present condition, the country was not ready for a transition to socialism. But the mob on Petrograd's streets had no use for the fine points of political doctrine. It was impatient to transform the Russian revolution into a social revolution rather than a political one. The Bolshevik slogan clearly stated, "All power to the Soviets!" and the mob wanted to put it into effect without delay. Surrounding the Tauride Palace, headquarters of the Soviet, the crowds loudly demanded that it assume all power.

A prominent participant in the current Soviet session was the Socialist Revolutionary Victor Chernov, then Minister of Agriculture in the Provisional Government. When he came out into the street from the Tauride Palace to reason with the crowd, a hulking brute of a fellow thrust his fist under Chernov's nose crying, "Take the power, you son of a bitch, as long as it's given to you!" [1] This single gesture was symbolic of the rampaging mood of the mob.

With the support of some units of the Petrograd garrison, but mainly with the help of one reliable Cossack regiment and Petrograd's cadets, the July rebellion was quelled.

The Provisional Government decided to arrest the leaders of the Bolshevik party. While this action was being considered, however, Petrograd's attorney general, N. S. Karinksy, telephoned his friend the Bolshevik Bonch-Bruevich that Lenin was to be arrested and tried.[2] Lenin, of course, disappeared immediately. Zinoviev vanished with him. Nevertheless, the government succeeded in arresting Trotsky, Kamenev, and Lunacharsky.

A few days after the July uprising, the appalling news of the catastrophe which followed the Russian offensive became known throughout the country.

The reaction against the Bolsheviks resulting from their connection with the uprising seemed to point the way to the establishment of a firm national government. The advantages of a dictatorship were openly discussed. There being no other candidates, Kerensky became a natural choice for the role.

The Soviet's moderate socialists were certain that Kerensky would not betray "the conquests of the revolution." In fact, the Executive Committee of the Soviet approved a resolution that a government headed by Kerensky be named the Government for the Salvation of the Revolution. The liberal circles still had no candidate for the role of dictator. Their attitude toward

Kerensky was skeptical, but they were prepared to uphold him in the hope that the bitter experience of the last few days would prompt him to exchange his orgy of words for action.

The first steps that he took as Prime Minister seemed to justify this hope. The Bolshevik newspapers were suppressed; censorship was introduced (although, as it turned out, not enforced); and capital punishment at the front was reinstated, "for the duration of the war, for some exceptionally serious crimes committed by military personnel."

Some minor details, however, were also symptomatic. Having assumed the premiership, Kerensky took up residence in the Winter Palace, began to travel in what had been the Tsar's train, and adopted a negligent and supercilious manner with his subordinates. The lightning speed of his career went to his head, and ambition and vainglory in all their pettiness rose to the surface.

The events surrounding Kerensky's arrival at the *Stavka* for the conference of July 16 provided the first example of this personality change.

General Brusilov, who was swamped with operational work and preparations for the conference, did not meet Kerensky at the Mogilev station. Brusilov sent one of his generals to explain to the Prime Minister that he was detained by urgent work and to request him to proceed directly to the conference.

Kerensky blew up. The absence of a ceremonial welcome at the station, complete with honor guard and the presence of the Supreme Commander in Chief, was interpreted by him as an unfriendly demonstration. He telephoned a curt order to the *Stavka,* summoning Brusilov to report to him without delay in his train. He commented to Tereshchenko, who was with him, that under the tsars these generals would not have had the nerve to behave so impudently, but now they allowed themselves to ignore the head of the government.

Kerensky expressed his displeasure by receiving the Supreme Commander in a disdainful pose, lounging on a sofa in his parlor car and barely rising from it to greet the General.[3]

Kerensky underscored his feeling of importance by obliging other generals urgently summoned to Mogilev for the conference to wait for his appearance for over an hour.

Two days later, Brusilov was removed from the post of Supreme Commander in Chief and replaced by General Lavr Georgievich Kornilov. Denikin's statement at the conference that "senior military leaders, including commanders in chief, are being fired like domestics," had received one more confirmation.

No one played as vital and important a role in Denikin's life as did General Kornilov. The fascination of his severe personality had an extraordinary impact on the usually calm and steady Anton Ivanovich, then tortured, outraged, and uncertain. Denikin's regard for Kornilov was spontaneous and warm, and at that moment of crisis, the lives of those two outstanding Russians became inseparably linked in the desire to save their country from anarchy.

There was nothing outstanding at first sight about Kornilov's appearance. His figure was neither majestic nor heroic, but short, lean, and slightly bandy-legged. Mongolian blood showed clearly in his face with its slanted eyes, high cheekbones, yellowish skin, hanging moustache, and sparse beard which barely covered his chin. His hands were small, with long, thin, nervous fingers. His voice was often harsh. But his face was striking despite its plain features, and those who met him for the first time soon reacted to the impact of his outstanding personality. The casual visitor was impressed not by the brilliance of his thinking, but by the reserve of inner energy and will power he sensed under the General's dry, unsmiling façade. He was not talkative; his simple and direct conversation appealed to his listeners by its sincerity and honesty. Though an outstanding combat general, he was extremely inexperienced and naïve in political matters. He was trusting by nature and a poor psychologist.

General Kornilov was a Siberian Cossack, son of an ordinary peasant who had attained officer's rank through service in the army. As a young officer of the General Staff, Kornilov served in the Turkestan military district, made detailed studies of various regions on Russia's Asiatic border, became well known as a traveler and explorer of that area. He fought in the war against Japan; and during World War I, as commander of an infantry division, covered the retreat of Brusilov's army from the Carpathians, was surrounded by the enemy, gravely wounded, and taken prisoner by the Austrians in April, 1915. As soon as he recovered, Kornilov began to plan his escape. With luck and the help of accomplices, he acquired the uniform of an Austrian soldier as well as a set of false documents. Taking advantage of the diversity of races in the Austro-Hungarian Empire, Kornilov managed to board an eastbound train filled with soldiers. Fear of being recognized soon made him decide to leave the train, and he continued on foot in the direction of Rumania, which had not yet entered the war. Subsisting on whatever came his way, Kornilov hid in forests and fields during the day and walked eastward during the night, plotting his direction by the stars.

His fantastic plan of escape was successful. General Kornilov returned to Russia in July, 1916, a celebrity and a national hero.

Immediately after the revolution, he was offered the command of the Petrograd military district by the President of the State Duma, M. V. Rodzianko, who did not bother to clear this appointment with the *Stavka* and General Alekseev. Rodzianko's telegram played on Kornilov's patriotism, asking the "valiant combat general whose name is popular and carries authority with the population" not to refuse this post "in order to save the capital from anarchy." Kornilov accepted, but the unprecedented case of a nomination to a high military post without the knowledge and permission of the High Command deeply offended General Alekseev. In order to avoid controversy while expressing his disapproval, Alekseev issued the following order: "I admit Lieutenant General Kornilov to the temporary high command of the Petrograd military district." [4]

Denikin, who knew both generals intimately, noted that this was the first of a series of incidents which influenced the subsequent relations between Alekseev and Kornilov.

General Kornilov assumed his new duties, but soon became appalled by the growing influence of the Soviet on the amorphous government. A resolution of the Petrograd Soviet forbidding the troops to leave their barracks under arms without the Soviet's permission finally precipitated his resignation. In early May, he accepted the command of the Eighth Army, already distinguished by the exploits of Brusilov, Kaledin, Denikin, and Kornilov himself. In early July, he was urgently dispatched to assume the command of the southwestern front. As soon as he arrived at his new post, Kornilov telegraphed the Provisional Government demanding restoration of capital punishment at the front and the immediate interruption of the offensive on all fronts so that the army could be reorganized. Without waiting for an answer, he gave the order to shoot deserters and looters, and formed elite units of volunteers for controlling the excesses at the front. The Provisional Government restored the death penalty at the front on July 12, the day following Kornilov's telegram.

Kerensky watched Kornilov's career with mounting interest. He was impressed by Kornilov's forceful fight against anarchy, and by the report which Kornilov sent to the conference at the *Stavka*. The suggestion for strengthening the role of the commissars and "purging" the army command particularly pleased Kerensky.

Although Kornilov had given Kerensky a very cold reception when the latter toured the Eighth Army with his exalted speeches before the offensive, Savinkov's insistence decided the matter in Kornilov's favor. Conditions at the front were catastrophic. A resolute and courageous leader at the head of the army was imperative. Denikin's command experience and his former position as chief of staff of the High Command, seemed to fit him for that role. However, he had antagonized the Petrograd Soviet and the socialist ministers by his straightforwardness. What is more, in his blunt speeches, he had wounded the vulnerable feelings of the Prime Minister himself. On the other hand, Kerensky still knew too little about Kornilov to realize that nothing could stop the latter from carrying out his decisions once his mind was made up.

It is possible, too, that Kerensky harbored the secret hope of using Kornilov as a lever in arresting the dissolution of the army and strengthening his own position, after which he could quietly dispose of the General as he had managed to dispose of his predecessors. This illusion, if it existed (and many thought it did), was dispelled the moment that Kornilov stepped into the position of Supreme Commander.

Before accepting this assignment, Kornilov had sent the government a telegram stating the conditions under which he was prepared to accept the High Command:

1. He would be responsible to his own conscience and to the people as a whole.

2. There would be no interference whatsoever in regard to his operational directives and, consequently, in his choice of senior commanders.

3. The measures recently enforced by him at the front would also apply to all sections in the rear where army reserves were stationed.

4. All measures advocated in his message to the *Stavka* conference of July 16 would be accepted.

"Having read Kornilov's conditions in the papers," wrote Denikin, "I was considerably surprised by the demands contained in Point One, which established a very original form of governmental and legal sovereignty of the High Command to be in effect until the meeting of the Constituent Assembly. I was impatient to learn the official response." [5]

The recently acquired freedom of speech and press in the Russia of 1917 made the publication of such sensitive documents possible. Everyone was on the alert to hear the government's reaction and to find out whether it was prepared to join with the High Command in its pursuit of firm authority, or would continue its former pattern of following the lead of the Petrograd Soviet.

There was obviously some complicated maneuvering behind the scenes. All indications seemed to point to some conflict between Kornilov and the government. This is what actually happened:

Kerensky was infuriated by Kornilov's first condition and wanted to remove him immediately from the High Command, but was prevented from doing so by Boris Savinkov and some other members of the government.

Kerensky was undoubtedly impressed by Savinkov's revolutionary exploits. He was a newcomer in the Socialist Revolutionary party, whereas Savinkov was a veteran with an impressive record of political arrests, exile, and escape from tsarist prisons, dating as far back as the last years of the nineteenth century. He had been engaged in terrorist activity since 1903, and admitted himself that he had "participated in the assassinations of Minister of the Interior Plehve and of Grand Duke Sergei Aleksandrovich, in preparing the attempt on the life of Admiral Dubasov, and in many other terrorist acts, including several unsuccessful attempts on the life of Nicholas II." [6]

Kerensky undoubtedly counted on Savinkov's nomination to the post of Acting Minister of War as a sort of insurance for his regime. The Ministry of War would be in firm though "revolutionary" hands; but at the same time, if the need arose, Savinkov would not hesitate to take drastic measures against any form of "counterrevolution" wherever it came from. The left wing of the Petrograd Soviet fully realized this. It disliked

Savinkov, did not fully trust him, yet feared and respected him. Thus, in theory, Savinkov's inclusion in the government could serve as a restraining force for rightist and leftist elements alike.

At Savinkov's insistence, Kerensky gave in partially to Kornilov's demands. Without mentioning his other points, he conceded to him the right to nominate his senior commanders. Despite this, however, Kornilov learned that Kerensky had chosen his successor at the southwestern front, General Cheremisov, without consulting him.

It was Kornilov's turn to be indignant at this complete negation of the prerogative he had just received. He refused to accept the High Command unless Cheremisov was immediately removed from his new post.

One of the chief military commissars, Maximilian Filonenko, was sent to Kornilov in the hope of resolving the conflict. He explained that Cheremisov's assignment to his new post had coincided with Kornilov's nomination, but that he would be transferred to Petrograd in consideration of Kornilov's wishes. Filonenko assured Kornilov that his other conditions would be studied in detail in the immediate future.

Asked what exactly he meant by his assertion that he would be responsible to his own conscience and to the people as a whole, Kornilov replied that he meant responsibility before a Provisional Government invested with the people's confidence. This nebulous explanation was neither opposed nor questioned any further, although it hinted plainly at the fact that Kornilov did not consider the present members of the government to be truly representative of the people's wishes. Nevertheless, the government informed the press that it had reached an accord with General Kornilov.

One could hardly expect this compromise agreement, in which neither party had fully stated its position, to result in a constructive collaboration.

On July 24, General Kornilov finally assumed the High Command. At the end of July, the *Stavka* offered the position of commander in chief of the southwestern front to General Denikin. He was surprised by this unforeseen move and anxious to know the reason for his transfer from one front to another. General Kornilov's chief of staff assured Denikin that his transfer was necessitated solely by current plans for a new strategic operation at the southwestern front.

En route to his new command post, Denikin stopped off at Mogilev. He was accompanied by his faithful friend and assistant General Sergei Leonidovich Markov. The latter had followed in Denikin's wake since the time when he was an outstanding officer in the Iron Division. He was Denikin's second deputy chief of staff at the *Stavka,* followed him to the western front as chief of staff, and was now on his way to assume the same function in Berdichev, a district town of the Kiev province, where the headquarters of the southwestern front was located.

Denikin gave a detailed account of his meeting with the Supreme Commander, which he considered important in the light of later events. Several of Kornilov's remarks stand out in this interview, in which no concrete plans were made for the future, but the helplessness of the Provisional Government was stressed. "The members of the government realize that they are helpless to do anything. They want me to join the government. . . . Oh no! These gentlemen are too dependent on the Soviet and can't decide anything by themselves. I say to them: Give me power and I shall engage in a decisive struggle. We must help Russia as far as the Constituent Assembly, and after that they can do as they like: I won't interfere with anything. In this, Anton Ivanovich, may I count on your support? To the fullest extent [answered Denikin]" [7]

The thought of restoring the Romanovs never crossed Kornilov's mind. Nevertheless, by the end of July, he had firmly decided to restore order in the nation and discipline in the army. Realizing that, helpless as it was, the Provisional Government still was the only symbol of lawful power in the country, he had no intention of overturning it, though he unquestionably planned to reform and purge it of undesirable elements. Kornilov's aim was to liberate the government from the oppression of self-elected revolutionary organizations pursuing narrow class interests, and to clear the way for the Constituent Assembly. After this, as he said, "they can do as they like." He planned to begin by getting rid of the Bolshevik leaders, then disbanding the Petrograd Soviet, all of which would unquestionably require the use of armed force.

Kornilov hoped to obtain the consent and cooperation of Kerensky and Savinkov, in order to achieve these changes as "legally" as possible, i.e., through a collaboration between the High Command and certain representatives of the civilian government. In his opinion, the reorganized government—be it a directory or a dictatorship—would have to include (at least temporarily) both Kerensky and Savinkov.

IX

TRANSITIONAL

PHASE

———◆◆———

Denikin remained in command at the southwestern front for less than a month. We know little about his day-to-day activities at that time. The scope of events which took place at the end of August left no place in his memory for the routine details of life. The following incident, however, described in the General's unpublished papers, must have appealed to his sense of humor:

Once, on a great holiday, I went to mass in the city cathedral (in Berdichev). The church was so full that, as the saying goes, there was not room for an apple to fall. My aide-de-camp and I stood in the thick of the congregation. The presence of the commander in chief apparently impressed the clergy. The *starosta* [head vestryman] emerged from the altar and fought his way to us through the crowd . . . carrying a small rug which he intended to place under my feet. Imagine that in the midst of revolution and democratization! I whisper to my aide, and the rug is removed. A few minutes later, the *starosta* again pushes his way through the crowd and whispers into my aide's ear. "What now?"—"He wants to know your name."—"Tell him to leave me alone." A short time passes, and the *starosta* is back. This time he invites us to move to the choir, which is less crowded. Well, this at least makes sense and we proceed to the right-hand choir. The priests come out of the altar for the Great Entrance. . . . After prayers for "The Russian nation and its God-fearing government," one of them turns toward the right choir and proclaims, in defiance of all church rules and tradition: "May the Lord God in his kingdom remember his servant Anton, commander in chief of the southwestern front, now and ever, and unto the ages of ages."
I was terribly embarrassed.[1]

Denikin was pessimistic about military conditions at the southwestern front. He found there "the same strained relationship between officers and soldiers, the same neglect of military duties, desertions, and an undisguised refusal to fight, all of which were still in a latent condition only because of the lull in combat activity. Finally, there was the same Bolshevik propaganda, but in a much stronger form." [2]

In Petrograd, the Bolsheviks had temporarily quieted down after the July events. But at the southwestern front, and particularly in Berdichev, they agitated with complete impunity. The Bolshevik paper *Free Thought,* printed in Berdichev, openly prophesied "a blood bath for the officers."

Far from improving, Denikin's relations with the committees and commissars were becoming more inimical. "As before," wrote the General, "I had no recourse to the cooperation of the commissariat, and sent word to the committee that I could consider dealing with it only when its activity would be carried out within a strictly legal framework." [3]

A letter arrived from General Alekseev: "My thoughts are with you in your new post. My opinion is that you have been assigned a heroic task. . . . Nothing has been done, even after July 16, by Russia's greatest chatterbox. The authority of our commanders is being increasingly curtailed." [4]

Denikin recognized the truth of this pessimistic letter, but in his heart he was still hoping. He expected that in the end, Kornilov's program for rehabilitating the army would be accepted by the government. The government, however, having approved the one condition concerning the nominations of senior commanders by the Supreme Commander, kept an obdurate silence about the other points of the program. The *Stavka,* too, was silent. News reached Denikin only through the papers. Gossip and hearsay were raising excited expectations among the officers.

In this tense atmosphere, Anton Ivanovich was preoccupied with uncertainties and with speculation. Kornilov's program was still unannounced. A conflict was unquestionably taking place. There was still hope of an acceptable solution in Petrograd. But how would it be put in practice in real life? What opposition would it encounter at the front—in regiments and committees? These questions haunted him continuously.

The only person with whom he could share his doubts, hopes, and anxiety was his close friend and chief of staff, Markov, from whom Denikin had no secrets. Together they discussed their certainty of an approaching crisis and of an unavoidable clash with the Petrograd Soviet.

In the meantime, tension in the capital was rapidly approaching a climax.

Denikin knew that Kornilov had gone to Petrograd twice, on August 3 and August 10. The information that reached him in Berdichev concerning these two visits was fragmentary and vague. Only one thing seemed clear: The solution of the crucial question was being deliberately postponed and had obviously met with stubborn resistance on someone's part. Denikin, for one, had no doubt that this resistance emanated from Kerensky.

He did not know at the time that during Kornilov's first visit to the capital, the report he had prepared at the *Stavka* after assuming the High Command was not submitted to the government. It was read only by Savinkov, Filonenko, and Kerensky who decided that it was much too harsh in form and content to be shown to the government's socialist members. They decided, with Kornilov's consent, to rewrite the report at the Ministry of War, along the same lines but in a form more acceptable to all concerned. Thus a discussion of the measures proposed by Kornilov was again being postponed. Kerensky, however, suggested that the Supreme Commander make use of his presence in Petrograd to report personally to the government on conditions at the front, but without referring to his proposed program.

In describing this occasion at a later date, Boris Savinkov mentioned an incident which led to serious consequences, as it influenced Kornilov's subsequent attitude toward the Provisional Government.

When he [Kornilov], addressing the government session, touched on our own and the Allies' strategic plans, I wrote Kerensky approximately the following note: "Is the Prime Minister certain that the state and Allied secrets being communicated to us by the Supreme Commander will not be leaked out to the enemy in friendly confidence?" I wrote this note because I knew that the Petrograd Soviet of Workers' and Soldiers' Deputies included people who had dealings with the enmy and who were at the same time on comradely terms with some members of the Provisional Government. Kerensky read my note and passed it to Kornilov. General Kornilov curtailed his report and asked me after the meeting whether I had been referring specifically to Minister of Agriculture Chernov.[5]

Savinkov made no mention of his answer to Kornilov. The latter, however, remained convinced that the person both Kerensky and Savinkov had in mind was Victor Chernov, the political émigré and "defeatist" of prerevolutionary times.

The term "defeatist" had been applied to those left-wing socialists who, before the collapse of the monarchy, hoped that Russia's defeat in the war would lead to a revolution and a transition to socialism. By contrast, the moderate socialists, nicknamed "defenders," adopted a patriotic platform and advocated pursuing the war to a victorious end.

Kornilov was dumbfounded. He burned with indignation at the thought that among the ministers of the Provisional Government was one whose loyalty was suspect to the Prime Minister and the Acting Minister of War, both of whom were comrades of Chernov's in the Socialist Revolutionary party.

Kornilov left for the *Stavka* the same night, with the understanding that he was to return in a week when his report, edited by the Ministry of War, would be ready for the consideration of the government.

But some mysterious subversive force, with access to the government's secret files, acted with lightning rapidity. On the following day, August

4, Kornilov's report, which had not been shown even to the members of the cabinet, was already in the editorial office of the Soviet newspaper *Izvestia*. A day later, *Izvestia* published excerpts from the report, with slanderous comments about the High Command and with the demand that Kornilov be dismissed.

General Denikin was deeply disturbed by these developments. He could not figure out Savinkov's role in them and had no way of knowing that a serious conflict was brewing backstage between Savinkov and Kerensky. It did not take Savinkov long to find out that "Minister of War Kerensky's policy was not shaped solely by the interests of the armed forces, but also by the moods and decisions of the Petrograd Soviet, a large part of which consisted of members with Bolshevik . . . leanings, to whom motherland, love of country, and the defense of the Russian front were empty words." [6]

For several days Savinkov tried in vain to obtain Kerensky's endorsement of the version of Kornilov's report edited by the Ministry of War. Kerensky's signature, in his capacity as Minister of War was indispensable before the report could be submitted to the government as a whole. The principal point of the report was the projected legal sanctioning of the death penalty for war crimes committed at the rear. Kerensky did everything to delay this decision and to postpone its discussion.

In general [wrote Savinkov], there was a divergence of opinion between Kerensky and myself from the day that I assumed my new duties. And it was not limited to differences of principle. Suffice it to say that Kerensky returned almost every day to the possibility of relieving Kornilov from the post of Supreme Commander, with the implication that this position would be assumed by Kerensky himself. Almost every day, therefore, I had to defend the argument that Kornilov was the only man in Russia who could restore the military effectiveness of the army.

On the night of August 8 . . . I requested a private interview with Kerensky. I said that the report had been completed by Filonenko and asked Kerensky if he would sign it. He replied that at no time and under no circumstances would he agree to sign a law sanctioning the death penalty at the rear. I then stated that this answer, as well as Kerensky's and [Minister of the Interior] Avksentiev's refusal to sign the list of Bolsheviks to be arrested, compiled by the Ministry of War, convinced me that my views diverged so widely from those of the Provisional Government that I was compelled to hand in my resignation. . . . My resignation was not accepted.[7]

Kornilov came to Petrograd for the second time on August 10. It was clear from newspaper reports that the Supreme Commander had little trust in the government and even less in the Soviet. The personnel of the *Stavka* feared an attempt on Kornilov's life, and he left for the capital with an armed escort of his faithful Tekintsy [members of a Turkmen tribe].

As a precaution, the Tekintsy set up their machine guns in the entrance hall of the Winter Palace, where the interview between the Supreme Commander and the Prime Minister was taking place. A specific account of Kornilov's second meeting with Kerensky was unavailable to Denikin at the time. But even the superficial newspaper reporting of those days suggested the cold atmosphere of the encounter. In any case, the meeting brought no tangible results and Kornilov's program remained suspended in midair.

The third and final meeting of Kornilov and Kerensky took place on August 14 at the State Conference in Moscow.

Kerensky initiated this conference and invited to it the representatives of all classes and political orientations in order to put before them his government's aims and problems, and "to feel the pulse of the country." [8]

The conference was held in Moscow's Bolshoi Theater. The right half of the great red-and-gold amphitheater was occupied by nonsocialists. These included representatives of commerce and industry, professorial and literary intelligentsia, former members of the State Duma, Cossack delegations, and eminent military authorities. The socialist wing occupied the left side of the house. The extreme right was not represented, and neither were the Bolsheviks.

Participants in the conference reported later that when one side of the theater applauded a speaker, the other side was either silent or booing.[9]

In the opinion of representatives of the Cadet party at the Moscow Conference, "the government was reviewing the conflicting forces and pitting the right against the left in the hope that this would help it survive at the center." They described Kerensky as "continuing to teeter between both sides in order to preserve his personal power." [10]

Kerensky was conscious of the growing anger of the military against him and could not disguise his fear of Kornilov, who was being promoted for the role of dictator by bourgeois and officer circles. His fear, combined with the desire to dominate, resulted in a veritable torrent of hysterical rhetoric and threats.

Kerensky's frenzied oratory was described by Milyukov, a participant in the conference: "By the expression of his eyes, the tense gesturing of his hands, the intonations of his voice, which rose to a scream for whole periods, then fell to a tragic whisper, by his measured phrases and calculated pauses, this man seemingly wanted to instill fear and to create an impression of force and power in the old style. The actual effect was pitiful." [11]

"Let everyone know," shrieked Kerensky, "let all those who have already attempted to lift an arm against the rule of the people, know that such attempts will be stopped with blood and iron." [12]

"And whatever ultimatums we receive and whoever issues them, I shall know how to make them submit to the governing power and to myself—the head of it." [13]

In addition to invoking blood and iron, he threatened to become piti-less and inexorable, to pluck the flowers from his soul and trample them, and to turn his heart to stone.

A hysterical cry from a woman in the audience responded to Keren-sky's ranting: "No, no Alexander Fedorivich, you can't do that!"

"And the orator, in the throes of passion or of a nervous fit, went on and on without being able to end his speech." [14]

The stage of the Bolshoi Theater presented a strange spectacle. In full view of the public, the producer and principal actor, having lost all con-trol over himself, was rapidly losing that which he coveted most—the support of both the left and the right wing of his audience.

Kornilov's arrival in Moscow for the conference was surrounded by pomp. He was greeted with speeches and shouts of acclaim. His entrance at the Bolshoi Theater was met with an ovation in which all the non-socialist groupings seemed to unite. The General's dry but forceful speech was very restrained and contained no sharp criticisms of the government.

"To my deep regret I must frankly admit my uncertainty that the Rus-sian army will unflinchingly carry out its duty to its country . . . ," said Kornilov. "The enemy is already knocking at the gates of Riga, and if the instability of our army does not allow us to hold the littoral of the Gulf of Riga, the road to Petrograd will be exposed." [15] Kornilov presented the essence of his program, emphasizing the need to implement it immediately. "We cannot become resolute . . . only under pressure of defeat and loss of national territory. If it took the rout of Tarnopol and the loss of Galicia and Bukovina to induce firm measures for preserving discipline at the front, we cannot admit that restoring order at the rear should be paid for by the loss of Riga." [16]

Riga was occupied by German troops on August 20. The leftist press, which had been clamoring for Kornilov's dismissal, took this occasion to accuse him of treason. "The *Stavka*," wrote *Izvestia*, "is trying to terrorize the Provisional Government by grave events at the front and force it to approve a series of measures aimed directly or obliquely against revolu-tionary democracy and its organizations." [17]

Denikin noted down the repercussions of the August, 1917, events which affected him directly at the front:

On August 7, he was ordered by the *Stavka* to detach from his front and move in a northward direction a native Caucasian unit known as the "Wild Division." It consisted of Cherkes, Chechen, Ingush, and Dagestan mountaineers from the northern parts of the Caucasus. In Denikin's words, "Its riders combined bravery with primitive customs and extremely elastic standards in relation to the spoils of war."

On August 12, Denikin was ordered to move to the north the Third Cavalry Corps, which had been in reserve. A few days later, a similar order came for the so-called "Kornilov Shock Regiment."

"As usual, the destination of the troops was not given," wrote the General. "The direction in which they were sent could indicate the northern front, which was seriously threatened at the time, as well as . . . Petrograd."

En route to the north, General Krymov, commander of the Third Cavalry Corps, called on Denikin. The two generals knew each other well. Krymov was recognized as a brave and determined man. He made no secret of his point of view about current events and considered that the country could be saved only by "a stunning blow at the Soviets." He did not discuss his new orders with Denikin but, wrote the latter, "Neither of us doubted that his mission was connected with the new turn in military policy we both expected. . . ."

At long last [Denikin continued], about August 20, the situation became somewhat clearer. An officer arrived in Berdichev and handed me a letter in Kornilov's own writing, requesting me to hear his emissary's verbal report.

The officer related that, according to reliable sources, there would be a Bolshevik uprising in Petrograd at the end of August. By that time the Third Cavalry Corps led by Krymov would reach the capital, quell the uprising, and make an end of the Soviets. Concurrently, a state of emergency would be declared in Petrograd, accompanied by the publication of new laws based on the "Kornilov Program." The only thing the Supreme Commander asked me to do was to dispatch to the *Stavka* a score or two of reliable officers, ostensibly "for trench-mortar instruction." In reality, they would be sent to join an officer detachment in Petrograd. In the course of our conversation the officer gave me various news of the *Stavka* and of its generally optimistic mood. Among other things, he mentioned rumors concerning the forthcoming nominations of new military commanders in Kiev, Odessa, and Moscow, and concerning projected changes in the cabinet which would include some of the present ministers as well as some new ones completely unknown to me. The role which the Provisional Government and Kerensky in particular were to play in all this was not very clear. It was hard to tell whether Kerensky would decide in favor of a drastic change in military policy, or resign, or be swept away by the force of events whose development and consequences could not be foreseen at this point either by pure logic or by the most astute mind.[18]

Despite the optimism of Kornilov's messenger, Denikin was obsessed by doubts. Did the *Stavka* really have a chance, or was its intrepid behavior the result of cold desperation?

Denikin's state of mind was reflected in the letters he wrote to his fiancée:

August 17
The conflict continues. . . . I am in a state of extreme nervous tension and terribly tired. The government is still procrastinating and putting off the reorganization of the army. I am depressed. Especially now that I feel almost completely alone.

August 23
This is a time of absolute tension, unlimited possibilities, great anxiety.

X

"NIGHT FELL—
A LONG,
SLEEPLESS NIGHT"

————◄———►————

A few days later occurred an event of incalculable importance:

In the evening of August 27 [related Denikin in his memoirs], I was thunder-
struck by a communication from the *Stavka* announcing the dismissal of General Kornilov from the post of Supreme Commander in Chief.

An unnumbered telegram signed "Kerensky" summoned General Kornilov
to hand over his functions as Supreme Commander temporarily to General
Lukomsky [Kornilov's chief of staff], and to leave for Petrograd without awaiting the arrival of a new Supreme Commander. This was a completely illegal
order, which the recipient was not obliged to obey, since the Supreme Commander was not subject to the individual authority of either the Minister of
War or the Prime Minister, and certainly not to that of plain Comrade
Kerensky.

Only the Provisional Government had the legal right to relieve the
Supreme Commander of his post. Strangely enough, this important point
escaped the attention of everyone at the *Stavka*.

Next, General Denikin received a copy of the telegram sent by General
Lukomsky to Prime Minister Kerensky, in which Lukomsky refused to
take over the functions of the Supreme Commander. His telegram concluded with the following words: "For the sake of Russia's salvation, you
must join forces with General Kornilov rather than dismiss him. The dismissal of General Kornilov will bring about horrors of a kind Russia has
never yet experienced. Personally, I cannot take upon myself the responsibility for the army even for a short period. I consider it impossible to

assume Kornilov's functions, as this will be followed by an explosion in the army which will be fatal to Russia."

Denikin fully realized the danger of this break between Kornilov and Kerensky, barring the remote possibility that Krymov's corps (the Third Cavalry Corps, ordered north from Denikin's front) could save the situation.

At the same time [wrote Denikin], I did not for a single day or a single hour find it possible to identify myself in principle with the Provisional Government, which I considered criminal and to which I therefore immediately dispatched the following telegram:

"I am a soldier and not used to playing hide-and-seek. July 16, at a conference with members of the Provisional Government, I stated that this government, by a series of military measures, had ruined and corrupted the army and trampled our battle banners in the mud. At that time I interpreted my being left at my post of commander in chief as the Provisional Government's admission of its grave crime against Russia and of its desire to mitigate the harm it had perpetrated. Today I received the news that General Kornilov has been removed from the post of Supreme Commander after having made certain demands [the Kornilov report] which could still save the country and the army. Interpreting this as the government's return to its former policy of systematic destruction of the army and, consequently, of the whole country, I am in duty bound to notify the Provisional Government that I shall not be a partner to its actions. No. 145. DENIKIN."

Denikin ordered that copies of his telegram be sent to all the commanders in chief and army commanders of the southwestern front, as well as to its quartermaster general. At the same time, he took measures "to isolate the front from receiving any kind of information concerning the events at hand without the knowledge of the General Staff, until the conflict was settled." Under prevailing conditions, however, no preventive measures could successfully conceal from the troops that a break had occurred between the government and the army command.

Denikin asked the *Stavka* if there was any way in which he could assist General Kornilov. "He knew," noted Denikin sadly, "that apart from moral support, I had no real means of helping him. And so, having thanked me for that support, he asked nothing else of me." [1]

The text of two other documents reached Denikin's headquarters on the night of August 28. One was a radiotelegram from Kerensky to all government officials, commissars, committees, and the like, for immediate release to the army and the population. The other was General Kornilov's appeal to the nation, made in response to Kerensky's telegram.

Kerensky's message asserted that on August 26, Vladimir Lvov, a former member of the State Duma, was sent to him by Kornilov with the demand that the Provisional Government surrender its full civilian and military authority to General Kornilov, who would then proceed to form a new government personally selected by him. Kerensky asserted further that in a conversation conducted by teleprinter, Kornilov had confirmed to him that he had officially authorized Lvov to convey this proposal. Having perceived in Kornilov's demands an attempt to establish a form of government opposed to the conquests of the revolution, the Provisional Government—in order to save the country, its freedom, and the republican regime—had authorized Kerensky to use every means of suppressing any attempt to encroach on the power of the government and on the rights which the citizens had achieved by the revolution.

The telegram ordered Kornilov to surrender his post to General Klembovsky, the commander in chief of the northern front. It declared martial law in Petrograd.

General Kornilov responded by the following proclamation: "The Prime Minister's telegram No. 4163, in its entire first part, consists entirely of lies. It was not I who sent State Duma member Vladimir Lvov to the Provisional Government, but he who came to me as the envoy of the Prime Minister. . . . In this manner, a major act of provocation was perpetrated, jeopardizing the fate of our country." In his highly emotional proclamation, Kornilov declared "that the Provisional Government, under pressure of the Bolshevik majority of the Soviets and acting in complete accord with the plans of the German General Staff . . . is destroying the army and undermining the foundations of the country."

He appealed to the people of Russia to rescue their "dying motherland," and stated that he would lead the people to the Constituent Assembly, where they could settle their own fate and decide on a form of government of their own choice. Kornilov concluded by declaring, "I refuse to hand Russia over to her age-old enemy—the German race—and to make the Russian people slaves of the Germans. I prefer to die with honor on the field of battle, so as not to witness the downfall and shame of the Russian land." [2]

This proclamation was dated August 27, 1917.

Anton Ivanovich realized that the Kornilov proclamation he had just read was "the voice of despair."

"Night fell—a long, sleepless night filled with anxious expectation and harrowing thoughts," wrote Denikin about this eerie vigil. "Never before had our country's future appeared so dark and our helplessness more frustrating and hard to bear. The historic drama unfolding in the distance was like a thunderstorm whose streaks of lightning raked the dark clouds gathered over Russia. And so we waited. . . . This night will never be forgotten." [3]

It was clear to the General that an irreparable, major disaster had occurred. But had not the Prime Minister himself sought the support of the military against the Bolsheviks? Were not the parties involved engaged in some sort of secret negotiations through the intermediary of Savinkov? Kornilov would not have flung his accusation of a "major act of provocation" unless it was founded! Who was Vladimir Lvov? How and by whom was he authorized to act as intermediary between Kerensky and

Kornilov? Denikin saw very well that the personalities of the principal actors were incompatible. But surely they were well aware of this themselves and accustomed to the fact. What then had precipitated the clash between them? Misunderstanding, intrigue, personal ambition, thoughtlessness, irresponsibility, gullibility? . . . There was to be no answer to these speculations for some time to come.

On the following day, all communications between Denikin's headquarters and the outside world were severed.

In the meantime, the committees of the southwestern front were feverishly stirring up the already mutinous soldier masses. They passed resolutions accusing General Denikin of treason, of preparing to open the front to the Germans, of wishing to restore Nicholas II to the throne. Printed proclamations calling for the arrest of Denikin and his staff were posted on walls and scattered throughout the city. At various meetings, crowds of soldiers aroused by this propaganda clamored for retribution against the commander in chief.

Denikin saw from his windows the huge throng of armed soldiers gathering for a meeting on "Bald Mountain," near the city. The meeting over, he watched the crowd, with its red banners and armored cars, set off in the direction of his headquarters.

The house was surrounded by revolutionary guards, and the committee of the front telegraphed Petrograd that General Denikin and his entire General Staff were being detained at headquarters under personal arrest. Putting up resistance would have been futile, since all the local military units had already been won over by propaganda.

The following day, August 29, Anton Ivanovich was able to send a letter to his fiancée in Kiev by a trusted messenger:

My dear, this is a new catastrophic period in Russian history. Our unfortunate country is caught in a net of falsehood, provocation, and helplessness.

No use talking about my state of mind. My "High Command" is fictitious, being under the control of commissars and committees.

Despite these unbelievable conditions, I shall remain at my post to the end and have instructed my subordinate commanders to do the same.

They claim to be saving the revolution, but are destroying the army and ruining the country!

I have once more quite openly declared to the Provisional Government that it is following a path of destruction for the nation and the army. I cannot understand the psychology of those people. They are fully cognizant of my point of view, they do not dismiss me, and at the same time they do not allow me to work as my duty commands me to do.

Am physically fit. My heart aches. My soul suffers.

Obviously, this undetermined state cannot last. God preserve Russia from new and terrible upheavals!

Don't worry about me, my love; my way is perfectly clear and straight.

DENIKIN

Denikin was unaware that on the same day his letter was written the following decree had been issued by the Provisional Government: "The commander in chief of the armies at the southwestern front, Lieutenant General Denikin, is hereby removed from the post of commander in chief and will be brought to trial for mutiny." The decree was signed by Prime Minister Kerensky and Acting Minister of War Savinkov.

This was followed by an order issued in Berdichev by the commissar of the southwestern front, Iordansky, for the arrest of General Denikin, of his chief of staff, General Markov, and of Deputy Chief of Staff Orlov. All of them were accused of "attempting an armed uprising against the Provisional Government."

The three generals were driven to the guardhouse in an automobile escorted by armored cars. They were met with hatred and jeers by a crowd of about a hundred assembled near the prison.

The generals were placed in separate cells. Their imprisonment in Berdichev was to last nearly a month, with each day holding the threat of lawless reprisal from the aroused mob. Denikin's account of this trying period is remarkable in its simplicity and strength:

Ward No. 1. Seven square feet of floor space. Iron bars on the window. A small peephole in the door. A plank bed, a table, a stool. Breathing is made painful by the stench of the privy next door. On the other side is No. 2, where Markov is pacing with long nervous steps. For some reason I still remember that he takes three steps from wall to wall, whereas I manage to take seven on the diagonal. The jail is full of vague noises. My sharpened hearing has learned to tell them apart and gradually enables me to reconstruct the routine of life around and even the mood of the moment. The guards, who I think belong to the prison guard company, are rude and vengeful fellows.

It is early morning. I hear voices. Where do they come from? Two soldiers are outside my window, hanging onto the iron bars. They stare at me with hatred and scream obscenities. They have thrown in some unspeakable object through the open window. I cannot escape their gaze. Turning to the door, I meet another pair of eyes watching with hatred through the peephole, and hear another string of curses. I lie down on the plank bed and cover my head with my army greatcoat. I remain this way for hours. . . . The small airless cubbyhole is continuously filled with a stream of unprintable words, screams, and curses. . . . I feel as if my soul were covered with drunken vomit, and there is no salvation, no escape from this moral torture. What is it they are saying? "He wanted to expose the front" . . . "sold himself to the Germans." . . . They even mention the amount—twenty thousand rubles. . . . "Wanted to deprive us of our land and freedom." . . . All this is not their thinking, but the committees'. "Commander in chief, general, *barin* [gentleman]"—now *that* is spoken, naturally, in their language. As is, "You've had your fill of bloodsucking, ordering us about, letting us rot in jail; take your turn sitting behind bars, now that we have the upper hand. . . . You've taken it easy driving around in cars—now see how you like the plank bed, you son of a bitch. You haven't much time left. . . . We won't wait for you to run away—we'll strangle you with our own hands first." . . .

I lay there with my greatcoat over my head, under a torrent of abuse, and tried to determine objectively whether I had deserved this.

Mentally, Anton Ivanovich passed his whole life in review. His father —a serf, then a soldier under the severe regime of Nicholas I, achieving officer's rank through his service. His pitiful pension. Anton Ivanovich's harsh and joyless childhood. His father's death and the family's poverty. A youth spent in study and bread-winning. Then, service as a volunteer in the barracks on soldiers' rations. Life as an officer; the Academy of the General Staff; his complaint to the Tsar against the minister of war. Return to the Second Field Artillery Brigade. Nomination to the General Staff; the Japanese war; the articles he wrote against obsolete military customs and arbitrary rule in the army. His endeavors to improve the condition of the soldiers and to have their human dignity respected. The war of 1914. The Iron Division. His constant presence in the front lines, sharing the dangers, joys, and sorrows of the soldiers. His intimate rapport with his riflemen.

No [decided Denikin], I have never been a foe to the soldier.
I threw off my greatcoat, jumped off the bed, and went to the window to whose bars clung a vituperating private.
"Soldier, you lie! You are not speaking your own mind. If you were not a coward hiding in the rear, if you have been in action, you saw that your officers knew how to die. You say that they . . ."
The hands let go off the bars and the man disappeared. I suspect that he was simply driven off by the harsh tone of my reprimand, which had its atavistic effect despite the helplessness of the prisoner delivering it. . . .
Soon the duty of guarding us was assigned to the cadets of the Second Zhitomir Officer Candidate School. This brought considerable moral relief. They not only guarded the prisoners but protected them from the crowd which gathered at the guardhouse on several occasions, roaring its hatred and threatening to lynch us. When this happened, the cadet company on duty rapidly gathered at a house diagonally across the street from us, with machine guns ready. I remember that in a moment of calm and clear realization of danger, when the mob was especially violent, I devised my own means of self-defense: There was a heavy carafe of water on the table, which could be used to smash the skull of the first attacker who broke into the cell; the other "comrades," excited and angered by the sight of blood, would kill me immediately without subjecting me to torture. . . .
With the exception of such unpleasant interludes, however, our life in prison followed a regular, methodical routine. . . . The physical discomforts of prison life meant little to us compared to the campaign hardships and moral suffering we had previously experienced. . . .
And every day, when I opened my window, someone's high tenor voice across the street (was it a friend's or a foe's?) intoned the song:
This is the last, the final day
That I can feast with you my friends.[4]

Following Denikin and his staff, Generals Erdeli, Vannovsky, and Selivachev, each of whom had commanded an army at the southwestern front, and General Elsner, who was its quartermaster general, were also brought to the Berdichev prison. They were accused of having approved the contents of the telegram sent by Denikin to the Provisional Government. Several other generals and officers were arrested at the same time, but soon released.

A while later, the Berdichev prisoners had access to some newspapers. They learned of the arrests of General Kornilov, Chief of Staff Lukomsky, Deputy Chief of Staff Romanovsky, and other officers at the *Stavka,* and of their confinement in the prison of Bykhov, a district town of Mogilev province.

A judicial investigation of the case of the arrested generals began even before they had received this news. It was held by the committee of inquiry of the southwestern front under the chairmanship of the assistant commissar of the front.

My testimony was perforce extremely brief [recollected Denikin]. It boiled down to the following postulates: 1. None of the persons arrested with me had participated in any activities directed against the government. 2. All orders given at headquarters in connection with General Kornilov's actions were issued by me personally. 3. I considered then, and still consider, that the course of action of the Provisional Government was criminal and fatal to Russia; nevertheless I had not fomented an uprising against it, but having dispatched my telegram No. 145, left it up to the Provisional Government to dispose of me as it saw fit.[5]

The commissar of the southwestern front, Iordansky, was anxious to get on with the case. On September 1, he queried the government whether, in conducting this case, he should be guided by political considerations or proceed according to law, bearing in mind local conditions. He also advised the government of having uncovered documents proving the existence of a conspiracy. The government's reply instructed him to proceed strictly according to law . . . bearing in mind local conditions. In the circumstances which prevailed at that time, the phrase "bearing in mind local conditions" could have only one interpretation —that of allowing the mob to interfere with the process of justice and predetermine its outcome.

There is no doubt that this was precisely Iordansky's aim. His scheming, however, received an unexpected setback from the Extraordinary Commission of Inquiry into the Kornilov Affair which had been hastily formed in Petrograd on the night of August 30.

Since the Extraordinary Commission of Inquiry considered that the Denikin case was linked to the Kornilov affair, it opposed Iordansky's insistence that Denikin be tried separately by a court-martial.

I. S. Shablovsky, chief prosecutor for the army and navy, was chosen to preside over the Extraordinary Commission of Inquiry. He had practiced law in Riga before the revolution, and following the 1905 uprisings, had acted as defense attorney in political cases involving riots, civil commotions, and other subversive activities in the Baltic provinces. It was there that he met and became friendly with Kerensky, who was acting in the same capacity. In March, 1917, Shablovsky's personal acquaintance with Kerensky unexpectedly brought him the nomination to the highest post in the judiciary department of the army and navy.

In the first days of September, Kerensky advised the members of the Commission that Commissar Iordansky had requested his permission to bring General Denikin and the members of his staff before a court-martial in Berdichev, as partners in crime with General Kornilov. Kerensky submitted the question to the decision of the Commission. The latter refused Iordansky's request because from a legal point of view it was inconceivable to judge accessories in a crime before judging its principal perpetrators, and in this case the investigation which might or might not indicate guilt and thus lead to indictment and trial had not yet begun. In addition, the Commission pointed out, satisfying Iordansky's demand would lend a new, extremely serious aspect to the case, since a verdict of guilty pronounced by a court-martial automatically carried with it the penalty of death.

Less than twenty-four hours later, Kerensky told Shablovsky that Iordansky insisted on having Denikin and the other generals of the southwestern front brought before a court-martial without delay. "Otherwise the Commissar could not be answerable for the situation at the front for a single day." The Commission's members commented later that this veiled threat "was repeated several times and that the lives of the accused were literally hanging by a thread." In their opinion, Kerensky was unquestionably "trying to pressure Shablovsky into changing the Commission's decision to conform with Iordansky's wishes." [6]

The following excerpts from the little-known but very valuable testimony on the subject by a member of the Extraordinary Commission of Inquiry, the military lawyer Colonel Ukraintsev, shed additional light on the controversy:

Having failed to make Shablovsky change his mind, Kerensky asked the members of the Commission to discuss the problem with Iordansky at a meeting to be held in Mogilev on the following day.

The encounter took place at the station in Kerensky's railroad carriage. Iordansky reasserted that he could not accept reponsibility for the front for a single day, unless the unanimous demand of its troops for bringing the incriminated generals before a court-martial was satisfied. He emphasized particularly that he was merely voicing the wishes of the entire front. It was noteworthy that Iordansky said almost nothing about the actual nature of the crime of which the commanding generals of the front were accused, and the little he said sounded extremely vague. . . .

Iordansky's argument evoked a series of objections on our part. Shablovsky expressed his doubt of the assertion that the entire front demanded that the generals be brought to trial.

[In the ensuing argument], . . . as Iordansky became more insistent, our resistance stiffened, so that the only advantage finally derived by the commissar from this meeting was the right to claim that he had performed his duty and alerted us to the danger threatening the front. "If you are willing to be responsible for this situation," he told Kerensky, "I wash my hands of it." In short, Iordansky presented the case in such a way that only one conclusion remained possible: The most important thing for the front, i.e., the soldier masses, was to see the recently established courts-martial and death penalty applied against the very people who were responsible for their introduction. "The front must have proof of the political integrity of the lawmakers."

Kerensky listened to the arguments of both sides with equal attention. . . . One felt, however, that he was definitely biased in Iordansky's favor . . . which he proved by addressing Shablovsky in roughly the following terms: 'You are well aware, Iosif Sigismundovich, that I am against military courts-martial and death penalty and you must realize, therefore, how painful this whole matter is to me and how difficult I find it to agree with Nikolai Ivanovich [Iordansky]. But please understand—how can I gamble with the stability of an entire front, and perhaps, with the fate of the whole country? Grave reasons of state oblige us to arrive at a painful decision. Grant Iordansky's request, and I promise you not to confirm the death penalty if it is imposed."

I repeat [wrote Ukraintsev], that I am rendering the exact meaning and tone of Kerensky's address but, of course, not quoting it word for word.

At this point, Shablovsky, who like the rest of us had been seated during the conference, rose to his feet and addressed Kerensky in a firm, even somewhat theatrical voice: "Alexander Fedorovich, how many times both you and I, in our court appearances, unflinchingly stood up for *legality* and refuted all considerations of expediency and tactics. Is it possible that now that the decision is in our hands, we shall embark on a course that we had always condemned? I don't believe that the entire southwestern front is actually demanding that its commanders be court-martialed, but even if this were true, the duty of a government commissar is not to cater to the unenlightened and stirred-up masses, but to explain to them the necessity of observing the law. I do not consent to the court-martialing of the generals of the southwestern front."

Shablovsky's words visibly upset Kerensky. After a prolonged silence, he proposed that we leave immediately for Berdichev to clarify the actual state of affairs on the spot and to bring out a decision in conformity with our observations. Both we and Iordansky accepted the proposal.

. . . We held different opinions regarding Kerensky's readiness to give in to Iordansky, but we were unanimous on one point: We could not trust Kerensky's promise not to confirm a verdict of the death penalty. That the military court-martial would reach this verdict under Iordansky's influence was a foregone conclusion. Even if Kerensky did not wish to confirm the verdict, there would be forces which would compel him to do so. It was absolutely clear that in this trial, which held the attention of the entire country, the life of the numerous defendants was actually at stake.[7]

The Commission left for Berdichev. There, Iordansky instructed its members to wait for the automobile which was to fetch them and not to leave for the prison unaccompanied. Time passed. Iordansky telephoned several times reiterating his request not to leave under any conditions until the car arrived. Nearly five hours went by before it came. The Commission's members were furious and wanted to know the cause of this delay. Its reasons became apparent as soon as they approached the prison. In order to create an impression of popular wrath, Iordansky had spent the intervening hours in assembling a crowd of several thousand soldiers near Denikin's place of detention. The crowd surrounded it on all sides; it was difficult to fight one's way through. The roar of the mob would drown out any conversations with the prisoners; one had to shout in order to hear one's own voice. The situation was threatening. The only thing which kept the mob from storming the guardhouse was a machine gun set up at its entrance and manned by the military cadet guard. Any questioning of the prisoners was obviously impossible and would have to be postponed to another day. Nevertheless, the members of the Commission did not want to leave without seeing General Denikin. This was the impression of the encounter:

We stopped to see General Denikin. He was in a solitary cell. Near the wall stood a neatly covered cot with a small icon hanging over it. The General met us standing; his whole appearance spoke of good military bearing and personal dignity. He behaved with absolute calm.

Shablovsky told the general that we had intended to question him but found it impossible to do so in the conditions prevailing around the prison. He then asked if the General had any complaints or wishes and was answered in the negative. We were impressed by the complete calm of Denikin, who could hear very well the clamor of voices outside and knew through a series of sad examples what an officer could expect from a mob of soldiers aroused by revolutionary slogans.

It was even harder to fight a path from the prison to the car. Rumors had been spread among the soldiers about "the wicked designs of the Commission." The crowd pressed against us so closely that we could only take a small step forward from time to time and were very soon separated from each other. The many-headed monster growled, bellowed, and threatened. Glancing back, I saw a pale-faced Shablovsky attempting to smile. Keep calm, I kept saying to myself, or we are done for. Dozens of times, in an intentionally tranquil voice, I repeated to the excited soldiers who swarmed around me, that we had come especially to learn what the front wanted and that we asked all those present to come tomorrow to the session of the Soviet, which we would also attend in order to hear the demands of the front. . . .

Need I emphasize that the entire incident was Iordansky's work? It was the most shameless provocation as well as a very primitive and unsubtle one.[8]

Complete quiet surrounded the guardhouse on the next day. There was no crowd, and the questioning of the prisoners proceeded without incident.

Shablovsky explained to Denikin that his Commission considered it imperative that a single trial be held for all the participants in Kornilov's action, and deemed it unthinkable to subject Denikin and his subordinate generals to a separate judgment. He stated that the Commission's aim was to transfer the prisoners from Berdichev to Bykhov, as the mood of the masses in Berdichev excluded the possibility of justice and threatened the accused with savage reprisals.

Also, with great difficulty, Shablovsky persuaded the Berdichev Soviet of the necessity of transferring the case to the highest appellate jurisdiction: the military department of the Central Executive Committee of the Soviet of Workers' and Soldiers' Deputies in Petrograd.

This change of venue represented the Commission's most important move on the bureaucratic chessboard of the then-existing system of Soviets, and the fate of the Berdichev prisoners was to depend on it.

From its inception, the Soviet had been inimical to the officer class. One could, therefore, hardly expect it to adopt an objective attitude toward the generals accused of counterrevolution. Fortunately, the military department of the Central Executive Committee of the Petrograd Soviet had fewer than ten members, and this allowed Shablovsky and his associates to establish a fairly personal relationship with them. The case was discussed on September 14 at the Smolny Institute, to which the Soviet had moved from the Tauride Palace after the July uprising. By outlining their case and explaining its legal aspects with calm and logic, the members of the Extraordinary Commission of Inquiry succeeded in achieving their aim. The military department of the Petrograd Soviet decided by a majority vote to postpone the trial of General Denikin and his companions until the completion of General Kornilov's investigation, and to transfer them in the interim from Berdichev to Bykhov.

Commissar Iordansky lost the round, but made the prisoners pay dearly for his discomfiture.

Thus [wrote Denikin], the threat of a trumped-up trial was avoided. But the Berdichev revolutionary organizations had up their sleeve another way of liquidating our group, a way at once easy and devoid of personal responsibility —"explosion of popular wrath." . . .

The departure for Bykhov was scheduled for 5 P.M. on September 27, from the Berdichev station.

A quiet removal of the prisoners [continued Denikin] presented no problem. . . . But this was not the way the commissars and committees had planned it. A great deal of publicity and an unhealthy atmosphere of curiosity and expectancy, artificially created by them, preceded the event. . . . From early morning on, the commissariat toured all the units of the garrison to obtain their consent for our transfer. The committee called a meeting of the entire garrison for 2 P.M., i.e., three hours before our projected departure. Moreover, the meeting was to be held in a field directly adjoining our prison. A colossal crowd assembled. Representatives of the commissariat and the committee of the front advised it of the order for our removal to Bykhov, took the trouble of indicating the exact hour of our departure . . . then appealed to the garrison to act with restraint. No one agreed to leave, of course, and the meeting went on and on. As the hour of five approached, an excited crowd of many thousands surrounded the guardhouse. We could hear its dull roar in our cells.

One of the officers of the cadet battalion of the Second Zhitomir Officer Candidate School which guarded us on that day was Captain Betling, a war invalid who had served before the war in the Seventeenth Infantry Arkhangelogorod regiment which I commanded. Betling asked permission of his superiors at the school to substitute his own half company for the unit designated to escort us to the station. We all got dressed and came out into the corridor. We waited. One hour . . . two. . . .

The meeting continued. Numerous orators incited the mob to take the law into its hands. . . . A soldier who had been wounded by Lieutenant Kletsando [9] screamed hysterically, demanding his head. . . . Assistant Commissars Kostitsyn and Grigoriev tried to pacify the crowd from the porch of the guardhouse. The good Betling also spoke to them several times, hotly and passionately. We could not hear his words.

At long last, Betling and Kostitsyn, both of them pale and distraught, came to me.

"What is your decision? The crowd has promised not to molest anyone; it demands only that you go to the station on foot. We can't be sure of anything, however."

I answered, "Let's go."

I removed my cap and made the sign of the cross: "God help us!"

[In the unpublished notes of Mrs. Xenia Denikin, we find the following: "Anton Ivanovich told me that he was certain that they would not be taken anywhere, but massacred by the mob on their way. There was only one wish in his chilled consciousness, that they finish them off quickly, without torture, without taunting them too long. He knew also that he would have the strength not to flinch before death." [10]]

The mob was raging. The seven of us, surrounded by the handful of cadets commanded by Betling, who walked by my side with drawn sword, entered a narrow passage in the sea of humanity which surged on all sides. Kostitsyn and twelve to fifteen delegates chosen by the garrison to convoy us, walked in front. Night was falling. In its eerie darkness, pierced from time to time by the armored car's searchlight, moved the demented mob. It expanded and rolled forward like burning lava. The air was full of its deafening roar, hysterical screams, and obscene curses. . . . Occasionally, Betling's loud, worried voice broke the din:

"Comrades, you promised! . . . Comrades, you promised! . . ."

The cadets, fine young fellows, were jostled from all sides. They shielded us from the surging crowd with their own bodies and could barely hold their thin chain together. Soldiers, splashing through the puddles left by yesterday's rain, collected handfuls of mud and flung them at us. Our faces, eyes, and ears were covered with the malodorous, slimy liquid. Cobblestones began to rain on us. Poor crippled General Orlov's face was badly smashed, Erdeli was also hit, and I received stones in the back and head.

We exchanged short remarks along the way. "Is this the end, my dear professor?" I asked Markov.[11]

"Evidently . . ."

The crowd does not allow us to take the direct way to the station. We follow a circuitous route, some five kilometers in all, along the town's principal streets. The crowd keeps growing. The curious fill the balconies of Berdichev's houses. Women wave handkerchiefs and animated guttural voices exclaim, "Long live freedom."

The station is flooded with light. Another huge crowd of several thousand people awaits us there. A great, raging, roaring sea engulfs everything. We thread our way through it with immense difficulty, pursued by vengeful looks and curses. We enter the carriage. I have a glimpse of Elsner's officer son, wracked with sobs, shouting senseless threats to the crowd, and of his orderly tenderly consoling him and taking away his revolver; of two women petrified with fear—Kletsando's wife and sister who had rashly decided to see him off. . . . An hour passes, then another. The train is not allowed to leave as the crowd wants us in a prison carriage and the station doesn't have one. The crowd threatens to lynch the commissars. They've ruffled Kostitsyn a bit. A freight car arrives at the platform, all filthy with horse dung. How little this matters! We have to climb in without steps. Poor Orlov is pushed in with difficulty. Hundreds of hands still try to reach us through the intrepid and firm barrier of cadets. . . . It is already ten o'clock. . . . The locomotive gives a wrench. The mob roars louder. Two shots are fired. The train moves off.

The noise grows less and less, the lights are dimming. Goodbye Berdichev!

Kerensky shed a tear of emotion, so moved was he by the selfless devotion of "our saviors," a term he used not for the cadets, but for the commissars and committee members. "What irony of fate!" exclaimed Kerensky [in his book *Delo Kornilova* (*The Kornilov Affair*)] "that General Denikin, arrested as an accomplice of Kornilov, should be rescued from the wrath of enraged soldiers by the members of the executive committee of the southwestern front and the commissars of the Provisional Government." [12]

THE KORNILOV
AFFAIR, I

What were the essential facts of the action ascribed to General Kornilov which led to such momentous consequences in General Denikin's life?

As has been mentioned, Kornilov's aim was to reform the Provisional Government, preferably with the cooperation of Kerensky and Savinkov, by liberating it from the oppression of self-elected revolutionary organizations. He wanted to disband the Petrograd Soviet, to suppress the Bolshevik party, and to introduce strict discipline in the army. Denikin had only an overall idea of the Supreme Commander's plans, but no detailed knowledge of them. He deferred willingly to Kornilov's heroic personality, with complete awareness of the risk involved in their common endeavor, but also with the conviction that the plans for rehabilitating the army and the nation were in competent hands. There could be no other approach within the traditions of army life. Besides, Denikin's headquarters were too distant from the *Stavka* to allow for regular communication. It was dangerous to resort to the telegraph, or even to written orders, in so delicate a situation. These could be easily intercepted by the commissars and committees which kept the High Command and especially its political activity under close surveillance.

Unfortunately, the assumption that the conduct of the affair was in competent hands was unjustified. Denikin gave in restrospect an appraisal of Kornilov's personality which explains to a certain extent the series of events we are about to examine.

Kornilov was a soldier and military leader. He was proud of this and considered it the principal motivation of his life. We cannot see into other people's souls. His actions and some of his words, spoken in confidence with complete frankness, defined quite clearly his own conception of the role he was destined to play: He had no illusions as to his qualifications for political leadership, but saw himself rather as a mighty battering ram that would break through the vicious circle which surrounded the government and rendered it irresponsible and helpless. He had to cleanse the governing power of its unstatesmanlike and anti-national elements . . . had to protect that power until the true wishes of the Russian people could be expressed and implemented.

But his nature, perhaps too indulgent, trusting, and lacking in discernment, prevented him from noticing that from the very beginning, unstatesmanlike and even unprincipled elements also attached themselves to his plan of action. This was the great tragedy of the Kornilov movement.

Kornilov's political image still remains unclear for many people. It is surrounded by a web of legends based on the nature of his entourage, which often acted arbitrarily in the General's name. . . .

The truth is that Kornilov was neither a socialist nor a reactionary, but it would be futile, within these broad confines, to stamp him with a specific allegiance to one party. Like the majority of officers and army commanders, any kind of party dogmatism was alien to him. His general outlook and convictions were those of a widespread majority of liberal democrats.

. . . Neither before, nor during, nor after the affair under discussion, nor even in private confidence, did Kornilov enunciate a definite political program. He had none. . . . It is rather unexpected to find this complete absence of a clear-cut political attitude in a leader prepared to take over temporarily the helm of the ship of state. But the havoc which prevailed in Russian social consciousness and political orientation by the fall of 1917 seemed to indicate that only a neutral force, aided by propitious circumstances, had a chance to succeed in unifying the immensely numerous but intellectually uncoordinated popular masses which stood beyond the framework of "revolutionary democracy." [1]

Thus spoke the associate of General Kornilov who, of all people, had the closest spiritual ties with his leader.

It would be vain to look for a harsh judgment on Kornilov in Denikin's writings. Having entrusted his fate to Kornilov once and for all, Anton Ivanovich thought and wrote of him for the rest of his life with profound love and devotion. It would have been unlike Denikin to behave differently. Nevertheless, he did not gloss over or deny the negative aspects of the Kornilov movement or excuse its mistakes. From his conversations in the Bykhov prison with Generals Kornilov, Lukomsky, and Romanovsky, and his subsequent talks with General Alekseev and many others, Denikin learned every detail of the affair and understood the whole unforgivably thoughtless, inexcusable sequence of errors made at that time.

Kornilov, a splendid combat general and a born hero, was an absolute child in political matters. He sought a way out of the labyrinth of harrowing problems besetting postrevolutionary Russia with a soldier's simplicity and straightforwardness.

With his innate sense of responsibility before history, General Denikin has left us a truthful testimony of this important page of the revolutionary period which became the prologue to the Bolshevik seizure of power.

As we already know, the three essential aims which Kornilov intended to carry out in Petrograd were the liquidation of the Bolsheviks, the dissolution of the Soviets, and the transformation of the Provisional Government into an effective national governing power.

With respect to the first two objectives, he could hope to reach some sort of understanding with the head of the Provisional Government, Kerensky. That he could do so with respect to his third objective, however, was extremely doubtful, and not only by reason of Kornilov's and Kerensky's mutual antipathy. If Kornilov became part of a "strong" government, supported by officers and nonsocialist circles, he would inevitably acquire a decisive role in it. This would threaten Kerensky with elimination from the government or, at best, with demotion to a second-rate ministerial function, a prospect with little appeal for the Prime Minister. Kerensky held on to his power with dogged persistence; all his defenses were alerted against his potential competitor, whom he observed with jealous enmity. Even half a century later, the mere thought of Kornilov daring to offer him the portfolio of Justice through V. N. Lvov's intermediary, could enrage the eighty-six-year-old Kerensky.[2]

We have already seen the initial series of misunderstandings and clashes between Kerensky and Kornilov. Taking into consideration the possibility that an accord with the former would not materialize, General Kornilov, despite his desire to enter the government by legal means, undertook a series of measures which would ensure his success in case of emergency, with or without Kerensky's consent.

As we know, on August 7, he ordered General Denikin to detach from the southwestern front and move in a northward direction the native Caucasian unit known as the Wild Division. On August 12 he ordered Denikin to move to the north the Third Cavalry Corps, headed by General Krymov, and a few days later Denikin received a similar order for the Kornilov Shock Regiment. Finally, about August 20, a messenger from General Kornilov asked Denikin to send to the *Stavka* "a score or two" of reliable officers, ostensibly for trench-mortar instructions, but actually to join an officer detachment in Petrograd.

But even before Kornilov had assumed the High Command and become, as Denikin expressed it, "the banner of the movement," certain individuals and political circles had formed a number of conspiratorial cells. These were independent of each other at first, but were later united under Kornilov's leadership. The elements which formed these units had differing political orientations, but all of them were opposed to socialism. The aim of most of them was to establish a military dictatorship. The possibility of restoring the monarchy, however, had never been discussed.

One of the first conspiratorial organizations of this kind, composed of officers stationed at the southwestern front, was founded by General Krymov, whom Kornilov had designated to lead the Third Cavalry Corps to Petrograd. It is doubtful that Krymov had any monarchist leanings. He had conspired with Guchkov against the Tsar in preparing a palace *coup* which was planned for March 1 but was superseded by the February revolution. Subsequently, Krymov apparently had no aims beyond the liquidation of the Soviets. "The future will determine our form of government," he told one of his associates; "personally, however, I have little affection for the dynasty." [3]

Krymov's organization consisted mainly of officers of his Third Cavalry Corps. It also included some officers of the Guards Cavalry which was stationed at the southwestern front at the time, as well as the officers of the garrison of Kiev and its military academies.

Krymov's idea was to make Kiev the center of future military resistance. "General Krymov," wrote Denikin, "had no hope of preserving the front. . . . In the event of its fall, his plan consisted of moving his troops by forced marches to Kiev, and after occupying and consolidating the city 'issuing a call to arms.' " [4]

Concurrently with Krymov's organization, but independently of it, several secret associations opposed to the Soviet and the government were created in Petrograd. These cells, which had no definite program, no funds, and no central authority, were, in Denikin's words "more like bands of captious young people playing at conspiracy."

Eventually, some of these cells became part of the Republican Center, an organization which tried to unify and channel their activities in a single direction. The Republican Center was formed in Petrograd in May, 1917, for the purpose of defending the country against Bolshevism. The future form of government did not enter into its considerations. Even its name was chosen almost accidentally. The monarchy had fallen, and it seemed logical that it would be supplanted by a republic; no one raised any objections to the proposed appellation.

According to Denikin, this group had the great advantage over all others of having certain financial means at its disposal. The funds were contributed in a roundabout way by leaders of the moneyed bourgeoisie, representatives of the banking and industrial aristocracy, all of whom, however, wished not to be personally involved in the organization, so as to avoid being compromised if it failed. The Republican Center paid particular attention to the formation of its military section. At the beginning of August, Colonel Sidorin, a member of the Alliance of Army and Navy Officers, was placed at its head. At a secret conference in Mogilev, presided over by General Krymov, plans were discussed for a possible military occupation of Petrograd. Sidorin affirmed that so far as he was concerned, everything in Petrograd was ready, which was completely untrue. In Denikin's opinion, Sidorin's "technical preparation" in Petrograd lacked seriousness. The conspiratorial meetings took place in popular restaurants and often turned into convivial parties.

At first, Kornilov may not have known everything that went on in Petrograd. From the moment that he assumed the High Command, however, all these diverse organizations sought his authority as that of their recognized leader.

When General Kornilov—already swamped with purely military questions and the overwhelming problem of arresting the complete disintegration of the front—found himself involved in the unfamiliar business of conspiracy, he delegated the latter activity to his entourage. The entourage, unfortunately, proved fatal to the whole movement which Kornilov had undertaken to lead. We turn once more to Denikin for the details of this development.

The strangest and least comprehensible aspect [wrote the General], was the influence on the course of events exercised by the [unknown and untrustworthy] politicians who surrounded Kornilov: Zavoiko [an ensign and personal aide to Kornilov], Filonenko, Alad'in, Dobrynsky, etc. . . . Their presence around Kornilov injected a certain element of adventurism and superficiality which was reflected in the whole movement bearing his name.

. . . Kornilov was a poor judge of character. This is not all, however. Once, at a later date, he answered my question about his former associates by saying, "I was alone. I knew those people very little. But they, at least, were willing to work and were not afraid to do so."

. . . It is true that Kornilov was alone. All the social and political figures who had supported, if not inspired, his movement, preferred to remain in the shade until the conflict was resolved.

As regards Savinkov—Kornilov never knew exactly whom Savinkov proposed "to knife in the back"—himself or Kerensky.[5]

If the right wing of Kornilov's entourage consisted mainly of unknown and insignificant nonentities, the left wing included, besides the *Stavka*'s unscrupulous commissar Filonenko, the mysterious and unusual figure of Boris Savinkov, who stood out in marked contrast to the mediocrities surrounding him.

Much has been written about Savinkov, but to this day no one has been able to decipher completely the complicated life, psychology, character, and aims of this strange man. Winston Churchill drew an intriguing portrait of him in his *Great Contemporaries*.

Churchill met Savinkov in 1919, in London, and was greatly impressed by him. A romantic at heart and a lover of adventure in the best and highest sense of that word, Churchill appears to have been fascinated by a certain Robin Hood aspect of Savinkov's character. "Boris Savinkov's whole life had been spent in conspiracy," wrote Churchill. "Without religion as the churches teach it; without morals as men prescribe them; without home or country; without wife or child, or kith or kin; without friend; without fear; hunter and hunted; implacable, unconquerable, alone."

Churchill devoted a whole brilliantly written chapter to Savinkov, including a remarkable physical description: "Small in stature; moving as little as possible, and that noiselessly and with deliberation; remarkable grey-green eyes in a face of almost deathly pallor; speaking in calm, low, even voice, almost a monotone; innumerable cigarettes."

As regards Savinkov's peculiar political role and behavior, Churchill compressed them into one exceptionally apt phrase: "He was that extraordinary product—a Terrorist for moderate aims." And, in truth, there was no hint of utopia in Savinkov's aims. In the final analysis, what he tried to attain by dynamite, murder, and blood, was nothing more than the reasonable norms of freedom and toleration as they were practiced in the Western world.

At a meeting arranged by Churchill between Savinkov and Prime Minister Lloyd George, the latter embarked on his theory "that revolutions like diseases run a regular course, that the worst was already over in Russia [this in the midst of the civil war!] . . . that by successive convulsions a more tolerable regime would be established.

" 'Mr. Prime Minister' said Savinkov in his formal way, 'you will permit me the honor of observing that after the fall of the Roman Empire there ensued The Dark Ages.' " [6] This was a revealing answer; by July, 1917, Savinkov was already profoundly disappointed in the course taken by the Russian revolution.

Of no less interest are the pages devoted to Savinkov—particularly in relation to the Kornilov affair—by Professor F. A. Stepun in his memoirs entitled *Byvshee i Nesbyvsheesia* (*The Past, and the Past that Never Came to Be*).

After the February revolution, Stepun engaged in political work with Savinkov, and served under him in the responsible position of chief of the Political Department of the Ministry of War. He wrote in his memoirs that Savinkov was puzzled by Kerensky, and called him a "self-infatuated *jeune premier* of the revolution." Savinkov related to Stepun with undisguised aversion how Kerensky in the summer of 1917 was showing one of the former Tsar's residences to the representatives of Western European democracies, and while talking to his guests, carelessly plucked at a button on the uniform of the former Tsar. "That was disgusting, I must tell you," concluded Savinkov. "Tsars may be killed, but familiarity even with the uniform of a dead Tsar cannot be tolerated." [7]

This was an extraordinary statement for a revolutionary of Savinkov's caliber. In his unformulated political philosophy, the socialist Savinkov may well have been the precursor of those other former socialists who, a few years later, founded the Fascist movement. In talking with his intimates, Savinkov referred to the Soviet and the "comrades" with the disgusted expression of a person with a sour taste in his mouth.[8]

From Savinkov's own writings and from accounts of people who knew him, it is evident that he had nothing but contempt for Kerensky, whereas in his own way he respected and even liked Kornilov. It is fair to assume that to him Kornilov represented a means of establishing a strong revolutionary government in which Savinkov would take over the leadership of the nation, after removing Kerensky and reducing Kornilov's role to a purely military one. Savinkov played an intricate game, and although the Supreme Commander was exceedingly wary of him, succeeded in persuading Kornilov that his program of changes in the capital had the full approval and sympathy of Kerensky.

On August 20, Savinkov finally obtained Kerensky's consent for dispatching the Third Cavalry Corps to Petrograd. Its arrival was to coincide with a declaration of martial law in the capital and its environs. Both moves were part of a plan for overcoming the Bolsheviks.

On August 24, Savinkov, accompanied by Colonel Baranovsky, Kerensky's brother-in-law and military adviser, arrived at the *Stavka* to settle the final details of the operation.

A protocol of the meeting between Acting War Minister Savinkov and General Kornilov was drawn up at the *Stavka* at that time, and a copy of this document is at present in the Columbia University Russian Archive. The document states that Savinkov assured Kornilov that his "demands will be met by the Provisional Government within the next few days." He pointed out, however, that the government feared that this would bring about a Bolshevik uprising and a strong reaction of the Petrograd Soviet, which "may also come out against the government." In this event, the Provisional Government could not count on the loyalty of the troops stationed in the capital. In order to ensure law and order, Savinkov, in the name of the Provisional Government, asked to place at its disposal by late August the Third Cavalry Corps by concentrating it in the vicinity of Petrograd. This would enable the government to declare martial law and to announce the new legislation. "I am asking only," said Savinkov, "that you not send General Krymov at the head of the Third Cavalry Corps, as we don't consider him very desirable. He is a fine combat general, but we doubt that he is qualified for this type of operation." (This request apparently was based on the apprehension that Krymov might deal ruthlessly with some of the socialist members of the government.) In conclusion, Savinkov emphasized that "the most drastic and pitiless measures should be taken" against the Bolsheviks and the Petrograd Soviet should the latter turn against the Provisional Government.

In order to notify the government when to declare martial law, Savinkov asked General Kornilov to telegraph him personally the estimated time of the cavalry corps' arrival in Petrograd.

It should be noted that General Kornilov did not mention to Savinkov that he had already designated the Third Cavalry Corps for the march on Petrograd, that it was headed by General Krymov, whom the government considered undesirable, and that it now included among its units the Wild Division of Caucasian natives, which also did not meet with the government's approval.

Kornilov felt greatly relieved after Savinkov's visit. Various steps undertaken by the *Stavka* without the government's knowledge suddenly appeared to be not only sanctioned, but enthusiastically approved by the Prime Minister and the Acting Minister of War. The "legality" of Kornilov's activity seemed almost assured.

Kornilov was not aware at that moment that a short time before Savinkov's visit to the *Stavka* something had happened which in a few days would bring about a complete change in the situation.

On August 22, Kerensky received a friendly call at his Winter Palace office from Vladimir Nikolaevich Lvov. (The latter was not related to Prince G. E. Lvov and had no title.) Formerly a member of the State Duma, he was Procurator of the Holy Synod in the Provisional Government. He was known as an honest idealist, but also as a muddleheaded dreamer of limited intelligence. Like most Russian liberals at that time, he felt the need for establishing a firm governing power in the country. To this end he decided to do everything possible to pair off the "weak" Kerensky with the "firm" Kornilov, in the hope that their combined effort would pull Russia out of revolutionary chaos onto the firm road of government reorganization.[9]

When Lvov was shown into the Imperial Library, where Kerensky received his visitors, the latter was sitting behind a huge desk (or *pupitre,* as Lvov described it) which completely masked him from sight.

"Alexander Fedorovich," said Lvov, "what a strange way to sit; I can't talk to you unless I see you. Why don't we move to some other place?"

"No, no," muttered Kerensky; "it really doesn't matter at all."

"Then let me stand," said Lvov, rising.

According to Lvov, the interview then continued as follows: "Kerensky immediately sprang toward me and felt both my pockets at the same time with his two hands. Having done so, he calmed down. Funny, thought I, can he be thinking that I came to shoot him?"

(Rumors of a conspiracy against Kerensky, which were rampant in the latter half of August, must have made him nervous to the point of frisking even the totally harmless and friendly Lvov.)

" 'Did you rid all the bishoprics of Rasputin's followers?' asked Kerensky, turning to me.

" 'This is not the subject I came to discuss with you,' I replied. 'Forget about it. I am here to talk on a very important matter.' "[10]

Mysteriously referring to a "mission" entrusted to him by "someone" whose name he was not at liberty to disclose, Lvov proceeded to entreat Kerensky in vague and nebulous terms, begging him to extend the hand of friendship to those whom he rejected and to reorganize the government to include in it rightist liberals and patriotic socialists instead of giving it up wholly to the Soviets.

"Tell me please, on whose support are you counting?" inquired Lvov, and without waiting for an answer, asserted that Kerensky leaned on the

Petrograd Soviet, which (Lvov believed) was already predominantly composed of Bolsheviks, while public opinion against the Soviet was rising
⌐nd would result in a massacre.

"Splendid!" retorted Kerensky, jumping up and rubbing his hands. "We
shall say then that we were unable to curb the populace, wash our hands
of the whole thing, and deny all responsibility." [11]

"This 'fall from grace' of Kerensky made a big impression in Soviet
circles when it was discovered in the course of Kornilov's interrogation in
Bykhov," wrote Denikin, concerning Kerensky's attitude toward the peo-
ple as revealed in this exchange. "Having learned of it, a member of the
Commission of Inquiry, Lieber,[12] clutched at his head exclaiming, 'My
God, but this is pure provocation!' " [13]

During Lvov's interview with Kerensky, the Prime Minister was thoroughly aroused by Lvov's hints that his friends disposed of "tangible
forces." He was afraid of the rumored conspiracy and the possibility of
hostile action directed against him, suspecting the Alliance of Army and
Navy Officers and the *Stavka,* but not General Kornilov himself. In view
of all this, Kerensky decided to make use of the simpleminded Lvov for
his own probe of the situation.

"Very well, I agree," he said. "I am even willing to resign if necessary,
but you must understand that I can't abandon control of the government:
I must hand it over to someone else." [14]

Milyukov was undoubtedly right when he wrote that "the good-natured
Lvov accepted this speech at its face value. . . . Having convinced himself that Kerensky was genuinely prepared to give in, he disclosed the real
purpose of his visit. 'Entrust me with the mission of entering into negotiations in your name, with all the parties whom I consider essential,'
he entreated Kerensky." [15]

And despite the subsequent controversy as to who said what, there is
no doubt that at this point Kerensky, in some nebulous way, must have
given Lvov the authorization to speak in his name.

"Where are you off to?" he asked casually as Lvov was preparing to
leave. But the would-be conspirator was wary: "I am going whence I
came," he answered, smiling. Then, he later reported, Kerensky showed
him out and stood a long time at the door of his office, waving.[16]

The long and short of it was that V. N. Lvov was certain of being empowered to enter into negotiations with parties he had not named, but
visualized as Kornilov and the *Stavka.* Having assumed the role of intermediary, Lvov ascribed his own ideas to Kerensky, completely distorted
the meaning of his subsequent conversation with Kornilov, and proceeded with his "mission," which was to culminate in an unimaginable
scandal.

Lvov left for the *Stavka,* where he remained for two days (August 24–
25) and had two interviews with the Supreme Commander. The first took

place on August 24 at 10 P.M., about three or four hours after Savinkov left by train for Petrograd. The second interview was on August 25, in the morning.

The lengthy and confusing conversations which took place at the *Stavka* between Lvov and Kornilov can be summarized as follows:

Lvov communicated to Kornilov that he had come at Kerensky's request, that Kerensky was not anxious to remain in power and was prepared to resign. If, however, the Prime Minister could be assured of Kornilov's support, he would be willing to remain at his post. Lvov then outlined three possible forms of government that could be adopted in the future:

1. A reorganized government in which Kerensky would retain the primary role.

2. A government in which all cabinet members would have equal power.

3. A government in which the dominating role would belong to the Supreme Commander.

After describing to Lvov the state of affairs in the nation and the army, General Kornilov stated that in his opinion the only way out of the existing situation was a dictatorship, and added that if the role of dictator was offered to him, he would not refuse it. Lvov asked whether Kornilov would be in favor of including Kerensky and Savinkov in the cabinet in case of a military dictatorship, and Kornilov admitted that, although his personal feelings toward them were negative, he considered their participation in the government indispensable. In discussing possible future cabinet members, Kornilov slated the Ministry of Justice for Kerensky and the Ministry of War for Savinkov. During the interview of August 25 he told Lvov that feelings against Kerensky were running so high among the officers that he could guarantee his safety only in Mogilev. Moreover, in view of the expected Bolshevik uprising in Petrograd, Kornilov felt that it was dangerous for the Provisional Government to remain in the capital. Therefore, he asked Lvov to convey to Kerensky and Savinkov his urgent request to come to the *Stavka,* where he, Kornilov, was ready to guarantee that nothing would happen to them.[17]

Kornilov knew very little about Lvov apart from his reputation as a person of integrity but of limited intelligence. He knew that Lvov had been in the Duma with Kerensky and that both were members of the Provisional Government. It simply could not occur to Kornilov that everything that Lvov relayed to him in such definite and inalterable terms as coming from Kerensky was nothing but the product of Lvov's personal fantasy. Lvov had asked him definite questions, and he had answered them. In doing so, he had not laid down any conditions or posed any ultimatums.

After leaving Kornilov, Lvov found himself in the midst of the General's entourage. There, according to Denikin, "he completely lost all sense of

proportion in estimating the importance, influence and role of his inter-
locutors. According to him, 'Dobrynsky could muster up to forty thousand
Caucasian mountaineers at a minute's notice and dispatch them to any destination.' . . . Alad'in was purported to be sending a telegram from Kornilov
to General Kaledin, *Ataman* of the Don Cossacks, ordering the latter to
move his troops in the direction of Moscow. . . . The same Alad'in demanding of him that no cabinet changes be made without consulting the
Stavka. . . . Zavoiko selecting future ministers and 'planning to convene
a national assembly!' . . . Professor Yakovlev evolving some unheard-of
agrarian program." [18]

Lvov hopelessly confused his conversations with Kornilov with the irresponsible bragging of various Dobrynskys, Alad'ins, Yakovlevs, and
Zavoikos who were swarming around the *Stavka.*

He showed up for the second time at the Winter Palace office of the
Prime Minister at 6 P.M. on August 26. Instead of accurately repeating
to Kerensky his conversation with Kornilov and admitting that the whole
idea of mediating between them was his own invention, Lvov ascribed to
Kornilov words which he had actually heard from Zavoiko.

Assuming this time the role of Kornilov's emissary, Lvov dictated some
demands to Kerensky in Kornilov's name. Kerensky was so taken aback
by them that he could not decide at first whether Lvov had lost his mind
or whether something extremely serious was indeed happening.

The proposals consisted of the following points:

1. Martial law to be declared in Petrograd.

2. All military and civilian power to be transferred to the Supreme
Commander in Chief.

3. All ministers, including the Prime Minister, to hand in their resigna-
tions. The executive power to be temporarily delegated to the deputy
ministers until a new government was formed by the Supreme Commander.

According to Kerensky's testimony, Lvov insisted in Kornilov's name
that these conditions be communicated to the Provisional Government
without delay, and that Kerensky and Savinkov leave for the *Stavka* on
the same night.

As I considered that V. N. Lvov's assertions were simply unbelievable [tes-
tified Kerensky], I answered that I found it impossible to convey such demands
to the Provisional Government as being from General Kornilov without their
being substantiated. At this, V. N. Lvov expressed his readiness to put down
in writing the various points he had relayed to me, and wrote them down in
his own hand on a piece of paper. . . . Having accepted this written declaration from V. N. Lvov, I was still unable to overcome my doubts. I therefore
suggested to Lvov, of my own accord, calling Kornilov by direct wire so that
both Lvov and myself could speak with him and (in the presence of a third
party), verify Lvov's authority to speak in Kornilov's name. Lvov agreed to
this second proposal also.[19]

During his stay in Mogilev, Lvov had gained the impression that although Kornilov himself wanted to protect Kerensky from a possible attempt on his life, the officers at the *Stavka* were seeking an occasion to do away with the Prime Minister. This helped to completely unbalance Lvov. It influenced his second interview with Kerensky, who, obviously, could not guess that Lvov was not relaying to him an "ultimatum" from Kornilov, but merely Kornilov's consent to the measures which he, Lvov, in the guise of the Prime Minister's emissary, had proposed to Kornilov as coming directly from Kerensky.

Rumors of a conspiracy had been rampant for several weeks, but Kerensky had no concrete information about it. By disbanding the police and other security agencies in March, the Provisional Government had condemned itself to complete helplessness and lack of protection in the event of a conspiracy directed against itself.

"You know our present situation," said Kerensky at one point. "Without a real security organization, we are like blind puppies. We can be fooled on all sides without seeing a damn thing." [20]

On the preceding day, Savinkov, just returned from the *Stavka,* had tried to reassure Kerensky by vouching for the Supreme Commander's complete loyalty. Then, at the very time when Kornilov at the *Stavka* felt relieved and reassured by an apparent approval of his activity, harrowing doubts and a terrible fear for his future assailed Kerensky. Could a double-faced Savinkov have deliberately tried to take him off his guard?

"The extent of my emotional disturbances can be confirmed by all those who saw me at that time," wrote Kerensky of his conversation with Lvov. "I ran up and down the huge office, trying to disentangle and understand the essence of the whole affair, why Lvov, etc. . . . It was necessary to obtain immediately sufficient proof of Lvov's formal connection with Kornilov in order to enable the Provisional Government to take drastic measures on the same evening." [21]

Kerensky's feelings and fears had reached such an emotional pitch, his instinct of self-preservation and his desire to immediately assemble enough evidence to incriminate, arrest, and convict Kornilov for "military insurrection" were so strong, that he seems to have lost all sense of proportion.

Having snatched the "piece of paper" with Kornilov's "demands" from Lvov, Kerensky assumed the dual role of investigator and detective and proceeded with the second phase of his inquiry. By means of the Hughes teleprinting apparatus, he placed a call to General Kornilov in order to receive the Supreme Commander's confirmation, "in the presence of a third party," that Lvov was acting as his official spokesman.

The third party chosen by Kerensky was V. V. Vyrubov, who was closely connected with him at that time. As for the second party, V. N. Lvov, he had absented himself from the Winter Palace for an hour and found on his return that the dialogue by direct wire to the *Stavka* had already taken place. In his absence, Kerensky had used Lvov's name and impersonated him in speaking to Kornilov. Kerensky's own translation of this strange conversation, recorded on the teleprinter, follows:

KERENSKY: Prime Minister Kerensky on the line. We are waiting for General Kornilov.

KORNILOV: This is General Kornilov.

KERENSKY: How do you do, General. Vladimir Nikolaevich Lvov and Kerensky are speaking. May we ask you to confirm that Kerensky can proceed according to the information transmitted by Vladimir Nikolaevich.

KORNILOV: Hello, Alexander Fedorovich, hello, Vladimir Nikolaevich. I am reconfirming the message on the situation in the country and in the army as told to Vladimir Nikolaevich with the request to transmit it to you; let me reiterate that recent developments and the course of events make resolute and immediate action imperative.

KERENSKY: This is Vladimir Nikolaevich asking you whether or not that certain decision I was to communicate to Alexander Fedorovich personally has to be implemented? Without your final confirmation Alexander Fedorovich is hesitant to trust me entirely.

KORNILOV: Yes, this is to confirm that I have asked you to transmit to Alexander Fedorovich my urgent request that he come to Mogilev.

KERENSKY: This is Alexander Fedorovich. Do I understand that you are confirming the message transmitted to me through Vladimir Nikolaevich? Today, it cannot be done, and I cannot leave. I hope to be able to leave tomorrow. Do you need Savinkov?

KORNILOV: I urgently request that Boris Viktorovich [Savinkov] accompany you. My message transmitted through Vladimir Nikolaevich applies in equal measure to Boris Viktorovich. Please don't delay your departure beyond tomorrow. Believe me that only awareness of the responsibility involved accounts for the urgency of my request.

KERENSKY: Shall we come only in the case of events which are subject to current rumors, or in any case?

KORNILOV: In any case.

KERENSKY: Goodbye, see you soon.

KORNILOV: Goodbye.[22]

The *Stavka*'s commissar, M. M. Filonenko, was dumbfounded when he read the record of this conversation on the following morning. He could not understand how Kornilov could so thoughtlessly confirm Lvov's statements, whose content was unknown to him. Filonenko considered that "the way in which Kerensky's question was formulated and the way Kornilov answered was absolutely inadmissible in any serious business dealing, particularly in a decision of great national importance, as Kerensky did not specify the exact nature of his question, while General Kornilov did not know to what exactly he was replying."[23]

Denikin's judgment was no less severe: "This conversation fully reveals Kerensky's moral profile, Kornilov's extraordinary imprudence, and the questionable role of the 'honorable witness' Vyrubov."[24]

Kerensky, a lawyer and political attorney, could not help knowing that from a legal point of view his conversation with Kornilov was totally invalid. It proved nothing, confirmed nothing, and did not even verify whether Kornilov had made the ultimative demands ascribed to him by Lvov. The dialogue on both sides could be interpreted differently by each participant, depending on his inclinations. On the basis of his own guesswork, however, Kerensky decided to use the record of his talk with Kornilov as proof of the latter's "treachery."

The comedy of errors begun by Lvov's naïve attempt to unite, by hook or crook, Russia's two chief protagonists, was assuming alarming proportions.

In order to round out his detective work and to have "an official witness" of his conversation with Lvov, Kerensky had hidden, behind a curtain in his office, the assistant director of militia, S. A. Balavinsky. Upon his return to the Winter Palace, the unsuspecting Lvov answered good-naturedly, in the presence of a hidden witness, the same questions that Kerensky had asked him two hours earlier.

On the following day, Balavinsky's written record of the conversation was already handed to the Department of Judicial Investigation.

Subsequently, Lvov denied Kerensky's version with regard to his having transmitted ultimative demands in Kornilov's name. "I could not and did not transmit any ultimative demands to him [Kerensky]," wrote Lvov, "but he asked me to put down my ideas on paper. When I did so, he arrested me. I had not even time to reread my paper when Kerensky snatched it from me and put it in his pocket." [25] (Lvov was arrested on August 26, late in the evening.)

Under arrest at the Winter Palace, where he was guarded by two sentinels, Lvov "listened with indignation as a triumphant Kerensky sang trills from operas in the adjoining room, which formerly belonged to Tsar Alexander III, and prevented him from sleeping." [26]

Milyukov affirmed that from that time on, Kerensky's actions were no longer dictated by logic or state considerations, but by the uncontrollable urge of a man passionately defending his power.

There was also, of course, a vindictive desire to downgrade Kornilov, who had dared to offer him the post of Minister of Justice. "Can you really believe that I could be Minister of Justice under Kornilov?" he asked Lvov haughtily, after drawing out of him the necessary testimony against Kornilov.

"I shall not give up the revolution," he announced to his deputy and Minister of Finance, Nekrasov, who gave him his assurance of opposing Kornilov "to the end." After a tumultuous session of the Provisional Government, Kerensky dispatched to Kornilov the telegram, whose contents we already know, removing the Supreme Commander from his post, summoning him instantly to Petrograd, and ordering him to surrender his functions temporarily to his chief of staff, General Lukomsky. As we have seen, Lukomsky refused to take over these functions and pronounced himself firmly against Kornilov's demotion.

This was the first sign of insubordination to the Provisional Government on the part of the *Stavka*.

Kerensky did not trust Savinkov sufficiently to advise him of these events before deciding with Nekrasov to oppose Kornilov "to the end" and to remove him from his post.

Amazed by these unexpected developments, Savinkov immediately attempted to prove that the entire incident was based on a misunderstanding. Kerensky at first rejected Savinkov's advice to try to settle the affair by means of peaceful discussions, before allowing it to become public property. However, on August 27 Kerensky gave Savinkov permission to communicate with Kornilov by direct wire. He also agreed to withhold publication of information incriminating the Supreme Commander, which was already prepared for release, until he learned the results of Savinkov's negotiations.

Despite this promise, and disregarding the possibility that Savinkov's attempt could still prevent the conflict from spreading, Nekrasov released the contents of Kerensky's radiotelegram to the press without waiting for the results of the Savinkov–Kornilov exchange.

As we have seen, Kerensky's message advised the public at large that Kornilov had sent to him a former member of the State Duma, V. N. Lvov, "with the demand that the Provisional Government surrender its full civilian and military authority to General Kornilov"; that Kornilov's aim was to establish in the nation a regime opposed to the conquests of the revolution; that to ensure the safety of the country, its liberty, and the republican regime, the Provisional Government had authorized him, Kerensky, to take drastic measures against General Kornilov, and so on.

Concurrently with this telegram, an appeal signed by Kerensky was addressed to railroad employees, summoning them to halt the movement of Kornilov's troops toward the capital and authorizing them to break up railroad tracks and derail trains if necessary.

Another order, addressed to the Petrograd garrison, stated that "General Kornilov, who boasted of his patriotism, . . . has now given us proof of his treachery. He has withdrawn regiments from the front, thus weakening its resistance to our sworn enemies the Germans, and moved these regiments against Petrograd."

"Kerensky," remarked Leon Trotsky with some irony, "wisely refrained from saying that the troops were withdrawn from the front not only with his knowledge but at his express order, for the purpose of purging the selfsame garrison which he was now advising of Kornilov's treason." [27]

Kerensky exhorted the troops to demonstrate their allegiance to "freedom and the revolution" and to stand firmly in defense of the "revolutionary government." [28]

An extremely odd aspect of the whole situation was that, having demoted Kornilov from his post and proclaimed him a rebel and traitor who had opened the front to the Germans, Kerensky had left the operative command of all the armies in his hands.

Having become suspicious of all nonsocialist elements, Kerensky openly appealed for support and help to the Petrograd Soviet of Workers' and Soldiers' Deputies.

A few days later, Trotsky was released from prison.

"One wonders if Kerensky realized at that moment that by declaring himself Kornilov's enemy, he was handing over both himself and Russia to Lenin?" wrote Milyukov. "Did he realize that this was the last chance the government had of overcoming the Bolsheviks? He had to relinquish too much if he brought himself to realize this. Kerensky's tragedy, which showed up very clearly in this decision, was that, though he already understood a great deal, he was unable to give up anything. . . . If Kerensky's 'crime' before Russia, which has so often been discussed, could be concentrated at one chronological point, then his 'crime' was performed at that moment, on the evening of August 26." [29]

XII

THE KORNILOV

AFFAIR, II

All was calm at the Supreme Commander's *Stavka* on the night of August 26, in the assurance that the changes Kornilov planned to bring about in the capital had finally obtained the full approval of the Prime Minister.

Carrying out the procedure agreed upon with Savinkov during their conference of August 24 at the *Stavka,* Kornilov telegraphed the latter, indicating the day on which the Third Cavalry Corps would be concentrated near Petrograd. On that day, the Provisional Government was to declare martial law in the capital and promulgate Kornilov's program into law.

There was indeed little reason to worry after the recent exchanges with Savinkov, Lvov, and Kerensky himself, and especially after the latter's communication by direct wire of a few hours ago, in which he promised to arrive in Mogilev and concluded with the words, "Goodbye, see you soon."

But in addition, several other factors served to reinforce Kornilov's conviction that at that moment a collaboration with Kerensky was possible, at least in the initial phase of his project.

A tremendous explosion had occurred on August 14 in the powder and ammunition depots of Kazan, destroying up to a million artillery shells and twelve thousand machine guns. At almost the same time, there were several cases of arson and explosions in Petrograd, including the Westinghouse plant and a large stockpile of ammunition at the suburb of Malaya Okhta. These were no accidents. Massive destruction on such a scale was due both to the activity of German agents and to the complete negligence of the troops guarding armament factories and depots. A tightening of army discipline in the rear was urgently needed.

On August 20, the occupation of Riga by the Germans made the need of drastic measures for regenerating the army more obvious than ever. Kerensky was fully aware of this and had no choice but to agree with Savinkov that under existing conditions, Kornilov's intervention was indispensable.

One should bear in mind, moreover, that there was no disagreement between Kornilov and Kerensky in relation to the past. Neither of them desired the restoration of the monarchy, and both of them envisaged a future government conducted along strictly democratic lines after a measure of order had been restored to the country. It was therefore possible to hope that their differences of character, temperament, and outlook, and their conflicting opinions, could all be overcome, at least temporarily, with sufficient good will on both sides.

For all these reasons, Kerensky's telegram to Kornilov, depriving him of the post of Supreme Commander, took the *Stavka* completely by surprise.

By the time Kerensky's other announcements, orders, and proclamations had reached the *Stavka,* doubts concerning the Prime Minister's sincerity had changed to the certitude that Lvov's intercession and Kerensky's promise to come to Mogilev were all part of a carefully planned provocation. It was this certitude which determined General Kornilov's reply to Kerensky's telegram.

Kornilov countered with his equally drastic appeal to the population and his refusal to submit to the orders of the Provisional Government. In his message, which has been quoted in a preceding chapter, Kornilov denied Kerensky's charges and returned them in kind, actually accusing him of treason.

Besides the bitterness engendered on both sides of this controversy, Kornilov had other, more serious reasons for casting his accusation at Kerensky and for refusing to relinquish the Supreme Command.

In his conversation of August 27 by direct wire with Savinkov, he had said:

I received today the telegram recalling me from my post. I repeat again that the interests of my country and the preservation of the army's military might are more important to me than anything else. I have proved my love for my country by risking my life many times and it is not for you or your fellow ministers to remind me of my duty to the motherland.

I am convinced that the completely unexpected decision of the government was reached under pressure from the Soviet of Workers' and Soldiers' Deputies, among whom are many people soiled by treason and betrayal. I consider abandoning my post under pressure from those people tantamount to leaving the battlefield in deference to the enemy. Therefore, in full awareness of my responsibility to my country, to history and to my conscience, I firmly declare that I will not leave my post in this dark hour of our motherland.[1]

There was obviously no hope for a reconciliation. The rift between the government and the *Stavka* had become an impassable breach. The secret military plans, which had initially included the intention and possibility of

a negotiated agreement with the government, had turned into open rebellion against it.

People of diverse political orientations were involved in the secret plans,
including some persons with reactionary tendencies. But Kornilov's movement as a whole did not pursue reactionary aims. Its aim was to consolidate
the positive achievements of the February revolution after ridding it of its
most harmful excesses.

Savinkov knew this better than anyone and ignored it with utter shame-
lessness in his appeal to the masses of August 28: "Fellow citizens, in this
hour of danger for our country, when the enemy has broken through our
front and taken Riga, General Kornilov has instigated a rebellion against
the Provisional Government and the revolution, and joined the ranks of
the latter's foes. . . . Regardless of his position, whoever attempts to undermine the conquests of the revolution will be dealt with as a traitor." [2]

Quite obviously, Savinkov realized at once that Kornilov's game was up,
and in his own words, "did not believe in the success of his movement."
Savinkov knew that the demoralization reigning in the capital would inevitably spread to Kornilov's troops, particularly when they realized that
they were there not to quell the Bolshevik uprising (which its leaders had
the foresight to cancel), but to make war against the government which
had refused to cooperate with Kornilov. The last thing Savinkov wanted
was to find himself on the losing side.

Savinkov's prognosis proved to be correct. As they approached the capital, the morale of Kornilov's men weakened, and an increasing number of
them deserted. A concerted effort to subvert the soldiers of the Third
Cavalry Corps was made by soldiers' committees, Soviets, railroad workers,
and particularly the Bolsheviks. They all realized that a Kornilov victory
would threaten their very existence, and they put up a bitter fight—armed
not with guns but with propaganda and proclamations which described
Kornilov as the leader of landowners and capitalists whose aim was to bring
back the Tsar and enslave the peasants and workers.

In its primitive simplicity, this sort of propaganda was easily absorbed
even by the most illiterate soldiers. Individuals clad in khaki scurried
through the ranks of the regiments marching on Petrograd, addressing them
whenever their officers were out of sight: "Comrades! Kerensky took away
the stick from your officers, he gave you freedom, and here you are again
buckling down to the officers' authority. Kerensky is for freedom and the
happiness of the people, and Kornilov is for discipline and the death penalty. Can it be that you are for Kornilov? Kornilov is a traitor to Russia and
wants to lead you into battle to defend foreign capitalism. He's been given
a large sum of money for this, whereas all Kerensky wants is peace!" [3]

Even the Caucasian natives of the Wild Division, who knew hardly any
Russian, were met, by Moslem representatives of revolutionary organizations who spoke their languages and quickly succeeded in undermining their
martial spirit.

The persons in charge of various cells of the secret officers' organization in Petrograd, proved totally incapable of coping with the situation. Some of them went into hiding; some were arrested. No demonstration of military strength took place in the capital.

In the meantime, General Krymov, on whose firmness and energy so many people were counting, was delaying his departure from the *Stavka,* instead of immediately rejoining his troops, whose units were now strung out along hundreds of miles of the railroads leading to Petrograd.

A great change had come over him. He was apparently extremely worried by the influence exercised over Kornilov by all the civilian and semi-civilian personnel which had attached themselves to the *Stavka.* "I must, of course, fulfill my commitment to the end," he told one of his friends. "I surrender my life to the cause. But the chances of failure are ninety percent. It is imperative that I rejoin the corps, but I fear that as soon as I leave Mogilev, things will go all awry here." [4]

Krymov continued to be pessimistic after rejoining his troops. Cut off from Kornilov and aware of the hopelessness of his mission, he accepted Kerensky's invitation to come to Petrograd for negotiations, which a fellow officer transmitted to him. The offer guaranteed the General complete safety and immunity.

On August 31, in Petrograd, Krymov first went to see General Alekseev, then had a stormy interview with Kerensky. He took his life on the same day, by a revolver shot in the chest, after writing a letter to Kornilov and dispatching it to the Stavka with his aide. The contents of the letter never became known; General Kornilov destroyed it.

The Kornilov movement spread panic in the circles connected with the Petrograd Soviet and among some of Kerensky's associates. They were mortally afraid of the Wild Division—while they were engaged in various discussions, all these Circassians, Ingushes, and Ossetians could massacre them. The most timorous secretly prepared their passports, ready to flee at a moment's notice across the Finnish border. This mood prevailed for the first two days. Then the tide began to run in the opposite direction. It was at that moment that political propaganda first proved its immense power as an instrument of class warfare.

On whose support could General Kornilov count at that time?

His isolated position at the *Stavka* had prevented him from having a complete and truthful picture of the situation. Enthusiastic letters and telegrams expressing loyalty and support had poured in to him from bourgeois-liberal circles, representatives of the Cadet party, merchants and industrialists, the officer corps, Cossack organizations, and the army command. He knew from the representatives of the Allied countries that their governments had lost faith in Kerensky and were pinning their hopes on him, General Kornilov, as the only man who could save the army and the nation from complete disintegration.

The welcome accorded him on August 14 at the State Conference in Moscow also seemed to indicate that the sympathies of all nonsocialists were on his side. The triumphant reception at the State Conference and the huge enthusiastic crowds in the streets of Moscow seemed to point that way, as did the words of the famed State Duma orator Rodichev: "You have become the symbol of our unity. All of us, all of Moscow, are united by our faith in you!"

And the telegram signed by M. V. Rodzianko: "The Conference of Leading Public Figures welcomes you, the supreme leader of the Russian army. The Conference affirms that it considers criminal any attempts to undermine your authority in the army and in Russia. . . . In this dark hour of trouble all Russians capable of thinking look up to you with hope and confidence. . . ."

Only one person—Cadet party member Maklakov—had the honesty and courage to convey a warning to Kornilov through the president of the Alliance of Army and Navy Officers, Colonel Novosiltsev: "Tell General Kornilov that he is, in fact, being misled by all of us, especially by Milyukov. No one will lend his support to Kornilov, everyone will go into hiding. . . ." [5]

And this was exactly what happened. Kornilov was abandoned. Only his faithful generals and officers supported him. Many of them were arrested and imprisoned at the same time as Kornilov.

The *Stavka*'s commissar, Captain Maximilian Filonenko, proved particularly inventive in warding off the onus of his close association with the Supreme Commander. A right-wing Socialist Revolutionary and a close collaborator of Savinkov's, Filonenko was in favor of Kornilov's program. When the storm broke, the Provisional Government representative's position at the *Stavka* became very awkward indeed. To protect his reputation and ward off suspicion, Filonenko asked the Command of the *Stavka* to arrest him. They did him that favor, including the pretense of obtaining his verbal promise not to leave Mogilev. This clever device enabled Filonenko to announce two weeks later, in a press interview, that Kornilov's open insubordination began at the precise moment when he arrested the commissar of the Provisional Government. Filonenko further revealed his true colors at the end of the interview when he told the newspapermen, "I love and respect General Kornilov, . . . but it is necessary to have him shot." [6]

(Many years later Filonenko's name reappeared in the newpapers. He had become a French barrister and was defending Nadezhda Plevitskaia, accused of participating in the kidnapping of General Miller by Bolshevik agents. The Paris criminal court condemned his client to twenty years of hard labor.)

General Alekseev was in Petrograd during the Kerensky–Kornilov crisis. He was in despair at the turn events had taken. He sympathized with Kornilov's aims, but although informed of their general outline, was unaware of many of the details. Alekseev definitely was not in the center of the conspiracy, as Kerensky later asserted.

When Kornilov's plans were short-circuited, Alekseev tried to unravel the tangled web of misunderstandings that had led to his break with Kerensky, and insisted in vain on a peaceful solution to the conflict. Kerensky realized that Alekseev had great authority in military circles, and that no one else could at that moment successfully represent the Provisional Government in negotiating with Kornilov and obtaining from him the peaceful transfer of the High Command to a new candidate. Kerensky, by his own admission, tried for two days to pressure Alekseev into assuming the difficult role of intermediary and into agreeing to become, subsequently, his chief of staff. For by that time the Prime Minister had decided to reinforce his position with the added title of Supreme Commander.

Even a touch of blackmail was tried on the reluctant general. Denikin has written down a conversation with Alekseev, related to him by Captain Chaperon du Larré (who, in exile, married Kornilov's daughter Natalia). Chaperon belonged to a secret officers' organization in Petrograd and came to see Alekseev on August 29. He found him

in a state of great depression. The old man sat engrossed in thought and tears were streaming down his face. "Tereshchenko just left here," he said. "He tried to talk me into accepting the position of chief of staff with Kerensky as Supreme Commander. . . . If I refuse, they will nominate Cheremisov. . . . You know what that means? Kornilov and his followers will be shot the next day! . . . My forthcoming role is profoundly revolting to me, but what am I to do? . . .

Cheremisov, who was favorably viewed by the Petrograd Soviet, detested Kornilov, who had previously opposed his nomination to the post of commander in chief of the southwestern front.

On August 29 [continue Denikin's notes], Kerensky issued an order depriving General Kornilov and his senior associates of their positions and bringing them to justice for "rebellion."

On the night of August 30, events reached a turning point: In order to save the lives of the Kornilov group, General Alekseev bowed his gray head to dishonor and agreed to become Supreme Commander Kerensky's chief of staff. Kerensky's self-nomination to that post injected an element of cruel comedy into the problem of national defense. Later, Alekseev always spoke of this short-lived period of his career with profound emotion and sadness.[7]

On the afternoon of August 30, Alekseev communicated by telegraph to General Kornilov that "after a painful struggle with himself," he had accepted his new post in order to liquidate the affair without bloodshed. He stated that he would come to Mogilev only if he received General Kornilov's assurance that the High Command would bow to his decision and surrender its functions to him.

Alekseev's conditions were accepted, and the *Stavka* submitted to his authority. But having given Alekseev carte blanche to bring order to the *Stavka* without bloodshed, Kerensky continued to act on his own behind

Alekseev's back, and made plans to send a punitive expedition to Mogilev in order to quell and defeat the "counterrevolution." Alekseev learned of this move on his way to Mogilev. He indignantly sent his demand by direct wire for its immediate cancellation, threatening to renounce his mission if he was not obeyed.

Kerensky tried to justify his underhanded behavior by saying that he had approved sending the troops only in order to protect Alekseev himself from any possible danger, and to protect the members of the Extraordinary Commission of Inquiry, who were also on their way to Mogilev, to question the generals and officers of the *Stavka*.

The harsh words addressed to Alekseev by Kornilov upon the former's arrival in Mogilev, must have been partly due to the foregoing episode. "It will be hard for you to emerge with honor from the present situation," said Kornilov. "You will have to walk on the edge which separates the honorable from the dishonorable." [8]

The reproach was bitter and unjustified. With distress in his heart, General Alekseev was consciously sacrificing his good name and self-respect in order to save the Kornilov group and preserve the organization of the army's High Command.

He arrived in Mogilev on September 1, and had a long conversation with Kornilov and his chief of staff, General Lukomsky. That evening, he summoned the latter once more on an urgent matter. Kerensky, from Petrograd, was demanding the immediate arrest of Generals Kornilov, Lukomsky, Romanovsky, and others involved in the Kornilov affair, in order to pacify the populace.

Reporting the implementation of this order to Petrograd by direct wire, Alekseev concluded the teleprinted conversation with the words, "I see that you have fallen completely . . . into the grasping hands of the Soviets." [9]

In those difficult moments, when all his endeavors had collapsed, the thought of suicide inevitably came to Kornilov. He was on the brink of following the example of Krymov, who was equal to him in courage and had deliberately taken his life in similar circumstances. There was, moreover, an additional reason which preyed on Kornilov's mind. It was a reckless phrase in one of his appeals to the population composed by Zavoiko, which stated with appalling clarity, "I affirm to all the people of Russia that I prefer death to being deprived of the position of Supreme Commander."

This phrase left him no choice.

"His intentions," wrote Denikin, "were apprehended by his loyal friend and wife, who had shared his restless and difficult life for twenty-two years. . . . Another mystery was taking place in the room which had recently witnessed the torments of the Tsar on the eve of his abdication. The mystery of unbounded love pitted against the coldness of despair.

"The mother told her daughter when she left the room, 'Your father has no right to abandon the thousands of officers who have followed him. He has resolved to drink this cup to the dregs.' " [10]

At first, the arrested *Stavka* members were detained in Mogilev's Hotel Metropole. Then, on the night of September 11, they were taken to the district town of Bykhov fifty miles away.

In the confusion which followed Kornilov's arrest, Lenin, who was then in Finland, immediately perceived a unique opportunity which opened for him a perspective of unlimited action.

Despite its clumsy style, his letter of August 30, from which some excerpts follow, was a remarkable example of his outstanding gift for revolutionary strategy and tactics:

"These lines may come too late, as events are developing with truly vertiginous speed. . . . Kornilov's revolt is a completely unexpected and quite unbelievably abrupt turn of events.

"Like any sharp turn, it calls for a revision and change of tactics. And as with every revision, one should be ultra-careful not to betray one's principles."

Lenin pointed out that this was a unique opportunity for his followers to fight against Kornilov while not supporting Kerensky. "We shall fight, we are fighting Kornilov, as do Kerensky's troops, but far from upholding Kerensky, we are showing his weakness. . . . In what, then, do our tactics change following the Kornilov revolt? In that we are changing the *structure* of our struggle against Kerensky. . . . We must choose the right moment, we shall not overthrow Kerensky now, we shall approach the problem of combating him *differently*. Namely, by explaining to the population . . . the weaknesses and *vacillations* of Kerensky. . . . And agitate we must this minute, not so much directly against Kerensky, as *indirectly,* always against him but indirectly [italics Lenin's]."

By demanding a "truly revolutionary war on Kornilov," by arousing the masses and "firing their insurgent spirit," Lenin was actually aiming at the overthrow of Kerensky. "Only the development of such a war can bring *us* to power, but we shall mention this as little as possible in our propaganda (let us keep firmly in mind, however, that events may bring us to power any day and that at that time we shall not let it escape us)." [11]

Someone has said of Lenin that he shaped his thoughts with an axe and presented them in a primitively simplified form. Lenin's incredible strength was precisely in this ability to hew his ideas into the simplest of shapes. His slogans were clear to the popular masses. He knew how to lead them.

Meanwhile, the Prime Minister was attributing his victory over his opponent to his personal ability, without a thought for the elemental forces which were already engaged in the struggle without his volition. Let them see now, he thought, how the "spineless" Kerensky has dealt with the "strong" Kornilov.

He had a typical exchange on this subject with Savinkov, who asked him whether he understood that the army would never recover from this final blow. "On the contrary," retorted Kerensky, "far from perishing, the army, elated by its victory over counterrevolution, will throw itself at the Germans and defeat them." [12]

Kerensky had no inkling that by his "victory" over Kornilov he had finished sawing off the limb to which he was clinging.

During all that time, the Extraordinary Commission of Inquiry into the Kornilov affair was methodically accumulating a vast amount of material: minutes of examinations of witnesses and accused, letters, telegrams, tele-printed records of conversations by direct wire, decrees, proclamations. By the end of October, 1917, the investigation was virtually completed. Still to be obtained was the testimony of Kerensky himself.

On August 27 he had testified before an investigator of the Petrograd District Court in order to establish Kornilov's guilt, but he had not so far been questioned by the Commission.

Kerensky's questioning took place in the second half of October [related Nicholas Ukraintsev, a former member of the Commission]. In preparing ourselves for it, we realized that we would run into many difficulties. After all, we were about to subject to an examination the leader of our government, who might attribute to our questions a lack of confidence in him or an expression of doubt in his words. We decided, therefore, to prepare a questionnaire formulated in a way that would not permit Kerensky to avoid answering each question directly, but worded in terms expressing our deep respect for the exalted position of our witness. The queries which might be particularly unwelcome to the Prime Minister were to be placed at the end of the list.

. . . Due to the carelessness or lack of restraint of one of the Commission's members, some information concerning the investigation was prematurely leaked out to the press. The Petrograd papers used this information against Kerensky, which, of course, could not fail to annoy him. . . .

. . . We did not expect an amiable welcome from Kerensky, but none of us could foresee that the meeting would end as disastrously as it did. . . .

. . . Kerensky received us in the imperial library at the Winter Palace. In the space between two large windows facing the Neva, stood a large carved armchair reminiscent of a throne. In front of it was a fairly long table at which we seated ourselves. Kerensky took up his place on the throne. If I were asked to describe his attitude on the throne, I would be obliged to say that he was "sprawling" on it. This was a detail, of course, but we immediately felt that it was intended to make us realize the distance separating us from the illustrious witness who had granted us the honor of this interview. Out of respect, Shablovsky conducted the inquiry standing. Tumanova, a veteran stenographer of the State Duma, invited by us, recorded the proceedings.

From the beginning, Kerensky's answers were so harsh and delivered with such haughtiness that Shablovsky was at a loss how to react. . . . The first one to lose patience was Raupakh, who rose and asked Kerensky to reformulate an answer with more precision. Lieber followed suit. At this, Kerensky completely lost control of himself. He sprang up and literally shouted at us. We silently

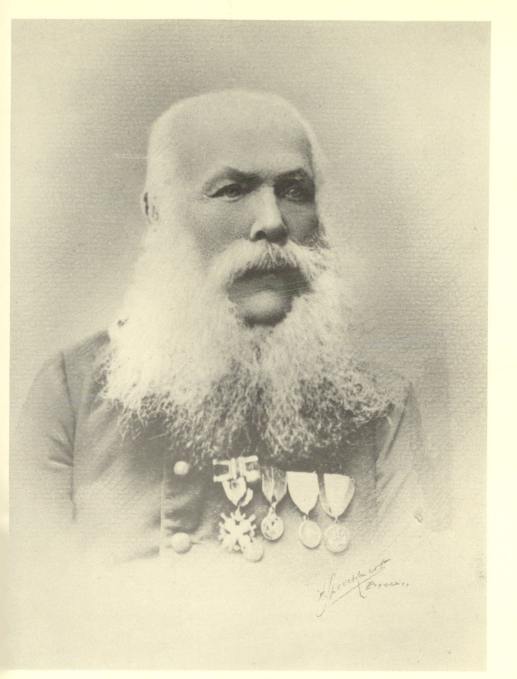

Ivan Efimovich Denikin (1807–1885), Anton Denikin's father.

Elizaveta Fedorovna Denikin, née Vrĵesinski (1843–1916), Anton Denikin's mother.

Xenia Chizh, Anton Denikin's future wife, at age sixteen in a gypsy costume.

Anton Denikin as a lieutenant, circa 1893.

Anton Denikin as a colonel and commander of the 17th Infantry
Arkhangelgorod Regiment, circa 1911.

Prime Minister Peter A. Stolypin (1862–1911).

General A. A. Brusilov.

Major General Anton Denikin, commander of the "Iron Brigade," with his chief of staff, Colonel Sergei L. Markov at the Austro-Hungarian front in December, 1914.

General Lavr G. Kornilov with his troops in World War I.

Alexander Kerensky, Minister of Justice in the Provisional Government, March, 1917. PHOTOWORLD.

Supreme Commander, General M. V. Alekseev in Mogilev, April, 1917. At his right, his chief of staff, General Anton Denikin.

War Minister A. F. Kerensky with the commander in chief of the western front, General Anton Denikin, June, 1917.

General Kornilov with Boris V. Savinkov, summer, 1917.

Group of arrested officers of the southwestern front confined in the prison of Bykhov. From left to right: a lieutenant, Generals Elsner, Vannovsky, Denikin, Erdeli, Markov, and Orlov. End of September, 1917.

A false identification issued to General Denikin on November 17, 1917, by the Polish riflemen division in the name of "Aleksandr Dombrovsky, assistant to the director of the 73rd Polish first-aid unit." This was used by Denikin in his escape from Bykhov prison.

Ataman of the Don Cossa
General A. M. Kaledin.

Colonel M. G. Drozdovsky, who, at the end of April, 1918, led a volunteer detachment from Rumania to join Denikin's army.

Denikin and his closest aides. From left to right: Generals Denikin, Lukomsky, Dragomirov, Romanovsky (partly hidden by entrance gate). Behind them: the French representative, Captain Fouguet, and Colonel Chaperon du Larré.

Lenin, the master propagandist, addressing a crowd.

Trotsky, War Commissar and chief organizer of the Red Army.

February 3, 1919, in Novocherkassk, capital of the Don Cossack region. Left to right: A. P. Bogaevsky, newly elected *Ataman* of the Don Cossacks; General Denikin, commander in chief of the Armed Forces of South Russia; P. N. Krasnov, former *Ataman* of the Don Cossacks; General I. P. Romanovsky, Denikin's chief of staff.

At the laying of a wreath in the name of France on the grave of General Alekseev in the crypt of the cathedral of Ekaterinodar. Left to right: Filimonov, *Ataman* of the Kuban Cossacks, General Denikin, General Markov's widow, French representative Captain Fouquet.

exchanged glances with Shablovsky, and he resolutely announced a recess. At this moment Tumanova rose from her seat and said in a loud voice, addressing Kerensky: "I am ashamed of you, Alexander Fedorovich, ashamed of the way you allow yourself to behave toward the Commission which is carrying out its duty."

This was the last act performed by our commission. Unanimously, as in its preceding action, . . . we reached the conclusion that although Kerensky's explanations were essential, we had to stand up for our dignity as an instrument of judicial authority and could not allow ourselves to be treated in the way we had been treated by Kerensky. . . . We separated on this decision. October 25 [the day of the Bolshevik revolution] was but a few days away.[13]

The Commission was disbanded after the Bolshevik *coup* without ever receiving Kerensky's answers to a number of ticklish questions. This prevented the Commission from summing up the results of its investigation and reaching an official conclusion.

Kerensky attempted to do this himself a few months later. After his escape from Petrograd during the Bolshevik uprising, he managed somehow to obtain the stenographic record of his interview with the Commission. The document, personally edited by Kerensky, with his own additions, cuts, corrections and commentary, was published by Zadruga in Moscow in 1918, under the title *Delo Kornilova* (*The Kornilov Affair*).

Kerensky has often returned to this painful subject in the numerous works written by him during his long years of exile. He has always treated it, as Melgunov has said, with remarkable inexactness in his statement of facts, presenting them always one-sidedly from the viewpoint of the self-excusing memoirist.

Half a century later, after an abundance of historical material has come to the surface, the Kornilov affair assumes a completely different aspect from the one initially given it by Alexander Kerensky.

Both Kornilov and Kerensky saw the danger of divided power. Both knew that the weakness of the Provisional Government and the irresponsible power of the Soviet of Workers' and Soldiers' Deputies were driving the nation toward anarchy.

Kornilov was for drastic measures to destroy the Bolshevik menace, disband the Soviets, and establish a firm government which would continue the war and govern Russia until a Constituent Assembly could be called. In pursuing these aims, he engaged in conspiratorial activity which he concealed from Kerensky, whose sincerity he doubted.

Kerensky had aims very similar to Kornilov's, but lacked the courage to state them openly. Having assumed a position of leadership, he too desired to establish a firm governing power, which would be concentrated in his hands. The Soviets' continuous interference in government affairs irritated him. Though he still held the title of deputy chairman of the Soviet, Kerensky expressed his disapproval of it by no longer participating in its meetings. His retort to Lvov: "Splendid! We shall say then that we were unable to curb the populace, wash our hands of the whole thing, and deny all responsibility," clearly revealed Kerensky's desire to get rid of the Soviets, or at the very least, drastically curtail their activity. But he could only pursue this aim indirectly, for fear of compromising his revolutionary reputation. He would have welcomed the suppression of the Soviets provided it took place without his participation, and even better, seemingly against his wishes, without involving him in an armed enforcement of power.

It was to achieve this result that, through Savinkov, an agreement to bring the Third Cavalry Corps to Petrograd had been reached between the Prime Minister and the Supreme Commander. The corps was also to disarm and bring to order the Petrograd garrison and the mutinous Kronstadt sailors.

This was as far as the "agreement" went. Like the rest of Kerensky's and Kornilov's short collaboration, it suffered from the absence of explicit conditions and mutual confidence and left the doors wide open to misunderstandings.

One of the principal sources of misunderstanding was Savinkov. Always pursuing his personal aim of taking the leadership of the revolution into his own hands, he played an intricate game in order to secure the collaboration of Kerensky and Kornilov in the government, misleading each of the protagonists as to the other's real aims. He behaved like a true gambler, and having lost the game, not only washed his hands of the deal but threw a false accusation at a man whom, in his own way, he liked and respected.

Neither Kerensky, nor Kornilov, nor Savinkov ever lost sight of his private aim—to achieve power, and subsequently, eliminate or subdue to his will the two other rivals.

Kerensky unquestionably hoped to exclude Kornilov from the government as soon as possible, after having used him to strengthen his own position. The revelation that his willful partner had violated their agreement by placing General Krymov at the head of the Petrograd-bound troops and including among them the Wild Division shocked Kerensky. But the added realization that Kornilov actually intended to assume control of the government, leaving to Kerensky a secondary post in his cabinet, almost drove him out of his mind. His jealous fear for his own future drove all other considerations from his consciousness.

The bitterness of conflicting accusations and justifications, rivalry, and mutual dislike between Kerensky and the Kornilov faction has persisted for years. But these personal elements are overshadowed by the awesome historical consequences of the Kornilov affair. Notwithstanding all the mistakes made by Kornilov, it is impossible to accept at its face value Kerensky's accusation that it was Kornilov who gave the Bolsheviks the opportunity to bring off their coup. Instead, after weighing the testimony of the participants, witnesses, and contemporaries of the affair, one must agree with the conclusion already reached by Milyukov and Melgunov.

The opinion of these two outstanding authorities on the Russian revolution was that not the Kornilov revolt in itself, but the measures taken by the government for its liquidation, precipitated the Bolshevik seizure of power. [14]

Despite the accusing stance assumed by him, Kerensky stands before history not only as a deeply involved witness in the Kornilov affair, but also as a defendant.*

* For a special bibliography on the Kornilov affair, see the notes to this chapter.

XIII

CONFINEMENT
IN BYKHOV

———————◄ ►———————

Having achieved his aim of liquidating the Kornilov revolt without bloodshed, General Alekseev did not wish to remain in the position of chief of staff to Kerensky, whom he did not trust, and handed his resignation to the government on September 10.

Alekseev's attempts to improve the fate of the arrested generals by obtaining their "pardon" from the government were sharply criticized by Kornilov. He insisted on being vindicated, not amnestied. "We considered ourselves morally, if not legally, in the right in relation to our country," wrote Denikin. "We desired and expected a trial." [1]

Alekseev's moral fiber came to the fore remarkably in this difficult period. He brushed aside all feelings and manifestations of human smallness which could have influenced his reaction to the personal criticisms and caustic remarks expressed about him. He consciously sacrificed his good name and reputation in the pursuit of a single goal: the preservation at all cost of the lives of the imprisoned generals for the purpose of combating the threat of approaching anarchy. He respected Kornilov but did not like him. Nevertheless, Kornilov was the symbol which could attract and unify patriotic Russians, and as such, had to be protected and preserved. The officers were for Kornilov. Many of them had been arrested and deprived of their pay at Kerensky's orders; their families were destitute and hungry. In order to assist them, but mainly to save the life of Denikin, who was imprisoned in Berdichev, Alekseev appealed for help to P. N. Milyukov in a letter dated September 12. Written two days after Alekseev resigned as chief of staff to the Supreme Commander, the letter is of considerable historical interest, and we are therefore quoting it at some length:

The reason which determined my resignation is my basic disagreement with the direction of the case against Kornilov and especially against Denikin and the persons accused with them.

The efforts of the members of the government are concentrated on persuading all of Russia that the events of August 27–31 were brought on by the rebellion and adventurism of a group of unruly generals and officers striving to *overthrow the existing order of government* and take over the administration of the country. They try to make it sound simple and uncomplicated, describing the accused as a small band of rebels, devoid of sympathy and support from any quarter, engaged in betrayal and rebellion. Subject, therefore, to the most primitive of all trials—trial by a *revolutionary court-martial,* and deserving of the *death penalty*. The purpose of this rapid judgment and sentence is to dissimulate the entire truth, the real aim of the movement, and the involvement of government members in the affair. To make this easier, they resort to the despicable trick of treating as separate cases the eight persons held in Berdichev: Denikin, Markov, Elsner, Erdeli, Vannovsky, and three others. On the basis of the contention that the investigation is completed, they want to subject them *on the spot to a revolutionary court-martial.* [All italics are Alekseev's.]

. . . An outrageous deed is being perpetrated, while the national conscience slumbers and the honest press does nothing to awaken it and remains silent. . . .

I affirm that the passions of the mob and soldiers in Berdichev were artificially stimulated and fanned into hatred by the demagogy of the dishonest and worthless membership of the committee, which had accounts to settle with Denikin and Markov who had put a stop to its shameless dipping into official funds. The pettily vengeful and morally abject Iordansky also had some run-ins with Denikin and Markov.

Alekseev stressed the point that the aim of the Kornilov movement was not to change the existing form of government, that Kornilov's plans were discussed with Savinkov and Filonenko, and through them, with Kerensky.

Only the most primitive revolutionary court-martial is capable of concealing the participation of these individuals in the preliminary discussions and agreement. . . . Kerensky's participation cannot be denied.

General Alekseev insisted that a detailed and comprehensive inquiry into the whole affair should take place, and that eventually it would disclose these facts.

There will be other work then for the Messrs. Filonenko, than to doff their hats before Kornilov's grave; they will have to take the stand next to the general. . . . [Apparently, in the early part of September Alekseev did not have too much faith in the Extraordinary Commission of Inquiry headed by Shablovsky.]

Alekseev appealed to Milyukov to prod the "honest press" into action. He also asked Milyukov to get in touch with some of the leaders of Russia's industrial and financial bourgeoisie and to collect from them 300,000 rubles for the families of the arrested officers, who were deprived of their pay.[2]

The Bolsheviks found Alekseev's letter, after they came to power, in the course of a search through Milyukov's papers, and published it in the newspaper *Izvestia* in December, 1917.

Neither Milyukov nor Alekseev expected this letter to be published. It therefore has the special interest of a confidential document expressing its author's undisguised point of view on the Kornilov action. The fact that in this letter Alekseev had no reason to attribute to Kornilov purposes other than the ones he was actually pursuing lends importance to Alekseev's affirmation that the Kornilov movement had never been directed against the February revolution, as Kerensky then, and later, affirmed it to be.

We parted with General Denikin and his fellow prisoners as they left Berdichev on September 27 in a filthy boxcar, heading for Bykhov, where the trial of all the participants in the Kornilov movement was to take place.

The Bykhov prisoners were confined in a forbidding, ancient two-storied building which had formerly housed a Catholic monastery, and then a girls' school, and had now been converted into a prison. It stood next to a Catholic church, or *Kosciel*. Its courtyard was surrounded by a fence with tall iron gates. A wooden sidewalk ran along its sides, providing a passage across the liquid mud which filled it on rainy days. The house had deeply recessed windows protected by iron grills, a massive wooden entrance door, a dark stairway, rooms with low, vaulted ceilings. In cheerless surroundings, the prisoners arrested several weeks before at the *Stavka* anxiously awaited the arrival of General Denikin and his companions. They had heard of the rioting in Berdichev and were haunted by fear for Denikin's safety. A sigh of relief went up when he appeared.

In Bykhov, Anton Ivanovich saw his fiancée for the first time since the middle of August. She had wanted to rejoin him in Berdichev, but he was afraid for her safety and forbade her to come there. So she remained in Kiev, in the former apartment of Denikin's mother. Terrified at what was happening to Anton Ivanovich, she set about organizing his defense in a very intelligent and businesslike manner. She engaged the well-known lawyer and orator V. A. Maklakov, who had been the defender of Beylis in a celebrated lawsuit. Maklakov, however, was in Moscow, and the commissar of the southwestern front, Iordansky, was rushing Denikin's case toward a court-martial. There was no time to lose, therefore, and Xenia Vasilievna also engaged a group of well-known Kiev defense lawyers of various political affiliations. A car was held in readiness in Kiev at the insistence of the defense lawyers, who feared that both "judgment" and sentence might be carried out with such speed that they could not afford the risk of delay in arriving. Fortunately, these precautions turned out to be unnecessary.

"I entered the ward and . . . was overcome with confusion," related Xenia Vasilievna of her reunion with Denikin. "It was full of people and they were all looking at me. My general smiled at me with his kind, shy smile. And all I wanted was to kiss his hands and cry. . . ." [3]

The conditions of the Bykhov imprisonment were quite different from those in Berdichev.

The prisoners had complete freedom of movement indoors, where they were guarded by Kornilov's loyal and faithful Tekintsy. A company of soldiers of the regiment of St. George guarded the building on the outside.

"Officially," wrote General Lukomsky, "we were expected to keep to our rooms except for meals and our daily walks; but in reality we were completely free in our movements inside the building and visited each other whenever we wanted to. We had no cash allowance, but were entitled to receive, at the government's expense, the same quality of food that was served in officers' messes. The *Stavka* had sent one of its cooks to Bykhov and we were fed quite decently. . . .

"We were allowed to walk twice a day in the courtyard surrounding the *Kosciel.* Later, a large garden which adjoined our building was also allocated to us for that purpose." [4]

The prisoners' wives were permitted to live in Bykhov and to visit them every day. In a word, after Berdichev, the limitations of Bykhov seemed a mere formality. "We had the queer impression," wrote Denikin, "that everyone was embarrassed at having to act as our 'jailers'." [5]

Mrs. Denikin has described the room which Denikin shared with Generals Markov and Romanovsky:

Two windows. Between them the only table, on which stands a small, battered, smoky kerosene lamp. Only two chairs, so that everyone sits on the beds. I seat myself next to Anton Ivanovich on his hard bed covered with a soldier's blanket and we begin to talk quietly under cover of the loud voices in the room. For over a month after this, I came to the prison twice every day. I spent virtually all my time there.

I went there after breakfast, returned home for lunch, then went a second time and came back for dinner. In this way I came to know and form an opinion on all the Bykhov prisoners. . . . Kornilov lived next door to us. . . . Across the corridor from him were Lukomsky and Erdeli, next to them Elsner and Vannovsky, and farther on Kisliakov and Orlov. Some of the younger officers occupied bedrooms on our floor, and the remainder were quartered downstairs near the dining room. All the generals usually gathered in our room, partly because it was larger and partly because the presence of women brought it some animation. General Romanovsky's wife Elena Mikhailovna, was especially lively and witty. Also present was General Lukomsky's wife. We sat on beds, trunks, and suitcases pulled out from under the beds. [6]

General Denikin made a list of the generals and officers who were confined in Bykhov by October 2. There were twenty-four men altogether. All of them, as Denikin said, "people of the most varied viewpoints, the majority of whom had no interest in politics and had been brought together solely by some degree of commitment to the Kornilov cause and by their unquestionable belief in it." [7]

If before the Kornilov revolt there had been a semblance of hope in the possibility of restoring order in the nation, that hope was irretrievably lost by September, 1917. Unrest among the troops, refusal to submit to the "brass," and reprisals against officers spread to every part of the army and became completely uncontrollable. Desertions multiplied; soldiers left their units, and using every means of transportation available, headed toward their home villages and hamlets scattered across the immeasurable vastness of Russia. They hastened home so as not to miss out on the division of landowners' holdings promised them by the Soviets. On their way, they looted not only the estates of the gentry but the villages and farms of their fellow peasants. They destroyed crops, cattle, and domestic fowl, and raided the government's liquor warehouses. Trains overflowed with unruly, drunken soldiers. Those who could not get in climbed on the car-tops, where they camped like gypsies. A tidal wave of deserting soldiers broke over the country, leaving chaos in its wake.

On September 10, General Alekseev was replaced in the post of chief of staff to the Supreme Commander by General N. N. Dukhonin, an honest and honorable man who was prepared, as Alekseev had been, to jeopardize his reputation to preserve the administrative framework of the army. The captives in Bykhov included him in their criticism of all those who continued to collaborate with Kerensky. Disregarding this attitude, Dukhonin did everything in his power to improve the condition of the prisoners and to surround them with troops that would protect them from being molested.

It was for this purpose that (in addition to the Tekintsy and the company of the regiment of St. George) the *Stavka* assigned to Bykhov in the latter part of September a number of Polish units from the recently formed Polish corps, under the command of General Dovbor-Musnitsky. The general and all his officers and soldiers were natives of the part of Poland which formerly belonged to the Russian Empire.

"The attitude of the Poles toward the Bykhov prisoners was truly chivalrous," wrote Denikin in one of his unpublished manuscripts.[8] Though he submitted to the orders of the *Stavka,* General Dovbor-Musnitsky considered his troops to be nationally independent. He instructed them, therefore, to keep out of Russia's internal strife, but ordered them to protect the arrested Russian generals even if it became necessary to do so by the force of arms.

A regular liaison between Bykhov and the *Stavka* was maintained by two officers who had formerly served under Denikin and were devoted to him—Colonels Kvashnin-Samarin and Timanovsky. These officers kept the Bykhov generals informed of the events at the *Stavka* and throughout the country. To all appearances, these events were going from bad to worse.

By mid-October only the blind and the deaf could have failed to observe that the Bolsheviks were preparing to seize power. Indeed, they made no secret of it. On October 16, Trotsky organized the Military-Revolutionary Committee, through which he planned to assume control of the Petrograd garrison. A day later, the Military-Revolutionary Committee ordered the distribution of arms and ammunition to the workers of the Putilov factory and other large plants. The procedure was simple: A warrant from the Committee was presented to the employees of the arms depots, who delivered rifles and cartridges to the workers without a word of protest. The proletariat was arming itself with no attempt at secrecy.

This time the slogan "All power to the Soviets!" acquired its true meaning, which it had lacked in the July uprising, before the Soviets had fallen into Bolshevik hands.

One of those who seemed not to realize the approaching danger was Prime Minister Kerensky, as indicated in the following episode related by Nabokov: "Four or five days before the Bolsheviks' October insurrection, during one of our sessions at the Winter Palace, I asked him [Kerensky] directly what his attitude was regarding the possibility of a Bolshevik move, which everyone was discussing at that time. 'I would be prepared to hold public prayers to bring about such a move,' he answered. 'But are you sure of being able to control it?' 'I have more forces than necessary. They will be definitely crushed.' " [9]

Alas, the "more forces than necessary" were simply nonexistent, and all the members of the Provisional Government, with the exception of its Prime Minister, understood this very well.

During the night of October 24, the Red Guards (armed factory workers who had joined the Bolshevik party) occupied in Petrograd the General Post Office, the telephone and telegraph exchanges, the railroad terminals, and the State Bank. The military leadership of the insurrection was in the hands of Antonov-Ovseenko, Podvoisky, and other old-time Bolsheviks. The garrison of the capital, which played such an important role in the February revolution, was sympathetic or at least neutral with regard to the Bolshevik *coup*. On October 25, the Military-Revolutionary Committee announced the downfall of the Provisional Government. Despite the striking success of the insurrection, this announcement was slightly premature, because the capture of the Winter Palace, where members of the government were in session, did not take place until the following morning.

On October 25, the Provisional Government, fully realizing its helplessness before the Bolshevik uprising, addressed an appeal to the population, informing it that the Petrograd Soviet demanded the surrender of power by the Provisional Government, and if it refused to comply, threatened to bombard the Winter Palace from the Fortress of Peter and Paul and from the cruiser *Aurora,* stationed in the Neva. "The Government can surrender its power to no one except the Constituent Assembly," continued the appeal; "it has, therefore, resolved not to surrender and to place itself under the protection of the population and the army." [10] This was tantamount to an admission that the situation was hopeless.

On October 26, at 2:10 A.M., all the ministers of the Provisional Government (with the exception of Kerensky and one other minister) were arrested and marched by the Red Guards across a bridge of the river Neva to the Fortress of Peter and Paul. There they joined the ministers of the tsarist government, held in the dungeons of that fortress-prison since the end of February. Compared to the February revolution and the uprising of July 3–5, the Bolshevik *coup d'état* was relatively bloodless.

In the early hours of October 26, Lenin, who had spent a sleepless night with Trotsky in a small room of the Smolny Institute in Petrograd, turned to his companion with the remark that such a sudden transition to power from a state of illegality made him feel dizzy. Having said this, Lenin—the militant atheist—gratefully made the sign of the cross.[11]

Meanwhile, the city was filling with rumors. News spread that on October 25, Kerensky had been seen speeding along the Voskresenski Prospect in a car which disappeared in the direction of Gatchina. Some said that distrusting the local garrison, he had left to muster troops loyal to the government and lead them to Petrograd to fight the rebellious Bolsheviks. Others cynically compared him to a rat leaving a sinking ship.

Having left Petrograd on the morning of October 25, by nighttime Kerensky reached the city of Pskov, headquarters of General Cheremisov, commander in chief of the northern front. Kerensky appealed to him for help, but Cheremisov did not lift a finger in response to his appeal. The following morning (October 26) only seven hundred mounted Cossacks from the Third Cavalry Corps halfheartedly joined Kerensky in the "March on Petrograd." The detachment was led by General Peter N. Krasnov, the corps commander who succeeded General Krymov and who disliked Kerensky and had little faith in the success of the enterprise.

As in the days of the Kornilov revolt, the nearer the troops came to the capital, the more reluctant they grew to risk their lives in combat. They crossed Luga and Gatchina, and having arrived at Tsarskoie Selo, decided against participating in a "fratricidal war." Only a few of the officer candidates in the capital, and the women's battalion, attempted to defend the government against the approaching Bolshevik wave.

On October 31, the Cossacks opened negotiations for a truce with the Bolsheviks. Sensing the antagonism of the officers and Cossacks in the Krasnov detachment, and fearing that they would hand him over to the Bolsheviks, Kerensky decided to flee. On the morning of November 1, he disappeared without a trace, and he remained in hiding for eight months. This marked the end of his historic role.

In view of Kerensky's disappearance, the High Command was assumed by General Dukhonin. He proclaimed on November 1 that according to General Krasnov's reports, Supreme Commander Kerensky had left the detachment and his whereabouts were unknown. Therefore, on the basis of the statute for the command of troops in the field, he, General Dukhonin,

was temporarily assuming the duties of Supreme Commander, and ordering a halt of further troop movements to Petrograd.[12]

A week later, the Council of People's Commissars, representing the new
Bolshevik government, ordered General Dukhonin to initiate parleys with
the German army command with regard to a cease-fire leading to the opening of peace negotiations. Dukhonin replied that only a government supported by the army and the entire nation was empowered to issue such an
order. He was relieved of his position for insubordination on the same
day, but ordered to continue in the performance of his duties until the
arrival at the *Stavka* of the new Bolshevik Supreme Commander—Nikolai
Vasilievich Krylenko.

Foreseeing the collapse of the Provisional Government and the massacre
to which it would inevitably lead, the Bykhov prisoners had been evolving a plan of action. The territory of the Don Cossacks appeared to them
to be the only refuge from which they could hope to initiate a struggle
against the approaching anarchy.

They did not expect too much difficulty in escaping and were already
provided with revolvers and fake documents. The fact that Shablovsky's
Commission and the *Stavka* had gradually obtained the release of most of
the prisoners also simplified the problem for the five generals remaining
in Bykhov at the end of October. They were Kornilov, Denikin, Lukomsky,
Romanovsky, and Markov.

After the Bolshevik *coup,* the generals knew that it was both senseless
and dangerous to put off their escape. "On the morning of November 19,"
recollected Denikin, "Colonel of the General Staff Kusonsky arrived from
the *Stavka* and reported to General Kornilov, 'Four hours from now Krylenko will arrive in Mogilev, which the *Stavka* will surrender without resistance. General Dukhonin ordered me to report to you that it is essential
for all the captives to leave Bykhov immediately.' " [13]

General Dukhonin had sent Colonel Kusonsky to Bykhov and ordered
him to liberate its prisoners, with the full awareness that by this action
he was signing his own death warrant. He could have gone into hiding
himself but refused to do so. "I know," he told his close associates, "that
Krylenko will arrest me and perhaps even have me shot. But that is a
soldier's death." He was the captain of the sinking ship and made up his
mind not to leave it. "On the following day," wrote Denikin, "a mob of
sailors, gone berserk with unchained fury, literally tore Dukhonin to pieces
in front of Krylenko, committing every outrage over his body. . . . True
to their 'apolitical' tradition," concluded Denikin bitterly, "the leaders of
the '*Stavka*'s bureaucrats' formally welcomed the new Supreme Commander . . . on the day that his predecessor had been lynched by the
mob." [14]

It would have been unlike Denikin to sympathize with Dukhonin's attitude of nonresistance to evil. Nevertheless, he viewed Dukhonin as a man of irreproachable integrity and remembered him with deep respect.

After hearing Kusonsky's report, Kornilov immediately ordered his faithful Tekintsy cavalry regiment to be ready to march out of Bykhov by midnight of the same day (November 19). It would have been easier and safer for Kornilov to escape by himself in a suitable disguise, but he decided to go with the regiment. He was deeply attached to the Tekintsy and wanted to be with them in this moment of danger. Denikin noted later that this decision almost cost him his life.

The company of the regiment of St. George learned of the generals' liberation without questioning or protest. On the contrary, they wished them Godspeed and asked to be remembered without rancor.

The other four generals agreed to meet in Novocherkassk, in the Don region, and proceeded to change their clothing and alter their appearance— an indispensable precaution, as each of them was a familiar figure in the army and could easily be recognized. Denikin and Lukomsky were to set out separately on this long and dangerous journey. Romanovsky and Markov decided to go together, and accepted Kusonsky's offer to ride on his locomotive as far as Kiev, where he was being sent on a special mission. Romanovsky remained in his officer's uniform after changing his general's shoulder straps for an ensign's. Markov put on a soldier's uniform and assumed the role of Romanovsky's orderly, convincingly imitating the uncouth manners of the "comrades."

General Lukomsky impersonated a "German colonist," * while Denikin obtained from the chief of staff of the Polish riflemen an identification "certifying that he was Aleksandr Dombrovsky, assistant to the director of the Seventy-third Polish first-aid unit."

In his guise as a Polish bourgeois, Anton Ivanovich went to the Bykhov station, bought a ticket, and having found out that the train for Rostov was leaving in five hours, decided to wait at the headquarters of the Polish riflemen rather than attract attention at the station.

As luck would have it, a Polish officer at headquarters was also leaving on the same train. "The presence of this young officer, Liubokonsky, proved of immense help to me," recollected Denikin, "relieving my anxiety by his pleasant company and surrounding me with his care throughout the journey."

"The train was delayed by six hours," continued Denikin. "After an endless wait, we finally left at ten thirty in the evening.

"For the first time in my life I was a conspirator, in disguise and with a false passport. I realized at once that conspiracy was not my dish. I was depressed, anxious, totally unimaginative. I was disguised as a Pole and talking Polish with Liubokonsky, and yet, when a soldier asked me what

---

* German colonists were the descendants of German farmers invited by Catherine the Great to settle in sparsely populated areas in south Russia and along the Volga River. They retained their language, their religion, and all their old customs.

province I came from, automatically answered, Saratov. I had quite a bit of trouble explaining how a Pole happened to come from the Saratov province." (Although Denikin was born in Russian Poland, his father had come from the Saratov province, and Anton Ivanovich had considered it his country of origin from childhood.)

On the following day, Denikin noticed that all the railroad stations displayed huge posters announcing the escape of Kornilov, Denikin, and the other Bykhov generals. The Military-Revolutionary Committee appealed to the population to quell without mercy any counterrevolutionary attempts and to assist in the capture of the generals. The poster said that Kornilov had left with a detachment of four hundred Tekintsy.

Several times, Red Guard patrols carefully checked the documents of all the passengers on the train, which was filled to overflowing with privates. They were obviously looking for someone. Each time they appeared, Denikin's hand sought the handle of the revolver in his pocket. Only much later, he found out that the gun was worthless.

To avoid conversations and the possibility of being recognized by one of the soldiers, Denikin stretched out on the upper berth of the compartment, turned to the wall, and pretended to be asleep.

"I stayed there so long," he related, "that the other passengers became suspicious. 'He's been there half a day without showing his mug,' they said, 'maybe it's Kerensky himself. . . . Turn him around!'

"Someone pulled at my sleeve, I turned over and lowered my head from the bunk. The soldiers burst out laughing, so little did I resemble what they expected. They even made up for the disturbance by offering me some tea."

In the course of this exceedingly slow journey, with its numerous and protracted stops, Denikin was immersed in the thick of the revolutionized population and the soldier masses.

I saw at close range what life had become like, and was horrified [he related]. First of all, by the unbounded hatred toward people and ideas which I felt all around me. Hatred toward anything, including inanimate objects, which was socially or mentally above the crowd and bore the slightest trace of prosperity or culture unfamiliar or incomprehensible to the mob. This feeling reflected centuries of accumulated resentment, the revolt against three years of warfare, and the hysteria spread by revolutionary leaders. With equal thoroughness and brute satisfaction, this hatred destroyed the foundations of government, threw a "bourgeois" out the window, broke the stationmaster's skull, or tore to shreds the velvet upholstery in the compartment. The psychology of the mob did not aspire to achieve a higher level of existence; it vented itself in a single desire— to grab or to destroy. Its aim seemed to be not to rise, but to pull down, to its own level, anything that stood out or appeared different.[15]

Denikin realized that the errors of the past, but especially the disastrous war, had brought on an epoch of mass destruction and lawlessness; they had sharpened to a climax the envy of the have-nots toward the haves, of the illiterate toward the literate, and aroused a wild protest against every form of law and order.

He was incapable of remaining a neutral spectator of this drama. And the longer he meditated on the painful problem, the firmer became his resolve to fight at all costs and as soon as possible the chaos raging in his motherland. That which the Bolsheviks had named the dawn of a new life appeared to Denikin as a mockery of common sense and the dignity of human beings.

During a change of trains in the Kharkov station, Anton Ivanovich saw in the crowd the familiar figures of Romanovsky and Markov. They boarded different carriages in the same train. Carefully threading his way through soldiers sleeping or sitting on the floor, Denikin finally rejoined his friends. They had much to tell each other, but had to be careful not to step out of their respective roles. Markov, like a good orderly, fetched boiling water for the tea whenever the train stopped at a station. A lieutenant, on his way to Tiflis, kept trying to remember the exact circumstances of his meeting with Aleksandr Dombrovsky at the Rumanian front in 1916. "Your face is so familiar," he repeated. But Polish citizen Dombrovsky obstinately maintained the impossibility of such an encounter. Only when they were parting at the Rostov station did Denikin admit that he was indeed familiar with the Second Division, in which the lieutenant had served, having fought alongside it in the battle of Rymnik. The lieutenant was petrified with astonishment at discovering that his traveling companion was General Denikin, who, like Kornilov, was being sought all over Russia by the Bolsheviks.

In the meantime, at 1 A.M. on November 20, the Tekintsy regiment led by Kornilov set out from Bykhov in a southwesterly direction. By speedy marches, hastening to increase their distance from the *Stavka* as quickly as possible, fearful of being pursued and attacked, the regiment covered approximately 375 kilometers in the first week. Bitter frost had set in. Yet it was necessary to march by night, keeping away from railroad tracks, going through woods and frozen marshes and across fields deeply piled with snow. The riders suffered from the cold; their horses were nearing exhaustion. In the villages, the exotic-looking Tekintsy were met with fear by the natives, already terrified by the pillaging of the deserters, and were seen off with astonishment after having paid for everything and molested no one.

Denikin has described this march after hearing the stories of its participants:

Ahead—was a long journey into the unknown. . . .

On the seventh day of the march (November 26) a peasant who had volunteered to guide the Tekintsy led them to a Bolshevik ambush. On reaching the edge of a wood, they were met almost point-blank with rifle fire. . . . At about 2 P.M. the detachment was approaching the Moscow–Brest railway line near the station of Peschaniki. A train suddenly appeared around the bend and opened fire with the machine guns and cannons of its armored platforms. The leading squadron wheeled sharply and galloped away; several horsemen fell; Kornilov's horse was shot from under him; the regiment scattered. . . .

Kornilov understood that he would never reach the Don with his regiment and that the Tekintsy had a better chance to save themselves without him. He parted from his men and made his way to the south alone. Some days later, on a station platform in Konotop, a young officer met in the crowd a lame old man, dressed in rags and old felt boots, and recognized Kornilov.

On December 6 [wrote Denikin], an old man bearing a passport in the name of Larion Ivánov, refugee from Rumania, arrived in the city of Novocherkassk, where he was anxiously awaited by his family and his companions in arms.[16]

In roundabout ways, with false documents, borrowed clothes, and altered appearances, the future leaders of the White movement were gradually reaching the Don.

XIV

BIRTH OF THE
WHITE MOVEMENT

———————◆ ◆———————

The Don Cossack Territory, a vast area in the southeastern part of European Russia which covers over 144,000 square kilometers, is located mostly in the basin of the river Don, which empties into the northeastern part of the Sea of Azov. It had been a pasture land for nomadic bands of Scythians, Sarmathians, Huns, and Avars, and later of Khazars, Pechenegs, Polovtsy, and Tatars. The name "Cossack" was probably derived from a Tatar word meaning "freebooter" or "adventurer." *

At the end of the fifteenth century, the Don Cossack Territory began to attract freedom-loving fugitives from the Muscovite state. They took to the steppes to escape the burden of taxation placed upon them by the growing centralized power, the beginnings of serfdom, and other unjust or restricting measures. Having shaken off the oppression of the ruling classes and tasted freedom, these strong and enterprising people gradually evolved their own Cossack way of life along strictly democratic lines. All the members of their communes had equal rights, and they were governed by an *Ataman* elected for a certain period by the *Krug,* or Cossack general assembly, which later became the Cossack parliament. The people of the Cossack communes established at the southern limits of the Muscovite state, in the proximity of alien nomads and under constant menace from their mighty non-Christian neighbors, the Tatars and Turks, gradually ac-

* The term "Cossack," describes a peculiarly Russian phenomenon. It was applied to settlers in the border areas of Russia, who were endowed with certain privileges and a certain degree of autonomy in return for obligatory military service for all men. The Cossacks formed eleven separate territorial groups, each with its own armed force, or *Voisko.* They were the Cossacks of the Don, Kuban, Terek, Astrakhan, Ural, Orenburg, Siberia, Semirechensk, Amur, Ussuri, and Zabaikalie.

quired the characteristics of a military class or militant order of knighthood. This "order" was destined gradually to colonize the outlying regions of the Muscovite state, and later, to defend the borders of Russia from enemy incursions.

At first the central government did not interfere too much in the internal affairs of the Cossacks, and the Don region was autonomous. With the passage of time, however, and especially after the Muscovite tsardom became the Russian Empire, the government began to draw tighter the reins of power. It strove to acquire better control over the freedom-loving Cossacks and to deprive them of some of their privileges. Attempts were made to appoint the *Atamans* rather than to allow the population to elect them. In 1671, in the reign of Tsar Alexis Mikhailovich, the Don Cossacks began to swear allegiance to the rulers of Russia.

The Don Cossacks included some unruly, anarchistic elements who resented Moscow's rule. Gradually, however, a new class of well-to-do, home-owning Cossacks began to evolve and acquire strength on the Don; and their well-being inevitably helped to evolve more conservative attitudes and views and a desire for closer ties with the tsarist government, which could, in case of need, give military as well as material assistance to the Cossacks.

On their part, the Don Cossacks were in a position to make an important contribution to Russia's armed might. Their vulnerable geographical location had made general military service traditional from time immemorial, so that the region's male population formed a huge army reserve ready to serve in any emergency.

In the course of World War I, the Don territory gave to the Russian army sixty cavalry regiments, which, incidentally, had no instances of desertion. The Don Cossacks were the only troops which joined the army equipped with their own horses, uniforms, and military gear. Only their firearms were provided by the crown.

The Cossacks came to be considered reliable and staunch supporters of the regime. Cossack units played a considerable part in quelling the agrarian and political uprisings of the 1905–6 revolution. After the February, 1917, revolution, the insistence of newly formed revolutionary organizations on leveling all land holdings in the Don territory put the Cossacks on the defensive. They began to view with suspicion the events taking place throughout the country. They also had plenty to worry about at home. At the advent of the revolution, the Don territory's population of over four million included, in addition to hereditary Cossacks, an even larger percentage of so-called *inogorodni,* or outlanders, who did not possess the Cossack privileges and represented the region's land proletariat. They eyed the rich Cossack holdings with envy. Later, during the civil war period, the *inogorodni* proved to be the Cossacks' most bitter enemies.

The Provisional Government under Kerensky reciprocated the suspicious attitude of the Cossacks. Kerensky distrusted them, and his distrust increased with the election of General Kaledin to the post of *Ataman* of the Don Cossacks.

Like most of the leaders of the White movement initiated in the late fall of 1917, General Aleksei Maksimovich Kaledin served at the southwestern front during World War I. Denikin had known him even before the war, when they both served in the Kiev military district. Kaledin was a taciturn, intelligent, profoundly honest individual. Like Denikin, he was sparing with his words but could be an excellent and forceful speaker when the occasion arose.

We have already had a glimpse of Kaledin on a rocky crag in the Carpathians, sitting beside Denikin and calmly observing the course of the battle in full view of the fiercely firing Austrians. This was at the beginning of 1915, when he was commanding the Twelfth Cavalry Division. Later, Kaledin replaced Brusilov as commander of the Eighth Army, which he led in the famous Russian spring and summer offensive of 1916—the offensive which began with Denikin's spectacular breakthrough at Lutsk. Brusilov's attitude towards Kaledin was negative, and when he became Supreme Commander, he obtained Kaledin's removal from the command of the Eighth Army.

In June, 1917, the Don Cossack *Krug* elected Kaledin as its *Ataman*. At the State Conference held in Moscow in mid-August, Kaledin spoke after Kornilov in the name of all the Cossack troops in Russia. His speech made a great impression. He pointed out "with profound sorrow" the role played in internal politics by private, class, and party interests to the detriment of the nation as a whole, and expressed the hope that the Provisional Government could rise above these unhealthy influences. He went even further than Kornilov in his demand that all Soviets and committees be abolished.

When the Kornilov revolt broke out late in August, Kerensky accused *Ataman* Kaledin of rebellion and charged him with threatening to disrupt communications between Moscow and the south of Russia. His accusations were based on unfounded rumors in certain newspapers. Kaledin sympathized with Kornilov but had no part in the conspiracy. Kerensky, however, advised the entire country by telegraph that Kaledin had been stripped of his position and summoned to the *Stavka* for questioning by the Commission of Inquiry in the Kornilov affair. The new Minister of War, Colonel Verkhovsky (then and there promoted to the rank of general), was asking for Kaledin's immediate arrest.

This stirred the Cossacks to a high pitch of excitement. All the persons who were close to Kaledin knew that the accusations against him were pure invention. The Don Cossack *Krug* assembled in haste to examine the matter.

The investigation began September 5 and lasted a week, at the end of which the *Krug* concluded that the accusations against Kaledin were entirely false and unfounded. A great scandal resulted. The Don Cossack leaders felt gravely insulted by the fact that the Provisional Government dared to order the dismissal and arrest on his own territory of a duly elected and highly respected Cossack chief. The *Krug* accused the government of gross violation of the principle of popular rule, and urgently demanded the refutation of its allegations concerning a rebellion in the Don region, and an immediate investigation and prosecution of the parties guilty of spreading misinformation. The whole affair of an alleged rebellion was characterized as either a provocation or the product of a deranged mind.

Kerensky expressed his deep regret that "a misunderstanding" had arisen between him and the Cossacks. Only the chaotic conditions which engulfed the entire country at this point can explain the fact that the Prime Minister and his advisers were not brought to task for the slander which could have cost Kaledin his life.

General Alekseev, who knew Kaledin and expected the Don Cossacks' attitude toward Bolshevism to be completely negative, left Petrograd for Novocherkassk, arriving on November 2. Alekseev immediately set to work creating the nucleus which was destined to grow into the leading White army of the Russian civil war. The majority of the officers had a high regard for Alekseev, the leaders of the liberal Russian intelligentsia considered him as an outstanding soldier-statesman, and his misunderstandings with Kornilov were known at that time only to a very small group of people.

By the end of 1917, the non-Russian nationalities on the borders of the former empire were striving to break away from it and declare their independence in the hope of warding off the Bolshevik contamination. To Alekseev and his future collaborators, Kornilov and Denikin, the Don appeared to be the only safe location from which their action could be initiated. Unlike those of most of the other border areas, the men of the Don region had a solid military training, and the people were mostly of Russian origin, spoke Russian, belonged to the Russian Orthodox Church, and were comparatively well off.

The generals had no great hopes that the Cossacks would go out of their way in helping their cause, but they did expect the Cossacks "to stand up for their own territory and property." [1]

The future leaders of the White movement overestimated the possibilities which the Don territory appeared to offer. Their presence in the Don, and the continuous flow of officers arriving there, aroused the Cossacks' fears of possible interference and invasion by Bolshevik troops. The sailors of the Black Sea fleet threatened reprisals. The industrial workers loudly and insistently demanded that the "counterrevolutionaries" be liquidated. Friction between the Cossacks and the *inogorodni,* who had fallen prey to Bolshevik propaganda, became more pronounced every day, thereby

heightening the atmosphere of tension and suspicion on all sides. *Ataman*
Kaledin's position was becoming extremely difficult, and that of his unin-
vited guests—even worse.

Kaledin knew that the lives of the generals and officers assembled at the
Don would be threatened anywhere else in Russia. He could not deprive
them of refuge, and assisted many of them with his personal funds. To
those who criticized him he quoted an old Cossack saying, "There is no
extradition from the Don." At the same time, however, the local situation was becoming so serious that he requested Alekseev to use the utmost
discretion in recruiting volunteers, and advised the General to transfer his
organization to points such as Stavropol or Kamyshin, which though outside the boundaries of the Don territory, were protected by it from central
Russia. However, for many reasons Alekseev was neither willing nor able
to follow this advice.

Meanwhile, singly and in groups, volunteers continued to arrive at the
Don, drawn by the presence there of their recognized leaders. Alekseev
and Kornilov had been their Supreme Commanders; Denikin had been
commander in chief at the western and the southwestern fronts, and
Kaledin was respected by all as the former commander of the Eighth Army
and the present *Ataman* of the Don Cossacks. There was an added attraction for many in the humble origins from which Alekseev, Kornilov, and
Denikin had risen to their positions.

Early in November, a small part of the regiment of St. George came to
Novocherkassk from Kiev. And in December, after an adventurous and
difficult journey, arrived an echelon of the shock regiment named for
Kornilov, who had organized it during the past summer at the southwestern front. At the risk of being recognized on the way and in constant
danger of being shot on the spot or tortured by Bolshevik patrols, officers,
officer candidates, cadets, and university students were also making their
way south.

Several years later, General Denikin gave the following summation of
the movement's initial phase: "If at that tragic moment of our history the
Russian people had not produced men prepared to rise against the madness and crimes of Bolshevik power and give their lifeblood for their
country threatened by destruction—they would not have been a people,
but dung to be spread on the vast reaches of the old continent, fit only to
be colonized by conquerors from west and east.

"Fortunately, we belong to the martyred but great Russian people." [2]

General Alekseev had no funds to maintain his organization and provide the arriving volunteers with the bare necessities of life. This man who
had recently been in charge of the billion-ruble Russian war budget was,
as Denikin put it, "scurrying and bustling around in great agitation in
order to get hold of a dozen beds, a few sacks of sugar, and some infini-
tesimal sum of money, needed to shelter and feed some homeless, persecuted people. . . . Alekseev wore himself out forcing the deaf to listen and

the sleeping to awaken, demanding help and giving in this way all his remaining energy and strength to 'his last labor on earth.' " [3]

Denikin reached Novocherkassk at the end of November and immediately called on *Ataman* Kaledin, who gave a warm welcome to his old comrade-in-arms. Anton Ivanovich asked Kaledin point-blank whether his arrival and the expected arrival of Kornilov would lead to further complications between the *Ataman* and the revolutionary organizations. "The Don will always provide you with a haven, answered Kaledin. But quite frankly, it would be better for you to sit it out somewhere in the Caucasus or in the Kuban *stanitsy* [villages] until the situation becomes clearer." [4] He outlined the conditions and public sentiments prevailing in the Don region, which obviously boded no good. Denikin was struck by the change in his host's appearance. He looked pinched, "as if weighted down by the burden of an inescapable grief," and his sad, tired eyes seemed to reflect all the pain of the catastrophe which had struck Russia and was moving in on the Don.

Denikin accepted Kaledin's advice without hesitation and without the least resentment. He took himself off to the Kuban, with Markov, until such time as Kornilov would arrive in Novocherkassk. He remained in hiding for approximately two weeks in the *stanitsa* Slavianskaia and in Ekaterinodar, under the name of Polish citizen Aleksandr Dombrovsky.

On December 6, as soon as the anxiously awaited Kornilov arrived in Novocherkassk, agents of the Alekseev organization transmitted the news to Denikin and the other generals who were in hiding in the Caucasus and the Kuban. They all immediately returned to Novocherkassk. In the meantime, representatives of the Moscow Center had also arrived in the city. This organization, formed in the fall of 1917 for the purpose of resisting Bolshevism, consisted of various nonsocialist groups—members of the Cadet party, representatives of commerce and industry and of other liberal-bourgeois circles. Among them were some prominent public figures, all of whom arrived in disguise: P. N. Milyukov, Peter B. Struve, the Cadet Mikhail Fedorov, Prince Grigori Troubetzkoy, and former State Duma President M. V. Rodzianko.

The leftist camp was quite unexpectedly represented in the person of Boris Savinkov. His arrival in Novocherkassk disconcerted the generals. He had never enjoyed their confidence, and his role in the Kornilov affair had completely discredited him in their eyes.

Savinkov's conduct during the Bolshevik *coup* had also been very strange: On October 26 he appeared at the secret apartment in which General Alekseev was then in hiding. Striking a theatrical pose, with arms crossed on his chest, Savinkov admonished Alekseev "to fulfill his duty to his motherland" and lead the Don Cossacks of the Third Cavalry Corps to the rescue of the Provisional Government in the capital. Realizing the futility of such a move, Alekseev refused. Savinkov then exclaimed with pathos, "If a Russian general refuses to do his duty, then I, a civilian, will carry it out!"

On the following day, Savinkov turned up in Gatchina, to which Kerensky had fled from Petrograd seeking the protection and help of General Krasnov. Kerensky met Savinkov with surprise and apprehension. His fears were not unfounded. In the course of this visit, Savinkov suggested to Krasnov that he arrest Kerensky and then lead his troops on Petrograd.[5]

Upon his arrival in Novocherkassk, Savinkov called on Kaledin and Alekseev. He tried to prove to them with great insistence that it would be a serious mistake to conduct the anti-Bolshevik struggle exclusively under military leadership. Such a struggle, he maintained, would be doomed to failure because it would give the Bolshevik-oriented masses the impression of being a counterrevolutionary movement bent on restoring the old regime. On the other hand, if a recognized veteran revolutionary such as Savinkov himself took part in the creation of the Volunteer Army, conferring on political matters with Alekseev and later collaborating with Kornilov, the impression would be of a widely comprehensive democratic endeavor with no trace of counterrevolution about it.

The generals viewed with suspicion the moral and political fluctuations of Savinkov's career. In this instance, however, his arguments impressed both Alekseev and Kaledin who, in principle, considered it useful to attract some "leftist" elements to their cause. Kornilov at first rejected Savinkov's offer, but changed his mind out of fear that by refusing Savinkov, he could be accused of placing his personal resentment above the overall interests of the cause. He was also reluctant to acquire an additional foe.

Alone among the senior generals, Denikin refused to act against his innermost convictions. Considering Savinkov to be completely amoral, he simply declared that he would have no truck with him and would refuse to shake his hand if they met. It took all of Alekseev's diplomatic talent to avoid a meeting between Denikin and Savinkov. The tension did not last long, however, as in January, 1918, Savinkov left Novocherkassk for Moscow, where he engaged in underground activity against the Bolsheviks.

Looking back at Savinkov's fleeting appearance in the south of Russia, General Denikin wrote, "The participation of Savinkov and his group failed to add a single soldier or a single ruble to the army, or to bring back to reason a single Don Cossack; all it did was to spread consternation among the officers."[6]

There were persistent rumors that Kerensky, too, had come to the Don territory in the hope of making his peace with Kaledin and obtaining from him an invitation to join forces. Denikin himself was convinced of the veracity of these rumors. He wrote, "By a bitter irony of fate the 'rebels' in Rostov were joined by Russia's former dictator and Supreme Commander of the army and navy, Kerensky, who arrived in disguise and make-up, hiding in fear from the self-same crowd which so recently carried him aloft in its arms as its chosen leader." [7] Kerensky, however, denied later that he had come to the Don territory.

A future biographer of Kerensky may succeed in retracing the wanderings of the former Prime Minister during his eight months of hiding from the Bolsheviks in Russia. He may then be able to establish the truth concerning the above episode in a period regarding which Kerensky has been both reticent and vague.

One distressing circumstance became clear with Kornilov's arrival—his relationship with Alekseev had deteriorated to a point which made constructive collaboration between them extremely difficult.

I do not know what they discussed [wrote Denikin about their first meeting in Novocherkassk], but those who were present had the feeling that they separated in the darkest of moods. . . .

Within a short time there was a meeting of the senior generals and the prominent public figures who had arrived from Moscow.

The essential purpose of the meeting [wrote Denikin], was to define the respective functions of the two generals, Alekseev and Kornilov, and their interrelationship. . . .

A distressing altercation took place. Kornilov demanded full control of the army, maintaining that any different way of administering it was impossible. If his conditions were not accepted, he planned to leave the Don and move to Siberia. For his part, Alekseev obviously found it difficult to give up his participation in a project which he had created with his own hands. Their curt, nervous exchanges were intermixed with the speeches of various prominent civilians who spoke of self-sacrifice and the national need for a concerted effort. [8]

In order to dispel the tension and bring about conditions in which a common goal could be pursued, General Denikin offered a compromise solution: to entrust the military power to General Kornilov, the civilian power and foreign relations to General Alekseev, and all problems connected with the administration of the Don territory to General Kaledin.

Denikin's suggestion was approved and accepted. The triumvirate thus created formed, as Denikin observed, the first anti-Bolshevik government in embryonic form.

On Christmas Day of 1917, General Kornilov assumed the command of the Volunteer Army.

At the moment, this "army" was not only ridiculously small but unarmed and completely devoid of funds.

The first contribution received by the Alekseev organization in November amounted to 400 rubles. Somewhat later, the moneyed bourgeoisie of Moscow sent 800,000 rubles. With the strengthening of the Soviet power, however, assistance from that quarter was soon cut off. Considerable pressure had to be exerted on the financial circles of Rostov and Novocherkassk, which reluctantly subscribed a few million rubles to the cause.

Finally, by agreement with the government of the Don territory, all the funds in the territory belonging to the Russian Treasury were divided between the Don Cossack Army and the Volunteer Army. Each received from the local State Bank and Treasury Department approximately 15 million rubles.[9]

In the meantime, the cost of living was rising daily and the value of money decreasing in the spiral of a rapid inflation.

At the end of December, the representatives of the British and French military missions succeeded in making their way from Moscow to Novocherkassk. They studied the situation at the Don and promised General Alekseev financial assistance amounting to 100 million rubles, payable at the rate of 10 million rubles per month. But the movement of German troops into the southern provinces of Russia, which occurred shortly thereafter, and the chaotic conditions which ensued, severed communcations between the Allies and the White Army. Assistance from that quarter became available only much later.

At the beginning of February, 1918, the army did not exceed three or four thousand people. "The recruiting was on a voluntary basis," wrote Denikin; "each volunteer signed up for a period of four months and committed himself unquestioningly to the orders of the army command."

Between November, 1917, and January, 1918, none of the volunteers received any pay, simply because there was no money. They were scantily fed and miserably housed. Regardless of their former army status, the volunteers occupying officers' positions began to receive 150 rubles a month in January, 1918; and the rank and file, 50 rubles a month. The ruble had fallen so low by that time that these salaries amounted to mere pittances.

"In the officer battalions and in some batteries, officers served as privates in conditions of extreme material need," related Denikin. "The Don Cossack military depots contained enormous quantities of supplies to which we had no access other than through stealing and bribery. The troops lacked literally everything: arms and ammunition, transport, field kitchens, warm clothing, boots. . . . And there was not enough money to satisfy the Cossack committees, who were prepared to sell anything on the side, including their conscience." [10]

The Volunteer Army acquired its artillery in rather unusual ways. For example, two field guns were obtained from a division which had defected from the Caucasian Turkish front and was engaged in looting in Stavropol province, approximately 160 kilometers from Novocherkassk. A detachment of Volunteers raided the division at night and captured the guns. Two cannon were stolen from a Don Cossack depot. An entire battery was "purchased" from the Cossacks returning with it from the front. The deal involved a quantity of vodka and some five thousand rubles.

Thus the future cadres of the Volunteer Army gradually came into existence. At first General Denikin was put in command of the "Volunteer division," with General Markov as chief of staff. Later, however, there were many changes at the top command level, and by the time the army set out on its first campaign, Denikin had become deputy commander of the Volunteer Army, General Romanovsky replaced General Lukomsky as Kornilov's chief of staff, and General Markov assumed the command of the First Officers' Regiment.

The aims of the newly formed army excluded any possibility of compromise with the Central Powers. The Bolsheviks and the Germans were regarded as equally destructive and dangerous to the national interests of Russia. The struggle against Bolshevism, therefore, was a continuation of the struggle against German imperialism. The ideal of loyalty to the Allies became a symbol of faith in their own cause to both the Volunteers and their leaders. The Allies were blindly idealized, and the highest moral principles and chivalrous impulses were ascribed to them.

It was, of course, impossible for a scarcely armed handful of people to think of engaging the German army. The Volunteer Army command, therefore, adopted a policy of "armed neutrality" in relation to the Austro-Germans, and avoided the risk of armed clashes with them.

Their openly expressed views inevitably affected the policy of the German command, which a few months later, obtained complete mastery of the Ukraine and the Crimea.

Xenia Vasilievna Chizh arrived in Novocherkassk ahead of her fiancé. While still in Bykhov, Anton Ivanovich had given her letters to Kaledin and Alekseev, introducing his fiancée and asking them to assist her. Both generals went out of their way to welcome Xenia Vasilievna, and Kaledin installed her in the house of some personal friends.

In the grim winter of 1917 there seemed to be no point in putting off Denikin's wedding to better days, and the couple decided to get married as soon as possible. They were obliged to wait until the pre-Christmas fast and Christmas holidays were over and marriage ceremonies could be performed in the Orthodox Church. They were married on January 7, a cold, gloomy day. There was unrest and shooting in the streets of Novocherkassk. It was thought safer to perform the ceremony in one of the smaller churches rather than in the cathedral. In order not to attract attention and undesirable spectators, the priest decided not to light the church chandelier, and the marriage took place by the flickering light of wax candles. There were no guests, no choir; only the priest and four witnesses who held the wedding crowns over the couple: General Markov, Colonel Timanovsky and Denikin's and Markov's aides-de-camp. *Ataman* Kaledin offered to give a small reception for the newlyweds, but the restless mood of the city obliged Anton Ivanovich gratefully to decline his invitation.[11]

Thus began the Denikin's family life. Like the modest marriage itself, all its years were to be marked by poverty.

Despite the isolated position of the Don territory, news of Soviet activity in the interior of Russia reached Novocherkassk and Rostov fairly regularly, brought mainly by the officers and intellectuals who were making their way to the Don.

From the moment they seized power, the Bolsheviks lost no time in issuing a series of decrees designed to break up the foundations of the country's former way of life. Among the many Soviet improvisations, certain events struck Denikin as exceptionally important.

Elections of representatives to the Constituent Assembly were held in mid-November, 1917. Although the Bolsheviks had already seized power, they received less than one-fourth of the popular vote. (Of 41,700,000 votes cast throughout the country, 9,800,000 were for the Bolsheviks.) When the Constituent Assembly convened on Jaunary 5, 1918, the Bolsheviks dispersed it. In the days preceding the Assembly, they had declared the Cadet party an "enemy of the people" and arrested some of its members in Petrograd. Two of them—Kokoshkin and Shingarev—who had been elected to the Constituent Assembly, were brutally murdered by them.

In December, the Soviets organized the "Extraordinary All-Russian Commission for Struggle against Counterrevolution and Sabotage," which later became known throughout the world as the *Cheka*. The extermination of dissenting elements and "class enemies" was assuming an organized form.

In December, 1917, the Soviet government initiated peace talks with the Central Powers at Brest-Litovsk. These were to last for three months, but as early as January, Denikin perceived that the Bolsheviks would make any concessions in order to remain in power, and that their negotiations with the Germans would result in disgrace, economic servitude, and huge territorial losses for Russia.

Finally, in mid-January, 1918, the Bolsheviks published a decree announcing the formation of a worker-peasant army composed of "the most class-conscious and organized elements of the working classes."

The nucleus of the Red Army consisted of the Red Guard units formed by the Bolsheviks at the time of their struggle against the Provisional Government. These were joined by revolutionary-minded workers from Petrograd, Moscow, Ivanovo-Vosnesensk, Kharkov, and the Donets coal basin. Later, former soldiers of the army and reserves who had been thoroughly indoctrinated by Bolshevik propaganda were also added to the Red forces.

At the beginning, the White and Red armies alike were made up of volunteers. As time went on and they grew stronger, both armies adopted a system of mobilization for increasing their ranks.

"In creating an army of the proletarian state," says a Soviet history of the civil war, "the Communist Party attached the highest importance to the political enlightenment of its fighting men. Political education was intended to help them develop a profound understanding of the function of the victorious proletariat's army and to appreciate the importance of their sublime duty before the Soviet motherland which had raised the banner of liberation of all the working people." [12]

Political education (or, more simply, Bolshevik propaganda among the soldiers) unquestionably influenced the Red Army, but in a somewhat different way from the spirit of high idealism and revolutionary pathos ascribed to it by official Soviet historians. The slogans coined at that time for arousing the mob—"Loot the looters!" "Murder the bourgeoisie!" "Put an end to their bloodsucking!"—attracted to the Red Army not only ordinary proletarians but also criminals released from prison by the Soviet regime. In the initial period of the civil war, the heroic members of the Red Army were overshadowed by a strong admixture of criminal elements.

As to the moral image of the White Army in the first months of its existence, General Denikin has left us a thoughtful and fundamentally just description of it, which captures the motivation of the volunteers. He also depicts the process of moral corruption that soon began—on the White as on the Red side—and added greatly to the cruelty of the war:

Much has been and still more will be written about the spiritual aspect of the Volunteer Army. Those who surrounded it with an aureole of sacrifice and martyrdom were right. And many of those who pointed to the grime which stained the purity of our banners were also sincere. It is important to present a correct synthesis of a number of complex factors in the life of the army which were brought on by the war and the revolution. . . . Our peculiar Cossack-like community attracted all those who sympathized with our struggle and were capable of enduring its hardships. These included both the good and the bad. Four years of war and the nightmare of the revolution had left their mark on everyone, divesting people of their surface coating of culture and bringing to a high pitch of tension their positive and negative tendencies. . . . There were high achievements and there was dirt. Heroism and cruelty. Pity and hatred. Social tolerance and exaggerated class consciousness. The first were encouraged and the second had to be counteracted. But the negative aspects were far from predominant.

The Volunteers were indifferent to politics, faithful to the idea of their country's salvation, brave in combat and loyal to Kornilov. The future held in store for them disabling wounds, a nomadic existence, and in many cases, death; and victory could only be envisaged in a very distant future. . . .

We soon learned that the Bolsheviks killed all the Volunteers whom they took prisoner, after subjecting them to inhuman torture. There were no possible doubts regarding this. In locations which had changed hands several times, the Volunteers had repeatedly found the mutilated bodies of their war comrades and heard the bloodcurdling descriptions of their murders, from those who had miraculously escaped the Bolshevik reprisals. I shall never forget the fearful impression made on me when I saw for the first time the bodies of eight Volunteers martyred in Bataisk. They had been slashed and stabbed, and their faces were disfigured to such an extent that their grief-stricken relatives were barely able to recognize them. . . . Late at night, in a distant backyard of the freight depot, in a maze of stationary trains, I found the carriage containing the bodies, which had been shunted there by order of the Rostov authorities "to avoid incidents." When by the dim light of wax candles, the timorously watchful priest prayed "for eternal memory to the slain," my heart contracted with pain and there was no forgiving the torturers. . . .

From the very beginning, the Bolsheviks' aims in the civil war were determined by the one word—annihilation.

The Soviet *oprichnina* * killed and tortured indiscriminately, driven less by the animal instincts aroused in fighting than by the deliberate instigation of its leaders, who had developed terror into a system which they believed to be the only means of preserving their power in the nation. They did not attempt to pass off terrorism as an "elemental force," as "popular ire" and other uncontrollable manifestations of mass psychosis. They overtly and unashamedly enforced it. . . .

There was no choice as to the means of counteracting a like system of warfare. The conditions in which the Volunteer Army operated, involving its almost constant tactical encirclement, its lack of home territory, military rear, and bases, left only two possible alternatives: to release the captured Bolsheviks or to "take no prisoners." . . .

Only much later, when the Soviet government organized its regular army after adding the mobilized mass of the people to its Red Guard *oprichnina,* and the Volunteer Army began to assume a governmental structure with a certain territory and a civilian administration, did it become possible gradually to introduce a more civilized and humane approach to the limited extent possible in the amoral climate of a civil war.

Not only bodies but souls were cruelly deformed by it.[13]

By the end of January, 1918, the disintegration of the Don Cossacks had reached such proportions that *Ataman* Kaledin found himself completely helpless and unsupported. Uprisings of Cossack soldiers broke out throughout the territory. Officers were killed, and to quote Kaledin, "proof was established that in some of the Don regiments, Cossacks sold their officers to the Bolsheviks for money."[14] The tragedy of Kaledin was that though they elected him, the Cossacks did not follow his lead and he was left powerless and helpless in their midst.

In the face of the Cossacks' refusal to fight the approaching bands of Red Guards, Kornilov decided in the middle of January, to transfer all the units of the Volunteer Army from Novocherkassk to Rostov, a large and prosperous city situated on the Don River, about thirty-five kilometers from its mouth in the Sea of Azov. He respected Kaledin and sincerely sympathized with him, but the whole political atmosphere of the Don irritated him, and he wanted to get away from its capital.

Whatever hopes Kornilov may have had in moving to Rostov, they were not justified. The city's numerous workmen received Kornilov's troops with antagonism, and its bourgeoisie failed to respond to his call to arms. Only the children responded.

---

* "Oprichnina" is a reference to the special troops organized by Ivan the Terrible about 1565 for the purpose of strengthening the power of the Tsar. In Russia, the terms *oprichnina* and *oprichniki* are still connected with the idea of lawlessness and cruelty.

Anton Ivanovich happened to witness the attempts of some of them to enroll as volunteers: "Some comic and at the same time deeply moving scenes could be observed in General Borovsky's battalion. A sobbing young fighter trying to prove that he was sixteen (the minimum recruiting age), or another one hiding under a bed from his parents, who were searching for him and in whose name, incidentally, he had produced a forged permission to enlist."[15] Many such children did succeed in enlisting. They fought and died as bravely as the grown-ups.

Shortly after transferring to Rostov, General Kornilov decided to move the Volunteer Army out of the Don territory. Denikin described this event and its tragic sequel in Novocherkassk:

At the end of January, General Kornilov came to the final conclusion that it was impossible for the Volunteer Army to remain at the Don any longer, as the complete lack of support on the part of the Cossacks threatened it with extinction. He decided, therefore, to move the army to the Kuban region, which seemed to be more sympathetic to the anti-Bolshevik cause. . . . On January 28 he advised General Kaledin by telegram of his decision.

On the twenty-ninth, Kaledin called together the members of his government and read to them the telegrams received from Generals Alekseev and Kornilov. He advised them that only 147 bayonets could be mustered for the defense of the Don territory and suggested that the government hand in its resignation.

"Our position is hopeless. I am resigning my position as *Ataman* of the Don Cossacks."

During the ensuing discussion he added, "Gentlemen, make it shorter. Time is flying. Remember, it was through chatter that Russia perished!"

On the same day, General Kaledin shot himself through the heart.[16]

This dramatic act brought a temporary revival of hope that the shock of their leader's death would spur the Cossack resistance to Bolshevism. It lasted but a few days. Because of Kaledin's death, Kornilov delayed his departure for a short period. But on February 9 he gave the order to cross the Don River and move to the nearby *stanitsa* Olginskaia. His plans were not definite beyond that point. The Volunteer Army might head for the Kuban or for the Don Cossacks' "winter quarters," the farmsteads scattered along the southeastern section of the Don region, to which the horse breeders drove their studs in the winter to provide them with shelter and food.

Bolshevik troops under the command of Antonov-Ovseenko were moving into the Don region; and some of their detachments, led by R. F. Sivers, were gradually occupying Rostov. An uprising started in one of its industrial suburbs.

"The lights of the inhospitable city we were abandoning shimmered in the dark," wrote Denikin, "solitary shots went off in the night. We moved silently, engrossed in our uneasy thoughts. Where were we going? What was in store for us?

"It was as if Kornilov foresaw the fate that awaited him. A letter to his friends, sent on the eve of the march, spoke of his fears for his family, left without protection among strangers, and of the probability that they would never meet." [17]

Anton Ivanovich was too reserved in his personal life to confide to anyone the fear and pain he must have felt at leaving his young bride. His wife, however, has shared the following memory with us: Before the departure of the Volunteers, Xenia Vasilievna begged her husband to take her with him, but he flatly refused. On the same day, she chanced to meet Kornilov. Seeing her distraught and in tears, he asked what was the matter, and having heard her answer, promised to speak to Denikin. Anton Ivanovich remained adamant. He explained to Kornilov that the presence of his wife in the transport, which risked continuously being surrounded by the Bolshevks, would tie him hand and foot at a time when all his energy and strength should be concentrated on fighting the enemy. Kornilov understood and did not pursue the subject.

Xenia Vasilievna, using her maiden name and passport, took a room in the house of some wealthy Armenians. She was in constant fear for her husband and completely alone, knowing no one in Rostov. Fortunately for her, neither did any of the townspeople know that she was General Denikin's wife.[18]

Some lines in a letter written by General Alekseev before leaving Rostov seem to express the ultimate meaning of the Volunteer movement for those who had done the most to create it: "We are leaving for the steppes. Only the grace of God may enable us to return. But we must ignite the torch so that at least a glimmer of light will pierce the darkness that is engulfing Russia." [19]

The Volunteer Army was off on its first campaign—the most heroic chapter of its history.

XV

THE FIRST
KUBAN CAMPAIGN

———————————————

The Volunteer Army began its eerie trek into the unknown on the night of
February 9.

> We left [wrote General Denikin], and madness followed in our footsteps. It
> overran the cities we had abandoned, with reckless dissipation, hatred, robbery,
> and murder. The wounded we had left behind were dragged out of the hospital
> into the street and slaughtered. Our families who remained there were faced
> with the constant fear of Bolshevik reprisals should some unforeseen accident
> disclose their identity. We started the campaign in unheard-of circumstances:
> a handful of people lost in the vastness of the Don steppe, amidst the stormy
> sea which had engulfed our native land. In our midst: two Supreme Command-
> ers of the Russian army; the commander in chief of one of our fronts; dis-
> tinguished chiefs of staff, corps commanders, veteran colonels. They marched
> in a long column, up to their knees in snow, their rifles and kit bags contain-
> ing their scanty belongings slung over their shoulders. They were leaving un-
> relieved darkness and spiritual servitude for an unknown destination. . . . In
> quest of the "bluebird."
>
> All is not lost while there is life and strength. Our faintly shining torch will
> be seen and the call to arms will be heard by those who have not yet awakened.
> Therein lay the innermost meaning of the First Kuban Campaign. It is point-
> less to approach with cold political and strategic reasoning a phenomenon which
> belongs completely in the realm of the spirit and human devotion. Small in
> numbers, ragged, pursued, surrounded, the Volunteer Army wandering in the
> untrammeled steppes of the Don and Kuban was a symbol of persecuted Russia
> and its threatened statehood.
>
> In the whole vast expanse of the country, there remained only one place
> which openly displayed the tricolored national flag—it was Kornilov's head-
> quarters.[1]

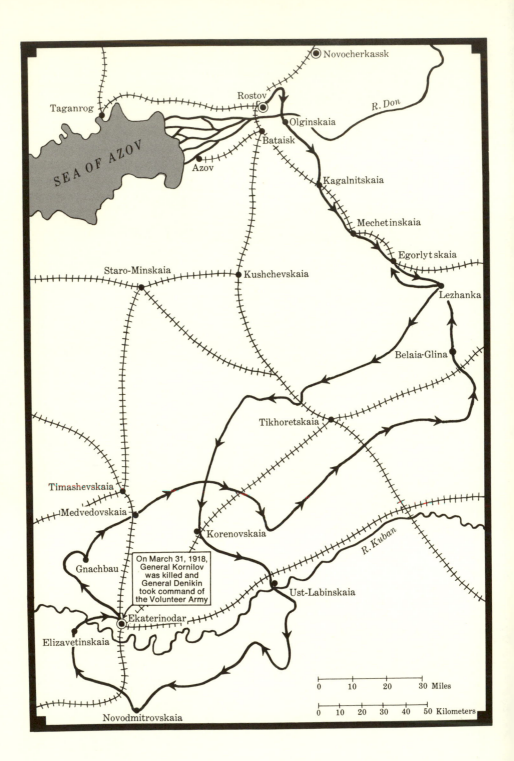

Novocherkassk

Taganrog

Rostov

SEA OF AZOV

Azov

R. Don

Olginskaia

Bataisk

Kagalnitskaia

Mechetinskaia

Egorlytskaia

Staro-Minskaia

Kushchevskaia

Lezhanka

Belaia-Glina

Tikhoretskaia

Timashevskaia

Medvedovskaia

Korenovskaia

R. Kuban

Gnachbau

On March 31, 1918,
General Kornilov
was killed and
General Denikin
took command of
the Volunteer Army

Ust-Labinskaia

Ekaterinodar

Elizavetinskaia

Novodmitrovskaia

0   10   20   30 Miles

0   10   20   30   40   50 Kilometers

All the senior commanders marched with the troops on the first day of the campaign. A cavalryman riding by offered his horse to General Kornilov, who thanked him but declined.

Kornilov wanted to make clear his determination to forgo any privileges and to share the hardships of the campaign with all its participants—with the young men as well as the veteran generals and colonels who were plodding in the deep snow as ordinary privates.

Kornilov walked at the head of the column in his tall *papakha,* or Caucasian sheepskin hat, and his white-collared sheepskin coat. All those who saw him examined him carefully, trying to guess whether this man was capable of leading them out of the dead end in which fate had trapped them.

Denikin too was studying Kornilov. He sensed the turbulent inner fire burning behind the general's somber and outwardly calm façade and noted "the innate dignity of his appearance, glance, and speech, which he retained in the most difficult days of his life."

Denikin, who was Kornilov's deputy army commander and would be his successor in case of emergency, walked beside him and the army's chief of staff, Romanovsky.

Anton Ivanovich had lost the suitcase containing his uniform and warm clothing. He strode gloomily through the snow in his light, frayed civilian suit, worn-out boots, and black hat, with a carbine slung over his shoulder. The suit was the one he had worn in escaping from Bykhov. As a result of exposure on that first day, he caught a cold which soon developed into a bad case of bronchitis, and was obliged to spend the next few days riding in one of the carts at the tail end of the baggage train.

General Alekseev also rode in the baggage train, carrying with him the suitcase containing the army's meager financial resources—some six million rubles in currency and Treasury notes. "Will it last to the end of the campaign?" worried Alekseev. He was suffering more and more from the disease which had first attacked him in the fall of 1916, when he was chief of staff to the Tsar; at that time, the illness had obliged him to leave Mogilev for a cure in the Crimea. Now the bouts of uremia had become so strong that sometimes he lost consciousness. The General was to die of it a few months later, in September, 1918.

The Volunteers were followed by a long line of vehicles carrying ordnance, forage, a field hospital, nurses, and refugees who could not risk falling into Bolshevik hands. The line stretched out for several kilometers and was occasionally broken by a marching column. The ranks exhibited an extraordinary variety of worn-out, ill-assorted clothing—civilian overcoats, military greatcoats, schoolboys' regulation caps, shoes, felt boots, puttees—but they marched cheerfully and in good formation, with firm confidence in their leader. In number they did not exceed 3,500 men—the equivalent of a wartime infantry regiment. They were followed, however, by almost a thousand noncombatants: the wounded, the refugees, the aged, and the drivers of the baggage train. The supply of cartridges was very small, and there were only some six or seven hundred artillery shells. "There was only one way to get additonal supplies," wrote Denikin, "by seizing them in battle from the Bolsheviks at the cost of blood."

The number of cavalry horses was also small. Additional ones were bought at a high price from the Cossacks, in the course of the march. At that early stage, the Volunteer Army had not yet begun requisitioning from the local population.

The army's first halt was to be in *stanitsa* Aksaiskaia. The billeting party sent there returned with the news that the local Cossacks were too afraid of the Bolsheviks and their reprisals to let the Volunteers spend the night in their village. Kornilov still hoped that the Cossacks would eventually come over to his side, after having their fill of Bolshevik rule, and lend their support to his army. He was, therefore, extremely careful not to antagonize the *stanitsy*. In this case, he delegated Denikin and Romanovsky to discuss the matter with the villagers, who finally gave their consent after protracted arguments. Only later did Denikin find out what had really settled the matter: One of his aides became tired of the endless negotiations. He drew aside the most aggressive of the Cossacks and hinted that dealing with Kornilov was no laughing matter. He advised the Cossacks to reach an agreement rapidly, as otherwise Kornilov was capable of hanging a few people and destroying the *stanitsa*.

In this area, control of the villages frequently changed hands, from the Reds to the Whites or vice versa, and the peasants were extremely wary and suspicious of both sides. They tried to maintain a neutral attitude until they could be sure which party was likely to win.

Denikin was gravely concerned with the attitudes prevailing among the peasants in that period.

Quite against our will [wrote the General], we were drawn into the vortex of the pervading social struggle. Here, as everywhere else where the Volunteer Army passed, it was secretly or openly upheld by the more secure and prosperous part of the population, anxious to restore order and the normal conditions of life. Conversely, the other part, which hoped to profit justly or unjustly from the general upheaval and lawlessness, was antagonistic to us, and there was simply no way to break this vicious circle and make them understand the real aims of our army. Demonstrate them by deeds? What could an army reduced to bloody fighting for its right to survival do for the local population? Convince them by words? Not when each word was blocked by an impenetrable wall of mistrust, fear, and servility.[2]

The Volunteer Army's command with (in the phraseology of the Bolsheviks) its "outdated concepts of bourgeois morality" was incapable of waging a verbal fight against Bolshevik propaganda, which consciously falsified facts and systematically fed deceptive but always tempting promises to the population.

The army halted for the second time in *stanitsa* Olginskaia. As it had not been pursued by Bolshevik troops, Kornilov gave the Volunteers a four-day rest. He used the time for drawing up an inventory of military supplies and reorganizing his men into larger units.

The Volunteer Army was re-formed as follows: First Officers' Regiment (commander, General Markov), Kornilov Shock Regiment (commander, Colonel Nezhintsev), Partisan Regiment (commander, General Bogaevsky), *Junker* Battalion (commander, General Borovsky), an artillery battalion of four batteries, each armed with two field guns, and a Czechoslovak engineers' battalion (commander, Captain Nemetchik). In addition, there were three small cavalry units totaling less than six hundred horsemen. From this time on, General Markov with his regiment usually marched in front, while the Partisan Regiment protected the rear of the column. During the halt at Olginskaia, Kornilov called a military council in order to discuss the future moves of the Volunteer Army. The opinions of the generals on this subject were divided, and the decision finally adopted by them was far from unanimous. Two possible plans of action were discussed:

The first plan favored moving eastward to the Don Cossacks' "winter quarters." The purpose of the plan was to draw away from the railroads along which the Bolsheviks were moving their troops and give the Volunteers a chance to rest, acquire fresh horses, and renew their supplies. In other words, the army was to assume a temporizing position for a month or two before deciding on a course of action in accordance with the latest developments.

The second plan proposed marching in the direction of the Kuban capital, Ekaterinodar, which had not yet been occupied by the Bolsheviks. The Kuban had rich reserves of foodstuffs, and it was hoped that its population, whom rumor described as anti-Soviet, would provide a good number of volunteers, especially mounted ones.

Generals Kornilov and Lukomsky were in favor of the first plan. They had recently learned that approximately 1,500 horsemen who refused to remain under Soviet rule had set out toward the "winter quarters" beyond the Don. They were led by the Don Cossack general Popov and had managed to capture on their way five cannon and forty machine guns. This unexpected flare-up of protest among the Cossacks, who had only recently refused to support *Ataman* Kaledin, gave rise to a new hope that Popov's detachment might become the nucleus of anti-Bolshevik resistance in the Don region.

In addition, Lukomsky argued that in view of the lack of information concerning events in the Kuban region, the expectation of an anti-Bolshevik uprising among the local Cossacks could prove to be completely erroneous. The principal danger of a march to Ekaterinodar, however, was the unavoidable necessity of twice crossing the railroad lines along which the Bolsheviks could move their troops and armored trains to cut off the advance of the Volunteer Army.[3]

Alekseev and Denikin nevertheless defended the project of moving into the Kuban region, as did most of the other generals.

General Alekseev stated his objections to the idea of withdrawing to the steppes beyond the Don in a memorandum addressed to General Kornilov. (Because of their strained relations, he often preferred to communicate with Kornilov in writing.) He argued, "In the 'winter quarters' our troops would soon be constricted by the spring flooding of the Don River on one side and by the Tsaritsin–Torgovaia–Tikhoretskaia–Bataisk railroad on the other side. Moreover, by that time, all railroad junctions and road exits would be occupied by the Bolsheviks, precluding all possibility of replenishing the army with men and supplies; not to mention the fact that remaining in the steppes would isolate us from the general march of events in the nation." [4]

Denikin's opinion was later summed up by him as follows:

The steppe region, though well suited for partisan activity by small units, would present great difficulties in maintaining the life of the Volunteer Army, with five thousand people to feed. The winter cabins scattered at wide distances from each other did not provide sufficient living quarters and fuel. The fact that the troops could be quartered only in small fragmented units, combined with our lack of technical communications equipment, would make a unified administration of the army extremely difficult. The steppe region could provide nothing for the needs of the army except unmilled grain, hay, and cattle. Finally, we could hardly expect the Bolsheviks to leave us in peace and not to attempt exterminating our scattered detachments one by one.

The Kuban, on the contrary, was not only a rich and well-provided region, but unlike the Don, held the promise of a sympathetic attitude, a militant government, and the potential of new volunteers, whose number had been greatly exaggerated by rumor. Finally, the capital city of Ekaterinodar, which had escaped Bolshevik occupation, offered the possibility of new and extensive organizational activity.[5]

Alekseev's and Denikin's arguments convinced Kornilov and he decided to march to the Kuban.

Both of the plans discussed by the military council were based solely on theory and guesswork, as the generals had no factual information on the conditions prevailing beyond their minute, circumscribed sphere of activity. They were without the technical prerequisites for military intelligence. The lack of cavalry precluded far-reaching reconnaissance parties. Secret agents sent out by Kornilov's general staff seldom returned—most of them were caught and exterminated by the Bolsheviks. The army command was left to rely on its intuition, and the results were often far from satisfactory.

General Popov was invited to join forces with the Volunteer Army, but he declined, saying that his Cossacks were reluctant to leave the Don. This refusal deprived the Volunteers of a much-needed cavalry reinforcement.

In order to reach the political center of the Kuban region as quickly as possible, Kornilov led his troops by forced marches in a southeasterly direction, trying to avoid Bolshevik units and possible armed engagements with them. The first clash occurred on February 27, near the large village of Lezhanka, after the army had crossed from the Don into the province of Stavropol. There, as happened often in all their subsequent progress, Kornilov's men stumbled into a "veritable wasp's nest," as Denikin put it.

The Volunteers found themselves in the path of a horde of several thousand soldiers who had left the Russo-Turkish front in the Caucasus and were heading for their homes in the faraway northern reaches of Russia. The majority of these soldiers did not march in isolated groups. After being thoroughly indoctrinated by revolutionary propaganda, they had remained in their army units, whose leadership had passed into Bolshevik hands. They were transporting an immense amount of stolen army and government inventory—quantities of rifles, cartridges, cannon, and shells; and carloads of salt, sugar, and manufactured goods. The latter were sold or bartered for food along the way, and if the soldiers found no buyers for their wares, they simply robbed the local population. As notorious enemies of the revolution, the first to suffer were of course the town "bourgeoisie"; they were not only robbed but exterminated. Then came the turn of the well-to-do Cossack farmers, in whose persecution the vengeful *inogorodni* took an active part.

The masses of soldiers wound their way along the railroads, and the Bolsheviks decided to make use of them in combating Kornilov's "counterrevolution." Near the village of Lezhanka, units of the Thirty-ninth Infantry Division, returning from the Turkish front, barred the way to the Volunteer Army.

It was a clear, slightly frosty day [recollected Denikin]. The Officers' Regiment marched in the vanguard. It was a mixture of old and young, with colonels commanding the squads. Never has such an army been seen. At the head of the regiment strides its deputy commander, Colonel Timanovsky, a victim of numerous wounds and serious injuries of the spinal vertebrae, leaning on his cane and smoking his perennial pipe. . . . One of the companies is led by Colonel Kutepov, former commander of the Preobrazhenski regiment. He is lean, strong, controlled; his military hat is pushed to the back; his orders come in short, clipped phrases. [This was the same Kutepov who was kidnapped by Soviet agents in Paris in 1930.] The ranks are filled with beardless youths— carefree and exuberant. General Markov canters by. He has turned his head toward us and said something that we can't make out, has reprimanded someone without slowing down, and sped on to the main detachment.

A dull boom, and way, way up, an explosion of shrapnel. This is it! The Officers' Regiment deploys and begins to advance, calmly, without breaking its march, directly on the village. It disappears over a ridge. Alekseev rides up, and we both walk forward. A wide view opens up from the ridge. The large sprawling village below us is surrounded by lines of trenches. Near the church stands a Bolshevik battery whose haphazard fire scatters shells along the roadside. Rifle and machine-gun firing intensifies. Our lines have halted and dropped to the ground; they are faced by a marshy, unfrozen stream which we will have to circumvent. The Kornilov Regiment has already begun to do so on the right-hand side. It is overtaken by a group of riders with the tricolored banner unfurled—Kornilov!

Excitement sweeps the ranks. All eyes are fixed on the distant figure of the commander. Meanwhile, Colonel Mionchinsky's officer candidates, under enemy machine-gun fire, roll their cannons up to the front lines. Their firing stirs up a commotion in the enemy ranks. But for some reason our advance is held back.

The Officers' Regiment can't stand the strain any longer; one of its companies rushes into the cold, cloying mud of the stream and fords it to the other side. All is confusion over there, and soon the field is dotted with running panic-stricken figures, fleeing carts, and the rapidly retreating battery. The Officers' and Kornilov regiments, which have reached the village from the west after crossing the dam, pursue the enemy.

We enter the totally deserted village. The streets are strewn with bodies. The silence is eerie. But for a long time it is broken by the dry rattle of rifle fire: The Bolsheviks are being "liquidated" . . . and there are many.[6]

The "war of annihilation" between ideological foes was becoming systematic on the White side as well as on the side of the Bolsheviks.

The Volunteers' first campaign lasted eighty days. Having left Rostov on February 9, they traversed a distance of 1,200 kilometers, and by April 30 were back near their point of departure, in *stanitsy* Mechetinskaia and Egorlytskaia of the Don region. They had made a large loop around the flat steppes of the Kuban, reaching as far as some of the villages in the North Caucasus. Forty-four of the eighty days had been spent in fierce combat; up to four hundred men were buried in the Kuban, and over 1,500 wounded were brought back by the Volunteer Army. At its return, the army, which now included Kuban Cossacks, numbered five thousand men. The Volunteers had continuously renewed their reserves of shells, cartridges, and other supplies by capturing them from the Bolsheviks. They had moved without a rest or breathing period, always surrounded by enemy troops—through rain and snow, fording the icy rivers in water up to their chests, often spending the night without cover on the freezing open steppe. The Volunteers had had to overcome physical and moral obstacles of a kind seldom experienced by any army. The whole campaign was characterized by Denikin as one of almost insane courage. The Volunteers managed to break through all encirclements, even when they were greatly outnumbered by the Bolsheviks, but it was dangerous for them to stay in any place for more than a few days. As soon as they moved on, the Red wave broke out once more over the ground they had covered. The campaign achieved no important political or strategic aims; it did not incite any serious anti-Bolshevik uprisings among the Kuban Cossacks and did not liberate the Kuban capital of Ekaterinodar, captured by the Reds on March 1. The First Campaign succeeded, however, in keeping together and preserving from destruction the cadres of intrepid people from which the most important anti-Bolshevik movement was soon to develop. The achievement of the campaign was in its victory of spirit over flesh. And this proved possible only because the leaders knew what they could expect of their men, and because the men had complete faith in their commanders.

The Communist writers who deny the heroism and devotion of the First Campaign are mistaken. They are wrong in maintaining that the Volunteers, trapped like animals and threatened with destruction, had no other choice but to fight to the last limit. They did have a choice: Each of the Volunteers could have behaved like the hundreds of thousands of people who hated Bolshevism but valued their lives even more and went into temporary hiding instead of responding to Alekseev's and Kornilov's call to arms. They consciously chose not to do so.

The Volunteer Army had to adapt itself to new and peculiar conditions of combat. It lacked most of the technical equipment of a regular army and soon adopted the methods of partisan warfare. The command was quick to evolve a tactical approach suited to these unusual conditions. This consisted of dealing a stunning forward blow to the enemy by means of a direct frontal attack in which the Volunteers, though inadequately protected by their limited artillery, advanced in close, unwavering lines. The recently organized Red troops were seldom able to withstand the impact of this frontal advance, and their unprotected flanks and rear allowed Kornilov, and later Denikin, to maneuver the forces with maximum effectiveness.

This shock tactic, so different from the principle of methodic offensive which prevailed in World War I, enabled the Volunteers to break through recurrent enemy encirclements and to continue moving.

To the roster of outstanding Volunteer leaders was soon added the name of General Markov. He inspired the officers with his fearless example. Denikin gave a good illustration of Markov's leadership in describing a battle which took place on March 15 near *stanitsa* Novo-Dimitrievskaia:

Rain fell throughout the night and was still coming down in the morning. The army advanced through water and liquid mud along roads and across fields. Water had soaked our clothing and ran in icy rivulets into our collars and down our necks. The men walked slowly, shivering with cold and dragging their feet, whose boots were swollen and filled with water.

At long last, the troops approached a small river beyond which, at a distance of about three kilometers, lay *stanitsa* Novo-Dimitrievskaia. The rains had turned the river into a wide, turbulent stream. The bridge across the stream had been washed away, and scouts were sent out to look for a ford. Markov crossed the icy stream with them. His white *papakha* [the tall Caucasian sheepskin hat] appeared on the opposite shore, and his loud voice was heard shouting to lead up the horses and start ferrying the officers across on their backs.

Meanwhile, the weather changed anew. The temperature fell drastically, the wind intensified, and a blizzard set in. Men and horses were soon covered with a coating of ice. We felt frozen to the marrow of our bones. Our clothing stiffened to the solidity of wood, immobilizing our bodies; it was difficult to turn one's head or to lift a leg into the stirrup.[7]

Braving every difficulty, Markov succeeded in transporting the Officers' Regiment across the river. Darkness fell, and in it the remaining units continued to cross as best they could.

Markov realized the futility of waiting for additional support. "We can't stay here to die in this weather," he told the officers, "forward to the *stanitsa!*" He ordered them not to shoot, but to move to the attack with bayonets at the ready. The freezing men started off at a run behind their commander. Clutching their rifles in their numbed hands, they rushed into the *stanitsa* and engaged the Bolsheviks in hand-to-hand fighting. The latter had not expected an attack in such inclement weather. Firing broke out from all the windows in the village, but the Reds were unable to pull their forces together. They started moving off singly and in groups to the opposite end of the village. Markov's officers, up to their knees in a liquid mass of snow, ice, and mud, staggered after them, shouting "Hurrah!"

Legend has it that on the next morning an army nurse, meeting Markov in the street, said to him, "This was really a march of the iced—an icy march!" "Yes, yes," rejoined Markov, "that's exactly what it was." True or not, the fact remains that from that day on, the entire first eighty-day campaign of the Volunteer Army became known as the "Icy March." [8]

A severe blow was dealt to Kornilov's original plan of campaign when news reached him that on March 1 Ekaterinodar had been taken by the Bolsheviks. A detachment of Kuban volunteers commanded by Colonel Pokrovsky, the Kuban Cossacks' *Ataman,* Filimonov, and the members of the Kuban parliament, or *Rada,* had escaped to the North Caucasus.

In view of Ekaterinodar's fall and of the heavy losses and extreme fatigue of his troops, General Kornilov decided to postpone moving toward the Kuban capital to a more favorable time. Instead, having crossed the Kuban river, he bypassed Ekaterinodar in a southerly direction and led the army toward the Circassian mountain villages, or *aouls.* There he hoped to rejoin Pokrovsky's volunteers and to give his own men a much-needed rest from continuous fighting and the danger of being encircled. The first hope was soon fulfilled, but the army never got a chance to have a real rest, as the North Caucasus region was swarming with troops deserting from the Turkish front. They had looted and ransacked the Circassian *aouls,* which the Volunteers found totally devastated. "The unfortunate Circassians greeted us as their deliverers," wrote Denikin, "surrounded us with attention, and saw us off with alarm. Their primitive minds interpreted recent events very simply: Authority had left and been replaced by brigands (Bolsheviks) who looted the *aouls* and killed their people. There was not a trace of revolutionary influence to be found in their outlook." [9]

On March 14 a meeting was held between the Volunteer Army command and Pokrovsky, whom the Kuban *Rada* had promoted to the rank of general on the preceding day. In addition to Kornilov, the meeting was attended by Generals Alekseev, Denikin, Erdeli, and Romanovsky.

Pokrovsky was not a Cossack by birth. He was a former flier, decorated with the Cross of St. George, but young and completely unknown. Denikin described him as "fiercely energetic, courageous, cruel, despotic, and not too seriously concerned with 'moral prejudices.' He was typical of the kind of people who in peacetime are sucked in by the mire of provincial army life in the sticks, but who emerge for a short-lived but turbulent period of activity in popular upheavals. Be that as it may, he achieved something in which more substantial and experienced people had failed, by assembling the only detachment [in the Kuban] which represented an actual force capable of combating and defeating the Bolsheviks." [10]

The impression made by Pokrovsky on the other generals was apparently similar to the one received by Denikin. They reacted to him with cold restraint, especially after Pokrovsky, expressing the fear that various changes might cause unrest among his troops, insisted on preserving the autonomy of his detachment, which he wished to submit to General Kornilov's authority only in military operations. Even the usually restrained Alekseev lost his patience. "Now, now, Colonel," he exploded, "forgive me, I don't even know by what title to address you. Your troops have nothing to do with this—we are fully aware of their opinion on the subject—you are simply standing on your dignity."

The recent negotiations with Popov, the Don Cossack general, concerning the submission of his detachment to Kornilov were still fresh and rankling in the memory of the Volunteer commanders. And to them, Pokrovsky's attitude smacked of the same indulgence of personal vanity at the expense of the common good.

The ensuing discussion was ended by Kornilov: "One army and one commander," he cut in abruptly. "I refuse to tolerate any other situation. Kindly convey this to your government." [11]

A few days later, Pokrovsky arrived once more for a conference with the Volunteer Army's commanders. He was accompanied by *Ataman* Filimonov, by the head of the Kuban government, and by members of the *Rada*. After a lengthy discussion, the Kuban representatives finally agreed to subordinate their detachment completely to General Kornilov, giving him the right to reorganize it as he saw fit.

The Kubantsy undertook to cooperate to the fullest extent in carrying out the army's military objectives. The chief of the Kuban region's troops (Pokrovsky) was to rejoin the Kuban government and proceed with the formation of a Kuban army.

General Kornilov lost no time in incorporating and mingling the Kuban units (some 2,500 men) with the Volunteers, which brought the total number of men under his command to approximately 6,000. At this point, the Volunteer Army consisted of some 9,000 people, including the attendants and refugees in its train. There were about 4,000 horses and 660 carts.

Among those who fled from Ekaterinodar with Pokrovsky's detachment was the former President of the State Duma, M. V. Rodzianko. He joined the wagon train of Kornilov's army for the rest of the campaign.

This train carried all the ammunition and supplies of the ambulant army, as well as its wounded, whose number increased every day. Their condition was desperate. Deprived of drugs, bandages, and antiseptics, they suffered horribly and often died of infections caused by slight wounds which would have easily healed under normal conditions. The doctors and nurses looked after the wounded with complete self-abnegation, but could give them little except moral assistance.

As Kornilov's men were continuously encircled by Bolshevik troops and in constant danger of being captured, the army command allowed the wounded to retain their arms. "The right to dispose of their lives at the last, fateful moment," said Denikin, "was the inalienable privilege of the Volunteers."

The coffers of the Volunteer Army were nearly empty, there were too few field kitchens, and the men were obliged to obtain their food from the local population. Many of them—poorly clothed, shoeless, hungry, and disoriented by the fighting conditions of the civil war—began to lose all respect for private property.

During a short halt, Denikin was billeted in a house abandoned by its owners, most of the village's pro-Bolshevik population having fled to the steppe with their horses and cattle. Anton Ivanovich found his Tekinets orderly busily searching the absent owner's trunk and putting aside the things which he found useful. Denikin reprimanded him indignantly and ordered him out of the storage room. The poor soldier, however, was completely unable to understand why his general made such a fuss over the property of people who were clearly inimical to the White Army.

Another time, during a march, the Volunteers were surprised by the sight of a man, clad in the Caucasian *cherkeska* (a coat worn in Circassia), running past the Officers' Regiment as if his life depended on it. General Markov, in hot pursuit, belabored the man's back with his *nagayka,* or Cossack whip, shouting "That'll teach you to steal, you son of a bitch! That'll teach you!" [12]

Stealing was continuously prosecuted in the White Army, but proved impossible to eliminate.

After Pokrovsky's detachment joined the Volunteer Army, the Kuban capital of Ekaterinodar once more became the goal of Kornilov's campaign.

At that time, the army was south of the capital on the left bank of the Kuban River, one of the four principal streams of the Caucasian region. Kornilov chose to avoid its bridges and to surprise the enemy by ferrying his troops across near *stanitsa* Elizavetinskaia, west of the city. It was from that direction that he planned to attack Ekaterinodar.

The crossing took place according to plan, and on March 28, Kornilov established his headquarters at a model farm of the Ekaterinodar agricultural association at a distance of three or four kilometers from the city. The farm, which overlooked the high sheer banks of the river, afforded an excellent view of the Kuban capital. The contours of its houses, railroad station, and cemetery were clearly visible, as were the rows of Bolshevik trenches lying between the farm and the city.

The farm's small whitewashed house could also be clearly seen by the enemy, to whom it afforded an excellent target. Its four rooms were occupied by Kornilov, Denikin, Romanovsky, and the staff, the army's liaison, and a first-aid station. The groans of the wounded could be heard in every part of the house.

On the following morning the enemy began to concentrate its fire on the farm, which it showered with shells for the next three days. In the meantime, the Volunteers started their advance on the city. They took its suburbs, then the railroad station and the artillery barracks. One detachment even penetrated to the center of town, but lack of support obliged it to fight its way back to the periphery. The enemy's numerical and technical superiority was making itself felt. Denikin wrote that Kornilov's scouts "estimated up to eighteen thousand men in the enemy battle lines, with two or three armored trains, two to four howitzers, and eight to ten field guns." [13]

The Soviet command was drawing up reinforcements to Ekaterinodar from every direction. The enemy's strength increased continuously, and its resistance became proportionately stiffer. On the other hand, the losses of the Volunteers grew with appalling rapidity: Over 1,500 wounded filled the first-aid stations, and several outstanding officers were killed, including Colonel Nezhentsev, commander of the Kornilov Regiment, who was replaced by Colonel Kutepov. Kornilov was deeply affected by Nezhentsev's death. He felt that his luck was failing him. His supplies were coming to an end, and his troops were nearing physical collapse. And the enemy's stock of shells and cartridges appeared inexhaustible.

For the first time since the halt at Olginskaia, Kornilov called a military council, summoning Generals Alekseev, Denikin, Romanovsky, Markov, and Bogaevsky, as well as the Kuban Cossack *Ataman,* Colonel Filimonov. The room contained nothing but a table, a bed, and a wooden bench, so some of the commanders sat on the straw-covered floor.

"The situation is very serious indeed," said Kornilov. "I see no way out of it except by taking Ekaterinodar. I have planned, therefore, to attack tomorrow at dawn along the entire front. What is your opinion, gentlemen?" Kornilov's tone clearly indicated that he had already decided the question. Nevertheless, all the generals except Alekseev pronounced themselves against the attack. They argued that there was a limit to human endurance, that the army would be shattered in the attempt, and that the consequences of an unsuccessful attack would be catastrophic. Finally, they said that even if the capital were taken, at a great cost in lives, the weakened troops would have to be spread too thin in an attempt to defend the large, sprawling city.[14]

General Alekseev offered a compromise decision—postponement of storming the city for twenty-four hours. Kornilov agreed to the delay without, however, modifying the rest of his plan.

General Markov, who had not rested for two days, fell asleep at the meeting but woke up in time to hear the final decision. "Put on clean underwear if you have any," he later told Colonel Timanovsky and the other officers who were in his quarters. "We shall storm Ekaterinodar. We won't take it, and even if we do, we shall perish in the act."

Denikin remained alone with Kornilov when the meeting was over.

"Lavr Georgievich [he asked], why are you so adamant in this decision?"

"It's the only way out, Anton Ivanovich. If we fail to capture Ekaterinodar, the only thing left for me will be to shoot myself."

"This you cannot do. Think of the thousands of human lives you would abandon to their fate. Why can't we leave Ekaterinodar in order to have a real rest, reorganize, and plan a new operation? You know that if our attack is unsuccessful, we will hardly be able to retreat."

"You will lead them——"

I rose and said with emotion, "Your excellency! If General Kornilov commits suicide, no one will be able to lead out the army—all of it will perish." [15]

The farm was under such intense fire that Kornilov's entourage tried to talk him into moving out of it with his staff, but the general flatly refused to do so. The next morning, March 31, at 7:30 A.M., as he sat at a table next to a window, Kornilov was killed by an enemy grenade which penetrated the wall.

At that moment, Denikin was observing the course of the battle from the high bank of the river near the farm. He was immersed in thought. Grenades whistled over his head. One of them landed in the wood adjoining the farm; another hit the house itself. A few minutes later an aide-de-camp came running toward him: "Your Excellency, General Kornilov . . ." Denikin understood immediately. His first impulse was to rush to the house, but he saw Romanovsky and several other officers approaching with a stretcher, which they set down next to him. The motionless figure of Kornilov lay on it. He was bleeding slightly from a small wound in the temple and profusely from his fractured right hip. He was still alive but his breathing was rapidly growing weaker. Denikin knelt, and trying to control his emotions, pressed his face to the hand of the dying leader.

"Will you accept the command of the army?" asked the chief of staff, and Denikin unhesitatingly answered, "Yes." There was no time for hesitation and no possibility of refusing. As deputy commander, General Denikin was in duty bound to replace Kornilov, yet, out of his great respect for the founder of the movement, Denikin sincerely believed at that time that he was assuming the command "only temporarily—here, on the battle-field." "For this reason," he related, "when I was asked to sign a short communiqué addressed to General Alekseev at *stanitsa* Elizavetinskaia, advising him of the event and asking him to come to the farm, I inserted the words, 'I beg to report . . .' at the beginning of the message. I wished to make it clear that I recognized Alekseev's unquestionable right to head our organization, and consequently, to name a permanent successor to our slain commander in chief." [16]

When Alekseev arrived, he turned to Denikin with the words, "Please accept this painful inheritance, Anton Ivanovich. May God help you!"

The question arose of how to word the announcement that General Denikin was succeeding Kornilov in the command of the Volunteer Army. Alekseev and Romanovsky discussed the matter in low voices. In whose name was the order to be issued? In what official capacity was Alekseev to sign it? Up to this time, every order and directive to the army had been issued simply by "The Commander."

"Simply sign 'General of the Infantry Alekseev,'" said Romanovsky finally, "the whole army knows who you are." [17]

The news of Kornilov's death spread like wildfire through the ranks. Denikin described its harrowing effect on the Volunteers: "Soon everyone knew. The effect was overwhelming. The men sobbed aloud; they spoke to each other in whispers, as if the man who had ruled their thoughts were still invisibly among them. He had been the focal point in which all their determination to fight, their faith in victory and hope of salvation were concentrated. And with his disappearance, fear and harrowing doubt pene-trated their brave hearts for the first time. Increasingly disturbing rumors began to circulate: that new Bolshevik forces were encircling the army on all sides, that capture and death were inevitable, that everything was lost." [18]

Doubts as to whether Denikin would be able to rescue the army troubled even the staunchest members of the Officers' Regiment. They would have liked to see their own commander, Markov, at the head of the army. "Markov," they said, "was Kornilov's right hand, his sword, his rapier. . . . He is the only one who should be placed at the head of the army."

As if sensing the mood of his officers, General Markov rode up to them with these words: "General Denikin has accepted the command of the army. There is no cause to worry about its fate. I have more faith in this man than I have in myself!" [19] This put a stop to any further discussion of the matter.

The question of whether or not to storm Ekaterinodar was settled on the same day. Denikin decided against it. In order to save the army, he planned to move it out at nightfall and to lead it by forced marches, as speedily as possible, in a northeasterly direction, out of reach of the Bol-shevik troops concentrated around Ekaterinodar.

"The plan of the forthcoming march," wrote Denikin later, "consisted in breaking out of the close network of railroads by moving the army in an easterly direction. In order to carry it out, we had to fight our way across the Black Sea railroad line. I chose *stanitsa* Medvedovskaia as the site of our breakthrough." [20]

General Alekseev had set out at full speed toward headquarters as soon as he received the tragic news. On the way, he encountered the Tekintsy guard accompanying the cart on which lay Kornilov's remains. Alekseev got out of his carriage and stood for a long time, immersed in deep thought, looking at the dead general's face. He knelt, bowed to the ground, and kissed him on the forehead. Regardless of the reasons for the conflict which existed between these two very different people, they had been united in their "last labor on earth" by their equally strong love for their country.

General Kornilov's body was taken to *stanitsa* Elizavetinskaia and laid in a pine coffin. A priest nervously recited the office for the dead, praying for the repose of the slain warrior Lavr. (The clergyman's fears were well founded: in the spring of 1918, over twenty priests were tortured to death in the Kuban region for having performed religious rites at the Volunteers' request.) During the night the cart with the coffin, which was concealed under a cover of hay, moved out of the *stanitsa* with the retreating army. Kornilov was to be buried secretly to prevent the encircling Bolsheviks from finding his grave. The body was laid to rest on April 2 near the German colonists' village of Gnachbau by a few men of Kornilov's escort, who leveled the burial site with the surrounding ground. The commanding staff stayed away from the funeral, in order not to attract attention. Only Denikin went by the grave unnoticeably to give it a parting glance.

"Instead of a salute by his faithful soldiers, the slain Commander was laid to rest to the thunder of enemy guns shelling the village." [21]

The Bolsheviks occupied Gnachbau the following day. They were not yet aware of Kornilov's death, but were told that the Volunteers had buried something near the village. Hoping to find a cache of money or valuables, they began to search for the treasure and discovered the freshly dug grave.

They took Kornilov's body to Ekaterinodar and dumped it in the cathedral square; a mob of drunken soldiers beat it and trampled it with their feet. They tore off its clothing and hung the naked body from a tree. When the rope broke, the crowd continued to vent its fury on the already shapeless mass. It was finally taken to the town slaughterhouse and burned on a straw fire.

In order to save his troops, Denikin had to resort to drastic measures. He ordered the baggage train reduced to a minimum: The refugees were packed six to a wagon; nearly two hundred carts were destroyed; all superfluous baggage was liquidated. And since the army's remaining ammunition did not exceed thirty shells, the Volunteers, with bitter regret, disabled and discarded all but four of their field guns. They were now faced with the difficult task of crossing the railroad. The entire network was in the hands of the Bolsheviks, who used it to advantage for moving their troops rapidly to certain strategic points in order to encircle the retreating Volunteers. The problem was further complicated by the fact that the Volunteers' artillery and army train could only traverse the lines at level crossings and required several hours to do so.

It was still completely dark in the early hours of April 3, when General Markov, marching at the head of the column, noticed a distant light shining in the steppe. As the Volunteers approached, they saw that it came from a small railroad post next to a level crossing. Markov rode toward it with several scouts. He and three of the scouts dismounted at some distance, entered the hut, and arrested the two railroad guards in it. From them Markov learned that two echelons of Red Guards and an armored train were stationed a kilometer away, at Medvedovskaia. Impersonating one of the arrested railroad men, Markov engaged in a telephone conversation with the Bolsheviks on duty at Medvedovskaia station. He assured them that everything was quiet at his post. The Reds, however, advised him that they would move the armored train to the post as an extra precaution. "Do that, comrades," rejoined Markov, "that'll be much safer."

He sent one of the scouts back to Denikin at a gallop with the request that the column be moved up as fast as possible, silently and without smoking, and halted two hundred paces away from the crossing. Denikin soon joined Markov at the hut.

In a few minutes a huge mass loomed out of the darkness from the direction of the station—it was the armored train [wrote Denikin].

It slowly drew nearer, with all lights extinguished; only the reflected flames of its open furnace glided along the tracks, forcing our men to retreat soundlessly from their light. The train approached the crossing. General Alekseev, the army's commander and his staff, and Markov, were gathered near the post. One grenade, a few belts of machine-gun bullets and . . . some serious changes would have taken place in the army command.

Markov rushed to the locomotive, *nagayka* [whip] in hand. "Stop the train! You'll run us over, you son of a bitch! Can't you recognize your own?"

The train halted. Before the bemused engineer could regain his senses, Markov had snatched a hand grenade from one of the riflemen and thrown it into the engine. The occupants of the cars opened fire on us at once with rifles and machine guns. They had no time, however, to fire a single one of the guns on the train's open platforms.

In the meantime, Mionchinsky [a brilliant young artillery officer] rolled one of our guns to the corner of the hut, under a shower of bullets, and aimed it almost point-blank at the train.

"Get away from the train, drop down!" shouted Markov's loud voice. A shot resounded and a high-explosive shell hit the locomotive, whose front part collapsed with a shattering noise. A second and third shell hit the armored carriages. Then Markov and his men rushed at the train from all sides. They shot at its carriage walls, climbed onto the roofs, hacked holes in them with axes, and threw bombs into the openings; they brought resinous tow from the hut and set two of the cars afire. The Bolsheviks, throughout, behaved with great fortitude, refusing to surrender and firing continuously from their cars. A few of them jumped onto the tracks, only to be met by our bayonets. One could see the charred figures of men escaping through the burned-out floors of the smoke-filled carriages and crawling along the tracks.

Soon it was all over. Only the crackling explosions of cartridges continued in the fire.

I warmly embraced the perpetrator of this unprecedented action—"Are you unhurt?"

"God saved me from the Bolsheviks," laughed Markov. "But it was our own men who fired like crazy. One shot went off right by my ear. I still can't hear anything." [22]

While the action at the railroad crossing was taking place, a battalion of the Officers' Regiment was on its way to the station; the engineers' unit was sent to blow up the tracks south of the crossing, to forestall a possible armored train attack from the direction of Ekaterinodar; and a cavalry detachment rode to capture the nearby *stanitsa*.

Over four hundred shells and nearly 100,000 rounds of ammunition were taken on that day.

The Volunteers were jubilant. For the first time since Kornilov's death, Denikin noted the "eager responsiveness and impeccable discipline" of his troops. Clad in a civilian overcoat under which were visible his khaki field shirt and two Crosses of St. George, Denikin reviewed his troops on horseback, thanking them for their outstanding bravery.

General Denikin decided to move his troops from *stanitsa* Medvedovskaia first eastward, then northward. He saw that in order to escape the Bolshevik encirclement, it was imperative to speed up the army's marches to cover distances of fifty-five to sixty-five kilometers a day, thus upsetting the calculations of the Bolshevik command.

To achieve this, it was necessary to transport the infantry in the army's wagons, but most of these were occupied by the gravely wounded. The General called a meeting of senior commanders to decide the painful question, "whether to take all the wounded with them or to leave the most serious cases in the *stanitsa* after taking all possible measures to guarantee their safety." Generals Alekseev, Romanovsky, Markov, and most of the other senior officers bowed to the necessity of leaving the wounded.

Such a decision could not fail to have a depressing effect on the Volunteers. Many of them attempted to transport their seriously wounded comrades with the army, but most of these died on the way, unable to survive the hardships of the rapid marches.

The medical personnel (which by that time had completely run out of medicines and dressings) drew up a list of wounded who, in their opinion, could not survive the new marching conditions. The village council of *stanitsa* Diadkovskaia agreed to take under its protection 119 wounded. A doctor and a nurse, provided with a certain amount of money, stayed with them. Several important Bolsheviks who had been taken as hostages in Ekaterinodar were left in the *stanitsa*. The most prominent of them, Limansky, gave his word that he would protect the wounded, and as it turned out later, he faithfully kept his promise.

But Denikin was to suffer from this memory for the rest of his life. "In reliving the past," he said, "I vividly remember the mental torture of those days and how, in sharing it with Romanovsky, we came to the same conclusion: that our painful duty as commanders obliged us to sign the order; but that we would have preferred shooting ourselves to being left behind." [23]

Toward the middle of April, in the course of the army's northward march, Denikin received news of important anti-Bolshevik uprisings in the Don region. The news was verified, and the General decided to lead the Volunteer Army toward the Don. He soon received additional and totally unexpected information about the unusual nervousness of the Bolshevik troops at the Don, and the movement of their echelons through Rostov to the south. The near panic of their retreat could not be attributed solely to local uprisings. The Bolsheviks seemed to be driven by some mysterious force.

The unknown force which so puzzled Denikin proved to be the German army.

The General, who had been cut off from the outside world for more than two months, did not know that after signing the Brest-Litovsk Treaty with the Bolsheviks, the Germans, who needed the raw materials abounding in south Russia, had overrun the Ukraine and the Crimea and were now standing at the edges of the Don territory.

It is hard to imagine the extent of Russia's isolation from the outside world at this period. Chaos prevailed throughout the country. The disruption of public transportation and postal and telegraph services, the absence of the "bourgeois" newspapers abolished by the Bolsheviks, the expanding civil war—all these had brought back the conditions of some ancient, forgotten times when news traveled only by word of mouth and was usually distorted on the way. Some items appeared in Bolshevik propaganda leaflets, but these dealt mainly with the triumphs and victories of the proletariat. Even large metropolitan centers came to depend on rumor as their only source of information.

It was not surprising, therefore, that the small army of Volunteers wending its way in the Kuban steppe, surrounded on all sides by Bolshevik forces, was almost hermetically sealed off from the general course of events.

The reports of German penetration into south Russia overwhelmed Denikin: "Our small army, almost completely deprived of military supplies, was suddenly brought face to face with two warring factions—the Soviet power and the German invasion, a numerically strong Red Guard and several army corps of a first-rate European army." [24]

The chaotic retreat of Soviet troops with enormous quantities of military supplies created a bottleneck at the junction of the Rostov–Tikhoretskaia railway line. This seemed to present two possible courses of action: either to attempt the destruction of the Bolshevik echelons or to limit the Volunteers' activity to raiding the nearby stations in order to seize some much-needed supplies.

The first alternative threatened the poorly armed and weary Volunteers with innumerable losses. But there were other reasons which prevented Denikin from taking this risk: "I must admit," wrote the General later, "that I was reluctant to deal a serious blow to the rear of the Bolshevik troops which barred the way to a German invasion of the Caucasus: actuality had become so distorted that at times it gave brigands and traitors the appearance of upholding Russia's national idea." [25]

Denikin limited the army's activity to several raids on railroad stations, which resulted in the capture of quantities of war supplies. Among these were trains filled with rifles, machine guns, and military outfits.

At the end of April, the Bolsheviks were giving comparatively little trouble to the Volunteers. Their attention was concentrated on the advances of the German army. By determination and luck, and also thanks to the developments of the larger European war still raging, General Denikin had succeeded in carrying out his plan: He had broken through the Bolshevik encirclement and preserved the cadres of his army. He was now able to give his men a much-needed rest, evaluate the existing situation, and decide on a new plan of action.

On April 30 his troops took up quarters in two large *stanitsy* of the Don region—Mechetinskaia and Egorlytskaia, southeast of Rostov.

XVI

AFTER THE
FIRST CAMPAIGN

The general situation in Russia, as Denikin realized at the end of the Volunteers' First Campaign, was an extremely complex and confused one. He had to find his bearings in it without delay, and eagerly absorbed all the information on recent and current events of which he had been deprived during the campaign. The facts he learned concerning the Brest-Litovsk Treaty and its consequences dealt a shattering blow to the General's national pride.

On the west and south, Russia had lost everything it had acquired since the reign of Peter the Great. Besides losing all influence over Poland and Finland (which in any event occupied a special position) it had given up, at the stroke of a pen, the Ukraine, the Crimea, the Baltic provinces, Georgia, and the cities of Batum, Kars, and Ardagan. Also, while engaging in peace negotiations with the Bolsheviks, Germany had managed behind their backs to conclude a treaty with a group of Ukrainian separatists. Having recognized the Ukraine as an independent state, the Germans occupied it with their troops, ousted the Bolsheviks who were already in power, and installed in Kiev a government fully prepared to collaborate with them. The Ukrainian *Rada,* composed predominantly of socialists, was soon found unsuitable by the Germans, who dissolved it peremptorily in mid-April and replaced it with the conservative government of *Hetman* * Skoropadsky, a former general of the Russian army.

Russia's outlying components were breaking off and becoming economic and military bases for the Central Powers. Germany was now able to pump

---

* The *Hetman* was the ruler or chief of state of the Ukraine. The term was derived from the German *Hauptmann,* which came to the Ukraine through Lithuania and Poland.

out of Russia for use in the war against the Allies not only grain, raw materials, and military supplies, but also hundreds of thousands of well-trained soldiers—some German, but most Austro-Hungarian—who had been taken prisoners by the Russians in the course of the war. The Russian Ministry of War estimated that in September, 1917, there were more than two million war prisoners in Russia—several times as many as the Allies took in the entire war. Most of the war prisoners in Russia were employed in agricultural work. At the beginning of 1917, large numbers were also employed in various branches of industry and construction, many of them in areas eventually occupied by the Central Powers. By far the greatest concentrations of prisoners, however, were in the Volga region, and in Siberia and central Asia—all of which were out of reach of the Germans. The German government exerted great pressure on the Bolsheviks to obtain their return.[1]

It was clear to Denikin that the Allies would have to take drastic measures to prevent this flow of enemy manpower from reaching the Western Front.

In addition, enormous reserves of military supplies sent by the Western Allies had accumulated in Murmansk, Archangel, and Vladivostok, and had been lying idle in these ports since the Bolshevik take-over. It was possible that the Germans might decide at any moment to appropriate them. On the other hand, the Allies would also doubtless make every effort to prevent them from doing so. An added reason for possible Allied action was the proximity of Murmansk to Finland, where the Germans had already landed some troops in support of the "White" forces of General Mannerheim against the Finnish Bolsheviks.

In short, Anton Ivanovich came to realize quite clearly that Russia had become the arena of a violent conflict of interests between the Central Powers and the Allies. It seemed that the handful of Volunteers under his and Alekseev's command was the only remaining force willing to stand up in defense of Russia's honor and national interests.

One joyful event helped to relieve Denikin's painful contemplation of these problems. This was the arrival from Rumania of a splendidly disciplined and spirited detachment of volunteers which had left the demoralized troops at that front and marched to the Don with artillery, machine guns, armored cars, and even a radio station. The detachment consisted of 667 officers, 370 soldiers, and doctors and nurses. It had traversed a distance of over a thousand kilometers in two months, constantly battling Bolshevik detachments which had invaded the southern provinces bordering the Black and Azov seas, and often covering sixty or seventy kilometers a day in its marches. This detachment captured Rostov, then left it and moved on to assist the Don Cossacks in liberating their capital, Novocherkassk.

On April 25, the detachment's commander, Colonel Mikhail Gordeevich Drozdovsky, sent a report to General Denikin in *stanitsa* Mechetinskaia:

"Detachment . . . has arrived and is at your disposal. . . . Detachment is exhausted by uninterrupted march . . . but is prepared for immediate action in case of emergency. Awaiting orders." [2]

By the end of April, the Germans had occupied and cleared of Bolsheviks a huge territory along the southern and western boundaries of Russia, extending from Sebastopol to Pskov and from Rostov to Kiev. Life in the occupied territory soon regained a normal appearance. Trains ran on schedule: the refugees from Soviet-occupied central Russia could not believe their eyes at the abundance of food in the markets. What was more important—they were no longer afraid of being aroused at night by Soviet agents, robbed, arrested, imprisoned, killed. . . . Small wonder that the Volunteers who had relatives in that zone were irresistibly tempted to share with them, if only for a short time, the relief of a peaceful and normal existence.

For many Volunteers the four-month period of service for which they had signed up was expiring in May. Denikin decided, therefore, to allow a three-week furlough to all those who wished to leave. "They will return if they want to," he said, "and if they don't, they can take their pleasure." The temptation not to return was overwhelming, and Denikin was taking an enormous chance; the whole army might disperse and vanish. But his secret hope was fulfilled—at the expiration of the furlough, most of those who had left returned to continue the struggle.

The physical and moral weariness of his men were not the only problems with which Denikin had to cope. Two other extremely important and acute questions soon occupied his attention.

First, Germany's successes in the spring and summer of 1918 led many people to believe that its victory over the Allies was assured and that Russia, or what was left of it, would not only have to accept that fact but would be obliged to rebuild its whole national life in accordance with German wishes. A "German orientation" came into existence and was advocated with particular insistence by propaganda originating in the capital of the Ukraine—Kiev. As distinguished a personality as Professor P. N. Milyukov, leader of the Cadet party and former Minister of Foreign Affairs of the Provisional Government, became convinced of Germany's ultimate victory and actively joined the pro-German camp. The Volunteer Army command felt in duty bound to counteract this "heresy."

The second painful problem concerned the army's political credo. "A united and indivisible Russia" had been the only motto of the Volunteer Army. Denikin had offered it as a symbol of opposition to the fragmentation of Russia, was proud of it, and was convinced of its rightness. His officers strongly supported it. This slogan could not fail, however, to arouse a certain fear in the newly formed states on Russia's periphery.

Nor was it sufficiently explicit for a movement which counted on winning the support of all classes of the population. A more concrete political program had to be stated. And the process of evolving and formulating such a program brought up a number of questions which were extremely delicate and difficult to resolve.

The chaos brought on by the revolution had wrought great changes in the social and political thinking of the nation. A distinct shift to the right was evident. Many liberals who formerly championed the idea of a republic had come to the conclusion that only a monarchy would assure the unity and greatness of the country. This approach could not fail to evoke a response among the Volunteer Army's officers, many of whom were also shifting to the right. The officers waited impatiently for a clear and definite political commitment on the part of their leaders.

The Volunteer Army's high command, however, was far from being in agreement on that subject.

General Alekseev considered that "in the normal cause of events, Russia should arrive at a restoration of the monarchy." At the same time, the wary Alekseev found it impossible for the army to adopt overtly monarchist slogans: "A premature announcement of such a slogan may only hinder the achievement of more pressing national objectives." [3]

General Denikin had a different point of view, and his opinion was shared by Romanovsky and Markov. He explained it as follows:

The atmosphere in the army was becoming tense and it was imperative to relieve it by some sort of decision. If in doing so we submitted to the wishes of the officers . . . we would run the risk of a complete break with the popular masses and, in particular, with the Cossacks, whose attitude at that time was not merely negative but downright inimical to the monarchist idea. We decided to talk the problem over with the officers.

A meeting of all officers holding command positions, down to and including platoon commanders, was called in the administrative office of *stanitsa* Egorlytskaia. Although Alekseev and I had not compared notes beforehand, it so happened that he spoke on the German question and I discussed the monarchist idea.

General Alekseev stressed the point that under existing circumstances, any compromise arrangement between patriotic Russians and Germany was inadmissible. He described the Germans as a cruel and pitiless foe, as menacing to Russian national interests as the Bolsheviks. In short, he stated that for the Volunteer movement an alliance with Germany was morally unacceptable and politically inexpedient in view of Germany's colossal losses and small chances of victory. He said that for the time being the Volunteer position vis-à-vis Germany should be—neither peace nor war.

Denikin's address was short and blunt. He said that when not involved in politics, the Russian army knew how to die and how to win.

But when every soldier began to decide the questions of strategy, war and peace, monarchy and republic, the army fell apart. The process is apparently being repeated at this time. Our unique problem is fighting the Bolsheviks and liberating Russia from them. There are many, however, who are not satisfied with this position. They want to raise the banner of monarchy immediately. . . . What right have we, a small handful of people, to decide the fate of the nation without its knowledge, without the knowledge of the Russian people?

Denikin told the officers to have faith in their leaders:

Those who have faith in us will follow us, those who don't—will leave the army.

As far as I am personally concerned, I shall not fight for a form of government. My struggle is for Russia only. And have no fear: On the day when I clearly feel that the pulse of the army no longer beats in unison with mine, I shall leave my post immediately in order to continue the struggle differently, in a way which I shall judge honest and direct.[4]

Anton Ivanovich remained faithful to the views which he expressed at that time. Even the promise contained in the last phrase of his address, which then passed almost unnoticed, had a profound, and as it turned out, a prophetic meaning.

Several years later, in 1920, Winston Churchill returned to that disturbing problem—whether to favor a monarchy—at a lunch with Denikin in London.

"In the course of a discussion of the reasons for the White Army's failure in the south," wrote Denikin in one of his unpublished papers, "Churchill turned to me with something between a question and a reproach: 'Tell me, General, why didn't you proclaim a monarchy?'

"That I did not do so is not surprising," replied Denikin, "I was battling for Russia, not for its form of government. When I asked two of my aides—Dragomirov and Lukomsky—both of whom were monarchists, whether they considered it imperative to adopt a monarchist slogan, both of them answered No. Such a declaration would have brought on the collapse of the front much earlier." [5]

The question of restoring the monarchy placed the White Army leadership in a cleft stick. "If I raise the republican flag, I will lose one half [of the Volunteers]," Denikin wrote to General N. M. Tikhmenev in 1918, "and if I raise the monarchist flag—the other half will leave me. In the meantime our primary task is to save Russia." [6]

It was a vicious circle, and according to Denikin the only solution was to adopt an attitude of "non-predetermination." This was expressed in two declarations (issued in late April and early May, 1918), which presented the political aims of the Volunteer Army. They stated that the army was fighting Bolshevism for the deliverance and unity of a ruined and humiliated Russia, and in its desire to join in a common endeavor with all Russian people, the army would remain nonpartisan; that the question of a future form of government was not predetermined by the army's leaders; that in fact this question would represent the final stage of the struggle, reflecting the will of the people after it had been liberated from its enslavement.

The first declaration referred to the convocation of a Constituent Assembly after law and order had been restored in the country and stated that an elective system must take the place of mob rule.

The reference to a Constituent Assembly and an elective system caused such a stir among the officers that Markov felt obliged to report it to the commander. To many of the officers the terms "Constituent Assembly" and "elective system" were inseparable from the period of anarchy which prevailed in the country at the end of 1917 and in the early part of 1918. These terms, therefore, were not used in the second declaration, although it retained the "non-predetermination" attitude and all the general premises of the first one. On the other hand, the second declaration stated with utmost clarity that a relationship of any kind with the Germans was out of the question.

The news that his wife was safe and sound brought great joy to Denikin.

Xenia Vasilievna had spent a frightening period in Rostov during the Volunteer Army's First Campaign, living under her maiden name and keeping her real identity secret. As soon as the Germans occupied Rostov, however, she decided to leave it. She moved to Novocherkassk when it was liberated from the Bolsheviks and rented a modest furnished room there. An amusing incident occurred at this point. Several officers of Colonel Drozdovsky's detachment, which had occupied Novocherkassk, took up quarters in the same house as Mrs. Denikin. Feeling somewhat cramped in the space assigned to them, the officers decided to get rid of the "young girl" and take possession of her room. A youthful lieutenant knocked at her door and announced that, as he and his companions had just completed an exhausting march and were getting ready for a new campaign under General Denikin's leadership, they needed a good rest and wished to occupy her room. He requested in no uncertain terms that Xenia Vasilievna move out as soon as possible.

"How could you wish to dispossess the wife of your commander?" protested Mrs. Denikin.

"What do you mean?" queried the nonplussed officer.

"Simply this: I am General Denikin's wife."

The officer burst out laughing. "In that case, my dear young lady, I am the Shah of Persia! But enough is enough. Get going now; we are tired and you are keeping us waiting."

The young woman, known to the officers as Xenia Chizh, had quite a time proving to them, to their great embarrassment, that she really was the wife of the Volunteer Army's commander.

Mrs. Denikin had had another curious experience while she was still living in Rostov. The modest and attractive "refugee from Poland" caught the attention of a young Armenian student who was the nephew of her landlord. He introduced himself, and finding that she had no friends in town, decided to keep her company. He called on her frequently and ended by proposing marriage. Refusing to take no for an answer, the fiery

Armenian continued to plague her with his attentions until Xenia Vasilievna's move to Novocherkassk brought the one-sided romance to an end. But the unfortunate suitor became seriously frightened when he found out that the object of his love was General Denikin's wife. He fled Rostov, terrified of having aroused the stern general's ire, and only returned after his family relayed to him Xenia Vasilievna's assurance that the commander of the Volunteer Army was not contemplating revenge. Actually, Anton Ivanovich was vastly amused by the whole episode and often joked with his wife about her mysterious "adventures." [7]

Meanwhile, the Don territory was shaking off the Bolshevik yoke through a series of uprisings. These were triggered by the confusion that had beset the Bolshevik detachments at the approach of the German troops. The latter, after crossing the Don boundary, invaded the western part of the territory, to the Voronezh–Rostov railroad, and occupied the cities of Taganrog and Rostov. In order to protect Rostov on the east, they established outposts in the *stanitsy* Aksaiskaia and Olginskaia. The Germans did not touch Novocherkassk. On April 28 (when most of the territory was still in Bolshevik hands) a special assembly, the *Krug* for the Deliverance of the Don, had been formed in that city, and on May 3 it had elected General Peter Nikolaevich Krasnov as *Ataman* of the Don Cossacks.

Denikin had known Krasnov since February, 1904, but their acquaintance was very superficial. They had first met during the Russo-Japanese War, when both were traveling on the Trans-Siberian express to the theater of operations. Captain Denikin was on his way to active duty, and Cossack Captain Krasnov was going to the front as a correspondent of the *Russian Veteran,* the official paper of the Ministry of War. Later, Denikin read some of Krasnov's articles and was impressed by them. But having himself written on military subjects, and being well acquainted with army life, he was also somewhat shocked by the poetic fancy at the expense of the truth which often cropped up in Krasnov's reporting. He had noted the same tendency to mix fantasy and fact in the talks they had on their long Siberian journey. Denikin and Krasnov met two or three more times during World War I, when Denikin already occupied important posts in the army. Later, when he was in the Bykhov prison, Denikin read in the papers that Krasnov had been named to command the Third Cavalry Corps, succeeding General Krymov, and had been sent by Kerensky to fight the Bolsheviks, who had just seized power in Petrograd. He heard subsequently that Krasnov had been arrested by the Bolsheviks but had managed to escape to the Don.

After Krasnov was elected *Ataman* of the Don Cossacks, Denikin watched his activity closely. Krasnov worried him by his consistent tendency to collaborate with the Germans. Nevertheless, Denikin could not help recognizing the new *Ataman*'s remarkable energy and outstanding administrative ability. He observed with approval the speed with which

Krasnov set about forming a Don Cossack army. A capable and authoritarian man of forty-nine, he lost no time in gaining control of the local administration. Until the regular *Krug* was called in mid-August, he single-handedly governed the Don territory, which was gradually being liberated from the Bolsheviks. He abrogated all the laws introduced by the Provisional Government and the Soviet of People's Commissars, and the Don territory reverted to the laws of prerevolutionary Russia until such time as a new code of laws would be proclaimed. Krasnov conceived of the Don territory as an independent country with its own army, foreign policy, customs regulations, currency, flag, and national anthem. This did not please Denikin, whose motto was "A united and indivisible Russia."

Furthermore, the *Ataman* was of the opinion that the Don territory's future depended entirely on Germany, in whose victory over the Allies he firmly believed. Krasnov, therefore, frankly adopted a pro-German orientation. This second aspect of the *Ataman*'s policy pleased Denikin even less.

At Denikin's initiative, a meeting took place on May 15 between the Volunteer Army command and the *Ataman* of the Don Cossacks. The purpose of the meeting was to establish closer cooperation between the Volunteers and the Cossacks and to agree on a common plan of action. Besides Denikin and Krasnov, the meeting was attended by Generals Alekseev and Romanovsky, Kuban *Ataman* Filimonov, several officers, and General A. P. Bogaevsky, who had arrived with Krasnov. Bogaevsky, a participant in the Volunteers' First Campaign, had been appointed head of the Don Cossack government and its Minister of Foreign Affairs. General Alekseev's illness had progressed noticeably in the harsh conditions of the First Campaign. Ill and exhausted, he sat at the conference table silently, with closed eyes, arousing himself only to make an occasional remark.

Unfortunately, the conference served to emphasize the latent antagonism of the participants and brought to the fore not only the incompatibility of Denikin's and Krasnov's personalities, but also the complete divergence of their political orientations and strategic approaches.

Friction set in as soon as the conference opened. General Denikin criticized a disposition prepared by the *Ataman* for taking the village of Bataisk in cooperation with German troops; he stated very explicitly that the Volunteer Army would tolerate no relationship with the Germans.

Standing on his newly acquired dignity, "the *Ataman* gave General Denikin to understand that he was no longer the brigadier general whom Denikin had known during the war, but the representative of a free nation of five million people, and consequently, any conversations with him should be conducted in a somewhat different key."[8]

However, this phrase quoted from Krasnov's memoirs (which he wrote in the third person), did not produce the desired effect. All those present knew that Krasnov had been elected *Ataman* only twelve days ago by the small fraction of the Don territory already liberated from the Bolsheviks; that the *Krug* for the Deliverance of the Don, formed at random, was not truly representative of the territory; that more than half of the "five million people" were still under the Bolshevik yoke, and consequently, were not free; and that in any case the entire population of the Don territory (including the *inogorodni,* who opposed Krasnov) did not exceed four million. In short, the *Ataman* had again given in to his tendency to exaggerate.

The conferees also disagreed on the future plans of the Volunteer Army. The *Ataman* insisted that the army set aside its plan for a Kuban campaign and march instead in a northeasterly direction, toward the Volga city of Tsaritsin. He argued that the important armaments factories and enormous supplies of materiel in that city would render the army independent of Cossack help and provide it with an excellent purely Russian operational base.

None of the other participants in the conference knew at that time that on May 4 General Krasnov had dispatched a letter to *Hetman* Skoropadsky asking him to exert his influence on Field Marshal Eichhorn, the German commander in chief in Kiev, to have Tsaritsin occupied by German troops! [9]

Denikin's military plans were diametrically opposed to Krasnov's. For one thing, Krasnov's demand for immediate action was out of the question in view of the Volunteer Army's great need for rest, reorganization, and supplies. Denikin opposed the move north for strategic reasons as well. First, the Volunteer Army risked finding itself in trouble on three sides: In the west were the Germans; in the north, the Bolsheviks; and in the east, the natural barrier of the Volga, toward which the Germans could easily press it. Moreover, a movement to the north would deprive the army of its main sources of manpower—the Ukraine, the Kuban, the North Caucasus, and the Crimea. This applied particularly to officer volunteers, of whom there were very few from beyond the Volga. On the other hand, movement to the south, for the liberation of the Trans-Don and the Kuban, would protect from the Bolsheviks the entire four-hundred kilometer southern border of the Don territory. It promised a steady flow of new recruits, opened the way to the Black Sea, and in the event of an Allied victory, would provide a convenient meeting place with them in Novorossiisk. The rich Kuban region would be an excellent base for a future northward movement of the Volunteer Army.

General Denikin then proposed to establish a unified command which would place the Don Cossacks under his orders. Krasnov categorically declined this proposal, and countered with one of his own: he would agree to give the Volunteer Army six million rubles, according to a promise previously made by *Ataman* Kaledin, provided the Volunteer Army would submit to his authority.

Losing his patience, Denikin retorted that his army was serving a national cause and would never consider hiring itself out as a mercenary to regional interests. Shortly before the conference, Denikin had learned that Krasnov had been exerting pressure on Colonel Drozdovsky not to allow his detachment, recently arrived from Rumania, to leave the Don territory until a regular Don Cossack army had been formed. Denikin demanded the immediate incorporation of the Drozdovsky detachment into the Volunteer Army.

The attempt to establish closer ties between the Volunteer Army command and *Ataman* Krasnov was an almost complete failure. Nevertheless, an agreement was reached by which the Don government would transfer to the Volunteer Army part of the military equipment which it expected to receive from armament stockpiles in the Ukraine, originally intended for the Russian southwestern front. The Volunteers were also "loaned" six million rubles with the understanding that they would guarantee the safety of the Don territory's boundary with the Kuban.

Both Denikin and Krasnov were ignorant of the fact that just two days before their meeting, events of momentous importance had taken place and were developing rapidly in a different part of Russia: An army corps of approximately forty thousand men of Czechoslovak origin had refused to submit to Soviet authority. The corps (or Czech Legion, as it became known) was composed partly of Czechs residing in Russia, but mainly of Austrian war prisoners of Czech and Slovak origin who wanted to establish an independent state of Czechoslovakia to be carved out of the Austro-Hungarian Empire. At the insistent requests of Professor Thomas Masaryk and Eduard Beneš, the Provisional Government had agreed in the summer of 1917 to permit recruitment of volunteers among the Czechoslovak war prisoners of the Austrian army. Their plan was to organize them into an independent army corps which would fight against the Central Powers on the Russian front. It should be noted that the imperial government of Russia was reluctant to take such a "subversive step" against the imperial government of Austria-Hungary even though the two countries were at war. After the disintegration of the Russian army, Masaryk (whose headquarters were in Paris and whose nationalist aims were supported by the Allies) decided to remove the army corps from Russia to France. With the support of Clemenceau, who needed additional troops, Masaryk announced in January, 1918, that in France the corps would represent the nucleus of a future Czechoslovak army. Subsequently, this plan was also approved by the Supreme Allied War Council. However, events in Russia interfered with Masaryk's plans.

The Czech troops were already en route to Vladivostok, where they were to embark for the journey to France, by way of the Panama Canal. Their echelons were staggered along the immense length of the Trans-Siberian railroad, from the Volga to the Transbaikal region. Friction between the Czechs and Soviet authorities had existed for some time. But when it reached such proportions that the Bolsheviks decided to disarm the Czechs, the latter refused to submit. They suspected a trap which would deliver them to the Austro-Hungarian authorities, who regarded the men of the Czech Legion as traitors. Rather than run that risk, the Czechs decided to fight their way across Siberia to the Far East. Within a few days, with very little opposition, they gained control of the entire Trans-Siberian line. Their success was due not to their own strength, but to the weakness of the Soviet forces.

The unpremeditated and unforeseen revolt of the Czechs at that moment produced a radical change in the thinking of the Allies. Even before the uprising of the Czechs, the British War Office had been inclined to keep them in Russia, with the thought of eventually reestablishing an Eastern Front against the Germans. Now, Clemenceau reversed his previous stand and instructed the Quai d'Orsay to do everything possible to divert the action of the Czechs to the restoration of order in Siberia. Without consulting the Czechs and instead of sending them to France, the Allies had decided to detain the Czech Legion in Siberia. They realized that the seizure of the Trans-Siberian line by the Czechs prevented the repatriation of the Austro-German war prisoners from Siberia; that it threatened the Central Powers with the possibility of creating a new front against them in the east; and finally, that the Czech Legion could be used against the hated Soviet regime, which had repudiated all previous Russian debts to the Allies, signed a separate peace treaty with the enemy, and was regarded by government circles in London and Paris as a mere tool of German imperialism.

The revolt of the Czechs sparked off a series of uprisings along the Volga and in western Siberia. Some were spontaneous, others were instigated by underground officers' organizations which had been waiting for a chance to initiate anti-Bolshevik action.

Secret Socialist Revolutionary committees also took an active part in the anti-Bolshevik uprisings, appealing to the population to resist both the Soviets and the German occupation. Their influence on the Czechoslovaks was considerable, and this, in turn, had a bearing on the subsequent relationship of the Czechs with the officer corps and all the Russian political groups opposed to the Socialist Revolutionary program.

Many of the Czechoslovak war prisoners scattered throughout Siberia joined the Czech troops, bringing their number up to approximately sixty thousand. The Czech detachments were well organized in comparison with the Red Army. This superiority, however, was only relative, for the corruption which destroyed the Russian army had also affected the Czechoslovak units which formed part of it in 1917. They, too, had succumbed to "democratization," with its elected soldiers' committees and "revolutionary discipline."

The initiative of the Czechoslovak corps spurred on the beginning of Allied intervention. A small Japanese contingent in Vladivostok was soon joined by British, American, and additional Japanese units, and by a small detachment of French soldiers from Indo-China. By the end of 1918, Allied troops in the Far East numbered approximately 70,000 men (57,000 Japanese, 8,000 American, 2,500 British, 1,500 Italian, 1,000 French). In addition, 23,000 men had landed in the northern ports of Murmansk and Archangel (12,000 British and 11,000 of various other nationalities). Another 5,000 British penetrated into the Transcaspian region.[10]

The threat of a new anti-German front in the east could not fail to affect the attitude of the German command toward the Volunteer Army. Though too small and weak to present a threat to the Central Powers, Denikin's troops had nevertheless won the respect of Austro-German officers. They had seen how, at a time of complete moral disintegration, the Volunteers' officers had set an example of the moral and military qualities on which the officers of European armies had been brought up for generations. The German command in Kiev and Rostov, therefore, maintained a respectful attitude toward Alekseev and Denikin despite the Volunteer Army's undisguised pro-Allied sympathies, and tried to evoke a friendly attitude among its officers. The Germans did not oppose the Volunteers' recruiting activity in the Ukraine; their railroad-station commanders went out of their way to assist parties of officers en route to the Volunteer Army. The Germans also preferred to ignore the partial transfer to the Volunteer Army of ammunition obtained from them by *Ataman* Krasnov.

The attitude of the Germans toward Denikin's army changed drastically after the Czechoslovak *coup*. If an Eastern Front were established, Denikin's Volunteers could become a real nuisance to the Central Powers. The Volunteer recruiting center in Kiev was closed, and the officers operating it were arrested; echelons of officers crossing the Ukraine to join the Volunteer Army were detained. The German authorities demanded the immediate restoration of all war prisoners who were former Austro-Hungarian subjects. This included the three or four hundred Czechoslovaks in the Volunteer Army's engineers' battalion who had participated in the First Campaign. General Denikin assured the worried representatives of his Czech contingent that he considered himself in honor bound to defend his companions in arms, and would not hesitate to fight for them in case of emergency despite his desire to avoid an armed clash with the Germans.

Disturbing news was also secretly relayed to Denikin from loyal officers who had entered the service of the Soviet General Staff. In September, 1918, when Denikin was in the midst of fighting his Second Kuban Campaign, they informed him that Germany's Minister of Foreign Affairs had addressed a note to the Soviet government in which he demanded an immediate cessation of the Czechoslovak movement, the expulsion of Allied troops from Murmansk and Archangel, and "the suppression of General Alekseev's revolt." The secret report on German-Soviet negotiations received by Denikin from Moscow ended as follows: "If the Soviet government proves unable to achieve the above aims unassisted, it must not oppose the movement of German troops across Russian territory for these purposes. . . . The Germans see the gravest threat to themselves precisely in the Volunteer Army and General Alekseev." [11]

Thus, Denikin's fear of possible German intervention if his army moved on Tsaritsin proved to have been well founded. While they did not interfere with the army's liberation of the Kuban, the Germans would not have allowed it to move toward the Volga, where a new anti-Bolshevik front was already being formed and where the Volunteers could have found themselves trapped between the Bolsheviks and the Germans, if an anti-German front had come into existence.

Some members of *Ataman* Krasnov's entourage were not in sympathy with his pro-German leanings. They kept General Denikin's staff informed of the *Ataman*'s secret negotiations with high German government circles. The accounts of these negotiations seriously worried the Volunteer command.

The *Ataman* had sent two "handwritten letters" to Kaiser Wilhelm. The contents of the first letter was not particularly disturbing. The text of the second letter, however, aroused serious misgivings in Alekseev and Denikin. Giving way once more to poetic fancy at the expense of truth, Krasnov addressed the Kaiser not in the name of the Don Cossacks, but in the name of a nonexistent federation, a so-called "Don-Caucasus Alliance" composed, according to him, of the Don, Kuban, Terek, and Astrakhan Cossack armies; of the Kalmyks of Stavropol province; and of the North Caucasus mountain tribes. In fact, all of these regions, except the Don, were still occupied by the Bolsheviks. Their representatives in Novocherkassk, moreover, had firmly rejected Krasnov's idea of forming a Don-Caucasus federation.

Krasnov affirmed in this letter that the Don Cossacks would preserve complete neutrality for the duration of the world conflict and not permit any anti-German armed forces to enter the Don territory. This statement shocked Alekseev and Denikin, who found it impossible to reconcile Krasnov's efforts to move the Volunteer Army across the Don territory toward Tsaritsin with the assurance given by him to the Kaiser that no anti-German forces would be allowed to cross the Don border.

Nevertheless, despite the serious divergences of their views, the leaders of the Volunteer Army and the *Ataman* of the Don Cossacks continued to maintain an official relationship.

During the early months of 1918, economic life in the Soviet zone presented a grim picture. Cut off from the Ukraine, Moscow lost its main source of food. The railroad system, neglected during the war years and greatly abused in the second half of 1917, was rapidly deteriorating: The rolling stock was in a state of disrepair and almost half of the locomotives were disabled. The shortage of raw materials needed by the industry resulted in the closing of a number of factories and plants, which, in turn, was followed by increasing unemployment of the "industrial proletariat." The normal exchange of goods between towns and villages was paralyzed. Lack of manufactured items prevented the towns from offering them to the peasant population, and this prompted the peasants to hoard their food supplies, so desperately needed by the cities. In a number of towns, hungry crowds rioted against the new rulers, and the closing of factories brought about a mass return of industrial workers to their native villages. The Soviet leadership took harsh measures against the lower bourgeoisie of the cities and against the more prosperous peasants in the villages. Both groups were regarded as dangerous class enemies, with particular emphasis on the well-to-do peasants.

Reports reaching General Denikin seemed to indicate that the mood of the country was turning against the Bolsheviks. But it was imperative for the General to obtain definite and more reliable information on what was happening in the Soviet-occupied zone and particularly in Moscow, to which the Council of People's Commissars headed by Lenin had moved from Petrograd in February, 1918. For this purpose, and also in the hope of finding some financial support for his army, Denikin dispatched several of his officers to Moscow. Their mission was to establish a liaison with underground anti-Bolshevik organizations and to evaluate for Denikin their activity, importance, and political leanings. They were also instructed to find out if the Volunteer Army could count on any contributions from the former members of the moneyed bourgeoisie and the diplomatic representatives of the Allied countries.

The Soviets were only beginning to organize their internal security, and their agents had not yet penetrated all underground organizations. But if, despite all their conspiratorial experience, the Bolsheviks' secret police and counterintelligence were still at an embryonic stage, the Volunteers' approach to these intricate problems was quite incredibly naïve. A case in point is that of General Kazanovich, one of the emissaries chosen by Denikin. A brave combat officer, wounded several times in the war and still suffering from a wound received in the Volunteers' First Campaign, he appeared totally unsuited for conspiratorial activity. When Kazanovich was summoned by Denikin, he naturally assumed that the interview would concern his brigade. "Imagine my surprise," he related, "when, after giving me a brief summary of the situation, Generals Denikin and Romanovsky asked me whether I would agree to go to Moscow to seek means of support for the continued existence of the army. I answered that I would much rather stick to my real job of fighting the Bolsheviks, but that I would, of course, agree to any mission if they considered it indispensable for the army. . . . The generals did their best to convince me by arguing that there was no one else they could send."

The various documents which Kazanovich was instructed to take with him were a further proof of his superiors' lack of conspiratorial experience. He carried letters from Generals Alekseev and Denikin; an identification issued by the Volunteer Army "to be presented to persons from whom a sympathetic attitude might be expected"; a false passport with a fictitious name and a certificate from the Don Cossack government with yet another name. But despite all this incriminating evidence of his "counter-revolutionary" activity, Kazanovich managed to carry out his mission without being searched, and remained in Moscow unmolested for a whole month.[12]

Denikin had known of the existence of the Moscow Center (also known as the Rightist Center) even before he left Rostov on the First Volunteer campaign. The Center consisted of a coalition of conservative and liberal groups, i.e., of nonsocialist elements.

At the beginning of 1918, another organization, the Union of Regeneration, was also created in Moscow. The majority of its members were People's Socialists and right-wing Socialist Revolutionaries. The Center refused to recognize the Constituent Assembly dissolved by the Bolsheviks, whereas the Union still clung to it. The Center favored a one-man military dictatorship, and the Union proposed a directory of three persons.

The question of foreign orientation soon created friction at the Moscow Center. Many of its conservative members leaned to the side of the Germans and favored negotiating with them. Those who opposed a pro-German orientation broke away and formed a new association—the National Center.

The National Center established close ties with the Union of Regeneration, which also had a pro-Allied orientation. Together they reached the compromise decision that the future form of government would be established by a new Constituent Assembly elected after Russia was liberated from the Bolsheviks. In the interim, the country would be governed by a directory consisting of one general, one socialist, and one nonsocialist.

The representatives of the Allied nations insisted on the collaboration of the National Center and the Union of Regeneration and soon began to give them substantial financial help.

These alliances and centers were composed of public figures from the tsarist and Provisional Government periods. They met conspiratorially under the very nose of the Soviet government to discuss the future structure of the country's administration; argued and quarreled, though they had no real popular support, tried to prove to the members of Allied missions and the representatives of the Volunteer Army that the true wishes of the nation were being voiced through them. It was part of Kazanovich's assignment to evaluate the importance of the various anti-Bolshevik centers and to establish contact with them.

Quite separate and in a totally different category was the Union for the Defense of the Motherland and Freedom, organized by Savinkov. Having had underground experience, he was able to assemble a group of officers, which Denikin estimated as amounting to two to three thousand. According to Savinkov himself, it consisted of 5,500 men. Be that as it may, by flaunting the names of Alekseev and Kornilov and playing up his short stay at the Don, Savinkov succeeded in bringing together several thousand officers and in establishing a liaison with Masaryk and, later, with the Allies. Having impressed the latter by his mysterious past and by veiled hints of strong backing and great opportunities, he managed to secure considerable financial support from them. Even Denikin, who had little confidence in Savinkov, wrote later that his organization, though small, was the only real anti-Bolshevik force in central Russia at that time.

The most tragic weakness of the organization was its leader's incompetence in purely military matters. He was now faced not with the familiar problems of planned political murder, but with determining the detailed and far-reaching strategy of an armed *coup* involving several thousand people scattered in numerous cities, and with the task of coordinating their actions with the expected Allied landings in the northern Russian ports. Savinkov was informed by his agents that British troops were not expected to land in Archangel before early August. He nevertheless scheduled his action for July 6 and carried it out on that day in several towns in Moscow's vicinity—Iaroslavl, Rybinsk, Murom.[13]

Meeting General Kazanovich at a secret apartment in Moscow, Savinkov "spoke in rather nebulous terms of the uprisings prepared by him at a series of points northeast, east, and southeast of Moscow. He said that on the whole everything was ready and success was assured and that he intended to follow up the local victories with converging marches on Moscow."[14]

The uprising based on guesswork and wishful thinking rather than on well-founded calculations ended in a debacle: Savinkov's organization was destroyed, the officers exterminated and Savinkov himself obliged to flee to Siberia.

General Denikin was particularly interested in finding out what went on in the Bolshevik army at that period. He had seen the disorganization of Red units in the south. But information received from Moscow showed that great changes in military thinking were taking place in the new capital. They gave the impression that the Soviet government, having realized the complete inadequacy of the Red Guard, had decided on a new approach to the organization of its armed forces and was abandoning the principle of voluntary enrollment in favor of general mobilization. A Soviet decree, whose text reached Denikin, canceled all regimental committees and abrogated the elective system in the army. A series of further Bolshevik measures restored general military conscription, demanded the registration of all former officers, pressed all General Staff officers into active service, and instituted schools for the training of new Red Army officers.

The Soviet government was taking an enormous chance in mobilizing the officers of the former army, and the Bolsheviks were fully aware of the risk. The system of coercion and terror introduced by them to minimize the danger of bringing in these "specialists" was such that only people of exceptional courage and conviction dared to oppose it. The actions of each officer who was co-opted into the Soviet camp were guaranteed by a hostage system, with all the members of his family—parents, wife, brothers, sisters, and even children—held responsible. To ensure against possible sabotage, the Soviets created in March, 1918, the institute of military commissars entrusted with political control over the entire organization and life of the army. The commissars could not interfere with the military dispositions of the "specialists," but it was they who would bear the responsibility in case of treason on the part of the commanding officers in their units.

Besides officers, the Bolsheviks inducted into the Red Army, in 1918, approximately 130,000 former noncommissioned officers of the old army. These were to play quite an important part in the final outcome of the struggle.

By November, 1918, the Red Army numbered up to half a million officers and men. Many of the elements included in it through mobilization were very uncertain. But the Communist cells of all the detachments and units formed a firm and stabilizing core, as did the old soldiers and noncoms, for whom service in the army was a profession. The Letts, who had served in the old army and were now cut off from their country by the German occupation, were formed into separate regiments. They, too, turned out to be reliable supporters of the Soviet regime.

The detachments of "Internationalists" were also to play an important role. They included Hungarian, German, and some Slavic war prisoners, as well as approximately 200,000 Chinese and 20,000 Koreans. The latter had been brought over from the Far East by the tsarist government as unskilled labor. Finding themselves without employment after the Bolshevik *coup,* they enlisted in the Red Army, where they achieved an infamous notoriety by their extreme cruelty toward political and war prisoners.[15]

The events of the first half of 1918 were the background against which Denikin evolved his military plans for the new campaign, which was to become known as the Second Kuban Campaign.

XVII

THE SECOND
KUBAN CAMPAIGN

"We were few," wrote General Denikin about his army at the outset of the Second Kuban campaign, "only eight or nine thousand strong against eighty to one hundred thousand Bolsheviks, but we had the advantage of knowing the art of warfare. . . . Our army had determination, the consciousness of a just cause, confidence in its strength and hope in the future." [1]

The Volunteers had only twenty-one cannon and two armored cars, while the Reds possessed hundreds of cannon and large quantities of machine guns, artillery shells, and rifle cartridges. But the Soviet troops were poorly organized, and their leaders waged a cruel war against the civilian authorities and were torn by internal conflicts. By that time, three independent Soviet republics had been formed in the North Caucasus: the republics of Kuban, Black Sea, and Terek-Stavropol. At the beginning of June, 1918, these were unified under the name of the North Caucasus Soviet Republic.

These republics had not broken away from Moscow, but being cut off from the central seat of Soviet power, they had no choice but to act independently; and the German occupation of the Ukraine created an impression in some local Soviet military circles that Germany still remained an enemy.

Avtonomov, Sorokin, and other Soviet commanders labeled the Central Executive Committee members of these republics "provocateurs and German spies" and the civilian authorities retaliated by denouncing the Red commanders as "bandits and enemies of the people." Despite its almost complete lack of communications with the North Caucasus, the Moscow government managed to exert enough pressure to subdue the conflict temporarily and prevent the situation from reaching a breaking point.

The Moscow government soon removed the controversial Avtonomov to a less responsible post. Sorokin, however, retained his position and later played a fatal role in the fortunes of his own army.

The confusion was such that the North Caucasus Bolshevik forces "could not be properly assessed," as Denikin put it. Even the Soviet General Staff in Moscow lacked exact information about them. One aspect of the situation (which was generally favorable to the Volunteers) worried General Denikin: The troops from the former Russo-Turkish front were prevented by the general turmoil from leaving the narrow area between the Don and the Caucasian ridge and dissolving in the vastness of Russia with the same rapidity as the soldiers of the Russian armies from the European fronts. Denikin foresaw that they could become "an almost inexhaustible and well-prepared reserve for replenishing the Red Army of the North Caucasus." [2]

Despite its small size, General Denikin's army was divided into three infantry divisions, one cavalry division, and one mounted Kuban brigade. Superficially, the word "division" seemed grandiloquent in relation to the small number of men in the unit it denoted (each division was equal in numbers to a normal regiment). In reality, like the whole structure of the army, it was the result of deliberate and thoughtful planning. Each unit of the army, composed primarily of officers, became a cadre for future reinforcements, which flowed into its ranks during the campaign, recruited from the population of the Kuban, the peasants of Stavropol province, and war prisoners taken in the course of the fighting. In this way the Volunteer Army was prepared to absorb the influx of new soldiers, whose training was immediately taken over by the experienced officers who had formerly occupied the position of privates.

"The units of the Volunteer Army," wrote Denikin, "were formed, armed, drilled, educated, decimated, and replenished again under fire, in constant battle." [3]

The strategy of the Second Kuban Campaign was very different from that of the First. During the First Campaign railroads represented the threat of Bolshevik attack and consequently were avoided by the Volunteers whenever possible; while in the Second Campaign the capture of important railroad junctions became a means of liberating the territory of the Kuban Cossacks from the Reds.

In order to protect the rear of his army, Denikin decided to disrupt railway communications between central Russia and the North Caucasus. His strategy called for four operational stages: First, his troops were to occupy the railroad junction of Torgovaia, as well as the station of Velikokniazheskaia, northeast of it. His next aim was to turn sharply southwest in order to capture the important station of Tikhoretskaia, located at the intersection of two railroad lines—the main line from Moscow to the Caucasus, and the line between Tsaritsin and Novorossiisk. Third, he would secure the flanks of his army; and then the final operation was to be a frontal attack on the city of Ekaterinodar, the military and political center of the Kuban and the North Caucasus.

When this campaign was analyzed later, even the military historians whose attitude toward Denikin was negative agreed that "the complex plan of operation was based on the pattern of the railroad network as well as on the disposition of the enemy's forces"; [4] that Denkin proved himself a most able tactician; [5] and that the whole series of battles in the first two phases of the operation (from Torgovaia to Tikhoretskaia) "was a continuous Cannae, i.e., an encirclement of both enemy flanks by the Volunteer Army, which unfailingly resulted in the evacuation of all points by the Reds, who had taken them but were afraid of being surrounded." [6] The comparison with Cannae referred, of course, to Hannibal's famous battle in the Apulian plain in which his army surrounded and exterminated the twice as numerous Roman army of Gaius Terentius Varro.

The first phase of the campaign was completed in five days. The second lasted two weeks. On July 1 the Volunteers took Tikhoretskaia. Between June 10 and July 1, they captured over fifty cannon, a large quantity of rifles, machine guns, cartridges, shells, and supplies, three armored trains, and a great many railroad cars. They routed thirty thousand Soviet troops commanded by Kalnin and severed the connections between the other Red Army units. Kalnin's staff train was among the numerous trophies they captured at the Tikhoretskaia station. Kalnin managed to escape, alone and on foot, at the last minute. His chief of staff, a former colonel of the old army who feared reprisals, shot his wife and himself in a compartment of the staff train.

The cruelty on both sides knew no bounds. Wounded Volunteers who fell into the hands of the Reds were subjected to unbearable tortures before being killed. Their arms and legs were chopped off, stomachs ripped open, eyes gouged out, tongues and ears cut off. Some were soaked in kerosene and burned alive.

During one of the battles (near Belaia Glina), the troops of Colonel Drozdovsky's detachment came across the disfigured corpses of their fellow soldiers, and avenged themselves by shooting their Red prisoners. Denikin summoned Drozdovsky to tell him that "such cruel mass reprisals were inadmissible as well as clearly harmful to the army" and to demand that similar incidents never be repeated. The General was, nevertheless, sadly aware that Drozdovsky and others like him would implement his orders "only nominally."

"We needed time," wrote Denikin in his memoirs, "a great spiritual effort, and a change of psychology in order to overcome the bestial urge that possessed everyone—the Reds, the Whites, and the Russians not involved on either side. In the First Campaign we took no prisoners at all; in the Second—we took them by the thousand. Later, we would take them by tens of thousands, as a result not only of the enlarged scope of the struggle, but also of an evolution of the spirit." [7]

The first two phases of the campaign were completed perfectly, but one could hardly expect the plan of operations to proceed indefinitely according to schedule without some unforeseen obstacles.

Having occupied Tikhoretskaia, General Denikin, on July 3, moved his troops in three divergent directions on the 140-kilometer front. His main forces were directed toward the right flank, in order to capture the station of Kushchevka and defeat the Soviet troops commanded by Sorokin which occupied it. The division of General Borovsky was moved to the left flank in order to take the Kavkazskaia station; and Colonel Drozdovsky's division was to march forward to Ekaterinodar.

After the Volunteers had taken Kushchevka, Sorokin abandoned his military trains and supplies in an effort to escape rapidly from the encirclement which threatened his troops. This created the impression that his units were completely demoralized. Sorokin, however, succeeded not only in leading out his troops, but in getting them ready for a blow at the right flank and rear of the Volunteer units advancing on Ekaterinodar. Simultaneously, a part of the so-called "Taman army" (one of the well-organized Soviet units in the North Caucasus, which included many *inogorodni*), made a sortie out of Ekaterinodar and joined in the attack on the approaching Volunteers. The Bolsheviks were many times more numerous than the Whites. Led by Sorokin and Kovtiukh, who commanded the Taman forces in Ekaterinodar, they attempted a pincers movement against the Volunteers, who found themselves in serious danger. A series of fierce battles lasted for ten days. Denikin's strategic ability and the prowess of his men finally overcame the enemy, and on August 3 the Volunteer Army entered Ekaterinodar.

But at what cost! Between the beginning of the Second Campaign and the capture of Ekaterinodar, the army had lost hundreds of men and several outstanding leaders, and worst of all, it had lost General Markov.

Markov was fatally wounded on the evening of June 12, at the outset of the campaign, near the station of Shablievka.

The Red units were retreating [wrote Denikin]; their armored trains were also pulling out, firing a few parting salvos in the direction of the abandoned station. The next-to-last shell proved fatal. Markov fell covered with blood. [A shell fragment wounded the back of his head and tore off most of his left shoulder]. He was carried to a hut and did not suffer long. Occasionally he regained consciousness and took leave affectionately of his officer friends who stood around him speechless with grief.

Next morning the First Kuban Riflemen Regiment rendered the last honors to its beloved division commander. The regiment had never performed so badly before. When ordered to "present arms" to its general, rifles and bayonets faltered and fell; the officers and men wept unashamedly. . . .

At nightfall, the body was transported to Torgovaia. After a short funeral prayer, we carried the coffin on our shoulders to the Church of the Ascension between the lined-up ranks of Volunteer Army divisions. The long column of mourners moved slowly in the twilight through the silence which had descended on the village. A black banner with a cross, his banner, which had appeared so often in the critical areas of the battlefield, fluttered above the coffin. . . .

When the funeral service was over, I retreated to a dark corner of the church away from the people and gave way to my grief.[8]

Markov's remains were taken to Novocherkassk and buried in its military cemetery. Innumerable people came to pray for the fallen general. Among them were General Alekseev, *Ataman* Krasnov, and Markov's mother, wife, and children. General Alekseev pronounced a eulogy of the deceased in a voice choked with emotion. Then, unexpectedly, he went down on his knees and bowed to the ground before Markov's mother thanking her for having "raised and nurtured a faithful son of Russia." [9]

In an order of the day, General Denikin changed the name of the First Officers' Regiment, originally commanded by Markov, to the First Officers' General Markov Regiment. The regiment bore this name with pride and valor throughout the history of the White Movement.

The death of Markov—the man, friend, and brilliant military leader—was an irreparable loss for Anton Ivanovich. "It left a great void in the army, in its spiritual life and the pathos of its heroic endeavor," wrote Denikin. "So many plans and hopes were tied to his name. So many times, later, when we were looking for a man among a terrifying array of nonentities, we sadly repeated, If only Markov were here." [10]

The entry into Ekaterinodar on August 3 was a highly emotional moment for Denikin and all those who had taken part in the First Campaign of the Volunteer Army. The city had acquired a kind of mystical meaning for them. Four months earlier, the Volunteers, heartbroken by the death of their beloved leader, Kornilov, were grimly retreating toward an unknown destination, closely pursued by the Bolsheviks and with little hope of escaping from their encirclement. Now, like a phoenix risen from the ashes, they marched into Ekaterinodar full of new hope and vigor. The liberated city met them with delirious enthusiasm. "A bright and joyous feast reigned in the churches, streets and houses and in human hearts," remembered Denikin.[11]

But the surge of optimism was soon marred by the dull and irritating trivialities of life and by the demands which the representatives of the Kuban government, whom the Volunteer Army had enabled to return to its capital, immediately put forward.

Having arrived from the farthest rear of the army at the Tikhoretskaia station, the members of the Kuban government wished to be the first to enter Ekaterinodar, thus showing themselves "the true masters of the situation." They asked General Denikin to delay his entry with the excuse that this would allow them to prepare "a fitting welcome" for him.

"However," wrote the General, "divisions of Volunteers were converging on the city, fighting was still in progress on the opposite shore of the river, and I was obliged, willy-nilly, to move my headquarters to the Ekaterinodar station. I left it only toward evening, when I couldn't resist taking a quiet drive through the familiar city, barely recognizable after the filth and destruction of the Bolshevik occupation and still afraid to believe in its liberation."

Denikin was deeply offended when he learned later that this perfectly natural and understandable action was held against him.

"My crafty politicians," thought the General, "had I but known that this would so offend your sense of sovereignty, I would have refused your celebrations altogether. Besides, what was there to prevent the government and *Rada* from entering Ekaterinodar with our cavalry, for example, when it was storming the city?" [12]

Despite the byplay of political intrigue behind the scenes, the welcoming celebrations for Denikin and his army took place in an atmosphere of solemnity and high enthusiasm. All members of the Kuban government and *Rada* came to Ekaterinodar on August 4, the day following its liberation. All of them made speeches praising the Volunteer Army's achievements. *Ataman* Filimonov asserted that, after completing the liberation of their homeland, the Kuban Cossacks would continue to fight for "A united and indivisible Russia."

Unfortunately, the promises to continue fighting for the liberation of Russia were mere lip service on the part of most of the members of the Kuban government and *Rada*. All they wished for was to be let alone by the conflicting parties, naïvely thinking that this was possible in the midst of a civil war. The Kuban leaders were against the Soviet power, but refused to understand that only a close alliance with the Volunteer Army could protect them from the Bolsheviks. At the same time, the immediate future of the Volunteer Army depended on the replenishments in manpower and cavalry horses which only the Kuban could provide.

The region's territory was about 82,000 square kilometers, and its population consisted of two distinct groups—the Chernomortsy (Black Sea people) and the Lineitsy (First-Liners).

The more numerous Chernomortsy were descendants of the ancient freedom-loving Cossacks of the Zaporozhie, on the lower reaches of the Dnieper River. While the ancestors of the Don Cossacks were fugitives from Muscovy, the Zaporozhie army was founded in the middle of the sixteenth century by Little Russian, or Ukrainian, peasants who escaped the bondage of the then powerful Polish gentry. When in 1775 Catherine the

Great disbanded the turbulent Zaporozhie army, and Russian troops occupied its stronghold, the Zaporozhie Sech, part of the Cossack army, fled
to Turkey. Those who remained in Russia were reorganized a few years
later into the Chernomortsy Cossack detachments and settled on virgin
land in the Kuban with the assignment of protecting its border from the
raids of the Caucasian mountaineers. There they were joined by their compatriots who had originally fled to Turkey, and later, by Ukrainian peasants
who migrated to the region in the nineteenth century. In the middle of
the century, the Chernomortsy Cossacks were renamed Cossacks of the
Kuban. There existed a natural bond between the descendants of the
Zaporozhie and those of the Ukrainian peasants, with whom they shared
the language and traditions of their former Ukrainian motherland.

Some ancestors of the Lineitsy came from the Don region, and others
were peasants from the central provinces of Russia and the province of
Stavropol. They were named Lineitsy or First-Liners, because in the 1830's
they became Russia's first line of defense when they were transplanted to
the northern part of the Caucasian range to defend the newly conquered
region and protect its communications with Transcaucasia. The Chernomortsy settled on the lower reaches of the Kuban River, while the
Lineitsy occupied its upper and middle reaches. The physical type of the
Lineitsy was predominantly central Russian, as was their language.

The Chernomortsy's political center was Ekaterinodar and that of
the Lineitsy was Armavir. Politically, the Chernomortsy intelligentsia
leaned toward Ukrainian separatism, while the Lineitsy favored the idea
of a unified Russia. The Chernomortsy outnumbered the Lineitsy both in
the government and in the *Rada*. This, according to Denikin, "determined
the entire political orientation of the Kuban and its relationship with the
Volunteer Army." [13]

Denikin sincerely and openly recognized the "need for maximum autonomy in the component parts of the Russian nation and for the most
meticulous respect for the ancient traditions of the Cossacks.[14]

At the same time, he flatly refused to recognize the Kuban's right to
proclaim itself a sovereign state, to have its own customhouses and foreign
policy, and to send its own delegates to the international conference which
would be called upon the termination of the World War. The political
atmosphere in Ekaterinodar was tense with the conflict resulting from
Denikin's opposition to the Chernomortsy's increasingly insistent demands.

The least acceptable of these was the insistence of the Kuban government that all Kuban Cossacks be withdrawn from the Volunteer Army and
reorganized into an autonomous Kuban army, subordinate to General
Denikin only in operational matters. Behind this move was the Chernomortsy's desire to offset the power of the Volunteers by their own troops,
which would enable them to dictate their own terms to the Volunteer
Army command. The reasons they gave officially, however, were quite

different. They cited the example of the Don region, which had its own army, their fear for the fate of the Kuban if the Volunteers withdrew from it, and many other factors. Needless to say, such a demand was totally unacceptable to Denikin, as it would deprive his army of half its manpower, including most of its cavalry.

At that time, the Cossack rank and file had no part in the discord which affected their political leaders; they simply followed their officers. The Kuban officers, trained in Russian military academies, viewed the events in the same way as Russian officers, and worked hand in hand with the Volunteers. They were suspicious of the activities of their government. Many of them would have liked to rid themselves of the troublesome Chernomortsy leaders, and the latter were quite aware of this.

Despite all the moral and political importance of Ekaterinodar, its taking by the Volunteers did not solve their overall strategic problems. Part of the Kuban was still in Bolshevik hands. The next stage planned by Denikin in the Second Kuban Campaign included not only the liberation of the whole Kuban region, but "the protection of the entire liberated territory and all of the North Caucasus by secure geographical borders—the Black and Caspian seas and the Caucasian range." [15]

The Black Sea, said Denikin, opened a window on Europe. It promised the liaison with the Allies for which he so fervently hoped, especially now that the swiftly approaching defeat of the Germans had become apparent. The United States had replaced Russia among the Allies and was bearing down on Germany with all its numerical and technical might.

On the other hand, having the Caspian Sea as an outlet would help establish communictions with the anti-Bolshevik movement which began with the Czech insurrection and was rapidly expanding over the Volga region and Siberia. It would also assure continuous contact with the British detachments which had made their way through Persia to the Caspian port of Enzeli.

In proportion to its size, the losses of the Volunteer Army were enormous. Between the start of the First Campaign and the fall of 1918, it had lost nearly thirty thousand killed and wounded Volunteers and Cossacks. The greatest number of casualties occurred in the First Officers' General Markov Regiment and the Kornilov Regiment. By the end of October, the Kornilov Regiment numbered "barely five hundred soldiers, although over five thousand men had already gone through its ranks." [16]

By that time, the military complement of all the army's regiments had been renewed many times over. The wounded and slain were constantly replaced by Kuban Cossacks and new volunteers arriving mainly from German-occupied Ukraine. At the beginning of August, the army had to resort to mobilization in order to refill its ranks, and toward the end of the year it made wide use of another source of manpower by impressing Red

Army prisoners. The four-month agreements previously accorded to Volunteer Army officers were terminated at the end of October. From then on, all officers under forty years of age were subject to the draft.

Denikin noted in his memoirs how these changes altered the moral image of the army and dulled its initial brightness, and how the monolithic unity of the original Volunteers began to fade into the realm of legend.

In August, after the capture of Ekaterinodar, when General Denikin was getting ready to continue the campaign, his army no longer numbered eight or nine thousand, but consisted of thirty-five to forty thousand men, with eighty-six cannon, 256 machine guns, five armored trains, eight armored cars, and two aviation units, with seven airplanes. All of these arms and ammunition had been captured from the Bolsheviks.

The scope of the Volunteer Army's operations was widening. Its formerly restricted front now stretched out over three to four hundred kilometers. This expansion obliged Denikin to revise his system of command. He was no longer able to lead his army in person, as he had done in the preceding five months.

"The strategic role played by individual army commanders grew in importance, while my direct influence on the troops became proportionately smaller.

"I used to lead the army. Now I only commanded it." [17]

By mid-August, General Denikin had succeeded in liberating the western part of the Kuban and in occupying Novorossiisk, thus acquiring an outlet on the Black Sea.

The theater of operations now switched to the eastern part of the Kuban region, where the Red troops were commanded by Sorokin.

News of the Volunteer Army's successes soon reached every town and village in the North Caucasus. Armed uprisings flared up in many places as the army approached. These uprisings were motivated by the plundering of the Red troops and by the fact that the population of the area was comparatively well off.

In some cases, the insurgent Cossacks formed partisan detachments which operated in the Bolshevik rear, raiding stocks of military supplies and blowing up sections of the railroad. The most outstanding partisan detachment was under the command of Colonel Shkuró, whose name soon became legendary. He was advancing to meet the Volunteers, seizing small and large cities on his way.

The local bourgeoisie of Kislovodsk, one of the Caucasian spas, enthusiastically welcomed Shkuró as their liberator, but soon found out to their horror that rumor had exaggerated the strength of his detachment. Shkuró's partisans had made a flying raid on the city, which they did not have the means to defend. The returning Bolsheviks avenged themselves mercilessly on the well-to-do sections of the population.

Somewhat later, Shkuró moved his detachment in the direction of Stavropol, the administrative center of Stavropol province, which borders the Kuban region. As he approached Stavropol, Shkuró sent an ultimatum to its commissars and to the head of the Soviet garrison to evacuate the city, which he otherwise threatened to bombard with heavy artillery. The Bolsheviks, shaken by rumors of the famous partisan's successes, took the threat seriously and left the city. In actual fact, according to Shkuró, his detachment did not possess a single piece of heavy artillery.[18]

The Volunteer command had not planned to move on Stavropol at the beginning of August, intending to do so only in a later phase of the campaign. However, in order to safeguard that city's population from the tragic fate of the citizens of Kislovodsk, Denikin decided to send several units of his army to Stavropol in support of Shkuró's detachment. In doing so, he realized that he was becoming involved in events which would inevitably distract his forces and attention from more immediate, previously planned actions and would delay their execution.

But, besides the fate of Kislovodsk, he had on his mind the horrible repressions which had struck the town of Armavir after it had been "liberated" and later abandoned by General Borovsky's Volunteer division. There, the returning Bolsheviks avenged themselves by exterminating over 1,500 citizens suspected of pro-White sympathies.

"Behind the abstract propositions of strategy," wrote Denikin in his memoirs, "and between the lines of reports joyfully announcing victories or laconically understating defeats—stared the blood-stained, tortured-to-death face of the man in the street. This phantom often moved me to tip the wrong side of the scales in deciding to alter a given plan of operations originally prepared according to the principles of military science."[19]

Despite its heavy losses, Sorokin's army had also grown considerably in that period. Besides the Taman units, it had absorbed large numbers of demobiziled soldiers from the Russo-Turkish front, which brought its contingent to 150,000 men and two hundred artillery pieces. The army was gradually emerging from the state of demoralization to which it had been brought by a long series of defeats and reverses. The *inogorodni* from the Kuban who had joined its ranks had an important part in this regeneration.

The Red army command was swayed by controversy regarding its future campaign plans. There were personal conflicts between individual commanders and between them and representatives of the local Soviet civilian authority.

Commander in Chief Sorokin did not see eye to eye with the commander of the Taman group—Matveev. When the latter refused to submit to Sorokin's orders, he was brought before a revolutionary court-martial and executed, which turned the Taman troops against Sorokin. At the same time, a conflict developed between Sorokin and the Central Executive Committee of the North Caucasus Soviet Republic. Sorokin knew that the Committee distrusted him, accused him of exceeding his power and of assuming dictatorial attitudes, and wanted to get rid of him. To forestall any such move, he decided to bring off a *coup* in Piatigorsk, the seat of the Committee, and to concentrate all the power in his own hands. In mid-October, Sorokin had the most prominent of the Committee members arrested and shot in the outskirts of the city. Nevertheless, his attempt failed. Surviving members of the Committee made their way to the front lines, whose representatives, incensed by Sorokin's conduct, officially. "outlawed" him as an enemy of the revolution. Having lost the support of his troops, Sorokin fled. While escaping, he was recognized, arrested, and shot during the questioning, by the commander of one of the Taman regiments.

Sorokin's insurrection led to frightful reprisals against Piatigorsk's bourgeoisie and intelligentsia, though they had no connection whatsoever with Sorokin. On October 18th the local *Cheka* ordered over a hundred suspected "class enemies" to be shot in reprisal for the execution of some members of the Central Executive Committee. In the mounting wave of Red terror, the unfortunate victims were slaughtered on the mere suspicion of being hostile to the Soviet regime.

Among the victims of this holocaust were two outstanding generals of the old army: Radko-Dimitriev and Ruzsky. The latter had been the commander in chief of the northern front in whose headquarters in Pskov Tsar Nicholas II had signed his abdication. Both generals had been offered important command posts in the Red Army and had signed their own death warrants by refusing them.

The rift in the higher echelons of Soviet power had left the army of the North Caucasus virtually leaderless. However, the rank and file and their immediate superiors, from company to regimental commanders, showed great resistance and determination. They recaptured Armavir and Stavropol from the Volunteers, but after twenty-eight days of bitter fighting, were finally obliged to retreat, having suffered heavy losses.

By the beginning of November, the entire Kuban region was cleared of Bolsheviks and by February, 1919, the operation conceived by Denikin for liberating all of the North Caucasus was finally completed.

The great, fertile, rich territory extending from the Black Sea to the Caspian, bordered in the south by the Caucasian mountain range, was now in Denikin's hands. Denikin had become a national figure, able at last to contemplate the ultimate aim of the Volunteer movement—the ousting of the Soviet power in Moscow.

General Denikin's victory prompted Trotsky to make contemptuous remarks about the defeated North Caucasian Red forces. He accused them of using partisan methods of warfare and of a complete lack of military organization. While this criticism was undoubtedly justified. Trotsky's reference to the bad morale of the Red troops was unfair, and Denikin took exception to it. He summarized as follows the results of this campaign and its effect on the enemy:

The hundred-thousand-strong army of the North Caucasus Bolshevik front had ceased to exist. It left in our hands fifty thousand prisoners, not counting the sick and wounded, 150 heavy guns, 350 machine guns, and enormous quantities of various equipment. It had covered the fields of Stavropol and the Caucasian foothills with its corpses. . . . For seven and a half months it had concentrated on itself almost all the Volunteer forces in the south, and for that alone should have received some recognition from the rulers in Moscow. But they have driven an aspen stake into its coffin and nailed a disparaging label to it. Thus I—the enemy—am obliged to defend the memory of the destroyed army before history. . . .

There is no doubt that the North Caucasus army was subject to the same failings which beset the other Red armies. It was obvious, however, that despite the lack of central guidance from which it suffered, its martial spirit . . . was immeasurably stronger than that of other Red armies, for we found it harder to cope with, and fighting it cost us relatively higher losses. And more than once, when seemingly utterly beaten, it sprang back to life again and again to resist the onslaught of the Volunteers.[20]

Many Volunteer Army commanders distinguished themselves in the Second Kuban Campaign. The most spectacular advancement, however, was that of the recently arrived general, Baron Peter Nikolaevich Wrangel.

General Denikin realized the paramount importance of mobility and maneuverability in a civil war and knew that they could only be achieved by cavalry forces. He was looking for a man who could create a powerful cavalry in the Volunteer Army, but saw no one in his command to whom such a task could be entrusted. He decided, therefore, to try out the talents of the newly arrived general, who had a reputation of a gifted and determined cavalry commander.

Denikin's conversation with Wrangel when the latter reported to him for the first time at the end of August, made an excellent impression on the commander in chief.

"How can we make the best use of your ability?" asked Denikin. "I am at a loss as to what to offer you. After all, we have so few troops."

"As your Excellency knows," answered General Wrangel, "I was commanding a cavalry corps in 1917, but as recently as 1914, I was still a squadron commander. I haven't aged so much since then as to be unable to return to this position."

"Well, not a squadron. . . . How about a brigade?"

"At your service, your Excellency." [21]

Since the revolution, Denikin had seen so many people whose conceit and self-interest came before the interests of the nation that he was pleasantly surprised by Wrangel's reaction to his offer. He liked Wrangel and was very favorably impressed by him.

Little did he know at that time that a year later, General Wrangel, an imperious and hard-driving man, would stand in open opposition to him and become a candidate for the post of commander in chief.

From the very beginning, Wrangel's achievements in the army amply fulfilled Denikin's expectations. He proved to be an outstanding cavalry leader with acute military judgment, prepared to assume responsibility and to make instant decisions. General Denikin appreciated his qualities of leadership, his ability to maneuver, and his drive. He had complete confidence in Wrangel and took pleasure in fostering his spectacular advancement in the army.

Exceptionally tall, lean, and wiry, Wrangel towered over the troops and impressed them by his resonant voice, martial appearance, and authoritative manner. He succeeded in obtaining the submission of such willful and independent leaders as Shkuró and Pokrovsky. He played an important role in the liberation of eastern Kuban from the Bolsheviks and in the subsequent battles around Stavropol and military operations in the North Caucasus.

As the Volunteer Army's size and influence expanded, the role played in it by Wrangel grew proportionately more important.

XVIII

SUMMER
AND FALL, 1918

Despite the Volunteer Army's important gains in the south, the attention of the Soviet government in the fall of 1918 was concentrated mainly on events in the east of Russia, where unrest in the region of the Middle Volga was becoming a serious threat to its power.

The uprisings of underground officer organizations, stimulated by the revolt of the Czechoslovak troops, had no definite political program. Their plans did not go beyond the overthrow of the Bolsheviks. The same was not true of the Socialist Revolutionary party, which had a considerable network of cells in the towns bordering the Volga. In Samara, on the left bank of that river, the local members of the party formed a Committee of Members of the Constituent Assembly (*Komitet Chlenov Uchreditelnogo Sobrania*, or *Komuch* for short). Although the names of these party members were unknown outside of their towns and districts, they declared themselves to be the nucleus of the future Russian government and set out to form a "People's Army." Colonel Moller, a Volunteer officer sent to establish a liaison with the Czechs, reported to Generals Alekseev and Denikin upon his return to the Kuban at the beginning of August, that the state of affairs in the "People's Army" reminded him of the Kerensky period. Discipline was nonexistent; the red flag was officially displayed; soldiers' committees flourished in the military units; military decorations and insignia were abolished and the soldiers were required to salute only their direct superior and that only once a day. Small wonder that under such conditions the officers, who in this area as everywhere else were the principal anti-Bolshevik element, regarded the local civilian authority with suspicion. They hoped to join forces with the Volunteer Army and to serve under the command of its leaders. General Alekseev had asked Colonel

Moller to explore the possibilities of support on the part of the Czechs and the Ural Cossacks, who were active in the provinces of the Lower Volga, in case the Volunteer Army moved in their direction. A completely unknown Captain Galkin, whom the Socialist Revolutionaries had placed at the head of the "People's Army" general staff, announced to Moller, "The Volunteer Army will bring us dissent and we must therefore avoid merging with it." [1]

The Volunteer Army was equally suspicious of the Socialist Revolutionaries, especially after it had learned that the actual, though unofficial, leader of the *Komuch* was Victor Chernov, a former "defeatist," subsequently Minister of Agriculture in Kerensky's cabinet, for whom the White generals represented a greater evil than the Bolsheviks.

The recruiting of the "People's Army" was unsuccessful. The peasants did everything to avoid military service, while the officers and bourgeoisie were unfavorable to the socialists' domination.

Nevertheless, despite their dislike of the political aspects of the *Komuch,* some officers, such as Colonel V. O. Kappel, sacrificed their feelings to the primary aim of overthrowing the Soviet government. They succeeded in assembling small but well-disciplined detachments, which aided by the Czechs, took Ufa at the end of June, Simbirsk at the beginning of July, and Kazan at the end of that month. The taking of Kazan had important consequences, as that city was the depository of the Russian gold reserve, evacuated there from Petrograd at the approach of the Germans. The gold reserve (651,500,000 gold rubles) first fell into the hands of the *Komuch* and later into those of the various successors of the Samara government. Although considerably depleted by unscrupulous individuals,[2] the bulk of the gold reserve later provided a substantial financial basis for the anti-Bolshevik forces in Siberia, while the Volunteer army in the south remained destitute throughout its existence.

Several local governments, vying for power with each other, sprang up in Siberia and in the Urals. They were gradually overshadowed by the regional government of Omsk, in western Siberia, which came into existence at the beginning of July. It was a coalition of Socialist Revolutionaries and liberals and adopted a more moderate political platform than the *Komuch*. The Omsk government proceeded to form a new Siberian army, which was joined by the Orenburg and Ural Cossacks and others who had decided to leave the "People's Army."

Inevitably, severe conflicts arose between the Omsk government and the *Komuch*. The latter's pretensions of becoming the supreme all-Russian power irritated the political leaders in Omsk. Meanwhile, the *Komuch*'s military strength was waning and the Bolsheviks, taking the initiative, were occupying one by one the cities it had ruled.

In this hopeless situation and under pressure from the Czechs, whose aims were strictly national, but who sympathized with the Russian Socialist Revolutionaries and were worried by the lack of unity among anti-

Bolshevik Russians, the *Komuch* decided to call a "state conference" in Ufa, a city on the western slope of the Ural Mountains, to which representatives from Omsk were invited, for the purpose of achieving a unified policy. The conference resulted in a compromise decision (which satisfied neither side) to form a Directory. The five members of the Directory consisted of two rightist Socialist Revolutionaries, two nonsocialists, and one army man, Lieutenant General Boldyrev.

Immediately after his election to the Directory, General Boldyrev was named Supreme Commander of All Anti-Bolshevik Armed Forces. Like Denikin and Kornilov, he was a peasant's son who had achieved a distinguished military career. He had been commander of the Fifth Army when the Bolsheviks came to power. His political views were more radical than Denikin's. The latter disapproved of Boldyrev and of the close ties with the leaders of revolutionary democracy which had linked his fate with theirs. Boldyrev's participation in the Union of Regeneration after the October revolution was the main reason for his being placed at the head of the Siberian army, despite the fact that his name was not nationally known and carried no prestige with the officers.

In spite of its almost accidental origin and its limited, provincial field of action, the Directory declared itself to be the provisional all-Russian government and the only supreme power in the entire Russian nation. It considered itself responsible only to the Constituent Assembly, which had been dispersed by the Bolsheviks on January 5, 1918. The Directory resolved that the Constituent Assembly would reconvene either on January 1, 1919, with a quorum of not less than 250 delegates, or on February 1, with a quorum of 170 delegates.

The association of the Directory with the Socialist Revolutionary Constituent Assembly immediately provoked antagonism in the Siberian army. As the Ufa Directory was subordinate to the Constituent Assembly, and by the same token, to the Socialist Revolutionary party, the officer corps was reluctant to recognize it as an "all-Russian government." In the eyes of the officers, the Socialist Revolutionaries had been elected as a majority party to the Constituent Assembly in the days of national insanity after Lenin had seized power. The negative attitude to the S.R.'s was based on their terroristic activity and their reliance on a peasant uprising in the period preceding the February revolution, and on the lack of organizing ability displayed by them after the downfall of the Romanovs. The officers regarded them as a politically destructive element.

General Denikin's attitude to the Directory was negative for the same reasons.

By the end of October, the Red Army at the eastern front had undergone considerable changes and was no longer a conglomeration of ill-assorted and poorly organized units. At its head was an experienced officer of the old army, Colonel of the General Staff Sergei Kamenev, who later became commander in chief of the armed forces of the Soviet Union. Assuming the offensive, the Red troops took Kazan, Simbirsk, and Samara and moved toward Ufa, with approximately 100,000 men and three hundred pieces of ordnance.

In the meantime, unrest broke out among the Czech troops, and by the fall of 1918, they no longer participated in military operations against the Red Army. The whole brunt of the struggle was carried by the Siberian White Army. It consisted at the time of 90,000 to 120,000 men, including drafted soldiers, and 263 pieces of ordnance. During the short period of the Directory's existence, it was commanded by General Boldyrev. He recognized the strategic necessity of linking the activities of the Siberian army with those of the Volunteer Army. However, as a member of the Directory and under the influence of his colleagues, he was motivated by political rather than strategic reasoning, and he decided to advance northward toward Archangel, on the White Sea. The local civilian authority in this British-occupied port was headed by the former Populist N. V. Chaikovsky, who recognized the Directory as the all-Russian government, whereas in south Russia Boldyrev expected to find "ideological alienation" and suspected that the creation of the Directory "would be received there without special enthusiasm." [3]

"One need only remember," wrote the military historian A. Zaitsov, "that the distance from the Ural at Ekaterinburg to Archangel was . . . 1700 kilometers, while the left flank of the eastern front [the Siberian army] at Novouzensk [in the province of Samara, on the left bank of the Volga River] was only three hundred kilometers away from Tsaritsin, to realize how little General Boldyrev's plans were influenced by purely military considerations." [4]

In addition to many other complicated and involved problems, General Denikin was extremely worried and irritated by the relationship with the newly formed Transcaucasian republic of Georgia.

In the spring of 1918, the Transcaucasian region had become a theater of the conflicting interests of Germany, Turkey, and England. At first, the Germans and Turks acted in unison in their effort to bar the British (who were advancing from Baghdad to the Caspian by way of Persia) from the rich oil wells of Transcaucasia. The disproportionately expanding Turkish influence, however, provoked measures by the Germans intended to curb the appetite of their ally. By establishing a protectorate over Georgia, Germany hoped to gain access to the Caucasian riches independently of Turkey. In June, 1918, Germany recognized Georgia as an independent republic and sent a diplomatic mission and a small detachment of German troops to Tiflis. This move was made easier by the fear which the possibility of a Turkish invasion evoked in the local Christian population. The Georgians, Armenians, and other non-Moslem elements in Transcaucasia, hoped that the Germans would shield them from the violence and fanaticism of the Turks and the local Moslems.

Meanwhile, the Volunteers, having liberated Novorossiisk, were moving southward along the Black Sea coast and made contact with detachments of the Georgian army below Tuapse. In a letter to the detachment commander, written in mid-August, General Alekseev expressed his joy that "fate . . . has made us allies" and the hope that "this alliance will assume a more permanent and all-embracing character." He sincerely believed in the possibility of close collaboration between the Volunteers and the Georgians in the anti-Bolshevik struggle.[5]

In this instance, the habitually skeptical Alekseev succumbed to quite unfounded optimism. The Georgian government was headed by former Mensheviks who in 1917 had been most active in the Petrograd Soviet of Workers' and Soldiers' Deputies. They had been antagonistic to the officer corps, and had contributed substantially to the disintegration of the army. Now, as the spokesmen of Georgian nationalism, they were in a mood to reject anything Russian. The slogan "A united and indivisible Russia" appeared to threaten their independence, while the possibility of complete victory by the Volunteers harbored the ghost of a return to the pre-revolutionary order. Their road and that of the Russian generals could never merge; their motivations and ultimate aims were too different. The Georgians did not wish to share with Alekseev and Denikin the huge amount of materiel which fell into their hands when the former Caucasian front disintegrated. Nor would they part with any of the large cash deposits of the Russian government in the local branches of the State Bank and Treasury. Having entered the sphere of German influence, Georgia had no choice but to submit its foreign policy to the will of the Germans, and the latter had no desire to strengthen the Volunteer Army.

All this soon became clear to General Alekseev. Nevertheless, he continued in his efforts to find a *modus vivendi* with Georgia and to reach a mutual agreement on the most important questions. In mid-September, a short time before his death, Alekseev invited the representatives of the Georgian government to come to Ekaterinodar in order to discuss them.

He welcomed "a friendly and independent Georgia" in the person of its foreign minister, Gegechkori, whom he assured that the Volunteer command would not attempt to endanger Georgia's independence. Despite this friendly greeting, the atmosphere of the conference rapidly deteriorated. The generals demanded the return to Russia of the Black Sea province of the Sochi district, annexed by Georgia, which Gegechkori flatly refused to grant. The conference broke up in an inimical atmosphere. "As a result of the failure to reach an agreement," wrote Denikin, "though I took no hostile action against Georgia, I nevertheless closed our border with it. Our troops remained south of Tuapse." [6]

Denikin's army was neither at war nor at peace with Georgia, and this meant that its border had to be guarded by troops which, though not numerous, could have been used to better advantage elsewhere.

At the beginning of August, 1918, rumors of the slaying of the imperial family in Ekaterinburg reached the Volunteer Army, and they were soon proved to be correct. The impact of the news was overwhelming. Despite the systematic terror engaged in by the Soviet regime, despite the cruelties of the civil war, which had blunted the sensibility of many, this murder brought home with extraordinary force all the savagery of the lawlessness and arbitrary rule which was sweeping the country, with no mercy left for women and children.

General Denikin ordered memorial services to be held. Officers and men of the Volunteer Army prayed with fervent concentration for the souls of the imperial family, and even those who disapproved of the monarchy felt deep respect for the memory of the Tsar who paid with his life for his voluntary and involuntary transgressions against the Russian people. Among nonmilitary circles, however, in the so-called "revolutionary democracy" the order to hold memorial services was criticized and condemned.

In his memoirs, Denikin wrote that "the profoundly horrified national conscience placed the blame for this crime on the German authorities who had an unlimited influence on the Soviet of Commissars but did not choose to use it to save the Tsar's family." [7]

In fact, the Germans had not chosen to use their influence in this instance. But even if they had demanded the release of the imperial family by the Bolsheviks, Lenin's inventive mind would have found some loophole for not carrying out such an order. Many excuses could be used: popular ire, refusal to submit to the central government on the part of local authorities, and finally, resistance and attempted escape on the part of the prisoners.[8]

General Denikin's attitude toward Tsar Nicholas II underwent several phases. Originally, he considered that the old regime had been psychologically undermined by the Tsar's unsuccessful rule, and blamed him for the consequences suffered by Russia. The murder of the Tsar evoked in Denikin feelings of profound indignation and pity. Finally, several years later, when he learned in detail with what dignity, patriotism, and true Christian humility the former monarch faced the approaching catastrophe, Denikin expressed his opinion concerning the late ruler as follows: "The image of the Tsar and his family, in the sense of their high patriotism and purity of soul, has recently been firmly established by indisputable historical documents." [9] However, Denikin's personal sympathy for the imperial family did not change his political convictions.

The need to create a governmental apparatus for the civilian administration of the land liberated from the Bolsheviks by the Volunteer Army became evident in August, 1918. The governing organization, named the Special Council, consisted of a number of departments under the chairmanship of General Alekseev. A Provisional Statute was adopted for use in the provinces occupied by the Volunteer army, until an all-Russian government came into existence. The entire civilian authority was concentrated in the hands of Alekseev, who, as we have seen, was responsible for most of the nonstrategic and nonmilitary aspects of the army. After his death, the civilian authority, too, devolved upon Denikin.

The Provisional Statute restored all the laws effective in Russia prior to October 25, 1917, which meant that the legislation enacted by the Provisional Government after the February revolution remained in force. The Statute recognized equal rights for all citizens regardless of race, class, or religion. It also recognized the special rights and privileges traditionally belonging to the Cossacks. A note was added to the effect that enforced appropriation of land, when necessitated by government and public interests, would be carried out only with due process of law and for a suitable remuneration.

Understandably, this paragraph aroused the suspicion of peasants who had helped themselves to the land of former estate owners and were sufficiently literate to understand its implications. In 1919, with the sweeping advance of the Volunteer Army into the Ukraine, the agrarian problem assumed an extremely serious aspect.

The dominating role in the Special Council was played by the military— first by General A. M. Dragomirov (a former commander in chief of the northern front), then by General A. S. Lukomsky (chief of staff of the Supreme Commander under Kornilov). The Special Council proved to be merely an inert advisory group for the commander in chief. It lacked the element of courageous creativity which the exceptional seriousness of the moment required.

General Alekseev's health was rapidly waning. He continued to devote all his energy to "his last labor on earth," but Anton Ivanovich could see that the end was approaching.

A careful man, Alekseev had the mind of a statesman, a wide understanding of political matters, and the ability to deal diplomatically with people whose views differed from his own. Denikin lacked the latter quality and admitted frankly that he was no diplomat. He sincerely liked and deeply respected Alekseev and dreaded the profound solitude in which the old general's death would leave him. He realized how unprepared he was to assume the responsibilities of civilian administration, not to mention the increasingly complex problems of state which were bound to come up as the territory occupied by Volunteer troops grew in size.

General Alekseev died in Ekaterinodar on September 25, 1918.

"In the years of the great turmoil," wrote Anton Ivanovich, "at a time when people altered with incredible ease their moral outlook, views, and 'orientation'; when confused or slippery individuals followed dark and devious paths, he marched on with his firm, aging tread along a straight but stony path. His name was a banner which drew together people of the most different political aspirations, by its aura of wisdom, integrity, and patriotism." [10]

After Alekseev's death, Denikin assumed the title of commander in chief. Contrary to his wishes, fate compelled him to shoulder too heavy a burden—the combined responsibilities of the civilian administration and the high command of the army.

In the meantime, Denikin's most faithful collaborators were dying one by one. He wrote that the "ranks of old Volunteers were growing thin in continuous combat and from typhus, which raged in the army. New graves arose every day near the obscure villages and settlements of the Caucasus." [11] Colonel Mionchinsky, the valiant artillery commander, was killed in action; General Drozdovsky died of blood poisoning after being wounded near Stavropol. Many of Denikin's closest associates were taken in this way, leaving him alone in the face of a long and harrowing struggle.

Denikin's relations with General Drozdovsky, a nervous and hot-tempered man, had often been quite strained. Following a military operation which, in the commander's opinion, was badly planned by Drozdovsky, Denikin officially reprimanded him. Drozdovsky was offended and countered with a report couched in quite unacceptable terms. The tone of the report could not be tolerated from the point of view of military discipline. Yet, any harsh measures might have led to a complete break with Drozdovsky, which Denikin would not consider. The problem was solved by Denikin's chief of staff, General Romanovsky, who advised Drozdovsky that his report was couched in such harsh terms that he could not convey it to the army commander. Drozdovsky never raised that question again, but rumors concerning the incident reached the army and were later used to undermine the reputation of Romanovsky, who was accused of "withholding the truth" from General Denikin.

After Drozdovsky's death, Denikin renamed the regiment he had brought from Rumania to join the Volunteer army, the Drozdovsky Regiment. It was responsible for many of the outstanding feats in the history of the White movement.

About a month before General Alekseev's death, the latter's state of health forced General Denikin to assume the new role of political chief. He subsequently made two speeches, one in August and one in November, 1918, in which he outlined the general political premises of the Volunteers.

On August 26, during his first visit to Stavropol, he stated:

In the pursuance of its painful endeavor, the Volunteer Army desires the support of all nationally oriented layers of the population. It cannot become the instrument of any single political party or civic organization. But although the army does harbor some definite political tendencies, it will never become an executioner of other people's thoughts and conscience. It says openly and sincerely: Be you rightists or leftists, love your tormented motherland and help us save it. . . . The Volunteer Army is not concerned with social and class struggle. The hard and painful days in which we live, when Russia is reduced to mere shreds, are not the right time for solving social problems. And each different part of the Russian state cannot build Russian life according to its individual wishes. For this reason, members of the Volunteer Army, to whom fate has delegated the arduous task of governing, will under no conditions attempt to alter the fundamental laws of the country. Their role is only to bring about bearable conditions of life that will allow us to live and breathe until such time as all-Russian law-making institutions, representing the thinking and conscience of the Russian people, will channel its destiny along a new course—toward light and truth.[12]

Denikin's second speech concerning the attitude and policy of the Volunteer Army was delivered on November 1, the opening day of the Kuban *Rada* in Ekaterinodar. It called for unity and spoke of the Kuban's need to maintain a close relationship with the Volunteer Army in its own interest, as the latter was its only safeguard against a Bolshevik invasion from the north. Denikin pointed out that the cruel conditions of the civil war made it imperative to have a single army under one command. He also stated, "The Volunteer Army recognizes the present and future need for the most comprehensive autonomy of the component parts of the Russian state as well as the most careful consideration for the ancient traditions of Cossack life." [13] The rest of his address was more or less a restatement of his earlier speech.

It should be noted that General Denikin's views on the aims of his movement and its attitude toward a future form of government have never changed. At the end, as at the beginning of his command, he expressed the same ideas. For example, on January 16, 1920, at a session of the Supreme Cossack *Krug,* he declared: "My task is the liberation of Russia. The form of government is a secondary problem to me. And should a struggle arise with relation to the form of government at some future time, I shall not take part in it. In all good faith, however, I consider it equally possible to serve Russia honestly under a monarch or a republic, provided one is certain that such is the wish of the Russian people." [14]

Looking back at his past, Denikin wrote, "In spite of everything, our two basic premises—the refusal to predetermine the form of government and the refusal to consider the possibility of collaborating with the Germans—were in fact observed by us to the very end." [15]

"The idea that the struggle against Bolshevism was at the same time a struggle against Germany had a profound moral significance for the anti-Bolsheviks," wrote Milyukov. "And the whole attempt to separate the aim of the civil war from that of the Allied one was interpreted as treacherous with respect to the Allies. We shall see," wrote Milyukov with irony, "how the Allies repaid this loyalty." [16]

As the territory captured by the Volunteer Army grew larger, the chances of contact with German occupational forces increased. To forestall this possibility, Denikin issued concise instructions to the army leaders ordering them not to initiate hostile action against the Germans without provocation, but to avoid any possibility of contact and any intercourse with them. Nevertheless, those to whom these instructions were addressed were also advised that the army was prepared to buy military supplies from the Germans "in exchange for local products." [17]

German officers initiated several meetings with various Volunteer Army commanders, during which they behaved very correctly and politely. The courtesy which individual German officers continued to extend privately to members of the Volunteer Army command did not reflect the subsequent overall policy of the German government, which after unsuccessfully attempting to subvert the Volunteer leaders in its favor, decided on a different course of action. While officially it ignored the existence of the Volunteer Army, it now made every effort to undermine it. To stem the flow of volunteers from the Ukraine to Denikin's army, Germany decided to create some competition for it. It secretly financed the formation of two other anti-Bolshevik "armies"—the Astrakhan and Southern armies. The recruiting for them took place in Kiev. The armies were assembled on territories assigned for that purpose by *Ataman* Krasnov—on the Don for the Astrakhan army and in the southern section of Voronezh province (occupied at that time by Don Cossacks) for the Southern army. Both armies openly adopted monarchist slogans and slandered the leaders of the Volunteer movement, accusing General Alekseev of betraying the Tsar and calling the Volunteer Army "a republican undertaking."

Their recruiting, however, made little progress. Nevertheless, the Germans succeeded by these means in sowing political discord among officers and in temporarily discouraging a few thousand people from joining the ranks of the Volunteer Army.

During that whole period, General Denikin had only one official exchange with the German command: His representative in the Don region, General Elsner, communicated to him an official request of the German command to speed up the restoration of the Indo-European telegraph line, which passed through territory occupied by the Volunteers. The Germans offered to supply personnel for mending and servicing the line. General Elsner was instructed to reply that "no outside help was needed." Some three weeks later, the Germans renewed their demands in a more insistent form. They not only requested that the Indo-European line be placed at the disposal of the German command, but demanded a definite answer within five days. General Denikin replied through Elsner that "as the telegraph lines were gradually mended, they were placed at the service of the public." [18]

Fortunately for Denikin, this correspondence had no aftereffects, as a few days later Germany admitted its defeat in the World War, and there followed the incredibly rapid moral disintegration of the German troops.

XIX

HOPE AND

DISILLUSIONMENT

At some of the most difficult moments of his life—as when in July, 1917, his troops on the western front refused to obey his orders to advance, or when in September of the same year, a mob of soldiers, carried away by hate propaganda, was threatening to lynch him in Berdichev—strangely enough, at those moments, when he was literally facing death, Anton Ivanovich would sometimes think of Ludendorff, who had so efficiently assisted in the disintegration of the Russian army.

Denikin knew that he himself would have had the strength "not to flinch before death," and he was curious to know what Ludendorff, that monolith of Germany's war power, would do if fate happened to involve him in a similar situation.

His hypothetical question was answered very clearly after the fall of Germany: General Ludendorff fled to Sweden from the specter of a possible revolution, while the Kaiser (whom Denikin considered to be the principal initiator of World War I and who had not moved a finger to save the Russian Tsar and his family) escaped to Holland. These two men, confident in their ultimate victory, had gambled in 1914 with a countless number of human lives. But when the reckoning came and their game proved to be a losing one, they abandoned their country to save their own lives.

By contrast, Denikin had nothing but sincere sympathy for the officers of the German and Austro-Hungarian armies. He felt sorry for these men who through no fault of theirs had found themselves in the same situation as the Russian officers a year earlier. The disintegration of their troops went through the same stages as had that of the Russian army, but with an even more catastrophic rapidity. Following the Russian pattern, soviets of workers' and soldiers' deputies sprang up all over Germany like mushrooms. Mass desertion prevailed on the Austro-German Eastern Front. Soldiers refused to obey their officers and expressed their distrust of them at public meetings. Soldier mutinies, in which officers were humiliated and killed, flared up in various parts of the zone occupied by the Central Powers. Driven to despair by the chaos which raged in the Austrian divisions, the Austrian army commander in Odessa committed suicide. Austrian officers fled in all directions to escape from their soldiers. And in the meantime, Moscow's propaganda was doing its best to fan the fire of revolt by summoning the German proletariat to make short work of the officers and bourgeoisie and seize power in their own hands.

The fate of the vast territory occupied in south and west Russia by the Central Powers became an immediate and burning question as soon as their downfall set in.

Denikin's army was then concentrating all its efforts on the liberation of the North Caucasus and the regions east of the Kuban. Even if its efforts in this direction succeeded, the army was still too small and poorly armed to undertake the occupation of the Ukraine, Novorossia, and the Crimea. It needed a respite, during which the Red armies had to be prevented at all costs from invading the vast and rich areas abandoned by the Germans. Such a respite, in Denikin's opinion, could be provided only by Allied troops, functioning not as fighting forces, but solely as garrisons replacing the Austro-Germans in maintaining order and stemming the wave of anarchy which was already threatening the abandoned regions. Furthermore, the staying power afforded by the Allies would give the Volunteers a base for the formation of a Russian army and a springboard for its future operations. Denikin would thus be able to complement his troops by mobilizing the local population and to obtain supplies from the still-plentiful stockpile of materials assembled for the former Russian southwestern and Rumanian fronts. Finally, he would have time to complete preparations for the achievement of his principal aim: an offensive directed at the center of Russia.

The atmosphere of phenomenal changes—the triumph of the Allies and the downfall of Germany—seemed to hold great promise for Denikin. At the same time, however, he was troubled by the uncertainty and indefiniteness of the whole situation. He needed to know exactly to what extent he could count on the Allies' aid.

In an attempt to clarify this question, Denikin requested General Shcherbachev (the last Russian commander at the Rumanian front who had remained in that country) to approach the French General Berthelot, who had been sent to Bucharest as Commander in Chief of the Allied forces in Rumania, Transylvania, and South Russia.

Shcherbachev knew Berthelot quite well. He reported to Denikin on November 3, 1918, that the results of his interview with the French general had exceeded all expectations. According to him, General Berthelot, who enjoyed Clemenceau's support, was authorized "to plan and implement all political and military measures relating to the south of Russia and its safeguarding from anarchy." The agreement with General Berthelot, which Shcherbachev communicated to Denikin, contained the following principal points:

Twelve divisions will be sent as soon as possible to occupy the south of Russia. One of them is expected to reach Odessa within the next few days.

The divisions will consist of French and Greek troops.

At the request of the Allies and General Berthelot, I [General Shcherbachev] shall be attached to the latter and shall participate in all his decisions.

The Allied base is Odessa; Sebastopol will also be occupied without delay.

The Allied troops in south Russia will be commanded at first by General d'Anselme, with headquarters in Odessa.

Besides Odessa and Sebastopol, which they will undoubtedly have occupied by the time this letter reaches you, the Allies plan to occupy, soon after their arrival, Kiev and Kharkov, with the Krivoirog and Donets basins, the Don region, and the Kuban, in order to allow the Volunteer and Don Cossack armies the possibility of consolidating their strength and to leave them free to engage in wider active operations.

Odessa, as the principal Allied base, will receive huge quantities of war supplies of all kinds—arms ammunition, tanks, clothing, railroad and highway equipment, airplanes, foodstuffs, etc.

The rich stockpiles at the former Rumanian front, in Bessarabia and the Ukraine, as well as the ones at the Don, can from now on be considered at your complete disposal. . . .

"This precisely worded letter," remembered Denikin later, "finally put an end to mere speculation on our part. Its all-embracing and concrete treatment of the question opened up new and extremely favorable perspectives . . . in our anti-Bolshevik campaign." [1]

On November 10 (Julian calendar), an Allied fleet composed of two destroyers and two cruisers (*Ernest Renan* and *Liverpool*) arrived in Novorossiisk. "Novorossiisk, then Ekaterinodar," wrote Denikin, "greeted the Allies with boundless enthusiasm, with all the fire of the Russian temperament and all the passion of hearts that had been tortured by expectation, misgivings, and hopes. The streets of Ekaterinodar swarmed with people whose loud, spontaneous and wholehearted rejoicing could not fail to elicit a warm response in their guests." [2]

The speeches exchanged by the new arrivals and those who welcomed them emphasized their mutual friendship and their hopes for a speedy end to the Bolshevik oppression. General Denikin expressed his heartfelt wishes for the well-being of France and England, promising that Russia, "not this ragged and helpless one, but a new, strong, and united Russia, would never forget this disinterested and friendly assistance." In his answering speech, Great Britain's representative, General Poole, reminded his listeners of the first years of the World War: "We did not and never will forget how you saved us by your heroic efforts in 1914, when our situation was critical. We shall never forget that although you found yourselves in the direst circumstances, you did not throw in your lot with the Germans, but risked all and remained faithful to the end to your allies." General Poole went on to speak of the mutual aim and desire of his country and the Volunteers to re-create a united Russia. The French representative, Erlich, with characteristic French oratory and an excellent command of Russian, talked of the Kremlin towers, of the red flag steeped in the blood of innocent victims, and of his conviction that this flag would soon be superseded by the "glorious tricolored banner of a great, united, and indivisible Russia." He, also, promised France's assistance to the Volunteers.[3]

The promises of the Allies were not limited to the statements of Berthelot and of the military representatives of Great Britain and France in Ekaterinodar. A conference including participants from France, Great Britain, the United States, and Italy was called in the Rumanian city of Jassy, in November, 1918, in order to consult with the representatives of anti-Bolshevik public opinion in Russia.[4]

The Allies were fairly well informed by their military intelligence as to the aspirations of various Russian political groups in Kiev. They decided, nevertheless, to hear out at the Jassy conference the opinions of all militantly anti-Bolshevik parties, from the monarchists at the right, to the Socialist Revolutionaries at the left. For that purpose they invited the most prominent Russian political leaders from Kiev, and asked General Denikin to send a representative of the Volunteer Army to the conference.

As was to be expected, disagreements immediately sprang up among the delegates, concerning the future form of the Russian government. The monarchists insisted on a military dictatorship headed by Grand Duke Nicholas. The latter was living at that time in his brother's Crimean estate, Dulber. He led a very secluded life, completely devoid of politics, behaved with great dignity, and would have nothing to do with the German forces of occupation.

The National Center, headed by Milyukov and Fedorov, also advocated a dictatorship, but with General Denikin in the leading role. The leftist groups, however, though not objecting to Denikin's military leadership, were advocating a directory of three, which would include, besides Denikin, two prominent representatives of leftist political parties.

Disappointing the hopes of its participants, the Jassy conference brought no results. The French and British ambassadors, on the mistaken assumption that their governments were about to engage in massive intervention in Russia, had called the conference on their own initiative. The Russian delegates, encouraged by their hosts, entrusted six of their members with the task of conveying the good wishes and hopes of south Russia to the Allied governments. Their mission ended on a rather undignified note: When the group arrived in Paris, "Clemenceau not only refused to receive the Russian delegation, but expelled it from Paris because of the alleged 'pro-German' leanings of one of its members." The member who became *persona non grata* was Milyukov, from whose account we have just quoted.[5]

The failure of the Jassy conference was an example of the extent to which Allied policy vis-à-vis Russia was poorly planned and badly coordinated. Thus, the local Allied representatives, while acting in good faith, gave completely unjustified hopes to the anti-Bolshevik camp.

The armistice conditions between the Allies and Germany, called for the withdrawal of German troops from the Russian regions occupied by them, to the prewar borders of Russia. There was, however, no deadline for this evacuation. The population of the Ukraine never doubted that the Allies would replace the departing Germans, and were upheld in this conviction by the representatives of France who began to reach Kiev even before Germany's final defeat. Nevertheless, the timing of the Allies' arrival was of the utmost importance for the bourgeois population in the Ukraine, as a lapse of time between the withdrawal of the Germans and the arrival of the Allies would represent an acute danger for them. They feared not only the organized forces of the Bolsheviks but a reaction on the part of the peasants, who might very well avenge all the requisitions and repressions they had suffered at the hands of the Germans by storming and looting the towns which harbored the landowners and the bourgeoisie.

The mood of the Ukrainian peasantry was anarchistic. They were anxious to proceed as soon as possible with a redistribution of the land and a settling of accounts with the landowners who had been reinstated in their holdings by the Hetman's government. The peasant movement was stimulated and led by self-styled *atamans* and organizers of armed bands. They made good use of the arms hidden in the villages since the fall of 1917 by the masses of soldiers deserting from the front. They also bartered village produce for military supplies from the demoralized German occupational troops, thus acquiring army horses, firearms and even cannon.

Hetman Skoropadsky's government had held out solely through the help of the Germans' military prestige. While they made use of the *Hetman* for their own purposes, the Germans never allowed him to organize any independent military forces of significance. Left to his own devices, Skoropadsky was totally helpless.

In the meantime, the members of the Ukrainian *Rada,* the socialists whom the Germans had so unceremoniously dispersed in the spring of 1918 and replaced by the *Hetman,* were returning to power. They formed a Ukrainian directory whose members included V. K. Vinnichenko, a socialist and separatist who later went over to the Bolsheviks, and Simon Petliura, also a socialist, who assumed the title of Head *Ataman.*

Vinnichenko [wrote Denikin] issued decrees of a completely Bolshevik type, on socialization, nationalization, and the leveling of bourgeois property. His appeals fell on fertile soil in a countryside which had not yet experienced the whole gamut of Bolshevik rule, and gave rise to pogroms, arson, banditry, and murder. Again, as at the beginning of that year, the turbulence was not motivated by national considerations. The [Ukrainian] directory fanned the flames of social passions in the hope of gaining popular support, and was later unable to localize them. . . . Long before the directory assumed any semblance of control, those who observed conditions in the Ukraine at that time, were unanimous in their predictions that the directory would be but a short and inglorious period of transition to actual Bolshevism; and when that period finally came about, it was recognized as the most anarchical of all . . . the regimes that had succeeded each other in the Ukraine.[6]

The inhabitants of Kiev made frantic but ineffective attempts to organize officer detachments for their protection. The new French consul, Hénaud, arriving from Odessa with "emergency powers," assured them in the name of his government of the speedy arrival of Allied troops and affirmed that the Entente would never permit the entry of Petliura's bands into the Ukrainian capital.[7]

Time passed, and still the Allies did not come. By the end of November, 1918, panic in the city had reached a climax, and on December 1, *Hetman* Skoropadsky fled to Germany, disguised as a wounded German officer. On the same day, Petliura's bands invaded the unresisting city and began to massacre the officers.

The Germans did not choose to interfere with Petliura's activities. In fact, they rather welcomed them. Pleased with the loss of face of the Allies, who had failed so dismally to keep their promise, they observed with satisfaction how rapidly Allied prestige was falling among the terrified inhabitants of Kiev.

In the meantime, the Allies' victory over Germany necessitated a complete revision of their policy toward Russia. Their intervention in Russia in the summer of 1918 had been justifiable as a measure directed against the Central Powers. Since Germany's defeat, however, Russia could no longer be considered a tool to be used in combating that country. At this point, the problem of whether or not to continue the intervention became complex and debatable. On the one hand, the Allied armies were exhausted by four years of war, and the morale of the troops could be seriously affected if they were sent to a new front to participate in the remote, and to them incomprehensible, Russian civil strife. On the other hand, there were strong feelings in British and French government circles against the Bolsheviks, who had dared to confiscate foreign property in Russia, annul all Russian debts to the Allies, and publish the latter's secret agreements with the Tsarist government. Finally, the Bolsheviks brandished the far from empty threat of world revolution, which under prevailing conditions, could flare up in the vanquished countries and spread all over central Europe. These considerations were strengthened by sincere moral indignation provoked by the Red terror and the Bolsheviks' ruthless reprisals against all anti-Communists.

These conflicting considerations in the Allied camp were not conducive to an all-out anti-Bolshevik effort. At best, they led to half measures, such as supplying the Volunteer Army with materiel without involving any troops in actual armed intervention.

As a result of poor communications with Western Europe, Denikin was not aware of the fluctuations of opinion in the Allied capitals. Letters and telegrams were routed through Constantinople, with considerable delays. Denikin waited impatiently for the help which had been so definitely promised him, and could not understand why it was not forthcoming.

Meanwhile, one Ukrainian city after another fell into Petliura's hands. On November 28, three days before the fall of Kiev, one of his bands entered Odessa, which offered no resistance. This was the city which General Berthelot had chosen as the principal Allied base in south Russia!

At that time, Odessa harbored innumerable refugees, most of whom had fled Kiev in fear for their lives. Bourgeois and intellectuals, rich and poor alike, discovered to their dismay that their hopes for Allied protection were unfounded. Panic gripped the city with its multiracial population and influx of refugees.

Part of Odessa was declared a neutral zone under the French flag, and placed under the protection of a Polish detachment whose presence in the city was purely coincidental.[8] A detachment of local Volunteers, whose morale by that time was fairly low, was feverishly reorganized and armed. Its command was assumed by General A. N. Grishin-Almazov. This self-assured and ambitious young man had been a mere lieutenant colonel in 1917. After the Bolshevik *coup*, Grishin, under the assumed name of Almazov, became extremely active in underground officer organizations. He happened to be in Omsk when the Siberian Directory was organized, and in the absence of more experienced candidates, was offered the position of minister of war. Friction between him and his colleagues, however, soon led to his dismissal. In October, 1918, he made his way from Siberia to Ekaterinodar. General Denikin, who knew nothing about him, greeted him with restraint. He was impressed, however, with his report on the Siberian situation and decided to send him to Rumania to acquaint the Volunteer Army and Allied representatives there with the military and political state of affairs in Omsk. Grishin-Almazov arrived in Odessa on his way back to Ekaterinodar, at a time when lack of military leadership again placed him in a position of command. By drastic measures, he succeeded within a few days in getting a grip on the Volunteer detachment entrusted to him and whipping it into shape.

On December 4, Odessa's inhabitants, who by that time had lost all faith in the promises of the French, were surprised by the news that French troop carriers were approaching the port with landing forces consisting of an infantry brigade with artillery and a cavalry regiment. General Borius, who commanded these troops, ordered the Petliura forces to evacuate the city. Having received a negative answer, he readily agreed to Grishin-Almazov's proposal to force the enemy out of the city with his Volunteer detachment. This operation was successful. The Volunteers cleared the city in twenty-four hours, and the Petliura forces retreated some distance to the north where they encamped in a semicircle around Odessa.

General Borius, delighted that not a drop of French blood had been spilled, offered Grishin-Almazov the post of military governor of Odessa. Grishin-Almazov reported his acceptance of this offer to Denikin, assuring him at the same time of his complete loyalty and requesting the commander in chief to confirm him in his post, which would enable him to govern Odessa in the name of the Volunteer Army.

"This unexpected addition to our territory," wrote Denikin, "though it accorded with our idea of unifying south Russia, further complicated the difficult situation of the Volunteer Army by the added burden of moral responsibility for the fate of a great city surrounded by the enemy and requiring food and supplies. And even more importantly, a city with an extremely tense political atmosphere. But the Russian tricolor had already been raised over Odessa, and this committed us. I confirmed Grishin-Almazov as military governor of the city and its vicinity and instructed him to call its officers to arms." [9]

Thus, quite unexpectedly, and against his better judgment, General Denikin became involved in a joint enterprise with the French, whose command held the upper hand and with whom his own opinions carried little weight. France's political fluctuations, the remoteness of the French command from Paris, due to defective communications, and a similar remoteness of Odessa from Ekaterinodar, could hardly be expected to result in wholehearted collaboration between the French and the Russian Volunteers.

The French immediately came to grips with the complicated maze of Russian political factions—their dissensions, intrigues, and inability to reach a compromise. These tortuous political contradictions were further complicated by the problem of Ukrainian separatism, which its advocates tried to promote as a national movement. They were located outside of Odessa, and the French found it difficult to ascertain whether they really represented the wishes of the popular masses. All Russian circles, including right-wing Socialist Revolutionaries, stood for a unified Russia, and assured the French that the conception of an independent Ukraine did not reflect the wishes of the peasants, that the whole idea of separatism was alien and artificial, that the revolutionary unrest in the countryside (which had no nationalist overtones) was being exploited by the small group headed by Vinnichenko and Petliura, for its own purposes.

Neither the local French command nor its government in Paris had a definite plan of action. Declarations that Bolshevism must be combated to the bitter end were uttered in the same breath with the slogan that not one drop of French blood was going to be shed.

Grishin-Almazov advocated expanding the Allied zone around Odessa, which was cut off by Petliura's bands from its sources of food and forage. Even the city water supply was controlled by the enemy. However, General Borius, whose orders were limited to the occupation of Odessa, refused to take action. Moreover, he declined Grishin-Almazov's offer to perform the operation with the Volunteer detachment, which at that time consisted of 1,600 men and fifty-six officers, with ten pieces of ordnance.

Petliura's units were gradually becoming demoralized under the influence of Bolshevik propaganda, while Red Army units, taking advantage of the French command's indecision, advanced unopposed on Kharkov, Chernigov, and Kiev. These cities fell without a struggle, and the members of the Ukrainian directory were forced to flee to Vinnitsa. Realizing that his venture was doomed, and seeing how easily his troops defected to the Bolsheviks, Petliura sought the possibility of reaching an agreement with the French.

In the meantime, relations between the French command and the representatives of the Volunteer Army were becoming more and more strained. At the beginning of January, 1919, General d'Anselme replaced General Borius at the head of the French command. In political matters, he closely followed the advice of his chief of staff, Colonel Freidenberg. In the absence of clear directives from Paris, the French command had to improvise its own policy, and Freidenberg, to whom this role was delegated, immediately assumed a position opposed to the Volunteer Army. He rejected the offer to enlarge the Russian contingent by mobilization, and at the same time, entered into negotiations with representatives of the Ukrainian directory, which had already lost all its significance. The Volunteers were understandably nonplussed by this move, in which French policy blatantly contradicted the principle of Russian unity.

Nevertheless, Freidenberg's negotiations with the bands of Petliura (who clutched at this straw in pure desperation) led to the lifting of their blockade of Odessa and allowed the French command, gradually reinforced by the arrival of additional Allied troops, to extend the zone of occupation without any risk, incorporating from west to east the semicircle of Tiraspol, Birzula, Nikolaev, and Kherson. In the middle of March, 1919, Allied forces in the Odessa district consisted of two Greek divisions, one and a half French divisions, a Polish brigade, and a Volunteer brigade, totaling between 40,000 and 45,000 men.

By that time, despite Freidenberg's opposition, the Volunteer brigade had grown to five thousand men. Its cadres were those of several infantry regiments stationed in Odessa before the beginning of the World War. Its command was taken over by Major General Timanovsky, who had fought with Denikin in the Iron Brigade and in the First and Second Kuban campaigns, and whom the latter had sent to Odessa from Ekaterinodar. Ti-

manovsky became field commander of the Russian units in Odessa, whereas
Grishin-Almazov assumed certain administrative functions as well as
those of chief liaison officer between Ekaterinodar and the local French
command. In his efforts to arm the Volunteer brigade, Timanovsky encountered new difficulties put in his way by Colonel Freidenberg. He intended to use for the brigade the old Russian army's stockpiles of rifles,
cannon, and ammunition in Tiraspol and Nikolaev. Freidenberg, however,
declared that Tiraspol lay outside the zone assigned to the Volunteer Army
and that Nikolaev was in the zone of the Ukrainian directory. One can
imagine the reaction of the Volunteers to this declaration.[10]

Communications between Ekaterinodar and Odessa were extremely
poor and consisted almost entirely of correspondence carried by the rare
and irregular steamers cruising between Odessa and Novorossiisk.

Hence, the complicated picture of events in Odessa was never clearly
understood in Ekaterinodar, where the conflict of the Volunteers with
the French command in Odessa was partly blamed on the little-known
personality of Grishin-Almazov. The Volunteer command, therefore, decided to replace him with the well-known and respected General A. S.
Sannikov, who was in charge of the Volunteer Army's ordnance and
supplies department and had occupied the same position at the Rumanian front during the war. Since he had been governor of Odessa under
Hetman Skoropadsky, he was familiar with local conditions.

Upon his arrival in Odessa, Sannikov called on General d'Anselme and
discovered to his dismay that the French general was unable to understand by what right General Denikin "appointed people in a region
occupied by French troops." Freidenberg too showed no desire to cooperate with General Sannikov. Relations became even worse when the
French decided to form new military units, to be called "mixed brigades,"
which were to consist of Russians from the Odessa region commanded
by French officers. The French also demanded that General Sannikov
fully submit himself to the French command "with respect to the use of
Russian troops."

Upon learning this, General Denikin sent two sharply worded telegrams
to General Sannikov, who was to relay their content to the French command.

In the first telegram, Denikin instructed Sannikov to coordinate his
activity in every possible way with the French, and permitted him to
submit the Russian units to the French command in operational matters
only (this, in view of the numerical superiority of Allied troops in the
Odessa district). "In every other respect, military, political, or civic,"
read the telegram, "you are under my command and can receive orders
only from me."

The second telegram concerned the plan to form "mixed brigades,"
which provoked a sharp reaction from Denikin. He could not understand
how the French allies, who had come to Russia to join forces with him,

could fail to understand that the formation of such units would undermine the authority of the Volunteer Army and its command, how they could fail to take into consideration the fact that the French basic pay, when compared to the miserable salary of the Volunteers, would attract to the "mixed brigades" the less idealistic elements in the officer corps.

"I categorically forbid you to experiment with Russian troops at the dictation of foreigners," telegraphed Denikin to Sannikov. He also ordered him to circulate an official announcement in Odessa that any Russian officer who enrolled in the "mixed brigades" would be court-martialed.

At the same time, Denikin wrote a personal letter to General Berthelot, giving all the reasons which have just been mentioned and pointing to the "terrible consequences which would result from the measures contemplated by the French command." The letter ended with this question: "What was the purpose of the Allies' arrival? To lend their help to a mortally wounded Russia or to subject it to their occupation with all the dire consequences that we would have to suffer as its result?" [11]

Until that time, Denikin had counted on a mutual collaboration between his representatives and the French military authorities. He had never expected that the French would simply consider Odessa as their zone of occupation. Now, having lost all patience and restraint, he proceeded to express his opinions to the French command with soldierly simplicity. Quite naturally, Denikin's directness irritated the French, and General d'Anselme retorted in kind: *Comment voulez-vous travailler avec ce Dénikine qui ne fait que nous péter dans les jambes? Il nous reste à plier nos bagages et nous en aller.*[12] (*Péter* means both "to explode" and "to break wind." In less picturesque language, d'Anselme was asking, "How do you expect us to work with this Denikin who does nothing but spike our guns? We might as well pack up and leave.")

The project of "mixed brigades" was abandoned, but a short time later, the French gave vent to their irritation by barring the Volunteer representatives from all participation in the administration of the Odessa region.

The French commander in chief in the Orient, General (later Marshal of France) Franchet d'Esperey decided to visit Odessa. Upon his arrival, and without any previous communications with Ekaterinodar, Franchet d'Esperey decided to get rid of Generals Sannikov and Grishin-Almazov. He sent them out of Odessa with a letter to General Denikin stating that he was placing the two generals "at Denikin's disposal." A state of siege was declared in Odessa, and a new local government, composed of persons approved by Colonel Freidenberg, was formed, to be known as the council attached to the French Command.

At this point there occurred a phenomenon very rare in the period of the civil war: The members of every Russian political party in Odessa, including People's Socialists, right-wing Socialist Revolutionaries, and even Mensheviks, united in their indignation at the French command's cavalier behavior and lack of respect for Russian national dignity. The socialists, who held political views divergent from Denikin's, nevertheless recognized his integrity and patriotism. They submitted the following protest to General d'Anselme: "If the French command will replace the Volunteers' administration of Odessa by creating a government organ under its aegis, it will arouse the bitter discontent of Odessa's population. In the present conflict between the French and Volunteer Army commands, Odessa's duma and its most influential democratic and socialist organizations express their solidarity with the Volunteer Army in opposing any attempts of the French command to establish any kind of 'South-Russian government' bearing the earmarks of a colonial regime and running contrary to Russia's sovereignty." [13]

The fact that members of Russian leftist parties had friends in French socialist circles and in the Chamber of Deputies intimidated Colonel Freidenberg, the backstage operator of French politics in Odessa. The reference to a "colonial regime" particularly worried him. His superior, General d'Anselme, was obliged to resort to confused explanations and to declare in the local press that "the French command has not the least intention of cutting itself off from the Volunteer Army. On the contrary, we are constantly striving to achieve a closer collaboration with it, the better to realize our common goal—that of maintaining order and safeguarding the citizens." [14]

Meanwhile, moral deterioration was gaining momentum not only in Petliura's bands, but in the French units as well.

A Ukrainian chieftain, *Ataman* Grigoriev, and his detachment of 1,700 men, with three cannon, defected from Petliura to join the Bolsheviks. Somewhat later, he acquired a gruesome reputation as the perpetrator of a series of Jewish pogroms in a number of Ukrainian towns and villages. For the time being, he threatened to chase the French out of Odessa, to make short shrift of the town's bourgeoisie, and incidentally, to make a bass drum out of Grishin-Almazov's skin.

Red army units had come right up to the limits of the Allied zone near Odessa, but as yet, neither they nor Grigoriev's bands presented any real threat to the numerically superior Allied units. The French command, however, tended to exaggerate the danger, and in addition, was less and less confident in its own soldiers. The latter made no secret of their desire to get out of Russia and of their sympathy for the Bolsheviks, whom they considered fellow proletarians. Soviet agents conducted a skillful propaganda campaign among the French soldiers and sailors. An underground newspaper, *The Odessa Communist,* published in French, incited the rank and file to rebel against their officers.

The French abandoned Kherson to the insignificant forces of *Ataman* Grigoriev, gave up Nikolaev without any pressure on the part of the enemy, and disgraced themselves completely near the village of Berezovka, where two thousand French soldiers were routed by a few hundred Bolsheviks. They fled in panic, leaving behind six cannon, five tanks, their wounded, and their baggage trains, and stopped only when an indignant Greek detachment barred their retreat. One of the captured tanks was sent to Moscow and exhibited in Red Square. "We all appreciate this present," wrote Lenin, ". . . as it testifies to the complete downfall of the Entente which had appeared to be so strong." [15] When unrest broke out in the French Black Sea fleet, it became clear that the French adventure in south Russia was approaching its end.[16]

Yet, the end came unexpectedly to the people of Odessa. On April 2 (Gregorian calendar), General d'Anselme announced that the French would evacuate the city within forty-eight hours.

The French had pressed most of the ships into their service [wrote Denikin]; vast quantities of Allied and Russian war materiel were left behind, as well as the money and valuables deposited in branches of the State Bank and Treasury. . . . One emotion predominated in the excitement and panic which gripped the Odessans—it was their unanimous, burning hatred of the French. It raged indiscriminately among those who were lucky enough to be on board ship and those who made their way in an endless procession of pedestrians, carriages, and carts, to the Rumanian border; among the unfortunates who remained on the docks with their miserable belongings, having failed to board a ship; and, finally, in the ragged mob which pursued the departing French with whistles and catcalls from the top of Odessa's cliffs.[17]

But five days went by before the news of Odessa's evacuation reached General Denikin. "Only yesterday," read his telegram to General Franchet d'Esperey, "did I learn that the French troops were leaving Odessa, after setting an impossible deadline for its evacuation. . . . The French command did not even deem it necessary to forewarn me. It is not even possible at this time to foresee the enormous historical consequences of this move. I assume in any event that the Volunteer brigade is morally entitled to every assistance and first of all to being dispatched immediately by sea, with its full complement of men, artillery, and baggage trains, to rejoin the Russian army in Novorossiisk." [18]

General Denikin's assumption proved wrong. The Russian brigade commanded by General Timanovsky was left to its own devices. Some time earlier, General d'Anselme had refused Denikin's request to have the brigade transferred to the Crimea. Now, after the Allied troops were already on shipboard and most of the city was in Bolshevik hands, Timanovsky's men, outraged by the behavior of the French, set off along the Black Sea coast toward the Rumanian border. Having arrived there, they were interned by the Rumanians, at the request of the French High Command, and deprived of their arms, artillery, and horses. They underwent a month of humiliating ordeals before their first units were sent to Novorossiisk to rejoin the Volunteer Army.

France's intervention in the civil war in south Russia was not limited to

Odessa. It also took place in the Crimea, where it passed through the same stages of hesitations, mistakes, and revolutionary unrest among the French sailors, and terminated in a similar fiasco.

The French sailors who landed in Sebastopol, the principal seaport in the Crimea, had already been exposed to Communist propaganda and immediately organized a political demonstration. They tore off the red pompons from their berets and pinned them to their chests as revolutionary badges. Bearing red banners and singing the "Internationale," they advanced along the city streets until Greek military patrols dispersed them.[19]

Sebastopol was abandoned by the French three weeks after Odessa. The behavior of the French command in the Crimea was perhaps even more insulting to Denikin's pride than it had been in Odessa.

In order to fend off the spread of anarchy, already raging in the Ukraine, General Denikin had begun to move units of the Volunteer Army from the Kuban to the Crimea in November, 1918, landing them in Kerch and Yalta. They were limited in number, and even several months later, did not exceed a total of five thousand men. The commanding officers who succeeded each other at their head showed little ability for coping with the complicated situation which prevailed in the Crimea, and unfortunately for Denikin, the French command prevented the transfer from Odessa of the highly disciplined five-thousand-strong brigade of General Timanovsky. In the meantime, the entire Crimean peninsula was aswarm with bands of insurgents and brigands. In addition, a large percentage of those local people who had joined the Volunteer detachments discredited the army in the eyes of the local population by their arbitrary searches and personal vendettas. Complaints against their abuses reached both the French command in Sebastopol and General Denikin's headquarters in Ekaterinodar.

In view of these events and of the overall military and political situation, Denikin had decided as early as December, 1918, to move his headquarters from Ekaterinodar to Sebastopol. His decision was also influenced by his desire to escape the proximity of the Kuban government, which was a constant source of irritation to him. He had not yet experienced at that time the vagaries of French politics and did not imagine that being near the French base in Sebastopol might prove to be far more nerve-racking than his constant bickerings with the Kuban separatists.

He was, therefore, completely taken by surprise by the telegram which General Franchet d'Esperey dispatched on January 27, 1919 (Gregorian calendar), to the head of the French military mission in Ekaterinodar, and which the latter relayed to Denikin's headquarters: "Have received your communication regarding proposed transfer of General Denikin's headquarters to Sebastopol. I consider that General Denikin's place is with the Volunteer Army and not in Sebastopol where the French troops, which he does not command, are stationed." [20]

This unexpected and high-handed interference in the internal disposition of the Volunteer Army was completely unacceptable to General Denikin. This was all the more so because small sections of his army had been engaged in continuous military operations at the northern approaches to the Crimea, first on its northern isthmuses, and later, at Akmanai, on the Kerch isthmus, while the French calmly did garrison duty in Sebastopol. He was outraged and offended and responded in harsh tones to Franchet d'Esperey's message. At the same time, he asked a former Russian Foreign Minister, S. D. Sazonov, then residing in Paris, to point out to the French government that "neither the contents nor the tone of the French general's communication could be tolerated." [21]

"It seemed," wrote Denikin, "that in these days of national disaster, the official representatives of France did everything they could to fill the cup of Russian grief and humiliation to overflowing." [22]

By that time (January, 1919) events in Odessa had already aroused Denikin's fear for the future of his relations with the Allies, but Franchet d'Esperey's telegram brought into focus the extent of the misunderstandings between the two presumably allied armies. General Denikin made several attempts to obtain a personal interview with Berthelot, then with Franchet d'Esperey, but the French generals always found excuses for postponing these meetings, which never did materialize.

Only in June, 1919 (two months after the French departed from Odessa and a month and a half after they abandoned the Crimea), was General Denikin handed "for his information" a document which finally clarified for him the true aims of the Allies and showed how radically different they were from the principles proclaimed by the Volunteer Army.

This was the protocol of an agreement reached by the governments of France and Great Britain, as of April 11, 1919 (Gregorian calendar), concerning French intervention in south Russia. The protocol, handed to Denikin by the chief of the French mission in Ekaterinodar, Colonel Corbeil, specified that it represented an *amplification* of the "Franco-British agreement of December 23, 1917 (Gregorian calendar) outlining their zones of activity" (*l'accord Franco-Anglais du 23 décembre 1917, définissant les zones d'action française et anglaise*).

For the first time, Denikin realized that during all that period, the Allied governments had not bothered to acquaint him with a decision they had made as far back as the end of 1917 (i.e., shortly after the Bolshevik seizure of power), a decision that directly concerned the zone in which his army was operating. Their agreement divided south Russia into two spheres of influence. The French zone encompassed Bessarabia, the Ukraine, and the Crimea. In the British zone were the regions of the Kuban and Terek Cossacks and the Caucasus, including Georgia and Armenia. The Don Cossack Territory was cut in two, with its western part in the French zone and its eastern part in the British zone.

It was clear that the former Allies were guided in their decisions not by strategic, but by purely economic considerations. The French were safeguarding their prewar investments in the Donets Basin and the Ukraine, while the British concentrated on protecting their interests in the Russian oil industry.

Any remaining illusions regarding the Allies' chivalry and disinterested help evaporated. As for the protocol of April 11, 1919, concerning French intervention, arriving as it did after the intervention had dismally failed, it appeared not only bitterly ironic but devoid of all common sense in its approach to Russian reality.

The Allied conferences which gave birth to that document had taken place at the Quai d'Orsay in Paris after the French had left Odessa— that is, after relations between the French and Volunteer commands had almost reached the breaking point. Despite this fact, the protocol expressed the Allies' desire for complete cooperation with General Denikin and outlined the means by which this could be achieved. It specified that General Denikin and the French High Command would keep each other fully informed concerning their operations and needs, by means of liaison missions, and would lend support to each other to the best of their ability. This point seemed particularly inappropriate in view of the events that had immediately preceded its drafting.

Anton Ivanovich had a great desire to tell his former friends, whom he had so highly idealized, to go to hell. But he had to restrain himself. Without supplies, no large-scale operations directed at the center of Russia could be undertaken. "For considerations of state," he destroyed many a rough draft of a letter to Franchet d'Esperey, couched in too harsh a tone during a momentary outburst of indignation.

Denikin had learned to admire France from a distance in his youth. He was fired by its history and literature, which he read in translation; admired the brilliance of its great military leaders, and had studied the campaigns of the French army in minute detail. The logic of the French intellect fascinated him. And after this, to be faced with such complete absence of logic, such utter and unpardonable nonsense!

Yet Denikin was able to rise above his initial bitter reaction: "Although at first the French government was extremely careless in its choice of persons who were to represent it in south Russia," wrote the General, "and although these people displayed an extraordinary lack of understanding of Russian reality, a study of the conditions in which their activity took place will be a mitigating factor in their favor when they are judged by history." [23]

The "mitigating factor" was the complex and unfamiliar situation with which the French command, totally uninformed of conditions in south Russia, was faced upon arriving in Odessa—the clash of interests between the Russians and the Ukrainian separatists headed by Petliura, the lack of unity among various Russian political groups in Odessa, and finally the absence of clearly formulated instructions from the government in Paris.

Denikin further expressed his thoughts concerning the French intervention and its consequences as follows:

The page of Russo-French alliance was turned and the book suddenly and unexpectedly closed, leaving a persistent, oppressive feeling of bitterness, resentment, and indignation.

The attitude of the public, the press, and the army toward the French was becoming extremely touchy and sometimes arrogant, which could lead to diplomatic complications. I must admit that I did not find it easy myself to overcome my personal bitterness in deference to government considerations. The latter prevailed, and when, a while later, the chief of the French mission, Colonel Corbeil, came to see me, depressed by all that had happened and with no desire to justify anyone, but only to share with me the emotional distress of the members of the French mission in Ekaterinodar, I was able to tell him quite sincerely: "What can we do about it? The past cannot be undone. Let us join efforts in reestablishing the ties which were so fatally broken by certain people, but which are indispensable to the interests of both our nations." [24]

The fact that the French were mainly to blame for the strained relations between themselves and the Russians in the south, must not lead us to the conclusion that the White Army command in Ekaterinodar had been blameless in the affair.

National pride, exacerbated by the events of the past few years, prevented Denikin from delegating enough authority to his representative in Odessa to allow flexibility in dealings with the French command. The Denikin government interfered in all decisions, even the most insignificant ones. This attitude, although it stemmed from a commendable desire to uphold in the field of foreign relations Russian national dignity, as the General understood it, infinitely complicated an already delicate situation.

The representatives of Great Britain with whom Denikin had to deal from November, 1918, to the end of his command, presented a complete contrast to their French counterparts in Odessa. General Poole and his successors, Generals Briggs and Holman, were men of high caliber—of great nobility and soldierly straightforwardness, in Denikin's view. Having come to know Denikin well and to appreciate the same qualities in him, they trusted him and were prepared to assist in every way the movement which he headed. Despite the political controversy in the British government resulting from the different approaches to the Russian question of Secretary for War Churchill and Prime Minister Lloyd George, these British generals firmly defended the unity of Russia, tried to satisfy the military needs of Denikin's army, and did everything in their power to defend its interests.

The differences of opinion concerning Russia between Churchill and Lloyd George were deeply rooted and irreconcilable.

Churchill's personality reflected the chivalrous approach to questions of honor, an approach which also formed an integral part of Denikin's credo and which he had vainly hoped to find in all of Russia's former allies. Churchill remembered the immense services rendered by Russia to France, Great Britain, and Italy during the war. He found it inconceivable to abandon to their fate those Russians who, throughout their hardest ordeals, had kept their word, remained faithful to the alliance, and refused to compromise with the Germans. He also shared with Denikin a true understanding of the danger which Bolshevism presented to the entire world.

Having assumed the duties of Secretary for War in January, 1919, Churchill directed his tremendous energy and oratorical talent to combating the power of the Soviets. Much of what he said and wrote on Russian unity coincided with Denikin's own views. Churchill maintained that a policy of dismembering Russia could not have positive results; that it would only lead to a succession of wars out of which a united, militarist, anti-Western power would arise, be it under a Bolshevik or a reactionary standard. He insisted that Great Britain should make every effort to promote the creation of a federalized Russia, which while adhering to the principle of local autonomy, would still preserve its general unity.[25]

Churchill foresaw the possibility of revenge on the part of a regenerated Germany, and to oppose this menace he wanted the support in Eastern Europe not of a series of weak disparate states, but of a strong, united, and friendly Russia.

Prime Minister Lloyd George knew little about Russia's past history and was so vague about contemporary events in that country that, unable to tell a Russian general from a Russian city, he referred in one of his speeches in Parliament to the military assistance which Britain was extending to Generals Denikin and Kharkov. ("The 'General Kharkov' episode," wrote Anton Ivanovich, "remained for a long time the favorite joke of the south-Russian newspapers.") [26]

Lloyd George was trying to pick his way between the obligation to assist the anti-Bolshevik forces, his desire to engage in commerce with the Soviet government, and his inclination to uphold the independence of the newly formed states which had recently sprung up on the periphery of the former Russian Empire. He openly advocated the dismemberment of Russia, following in the footsteps of Disraeli, who had seen in a great and powerful Russia a menace to Great Britain's interests in India, Persia, and Afghanistan.

The British representatives in Ekaterinodar, however, had been selected by Churchill, shared his views, and did their best to carry out his policy.

The duality of Britain's Russian policy (especially with respect to Transcaucasia), the divergence between Churchill's pro-Russian approach and Lloyd George's anti-Russian one, the lack of a clearly thought-out program of action—all this greatly discouraged Denikin, and his customary frankness even drove him once to the point of asking the British "whether they had come to the Caucasus as friends or enemies." [27]

However, he had no complaints regarding the flow of British supplies to his army. Between March and September, 1919, it had received 558 pieces of ordnance, twelve tanks, 1,685,522 artillery shells, 160 million rifle cartridges, and 250,000 sets of military uniforms.[28]

After the failure of the White movement, when leftist circles in Great Britain accused Churchill of having wasted immense sums of money on Denikin's support, Churchill retorted that the rumors that a hundred million pounds sterling had been expended in south Russia were "an absurd exaggeration." The military supplies sent to Denikin, "though they had been most costly to produce, were only an unmarketable surplus of the Great War, to which no money value can be assigned. Had they been kept in our hands, till they mouldered," said Churchill, "they would only have involved additional charges for storage, care and maintenance."[29]

The rivalry which existed between the French and British forces of intervention had become evident at Denikin's headquarters as soon as their respective missions arrived in Ekaterinodar in November, 1918.

The question of precedence was a bone of contention for the French and British High Commands in Constantinople, whose heads were General Franchet d'Esperey (commander in chief of the Army of Salonika) and General Milne (commander in chief of the British Army in the Balkans).

"On March 11 [1919]," wrote Denikin, "I received a notification from General Franchet d'Esperey stating that the Allied forces operating in south Russia were under his command. This communication was immediately and categorically denied by the British mission."[30]

Another entry in Denikin's memoirs throws additional light on Franco-British relations at that time: "On one occasion, General Romanovsky was visited by a member of the British mission, who said to him, 'Why don't you drop your discussions with the French? They only promise, and will never deliver anything. Just give the order to have the lists of indispensable supplies for your army sent to us.' General Milne wrote me directly on the same subject, affirming that everything that was within his power to provide, would be prepared for us without delay."[31]

The most glaring example of the rivalry and complete lack of coordination between the British and the French in Russia was the so-called "Prinkipo" episode. While the French were still in Odessa, at Lloyd George's insistence and despite very strong opposition on the part of Winston Churchill, President Wilson at the end of January, 1919, prepared a proclamation in the name of the Allied powers inviting all the warring parties in the Russian civil war to send their representatives to a conference on the Turkish island of Prinkipo, near Constantinople, in order to reach an agreement and put an end to the hostilities. President Wilson designated February 15 (Gregorian calendar) as the opening day of the conference. With French troops in Odessa and the Crimea, Clemenceau was opposed to this step, but reluctantly agreed to it. Officials of the Quai d'Orsay, however, who cordially disliked Lloyd George and knew that he had masterminded Wilson's invitation but preferred to remain in the background for reasons of internal politics, advised the Paris representatives of the White regimes to ignore the invitation. It was accepted by the Soviet government, but categorically rejected by the leaders of the White movement, and as a result, the conference never took place.

The failure of Woodrow Wilson's initiative was no surprise to the State Department in Washington. According to George Kennan, a leading authority on Soviet-American relations, the then Secretary of State, Robert Lansing, wrote to his deputy in Washington that "nothing was likely to come of the proposal." [32]

The vacillations of the Allies, and in this instance, their unexpected offer to make peace with the Bolsheviks provoked amazement in anti-Bolshevik circles by its naïve ignorance of the fact that the civil war could not be resolved by a compromise.

XX

STRUGGLE FOR A UNIFIED COMMAND AND CHANGES IN SIBERIA

The fall of Germany had a disastrous effect on the situation of the Don Cossack army. By late November, 1918, the German troops had withdrawn from the Don region, leaving the extensive borderline which they had previously protected open to Bolshevik invasion. To compensate for this, the Don Cossack army, numbering approximately 52,000 men, had to be stretched out along the entire length of the front, from Lugansk to Tsaritsin and from Tsaritsin to Manych.[1]

General Denikin described as follows the situation in the Don region at that time: "The Don was fighting valiantly for survival in the face of an enemy that was twice as strong. . . . The Don army was unfailingly victorious, taking thousands of prisoners and valuable booty. . . . But in a civil war, more than in any other, morale is more important than all the other components of success. That which had been gained in the course of many months by moral elation as well as by the force of arms was lost in an instant when the army's spirits fell. The attitude of the Cossacks underwent another change, and this was cleverly exploited by Soviet propaganda." [2]

The Don army soon began to retreat. This again brought to the fore the question of a unified command for all anti-Bolshevik forces in south Russia and of a common plan of action issuing from one center. Either the Don army or the Volunteer Army could serve as such a center at the time. The Don army, however, represented mainly the local interests of its region, whereas the Volunteer Army was recognized as embodying Russia's national interests. Even the Socialist Revolutionaries (V. V. Rudnev, Abraham Gots, Mark Vishniak, and others) assembled for a convention in Simferopol in December, 1918, delegated to the Volunteer Army "the responsible role of serving in south Russia as the nucleus for the re-creation of a national Russian army." [3]

One other reason was strongly in favor of the Volunteer Army's leader-ship: The Allied governments, who had promised their assistance in combating Bolshevism and sent their military missions to Ekaterinodar, knew that Denikin had kept faith with them to the end, whereas Krasnov, in view of his recent pro-German orientation, was hardly to be trusted.

Though he realized perfectly well that he could not aspire to the leader-ship of both armies, Krasnov still hoped to preserve his power in the Don region. He did not wish to submit to Denikin, whom he intensely disliked, and hoped that the Allies could be persuaded to place some other military figure, acceptable to both the Volunteer and the Don Cossack armies, in the position of commander in chief. (General Shcherbachev was one of his candidates.) Krasnov was an outspoken admirer of the old regime, and regarded Denikin as a man with leftist political tendencies. He resented Denikin's blunt remarks during their meeting in May, 1918, and also the fact, mentioned by Krasnov himself, that Anton Ivanovich did not show enough deference to the high position of the new ruler of the Don Cossack region, but was inclined instead to treat him as a former brigade com-mander of the old imperial army.

Immediately after the German defeat, in November, 1918, Krasnov sent a delegation to confer with the French command in Jassy. The delegation made a negative impression on General Berthelot. The *Ataman*'s repre-sentatives not only did their best to discredit the Volunteer Army and its command, but found it necessary to hint that, should the Allies favor Denikin's leadership over Krasnov's, the Don army might seek an under-standing with the Bolsheviks. This exasperated Berthelot who retorted that it was disgraceful to sling mud at a friendly army. "Is the Don army more numerous than the Volunteer Army?" he asked, and added without waiting for a reply, "But even had General Denikin only a single soldier, our sympathies would still be on his side. He was one of the few generals who, in the hardest conditions, remained true to the idea of the alliance." [4]

The British military representative in Ekaterinodar handled the ques-tion with even greater directness. He came to see Denikin at the beginning of December, 1918, and asked him whether he considered it necessary to get rid of Krasnov in the general interests of the cause. "No," answered Denikin, "I would only like you to exert your influence in changing his attitude toward the Volunteer Army." "Very well," said Poole, "then we shall talk." [5]

An interview between the British General and the Don Cossack *Ataman* took place on December 13, 1918, at the station of Kushchevka. Krasnov's own description of it (in which he refers to himself in the third person) throws an interesting light on the *Ataman*'s personality and attitude:

The beginning of the meeting was frigid. General Poole insisted that the *Ataman* come first to see him in his railway carriage and that all discussions be held there. The *Ataman* refused this, and it appeared for a while that the interview would not take place. The British Colonel Keyes was dispatched to see the *Ataman*. "Tell General Poole," the *Ataman* told him, "that I am the elected head of a free people of five million, which asks nothing for itself. Nothing! Do you hear? It needs neither your guns, nor your rifles, nor your ammuniton; it has all that and it has rid itself of the Bolsheviks. Tomorrow it can make peace with the Bolsheviks and lead an excellent life. But we must save Russia, and it is for this that the help of the Allies is indispensable to us and that they are under an obligation to render it. General Poole will be speaking with the sovereign head of a strong and mighty people, who demands a certain amount of respect for his person. General Poole should come to me, and I shall return his call without delay."

The diplomatic impasse was resolved by Poole's agreeing to hold the discussions at Krasnov's quarters, and the *Ataman*'s agreeing to be Poole's guest at lunch. "The *Ataman* and General Poole met like two pompous, angry turkey-cocks," noted Krasnov in his memoirs.[6]

He knew, of course, that this encounter could only end by his giving in to a certain extent, if not capitulating completely, as his military situation was growing worse from day to day. Nevertheless, the *Ataman*'s arrogant behavior and the way he staged the whole episode so rattled and perplexed the straightforward Englishman as to make him agree to some very ambiguous conditions. These were, briefly, as follows:

First, the submission of the Don Cossack army to Denikin would not be announced until Krasnov judged that the minds of the Cossacks were sufficiently prepared for the necessity of such a move.

Second, the issuance of categorical directives involving the Don Cossacks would be avoided at the outset and replaced by "instructions" regarding a given operation, which could be revised by the *Ataman*.

Third, the Volunteer Army High Command would not interfere in the internal direction of the Don army, i.e., in nominations to command posts, promotions, the drafting of Cossacks, and the like.

"In effect," wrote Denikin, "these conditions reduced to nothing the concept of a unified command, but at least they recognized its existence, put the problem on the mat, and laid the ground for further discussions." [7]

These further discussions took place December 26 at Torgovaia station, at a time when the situation at the Don Cossack front had become critical. General Denikin presided at the meeting. In addition to himself, the Volunteer Army was represented by Generals Dragomirov, Shcherbachev (who had arrived from Rumania) and Romanovsky. On the side of the Don Cossacks were *Ataman* Krasnov, General Denisov and several other officers.

Denikin and Krasnov had not met since their conference at Manych-skaia in the middle of May. They disliked each other to such an extent that they had ceased to correspond, and had been communicating with each other through the representative of the Volunteer Army at the Don and his Don Cossack counterpart in Ekaterinodar. Denikin recognized the administrative talent and enormous energy with which the *Ataman* had created an impressive and well-armed army out of insignificant partisan detachments and knew that these qualities were invaluable in the anti-Bolshevik struggle. But he was irked by Krasnov's blatant careerism, which sometimes permitted his personal ambition to interfere with the pursuit of the common goal. The *Ataman*'s predilection for poetic fancy at the expense of truth also annoyed Denikin, as did his criticism of the Volunteer Army command for the naïve form and content of its statements, and its cynical views and motives. Such was the emotional climate in which their stormy interview took place. Denikin broke off the negotiations twice, and in each case *Ataman* Krasnov and General Shcherbachev persuaded him to resume them.

As a result of this painful meeting, Denikin was officially recognized as the Commander in Chief of the Armed Forces of South Russia, and the Don Cossack army was placed under his command. General Denikin announced his acceptance of his new position in an order of the day dated December 26, 1918.

In the meantime, great changes were taking place in the Soviet military establishment. Trotsky, more than anyone else in the Bolshevik camp, was responsible for transforming the originally weak and inefficient Red detachments into a workable fighting machine. By April, 1918, he had succeeded in enforcing his demands that a regular army with compulsory military service be reinstated to replace the existing forces recruited through volunteer enlistments, that soldiers' committees and meetings be abolished, that strict discipline be enforced, and that old army officers, under threat of merciless punishment in case of disloyalty, be drafted as "military experts" to work under the supervision of political commissars. Eligibility for military service was based on class origin. Only workers and peasants not employing hired help, and aged eighteen to forty, were drafted into the army. The former propertied classes and well-to-do peasants were mobilized as a labor force. At Trotsky's insistence, a Supreme War Council was created to supervise the reorganization of the army, and in September, 1918, the Revolutionary Military Council of the Republic was formed to direct military operations as well as administrative work.

Toward the fall of 1918, a struggle for a unified command was taking place on the Soviet side. Trotsky insisted on establishing a unified command for the Red Army and with Lenin's help achieved this goal, despite the strong opposition of all the prominent members of the party, who feared that it would lead to Bonapartism. A single commander in chief was appointed, and his authority was extended to all the fronts of the Red Army. The first two men to hold this post were former officers of the old army—I. Vatsetis and Sergei Kamenev. Trotsky wrote later that the unified command, achieved through his efforts, had saved the Red Army from defeat by giving it expert military knowledge which utilized to the full extent the central location of the Soviet zone and the communication lines controlled by it.

The numerical strength of the Red Army was rapidly increasing: It grew from 330,000 men at the end of July, 1918, to 800,000 men by the end of December.

Long before his conference with Krasnov, Denikin had become aware of the precarious position of the Don front, from which the Cossack units, with their men deserting, were retreating and melting away. On December 6, three weeks before the conference, a Volunteer detachment, transferred by Denikin's orders from the North Caucasus, had already arrived in the vicinity of Iuzovka. Its mission was to protect the left flank of the Don Cossack army and the Donets coal basin at the Ukrainian border. At the beginning, the detachment consisted of only 2,500 men, but gradually it absorbed the Kornilov, Markov, and Drozdovsky regiments, the First and Second Cavalry regiments, and by the end of May, the Alekseev Regiment (formerly the Partisan Regiment, now renamed in honor of the late general). This was still but a handful of people, as all the proud units which joined the detachment had lost most of their complement during the North Caucasus campaign; only later did it grow to 4,500. By its brilliant maneuvering, the detachment managed to hold at bay an enemy several times superior to it in numbers. The Volunteers came to grips with the insurgent bands of the anarchist Makhnó, who was to play an important role in the future course of the civil war, with some of Petliura's bands who had defected to the Reds, and with two divisions of the Red Army. There were days when the Volunteers' situation seemed hopeless, but they managed to hold out successfully until, at last, the military initiative passed to Denikin, and his army began to advance along a wide front toward the Ukraine and the north. The detachment was commanded by General Mai-Maevsky. His initial successes, for which he deserved full credit, led to his quick promotion by the White Army command. Unfortunately, these new responsibilities proved too great for a man who suffered from periodic bouts of hard drinking and whose weakness eventually had a deplorable effect on the conduct of his troops.

General Denikin meticulously avoided any interference in the Don's internal affairs. Meanwhile, the people of the Don were anxiously awaiting the arrival of the Allied troops which Berthelot had so thoughtlessly promised to Denikin. But the troops did not come, and the morale of the population deteriorated rapidly. Among the Don Cossack officers, and especially among the liberal intelligentsia, the latent and previously hidden discontent with *Ataman* Krasnov, finally broke through. It was rumored that the *Ataman*'s Germanophile record was responsible for the delay in the Allies' arrival. Krasnov's principal collaborator, General Denisov, who commanded the Don Cossack army, became a special target of popular discontent and was blamed for the military reverses of his army. At a meeting held February 1, 1919, in Novocherkassk, the Don Cossack *Krug* passed a vote of no confidence against General Denisov and his chief of staff, General Poliakov. Krasnov interpreted this vote as indirectly expressing no confidence in himself and asked the *Krug* to find him a successor, hoping that the delegates would not take him at his word. The *Krug,* however, accepted his resignation.

General Denikin had been invited to the session of the *Krug* in his capacity as Commander in Chief of the Armed Forces of South Russia, which included the Don Cossack army. He described what turned out to be his last encounter with Krasnov as follows:

Early in the morning of February 3, my train was approaching Kushchevka. There at the border of the Don region, I was met by the former *Ataman,* General Krasnov, who had arrived ahead of the leaders of the Don opposition who also wished to talk to me before I addressed the *Krug.* For the third time in the course of the struggle at the south, I met the man with whom fate had so abruptly confronted me on the seemingly wide Russian road. I no longer had before me the *Ataman* proud of his own and the Don Cossacks' achievements, but a man severely punished by fate for his own and other people's transgressions. A man unquestionably gifted, but with no control over his words and feelings, who had created his own opponents and enemies everywhere and was recklessly expending his strength in combating them. And there was no bitterness in my soul against him at that time. I expressed to Krasnov my regret at his withdrawal. He replied, "The *Krug* will submit to every word you say. . . ."

. . . But, in all conscience I was incapable of uttering the words that Krasnov expected from me.

"I cannot and will not be the judge in your internal strife," was all that I considered myself in the right to say to the *Ataman* and to the *Krug,* on the eve of the elections to the post of *Ataman,* which were to determine Krasnov's future.[8]

The new *Ataman* elected by the *Krug* was General A. P. Bogaevsky, who had taken part in the First Kuban Campaign and was at the time chairman of the Don government. He asked and received Denikin's consent to the nomination of General Sidorin to the command of the Don Cossack army, and of General Kelchevsky to the position of chief of staff.

Denikin and Krasnov were never to meet again. These two men whom fate had "so abruptly confronted . . . on the seemingly wide Russian road" continued to hold widely divergent views during the long years of their exile. During World War II, the political émigré Denikin, though carefully watched by the Gestapo in German-occupied France, nevertheless directed all his energies to anti-German propaganda; while the political émigré Krasnov, residing in Germany, collaborated with the Nazis, helped them to form Don Cossack detachments to fight against the Communists, and paid for this with his life. The Yalta agreement concluded by Roosevelt, Churchill, and Stalin, called for the surrender to the Moscow government of all present or former Russian nationals who had put on the German uniform in order to combat the Soviet Union. Krasnov was among them. He was handed over by the British army to the Soviet representatives in the Austrian town of Lienz in the spring of 1945, and executed in Moscow in 1947.

In the meantime, great changes were taking place in Siberia. By November, 1918, the relations between the officers in Omsk and the Directory had deteriorated to such an extent that the replacement of the collective government by a dictatorship was openly discussed. The candidate for the role of dictator was the recently arrived Admiral Alexander Vasilievich Kolchak.

He had come to Siberia with the intention of acquainting himself with its military-political situation and then making his way to the Kuban to place himself under the command of General Alekseev (of whose death he was not yet aware) and to participate in the anti-Bolshevik movement originated by him.

There were no men of national stature and authority in Siberia at that period. It was not surprising, therefore, that the rightist and the liberal elements in Omsk eagerly sought to place Admiral Kolchak in a position of power. His name was widely known as a result of his oceanographic studies of the Arctic waters, his active contribution to the re-creation of the Russian fleet after the Japanese war, and especially his outstanding record in the World War.

Kolchak was born in November, 1874, in the family of a naval artillery officer. His parents had no income except the father's meager salary. After graduating from the Naval Academy in 1894, Kolchak spent several years navigating in foreign waters, working at the same time on special projects in oceanography and hydrology. At the age of twenty-five, he had already published several scientific papers and had acquired such a reputation in his field that he was invited to join, as a hydrologist, a scientific expedition organized by the Russian Academy of Science under the leadership of Baron Toll, for the exploration and study of the Arctic Ocean island of Bennet. Upon his return to St. Petersburg, after two years spent in the polar region, Kolchak received the highest award of the Russian Imperial Geographic Society, a gold medal, for his scientific contributions in the fields of hydrology and magnetometry.

He volunteered for active service in the Russo-Japanese War, became an expert in mine laying, and blew up the Japanese cruiser *Takosado* in the vicinity of Port Arthur, for which he was awarded the Sword of St. George. After Russia's defeat in the Far East, he was one of the founders of the Army-Navy Circle, whose principal aim was the creation of a modern fleet equipped with the latest technical and military devices. At the insistence of Kolchak and the semiofficial circle of which he was the guiding spirit (and which enjoyed the approval of the Ministry of the Navy), a Naval General Staff was created in 1906. Kolchak joined it as chief of naval operations in the Baltic Sea. Foreseeing that a war with Germany was inevitable and realizing that the Russian fleet could not possibly compete with the German fleet, Kolchak came to the conclusion that the only means of defense against the latter lay in highly effective mining activity, and concentrated all his energy on its development.

On the eve of World War I, when Russia had not yet entered the conflict but was expected to do so at any moment, Captain Kolchak, without waiting for approval from St. Petersburg (but with the permission of the commander of the Baltic fleet), laid a minefield at the entrance of the Gulf of Finland, in order to prevent the German fleet from approaching St. Petersburg and Kronstadt. In the spring of 1915, Kolchak completed another brilliant operation with a fleet of four minelayers which he commanded, by mining the enemy waters on the approaches to Danzig, with the result that a whole series of German vessels was destroyed. By that time, Kolchak was widely recognized as an expert in mine laying, but he did not limit himself to activities in this field. In the spring of 1916, a fleet of several minelayers under his command attacked and sank a large German convoy transporting ore from Sweden to Germany. Kolchak, who was rapidly advancing in his naval career, received the Cross of St. George for valor, and in June, 1916, was given the command of the Black Sea fleet with the rank of Vice Admiral. Repeating his exploit in the Baltic Sea, Admiral Kolchak laid a network of minefields along the Turkish coast near the Bosphorus. This protected the Black Sea from the raids of German submarines and their high-speed cruisers *Goeben* and *Breslau*. By the end of the year, thanks to Kolchak, freighters could transport supplies to the Russo-Turkish front in the Transcaucasia without being molested.

After the fall of the monarchy, the sailors of the Baltic fleet treated their officers with exceptional savagery. Many navy officers were killed in Kronstadt and on board their ships in the days of the so-called "bloodless revolution." The Black Sea fleet arrived at this stage considerably later, but by June, 1917, its crews' insurgence also reached alarming proportions. The sailors started disarming their officers. They demanded that Kolchak surrender his arms, but he refused, and as a gesture of protest, threw his sword into the sea from the bridge of his flagship, *Georgi Pobedonosets*. He was outraged and did not wish to continue in his command, which he relinquished to the admiral next in rank, and left for Petrograd. Seeing the helplessness of the Provisional Government and finding no outlet for his military talents, Kolchak, with Kerensky's consent, accepted the invitation of the United States Department of the Navy to come to the United States for consultations on naval problems and particularly on mine-laying operations. Kolchak first traveled by way of Sweden and Norway to England, where he had several meetings with the First Lord of the Admiralty, Admiral Jellicoe, concerning the mining of the German coastline. Upon his arrival in the United States at the end of August, and during his entire stay there, Kolchak was treated with utmost courtesy and consideration, and he was invited to assist at the maneuvers of the American fleet in the Atlantic Ocean, on board the flagship *Pennsylvania*. He learned about the seizure of power by the Bolsheviks in San Francisco, on the first lap of his homeward journey. Arriving in Japan, he was advised of the Soviet-German negotiations in Brest-Litovsk. His reaction to this news was immediate. Kolchak called on the British ambassador in Tokyo and advised him that he considered himself in honor bound to continue carrying out Russia's obligations toward its allies. Kolchak asked the ambassador to convey to his government his request to be accepted into the British army in any capacity, even that of a private, as he wished to continue the fight against German imperialism at all costs. After some delay, the British proposed to the Admiral that he join their forces in Mesopotamia. On his way there, however, Kolchak was handed an urgent telegram from London by the commander of the British forces in Singapore. In it, the British government insistently requested Kolchak to leave for the Russian Far East by way of Peking, where he was to call on the Russian ambassador, Prince Kudashev. Kudashev discussed with Kolchak the activity of the Volunteer Army in south Russia and suggested that the time had come to create a similar armed movement in the Russian Far East and to restore law and order in that area.

This conversation set in motion a sequence of events which within a few months would place Admiral Kolchak at the head of the White movement.

Kolchak soon became disappointed in the leaders of the anti-Bolshevik movement in the Far East and in Siberia. He was anxious to leave the post of Minister of War in Omsk, with which he had been saddled against his will, as soon as possible, and rejoin the leaders of the White movement in south Russia, whose ideals and principles he shared. But fate decided differently. A *coup d'état* took place in Omsk on the night of November 17, 1918. The Directory was overthrown, and three of its Socialist Revolutionary members were arrested, provided with a substantial amount of money, and sent abroad under escort. The next day, Kolchak, who had had no part in the *coup,* was proclaimed Supreme Ruler.[9]

The distance separating the forces of Kolchak from those of Denikin was very great. At the start of 1919, the left flank of Kolchak's army (the Orenburg detachment), moving west from the region of the Ural Mountains, was separated by approximately nine hundred kilometers from the right flank of Denikin's forces, which were then fighting in the Don Cossack Territory, trying to stave off a Soviet offensive.

Communications between Siberia and south Russia were extremely irregular. They were carried out by couriers sent from both directions, but many of these were intercepted by the Bolsheviks. Denikin, therefore, had only a tenuous conception of the events unfolding in Omsk and at the Siberian front.

His attitude in regard to the change of government in Siberia was favorable: "I reacted with great satisfaction and complete acceptance to the replacement of the Directory by the single rule of Admiral Kolchak." [10] Denikin had never met Kolchak. He knew, however, that Kolchak was a distinguished naval officer and a brave and honorable man, and believed his honest and disinterested motives were not to be doubted.

XXI

DENIKIN'S
BIG OFFENSIVE

At the beginning of March, 1919, Denikin's northern front was over eight hundred kilometers in length. Against the 42,000 to 45,000 Whites at the front, the Bolsheviks concentrated five armies, totaling approximately 130,000 to 150,000 cavalry and infantry personnel.

The Soviet Tenth Army, numbering nearly 23,000 men and reinforced by the so-called "Steppe" forces of approximately 10,000, advanced against Denikin along the Tsaritsin-Tikhoretskaia railroad. It was commanded by a former lieutenant colonel who would later be a marshal of the Soviet Union, A. I. Egorov. At that time, he enjoyed the special good graces of Stalin and Voroshilov, who considered themselves the "organizers" of the defense of Tsaritsin.

Stalin's name was then known only to a small group of people at the top of the Soviet hierarchy.

The Soviet Ninth Army, of 28,000 men, was under the command of a former colonel, Vsevolodov; and the Soviet Eighth Army, of 27,000, under that of a former officer of the imperial guard, Captain M. N. Tukhachevsky, who was transferred to the front against Admiral Kolchak a short time later. Like Egorov, Tukhachevsky later was made a marshal of the Soviet Union, and in 1937 both men became victims of Stalin's devastating purge of the Red Army command. The Soviet Thirteenth Army was commanded by Kozhevnikov, and consisted of 20,000 to 25,000 men. There was also the Ukrainian Second Army (renamed a short time later the Fourteenth Army), whose command was assumed by Voroshilov. It included the insurgent bands of Makhnó, Opanasiuk, and other Ukrainian rebels. Further on, a special Crimean corps was disposed along the Berdiansk-Melitopol-Perekop line.

Denikin's situation was extremely grave. The Soviet troops, at least three times more numerous than his, were advancing along the entire front. Fighting was stubborn, fierce, and widespread. But the military good fortune of the Bolsheviks in the Ukraine and the Don region, which had lasted throughout the winter and the early spring of 1919, suddenly failed them at the beginning of May.

In those difficult months, two factors helped Denikin, as they had done a year earlier—his own combat experience and the valor and persistence of the best Volunteer units, the Kornilov, Markov, Drozdovsky, and Alekseev regiments, which fiercely defended the Donets Basin while suffering cruel losses. In order to divert some of the Bolshevik forces from them, General Shkuró attacked the enemy rear with his Kuban cavalry, pierced the Soviet front at Debaltsevo, and successfully continued his cavalry attack right to the Sea of Azov. The commander in chief personally conducted a complex operation in the direction of Manych, where the Soviet Tenth Army posed a threat to the rear of the White Army and its system of communications. Meanwhile, General Ulagai's cavalry, operating on the army's right flank, defeated the Steppe forces of the Tenth Army and the Red cavalry commanded by Dumenko, taking prisoner six Soviet regiments with their artillery, army trains, and staffs.[1] Finally, General Wrangel displayed his extraordinary talents as a cavalry leader in dealing the enemy a crushing blow with his mounted forces in the vicinity of Velikokniazheskaia.

Between April 22 and May 8, over fifteen thousand prisoners and fifty-five guns were captured from the Soviet Tenth Army.

By ceaseless maneuvering and a series of successful attacks, and by virtue of the superiority of his cavalry and the quality of its leaders, General Denikin succeeded in smashing the Red forces and taking the military initiative away from them.

Denikin's great asset was his cavalry. Trotsky was one of the first Soviet leaders to realize in full the threat presented by Denikin and the important role of the White Army's mounted forces. "Denikin . . . is unquestionably more dangerous to us than Kolchak," he declared.

The superiority of his cavalry in the first stages of the struggle was a great boon to Denikin and enabled him to deal us a series of smashing blows . . . [wrote Trotsky]. Cavalry played an enormous, sometimes decisive, role in our war of field maneuvering. One cannot improvise a cavalry in a short period of time. It requires specific human material, trained horses, and a corresponding quality of command. The cavalry command was composed either of members of aristocratic, predominantly noble families, or of the inhabitants of the Don and Kuban regions, where horsemanship is innate. . . . The formation of mounted units was always fraught with great difficulties for the revolutionary classes. It had not been easy for the Great Army of the French revolution, and was all the more difficult for us. If one reads the list of commanding officers who deserted from the Red Army to the White, one will find in it a very high percentage of cavalrymen.[2]

At that period, the Red cavalry barely existed. An unquestionable achievement of Trotsky in the revolutionary cause, made under the slogan "Proletarians to horse!" was the formation of a mighty cavalry attacking force, the First Cavalry Army, which later played a decisive role in the civil war.[3]

There were already serious conflicts between Trotsky and Stalin in those days, and their hatred for each other was beginning to grow. Nevertheless, it could not have occurred to Trotsky that among the countless indictments of sabotage preferred against him by Stalin would be the accusation that it was he, Trotsky, who had deliberately opposed the development of a Red cavalry.

In the spring of 1919, several major events that were totally unexpected by Denikin further enhanced his military position: Vsevolodov, the former colonel commanding the Soviet Ninth Army, defected from the Reds and joined the Volunteer Army, after deliberately snarling and disorganizing the operative plans of his troops. Also, huge uprisings flared up in the Soviet rear. The Cossacks of the Upper Don sector, recently occupied by the Red Army, rose against the Communists. The sympathy of these well-to-do farmers was definitely on the side of the Whites. The rebellion expanded, and by April there were thirty thousand insurgent Cossacks in arms.

An uprising in the Ukraine was instigated by *Ataman* Grigoriev, the same adventurer and freebooter who, a few months earlier, had abandoned Petliura for the Bolsheviks and fought against the French near Odessa, and who now decided to coordinate and lead the series of small anti-Bolshevik peasant revolts flaring up in the region. He had sixteen thousand men under his command. They were natives of the Kherson and Ekaterinoslav provinces, along with some from the provinces of Poltava and Kiev. They exterminated the Communists and representatives of the Soviet government in Cherkasy, Elizavetgrad, Aleksandria, Znamenka, and other towns and villages, perpetrating cruel pogroms against the Jewish population wherever they went.

Grigoriev's uprising confused all the plans of the Red Army command, forcing them to withdraw a large part of their troops from the Denikin front in order to quell it. Insurgent bands which recognized no one's authority were roaming the Ukraine. The ones led by the anarchist Makhnó elicited the particular fear and distrust of the Bolsheviks. Makhnó was a master of partisan warfare, and conducted his raids with extraordinary skill and fearlessness. He considered the "White generals" as the prime "enemies of the people" and collaborated for the time being with the Red Army. But the Bolsheviks foresaw that at a given moment all his energy and pitiless cruelty could be turned against them.

All these developments were in Denikin's favor, and by the beginning of May, enabled him to concentrate 50,500 troops against the remaining 95,000 to 105,000 of the Red Army. He also sent into action his recently arrived British tanks.

"Early May," wrote the General, "was a sharp turning point for the Armed Forces of South Russia. The Bolshevik front wavered, and all our armies, from the Caspian Sea to the Black Sea, were launched in a vigorous offensive." [4] This offensive, which continued uninterrupted for nearly six months, brought Denikin to the fore in the historic role of the principal and most dangerous foe of Soviet dictatorship in the civil-war period. By October, he had wrested from the enemy a territory of 820,000 square kilometers, with a population of 42 million people; the line of his front extended from Tsaritsin on the Volga, through Voronezh, Orel, Chernigov, and Kiev, to Odessa, and all of these cities were occupied by the White Army.

At the outset of the great offensive of May, 1919, the Armed Forces of South Russia consisted of three armies—the Volunteer, the Don Cossack, and the Caucasian—and of several independent detachments. General Mai-Maevsky was placed in command of the Volunteers, General Sidorin commanded the Don Cossacks and General Wrangel commanded the Caucasian forces.

The Volunteer Army included all the original, tried and tested Volunteer units—the Kornilov, Markov, Drozdovsky, and Alekseev regiments. The choice of Mai-Maevsky as commander of this army was based on the fact that he had successfully

borne the brunt of the entire six-month long defense of the Donets Basin . . . [during which, as Denikin put it] he conducted "a railroad war," applying a special tactical approach to offset the enemy's overwhelming numerical superiority. Using the dense network of railroad lines in the Donets Basin, Mai-Maevsky occupied the principal points of the front line with small detachments and kept armored trains filled with mobile reserve units at railroad junctions in the rear. These were rapidly thrown into action in any direction threatened by the enemy, and quite often, rerouted on the following or even the same day, to an opposite sector of the front. The enemy received the impression that we were uniformly strong in all directions, while in actual fact, the same people were fighting day in and day out, moving from point to point and resting on the train . . . physically exhausted but full of courage.[5]

The human material under Mai-Maevsky's command was of quite exceptional military caliber and spirit. But there is also no doubt that the General, though he later turned out to be an incurable alcoholic, managed at that time to keep himself in hand and to display outstanding military ability. He was rather repulsive physically. Small, obese, with a clean-shaven flabby face and a large fleshy nose surmounted by rimless eyeglasses, with tiny pig eyes, he looked more like a provincial actor gone to seed than like a fighting general, yet even General Wrangel, who was one of his harshest critics, had to recognize Mai-Maevsky's vast experience and military erudition. "Unquestionably an intelligent man . . . whose conversation was quite impressive," wrote Wrangel about him.[6]

The command of the Volunteer Army's First Army Corps was assumed by General A. P. Kutepov, a brave, determined, and firm man who had participated in all the Volunteer Army campaigns from the beginning.

The numerical strength of the Don Cossack army fluctuated throughout the entire course of the civil war, depending on the psychological conditions of the moment. In periods of success (as in the fall of 1918, under *Ataman* Krasnov) its numbers rose as high as fifty thousand. In periods of retreat, it melted away. Thus, by May, 1919, it had been reduced to fifteen thousand men; General Denikin's successes again revived the Don Cossacks' spirits, and they enthusiastically began to clear their region of Bolsheviks. By late June, 1919, the Don Cossack army had grown to forty thousand men.

General Wrangel's Caucasian army was mainly composed of cavalry units. The Kuban Cossacks formed its nucleus. The army consisted of three cavalry corps, commanded by Generals Ulagai, Pokrovsky, and Shatilov, the composite Don Cossack corps, the Sixth Infantry Division, and several smaller units.

The Volunteer Army was stationed at the left flank of the Armed Forces of South Russia; next came the Don Cossack army, and on the right flank, the Caucasian army. Even farther to the right, in the direction of Astrakhan, operated a detachment of five thousand men under General Erdeli.

In addition to these troops, some smaller units were located in the eastern part of the Crimean peninsula, to which they had been transferred by General Denikin considerably earlier, in November, 1918. Despite their small numbers, these units were at first impressively called the Crimea-Azov Volunteer Army; later, they were reorganized as a division. These units had moved forward to northern Taurida, but were soon forced back by Soviet troops, first toward Dzhankoi, then toward Kerch, where they succeeded in consolidating their position. They stopped sixty-five kilometers west of Kerch and occupied positions near Akmanai, along the narrow twenty-kilometer-wide part of the isthmus separating the Black Sea from the Sea of Azov. The situation of this small army, which had to fend off the attacks of vastly superior and better-armed Red troops, was extremely difficult. It became even worse when a well-organized Bolshevik uprising flared up at the rear among local longshoremen and quarry workers, who used as their base of operations the numerous quarries and catacombs in the vicinity of Kerch. The catacombs dated back to the times when the region was the site of the ancient Greek colony of Panticapaeum. Archaeologists had been exploring them since the preceding century, bringing to light many treasures of Hellenistic art—statues, urns, gold ornaments and sarcophagi which were transported to the Hermitage Museum in St. Petersburg. Besides the catacombs, the region was riddled with quarries containing vast underground labyrinths with innumerable entrances and exits. The insurgents made brilliant use of the location. Emerging from their underground hideouts, they captured Volunteer Army transports and men and terrorized the bourgeois elements of the population. A great deal of time and tremendous effort were required to quell the uprising while continuing the fight at the front and at the rear. The uprising was finally ended in the middle of May, and the Volunteer units were then able to plan an offensive. But in order to start it, they had to break through the well-fortified positions of the Reds on the Kerch isthmus near Akmanai. They were strongly supported in this undertaking by warships of the Allied fleet stationed nearby.[7]

A few weeks earlier, one of these warships, the British dreadnought H.M.S. *Marlborough*, had carried out a special mission at the request of the British royal family: At the beginning of April, 1919, the situation of the Crimea appeared hopeless and Soviet troops were moving unimpeded toward Sebastopol and Yalta, the area where most of the remaining members of the Russian imperial family were then residing. At that time, England's Dowager Queen Alexandra wrote her sister, the Dowager Empress Marie Fedorovna, imploring her to leave Russia before it was too late. The letter was entrusted to Captain Johnson, commander of the *Marlborough*, with instructions from the British Admiralty to give every assistance to the Empress Marie and the members of her family. Johnson's mission was successfully completed: H.M.S. *Marlborough* left the Crimea carrying aboard the mother of Russia's last Tsar, his sister Grand Duchess Xenia and her children, the former Supreme Commander of the Russian armies, Grand Duke Nicholas, and his brother Grand Duke Peter, with their families and numerous entourage.[8]

The successes of Denikin's troops were developing with extraordinary momentum along the entire front. In the first month of the offensive, the Volunteer Army, overcoming enemy resistance, moved forward on a wide front to a distance of over three hundred kilometers into the Ukraine. On June 10, General Kutepov took Belgorod. On June 11, Volunteer Army detachments occupied Kharkov. On June 16, General Shkuró's cavalry units stormed into Ekaterinoslav, and they were soon in control of the entire lower reaches of the Dnieper.

The Don Cossack army dealt crushing blows to the Eighth and Ninth Soviet armies. Pursuing the enemy, it joined forces with the insurgent Cossacks of the Upper Don district and liberated from the Bolsheviks the entire Don region. By early June, they had overrun its confines and advanced to the level of Balashov-Povorino-Novyi Oskol.

In the meantime, General Wrangel's Caucasian army was advancing on Tsaritsin. The Soviet government referred to the future city of Stalingrad as the "Red Verdun," and swore that it would never be surrendered to the enemy. General Wrangel's troops had to traverse hundreds of kilometers of unpopulated and often waterless steppe, under conditions of dire privation. The endless stretches of plain, overgrown with feather grass and interspersed with salt marshes, were intersected by the railroad branch connecting Velikokniazheskaia with Tsaritsin, which was supposed to supply the advancing army with war materiel and food. The retreating Soviet Tenth Army, however, destroyed tracks and blew up bridges on its way, greatly impeding the progress of the Whites. General Wrangel was faced with the choice of either waiting for the railroad and bridges to be repaired, or as General Denikin wrote later, "relying on the elements of speed and surprise, [to] pursue the enemy relentlessly and rush into Tsaritsin in its wake." Wrangel chose the latter course. Having reached Tsaritsin, he attacked its fortified approaches, engaging the enemy in a series of violent skirmishes which lasted several days and were perhaps the bloodiest of the civil war. Success shifted from one side to the other. The Reds resisted stubbornly and occasionally counterattacked. The Caucasian army suffered heavy losses. Among the killed and wounded were five division commanders, two brigade commanders, and eleven regimental commanders. While the battle for the city raged, however, the Whites worked feverishly at restoring the bridges and tracks, and the renewed functioning of the railroad finally saved the situation. Armored trains, cars, and tanks, as well as the Seventh Infantry Division, were moved up to the rescue, and on June 17, the Caucasian army broke through the Red Army fortifications and entered Tsaritsin.

The Seventh Infantry Division had been formed from the units, formerly commanded by General Timanovsky, which had been interned in Rumania following the surrender of Odessa by the French. They had just arrived by troopship at Novorossiisk, and were placed almost immediately at General Wrangel's disposal.

The march on Tsaritsin had lasted forty days. In its course, the Caucasian army captured forty thousand prisoners, seventy pieces of artillery, three hundred machine guns, two Red Army armored trains (*Lenin* and *Trotsky*), 131 locomotives, and nearly ten thousand railroad cars, 2,085 of which were loaded with artillery and commissary supplies.[9]

It was a great victory—Tsaritsin's economic and strategic importance to the Soviet government was quite exceptional. The city was the terminal point of the railroad which traversed the North Caucasus to Novorossiisk, thus linking the Volga region with the Black Sea ports. Moreover, the loss of Tsaritsin cut off central Russia from the lower reaches of the Volga and from the Caspian Sea. Important artillery and munitions factories and huge depots storing various military supplies were located in and around the city. It was also the closest point to Kolchak's armies reached by Denikin. By that time, however, the Admiral's troops were continuously retreating eastward under Bolshevik pressure, and the distance between the two White armies increased every day.

The Soviet Tenth Army, pursued by Kuban Cossack units, was rapidly withdrawing northward along the Volga. General Wrangel's popularity in south Russia grew every day. Generals Ulagai, Pokrovsky, and Shatilov had also distinguished themselves under his command in the Tsaritsin battles.

Meanwhile, the Volunteer units in the Crimea and the Kerch isthmus had overthrown the Reds, and by June 16, completely cleared the Bolsheviks from the Crimean peninsula.

Only General Erdeli's detachment, for reasons beyond his control, had remained unsuccessful, marking time in the region of Astrakhan without ever succeeding in capturing that city.

General Denikin arrived in Tsaritsin a day after its occupation. He was met by an honor guard, and thanked General Wrangel for his brilliant victory. Later, he attended a solemn *Te Deum* in the cathedral and reviewed the troops. The citizens of Tsaritsin gave its liberators an enthusiastic welcome. Jubilant crowds filled the cathedral square and all the streets adjoining it.

The rapid and successful advance of his troops opened up enormous possibilities for General Denikin. One of his closest associates, General Lukomsky, summed up the situation as follows:

> The first impression was that Bolshevik resistance had completely collapsed and that they no longer had the strength to resist the northward advance of our troops. But the commander in chief and his staff were fully aware that our position was far from secure, as the front of the Volunteer Army was inordinately extended, weak in every area, and lacking instantly available reserves. On the one hand, it was necessary to pause, replenish the gaps in our ranks, bring up reserves, and restore order in the rear. On the other hand, however, it was dangerous to grant the enemy a respite and there was the temptation to expand our success without giving the disorganized units of the Soviet army a chance to recover.[10]

Thus, two choices were open to Denikin—to stop and consolidate the newly occupied territory or to continue the northward offensive. As we shall see, it was not "the temptation to expand our success" which prompted the General to choose the second course, but a number of other considerations. Realizing the numerical insufficiency of his troops, he considered that the only way to achieve a final victory was to pursue the enemy forces, in order to demoralize them completely and break their resistance without letting them recuperate and regain their senses. Only by moving forward, reasoned Denikin, could his army be enlarged and revitalized. He hoped to recruit fresh forces in the Ukraine and knew that without them the balance of power would remain with the Reds, who would eventually crush him by their enormous numerical superiority.

Denikin considered the alternative of stopping the offensive in order to consolidate his position to be out of the question. In his opinion, this approach, which would be logical in fighting a foreign power, was unacceptable under the conditions of a civil war, in which the element of psychology plays a dominating role and every delay strengthens the enemy.

Since the beginning of May, General Denikin's forces had been advancing in a wide fanlike movement, spreading out in different directions. After the occupation of Tsaritsin, he decided to have his troops move from their widely scattered locations toward the center of Russia, along lines converging at a single point—Moscow. The flanks of his army would thus be pulled in to reinforce its center, and the main thrust on Moscow would be made by the Volunteer Army by the shortest route, through Kharkov, Kursk, Orel and Tula.

On June 20, General Denikin issued from Tsaritsin an order to his armies which later became widely known as the Moscow Directive:

Having as my ultimate aim the capture of the heart of Russia—Moscow, I hereby order:

1. General Wrangel to advance to the Saratov-Rtishchevo-Balashov front, replace the Don Cossack units in those sections, and continue to advance toward Penza, Ruzaevka, Arzamas, and later Nizhni-Novgorod, Vladimir, and Moscow.

2. General Sidorin—with his right flank, prior to the advance of General Wrangel's troops, to continue implementing his former assignment of advancing to the Kamyshin-Balashov front. Remaining units to develop thrust on Moscow in directions of a) Voronezh, Kozlov, Riazan, and b) Novyi Oskol, Elets, Volevo, Kashira.

3. General Mai-Maevsky to advance on Moscow in the direction of Kursk, Orel, Tula. In order to ensure protection from the west, advance to the line of the Dnieper and Desna rivers, after taking Kiev and other points of crossing in the Ekaterinoslav-Briansk sector.[11]

There followed five other instructions concerning less significant sections of the front.

Denikin's troops proceeded to carry out their orders. The territory occupied by the Armed Forces of South Russia grew larger every day. Kherson and Nikolaev were occupied early in August; Odessa, on August 10; and Kiev, on August 17. On September 7, the First Army Corps, commanded by General Kutepov, took Kursk; on September 17, General Shkuró's cavalry stormed into Voronezh; and on September 30, General Kutepov's units occupied Orel.

The Fifth Cavalry Corps, recently assembled from cadres of cavalry regiments of the prerevolutionary Russian army, was operating successfully in the direction of Chernigov. Its commander was General I. D. Iuzefovich, and its chief of staff was the recently promoted General Kusonsky. Having occupied Bakhmach, units of the corps captured Baturin, Nezhin, Konotop, Korop, Krolevets, and Glukhov, and were approaching the large gunpowder works of Shostka.

The White armies advanced so rapidly that their command could already imagine the joyous pealing of church bells in liberated Moscow.

At the beginning of August, the Reds made an unsuccessful attempt to wrest the initiative from the Whites, but Denikin retained his command of the situation. A Red Army group headed by Selivachev, a former general who served under Denikin in 1917 on the southwestern front, attempted a move on the cities of Kharkov and Belgorod, while another group, commanded by Shorin, advanced in the direction of Tsaritsin. However, skillful flanking maneuvers of the White command repulsed the troops of both Selivachev and Shorin.[12]

At approximately the same time, a special cavalry group of seven to eight thousand Don Cossacks was placed under the command of General Mamontov, whose mission was to disrupt the operations of the Bolsheviks' southern front and create panic at its rear. Breaking through the front, Mamontov carried out a month-long cavalry action, penetrating to the farthermost rear of the enemy. On his way, he alternately seized and abandoned such important points as Tambov, Kozlov, Lebedin, Elets, Griazi, and Kastornaia, destroying railroad bridges and war-supply depots.

Mamontov's operation greatly alarmed Moscow. It could have achieved important results for the White Army, had not Mamontov himself and his men succumbed to a passion for looting. The detachment turned into a band of marauders; its transport, filled with stolen goods, stretched out for sixty kilometers. All that the Cossacks wanted now was to bring their loot back to their *stanitsy* as soon as possible. This brought the detachment's military usefulness to an end.

The Moscow Directive unquestionably reflected tremendous optimism. After the failure of Denikin's epic offensive, it became the target of bitter criticism. The General was blamed not only for excessive optimism, but for overestimating his army's successes and underestimating the assets remaining at Moscow's disposal. One should bear in mind, however, that Denikin had ample grounds for optimism at that time. All the reports and information reaching him from the Soviet zone spoke of the alarm, and later the panic, which had seized the Soviet government, of the disintegration of Red Army troops and the mounting anger of a population continuously harassed by the requisitions and arbitrary rule of the Soviet power.

Moscow's nervousness, which grew rapidly with every advance of Denikin's forces, was reflected in the telegrams sent by Lenin, the letters of his closest collaborators, dispatches from the front, resolutions of the Central Committee of the Communist party, and other documents later published in the Soviet Union.

For example, in his telegram of April 22* to the Commander of the Ukrainian front, Lenin said that Denikin had made magnificent use of existing conditions and that "colossal danger" threatened from that direction.[13]

---

* All Soviet documents quoted in this chapter (beginning with April 22 and through September 30, 1919) are dated according to the Gregorian calendar.

Lenin was extremely worried and irritated by the Don Cossack uprising, which gathered momentum in April and May and proved impossible to suppress. In a series of telegrams to G. I. Sokolnikov, a member of the Revolutionary Military Council of the southern front (executed by Stalin in 1936 for antiparty activity and participation in the "Trotsky-Zinoviev" bloc), Lenin fumed at the delay in liquidating the uprising, and demanded immediate "fierce and pitiless reprisals" for the insurgents. "For us," wrote Lenin, "the most ruthless, immediate *coûte que coûte* suppression of the uprising is an absolute necessity. . . . End the uprising at all costs!"

The appearance of a French colloquialism in an official "proletarian" document strikes one as incongruous. The most interesting aspect of his telegrams, however, is the inclusion of two seemingly contradictory questions, which closely follow each other: "Should we send additional complements of *Chekists* [secret police agents]?" and "Couldn't we promise an amnesty, and at this cost, induce them to surrender their arms?" [14] Generous promises to the enemy were a form of bait widely and deliberately used by Lenin, who followed them up with ruthless reprisals.

Worry caused by Denikin's successes fills Lenin's teleprinted conversation (of May 28, 1919) with the President of the Ukrainian Council of People's Commissars, Rakovsky: "We are forced to resort to heroic measures, right up to dispatching to the south masses of command trainees, which may very soon deprive the Red Army of Red commanders. . . . For this reason the Central Committee of the Russian Communist party insists that it considers every minute of delay in extending military assistance to the southern front a crime for which Antonov [commander of the Ukrainian front] and Podvoisky [people's commissar for Ukrainian military affairs] will be held fully responsible."

Both N. I. Podvoisky and V. A. Antonov-Ovseenko were important party members, but at that time, they aroused undisguised irritation in Lenin, who complained in the same teleprinted conversation that "Antonov and Podvoisky get off by sending shallow and boastful telegrams." [15]

On August 10, Lenin wrote to the Revolutionary Military Council of the Republic, "Denikin's successes are enormous. . . . What happened? How could we have missed out so badly? . . . It is utterly unthinkable to delay with the offensive, as such a delay will deliver all of the Ukraine to Denikin and destroy us. You are answerable for every extra day and even hour of delay in the offensive." [16]

Despite Lenin's threats, Denikin's spectacular advance continued, eliciting desperate appeals for help to Moscow from the Soviet's southern front: "The Don Basin is under direct threat by Denikin," wrote Voroshilov on May 11. "We have abandoned Lugansk and Radkovo. The Communist workers of Kharkov and the Donets Basin have been mobilized. Grigoriev has started an uprising and approached Ekaterinoslav and Kremenchug. The downfall is near. Help with everything you can!" [17]

A report by the Red commander in chief, I. Vatsetis, delivered on June 24, 1919, painted a distressing picture for the Revolutionary Military Council of the Republic:

In all directions . . . particularly the Kharkov-Voronezh one and to the north of Tsaritsin, are operating large, high-quality cavalry forces of the enemy, whose maneuvering enables him to perform deep enveloping movements around our troops, which are weak in cavalry. . . . The situation at the southern front at this time is admittedly threatening, as, in addition to the instability of our troops, the enemy exceeds them numerically by 150 percent [an absurd exaggeration], has a vastly larger cavalry, and the morale of the entire Don Cossack army is at an unprecedentedly high level. The [enemy's] thrust is aimed at the weakest spot in our republic, in the direction of the Tula war works, located at the approaches to Moscow, and is forcing our southern armies toward its starving center.[18]

At long last, at the beginning of July, the Central Committee of the Communist party openly appealed to the public at large with a veritable outcry for help, headed by the slogan, "All out against Denikin!" The appeal was sent to all party organizations and cells and printed in the newspaper *Izvestia* on July 9. The danger could no longer be kept secret. It was approaching with incredible rapidity.

Comrades! [proclaimed the appeal], one of the most critical, perhaps even the most critical moment of the socialist revolution has arrived. The defenders of exploiters, landlords, and capitalists, both Russian and foreign (with the British and French at their head) are making a desperate attempt to reinstate the power of the despoilers of popular toil, the landowners and exploiters of Russia, in order to strengthen their declining power in the whole world. . . . Foreign capitalists are now making a desperate attempt to reestablish the capitalist yoke by Denikin's invasion. . . . The efforts of workers and peasants, all the efforts of the Soviet republic, must be concentrated on repulsing Denikin's invasion and overcoming him.

Along with its appeal for help, this lengthy document instructed the members of the Communist party in minute detail concerning the propaganda to be used at this critical moment (such as "acquainting the people with the truth concerning Kolchak and Denikin"), told them how to contend with desertion and counterrevolution in the rear, how to conduct a general mobilization, and so on. The main instrument to be applied throughout was terrorism:

Our business is to look facts in the face. Which is better? To seek out and imprison and sometimes even shoot hundreds of traitors among the Cadets, the politically neutral, the Mensheviks, and the Socialist Revolutionaries, who "act" (some with arms, some by agitating against mobilization, like the printers and railwaymen among the Mensheviks) *against* the Soviet government, *i.e., for Denikin?* [Italics in original] Or should we allow matters to reach the point of allowing Kolchak and Denikin to beat, shoot, and whip to death tens of thousands of workers and peasants? The choice is not difficult. There is one, and only one, way to solve the problem! [19]

The last part of the appeal had its effect. Terror enveloped all the Communist-controlled territory. Not "hundreds of traitors," but tens of thousands of innocent people were sought out and executed without investigation or trial.

"Denikin's offensive is an attack on the very existence of the Communist party," proclaimed another appeal of the Central Committee, dated September 30, 1919. "Every reserve of revolutionary energy possessed by our party must be used in the fight against Denikin. Our entire government apparatus must serve a single aim—to vanquish Denikin and destroy the forces of his White-guard bands." [20]

A month later Stalin, who had been appointed a member of the Revolutionary Military Council of the southern front, formulated with utmost clarity the idea of "exterminating the living forces" of the enemy. In speaking by direct wire with Ordzhonikidze, a member of the Fourteenth Army's Revolutionary Military Council, he demanded the physical extermination of Denikin's best regiments. "I repeat—exterminate, for we are speaking about extermination," were the concluding words of Stalin's instructions.[21]

On September 30, the Central Committee of the Communist party issued orders for organizing the immediate defense of Moscow and Tula: ". . . The immediate military as well as political problem of the forthcoming month is to repulse, by any means and at the cost of any sacrifices and losses, the advance of Denikin and to defend Tula, with its war works, and Moscow against him. Then, using the immense superiority of our infantry, to assume the offensive against Denikin's cavalry, which will be paralyzed by impassable roads and slush." As usual, the role of propaganda was heavily stressed: "It is imperative to create a state of mind which will immediately make Denikin's men feel that they are in enemy country." [22]

These documents show how close Denikin had come to that invisible psychological boundary whose crossing, in the climate of the civil war, could have resulted in the overthrow and total dissolution of the Bolsheviks' armed resistance.

XXII

COMMANDER IN CHIEF
OF THE ARMED FORCES
OF SOUTH RUSSIA

During the spring, summer, and autumn of 1919, the attention not only of south Russia but of the entire country was concentrated on General Denikin. He was discussed in every corner of the former Russian Empire—with hope by some and with hatred by others.

Denikin's nationwide reputation was founded on the exploits of his Iron Division in World War I, on his opposition to the demoralization of the old army under the Provisional Government, on his courageous and open declaration of support for General Kornilov, and on his forceful oratory. Everyone knew about the dangers the general had faced during his incarceration in Berdichev and his transfer as a prisoner from Berdichev to Bykhov; all had heard of his escape from Bykhov to the Don and of his role in the creation of the Volunteer Army, which he had rescued from the peril of Bolshevik encirclement after Kornilov's death. The liberation of the Kuban and the North Caucasus and the Volunteer Army's breakthrough on a wide front leading to central Russia, all these created a heroic aura around Denikin's person and made his name universally known.

In south Russia he was acclaimed as a hero by many, but he was criticized by many others for the absence of a definite political program in the movement which he headed and for his inexperience in politics and matters of state.[1] Some of his critics were politically inclined to the right and others to the left, but even their most severe and outspoken condemnations of Denikin's strategy and administration never detracted from his moral image or heroic stature—with the exception, of course, of the Bolsheviks' propaganda, which spared no efforts in attempting to demolish Denikin's character as well as his military reputation.

Anton Ivanovich wished that he could command the widespread support of various political factions, but their class and party selfishness repelled him. The rightist circles were bent on defending the interests of former landowners and industrialists. As for the Socialist Revolutionaries and Mensheviks, he considered them completely devoid of common sense after the events of 1917. His own political views brought him close to the Cadet party. But this party, also, had been too timorous and uncertain during the Kornilov crisis to command his respect.

Denikin was fully aware of the need for popular support for his cause. He was, however, faced with the insoluble dilemma of finding a policy that could satisfy and unite all classes. A major part of the population consisted of peasants, whose good will he could earn by recognizing and officially confirming their ownership of the land which they had expropriated from the landowners in the winter of 1917. Denikin himself, the son of a former serf, had never owned a home or a piece of land and had been in favor of a radical agrarian reform since Stolypin's time. But he refused to recognize violence and usurpation as the means of achieving it. He considered that the agrarian question in Russia should be resolved legally, by the majority vote of representatives of the entire country, in a national or constituent assembly called after the overthrow of the Soviet power.

In theory, General Denikin was vested with unlimited power. In actual fact, however, he had to consider the reaction of the Volunteers to his every move. His promise not to predetermine the future form of the Russian government was, therefore, not only a formula in which he sincerely believed, but also the only one which could retain both monarchists and republicans in the ranks of his army.

Politics frustrated Denikin. By preference, he surrounded himself mainly with military advisers, with whose help he hoped to terminate the civil war by purely military measures, culminating in the defeat of the Red Army and the downfall of the Soviet power.

Military operations, the complicated and unfamiliar problems of civilian administration, and the delicate relationships with the newly formed states on Russia's periphery, left Denikin little time for his personal life. What there was of it was extremely secluded. Only a small group of his closest colleagues penetrated his family circle. Unlike many present-day statesmen, Denikin firmly believed that his private life belonged to him and had no bearing on his public career. His solitude was mitigated by his close friendship with his chief of staff, Ivan Pavlovich Romanovsky, with whom he shared his interests, hopes, joys, and sorrows.

Denikin had not sought power. It had come to him unbidden and unwelcome, and only his sense of duty had made him accept and carry its heavy burden. Deep down, he longed for very different things: for the companionship of his wife, whom he rarely saw, and for the family life which circumstances had never allowed him to enjoy. He longed for privacy and the opportunity to continue his work in the field of military literature and history.

Denikin's wife was expecting a child. Her health was delicate, and she was ill during most of her pregnancy. While suffering all the anxiety of an elderly prospective father, Anton Ivanovich intensely hoped for a son, whom he had already decided to name Ivan. His quiet talks with his wife, during his infrequent visits to their home in Ekaterinodar, were all about the expected "Van'ka," as were Denikin's letters to Xenia Vasilievna from the front, from the combat zone at Stavropol, and from the various towns, *stanitsy* and villages where his presence was indispensable. "I am infinitely happy if it is true that my dream of Van'ka will be fulfilled," became the refrain of many letters.[2]

There was to be no Van'ka, however; instead, a daughter, Marina, was born on February 20, 1919. The delivery was difficult. Mrs. Denikin's physicians telegraphed the General at the front advising him that they might face a choice between preserving the life of the mother or that of her child and requesting instructions. After telegraphing the doctors to do everything in their power to save his wife's life, Denikin, tortured by anxiety, journeyed home as quickly as possible. Fortunately, all was well when he arrived.[3]

One of Denikin's dreams "when all this will be over" was to acquire a plot of land somewhere on Russia's southern shores. He was vague about the actual location of the spot, but wanted it to be near the sea, with a small garden and a field in the back in which he could plant cabbage. This dream of cabbage was often mentioned in his conversations with his wife and close friends and in his letters. It seemed to symbolize his desire to escape from the alien and unhealthy atmosphere of large urban centers and their complicated intrigues, and to revert to the life of his forefathers.

"My program," he announced one day to a group of Cadet party representatives, "consists of restoring Russia and then raising cabbage." [4]

"Oh dear, Assia," wrote the General to his wife, when will the time come for planting cabbage?" [5]

Anton Ivanovich was completely disinterested where money was concerned. He had known nothing but poverty since his youth, was used to it, and had come to the conclusion that wealth was not a condition of happiness. The important command positions he had achieved during the war had allowed him to maintain his mother in Kiev in comparative comfort. As for himself, he had spent those years of relative affluence in the trenches. When he became the ruler of south Russia, Denikin's habitual frugality was enhanced by the fear of being accused of extravagance. When, in the warm spring of 1919, the General was asked why he continued to wear his heavy Circassian coat, he answered quite frankly,

"My last pair of pants is torn and my summer uniform tunic isn't long enough to cover them."

At the outset of 1919, despite the General's exalted position, the Denikins lived in poverty. Xenia Vasilievna cooked the family's scanty meals, and her husband went about in patched trousers and worn-out boots. One of his close associates testified later that, because of his extreme scrupulousness, Denikin "contented himself with a salary which did not allow him to satisfy the essential requirements of an extremely modest way of life." [6] Fortunately, the arrival of uniforms from Great Britain at the beginning of the summer solved the General's clothing problem.

Anton Ivanovich expected his officers and civilian employees in south Russia to follow his example of abnegation. Professor K. N. Sokolov, then in charge of the propaganda department, wrote in his memoirs that the wretched salaries of these people reduced them to "a choice between heroic starving and the misuse of funds. . . . One of the reasons why graft and rapine developed so quickly in south Russia lay precisely in our system of starvation salaries." [7]

The insufficient pay provoked discontent, particularly when it was compared to the more generous salaries of the Don and Kuban armies. Denikin was labeled a miser. But he was first and foremost a miser in relation to himself. He wrote to his wife, "The Special Council fixed my salary at twelve thousand rubles a month. I crossed the amounts out for myself and others and reduced mine by one half. I hope that you won't scold me." [8]

This was in the days of catastrophic inflation, when the value of paper money issued without any backing fell, day by day, as the cost of living spiraled. Before the raise in question, Denikin had received a little over a thousand rubles a month, and his close associates got even less. In those inflationary days, such amounts could not even pay for the bare necessities of life.

Many of the commander in chief's advisers pointed out to him that "such economizing of state funds would lead to no good, as the officers' miserable salaries would drive them to looting." [9] The commander in chief, however, expected "self-sacrificing modesty" from his officers. He was to be disappointed in this as in many of his other hopes.

"There is no peace of mind," wrote the General to his wife. "Every day brings its quota of rapine, plunder, coercion, in the whole territory occupied by our armed forces. From the lowliest to the highest, the Russian people has fallen so low that I cannot foretell when it will be able to rise from the mire. There is no prospect of help in this matter from any direction. I threaten with penal servitude and hanging in impotent anger. . . . But I cannot be expected, after all, to catch and hang marauders at the front and at the rear single-handed." [10]

The situation called for Draconian laws, but the General, while rigorously strict concerning himself, had none of the traits of the true dictator.

We wrote drastic laws, which usually called for the death penalty. We sent generals invested with emergency powers and accompanied by committees of inquiry to the armies, to examine locally committed crimes. The army commanders and I issued orders designed to combat violence, looting, robbing of prisoners, etc. But these laws and decrees sometimes met with the obstinate resistance of elements which refused to recognize their moral significance and crucial need.

We should have started at the top, and instead of that, went after the rank and file. [11]

This frank admission gives us one of the reasons for the eventual failure of the White movement in south Russia.

Like Don Quixote, Denikin was divorced from historical reality. His courage, honor, and idealism, all that he believed in and professed but could not obtain from his subordinates, were part of the discord between dream and reality, spirit and matter, poetry and the prose of everyday life, which characterized Cervantes' famous hero. His very principles of patriotism, honor, and duty weakened Denikin's approach to a practical and drastic solution of the immediate problem. Theory, as he admitted himself, no longer agreed with practice.

A man of outstanding intellect but little flexibility, Denikin realized his mistakes when it was too late, and confessed them with his usual candor. The admission of these mistakes made in his five-volume *Ocherki Russkoi Smuty (The Russian Turmoil)* has the ring of profound tragedy; the memory of the black pages in the history of the White movement, and the thought that he had been incapable of coping with its shameful excesses, haunted Anton Ivanovich Denikin to the end of his life.

In 1919, Xenia Vasilievna's youth limited her to the role of affable hostess. She poured tea or served a modest repast, but as she herself admitted, at that time she took no part in the conversation, which was usually centered on political problems. Besides Denikin's closest collaborators and their wives, the only people who came to the Denikins' house in Ekaterinodar were Countess Sophie Panin, N. I. Astrov, and M. M. Fedorov, all active members of the Cadet party, and possibly two or three others.

The Denikin family's attention was concentrated on little Marina. Her christening was quite an event for her parents. It was performed by the Right Reverend Father George Shavelsky, former chaplain of the imperial army and navy, who was serving in the same capacity in south Russia. The godfather and godmother were General Lukomsky and the wife of General Romanovsky. The Denikins, Lukomskys, and Romanovskys had much to talk about and many memories to share with Father Shavelsky after the christening.

Anton Ivanovich had known the priest for many years, but their acquaintance had become more intimate in the spring of 1917, when Denikin was chief of staff of the Supreme Commander. Shavelsky particularly relished the memory of an incident which had posed a problem to him and Denikin in Mogilev.

The Reverend Father had on his staff an archdeacon named Speransky. He was an honest and kindly man whose thunderous bass and splendid rendering of prayers was greatly admired, especially when, at the end of the office for the dead, he intoned, "In blessed dormition give rest eternal, O Lord, to thy servant. . . ." One weakness, however, marred the good qualities of the archdeacon; he loved to down an extra shot of vodka when he was in convivial company. This was not easy, since the sale of alcoholic beverages had been prohibited during the war. But he found a way to circumvent the problem, and it was for this reason that Denikin had to summon Shavelsky.

"Look here, Father, your archdeacon has taken a whole pailful of pure alcohol from the depot for cleaning the church plate," said Anton Ivanovich. "Hell! This is inconceivable! They will all become inveterate drunkards."

Father Shavelsky investigated the matter. The archdeacon denied nothing, but stated in self-defense that the local Catholic priest had taken five pailfuls of alcohol "for cleaning the church plate," while he, Speransky, had modestly taken one. The cleric's guilelessness disarmed both church and army authorities. He was allowed to keep his pailful but warned that in the future he would have to find a different way of keeping the church plate clean.[12]

In the summer of 1919, the Denikin household grew by the addition of a soldier-cook, with primitive culinary talents, and a nurse, who quickly gained the upper hand in the nursery. Like most Russian *nianias,* she became totally devoted to the child, but treated the parents with jealous intolerance, especially the mother, to whom she was consistently rude. Xenia Vasilievna recollected without affection that "she had poisoned a good deal of my life." The General was not in the nurse's good graces either, but took a good-natured view of her despotic attitude and did not interfere in the nursery feuds between his wife and the *niania,* whom he nicknamed the Rural Tyrant.

Until May, 1919, the eastern front of the civil war had occupied the principal attention of the Soviet government. At the time of the Omsk *coup d'état* of November 17–18, 1918, which tumbled the Directory and proclaimed Admiral Kolchak Supreme Ruler, the strategic position of the White armies in Siberia was very precarious. The Red armies, under the overall command of former colonel S. Kamenev, were pressing against them along the entire front, which extended from north to south for over a thousand kilometers. The inclement Siberian winter, however, with its rigorous frosts, held up their forward movement, and in February, 1919, both sides, exhausted by marching conditions, became stationary along the approximate line of Perm-Ufa-Orenburg-Uralsk. In March and April, the military initiative passed from the Reds to the Whites. The balance of forces at that time favored Kolchak's army, which numbered 120,000 to 130,000 Whites, as against 110,000 Reds. It began to move westward in the direction of the Volga with unexpected rapidity, advancing almost six hundred kilometers in one month. But having come to within approximately a hundred kilometers from Simbirsk (Lenin's home town) and sixty kilometers from Samara, the White regiments first slowed down at the end of April, then began to roll back eastward with a speed equal to that of their offensive.

The reasons for Kolchak's rapid retreat were not clear to the members of Denikin's general staff, but they were not alarmed. There was practically no liaison with the theater of operations in the east. Details were lacking, and having become accustomed in the last few months to the tremendous shifts at the eastern front—from the Urals to the Volga and back—General Denikin had no way of knowing at the time that the current turn of the Admiral's military luck was the prologue to the downfall of the White movement in Siberia. Ironically, it was precisely at this period that he came to the final decision of submitting himself to Kolchak's authority and officially recognizing his supreme command, in the general interests of the cause.

In one of his first letters to Denikin, Kolchak had outlined his political views, which coincided in every respect with Denikin's:

I accepted the functions of ruler and commander without any predetermined views on the future form of the Russian government [wrote the Admiral], for I consider it impossible to discuss the future in the course of a harrowing civil war and before Bolshevism is liquidated. The extermination of Bolshevism and the establishment in the nation of conditions under which the solution of this problem can be approached—is the only practical aim at this moment. I have received . . . the general program of the Volunteer Army, with which I am in complete accord. As far as I can see, you, Anton Ivanovich, have assumed in south Russia approximately the same functions as I have. And we now bear the heavy burden of responsibility for the future of our Motherland. A close and coordinated collaboration, identical in aims and motivation, is essential between us.

In his long letter, the Admiral also declared that he considered indispensable a meeting between Denikin and himself as soon as the armies of south and east Russia came into contact, in order to decide the question of "a single government and command, the consolidation of government agencies, or in any case, a coordination of their activities." Kolchak stated that these decisions would be contingent on the strategic positions of the Siberian and south Russian armies, the respective territories occupied by them, and the political significance of the respective governments in relation to the Allies. He expressed his conviction that a decision concerning these important questions would be reached "without regard to personal interest, guided only by the well-being of our country and by state considerations concerning its advantages and interests." In describing the general situation in the east, Kolchak complained about the attitude of the Japanese, their policy of "predatory usurpation," and the support they gave to the bands of the self-styled *atamans* Semenov and Kalmykov.[13]

Japanese aims in the Russian Far East were of a strictly imperialist nature. Under the pretext of protecting the lives of their subjects in Vladivostok, the Japanese landed a small expeditionary force in that city in April, 1918. By the end of the year, this force grew to about seventy thousand. The Japanese wanted to obtain control of the entire Russian Maritime Province and to establish themselves as a ruling power over Siberia to the east of Lake Baikal. Strictly an army of occupation, their troops were not concerned with fighting the Bolsheviks.

Kolchak's letter, written on December 28, 1918, and sent by steamer from Vladivostok, reached Denikin only in mid-April of 1919, after circling the whole southern part of the Asian continent. Such was the system of postal communication between Siberia and south Russia at that time. Denikin immediately replied to the Admiral, and in order to speed up the delivery of his letter, entrusted it to General Grishin-Almazov, who had decided to leave for Siberia, crossing the Caspian Sea (from Petrovsk to Guriev) and continuing by land to Omsk.

"In my preceding letter, which you must surely have received by this time," wrote Denikin, "I expressed my view that after the juncture of our armies, it is indispensable to establish a single government uniting the east and the south. This thought was expressed in almost exactly the same terms as those you have used in your last letter. I am very glad. God willing—we shall meet in Saratov and resolve the problem in the best interest of our country."

The General concluded his letter with the following statement: "At the present time we receive extensive help in supplies from the British and extensive interference from the French. But all this is less important than our coming together, which I await with the greatest impatience." This statement, as Denikin later testified, was written "under the immediate impact of the evacuation of Odessa and the Crimea by the French." [14] It was to play a considerable role in the future relations between Paris and south Russia.

With luck, the itinerary chosen by Grishin-Almazov would take him to his destination in approximately three weeks. It was generally used by couriers between Omsk and Ekaterinodar, but these were often intercepted by Soviet detachments, and the same fate befell Grishin-Almazov. After being sent out of Odessa by General Franchet d'Esperey, Grishin-Almazov arrived in Ekaterinodar, where he received Denikin's permission to depart for Omsk in order to acquaint Admiral Kolchak with the situation in the south. On the first lap of the journey, the steam launch on which Grishin-Almazov was crossing the Caspian, was seized by a Soviet destroyer. Everything happened so unexpectedly and quickly that he did not have time to destroy the documents he was carrying. Seeing the hopelessness of the situation, he tried to take his life, and did succeed in mortally wounding himself. He died in his cabin, jeered at and insulted by the Red sailors who had captured him. All the mail that he was taking to Siberia, including Denikin's letter to Kolchak, fell into the hands of the Bolsheviks. The letter was immediately forwarded to Moscow. It was published in *Pravda* and reprinted in the French newspapers, to the intense irritation of the Paris government. Denikin's criticism of French behavior in Odessa and the Crimea particularly incensed Clemenceau, who unexpectedly detected in it a "Germanophile" attitude, of which he openly accused Denikin. The phrase referring to the future meeting of the two White leaders in Saratov led to a major concentration of Red Army forces in the direction of that city. As became evident later, the entire plan of Soviet operations at their southern front was henceforth based on the assumption of a White Army thrust on Saratov.

Kolchak's military successes in the spring of that year impressed the Allied governments, which at Clemenceau's initiative, sent a diplomatic note to the Admiral. The note stated that the past twelve months had convinced the Allies of the futility of further attempts to reach an agreement with the Soviet power. The Allies declared themselves prepared to help Kolchak in establishing his government as a national government, and offered material assistance to the Admiral and "all those who will join him." The offer, however, was circumscribed by the following conditions: the convening of a Constituent Assembly immediately following the taking of Moscow (if sufficient order to hold elections had not been established by that time, the assembly was to consist of the delegates elected in 1917); reestablishment of free elections and a democratic form of government; no return to former social privileges; recognition of Poland and Finland as independent countries; recognition of the autonomy of Estonia, Latvia, Lithuania, and the Caucasian and Transcaspian territories, with any debatable questions concerning their boundaries to be submitted to the League of Nations. The problem of the future of Bessarabia, which had been occupied by the Rumanians, would be decided at the Versailles peace conference.

The conditions stipulated in the Allied governments' note were mainly intended to pacify their countries' leftist elements, and it is doubtful that the Allies expected Kolchak to be completely sincere in accepting them. Nevertheless, Kolchak's reply (dated May 22, 1919), which satisfied the Allies, was a sincere expression of the Admiral's views and political program.

Kolchak began by recognizing all the foreign indebtedness of pre-Communist Russia. As for himself, he stated that he had sworn before the highest court of his government that he would transfer his powers to a Constituent Assembly legally elected after the fall of Bolshevism, but not to the 1917 Constituent Assembly "which was elected under the regime of Bolshevik oppression and most of whose members were in the ranks of the Bolsheviks." Kolchak confirmed the independence of Poland, "already proclaimed in 1917, by the Provisional Government, all of whose declarations and obligations we have assumed." He pointed out, however, that the establishment of the Russo-Polish border, and the future of Finland and Bessarabia, were subject to the decision of the Constituent Assembly. Kolchak recognized in principle the autonomy of Estonia, Latvia, Lithuania, the Caucasus and the Transcaspian region, but the extent of the autonomy of each ethnic group was to be decided separately. The advice of the League of Nations would be sought in case of disagreement. With regard to the internal policy of Russia, Kolchak wrote that "there can be no return to the regime which existed in Russia prior to February, 1917," that he recognized the equality of all classes of the population, regardless of race or creed, and that the peasants "would be guaranteed land to the full extent of their needs." [15]

The Allied note to Kolchak revived the hopes of all anti-Bolshevik elements except the Mensheviks and Socialist Revolutionaries who had their headquarters in Paris. It greatly stimulated the Political Council, a new organization formed in Paris under the leadership of Prince G. E. Lvov, the former Prime Minister of the Provisional Government. A number of political figures of widely divergent views came to join it at different periods of its existence, including the former terrorist Savinkov, the former Populist N. V. Chaikovsky, several liberals, and some died-in-the-wool conservatives, such as the former tsarist Minister of Foreign Affairs S. D. Sazonov. As Russia was not represented at the Versailles peace conference, the Political Council's members sought to exert their influence backstage, through their personal contacts in the Allied governments, on questions which concerned Russia.

The Political Council also attempted to unify around the person of Admiral Kolchak all the Russian armed forces engaged in combating the Soviet power on the different fronts. Some members of the Political Council hoped that as a result of so doing, they would play a leading role in the Russian government, should the White movement prove victorious. They sent a delegation from Paris to Ekaterinodar in the hope of bringing Denikin around to their views. Cut off as they were from south Russia, and unacquainted with Denikin's personality and thinking, they had no idea that the General had already decided some time ago, quite independently, to submit to the authority of Admiral Kolchak. He was waiting for the right moment to make public his decision, and considered that the occasion of the linking of the eastern and southern White fronts, which at that time seemed imminent, would be appropriate. However, this linking was much longer in coming than had been expected, and in the meantime, the possibility of Allied recognition of Kolchak as the ruler of Russia became apparent. After considerable reflection, Denikin decided that the time had come to announce his decision, thus lending political and moral support to the Admiral.

It is not surprising, therefore, that Denikin was annoyed by the interference of strangers and complete outsiders in a project of extreme importance concerning which he had already made up his mind. A man of Denikin's highly developed sense of duty found it hard to accept appeals to carry out his "duty" on behalf of his country from people who had been safely sitting it out in Paris and had never tasted the smell of gunpowder on the battlefield. The presence of V. V. Vyrubov among the delegates was another factor which irked Denikin. The fact that Vyrubov had been a close collaborator and trusted aide of Kerensky at the height of the Kornilov affair in August, 1917, did not inspire confidence in the General.

Denikin realized perfectly well that the delegates, who arrived in Ekaterinodar on May 28, were in a ticklish situation. They had to broach a delicate and sensitive subject and were faced with the embarrassing mission of convincing Denikin, who had engaged in battle with the Bolsheviks almost a year before Kolchak entered the White Movement, that he should submit to the Admiral's authority. The General did not lift a finger to facilitate their task. He listened to them in silence, gave no indication of his decision, and asked them to state their mission to the Special Council of south Russia, after which the Council would debate the question and submit its conclusion to the commander in chief.

Denikin knew full well that the Special Council would not react enthusiastically to the proposal, since his submitting to Kolchak's authority would automatically reduce the government of south Russia to a secondary role. In view of the reverses of the Kolchak forces in the past month and the spectacular successes of the south Russian forces during the same period, General Denikin's closest aides considered the problem of submission premature, to say the least.

As the purpose of the Paris delegation became known, the political circles in south Russia were rife with rumors and forecasts concerning whether he would submit. The leftist elements, who erroneously considered Kolchak's government to be more liberal than Denikin's, were for submitting. For the same reason, the rightist elements and the moderate liberals were against it. Meanwhile, Denikin was prepared to carry out his decision at a moment's notice. He had taken no one into his confidence except General Romanovsky, who knew how to keep a secret.

On May 30, in Ekaterinodar, General Denikin gave a farewell dinner for General Briggs, who was returning to Great Britain and was being replaced by General Holman, recently arrived from London. Briggs was greatly respected in south Russia. Denikin sincerely appreciated the British general's understanding and help. The farewell party was exceptionally warm and friendly, and continued long past midnight. Toward its end, the participants noticed that the commander in chief was writing something in pencil on a scrap of paper, bending over the table with intense concentration. It was the announcement of his submission to Kolchak's authority, which he had not had time to compose during the day. Denikin read it aloud as soon as it was written:

Due to the immeasurable feats of the Volunteer armies, the Kuban, Don, and Terek Cossacks, and the mountaineer people, the south of Russia has been liberated and Russian armies are relentlessly advancing toward the heart of the country.

The whole Russian people is watching the successes of the Russian armies with baited breath, with faith, hope, and love in their hearts. But along with military successes, far behind the front lines, treachery based on personal ambitions is trying to dismember our Great United Russia. Our country's salvation lies in a unified supreme power, which is inseparably linked with a unified Supreme Command.

It is with this profound conviction that, resolved to dedicate my life to the service of my dearly beloved country, whose happiness I prize above all else, I submit to Admiral Kolchak as the Supreme Ruler of the Russian nation and the Supreme Commander of the Russian armies.

May God bless his sacrificing endeavor and grant salvation to Russia.[16]

Having listened to several speeches in the course of the evening, the assembled guests had expected the commander in chief to say a final word of farewell to General Briggs. What happened instead came as a complete surprise to all of them except General Romanovsky. They were profoundly moved. "We all froze," wrote an eyewitness, "then our overflowing hearts and emotions burst out in a stream of rapturous exclamations and comments. General Denikin passed from embrace to embrace." [17] Carried away by his enthusiasm, I. P. Shipov, a member of the Special Council, kissed the General's hand. Foreigners and Russians alike felt the unique importance of the moment. They had witnessed an unprecedented event: At the zenith of his fame and military success, the commander in chief, disregarding all personal ambition, voluntarily and unconditionally submitted to the supreme authority of a man who was a total stranger to him, carrying out what he considered to be his duty. The moral impact of this gesture was tremendous. Generals Briggs and Holman retained a lifelong respect for the patriotism and chivalry evidenced by Denikin on this occasion.

The order of the day was immediately printed and circulated among the troops and population. A copy was handed to General Briggs and another dispatched to Siberia with Captain V. V. Perfiliev. The latter followed the same itinerary as Grishin-Almazov but was able to carry out his mission without falling into Bolshevik hands.[18]

In the unpublished papers of General Denikin we find the following entry: "I confirm once again that my recognition of Admiral Kolchak resulted from my personal conviction, which was influenced by no one and was somewhat contrary to general opinion. Likewise, that at the time, I did not discuss this subject with any of the political figures in the south." [19]

It should be noted that Denikin's recognition of Kolchak as the leader of the White movement did not in fact bring about any changes in the administration or governmental structure, or in the command of his armies. The unification and overall merger of the two White forces was supposed to be effected after the linking of their armies—which, however, never took place.

XXIII

"THE RING
AROUND MOSCOW"

During the summer of 1919, the Soviet Union was surrounded, on the periphery of the former Russian Empire, by a ring of hostile forces, most of which were engaged in open warfare with Moscow. True, in quality and strength the various parts of this ring were far from even. The hundreds of kilometers separating some of the anti-Bolshevik forces from each other prevented them from coordinating their actions. By contrast, Moscow's position at the center of a densely populated territory, with a network of railroads connecting it to the periphery, allowed the Soviets to move their troops with comparative ease. Nevertheless, by the middle of 1919, Moscow had been cut off from its supplies of raw materials, oil, and coal, and from the granaries of the Ukraine and Siberia. Its economic position appeared desperate.

Admiral Kolchak's armies formed the eastern links of the chain surrounding the Soviet republic. At the north, from Murmansk to Archangel, operated the troops landed by the Allies, which were later reinforced by Russian detachments. This area adjoined the border of Finland, which had proclaimed its independence. Although Finland observed an armed neutrality, its frankly hostile attitude toward Moscow kept Soviet troops on the alert along the border. West of Petrograd, another White army, commanded by General Iudenich, threatened the former capital. Farther south, extended the front of the Polish state, which was at war with the Soviet Union. Completing the circle at the south were General Denikin's forces, which represented the greatest danger threatening the Bolsheviks.

We shall see, in reviewing the other anti-Bolshevik fronts, on what shaky foundations General Denikin had based his optimistic outlook and some of his strategic planning.

Admiral Kolchak's front, which extended from north to south for over a thousand kilometers, was held by three armies. In the northern sector, on the level of Viatka, was the Siberian army, headed by a former Czech officer named Gaida. After the Czech troops had ceased to fight and abandoned the front in 1918, Gaida had joined the Whites and been promoted to lieutenant general by Kolchak. His army included detachments composed of the workmen of the Votkinsk and Izhevsk plants, who had rebelled to a man against the Soviet government.

The Votkinsk works, founded in 1759, manufactured railroad tracks, iron and steel ware, and the like. The Izhevsk works, established a year later, produced firearms and various types of steel ware. Both were located in the province of Viatka, were owned by the government, and controlled huge tracts of land (over 532,000 acres belonged to the Votkinsk works). The peasant population of this land worked in the factories, but devoted their spare time to agriculture and handicrafts. When these industrious and prosperous people took up arms, they proved to be some of the staunchest fighters against Communism. Their detachments were the only ones in all of the White armies, to be entirely composed of factory workers.

In the middle of Kolchak's line was the Southern Army, parts of whose cadres were former units of the "People's Army" that had been assembled under the *Komuch* government in the early summer of 1918. It was adjoined at the south by the Orenburg army, composed mainly of Orenburg Cossacks and commanded by their *Ataman,* General Dutov.

Soviet sources, using the statistics of the field staff of the Revolutionary Military Council of the Republic, estimated as of June 1, 1919, the ratio of Red forces at the eastern front with Admiral Kolchak's forces as follows: [1]

	Reds	*Whites*
Bayonets [infantry]	119,214	101,200
Swords [cavalry]	11,184	30,200
Machine guns	2,298	1,046
Cannon	367	280

A gifted and experienced naval officer, Admiral Kolchak was not well versed in the tactics and strategy of land warfare. When he replaced General Boldyrev in November, 1918, and became the Supreme Commander of the White armies, he had to depend to a large extent on the advice of the army generals surrounding him. The choice he made of his closest advisers was extremely unfortunate. By the force of circumstances, the south of Russia had attracted the flower of the Russian army's officers, leaving Siberia without experienced or talented commanders qualified for the leading posts in its armies. There were excellent officers in the field, but the headquarters were staffed with senior officers of mediocre ability. Kolchak's chief of staff was D. A. Lebedev, whom he had recently promoted from colonel to general. Lebedev was apparently a self-confident and imperious man, but he was deficient in both professional knowledge and

ARCTIC OCEAN

Murmansk

WHITE SEA

MILLER
(ALLIED FORCES IN
NORTHERN RUSSIA)
Farthest advance
Oct. 1919

Arkhangelsk

R. Dvina

NORWAY

SWEDEN

FINLAND

BALTIC SEA

Helsingfors

Revel

UDENICH
Farthest advance
Oct. 1919

Petrograd

Riga

Pskov

Viatka

Glazov

Perm

Izhevsk

KOLCHAK
Farthest advance
May 1919

Kazan

Ufa

R. Volga

★ MOSCOW

GERMANY

PILSUDSKI
(POLISH ARMY)
Farthest advance
Oct. 1919

Warsaw

Minsk

Mogilev

Tula

Orel

Chernigov

DENIKIN
Farthest advance
Oct. 1919

Kiev

Kursk

Voronezh

Samara

Orenburg

AUSTRIA
HUNGARY

Kharkov

R. Dnieper

R. Don

Saratov

R. Ural

R. Dniester

Ekaterinoslav

R. Donets

Odessa

Novocherkassk

Tsaritsin

RUMANIA

Rostov

R. Danube

SEA OF
AZOV

Ekaterinodar

Astrakhan

BULGARIA

Sebastopol

Novorossiisk

R. Kuban

BLACK SEA

CASPIAN SEA

TURKEY

Batum

TRANS-CAUCASIA

Baku

0   100   200   300 Miles

0   200   400 Kilometers

PERSIA

military experience. The great distance separating the headquarters at Omsk from the armies at the front made Lebedev's operational directives even less effective.

A very harmful influence on Admiral Kolchak was exerted by General Gaida. The continuous friction between him and Lebedev resulted in contradictory advice and decisions, making the Admiral's position extremely awkward.

Under pressure from the British military representative, General Knox, Gaida persuaded the Admiral to direct the main thrust of his forces to the north to rejoin the British troops landed at Archangel. The efforts of Kolchak's other advisers to persuade him of the urgent necessity of advancing southward, to join forces with the Volunteer Army, proved of no avail.[2]

There were those, later, who accused Kolchak of deliberately planning to avoid the junction with Denikin so that he could be credited with taking Moscow without his help. This accusation is groundless; even Kolchak's enemies recognized his disinterested and honorable motives. The sad truth was that the Admiral, an explorer and scientist by vocation, and a nervous and impressionable man, was easily influenced in an area of activity in which he had little experience. Gaida, supported by Knox, precipitated his decision by the alluring promise of a rapid and definitive success in the north.

Later, when Kolchak realized that Gaida's influence was harmful, he removed him from his service. But it was too late; the military decisions made by Kolchak at Gaida's behest had already jeopardized the future development of operations at the front.

General Lebedev turned out to be almost as bad a counselor as Gaida, and his decision to set a trap for the advancing Red forces near the city of Cheliabinsk (an important grain-trading center and the starting point of the Trans-Siberian railroad) led to disaster. Lebedev was dismissed. Kolchak's retreating armies reached Siberia at the end of July and continued to roll back eastward. The huge, uninhabited spaces of Siberia were a poor base for recruitment and setting up defenses. The entire economic life of the region was concentrated along the narrow line of the great Trans-Siberian railroad, which was also the only means of transporting replenishments, ordnance, and food to the front.

The vital main rail line, however, was interrupted in several places. From Novo-Nikolaevsk to Lake Baikal, all its principal stations were overrun by echelons of Czechoslovaks who had stopped fighting against the Bolsheviks at the end of 1918 and were awaiting repatriation. They were demoralized, angry, and exasperated by the delay in their departure. The Interallied Committee in the Russian Far East had attempted to occupy the armed Czech units by entrusting to them the defense of that section of the railroad. The consequences of that move were disastrous for the White army. Having commandeered thousands of railroad cars (and filled them with the property they had looted on their way from the Volga to the Urals), the Czechs paralyzed Kolchak's transport and later added to the confusion of his retreat.

Conditions on the Trans-Siberian railroad were equally bad east of Lake Baikal. The Transbaikal region was in the hands of *Ataman* Semenov, who, with Japanese assistance, had been its undisputed dictator. The Admiral had good reasons for suspecting the Japanese of planning to appropriate the eastern reaches of Siberia, and his relations with them were extremely strained.

The immediate rear of Kolchak's front harbored bands of insurgents who threatened his communications and the adjoining towns. There were practically no indigenous Siberians in those bands, which were composed partly of peasants who had migrated to the Ural area from central Russia after the 1905 revolution, and partly of criminal elements released from Siberian prisons in 1917. All of them were antagonistic to Kolchak's government, whose requisitions and mobilization they did their best to resist. Like their counterparts in the Ukraine, the Siberian insurgents considered every town to be a center of oppression as well as the place where the remainders of the bourgeoisie concealed their belongings.

"Kolchak and Siberia," wrote P. N. Milyukov, "were officially considered the mainstay of the White Movement. . . . This choice was not dictated by internal considerations, but by who would receive the earliest and amplest assistance from the Allies. In reality, the choice of Siberia as the center of the entire White Movement already exposed the latter to the risk of being defeated." [3]

The anti-Bolshevik struggle in the north of Russia began with the landing of a small Allied detachment near Murmansk in March, 1918. This was followed at the beginning of August by a larger landing operation in Archangel, involving approximately five British and Canadian battalions, an equal number of Americans, and single battalions of Frenchmen, Poles, Serbs, and Italians. The total number of Allied troops in Archangel never exceeded fifteen thousand men. Their overall command was entrusted to General Poole (until his departure for Ekaterinodar as Britain's military representative at Denikin's headquarters) and then to General Ironside. He was at that time virtually in charge of the situation at the north of Russia.

At first the Allied landings stirred great excitement in Soviet circles, but the Allies' passive behavior soon put it to rest. The Bolsheviks realized that in spite of its large area, this theater of operations would not be vitally important because of its climate, remoteness, poor communications, and difficult terrain.

General Denikin was of the same opinion. He had made a correct diagnosis of the Archangel operation as soon as he received the news of the Allied landing: "The very fact of sending [Allied] forces to such a distance and such wilderness, points more to the economic concern of the British than to the seriousness of their military plans." [4]

And in truth, Great Britain's principal motive was to safeguard from the Germans and the Soviets the materiel it had sent to Murmansk and Archangel before the Bolshevik revolution. To this was later added the project of extracting lumber from the densely wooded Russian north.

After their landing, the Allies undertook the formation of Russian detachments to supplement their forces, but the sparsely populated region provided few recruits. The detachments, whose total complement did not exceed three thousand men, were composed of a small number of officers who had been located in the region, and of peasant groups engaged in partisan warfare with the Bolsheviks. Their Russian commanders were successively Captain of the Navy Chaplin, Colonel Durov, General Marushevsky, and finally, General E. K. Miller, who arrived in Archangel at the beginning of 1919. All military initiative, however, was rigidly controlled by the British.

The civilian administration of the region was delegated to a "provisional government" presided over by the People's Socialist N. V. Chaikovsky. Unlike other White governments, this one had a comparatively leftist orientation, being composed of four Socialist Revolutionaries who had formerly been elected to represent the northern provinces at the Constituent Assembly. None of this pleased the local army officers, the government was overthrown, and its members were even confined for a while in the Solovetski monastery, from which they were soon liberated at the request of the Allies. The provisional government was reorganized with more acceptable members and continued to function until the beginning of 1919, when Chaikovsky resigned of his own accord in order to leave for Paris to join the recently formed Political Council. In April, 1919, the northern region recognized the supreme authority of Admiral Kolchak.

The decision to evacuate the Allied expeditionary forces from Archangel became known as early as July, and the operation was completed by the end of September, 1919. Eight months after Germany's defeat, the Allies no longer had to remain in the Arctic region of Russia to protect their munition stores from falling into German hands. Moreover, powerful political groups, especially in London, were getting tired of the involvement in Russian internal affairs. Before the evacuation of the Allied forces began, however, General Ironside had proposed to the Russian command, headed by General Miller, that all the Russian units be evacuated together with the Allied ones. He expressed the opinion that without Allied support the Russian undertaking was doomed to failure. The fact that the northern front was the only area of the civil war in which the anti-Bolshevik struggle was waged by predominantly Allied troops, with only auxiliary help from Russian detachments, gave weight to General Ironside's argument.

General Miller discussed the problem with the senior members of his staff and the commanding officers of all the units in the field. He asked their opinion on the following questions: Should the Russians remain in the region after the British departed? Would it be possible later (in case of defeat) to evacuate their troops successfully? Did they consider it possible to carry out an offensive operation without Allied support?

The representatives of the fighting forces unanimously answered all three questions in the negative.[5] They pointed out the shaky morale of their troops, which had by that time absorbed a considerable number of mobilized peasants and Red Army prisoners; the complete lack of protection at the rear; the icebound condition of the White Sea near Archangel which set in in early fall; the fact that the only ice-free port from which the troops could be evacuated was Murmansk, whose distance from Archangel was too great to be negotiated on foot or in sleighs.

But the chief of staff, General Kvintsinsky, insisted on continuing the fight. He spoke of military honor and of the anti-Bolshevik activity at other White Army fronts, and clinched the argument by quoting an order, allegedly received from Admiral Kolchak, "to defend the region to the end." Upon hearing this, the field commanders gloomily declared that if such was the case, any further discussions of the problem were pointless since they were in duty bound as officers to submit implicitly to the wishes of the Supreme Commander.

In reality, General Miller's staff conveyed to the officers an untruthful version of Kolchak's orders; the Admiral had left the decision of this difficult problem entirely to General Miller. Many episodes of this phase of the civil war remain obscure to this day, but it seems reasonable to assume that General Miller's decision to remain in the north was primarily based on the belief that Denikin was about to smash Bolshevik military resistance and to occupy Moscow, and the knowledge that Iudenich was almost in Petrograd. Consequently, a decision to abandon the struggle in the north at that moment could be interpreted as treason to the White cause.

General Miller's decision to remain in Archangel aroused the indignation of the British. General Ironside called it a criminal adventure, and one of his close aides told the Russian officers that their commander in chief would have displayed greater civic courage by leaving Archangel than by remaining in it.

The British departed, leaving the Russians in charge of a front whose winding line extended for several thousand kilometers from the Finnish border to the Pechora River, flowing into the Arctic Ocean. The front held out by inertia until February, 1920, when a rapid disintegration set in and resulted in its total collapse.

When at last General Miller realized that the predictions of the British and of his own officers were coming true, it was too late. The White Sea was icebound, and the way to Murmansk had been made impassable by snow. Only a few hundred men, including the commander in chief's staff, were lucky enough to make their escape from Archangel on the icebreaker *Minin*. The rest of the troops were abandoned to their fate and the bloody reprisals of the enemy.[6]

While the White front in the north played but a secondary role, the action of the northwestern front, which had been formed in the eastern section of the Baltic provinces, became increasingly important. The front's proximity to Petrograd gave it a special strategic importance. Its success, however, depended on the supplies provided by the Allies and on the assistance given by the British fleet to its activity along the Baltic coast.

A number of circumstances, local as well as international, interfered with the successful development of this undertaking.

When, after Germany's defeat, its troops were forced to withdraw from the Baltic provinces, and Estonia, Latvia, and Lithuania made haste to declare their independence, Soviet troops rushed in to fill the vacuum created by the retreating Germans. They occupied Riga and Mitava at the beginning of January, 1919, forcing the newly formed Latvian government to implore the Germans to slow down their retreat until Latvia itself could organize some semblance of armed resistance. An agreement was reached, according to which the Germans undertook to form detachments of volunteers from their army for Latvia's defense, and to provide them with supplies. In return, the Latvian government promised to grant the German volunteers all the rights of Latvian citizenship, which included an allotment of Latvian land for each soldier. This solution pleased both the Baltic landowners and the German government, which had always dreamed of colonizing the Baltic provinces.

The movement of Soviet troops toward the German border and the possibility of their coming to the assistance of German Communists appeared so threatening to the Entente governments that they decided to postpone the evacuation of the Baltic region by the Germans. A detachment of German volunteers was hastily formed, under the command of Major Bischof. A short time later, it became part of a larger military unit commanded by a Prussian general, Count Rüdiger von der Goltz. The Soviet advance to the west was arrested along the line of Vindava-Shavli-Kovno-Grodno-Luninets. In March, von der Goltz assumed the offensive, taking Vindava and Mitava, and he occupied Riga at the end of May. Officers of the local Baltic *Landwehr,* which had joined forces with the Germans, organized a *coup d'état* in Riga, overthrowing its pro-Allied socialist government and replacing it with a pro-German conservative one.

This event, combined with von der Goltz's military successes, created a commotion in Great Britain and France. The ghost of Germany's resurrected military might arose before the governments of the Entente, and their policy toward the Baltic nations underwent another change. The Allies forced von der Goltz to abandon Riga, and an anti-German government was reinstated with their approval.

Toward the end of summer, they demanded from Berlin the recall of von der Goltz to Germany. But the wily Germans found a different way of protecting their interests. They formed a "Russian" detachment, which absorbed the German volunteer and the Baltic *Landwehr* units. An individual named Bermont, who claimed to be a Russian colonel, was placed in command of the detachment. Having decided to assume a title, the new commander began to call himself Prince Avalov-Bermont. General Denikin considered him a typical adventurer.

A turmoil of intrigues, conflicts, and mutual distrust raged in the newly formed Baltic nations, around the clashing interests of Germany, Great Britain, and France.

The representatives of Denikin and Kolchak, and various Russian organizations in Paris and London, insisted on the necessity of forming an independent Russian armed force in the Baltic region. They had the further problem of finding for it a leader who would be acceptable not only to Omsk and Ekaterinodar, but also to the Allies, on whose material support the Russian units would depend. Finally, they had to find a political formula which, without conflicting with Denikin's and Kolchak's slogan, "A united and indivisible Russia," would secure, if not the support, then at least the noninterference of the Baltic nations which had just proclaimed their independence from Russia.

It was decided to assemble the Russian anti-Bolshevik force in Estonia, because this was the Baltic nation closest to Petrograd. The nucleus of the new army consisted of the Russian volunteer units which had already played a decisive role in liberating Estonia from the Bolsheviks. Despite their small numbers (less than three thousand men) they called themselves the Northern Corps. They were commanded first by Colonel Dzerozhinsky and later by General A. P. Rodzianko, an officer of great energy and initiative. In mid-May, 1919, he launched an offensive which took the Bolsheviks completely by surprise. The Soviet Seventh Army took a considerable beating from him, and many of its units voluntarily defected to his side. By early June, Rodzianko's forces which had been renamed the Northwestern army, numbered nearly thirteen thousand infantry and cavalry men, and after taking Pskov, stood at approximately twenty kilometers southeast of that city. The troops received no material help from anyone. Bootless and ragged, they had as their only source of supply the military loot they wrested from the Bolsheviks.

The question of appointing a commander in chief for the new army was a delicate one. Besides Rodzianko, another Russian detachment leader, Prince Lieven, had distinguished himself in the Baltic region. They were both courageous officers, but neither was sufficiently well known to the general public. Moreover, they were unknown in British and French official circles, and the Russian Political Council in Paris prevailed on Admiral Kolchak (who had already been recognized as Supreme Ruler by Denikin) to appoint as army commander a general whose name would carry weight in London and in Paris. The choice fell on General Iudenich, former commander in chief of the Russian forces at the Caucasian front against Turkey. Iudenich was in Finland at that time and was anxious to play a role in the anti-Bolshevik struggle and to link his name with the Northwestern army. He sought Denikin's support and advised Kolchak by telegraph, "All parties, from Cadets and to the right of them, have united around me. My program is identical with yours."

In the middle of June, Kolchak appointed Iudenich commander in chief of the northwestern front. The "front" at that time was still occupied by a single army, headed by General Rodzianko, who was not too well disposed toward the new commander thrust on him from outside. It was July when Iudenich finally arrived at his new post in Estonia, where the delicacy of his situation was immediately borne on him. Estonia, then engaged in peace negotiations with Moscow, required from Iudenich the recognition of its independence, and was supported in this by the military representatives of Great Britain in the Baltic region. The General's "Political Council" (consisting of several individuals he had appointed as his political advisers), under pressure from the British, agreed to the formation of a "government of the northwestern region" whose first official act was the recognition of Estonia's independence. Iudenich was faced with this *fait accompli* upon returning from a trip to the front. The British were not worried about any opposition on his part. In contrast to their attitude toward Denikin, which was always one of respect and cooperation, their treatment of Iudenich was unceremonious and even supercilious.

The Estonians accepted "with satisfaction" the recognition of their independence, but declined any collaboration with the Russian troops. They refused to sign an agreement, prepared by the British, according to which Estonia would agree to give military assistance to the Northwestern army in return for the recognition of its independence by the Russians.

Despite this difficult situation, Britain's representatives urged Iudenich to launch an offensive on Petrograd, promising to lend him the full support of their fleet in the Baltic for seizing the important strategic points of Krasnaia Gorka and Kronstadt. Iudenich yielded to their insistence, partly on account of other important considerations: His idle and badly paid troops were becoming restless, and Denikin's army, at the peak of its success, was already approaching Orel and diverting the best forces of the Red Army for a life-and-death struggle with their principal opponent in the south. The Soviets, therefore, could hardly be expected to withdraw forces of any significance from that front. Finally, the loss by the Reds of Petrograd—the "cradle of the Bolshevik revolution"—would have enormous repercussions in the entire country and abroad.

The Northwestern army, which numbered approximately 17,000 men at that time, was opposed by the Soviet Seventh Army, of 24,000 men.

The offensive started on September 15 and was completely successful for the first few days. By the beginning of October, the main forces of Iudenich had captured Krasnoie Selo, Gatchina, Pavlovsk, and Tsarskoie Selo. The break in the offensive came unexpectedly between October 10 and 12, when the advancing troops were already able to discern Petrograd in the distance.

The British and General Iudenich had tried in vain to persuade Bermont and his troops (which had grown by that time to an army of thirty thousand German and Baltic "volunteers") to join in the offensive. The former soldiers of the German army were willing to fight for the land allotments promised them in Latvia, but not for the liberation of Russia from the Bolsheviks. Instead of joining the offensive on Petrograd, Bermont unexpectedly wheeled around and marched on Riga, the capital of Latvia. Iudenich declared Bermont a traitor. Meanwhile, instead of keeping the promise to support Iudenich on the approaches to Petrograd, the British fleet about-faced and steamed off toward Riga to prevent Germanophile forces from seizing that city and overthrowing its pro-Allied government. Thus, while spending colossal sums on supplying the White armies, the British failed to give them the help they had promised in the vital march on Petrograd, and rushed off instead to liquidate a comparatively minor crisis in Riga with which they could have easily coped at a later date. They failed at the crucial moment, and Iudenich was defeated.

There were, of course, additional reasons for Iudenich's failure. For one thing, he did not command the respect of his subordinates; each of them wanted to be the first to enter Petrograd, and in their rush for the city they neglected to carry out his directive that the railroad between Petrograd and Moscow be destroyed, to cut communications between the two. Another—and most important—cause of Iudenich's failure lay in the efforts of Trotsky, who applied himself with desperate energy to the saving of an apparently lost cause. Even Lenin was resigned to giving up Petrograd at that time, rather than weakening the Soviet front against Denikin. But Trotsky, having taken upon himself the defense of Petrograd, appealed and threatened, and feverishly organized its resistance. He foresaw that the Estonians and Latvians would not lift a finger to help Iudenich, and leaving that front unprotected, removed the Soviet Fifteenth Army from their border and turned it toward Petrograd. The army took Luga and threatened to cut off the Whites from the means of retreat to their bases. Iudenich's army began to roll back, and this withdrawal signaled the end of its existence. As soon as the tide had turned, Estonia hastened to conclude a truce with the Bolsheviks. Upon its return to Estonia, the Iudenich army was disarmed, and its officers and men were interned in concentration camps.

A curious sidelight to these events may be found in the official Soviet history of the civil war: In December, 1929, Klimenti Voroshilov enhanced his career by proclaiming Stalin "Petrograd's savior." The legend took hold and became the official version of the events of that period, despite the fact that in September and October of 1919, during the Iudenich offensive, Stalin was at the southern front with the anti-Denikin forces and had nothing whatsoever to do with the defense of Petrograd. The Soviet chroniclers, for reasons other than historical, decided to overlook the fact that following a resolution of the Central Committee of the Communist party, Lenin himself had decorated Trotsky with the highest Soviet award —the Order of the Red Banner—"for saving Petrograd." [7]

A short time after the Bolshevik revolution, the government of Finland (part of the Russian Empire since 1809), declared that the state of anarchy in Russia obliged the Finnish people to liberate itself forever from any dependence on Russia. But the bloody anarchy raging in Russia swept into Finland, and civil war engulfed the little country. Like Russia, Finland was split into two rival camps—the Whites and the Reds. The White troops were led by a former officer of the Russian imperial guard, Baron Mannerheim. In March, 1918, almost simultaneously with their Ukrainian offensive, the Germans landed troops in Finland. By the middle of April the joint forces of Mannerheim and the German division commanded by Count Rüdiger von der Goltz (later active in the Baltic provinces) succeeded in liquidating the Finnish Communist units.

In bringing troops to Finland, the Germans had other aims besides furthering their political and economic interests in that country: Their troops presented a menace to Murmansk, with its important depots of Allied military supplies, and could also be easily moved in the direction of Petrograd. They took infinite pains to consolidate their influence in Helsingfors and were so successful that in October, 1918, the Finnish *Seim,* or parliament, voted to introduce a monarchist regime in Finland with Prince Friedrich Karl of Hesse at its head. With Germany's defeat, however, Finland made a complete political about-face and secured the full support of the Allied countries.

What was the strategic position of Finland in relation to Soviet Russia at that time? General Denikin described their position as follows:

It appeared to the Finns, and actually was, very advantageous to them. Finland controlled the fortified coastline and skerried waterways of the Gulf of Finland; its army was composed of three or four divisions, forty- to fifty-thousand strong, whose forward units stood at a distance of twenty-five kilometers from Petrograd and sixty to eighty kilometers from the Murmansk railroad, to the west of Petrozavodsk, presenting a direct threat to the Russian capital and to the rear of the Bolshevik army, protecting it against the troops of Generals Ironside and Miller. The Finnish army had against it the paralyzed Russian Baltic fleet and the numerically small Red Guard units protecting the capital and Petrozavodsk. The aggregate . . . of strategic conditions predetermined the direction of Finland's Russian policy: It preserved to the end (the conclusion of peace with the Bolsheviks) an "armed neutrality" equally maintained by the Russophobes Svinhufvud and Stahlberg and by the Russophile Mannerheim—the three government leaders who succeeded each other in the years 1917–1919.[8]

Denikin had the following reflections on Finland's independence and its involvement in the anti-Communist struggle: "The separation of Finland from Russia, not limited by any strategic guarantees, created impossible conditions for our national defense on land and at sea. From the very first, however, the new nation evidenced its determination to continue rounding out its borders at the parent state's expense." The General enumerated Finland's demands, which included the Aland Islands, eastern Karelia (whose loss would deprive Russia of a section of the railroad to Murmansk and cut it off from that ice-free Arctic port), the mouth of the river Pechenga, flowing into the Arctic Ocean near the Norwegian border, and finally, the immense quantity of Russian state property appropriated by Finland: army and navy supplies, arsenals, warehouses, naval bases, and commercial vessels.

"What kind of Russia and what kind of Russian government could agree to satisfy Finland's insatiable appetite?" Denikin asked.

"I, personally, did not exclude the possibility of support from the Finnish army in the anti-Bolshevik struggle. . . . But under the impression of Finland's demands, its treatment of the Russians, and the more than ambiguous politics of the Entente powers since the end of 1918, I definitely adopted the point of view that we would have paid too high a price for Finland's assistance and that the entrance of Finnish troops onto Russian territory was, therefore, inadmissible."

In May, 1919, Denikin communicated the following statement to the Allied governments, through their representatives at his headquarters: "Russia considers with complete sympathy the idea of Finland's independent development. However, the best interests of both nations insistently demand that their future relationship be founded on principles which can guarantee their mutual prosperity and safeguard their essential needs. From this point of view, the solution of the Finnish problem adopted independently from Russia and without consideration for its primary governmental interests, particularly the strategic ones, is unacceptable to the Russian people."[9]

Admiral Kolchak's attitude was similar to Denikin's. In his reply to the Allies, dated May 22, 1919 (described in the preceding chapter), he wrote, "We are prepared at this time . . . to recognize the present government of Finland, but the final decision concerning the Finnish question must be left to the Constituent Assembly."

Some Russian politicians favored adopting an opportunistic policy and recognizing the complete independence of Finland for the time being, leaving the future to take care of itself. But Denikin and Kolchak were men of their word and refused to take this attitude. They did not consider argrements as mere scraps of paper.

Consequently, having lived through its own internal struggle, Finland did not take up arms in the Russian civil war, but by its very presence, obliged Moscow to maintain a certain number of troops along its border.

The situation with regard to Poland was entirely different. In an official letter Admiral Kolchak, having assumed supreme authority over the White cause, advised the Supreme Allied War Council that his government considered the formation of a Polish state to be a natural and just consequence of the World War. "The Russian government," wrote Kolchak, "considers itself empowered to confirm the independence of Poland, declared in 1917 by the Provisional Government, all of whose declarations and obligations we have assumed." Nevertheless, Kolchak postponed the final determination of Poland's border with Russia until this question could be decided by the Constituent Assembly.[10]

The complete independence of Poland was thus unconditionally recognized except that its boundary with Russia remained unsettled. The leaders of the White movement thought that a temporary formula for defining Poland's territory, based on the ethnic composition of Poland and acceptable to that country, could be adopted at that time, and they could then join forces against the menace of Communism threatening all of Eastern Europe.

By 1919, Poland already had a fairly well-organized military force, composed of trained soldiers and experienced officers who had previously served in the German, Austrian, and Russian armies. It had at its disposal the ample military supplies of these three armies, which were rapidly being replenished by new armaments arriving from France. In the spring of 1919, the Polish troops, stretched out to a great distance from north to south, took the offensive against the Soviets. They occupied Vilna, approached Minsk, and by the end of summer, reached the level of Dvinsk, Bobruisk, and Kamenets-Podolsk, where their forward movement came to a halt.

General Denikin sincerely believed in the possibility of a collaboration with Poland.

In undertaking an offensive in the direction of Kiev [wrote the General], I had in mind the great importance of a junction between the Volunteer Army and the Polish forces advancing to the line of the Dnieper. Such a junction would automatically eliminate the whole western front and liberate a considerable portion of our forces in the Kiev and the southern Ukraine regions for operations in a northward direction. The advance of Polish troops toward the Dnieper would deflect the Bolshevik forces at the north and provide reliable protection from the west for our armies advancing on Moscow. Finally, a junction with the Poles would open up for us railroad communications to Western Europe— to the centers of political influence and power and the sources of supplies for the army.

Rostov on the Don, 1919. General Denikin speaking to General Bogaevsky, *Ataman* of the Don Cossacks. In back (with wrist watch on left hand), Denikin's deputy chief of staff, General Pliuschevsky-Pliuschik.

The people of liberated Tsaritsin greet General Denikin, June, 1919.

A *Te Deum* service in front of Tsaritsin's cathedral.

General Denikin reviewing a parade
in Tsaritsin, June, 1919.

General Denikin in 1919.

Admiral Alexander V. Kolchak, supreme leader of the White Movement.

General Aleksandr P. Kutepov.

General Baron Peter Wrangel.

Summer of 1919 in Taganrog. General Denikin with some of his advisers. Left to right: General Romanovsky, General Denikin, K. N. Sokolov. Standing: N. I. Astrov and N. V. Savich.

Commander of the Volunteer Army, General Mai-Maevsky, reviewing the Second Kornilov Regiment, summer of 1919.

Nestor Makhnó, anarchist and guerrilla leader.

General Romanovsky, Denikin's chief of staff (center), with General Pliuschevsky-Pliuschik, deputy chief of staff (to his right), and a staff officer.

Semen M. Budenny, Red cavalry leader and commander of the First Cavalry Army, 1919.

И. А. БУНИНЪ

ЧАША ЖИЗНИ

КНИГОИЗДАТЕЛЬСТВО РУССКАЯ ЗЕМЛЯ

ПАРИЖЪ

1921

Dedication on a book presented to General Denikin by the novelist and Nobel Prize winner, Ivan Bunin: "To Anton Ivanovich Denikin, in remembrance of the most beautiful day of my life—September 25, 1919, in Odessa, when I would have unhesitatingly and gladly died for him."

Denikin and his daughter, Marina, in front of their apartment house at 15 Rue Gallet in Sèvres, France, in 1933.

Mushroom hunting near Allemont, France, in 1935. Denikin and his wife.

Denikin fishing in the French countryside.

N. V. Skoblin, former commander of the
Kornilov Regiment, who became a Soviet
agent in France.

General Denikin in Paris, 1938.

Mrs. Xenia Denikin, with several compatriots, interned by the Germans in June, 1941, in German occupied France.

Kreiskdtr. Mont de Marsan/ Feldgendarmerie,   am 1. Juli 1941.

Bescheinigung.

Nxxx - Der - russischen Staatsangehörigen

.....Xenia..D.e.n.e.k.i.n.........

wohnhaft in .Mimizan.............. wird hiermit bescheinigt, dass

xX - sie - vom 15 Juni 1941 bis 1. Juli 1941 in Mont de Marsan inter-

niert war und nach Prüfung xxxxxx - ihrer - Persönlichkeit wieder nach

xxxxxx - Ihrem - Wohnort entlassen wurde.

Der Kreiskommandant.

A.B.

Knoth.

Stabsfeldwebel d. Feldgend.

Document certifying Mrs. Denikin's release by the German authorities.

The Denikins in Mimizan during the German occupation of France.

Passport photo of Denikin made in France before leaving for the United States in November, 1945.

Being personally completely in favor of the restoration of the Polish state, I did not expect the unavoidable difficulties of Russo-Polish relations to be insurmountable. In any event, I was convinced that our paths would be closely parallel in the near future, as both Poland's and Russia's fates were clearly and fatally threatened by the continued existence of the Soviet regime.[11]

Apart from its great strategic significance, the Polish question had a deep personal significance to Denikin, who was born and bred in Russian Poland. In September, 1919, Denikin greeted the representatives of Poland who had come from Warsaw to Taganrog to negotiate with him as the ruler of south Russia: "After many years of mutual misunderstandings and internecine strife, after the harrowing experiences of the World War and of general devastation, two Slavic sister nations emerge on the historic arena in a new relationship based on the identity of their national interests and on their facing the same opposing forces. My heartfelt wish is that our paths remain united. I raise my glass to the restoration of Poland and to our future blood relationship!" [12]

A postscript to this welcoming speech was written by Denikin in his memoirs when he was already in exile: "Never have I more bitterly regretted any words said by me." [13]

At the time he spoke them, however, neither he nor the Allies who were helping Poland knew that the head of the Polish state, General Pilsudski, had concluded a secret treaty with Moscow. The treaty stipulated temporary cessation of hostilities on the Polish-Soviet front. The Polish mission had been sent to Taganrog only to reassure Denikin, by engaging in fictitious negotiations. Pilsudski viewed Bolshevism, which had led to the weakening and dismemberment of Russia, as a lesser evil than the "united and indivisible" Russia whose restoration was Denikin's aim.

Pilsudski's secret double-dealing became known only after his death, with the publication of the memoirs of two of his associates—the chief of the Polish General Staff, General Haller, and the chief of operations of the Polish army, General Kutrzeba. According to them, Pilsudski's aim in 1919 was to prolong as much as possible the agony of the civil war in Russia, so that he could later enlarge his territory out of its ruins, and making a vassal state of the Ukraine, create a great Poland extending from the Baltic to the Black Sea. In 1937, in Paris, Denikin published a brochure with a complete exposé and analysis of Pilsudski's secret agreement with the Soviet government, based on materials published in Poland by Haller and Kutrzeba.[14]

At the beginning of his military reverses in the late fall of 1919, Denikin could not yet have been aware of the whole essence of the deed, but he already had his suspicions. On November 26, he sent Pilsudski a letter in which he frankly expressed his misgivings:

Some time ago, having welcomed with a feeling of complete satisfaction a shift in Russia's policy favoring the recognition of the rights of the Polish people, I believed that this shift would lead to the oblivion of past historical mistakes and the alliance of two related peoples. But I was mistaken.

In these harrowing days for Russia, you—the Poles—are repeating our mistakes and, possibly, even making greater ones. . . .

The eastern Polish army, which had been successfully advancing against the Bolsheviks and the bands of Petliura, halted its offensive almost three months ago, at the most difficult time for the Russian troops, giving the Bolsheviks the possibility of transferring over 43,000 infantry and cavalry men to my front. The Bolsheviks are so certain that the Polish front will remain passive, that they calmly turn their back on it in advancing on Kiev and Chernigov.[15]

The "past historical mistakes," mentioned in Denikin's letter, referred to the "Russification" policy which the imperial regime had tried to enforce in Russian Poland. It had shocked Anton Denikin years ago when he was studying in the *Realschule* in Wloclawek. And his reference to the Poles repeating the old Russian mistakes had to do with the "Polonization" policy practiced by Pilsudski's government with regard to Russian nationals residing in Poland and to the restrictive measures directed at the Russian Orthodox Church and its parishes in Poland.

Was Denikin possibly exaggerating his chances of completely defeating the Bolsheviks, provided that the Poles joined in the struggle? We have an answer to this question from no less an authority than the future Soviet marshal M. N. Tukhachevsky: "If only the Polish government had succeeded in coming to an agreement with Denikin before his defeat, Denikin's offensive on Moscow, upheld by a Polish offensive from the west, could have had a much worse ending for us, and it is even difficult to guess at its final results. But the complex combination of capitalistic and nationalistic interests did not allow this coalition to be formed, and the Red Army was able to face its foes one by one, which considerably lightened its task."[16]

XXIV

BEHIND
DENIKIN'S FRONT

In October, 1919, when Denikin's military successes were at their peak, the internal situation in the huge territory occupied by his army was becoming extremely precarious.

The ever-present friction between the White Army command and the Cossack governments was sharply accentuated after their territories had been liberated from the Bolsheviks. Don and Kuban Cossacks formed the largest part of Denikin's troops, and they wished to have a voice and an active role in policy decisions. Their main concern, however, was with the local interests of their regions. Many Cossack political leaders, of the Don and especially of the Kuban, felt that the conflict between the Cossacks and the Soviet government should cease as soon as their regions were completely freed from the Communists. General Denikin continued to expound the idea of "maximum autonomy in the component parts of the Russian nation and . . . the most meticulous respect for the ancient traditions of the Cossacks." But in actual fact, circumstances often obliged him to interfere in the internal affairs of the Cossack regions. This irritated local leaders and created an atmosphere of mutual ill will, which inevitably affected the Cossack troops and detracted from their fighting efficiency.

Conditions were even more precarious in the hitherto most reliable part of Denikin's forces—the Volunteer Army. Despite its name, it had not been a truly "volunteer" entity since the middle of 1918. The tragedy of the Volunteer Army was that alongside of the idealistic and dedicated officers, students, cadets, and some old army soldiers, it was gradually absorbing into its ranks criminals and mercenaries. This was particularly true of the replenishments absorbed by the army in the Ukraine.

Since the end of 1917, the Ukraine had been ruled by a series of fly-by-night governments. The *Rada,* the Bolsheviks, the *Rada* again, *Hetman* Skoropadsky, the directory, Petliura, and once more the Bolsheviks, succeeded each other with extraordinary rapidity. Each of these governments imposed requisitions of every kind, and none of them enjoyed the confidence or respect of the population. The cities, which harbored the remainders of the bourgeoisie and a large Jewish population, became the target of brigandage and looting by the villagers, who had no industrial resources of their own. Innumerable self-styled *atamans,* who had formed partisan groups of armed peasants (most of them former soldiers), raged all over the countryside. All of them—Shuba, Zeleny, Volynets, Struk, Sokolovsky, Palyi, Angel, Boshko, and especially *Ataman* Grigoriev— would swoop down on towns and Jewish settlements, wreaking vengeance for the requisitions of grain performed by the city authorities under the *Hetman,* the Soviets, or any other political regime. Makhnó's partisans (though fully as destructive as the others) played a distinctive role in the civil war and will be discussed separately in this chapter.

A wave of Jewish pogroms swept over the Ukraine. They were prompted partly by the desire to find a scapegoat for all the misfortunes of the period, but mainly by insistent talk, in all levels of the population, which connected the Jews with the Communist movement. The large percentage of Jews in the Communist party and the Soviet government was pointed out, and the names of prominent party members were cited, including Trotsky (whose real name was Bronstein), Zinoviev (Radomyslsky), Volodarsky (Goldstein), Kamenev (Rosenfeld), Litvinov (Meyer Wallach), Sokolnikov (Brilliant), Gusev (Drabkin), Sverdlov, Uritsky, Slutsky, Rakovsky, Joffe, and others. These were followed by the names of lesser-known Jews occupying leading posts in the provinces. They were labeled "the speculators of the revolution." The responsibility for their actions was blamed indiscriminately on the Jewish people as a whole, and the well-known slogan "Death to the bourgeois" was soon followed by "Death to the Jews," as well as by "Down with the *Katzapi* [Great Russians]" and "Death to the Communists." The partisan bands of the local *atamans,* wrought up by anti-Semitic agitation, clamored for a showdown. The resulting pogroms extended to urban merchants and tradespeople and did not spare the Jewish poor, none of whom had anything to do with politics. Their innocent blood was spilled in countless towns and settlements of the Ukraine, and trains of carts, loaded with looted Jewish property, wound their way from the towns to the outlying villages. At that time, it was the innocent who suffered, not the prominent Jewish members of the Communist party. These paid for their prominence later, in the 1930's, when Stalin, bent on strengthening his personal power, singled them out for their alleged "Trotskyism" and "antiparty activity."

By the time the Volunteer Army arrived in the Ukraine, the conception of government authority as an instrument of law and order, had been completely discredited, particularly in the minds of the peasants, whose mood was almost universally anarchic. As the army, penetrating deeper into the Ukraine, began to absorb these debauched freebooters into its ranks, the process of its demoralization was considerably speeded up.

But although this influx of undesirable elements unquestionably affected the army for the worse, it was by no means the only cause of its moral decline. By the middle of 1919, the army had grown from a handful of volunteers into a numerically impressive armed force. But it had not acquired the characteristics of a regular army and still retained many of its partisan ways. Most of its units continued to be assembled and armed on the march, in the course of campaigns. This system of recruiting had been justifiable a year earlier, when the army had a unified composition and spirit, and when a different system of recruiting was impracticable in any case. But now, with changed fighting conditions and the inclusion of tens of thousands of mobilized peasants and former Red Army soldiers in its ranks, a new and more systematic approach to mobilization was indispensable.

One of the evils which lowered army morale and antagonized the local population was the practice of "self-supplying," i.e., the requisitioning by armed units of food and forage along the entire front line. In addition, since most means of transport had been disrupted, the local people were obliged to bring up the supplies themselves, with their own horses and carts (which deprived them of their use in the fields), and often had to follow the advancing or retreating troops for weeks at a time. The Bolsheviks were using exactly the same system, which for the affected civilians reduced to nothing the difference between the Reds and the Whites. It is true that at first the Whites issued receipts for the supplies they commandeered, but even this gesture was gradually abandoned. One of the excuses advanced to justify the situation was the complete disruption of the railroads, which prevented the movement of adequate supplies to the front. But whatever the reason, "self-supplying" was a disaster for the local population. It also contributed to the demoralization of the troops, who often turned requisitioning into organized looting.

The army needed rigorous discipline, severe penalties for breaking this discipline, imposed without regard to rank or military valor, and ruthless punishments for looters and other lawbreakers. Unfortunately, the White Army command proved incapable of coping with this problem.

The moral disintegration of the army was hard to bear for the old Volunteers, and particularly for Denikin. As we have seen, despite his personal rigid self-discipline, he did not display enough firmness in requiring this quality from his generals and officers, and in looking back, he bitterly reproached himself for this weakness: "We should have started at the top, and instead of that, went after the rank and file."

When military crimes were reported to Denikin's headquarters, they were severely punished by various measures. But this kind of information rarely reached headquarters. Many of the senior commanders viewed such disorders lightly, took no drastic measures to curb them, and did not report them to their superiors, being themselves not loath to complement their own meager salaries at the expense of the "grateful population" and from the stores of government and private goods left behind by the Bolsheviks. The expression "from the grateful population" was widely and cynically used at that time with respect to foodstuffs, warm clothing, underwear, and other goods which the troops collected without payment from the local citizenry.

How could the commander in chief be unaware of what went on around him? He did know some of the facts, but far from all of them, and often learned them when it was too late. He wrote personally to the army commanders, stating the facts that had reached him, pointing out instances of looting at the front, and demanding that the officers take immediate and strict measures to put a stop to them and that the guilty parties be court-martialed. One such letter, written to General Mai-Maevsky on September 10, 1919, eventually fell into the Bolsheviks' hands and was published by them:

. . . There is robbery, on a grand scale, of government property captured from the Bolsheviks, and of the private belongings of the peaceful population, perpetrated by individual army men, small bands, and whole military units, who often operate with the connivance and even the approbation of their commanders. Tens of millions of rubles' worth of the most diversified merchandise, starting with army warehouses and ending with ladies' underwear, have been stolen and carted away or sold. Tanneries, warehouses of food and manufactured goods, thousands of tons of coal, coke, and iron, have been plundered. Our railroad control points stop railroad cars which transport enormous quantities of sugar, tea, glassware, office supplies, cosmetics, and textiles, in the guise of military cargo. We intercept horses captured from the enemy and sent to the captors' homes. . . .[1]

This letter was written on September 10. Mai-Maevsky, however, was not removed from his post until November 23. Why was a man whose army harbored such incredible misdeeds not removed earlier? Why were his actions, or his lack of action, not subjected to an earlier investigation?

Although, by that time, General Denikin had begun to distrust many of his political advisers, he still preserved a kind of naïve faith in his old volunteers who had no connection with politics. Their past valor in the field, at the inception of the White movement, seemed a guarantee of their sincere patriotism and honesty. As an old soldier, Denikin continued to believe that an element of honor and chivalry distinguished his former comrades in arms, not realizing that even they could succumb to the general dissoluteness of the period. He was to pay a steep price for his confidence and his lenient attitude toward them.

Denikin found out the full measure of Mai-Maevsky's shortcomings only after he had already removed him from the post of commander of the Volunteer Army.

Mai-Maevsky's ideas on the way to fight a civil war have been noted by General Wrangel. Just before the end of the Denikin period, a short time before Mai-Maevsky's death, Wrangel called on him at the Hotel Kist in Sebastopol; later, he described their interview:

> He [Mai-Maevsky] was visibly touched by my visit. . . . "To be successful in war," said he, "a commander must make use of all the motivations of his subordinates, not only the positive ones. The present war is particularly trying. If you require your officers and soldiers to behave like ascetics, they will refuse to fight."
>
> I was indignant [continued Wrangel]: "In that case, your Excellency, what difference is there between the Bolsheviks and ourselves?"
>
> General Mai-Maevsky was quick to retort, "That's just it—the Bolsheviks are winning," he concluded, obviously convinced that he had made his point.[2]

With respect to looting, the Don Cossack troops were every bit as bad as those of the Volunteer Army. They even transferred to the Don region the machinery of factories located in other territories. And there was the notorious raid behind the enemy rear of General Mamontov and his hand-picked mounted detachment. Returning from this raid, Mamontov telegraphed to the Don capital of Novocherkassk, "Greetings! We bring rich gifts to our relatives and friends; sixty million rubles for the Don treasury, precious icons and plate for the churches."

"In truth," wrote Denikin, "this telegram sounded like a death knell." [3]

Submerged in work, in the feverish atmosphere of the civil war, Denikin was unable to deal effectively with such problems. He dispatched committees to investigate abuses, appealed to honor and conscience, issued menacing decrees, expressed his indignation, threatened, and demanded. . . . And in the end, perceiving the fruitlessness of his efforts, wrote to his wife on April 29, 1919, "I cannot be expected, after all, to catch and hang marauders at the front and at the rear single-handed."

It was the despairing cry of a man burdened by fate with the role of dictator for which he had neither desire nor sufficient strength.

The pogroms of the Jews which took place in the Ukraine during the period of its occupation by Denikin's troops gave rise to rumors that the General was anti-Semitic, and tolerant of the pogrom movement. These allegations greatly distressed Anton Ivanovich. A man of deep religious convictions, who himself had experienced many injustices as well as insults and who had miraculously escaped death at the hands of a mob of soldiers in Berdichev, Denikin always defended justice as he understood it, and to him, the pogroms were absolutely inadmissible and inexcusable. He considered this brutal and bestial phenomenon to be in complete contradiction with the fundamental principles of Christianity.

Denikin's views and personal qualities were well known to the cultured Jewish circles in Russia, who had been in contact with him and were not blinded by political antagonism. They did not justify all of his policies, but they respected him as a person. In October, 1927, at the Palais de Justice in Paris, Samuel Schwartzbard was brought to trial for the assassination, in May, 1926, of Simon Petliura, whom he had killed to avenge the pogroms perpetrated by his troops in the Ukraine. The trial attracted the worldwide attention of the press. The newspapers reported in detail the testimony of witnesses and the speeches of Schwartzbard's distinguished defense attorney, Torres. When other excesses which took place in the Ukraine during the civil war were mentioned, and Denikin was named in connection with them, a number of formerly prominent public figures of Russian-Jewish origin disagreed. The well-known barrister M. L. Goldstein, G. V. Sliozberg, and others, asserted that in their opinion, Petliura instigated and inspired the pogroms, whereas Denikin, a man of unquestioned integrity, became their moral victim.

Denikin grimly recorded in his memoirs the depressing episodes which blackened the good name of his movement:

A wave of anti-Semitism swept over the south long before our armies penetrated beyond the Pale of Settlement. It manifested itself luridly, passionately, forcefully—at the top and at the bottom—among the intelligentsia, the common people, and the army; in the camps of Petliura, the rebel peasants, Makhnó, the Red Army, the Greens [insurgent bands of peasants and deserters], and the Whites. . . . The Armed Forces of South Russia did not escape the contagion and besmirched themselves by Jewish pogroms. . . .

There is no justification, absolutely none, for a phenomenon of this kind. . . .

The pogroms brought calamity on the Jewish population, and they also struck at the troops' own morale, corrupting their minds, destroying discipline, causing disintegration. Only the blind could fail to see it. And only blindness can explain a point of view, then quite current in Jewish circles, that "pogroms, as part and parcel of military life, are organically tied to the social and political program of the Volunteer Army." I can assure these persons that if in addition to the prevailing mood, anti-Semitic activity had been "programmed," if, in fact, the troops had only been given the least reason to believe that the high command approved of pogroms, the fate of the Jewish population in south Russia would have been incomparably more tragic.[4]

At the end of June, 1919, Denikin was visited at his headquarters in Taganrog, to which he had moved from Ekaterinodar, by representatives of the Jewish communities. "They painted a tragic picture of Jewish life," wrote Denikin, "and asked me to stop the pogroms by my 'powerful word.' I answered that 'I have no reason to regard the Jewish people with special sympathy. But out of considerations of Christian morality and government expediency, I will do everything I can to avert acts of violence toward the Jewish population.' "[5]

At Denikin's insistence, the commander of the Volunteer Army issued an order stating that "all citizens, regardless of their race or religion, will be guaranteed immunity and the inviolability of the individual, home, and private property." [6]

General Dragomirov, who was then Denikin's assistant, wrote in answer to a complaint from a prominent Jewish citizen, "The Volunteer Army rejects with equal indignation the persecution of any class, as well as of any nationality or race. The Volunteer Army remembers with special gratitude the aid extended to it, with your help, by Jewish citizens of south Russia, and it will never stoop so low as to hold an entire race responsible for the faults and crimes committed by separate irresponsible individuals." [7]

After the occupation of Kiev, Dragomirov became chief administrator of the Kiev region, whence he reported to Denikin, "The hatred of the troops toward the Jews attains a kind of insane fury. . . . Separate bands of bandits have started rummaging in the Jewish quarters and extorting money. A few blackguards, caught red-handed, were acquitted by the court-martial. . . . I called in its members and gave them a dressing down such as I have never given before. . . . After this, the court began to pronounce death sentences, all of which have been carried out." [8]

"Quantities of orders were written by me, Generals Dragomirov, Mai-Maevsky, Bredov, and others," remembered Denikin with bitterness, "condemning the pogroms and demanding drastic measures against them. These measures arrested the spread of pogroms, but did not completely eliminate them." [9]

Many representatives of the Jewish community asked the commander in chief to issue a special solemn proclamation condemning the pogroms. "They could not understand," wrote Denikin, "that words were ineffective in this matter, that any additional publicity around this problem only made the position of the Jews worse, exacerbating the masses and eliciting the usual accusation that I had 'sold myself to the Jews.' They could not understand that a special campaign for protecting the Jews was doomed to failure and that only a campaign based on general moral principles and the enforcement of overall military discipline could be effective, by condemning and severely punishing all brigandage, all violence to people, be they Orthodox, Mohammedan, or Jewish." [10]

And Denikin's fault, which spelled the doom of the White movement, was precisely his failure to impose an iron discipline on his troops, before it was too late, severely punishing "all brigandage, all violence to people, be they Orthodox, Mohammedan, or Jewish." He should have done this as early as the beginning of 1919, chastising the culprits, with great publicity and fanfare, with orders of the day and public announcements in which their names, misdeeds, and punishments were enumerated. Such measures would have made everyone, in the army and outside of it, conscious that the high command would not tolerate any undermining of its authority and the prestige of the movement it headed. Instead, the army meted out its punishments unskillfully, sporadically and secretively, as if ashamed to admit the presence of scoundrels in its ranks.

One of the few who rejected this policy of hushing up was General Wrangel. He had the looters in his army hung publicly. His record in this matter strengthened his later candidacy for the post of Supreme Commander.

The situation with regard to the peasants was also bad. Displeasure with Denikin's rule developed with extreme rapidity among the rural population. Requisitions and looting were contributing factors, but the principal reason lay in the agrarian problem, which the government of south Russia handled in an extraordinarily nearsighted manner.

Having seized after the revolution the landowners' land, agricultural implements, cattle, and horses, and for good measure, their clothing, furniture, china, silver, paintings, and books, the peasants anxiously awaited Denikin's pronouncement on that painful question. They would have welcomed a decision confirming their ownership of the land and forgiving all their past trespasses.

The government of south Russia made two attempts to formulate a policy of agrarian reform. The first version, prepared by Kolokoltsov, was so reactionary that General Denikin indignantly rejected it as "a desperate act of self-protection by a social class," and dismissed its author. The second project was developed by Tchelitchew (head of the Department of Justice) and Professor Bilimovich (head of the Department of Agriculture), but remained on paper. Many specialists on the agrarian problem in Russia commented later that the Bilimovich-Tchelitchew project would have represented an important reform in the period preceding the revolution. In 1919, however, it no longer had any value. Denikin himself had to admit that "since that time, the pendulum of popular expectations had swung a good deal further, and the new legislation could no longer have influenced events and was worthless, in any case, as a political weapon." [11] Thus, no agrarian legislation was promulgated during the existence of the Armed Forces of South Russia.

However, temporary rules, aimed at ensuring the harvesting of crops made it quite clear to the peasants (the de facto holders of the land) that the interests of their hated landlords would be properly safeguarded at harvest time. Specifically, in June, 1919, the government of south Russia decreed the following proportions in allocating the various harvests: fodder grass—half to the sower, half to the landlord; grain—two-thirds to the sower, one-third to the landlord; root crops—five-sixths to the sower, one-sixth to the landlord.* By autumn, these rules were modified in favor of the peasants. It is hard to believe that such decrees were being issued long after the Bolsheviks had proclaimed "All land to the peasants."

However, the effect of theoretical declarations and instructions was

---

* During the Bolshevik occupation of the Ukraine, the landlords fled from their estates. But upon the arrival of the Volunteer Army, some of them returned from their hiding places in nearby towns and cities, and were in a position to collect their allotted share.

nothing compared to what was actually taking place in many parts of the Ukraine. Here is what General Lukomsky had to say in his memoirs: "Every peasant, tilling land that had been seized from a landlord, expected from day to day to have it taken away from him or to be imprisoned himself as the usurper of someone else's property. There were, unfortunately, . . . cases where former landlords, assisted by sympathizing officers and members of local administrations, and protected by troops, not only recovered from the peasants the agricultural implements and cattle stolen from them, but vented their vengeance in reprisals." [12]

How could Denikin, who had always endeavored to keep his movement above class interests, and who was himself the son of a peasant, tolerate this state of affairs? Some answers may be found in the testimony of persons who were constantly in touch with him at that time.

In principle, Anton Ivanovich considered it right to let the peasants keep the land they had seized, in view, as he put it, of "the geological displacement that had occurred in Russia." [13] He also agreed with some of his advisers that this concession would have been a trump card in influencing the psychology of the masses. But he could not overcome his deep-seated revulsion before the arbitrary seizure of property and every kind of coercion and violence. The revolution had made him so allergic to revolutionary methods that he could not bring himself to proclaim an agrarian policy which would be clear and acceptable to the peasant for whom, after all, the whole meaning of the revolution lay in his gaining possession of the landlords' soil. The desires of the landlords did not influence Denikin. In fact, he was annoyed by their manifest class egoism.

Infuriated by the way his movement was being discredited, at the end of June, 1919, he sent the following telegram to all army commanders:

I am informed that in the wake of troops advancing to locations cleared of Bolsheviks, arrive the owners, who reinstate their rights violated at various periods. They frequently receive the support of military detachments and resort to actions which bear the earmarks of settling personal accounts and revenge. . . . Violators from either side shall be brought to trial. Any arbitrary, violent actions, by individuals or groups, must be stopped by the most drastic means. Otherwise, order will not be restored for a long time to come; mutual hatred will grow and the authority and popularity of the army will decline. One type of coercion will be replaced by another; the population will view the troops of the Volunteer Army not as their liberators from arbitrary rule, but as prejudiced champions of the interests of one class to the detriment of another.[14]

However, although full of righteous indignation, this telegram failed to give army commanders specific instructions concerning what to do in the endless peasant-landlord disputes which were taking place in the regions under direct army control.

In the meantime, the peasant unrest was taking concrete form. The Ukrainian partisan bands, which had subsided for awhile and were quietly sitting it out in the villages, began to revive. Their raids, brigandage, assassinations, and arson terrorized the local administration, the police, and the insignificant garrisons stationed in some of the towns. Insurgent detachments of peasants and deserters, nicknamed *Zelenyi* ("the Greens") because they hid in the greenery of the forests, sprang up in the mountains of the North Caucasus and along the Black Sea coast near Novorossiisk, Tuapse, and Sochi. (*Ataman* Zeleny, who operated in the Ukraine had no connection with them.)

The most important partisan unit was that of the anarchist Nestor Makhnó. Unlike other partisan groups, which had no formulated political policy, this one advanced an anarchist-Communist program. Makhnó's program presented a strange combination of the ideal of free, organized communes (which were to become the basis of a future society) with utterly arbitrary ruthlessness and violence.

Makhnó was the son of a peasant family of the large village of Guliai-Pole in the Aleksandrovski district of Ekaterinoslav province. He was born in 1889, and had been obliged to work since childhood. His father was a buyer of cattle and pigs for the butchers of Mariupol. Until he was ten, little Nestor helped him dress out the pigs' carcasses. At eleven, he was put to work as a salesman's apprentice in a haberdashery store. The salesman had most unpleasant memories of him: "He was a regular little polecat, taciturn and secretive. . . . He bore as much malice to the employees as to the boss and customers. In three months, I must have broken at least forty wooden yardsticks on his back, with no results whatsoever." [15] The boy bore the beatings stoically, but always took his revenge: He poured castor oil into the salesmen's tea, cut off the buttons of their suits, and once, when he was particularly angry, scalded his supervisor with boiling water. This put an end to young Makhnó's commercial career. He was properly flogged and returned to his father, who placed him, this time, in a printing house. The boy became interested in the typesetters' work and rather liked it. It was in the printing house that he met the anarchist Volin (V. M. Eichenbaum), who instructed him in the teachings of Bakunin and Kropotkin and got him interested in their theories. In Makhnó's mind, these boiled down to one simple formula: to destroy everything and recognize no one's authority.

During the 1905–6 revolution, Makhnó was tremendously impressed by the "expropriations." Though only sixteen years of age, he organized a raid on the district treasury in the town of Berdiansk. He disappeared with the cash after killing three employees, but was soon betrayed by one of his accomplices. He was tried and received a life sentence for robbery and murder. After 1908, he was confined in the Butirski prison in Moscow, where he met the anarchist Peter Arshinov, who was also serving a life sentence. The fact that both had committed acts of terrorism cemented their friendship. Arshinov became Makhnó's mentor and spiritual guide. He wrote later about his famous pupil, "No matter how hard and hopeless was our life in prison, Makhnó still tried to make the maximum use of his stay there to further his education. Prison was actually the only school where Makhnó acquired his historical and political knowledge, which was to be of immense help to him later, in his revolutionary activity." [16] This activity began in March, 1917, after the Provisional Government proclaimed a general amnesty for all "political" prisoners. Makhnó made a beeline for his home village of Guliai-Pole. By fall, he had organized his fellow villagers and had started raiding and murdering the local landlords and carting away their belongings. When the Ukraine was occupied by the armies of the Central Powers, Makhnó, in the fall of 1918, organized large detachments of partisans and undertook a series of raids on the smaller Austro-German garrisons. The raids were always unexpected. The enemy was caught off guard and disarmed and the officers, as well as any representatives of the *Hetman*'s government, were killed on the spot. Makhnó's first rule and basic policy was to exterminate ruthlessly the enemies of the peasants, i.e., all landlords and all officers, be they Russian, Austrian, or German. Arshinov, who became the historian of Makhnó's movement, noted with satisfaction that Makhnó was most successful in this respect, and destroyed in 1918 "hundreds of country estates and thousands of active enemies and oppressors of the people." [17] The German occupation of the Ukraine taught partisan warfare to Makhnó. He realized that the secret of success in this undertaking was to secure the confidence and support of the local people. Little by little, the neighborhood peasants became part of the small, but well-organized cadre of a permanent detachment which *Bat'ko* (Ukrainian for "Father") Makhnó could muster anywhere at short notice. The rest of the time, the peasants dispersed to their respective villages. They remained there, peaceful on the surface but actually armed to the teeth, with horses and carts at the ready, and with the weapons and experience accumulated during their service in the World War. A stranger arriving in such a village would never guess that he was in the midst of an armed camp. The camp usually came to life at night when, at Makhnó's orders, the whole countryside became filled with partisans and the nucleus of Makhnó's forces was transformed into an impressive armed unit.

His system of reconnaissance and espionage was also founded on the loyalty of the villagers. The peasants were his scouts and reconnoiterers. They kept Makhnó informed of everything that went on in the district, including the location, movements, numbers, and armament of enemy units.

The secret of success lay in the unexpectedness and rapidity of the attack. Marching by night, Makhnó turned up where he was least expected, seized weapons, ransacked private and government property, and dealt bloody reprisals to the local administration and well-off citizens. He set afire everything that he and his peasants could not carry away in their carts, and then disappeared.

Having explored the remote areas of Ekaterinoslav and Taurida provinces, he kept in them the nucleus of his peasant army. The rest of the partisans were quickly summoned from the villages. They moved from place to place in light, four-wheeled carts, which the Ukrainians nicknamed *tachanki*. This peasant infantry on its *tachanki* could travel almost as fast as cavalry, and sometimes covered as much as ninety or a hundred kilometers in twenty-four hours.

After Germany's defeat, Makhnó collaborated with the Bolshevik troops advancing on the Ukraine from the north. In March, 1919, his partisan units were officially incorporated into the Red Army. But friction set in after the first month and ended in a complete break in May, when Trotsky officially "outlawed" Makhnó.

In mid-July, 1919, a meeting between two leaders of the partisan movement, *Ataman* Grigoriev and *Bat'ko* Makhnó, took place near the town of Aleksandria in Kherson province. Grigoriev had sent Makhnó a short message: "*Bat'ko!* What's the point of looking at the Communists? Kill them!" The encounter took place in Makhnó's territory, and at his initiative, for the alleged purpose of setting up a joint plan of action. In reality, it was simply a trap which Makhnó set for Grigoriev.

According to Makhnó's biographer, "Semen Karetnik, Makhnó's closest assistant, felled Grigoriev by several shots from a Colt. Makhnó ran up, shouting 'Death to the *Ataman*,' and finished him off." [18]

In all probability, the principal motive for Grigoriev's murder was to get rid of a dangerous rival. This was the opinion of Denikin, who wrote of "two spiders in a jar, the struggle of two *atamans* for power and influence in the restricted space of the lower Dnieper region, to which they were relegated by fate and the advancing Armed Forces of South Russia." [19]

Denikin's offensive in the summer of 1919 was driving the Bolsheviks to the north, and Makhnó, who had broken with them, to the west. Cut off from their base, Guliai-Pole, Makhnó's men retreated continuously for four months, before Denikin's advancing troops. They traversed over six hundred kilometers of unfamiliar territory. By the end of September, tired, ragged, and hungry, they were ready to rebel against their leader, and sensing this, Makhnó made a totally unexpected decision. He suddenly about-faced, led a frontal attack on the pursuing Volunteers, and breaking through their lines, took off at full speed in the direction of home. On its way east, his army was once more replenished by peasants who left their villages in order to rejoin it.

In October, all the effort of Denikin's forces was focused on combating the Bolsheviks along an extremely wide front, extending through Zhitomir-Kiev-Chernigov-Orel-Elets-Voronezh-Liski-Tsaritsin. All the troops were concentrated at the front, leaving the rear of the army unprotected. *Bat'ko* Makhnó's partisans raced homeward on their light *tachanki*, along the flat, deserted steppe, without meeting any opposition. No one at Makhnó's headquarters bothered about statistics, and the actual size of his army was anybody's guess. Soviet sources estimated that in October, 1919, it had increased to 25,000 men. On their way, they blew up the depots of the Volunteer Army, liquidated the local administrations and garrisons and destroyed the railroads, wreaking chaos wherever they went. On about October 20, Makhnó unexpectedly stormed and thoroughly ransacked Ekaterinoslav, one of the most important cities in the Ukraine. The onslaught continued in the direction of Taganrog, where Denikin's headquarters were located.

To fend off this threat, the Armed Forces of South Russia had to withdraw some much-needed troops from the front, at the very moment when Denikin's military luck was beginning to waver. The Terek and Chechen divisions and a brigade of Don Cossacks, separated from General Shkuró's cavalry group, gave Makhnó's bands a thorough beating. But despite heavy losses the latter were rapidly replenished. The task of liquidating them was subsequently entrusted to infantry units transferred from the west, under the command of General Slashchev. They arrested the advance of Makhnó's units when they were eighty kilometers from Taganrog, and temporarily dispersed them. But they never succeeded in completely destroying Makhnó's bands, which were dispersed and reborn again and again. The peasants disappeared into their villages and *Bat'ko* Makhnó vanished into thin air, only to reappear at the opportune moment. A year later, they joined forces with the Reds in defeating General Wrangel's army in the Crimea.

Makhnó performed a great service for the Red Army, since his daring raid in the far rear of the Volunteer Army helped the Reds to wrest the military initiative from Denikin. But after Wrangel's defeat, having made full use of Makhnó's services, the Bolsheviks officially outlawed him once more, and this time, seriously applied themselves to his destruction.

The Red and the White leaders had exactly the same attitude toward the rebel bands: "The activity of rebel detachments," wrote General Denikin, "often seriously upset the strategy of all conflicting parties, weakening one or the other in turn, by creating chaos in the rear and deflecting troops from the front. Objectively speaking, the partisan movement was a positive factor for us while it operated in enemy-occupied territory, and became a negative one as soon as the territory fell into our hands." [20] Trotsky expressed similar views in one of his civil-war speeches: "Makhnó's volunteers undoubtedly represent a danger for Denikin, so long as Denikin dominates the Ukraine. . . . But tomorrow, when the Ukraine is liberated, Makhnó's followers will become a deadly danger to the worker-peasant state. The Makhnovite movement . . . is a national abscess of the Ukraine, which must be lanced once and for all." [21]

The problem of definitively lancing the "abscess" faced the Red command in November, 1920, after the civil war came to an end. It concentrated the attention of the Communists on a vast area whose center was marked by the tiny dot of Guliai-Pole. Makhnó became the object of a hunt on a national scale. Surrounded by thousands of Red Army troops, many times wounded, shot through the nape of the neck, his right cheek pierced by a bullet, he fought for his life like a trapped beast and continued to hold off the assaults of the enemy with a handful of followers, themselves facing hanging. Fighting continuously, Makhnó made his way across several hundred kilometers, from Guliai-Pole to the Rumanian border. After breaking through enemy lines in several places, he succeeded in crossing the Dniester River to Rumania, in late August, 1921. From there, he escaped to Poland, and after many trials and tribulations, finally settled down in Paris.

There, unexpectedly for himself and many others, this strange and fearless man and inveterate bandit, became a Russian political emigré, side by side with Bunin, Merezhkovsky, Aldanov, Berdyaev, Milyukov, Kerensky, Melgunov, Denikin, and countless others, whose throats he would have cheerfully cut at one time. Deprived of his habitual element —debauchery, drinking, violence, and constant danger—the semiliterate Makhnó found himself stranded in France, without money or the ability to speak the language. From time to time, he worked as a house painter. He wanted to write and publish his memoirs, with the help of fellow anarchists, in order to whitewash his personal role and impart an ideological character to his movement. In the process, however, he quarreled with all his literary collaborators. Lonely, vain, and embittered toward everything and everyone, he died of tuberculosis in 1935, in a suburb of Paris. Three notebooks of his unfinished memoirs, edited by Volin, were published after his death.

It was always a sore point to Makhnó that in their accounts of the civil war, the Bolsheviks deliberately belittled the role played by the Makhnovites in defeating the White Movement in the south of Russia.

It appears certain that a number of future leaders of partisan warfare carefully studied the methods evolved by Makhnó and made good use of them. They included, no doubt, Yugoslavia's future Marshal Tito, as well as Ho Chi Minh, both of whom received their revolutionary training in the Soviet Union.

XXV

EXTERNAL RELATIONS
AND INTERNAL
SETBACKS

By the fall of 1919, the powers of Western Europe were under the impression that the days of Soviet rule were numbered. The newspapers of European capitals were full of General Denikin's war triumphs, Iudenich's march on Petrograd, the disintegration of Red Army troops, and the atmosphere of panic in Moscow.

The Paris government, after the ignominious surrender of Odessa, was anxiously seeking ways and means of restoring friendly relations with Denikin, whose armies appeared to be inexorably moving on Moscow. At that time, the French government was engaged in revising all the aspects of its foreign policy, but its uncompromising attitude toward the Soviet regime remained unchanged. The French were grimly aware of the new isolationist mood in the United States, whose main intent was to keep out of European entanglements. They had little confidence in Great Britain, and were afraid of being left alone to face a possible revival of Germany's power. France was haunted by the thought that Germany might seek to join forces with Russia in the event that the Bolsheviks were overthrown. Some corrective measures were urgently needed to forestall this possibility, and a special French mission, led by General Mangin, was dispatched to General Denikin's headquarters, where it arrived at the beginning of October.

Shortly afterward, the military situation in south Russia changed for the worse, and so the mission's role in reestablishing friendly relations with Denikin lost much of its importance. Nevertheless, it did succeed in improving relations and in ironing out a number of painful incidents. It brought to an end the atmosphere of strain and distrust created by the French role in Odessa and the Crimea, which had led to friction in many areas, some of them quite unexpected.

For example, after the Allied landing at Archangel in August, 1918, the Bolsheviks took as hostages some members of the "Anglo-French bourgeoisie" in Petrograd and Moscow. They threatened to shoot them if the Allied troops captured the town of Vologda. The Allies did not venture that far inland, but continued their intervention in Russia, and the hostages remained captive in Soviet prisons. During Denikin's successful advance to the north, the French Ministry of Foreign Affairs addressed a rather unusual request to his headquarters (a fact not previously recorded in any books dealing with the Russian civil-war period). The French asked the Volunteer command to turn over to them a number of leading Bolsheviks (*à livrer à la France quelques Bolsheviks notables*) so that they could negotiate with Moscow for the release, in an exchange of hostages, of the French citizens imprisoned in Russia.

The response to this request was curt, to say the least. It simply stated that leading Bolsheviks were not taken prisoner, but executed on the spot, and that for this reason, the Volunteers could not provide France with the necessary hostages. (*Les Volontaires, fusillant immédiatement tous les Bolsheviks notables tombant entre leurs mains, ne peuvent en livrer comme otages à la France.*)

Without commenting on the wholesale execution of leading figures by either of the warring sides, the French government continued to pursue its objective through diplomatic channels. On November 19, 1919 (Gregorian calendar), after Mangin's arrival in Taganrog had somewhat improved Franco-Russian relations, the French Ministry of Foreign Affairs asked the representatives of Kolchak and Denikin at the Russian embassy in Paris (whom they customarily ignored) to intercede with General Denikin in favor of revising his original decision and making some exceptions to the general rule, on behalf of France. (*Le Ministère des Affaires Étrangères . . . espère qu'elle* [*l'Ambassade de Russie*] *voudra bien insister auprès du Général Denikine pour obtenir quelques exceptions qui faciliteraient grandement un échange auquel l'opinion française s'intéresse au plus haut point.*)[1] No answer to this curious letter is to be found in the archives of the period. Quite possibly, an answer was never written, since by the time the French note arrived, the armed forces of south Russia were already in full retreat before the onslaught of the Bolshevik armies.

Incidentally, the French were not alone in attempting to secure well-known Bolsheviks as hostages. The British did the same thing, except that instead of trying to obtain Denikin's help, they acted independently, and sometimes quite successfully. Thus, they were able to detain Maxim

Litvinov in London and exchange him for the British diplomat Bruce Lockhart, who had been arrested in Soviet Russia.

One of the important points of contention between Denikin's government and France had been successfully settled by the autumn of 1919. It concerned the Russian Black Sea fleet and the commercial vessels seized by the French in Odessa. When, early in 1918, the Germans occupied the Ukraine and the Crimea, the Russian fleet left Sebastopol for Novorossiisk, which was then in Soviet hands. The Germans demanded its surrender, in accordance with the conditions of the Brest-Litovsk Treaty. In the middle of June, 1918, Moscow sent two telegrams to Novorossiisk. One contained the order to surrender the ships to the Germans; the other, written in code, ordered that the ships be scuttled. The Red sailors disagreed on whether or not to obey the coded message. Some of them sailed to the Crimea and surrendered their warships to the Germans, while others sank their vessels near Novorossiisk. After Germany's defeat, the Allies took over the Russian vessels surrendered to the Germans. According to Denikin, these included a dreadnought, ten or more destroyers, several submarines, some old battleships, and many auxiliary vessels. Most of the battleships were in need of complete overhauling. The Allies manned them with their own sailors, under their own flags. Nevertheless, by the time Denikin's major offensives were launched, he already had at his disposal in the Black Sea the cruiser *Kagul* (renamed *General Kornilov*), five destroyers, four submarines, and a score of other armed vessels, boats, and barges. By the autumn of 1919, the continuing successes of the White armies determined the Allies to transfer to the Armed Forces of South Russia all the other military and commercial vessels held by them in the Black Sea, including twenty-two commercial steamers removed from Odessa by the French.[2]

The United States was represented in south Russia by a military mission headed by Admiral N. A. McCully, whose principal assistant was Colonel Clyde S. Ford. The United States mission had little connection with the other Allied missions, adopting the attitude of an aloof but benevolent observer. General Denikin described the American position in relation to south Russia as follows: "Our relations with the United States government were semiofficial. Their representatives, lacking the necessary authority, avoided any political entanglements. . . . Their assignment was 'to make a study of the situation in south Russia for the use of the peace conference. . . .' We received a modest quantity of the war supplies ordered in the United States by the former government of Russia, and purchased some others ourselves. The only, but extremely generous, outright help we received from the Americans was in medical and hospital supplies." [3]

When at the end of World War II the United States of America became the principal target of Communist propaganda, there evolved a whole literature accusing America of all the sins and conspiracies of international imperialism. The United States was described as the prime instigator of Allied intervention in the Russian civil war.

The facts are quite different. President Wilson was strongly opposed to any involvement in Russian internal affairs. American troops did participate in the Allied intervention in the north of Russia and in Siberia, but this involvement was due to a misconception on the part of the President and to an apparent lack of coordination with the Allied High Command.

The misconception concerned the Siberian episode. Woodrow Wilson was very much in favor of establishing an independent Czechoslovak state, and it seemed to him that the Czech Legion, stranded in Siberia, was in danger of being attacked by German and Austrian war prisoners there. This rumor possibly stemmed from the Czech lobby in Washington, headed at that time by Professor Masaryk, a personal friend of the President's. In any event, in July, 1918, a decision was taken in Washington to send about seven thousand American troops, commanded by Major General William S. Graves, to Vladivostok for the purpose of guarding the Czechoslovak line of communication on the Trans-Siberian railroad.

The American decision to send troops to the north of Russia was also made in July, 1918 (Gregorian calendar), under strong pressure from the British. Three untrained American battalions were dispatched from England, under British command, and reached their destination in September. They were not intended by President Wilson to engage in any military action against the Bolsheviks, but were supposed to guard the military supplies accumulated in that area, to prevent their falling into German hands. Yet, as soon as the Americans arrived, the British command rushed them to the front against Red detachments.

By the middle of 1919, when General Denikin launched his big offensive, President Wilson was sick and tired of his Allies and of their intervention efforts in Russia which involved American troops. Wilson's attempt, mentioned in a previous chapter, to bring together the warring parties in the Russian civil war on the island of Prinkipo in February, 1919, was a clear indication of his desire even then to bring American intervention to an end.

Serbia, which had suffered from the war more than any other country, was prepared to send volunteer detachments to Denikin's assistance. Regent Alexander (subsequently king of the newly formed Yugoslavia) offered to form a Serbian volunteer corps, thirty to forty thousand strong, and place it at the complete disposal of the commander in chief of the Armed Forces of South Russia. But Serbia itself had been so devastated that it could equip such a unit only with the help of the other Allies, and the discussions on this subject with the latter proved fruitless.

Regent Alexander, who had been educated in Russia, spoke the language perfectly, and was an ardent Russophile, wrote General Denikin from Belgrade: "I follow the movements of your heroic troops with extreme attention, and with all my heart, wish you success in your patriotic and historic endeavor, whose importance to all Slavic peoples is immeasurable. As a token of my respect for your personal valor and of my sympathy toward your great cause, I beg you to accept and wear the Order of the White Eagle, First Class, Decorated with Swords." [4]

Among the foreign distinctions received by General Denikin during the civil war was his appointment as a Knight Commander of the Order of the Bath. The British decoration was presented to him by General Holman, a man of gigantic stature, who had replaced General Briggs as head of the British military mission. At the same time, Holman handed Denikin a personal letter from Secretary for War Churchill. Unfortunately, we have the text of this letter only in an imperfect Russian translation made in Ekaterinodar for General Denikin. The retranslation into English undoubtedly fails to render the inimitable personal style of its writer: "The purpose of his [General Holman's] arrival," wrote Churchill, "is to assist you in every way in your effort to crush the Bolshevik tyranny. . . . I hope that you will accept him as a friend and comrade, with complete confidence, and will not fail to send news, through his intermediary, to me or to the chief of the General Staff of the Empire. In accordance with the policy of His Majesty's government, we shall do everything possible to help you in every way." [5] Churchill's promise was not an empty one. General Holman was directly subordinate to Churchill and carried out his instructions to the letter. General Denikin affirmed that the activity of the British military mission in south Russia was always "frank, straightforward, and friendly." [6]

Thus, by the fall of 1919, the relationship of the Armed Forces of South Russia with the outside world (excepting Poland) had become fairly satisfactory. The "outside world," of course, did not include Russia's enemies in the World War, and for the Volunteers its most important components were Great Britain and France. As for the defeated Central Powers, they were going through phases which seemed to follow the Russian pattern. Two important Communist uprisings occurred in Germany. The first one flared up in Berlin in January, and the second one, in April, spread through Bavaria. Both, however, were rapidly suppressed.

The state of affairs in Hungary was much more serious. Having lost Croatia, Slovenia, Transylvania, and a portion of its own territory as a result of the war, Hungary was crushed and demoralized and therefore most receptive to the Soviet propaganda which poured into it with the stream of Hungarian prisoners returning from Russia. The "democratic" regime of Károlyi, which closely followed Kerensky's unfortunate example, soon brought the country to Bolshevism. In late March, 1919, Hungary proclaimed itself a soviet republic and placed the Communist Béla Kun at the head of its government. He had returned a few months earlier from captivity in Russia, where he had been thoroughly indoctrinated and provided with ample means. The soviet regime in Hungary lasted from March 21 to August 1, 1919 (Gregorian calendar). It aroused hopes of a world revolution in Lenin, whose plans for breaking through Rumanian-occupied Bukovina and effecting a junction between Russian Soviet troops and the newly formed Hungarian Red army, were already being worked out by the Soviet military command.[7]

Denikin's offensive confused the Soviet planning and prevented its being carried out. The soviet government in Hungary was overturned, and its instigators, including Béla Kun, fled to Moscow. Thus, indirectly and quite unexpectedly, General Denikin came to play a decisive part in the future of Hungary.

The White Army command ran into great difficulties in establishing relationships with the parts of Russia which had proclaimed their independence. The basic reason for this was its uncompromising principle of "a united and indivisible Russia." The Bolsheviks at that time did not have this problem. They had under their control only central European Russia, with its homogeneous population, and for purposes of propaganda, they could make any seductive promises whatever. Eventually, when Stalin became the undisputed ruler of the country, the policy he practiced (without, of course, using Denikin's slogan) was that of a united and indivisible Russia.

As soon as the Volunteer Army stepped onto Ukrainian soil, it was faced with the problem of Ukrainian independence. In Denikin's opinion, the problem had been artificially created—inspired by the Germans who desired the dismemberment of Russia, and implemented by a small group of chauvinistic Ukrainian intellectuals not representative of the popular masses.

A brief excursion into the early period of Russian history will explain Denikin's point of view concerning the Ukrainian question. The cradle of the Russian people was the region of the middle Dnieper River, with Kiev, "the mother of Russian cities," as its administrative and cultural center. But countless migrations of nomadic races across the steppes of south Russia brought ruin to Kiev. Time and time again, the city was ransacked and pillaged by the nomads; its greatest misfortune occurred in the early thirteenth century with the invasion of the Tatars, who imposed their yoke on Russia. But even before the appearance of the Tatars, life in the Kiev region had become unbearable for the native Russian population. Streams of refugees, seeking safety, began to move in different directions. Some moved northeast, eventually occupying the vast area forming the center of European Russia, and in the middle of the twelfth century, founding the city of Moscow; they became known as the Great Russians. Some escaped in the direction of the Carpathians; they became known as the Little Russians (or Ukrainians). Later they expanded back eastward into the land of their ancestors—the region of the middle and lower Dnieper River and the vast virgin steppes of south Russia. A third group, which settled in northwestern Russia, became known as Belorussians. During the centuries that followed, the distinction between these three branches of the same people increased, as each intermixed with different races and tribes. Denikin was well versed in Russian history, and he firmly believed that the three major branches of the Russian people, "though differentiated by local characteristics, created their history in common." [8]

It was well-known that under the old regime there had been no trace of national injustice, let alone oppression, with respect to the Ukrainian people, and that any bureaucratic pressure emanating from St. Petersburg had affected the Ukrainians and the Great Russians in equal measure. In fact, the Ukrainian peasants had been better off than their Great Russian neighbors, and had always been free to speak their native language.

In the Ukrainian offensive, the Volunteer troops at first had only one enemy, the Red Army. As they approached Kiev, however, they encountered the Ukrainian units commanded by Simon Petliura.

Early in the winter of 1919, when the Ukraine had been overrun by the Bolsheviks, Petliura with some of his supporters and disorganized bands, had fled to Galicia, a Ukrainian region which formerly belonged to Austria-Hungary. There he found support in the "Galician army," which had been formed by former Austrian army officers and soldiers of local Ukrainian descent.

Petliura succeeded in unifying under his command the well-organized Galicians and the weakened bands which had fled with him from the Russian Ukraine. He proclaimed himself "generalissimo" of the two armies, placing Tarnavsky, a former Austrian officer, at the head of the Galician one, and *Ataman* Tiutiunnik, former chief of staff of *Ataman* Grigoriev, at the head of the Ukrainian one. By midsummer, he had up to 35,000 men under his command, of whom over 20,000 were Galicians. The relations between his two armies were strained. The Galicians maintained military discipline and held fairly conservative views. The Ukrainians, already demoralized by looting and pogroms, and tainted by anarchy, were thoroughly undisciplined. Each side had its own government, and quarreled with the other. The reasons for this precarious association were simple. Squeezed out of the Ukraine by the Bolsheviks, Petliura sought refuge in Galicia with its closely related race and language.

On their part, the Galicians, who hated the Poles and were afraid of being annexed by the new Polish state, wanted to reinforce their army with Petliura's bands. The attempt was doomed to failure.

The principal enemy for Petliura and his movement was Russia—any Russia, be it Red or White. He was prepared to support either of the warring sides in the civil war if doing so could weaken the other, and help him to obtain from the victor the recognition of the Ukraine's complete independence. The Galicians, however, bore no ill will toward Russia, to which they looked for protection against the possible Polonization of their region. They were not opposed, in principle, to the incorporation of the Ukraine and Galicia by the Russian state, as a single and fully autonomous component. This drastic difference in political approach led to a new stage in the controversy between Petliura and his new allies. The Galicians did not wish to fight against Denikin. Their government and command had faith in the Russian general's integrity, while their association at close quarters with the Ukrainian "generalissimo" had convinced them that he was an opportunist and an intriguer not to be trusted.

Denikin considered Petliura, who after the revolution had declared himself a Ukrainian separatist, to be a traitor; even a temporary agreement with a man of this sort was inadmissible to him. But the final, incontrovertible argument which made cooperation impossible, was that as a matter of principle, Denikin could not deal with a man whose aim was the dismemberment of Russia.

On August 3, Denikin communicated his uncompromising stand in this matter to the military representatives of the Allies. Concurrently, the Allies themselves (who had tried to convince Petliura of the necessity of cooperating with Denikin) arrived at the conclusion that further negotiation with Petliura would be futile. Denikin followed his announcement by an order of the day to his troops: "I do not recognize a separatist Ukraine. Petliura's followers can either become neutral, in which case they must immediately surrender their arms and disperse to their homes; or else join us and agree to our aims, one of which is to grant wide autonomy to the peripheral regions. If Petliura's followers refuse to carry out these conditions, they must be considered enemies in the same way as the Bolsheviks." [9]

Such was the political background when, on August 17, Denikin's troops, led by General Bredov, confronted Galician army units on the approaches to Kiev. Taking advantage of the disruption of the Red Army retreating before Denikin, Petliura moved his Galician units to the west of Kiev, so that he would be the first to enter the Ukrainian capital and would have a chance to consolidate his power in it. But as things turned out, Bredov and the Galicians entered Kiev at the same time. And to avoid any conflict with the Volunteers, the Galicians, accepting a proposal made by Bredov, withdrew to within a distance of a day's march from the city. The following day saw the publication of an agreement between

Bredov and the Galicians, who, unexpectedly for Petliura, had decided to act independently of him. A day later, Petliura surprised the Galicians in his turn by concluding a pact with Poland, to which he agreed to cede their Galician homeland. This resulted in a final break between the Galicians and Petliura. The Galicians recognized Denikin's supreme command. Petliura became the obedient instrument of the policy of Poland, whose aim was the weakening and dismemberment of Russia.

During the two months that followed, the Volunteers had several bloody skirmishes with Petliura's bands and gave them severe beatings near Uman, Gaisin, and Birsula. At the beginning of November, Petliura with his staff, government, and a small part of his troops, took refuge from the Volunteers behind the lines of the Polish army. But in spite of this, Denikin was obliged to continue stationing between eight and ten thousand men on the "Petliura front" to protect himself from a possible attack from this direction.

Because of its disagreements with Georgia (described in an earlier chapter) and its break with Petliura, the Volunteer Army was thus forced to maintain a certain number of troops in areas of secondary importance, instead of using them at the all-important anti-Bolshevik front.

Before the occupation of Kiev by the Volunteers, the commander in chief issued an appeal to the population of Little Russia. The declaration categorically precluded the possibility of Little Russia's separation from Russia, but promised the most careful consideration for the region's national characteristics, traditions, and language. "In view of the above," read the declaration, "the initiation of self-government and decentralization will be at the basis of reorganizing the provinces of south Russia with unfailing consideration for the special characteristics and traditions of local life." The declaration ended with the following statement: "While Russian will remain the official language in the entire territory of Russia, I consider inadmissible and forbid the persecution of the Little Russian national language. Little Russian may be spoken by everyone, anywhere —in local civic organizations, . . . government offices, and courts. Private schools, supported by private means, may teach in any language they wish. As regards public schools, lessons in the national Little Russian language and its literary classics may be organized for those who express the desire to study it. Likewise, there will be no limitations in the use of Little Russian by the press." [10]

The period of Denikin's rule in the Ukraine was too short to have an impact on the cultural life of the region, but his declaration was criticized by a section of the local intelligentsia. For example, M. P. Chubinsky (a former professor of the Imperial Alexander Lyceum, later Minister of Justice in *Hetman* Skoropadsky's government), who could not possibly be suspected of revolutionary tendencies, wrote that "General Denikin's appeal . . . was a painful blow not only to the separatists, but to all those who, while desiring the union of Russia with an autonomous Ukraine, and having the highest esteem for the Russian language as a vehicle of Russian culture, nevertheless desired the widest recognition for their own language, to which they were deeply attached." [11]

The unrest of the masses, already growing for the reasons previously enumerated, was exacerbated by the new administration established by the Whites in the provinces liberated from the Bolsheviks.

After their *coup,* the Bolsheviks had immediately realized that the old administrative apparatus had to be preserved if they were to retain control of the country. They had been able to coerce most of the original employees to remain in their civil-service posts. Having placed loyal party workers in key positions, they were able to set the old bureaucratic machine in motion and to operate it. Though antiquated and worn at the seams, it still worked.

Exactly the opposite occurred in Russia's outlying provinces. During the revolution and civil war, the government bureaucracy in these areas disintegrated completely. Denikin and Kolchak had been obliged to create local civic administrations from scratch. The task proved extremely difficult, and its results were far from satisfactory.

General Denikin had neither the time nor the experience to set up a civilian government, and delegated this task to his Department of the Interior. The head of the department, N. N. Chebyshev, decided to make use of the administrative experience of the former provincial governors who were in south Russia. It was an unfortunate decision. The persons he selected showed a complete lack of understanding of the enormous psychological changes undergone by the country. General Denikin painted a depressing picture of the civilian administration in south Russia under the Whites: "Everything was in the past for these people, and they attempted to revive this past both in spirit and letter. Their example was followed by underlings belonging to the old regime, some of whom had been frightened by the revolution, while others were filled with hatred and vengeance. They had to take over unfamiliar regions which had already been subjected to several changes of power, and whose populations had lost all respect for law and order and trusted no one. Their lives had been disrupted and filled with local antagonisms and class hatred." [12]

The urban population at the rear indulged in speculation on a grand scale. The speculators included many old army officers who for various reasons had landed in the Ukraine. Having undergone a number of regimes—the *Hetman's,* Petliura's, the Bolsheviks'—they had become experts in "survival" and had developed a cynical attitude toward life, in which ideology no longer played a part. Their energy was concentrated on adapting themselves to the rapidly changing conditions, and in this many of them had become remarkably adept.

Illegally acquired merchandise—foodstuffs, sugar, salt, canned goods, liquor, clothing, linen, uniforms from Great Britain, all these were sold and resold on the black market by speculators. Volunteers arriving in the rear wounded or on sick leave were disgusted by the drunken orgies and reckless spending that went on behind the lines, in contrast to the severe conditions at the front.

Denikin was both desperate and helpless in the face of these abuses about which he later wrote, "The Russian turmoil, while it brought forth such great examples of self-sacrifice, also stirred up all the muddy scum and low instincts latent in the depths of the human soul." [13] There were no men, complained Denikin, who understood that the internal situation could only be improved with the help of a leader of exceptional stature and experience, a man of Stolypin's caliber, to whom he could entrust the entire government of the occupied region. The General was only too aware of his own shortcomings in civilian administration, for which his previous career had in no way prepared him.

The circumstances of my life and military service, spent mainly in the provinces [wrote Denikin], afforded very few contacts with people in the worlds of government, politics, and social work, and this made it very difficult for me, later, to choose the right persons for the most responsible posts. At first, I tried the following system of verifying my decisions: When a candidate was proposed by the "rightists," I gathered information on him from the "leftists," and vice versa. Later, I established a more formal approach, whereby all suggestions for replacement and nominations to leading positions were examined by the Special Council, whose chairman advised me of its decision.[14]

As the Bolshevik threat drew farther away from the Kuban, the attitude of the *Rada* (the Kuban Cossack parliament) toward the high command of south Russia became increasingly provocative. We know that friction between them began considerably earlier, and that Denikin, at the end of 1918, already wanted to move his headquarters as far as possible from Ekaterinodar. At first, he thought of transferring to the Crimea, but circumstances prevented him from doing so. As his armies advanced farther north, he was finally able to move his headquarters to Taganrog, a port on the Sea of Azov, in which Tsar Alexander I had died in 1825. As Taganrog was too small to accommodate the numerous personnel of the various government agencies, all departments of the Special Council were transferred to Rostov. The disrupted condition of the railroad between the two cities, made communications between the general staff and the civilian government extremely difficult. Furthermore Denikin failed to foresee that upon his departure, the situation in Ekaterinodar would take a sharp turn for the worse. As soon as Denikin himself left the capital, the Kuban *Rada* openly resumed its separatist activity.

By the early autumn of 1919, the separatist campaign was in full swing. The *Rada* leaders openly criticized Denikin's government and systematically removed from office any Cossacks who sympathized with the ideas of the Volunteer Army. They also strove to undermine the Kuban *Ata-man*'s authority, accusing him of being Denikin's henchman. In open defiance of the White Army command, the separatists engaged in negotiations with Georgia and with Petliura and spread the opinion that *Bat'ko* Makhnó would bring true freedom to the people. The situation became increasingly tense, as this propaganda began to reach the ranks of Kuban Cossacks at the front. The Kuban officers, who firmly and loyally maintained a pro-Russian orientation, found it increasingly difficult to maintain discipline in the ranks, which by the fall of 1919 began to put up a passive resistance to authority. The men lost the desire to fight for the ideals proclaimed by General Denikin. They began to desert the army for their *stanitsy,* where the Kuban authorities deliberately let them alone. Other deserters joined the bands of Green partisans.

The Caucasian army, composed largely of Kuban Cossacks, was the first to suffer from the deteriorating morale in the Kuban region. It ceased to receive replenishments in manpower and horses, while its ranks grew thinner through desertion. "Fate had willed it so that the Kuban constituted our home front," wrote General Denikin. "It was the source of recruitment of the Caucasian army and the link uniting us with the Northern Caucasus, as well as with our only seaport—Novorossiisk. In October, Kuban units still formed 12 percent of the Armed Forces of South Russia. We were bound by undissoluble ties." [15]

The situation called for immediate action. The festering sore in the body of the army represented a deadly danger and required drastic measures. In the middle of October, General Denikin included the Kuban in the sector forming the rear of the Caucasian army. This gave the army's commander, General Wrangel, wide administrative powers in the region. Denikin entrusted Wrangel with the task of restoring order in his army rear, and with Wrangel's consent, placed General Pokrovsky, an energetic and determined man, in command of the troops in that sector.

On October 9, Denikin called General Wrangel to an urgent conference, in which General Lukomsky and Professor Sokolov also participated. The latter described it as follows in his memoirs:

General Lukomsky announced the arrival of the commander of the Caucasian army, and a very tall, lean military man, clad in a Caucasian coat and wearing a general's insignia and the Cross of St. George, strode rapidly into the study. General Wrangel took an armchair facing Denikin at his desk. It was interesting to observe these two heroes of the White movement next to each other: the one, short, stout, with a round, good-natured face, slow conversation, and charming, diffident smile; the other, lithe and elegant, quick of movement and speech, which he underscored by staccato gestures and vivid facial expressions. General Wrangel outlined his plan concisely, clearly, and accurately. The plan was very simple: Prior to the session of the *Rada,* scheduled to open around October 20, General Wrangel arrives in Ekaterinodar, where he is awaited by General Pokrovsky, who has at his disposal some trustworthy units, previously transferred "on furlough" from the front. As the commander of the Caucasian army,

General Wrangel attends the *Rada* session and ascends the rostrum. His speech describes the difficult situation of the army, ignored by the home front with its political games, and insists, on behalf of the front lines, on the indispensable revision of the region's constitution. Immediately following his speech, a group of *Rada* members proposes a previously prepared amendment. If it is accepted, General Wrangel takes his leave [and returns to the front]. If, however, the *Rada* categorically rejects the constitutional reform, General Wrangel goes out to address the troops and to acquaint them with the problem. . . .[16]

The proposed new Kuban constitution, according to which the *Ataman* would no longer be politically dependent on the *Rada,* was prepared beforehand by Professor Sokolov, but events turned out somewhat differently from General Wrangel's plan.

A few days before Wrangel's projected speech at the *Rada,* General Denikin received some news which deeply disturbed him. He knew that a delegation sent to Paris by the *Rada* was waging a campaign against the White Army command and promoting the Kuban's separation from Russia. But he had not learned until now that in July, the Kuban delegation in Paris had signed an agreement with the self-styled "Government of the Republic of the Mountaineer Peoples of the Caucasus." It claimed to be a government-in-exile of a republic which actually had never existed, and purported to represent the Ingushes, the Circassians, and various Dagestan tribes of the Caucasus. By a "solemn act," the signatories of the agreement mutually recognized the sovereignty and complete political independence of the Kuban and the "Republic of the Mountaineer Peoples of the Caucasus."

To Denikin, this was an act of treason, which would inevitably lead to complete political turmoil among the Kuban Cossacks. Under the circumstances, he considered a show of military force imperative. Without waiting for the implementation of Wrangel's plan, and even without notifying him, Denikin gave the order to court-martial as traitors all the signatories of the agreement as soon as they entered the territory of the Armed Forces of South Russia.

The decree created confusion in the *Rada.* Nevertheless, its members treated it as a vain threat, refused to condemn their Paris delegates, and were loud in their denunciations of Denikin and his government.

Wrangel's task had been considerably complicated, but he was determined to carry it out. He was invited to the meeting of the *Rada* in his capacity as commander of the Caucasian army, but after hearing the insults directed at his army superiors by its members, he telegraphed his refusal to come. He stationed himself in Kislovodsk, established communications by direct wire with General Pokrovsky, who had arrived in Ekaterinodar with his detachment, and ordered him to act immediately.

On November 5, Pokrovsky demanded that the *Rada* cease its campaign of defamation against the Volunteer Army and surrender to him Kalabukhov, the only member of the Paris delegation who had turned up in

Ekaterinodar. This gave rise to stormy debates in the *Rada*. A day later, Pokrovsky threatened the *Rada* with dire consequences if the time limit of his ultimatum was exceeded, and demanded the additional surrender of twelve members of the Kuban separatist faction. This time, the *Rada* gave in without a murmur. Kalabukhov was court-martialed and hung the next day. The twelve separatists were freed a few days later and exiled from Russia.

The belligerent mood of the *Rada* subsided. Yesterday's separatists, who had been so loud in denouncing the White command, were now on their best behavior. They loudly repented their past transgressions, promised to fight Bolshevism in complete unity with the White Army, stood during General Wrangel's address, which they received with ovations, and unanimously accepted the changes in the Kuban constitution proposed by him. No one had obliged them to listen standing to Wrangel's speech or to interrupt it with applause; indeed, they later regretted this show of enthusiasm, considering it a moment of weakness, and they held it against both Wrangel and Denikin.[17]

There is no doubt that the long-drawn-out antagonism in the Kuban had reached a stage which called for drastic action. But neither is there any doubt that better-planned and more timely measures could have spared the White Army command the necessity of resorting to force for its solution. The events in Ekaterinodar had serious repercussions among the Kuban units at the front. They were a blow to the Cossacks' self-esteem, and dampened their desire to continue the struggle. Later, Denikin concluded that one of the main reasons for the defeat of his movement lay in his relationship with the Kuban.

As a result of these events, *Ataman* Filimonov was obliged to resign. He was replaced by General Uspensky, a sincere supporter of Denikin, who died of typhus a short time later. His successor, General Bukretov (elected when the Red army was already approaching the Kuban) was a personal enemy of Denikin's.

To the difficulties and mistakes of the White movement in relation to the separatist tendencies of Russia's peripheral regions, must be added the harmful results of its uncompromisingly negative policy toward the old army officers who had joined the ranks of the Red Army.

In November, 1918, General Denikin issued a decree addressed to all former officers who had remained in the Bolshevik service. It condemned their collaboration and concluded with a threat: "All those who will not leave the ranks of the Red Army without delay, will be cursed by the people and subject to the severe and relentless court-martial of the Russian army." Denikin frankly admitted in retrospect how mistaken this policy had been. The Bolsheviks gave his decree the widest circulation, as propaganda against the Volunteer Army. "It had a crushing effect on those who, while serving in the Red ranks, were spiritually with us," wrote Anton Ivanovich.[18]

With the exception of a heroic minority who had deliberately and at the risk of their lives joined the Bolsheviks in order to engage in subversive action, most of the old army officers either had been pressed into the Red Army or had enlisted in it from sheer want, to provide for their starving families. Instead of being given sympathy and understanding, which would have secured their allegiance to the White cause, those who were taken prisoner were treated with utmost severity. The rehabilitation committees set up to investigate their activities under the Bolsheviks procrastinated endlessly and were often far from objective in their decisions. Even worse was the fact that not all of the officers taken prisoner were sent to the rear. Some fell victims to the inhuman hatred of the two sides for each other. There were cases of immediate execution on the spot of "Red" officers captured in battle. This fate befell a former army general, A. V. Stankevich, and a former captain of the imperial guard, A. A. Brusilov (son of the famous general), taken prisoner in the course of the bloody fighting near Orel, when the whole issue of the civil war was at stake and the Reds were slaughtering all the White officers who fell into their hands.

No wonder many of the former officers serving in the Red Army with the intention of joining the White side at the first opportunity later changed their attitude completely and became real enemies of the Volunteer Movement. The arbitrary executions of Stankevich and Brusilov were only two examples of the bestial instincts aroused by the civil war, which Denikin tried so unsuccessfully to curb.

Denikin's army was still advancing northward, the territory occupied by his troops was constantly becoming larger, and only some 250 miles separated the Volunteer Army's outposts from Moscow. And yet, from the middle of October, 1919, there was a growing feeling in some of the well-informed circles of south Russia that a turning point in General Denikin's military luck was close at hand. There was less and less hope that the Whites would succeed in defeating the Red Army before the approach of winter. The wave of peasant uprisings, Makhnó's guerrilla activity, disorganization in the rear of Denikin's forces, lack of discipline in his troops, the trouble with separatists in the Kuban—each of these, even taken separately, was sufficient reason for gloomy forebodings.

XXVI

THE TURNING

OF THE TIDE

The defeats at the southern front during the summer brought confusion and panic to the Soviet provinces, especially to those closest to the approaching White armies. At the same time, however, Moscow's central government responded to the situation with extraordinary energy and drive. The question had become one of mutual extermination—it was them or us. No other choice remained, and having realized that their personal lives and power were at stake, the leaders of Bolshevism—Lenin and the members of the Bolsheviks' Central Committee—displayed remarkable resourcefulness and perception in wresting the initiative from Denikin. They made full use of propaganda and terror throughout their territory (thousands of people were arrested and shot without trial on mere suspicion of harboring anti-Red feelings); they selected experienced party members to organize and lead rebel bands in the enemy rear (Bolsheviks left underground cells in the areas which they abandoned, and these cells kept in touch with Moscow, which directed their activity); they cleverly utilized the military experience of old army officers who had been pressed into the Soviet service. The latter were well aware by this time of the risks they could incur at the hands of a victorious White force.

Since the beginning of 1919, the importance of the White cavalry had become quite clear to the Bolsheviks, who understood its decisive strategic value not only as one of the fighting arms of the service but as an independent force. Denikin's superior cavalry threatened with annihilation the Red infantry assembled by mobilization, whose behavior under pressure was unpredictable. The formation of a Red cavalry was, therefore, an absolute and urgent necessity, a fact which Trotsky was the first to formulate—in his slogan "Proletarians to horse!"

Nevertheless, as we know, Trotsky feared that a lack of experienced horsemen would delay the formation of a Soviet cavalry. His fears proved unjustified. Many natives of regions where riding ability was inborn had already made their way into the Soviet zone to join the Reds. They were Cossacks from the Don, Kuban, and Terek, most of them *inogorodni,* —of the region's land proletariat—whose sympathies were with the Bolsheviks. Anxious to return to their *stanitsy* and villages, they became the nucleus of the Soviet cavalry, rapidly and efficiently formed in the spring and summer of 1919 and placed under the command of Semen Mikhailovich Budenny.

Budenny, born in 1883, came from a family of *inogorodni* peasants who had moved to the Don region from the province of Voronezh and settled near *stanitsa* Platovskaia, in the vicinity of the river Manych. Budenny was recruited into the army in 1903, took part in the Japanese war, then served in the Primorski Dragoon Regiment, from which he was sent in 1907 to the Officer Cavalry School in St. Petersburg. The school trained soldiers to become instructors in the breaking in of riding horses. Budenny seized with enthusiasm this opportunity to better himself. It could lead to his obtaining, at the end of his military service, the position of riding master at one of the prominent stud farms, and thus allow him to escape the routine of peasant life, to which he had no wish to return. Budenny graduated first in his class and returned to his regiment as a noncommissioned officer. At the start of the war in 1914, he was transferred to the Eighteenth Severski Dragoon Regiment and attached to a platoon commanded by Lieutenant Kuchuk Ulagai, who later became an outstanding cavalry general in Denikin's army.

At the end of 1914, the Caucasian cavalry division, which included Budenny's regiment, was transferred from the western front to the Caucasian front, where it engaged in fighting the Turks. There Budenny received all the awards of the Order of St. George which a soldier was entitled to receive for bravery or military valor. When the Bolsheviks came to power, Budenny embraced the Soviet cause, and he soon distinguished himself in the civil war as a cavalry leader. For Budenny, horses were more a military weapon than a means of locomotion. By the time the First Cavalry Corps, which later grew into the First Cavalry Army, was formed, Budenny had provided the units he commanded with the best handpicked mounts that could be obtained in the stud farms of central Russia.

In the course of the civil war, Budenny made friends with Klimenti Voroshilov, then a member of the Revolutionary Military Council of the Cavalry Army, and came into close contact with Stalin, a member of the Revolutionary Military Council of the southern front since the fall of 1919. However, Budenny never achieved a good rapport with Trotsky, a fact which proved greatly in his favor under Stalin's rule. Trotsky, who was then the Soviet Minister of War and in charge of assigning

important military positions, did not have a high opinion of the uneducated Budenny's intelligence. He appreciated the noncom's soldierly common sense, but doubted that this "illiterate Budenny" could cope with
the complex problem of leading a great cavalry force.[1] However, Trotsky
had no other reliable cavalry commanders, and there was also Budenny's
unquestionably proletarian origin to consider. Without enthusiasm, he assigned to Budenny the role of a Soviet Murat, making no secret of his
personal contemptuous attitude toward him. Budenny repaid Trotsky
many years later. His memoirs, published in 1958, blackened Trotsky's
name in the best traditions of the time, accusing him of willful sabotage
against the Soviet Union.

Whatever Budenny's qualities and weaknesses, he proved worthy of
the task entrusted to him. His Cavalry Army played a very significant
role in the defeat of the Armed Forces of South Russia.

At the beginning of October, while the bands of Makhnó and other
partisans raged at the rear of his armies, Denikin's front against the Reds
extended in a gigantic arch over a distance of 1,130 kilometers.[2]

It consisted of separate troop concentrations at the most vital points,
disposed from east to west as follows:

At the lower reaches of the Volga, opposite Astrakhan, operated the
detachment of General Dratsenko, composed of approximately 4,000 men
from the North Caucasus.

Farther on, in the region of Tsaritsin, came General Wrangel's Caucasian army, of 14,500 men.

To the left of Wrangel was the Don Cossack army of 50,000 men
commanded by General Sidorin. Its front extended from the confluence
of the Ilovl and Don rivers to Zadonsk, located eighty-five kilometers
from Voronezh in the province of that name.

General Mai-Maevsky's Volunteer Army, extending in a thin line over
a huge front between Voronezh and Chernigov, was advancing in the
direction of Moscow. It consisted of only 20,500 men, but these were
the staunchest and most reliable cadres of Denikin's army. At the most
important point, north of Orel, General Kutepov's First Army Corps drove
a sharp wedge in the direction of Moscow, dealing severe frontal as well
as lateral blows to the enemy. Advancing toward Elets was the Markov
division; to the north of Orel, the Kornilov division; and at its left, in
the direction of Briansk, the Drozdovsky division. To the right of Kutepov's corps, at the junction of the Don Cossack and Volunteer armies,
operated a mounted detachment of Mamontov's and Shkuró's Cossacks.
Kutepov's left flank was protected by the Fifth Cavalry Corps of General Iuzefovich, composed mainly of cadres of cavalry regiments of the
old army. Iuzefovich's cavalry (a part of the Volunteer Army) was scattered between the mouth of the river Seim and Khutor Mikhailovski.

To the west of it, along the river Desna, between Kiev and Chernigov,

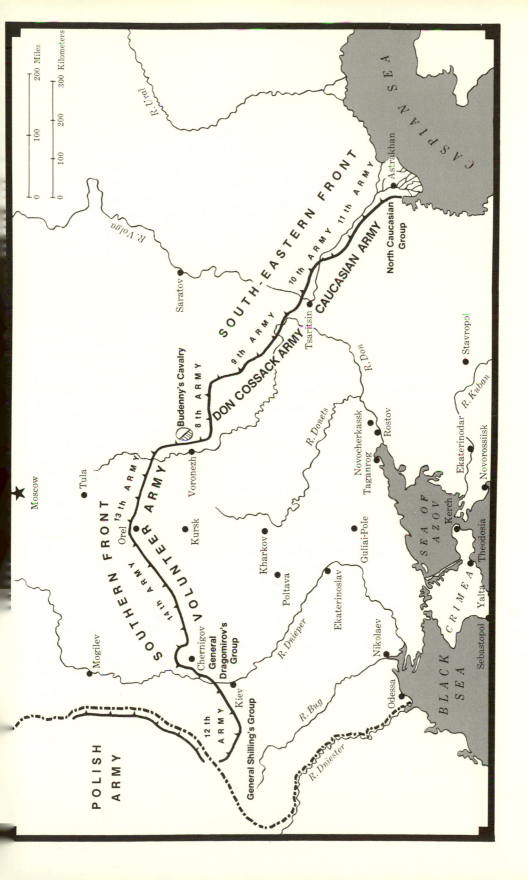

operated the troops of General Dragomirov, consisting of 9,000 men.

On their left flank, from the north to the southwest, in the general direction of Fastov, Berdichev, and Kamenets-Podolsk, General Shilling's group was engaged in fighting the bands of Petliura.

Thus (according to Denikin) in the first half of October, 1919, the Armed Forces of South Russia facing the Red Army (excluding Shilling's troops) attained a total of approximately 98,000 men.[3] Soviet sources indicate that at that time the Whites had at their disposal roughly 2,230 machine guns and 540 cannon. The same sources estimate the total number of Red troops directed against Denikin at 155,653 infantry and 21,215 cavalrymen, 4,416 machine guns, and 892 cannon.[4]

Consequently, at the decisive moment of the struggle, the Reds had an enormous numerical advantage in men and armament over Denikin's armies. Denikin, however, still had the advantage of a superior cavalry.[5]

To strengthen and improve the command of its armies against Denikin, the Revolutionary Military Council of the Republic, headed by Trotsky, at the end of September, 1919, divided its southern front into two sectors —the southern and southeastern fronts. A. I. Egorov was placed in command of the southern front. The member of the Revolutionary Military Council assigned to this front was Stalin. V. I. Shorin became the commander of the southeastern front; and V. A. Trifonov, the Revolutionary Military Council member assigned to it. S. S. Kamenev, who had been made commander in chief of the armed forces of the Soviet Union in July, 1919, was given the overall command of both fronts.

The principal hopes of the Soviet government were centered on the southern front. It was manned by four armies: the twelfth, fourteenth, thirteenth, and eighth, with a total of 104,074 infantrymen, 14,848 cavalrymen, 2,765 machine guns, and 607 cannon. Budenny's cavalry corps stood in reserve to the east of Voronezh, while the best Soviet army units were being rapidly transferred and concentrated against Kutepov's sector. In addition, 6,800 members of the Communist party and over 8,000 "sympathizers" were sent for the political supervision and military morale building of the troops at the southern front. Because of the secret understanding reached with Pilsudski's government, the Red command was able to transfer most of its forces stationed along its Polish front to the southern front, for use against Denikin. The Soviet southern front extended along the line of Zhitomir-Kiev-Orel-Voronezh, to Bobrov, a district town of Voronezh province located approximately a hundred kilometers southwest of its capital.

The Soviet southeastern front extended from Bobrov in the direction of Tsaritsin, then followed the left bank of the Volga. It included (from west to southeast) the ninth, tenth, and eleventh Soviet armies, totaling 51,579 infantrymen and 6,367 cavalrymen, armed with 1,651 machine guns and 285 cannon.[6]

The Communists were fully informed by their already well-established military intelligence and espionage systems of the disorder reigning in their opponent's territory. Nevertheless, the reports they received indicated that Denikin's forces still remained strong and dangerous, possessed of extensive combat experience and the ability to move rapidly and to deal unexpected and crushing blows. They came to the conclusion that only by an important victory at the front could they transform the incipient moral disintegration in the enemy camp into a major catastrophe.

At the beginning of October, the Red command completed its plan of military operations. The main blow, aimed at the Volunteer Army's flanks, was to achieve the strategic purpose of cutting off the Volunteer Army from the Don Cossack army at their point of junction. This would also achieve an important political purpose in permanently separating these two principal components of the White movement. The Soviet Fourteenth Army, enlarged and strengthened by reserves, was to attack, from Orel in the northwest, the left flank of General Kutepov's First Army Corps. Concurrently, Budenny's cavalry would advance from the east toward Voronezh and then Kastornaia (the railroad junction between Kursk and Voronezh), in order to break through to the rear of the Volunteer Army and cut it off from the Don Cossack army.

Although the disposition of the Soviet forces was known to General Denikin's staff, the danger they represented was greatly underestimated. The White Army leaders were too used to winning against uneven odds to be seriously intimidated by the enemy's numerical superiority. They also underestimated his growing strategic ability. The Soviet strategists Kamenev, Shorin, Egorov, had been unmercifully beaten by the Whites in the last few months. Denikin overlooked the fact that the bitter lessons his opponents had learned from him would in the long run contribute immeasurably to their military experience, and would eventually be used against his army. The Soviet commanders proved to be most able pupils in adopting the methods which the White leaders had been obliged to evolve as their movement developed in the harsh conditions of the civil war: the artful maneuvering, mobility, regrouping of troops, and especially the use of cavalry as an attacking and outflanking instrument, so different from the conventional strategy of World War I. The lessons they had learned determined their success, but unlike Peter the Great after his victory over the Swedes at Poltava, they did not render thanks to the enemy who had taught them how to win.

Meanwhile, General Denikin, confident in Kutepov's ability to deal with the Soviet offensive, decided not to slow down his movement to the north of Orel. Denikin's principal concern was Budenny's cavalry, which he saw as a threat not so much to the Volunteer right flank as to the left flank of the larger but less steadfast Don Cossack army. Accordingly, he moved to strengthen the Cossack left by adding to it General Shkuró's cavalry units.

The strategy contemplated by Denikin at that time for fending off the blows of a numerically superior Soviet army called for a rapid regrouping of his troops into powerful attacking forces which could be launched against the enemy at any given sector of the front. The implementation of this plan, however, met with a whole series of obstacles.

Partisan warfare was raging at the rear of Denikin's armies. The activity of Makhnó's insurgents and of other rebel bands in the Ukraine necessitated the transfer of a large number of troops from the front, weakening it at the most critical moment. At the same time, the reserves and reinforcements on which Denikin counted did not come up to expectations. Some of them were absorbed by the antirebel struggle, and the general lack of organization in the territory of south Russia made mobilization of recruits difficult.

General Lukomsky (who then combined the post of chairman of the Special Council with that of Minister of War) wrote in his memoirs that there were two methods of utilizing newly mobilized troops: the formation of fresh units at the rear, and the reinforcement and enlargement of existing units at the front. In reality, because of the excessive length of the front and the numerical weakness of the forces there, the second method was applied almost exclusively. For example, when the Kornilov, Markov, and Drozdovsky regiments received reinforcements at the front (regardless of whether these were mobilized soldiers or war prisoners from the Red Army), they immediately formed them into additional regiments, with their own men as officers and noncoms, eventually enlarging their units to the size of brigades and divisions.

The weakness of this system was noted by Lukomsky, who wrote, "A newly formed regiment composed of reinforcements from reserve battalions at the rear and of recently captured Red Army men, would go into action within a few days, and having as yet no unity, would suffer heavy losses in deserters and prisoners at the slightest military upset." [7] General Mai-Maevsky's army presented the most glaring example of the inadequacy of this procedure.

Denikin's reliance on the Cossack cavalry of Generals Mamontov and Shkuró also proved unjustified. On the surface, Mamontov's Don Cossack regiments seemed to represent an excellent cavalry force capable of impressive combat action. In reality, their morale had been seriously affected by Mamontov's raid behind the enemy lines the preceding month. The wholesale looting had done untold harm to Mamontov's detachment by accustoming its men to brigandage.

Shkuró's cavalry had been weakened by the separation of several units directed against Makhnó; the Kuban Cossacks, who formed its nucleus, also succumbed to the temptation of plundering and to the anti-Denikin propaganda of the Kuban separatists. Shkuró himself related that many of his Cossacks began to desert at that time, taking with them horses and the loot they had accumulated.[8]

In short, the sharp Cossack sword, so bravely wielded but a short time ago, had become considerably blunted.

Such were the general conditions when the opposing forces began to engage each other. The fighting, concentrated at first at the center, around General Kutepov's corps, soon spread along the entire front. Both the White and the Red command were fully aware that this enormous battle was to decide the issue of the entire campaign.

Kutepov's troops fought fiercely, with tremendous persistence. Villages were lost and recaptured constantly in hand-to-hand combat. At this point the advantage of the enemy's numerical superiority became fully evident. It advanced in close, continuous lines along the wide front, against the scattered battalions and squads of the Markov, Kornilov, and Drozdovsky units, in order to rout them and encircle their flanks. The Whites defended themselves valiantly, dealing heavy counterblows to the Reds, but Kutepov's units were melting away, with no reserves of manpower to fall back on.

In the meantime, Budenny's cavalry, stationed behind the junction of the Eighth and Thirteenth Soviet armies northwest of Voronezh, assumed the offensive. Aiming to take Voronezh, capture the railroad station of Kastornaia, and carry the fight in the general direction of Kursk, it dealt some nasty blows to Shkuró's units and threatened the rear of Kutepov's corps. The savage and stubborn fighting lasted for thirty days, during which the Whites were gradually forced to retreat and abandon one by one the towns, villages, and settlements they had captured so recently and with such hope for a final victory.

The situation at the front was growing extremely serious, but Denikin had lived through worse. He realized that only by crushing Budenny's corps could he recapture the initiative, the possibility of maneuvering and of a large-scale offensive, and knew that this could only be achieved by assembling a powerful military force. He drew out his last reserves from the North Caucasus and the Georgian border. By mid-November he had concentrated near Volchansk-Valuiki a special task force. Its nucleus consisted of General Mamontov's cavalry (a detachment of seven thousand cavalrymen), three thousand infantrymen, and fifty-eight cannon, along with tanks armored trains, and several airplanes.

By that time Mai-Maevsky had already been relieved of his post. "Wishing to utilize the cavalry talents of General Wrangel," Denikin gave him the command of the Volunteer Army, into which the new task force was incorporated.

We shall let Denikin himself relate how the plans on which he had based such high hopes came to be disrupted:

Before leaving Taganrog for the Volunteer Army, General Wrangel advised me that he would not tolerate the presence in it of Generals Shkuró and Mamontov, whom he considered the principal culprits in the disintegration of the cavalry corps. General Shkuró was then on sick leave in the Kuban. As regards

Mamontov, I warned Wrangel against drastic action against a person who, for better or worse, enjoyed great popularity in the Don.

Upon rejoining the army, General Wrangel placed General Ulagai, a highly esteemed and valiant Kuban officer, in command of the Cossack cavalry detachment. Despite the fact that this was a temporary formation, and the choice of its leader, which depended entirely on the army commander, did not have to be based on precedence, the nomination gave rise to a serious incident: Mamontov took offense and advised all and sundry by telegram that "considering the composition of the cavalry group, I find my unwarranted replacement as commander of the cavalry group by a person who does not belong to the Don Cossack army and ranks below me in the service, to be lacking in consideration for the dignity of the Don Cossack army and insulting to myself. For the above reasons, I consider it impossible to remain at the post of commander of the Fourth Don Cossack Corps." Mamontov sent copies of this telegram to all his regiments. On the next day, as he took his unauthorized leave from the corps, Mamontov reported, not without malice, the rout of his regiments under enemy pressure.

This unheard-of action was not, however, criticized in the Don. My orders to deprive Mamontov of his command met with unexpected opposition from the Don Cossack *Ataman* and General Sidorin. They pointed out that in addition to the negative effect Mamontov's dismissal would have on the Don Cossack army, the entire Fourth Corps was disintegrating and could only be reassembled by Mamontov. In effect, as soon as the corps was returned to the Don Cossack army, Mamontov resumed its command and reassembled an impressive number of cavalrymen. Later, the corps dealt some heavy blows to Budenny's cavalry in the fighting beyond the Don.

These successes could not alter the general situation and did not compensate for the grave blow to military discipline.[9]

One should note also a typical phenomenon of the civil war which affected the Reds and the Whites in equal measure: The advancing side never had any trouble in acquiring reinforcements of war prisoners and locally mobilized men, whereas the retreating side immediately began to lose its draftees. They deserted as soon as their home villages were recaptured by the enemy. This characteristic of the civil war was noted by the future Soviet marshal M. N. Tukhachevsky: "The natives of districts being abandoned desert in order to remain near their homes. Thus, during an offensive, the advancing party is continuously strengthened, while the retreating party is continuously weakened."[10]

True to this pattern, Denikin's retreating troops were melting away. The hundreds of victims of the typhus epidemic which had spread throughout south Russia, and the early setting in of a particularly harsh winter, further speeded up the process. Thousands of soldiers and officers were disabled not only by wounds, but also by severely frostbitten feet and hands.

At first, the infantry suffered most of all. Later, the muddy autumn roads, which soon became crusted with ice, then covered with snowdrifts, became impassable for the cavalry and especially for the artillery. The artillerymen could no longer cope with their burdens.

Early in December, the Fifth Cavalry Corps of the Volunteer Army became so depleted that it was reduced to a division. Its temporary commander, General Chekotovsky, reported on December 4 to General Wrangel:

The division's cavalry complement has reached complete exhaustion. Since the beginning of the campaign in June, the division has been stationary for only five or six days. . . . If a few horses have been shoed in this half year, they were exceptions. Reshoeing for the winter was out of the question. At present, the horse has become a burden to its rider, slipping and falling at every step, for road surfaces are like glass and the frozen plowed-up fields are impassable. The regiments move at three versts [a little over three kilometers] an hour. Artillery guns are being pulled by all available means, including the horses of the officers, who follow on foot. . . . If people think that there are still considerable reinforcements at the rear . . . they are mistaken. . . . In order not to confuse the high command with such grand terms as "brigade" and "division," which would call for correspondingly important assignments, I deem it my duty to report that the First Cavalry Division no longer represents a combat force capable of carrying out military assignments, but has become a small exhausted unit, lower in numbers than a small-size regiment.[11]

At the same time, Budenny's cavalry, mounted on well-shoed horses, was wedging in deeper between the Volunteers and the Don Cossacks. Insurrections threatened the rear of Denikin's forces, and criticism inevitably followed the military reverses. Timidly at first, but soon loudly and openly, certain elements began to sponsor a new candidate for the role of commander in chief. This candidate was General Peter Wrangel.

XXVII

STRUGGLE FOR POWER
IN THE WHITE CAMP

The loss of military discipline in the lower echelons of the White Army was immediately obvious to the general population; less evident but equally serious was a corresponding slackening of military traditions among members of the high command.

"Serious internal conflicts accompanied our military operations," wrote General Denikin. "The numerical weakness of our forces, and our desperate lack of technical equipment and supplies, created a chronic state of insufficiency at all the fronts and in all the armies. It was, therefore, extremely difficult to separate any troops for inclusion in the commander in chief's reserve. Each commander considered his front to be of primary importance. Every strategic transfer of troops gave rise to conflicts of interests, resentment, and delays."

Headquarters had to consider not only the individual psychology and personal relationships of the senior commanders, but even their vagaries, which, as in Mamontov's case, were often of paramount importance. True, the Mamontov affair was complicated by the problem of the Don Cossacks' national pride. As regards other recalcitrant generals, the supreme headquarters, or *Stavka,* was unquestionably guilty of not enforcing its authority over them before it was too late.

While, according to Denikin, the exchanges between his headquarters and the commanders of the Volunteer and Don Cossack armies "mainly concerned operational plans and never infringed upon military discipline and subordination," the relationship between the *Stavka* and General Wrangel, commander of the Caucasian army, was altogether different.

"Not a day passed," wrote Denikin, "without the *Stavka* or myself receiving nervous, demanding, peremptory and sometimes offensive telegrams from Wrangel, aimed at proving the superiority of his strategic and tactical plans, our deliberate neglect of his army, and our responsibility for the delays and failures of his operations. . . . This systematic internal strife created a painful atmosphere of antagonism. The mood communicated itself to the various staffs and through them to the army and citizenry. . . . This relationship between commander and subordinate, obviously ruled out in any normally formed and constituted army, had come about as a result of the loss of an established succession of power and of military tradition." [1]

By mid-November, 1919, the differences between Denikin and Wrangel had placed the latter at the center of the political opposition to Denikin, which had secretly existed in rightist circles since the end of the preceding year. With the growing White reverses, this opposition had finally found in General Wrangel a spokesman for expressing its discontent and undermining the authority of the commander in chief and his staff.

By that time, General Wrangel had become widely known as an outstanding cavalry leader. He had many enthusiastic admirers, not only among the officers but also in the civilian population, where he was considered more flexible than Denikin in his approach to the aims of the White Movement, to its relationship with the newly formed peripheral states, and to a whole series of other questions of principle. Wrangel's determination, his success in curbing army disorders through drastic measures, his unquestionable desire to concentrate power in his own hands, all made him a likely candidate for the leadership of the White Movement.

It is difficult to imagine two people more unlike than Wrangel and Denikin. Accompanying the difference in their family origins—the privileged background of the one and the modest origins of the other—was the difference in their personalities. Wrangel had the dash and worldly glamor of an officer in a distinguished regiment of the old imperial guard, while Denikin lacked these surface qualities. Wrangel was imperious and abrupt, but was at the same time a practical realist possessed of great elasticity in political matters. Denikin, on the other hand, lacked flexibility and was restrained in manner and in speech. Despite his many trials and his disappointment in many of his aides, Denikin retained certain traits of the romantic idealist. He remained true to his innermost principles and world concepts, which were unfortunately quite divorced from the reality around him. Wrangel was a born leader who would not hesitate to assume dictatorial powers; Denikin viewed dictatorship as a temporary if unavoidable phase of the civil-war strife. It is not surprising, therefore, that his so-called dictatorship was far from effective. General Wrangel chose his subordinates without regard for their seniority and former record and rejected anyone who did not suit him. Denikin's attitude was quite different. He was hamstrung by his loyal consideration for the former services of his brothers in arms. Wrangel noted this trait in his memoirs: "The seemingly firm and implacable General Denikin

proved extraordinarily soft in regard to the senior commanders subordi-
nated to him. A true soldier, strict in relation to himself, whose austere
way of life was an example to all, he seemed hesitant to demand the
same from his subordinates." [2]

The disagreements between the two generals began in April, 1919,
shortly after General Wrangel recovered from typhus, and were at first
known to very few people. They concerned the choice of the main direction of the offensive by the Armed Forces of South Russia. In a series
of letters and reports, Wrangel insisted that the main thrust should be
aimed at Tsaritsin, for the purpose of capturing the lower reaches of the
Volga and establishing a liaison with the forces of Admiral Kolchak.

This had also been Denikin's early opinion, which he had arrived at
independently, before hearing Wrangel's proposal. While completing the
Second Kuban Campaign and the liberation of the North Caucasus early
in 1919, he had sketched out a plan for moving the Caucasian army
(known at that time as the Caucasian Volunteer army) in the direction
of Tsaritsin.

> But by the beginning of February [he wrote], when the transfer of these troops
> would have been possible, the general situation had undergone a drastic change.
> The Don army, in complete disarray, was retreating toward the Don, pressed
> by the superior forces of the Reds. The Soviet troops were advancing almost
> continuously in the direction of Novocherkassk. The *Krug,* the *Ataman,* and
> the government pointed out the deadly menace to the Don region. Meanwhile,
> on the left flank of the Don Cossacks, the Volunteer corps commanded by
> General Mai-Maevsky was still fending off the attacks of large enemy forces,
> and blocking the way to the Donets coal basin, which was vital to us and
> "desperately needed" by the Bolsheviks, as Trotsky expressed it in his ap-
> peals. . . .
>
> I was faced by a dilemma: Should I forsake the Don region and surrender
> the coal basin to the Bolsheviks by moving the army toward Tsaritsin, or should
> I, while securing the Tsaritsin direction with part of the troops, save the
> Donets bridgehead and preserve the Don Cossack army from disintegration?
>
> I chose the second alternative without hesitation.

(As regards the possibility of operating a junction with Kolchak's
armies, they were at that time separated from Denikin's forces by approximately seven hundred kilometers.)

In the meantime, General Wrangel continued to insist on his plan of
action, proposing to sacrifice the coal region, whose defense he considered
hopeless, and to move the Caucasian army in the direction of Tsaritsin.

"His plan," wrote Denikin, "would have resulted in the loss not only
of the coal basin, but of the entire right-bank section of the Don region,
with Rostov and Novocherkassk, and in the destruction of the rebellious
Cossacks [thirty thousand] of the Upper Don district."

"My plan was different. I considered it possible to attack or at least
arrest the activity of the four Bolshevik armies to the north of the Don

and to defeat at the same time the Tenth Army, in the direction of Tsaritsin. Our victorious advance, by diverting large forces and supplies of the Soviets, would ease the pressure on other White Army fronts." [3]

The immediate future proved that Denikin's plan had definite possibilities of succeeding. The advance on Tsaritsin, at the time when it was proposed by Wrangel, did not, therefore, represent the only correct solution to the problem, as some sources tried to make it appear later.

In mid-June of 1919, the letters and reports of General Wrangel to Denikin took on the aspect of pamphlets directed at the general reader. General Wrangel divulged their contents to his aides and to some public figures, through whom they eventually reached both officers and civilians. The communication to outsiders of these letters and reports, with their harshly stated demands and criticisms of the *Stavka's* activity, did a great deal to undermine the authority of the commander in chief.

As he had in 1918 with respect to General Drozdovsky, Denikin placed General Wrangel's military merit above his personal feelings for him. These had been consistently friendly until now, but were marred by resentment at the contents of Wrangel's letters and especially at the fact that the letters had been circulated among outsiders. "Nevertheless," wrote Denikin, "I armed myself with patience, remembering General Wrangel's services, bearing in mind his inherent nervousness and not wishing to deprive the army of a gifted cavalry leader and to expose the *Stavka* to accusations of partiality." [4]

During the victorious northward advance of Denikin's forces, the Tsaritsin controversy was temporarily forgotten. It was revived, however, when the fortunes of war turned against the White Army, and became an ace in the hands of the anti-Denikin movement. By that time, the strategic reasons for his decision were no longer remembered by the general public. He was blamed for not taking Wrangel's advice, for failing to achieve a junction with Kolchak's forces ("a precious opportunity missed"), for being guided by personal ambition ("a vain man intoxicated with power"), for wanting to be the first to be greeted by the church bells of a liberated Moscow. Even Denikin's sincerity in making the decision to submit to Kolchak was questioned, and to cap all, a final accusation was made: "Admiral Kolchak's forces, treacherously abandoned by us, were defeated. . . ." [5]

While Denikin, in the south of Russia, was being accused of betraying Kolchak, the Admiral, in Siberia, was being blamed for betraying Denikin. In order to undermine further the Admiral's authority, already shaky since the autumn of 1919, certain elements in Omsk were circulating pamphlets accusing him of deliberately avoiding a junction with Denikin's armies.[6]

Only blind hatred or the deliberate distortion of truth could have engendered so gross a calumny against these two men, whose mistakes were many, but whose integrity and honor were beyond question.

At the end of November, 1919, Mai-Maevsky was relieved of his post as commander of the Volunteer Army and replaced, at Denikin's insistence, by General Wrangel. The latter's position at the head of the Caucasian army was assumed by General Pokrovsky. Denikin's decision to choose Wrangel for this post and to place Mamontov's large mounted unit under his orders, despite the friction of the preceding months, was determined by his desire to utilize Wrangel's talents as a cavalry leader.

As we already know, General Wrangel placed Ulagai at the head of his mounted troops, which offended Mamontov, brought on his ostentatious withdrawal, and contributed to the final disintegration of his cavalry units. The *Stavka*'s plans, based to a large extent on the performance of the cavalry, resulted in failure. The ensuing redistribution of command posts aggravated the incipient conflict between Denikin and Wrangel.

Wrangel's nomination to his new post [wrote Denikin], added further complications to the atmosphere of internal dissension which was particularly hard to bear on top of the reverses that the armies and I were undergoing at the time. First came a report exposing our neglect of the basic principles of warfare in the past and underscoring the superiority of General Wrangel's strategic theories. This report, also, had been communicated to the senior officers. . . . The new army commander painted a harrowing picture of the legacy left him by General Mai-Maevsky: a system of "self-supplying" which had transformed "warfare into a gainful pursuit and the use of local commodities into looting and speculation" . . . troops depraved by this system and the example of some senior commanders . . . huge conglomerations at the rear blocking all means of communication . . . a chaotic evacuation, complicated by a wave of refugees. . . . And, in conclusion: "The army no longer exists as a combat force!" [7]

Denikin categorically rejected this conclusion. The memory of the first heroic campaigns of the Volunteer Army would not let him accept it. "An army," he said, "which had resisted the blows of an enemy almost three times stronger than itself . . . and over a distance of four hundred versts [about 427 kilometers] between Orel and Kharkov, [and] was still able despite the loss of 50 percent of its complement to counter the enemy onslaught, maneuver, parry, and launch attacks successfully—such an army was not dead." [8]

Denikin's reaction to Wrangel's report was more emotional than realistic. In spite of the heroic record of the Volunteer Army, the defeats and continuous retreat of late 1919, following the elation of almost certain victory, had shaken the faith of even its staunchest fighters in the ultimate success of their endeavor.

General Wrangel's report was sent on December 9, after he had familiarized himself with conditions at the front to which he had been assigned. He stated that at the time of his arrival (the end of November), there remained approximately 3,600 infantrymen and 4,700 cavalrymen in the entire army; the Kuban corps had been reduced to a brigade, and the Kornilov regiments to battalions; the Markov regiments retained only their cadres and the Drozdovsky division had dwindled to three squads.[9]

General Wrangel's report was essentially correct in its description of the disastrous situation at the front and of its causes. At the same time, unfortunately, it was couched in excessively harsh and provocative terms, more in the style of an aggressive newspaper attack than of a report from a subordinate general to his commander in chief. When General Denikin learned that copies of this report also had been sent by General Wrangel to several people and its substance "confidentially communicated" to a number of others, his suspicions were definitely aroused.[10]

Denikin had known since June that certain of General Wrangel's reports, letters, and telegrams were being circulated among outsiders. At that time, however, he did not interpret Wrangel's conduct as a sign of a struggle for power, but ascribed it to his quick and nervous temperament. Now, however, in the midst of reverses, he saw it in an entirely different light, not only as a breach of military discipline, but as a political gambit directed against the commander in chief. Yet, to use his own expression, Denikin silently continued to bear with immeasurable, endless patience the controversy developing around the *Stavka*. Later, he blamed himself bitterly for keeping silent at that time.

Almost immediately after Wrangel assumed the command of the Volunteer Army, serious disagreements with regard to strategy arose between him and the *Stavka*. The Red cavalry had already cut a deep swath in the White Army front, forcing the Armed Forces of South Russia to retreat in two separate sections, one moving southeast, and the other, southwest. General Wrangel believed that the Don Cossack army should remain and form a front in the Don region. Simultaneously, he proposed to separate the Volunteer Army from the Don Cossack army and direct it toward the Crimea, whose access it would defend while effecting a junction with the units of Generals Shilling and Bredov, who were then retreating from Kiev toward Odessa. Wrangel also pointed out that a retreat of the Volunteer Army toward the Don would involve a very complicated and dangerous flank movement which would expose his troops to continuous enemy attacks.

General Denikin categorically rejected Wrangel's proposal. He considered it unthinkable to separate the Volunteers from the Don Cossacks. He therefore ordered the Volunteers, if they found it impossible to hold their positions, to retreat only together with the Don Cossack army, regardless of the sacrifices this could involve.

"The departure of the Volunteer Army for the Crimea," said the General, "would result in the inevitable and immediate collapse of the entire Don Cossack and Kuban fronts, bringing dire hardship and possible death to tens of thousands of sick and wounded soldiers . . . scattered in the territory of the Don and the North Caucasus. No strategic considerations could justify such a step in the eyes of the Cossacks, who would consider it a betrayal on our part." [11]

There is no doubt that the General's analysis of the situation in this particular instance was correct: From the very beginning of the civil war, the Volunteer Army was the backbone of the White movement. Despite everything, it still represented a serious fighting force, while the morale of the Cossacks had been sapped by the retreat. Withdrawal of the Volunteers from Cossack territory to the Crimea would have threatened to bring about a complete collapse of Cossack resistance.

In view of the smallness of the Volunteer Army, General Wrangel suggested reducing it to an army corps. As for himself, he requested permission to leave for the Kuban, where he planned to assemble a cavalry army. Both proposals were approved by the *Stavka*. General Kutepov was placed in command of the Volunteer corps, and General Wrangel was dispatched to the Kuban.

In the meantime, however, the relationship of Denikin and Wrangel continued to deteriorate. On December 11, Generals Wrangel and Sidorin met for a conference at Iasinovataia station, allegedly to work out the details of a complex flank operation which would enable the Volunteers to rejoin the Don Cossack army. Denikin had not only allowed this interview, but insisted on its taking place. He was completely taken aback, however, when Wrangel afterward summoned by telegram the commanders of the Don Cossack and Caucasian armies (Generals Sidorin and Pokrovsky) to meet in conference with him. Denikin learned of the proposed meeting by chance when a copy of Wrangel's telegram was forwarded to the *Stavka*. This time he lost his temper. "The very fact," he later wrote, "of summoning the army commanders without the commander in chief's authorization, constituted an unprecedented breach of military tradition and military discipline." [12]

In a peremptory telegram addressed to the three army commanders, Denikin pointed out that some of the army leaders allowed themselves to take unacceptable liberties in making their requests, stated that he would no longer tolerate such conduct, and demanded unquestioning obedience from his subordinates. In a second telegram, he forbade the meeting convoked by General Wrangel, calling such action unpermissible, and enjoined the commanders from leaving their armies without his permission.

In his memoirs, General Wrangel referred to this episode as follows: "Apparently, General Denikin saw in my telegram a preparation for some kind of 'plot' in which his closest assistants were about to engage." [13]

Although at that moment Denikin had no proof that a "plot" was being fomented, he was to receive, within the next few weeks, ample evidence confirming that General Wrangel had been discussing with some of the senior army leaders the possibility of removing Denikin from the post of commander in chief and replacing him by another officer. On the strength of the testimony collected at that time, General Denikin had every reason to affirm at a later date several facts: First, in his meeting of December 11, 1919, with General Sidorin, General Wrangel had "harshly criticized the strategy and policy of the *Stavka* and raised the question of removing Denikin from the post of commander in chief and replacing him by another person"; and furthermore, General Wrangel had decided to call a conference of the three army commanders (Wrangel, Sidorin, Pokrovsky) precisely "to decide this question and other questions connected with it." [14] Second, around December 20, 1919, during his stay in the Kuban for the purpose of forming a cavalry army, General Wrangel engaged in secret discussions on how to force General Denikin to relinquish his post.

Among those Wrangel approached were General Shkuró, General Vdovenko (the *Ataman* of the Terek Cossacks), P. D. Gubarev (the chairman of the Terek *Krug*), and General Erdeli.[15] They subsequently notified General Denikin of Wrangel's overtures. They flatly refused any part in the project, basing their refusal on their loyalty to the commander in chief as well as their conviction that a "generals' uprising" at such a critical time would lead to the collapse of the front. They also argued that General Denikin's name was irreplaceable as a symbol of leadership in the White movement. A special courier was urgently dispatched by them to notify General Denikin of everything that had taken place.

Generals Denikin and Wrangel saw each other for the last time on December 27, 1919, at a gathering attended by other officers. "In the course of the general conversation," wrote Wrangel, "General Denikin did not address a single word to me." [16]

However, the final break between them did not occur until February, 1920.

A complete analysis of the Denikin–Wrangel relationship has yet to be written. At present, it is enough to say that at a certain moment, General Wrangel—a brilliant military leader whose achievements in the White movement were outstanding—lost faith in Denikin's leadership. Considering his command detrimental to the cause, he sought to remedy the situation by organizing a "palace revolution," preceded by the secret negotiations that such an undertaking requires. At the same time, both the course of events and Wrangel's own activity were building him up as Denikin's successor in the White Army command.

It was hard for Denikin to witness and silently bear the power play led by a man whom he had valued so highly and promoted so consistently. Nevertheless, the answers which he gave many years later to the accusations leveled at him at that time were characterized by restraint and were always based on scrupulously verified facts. This subject was treated by General Denikin in Volume V of *Ocherki Russkoi Smuty* (*The Russian Turmoil*).

In his unpublished papers he left the following note: "It was always hard for me to write about our conflict, especially as the last thing I wanted was to discredit my successor, to the enjoyment of the Bolsheviks. . . . Let history be the judge. . . ." [17]

XXVIII

CALUMNY

———◄──── ────►———

Even before any reversals at the front, while Denikin's prestige was still high, unfavorable comments concerning his chief of staff, General Romanovsky, were being made in some political circles in south Russia. Romanovsky's close association with Denikin, begun at the time of their incarceration in Bykhov after the Kornilov affair, had developed into an exceptional friendship, which gave rise to the suspicion that Romanovsky might use his influence on Denikin for his personal gain. Some called Romanovsky the "gray eminence," others bluntly accused him of being Denikin's "evil genius."

Romanovsky was described as very ambitious, and jealous of his exclusive position. He was suspected of hiding the real state of affairs from the commander in chief.[1] In the historical perspective of half a century most of those accusations appear groundless. There is no doubt that Ramanovsky's devotion to Denikin was genuine and devoid of excessive ambition. On the contrary, he kept himself in the background and avoided publicity.

He did his best to protect Denkin from unnecessary trouble, as in the episode, described in an earlier chapter, in which General Drozdovsky sent the commander a report couched in unacceptable terms, and Romanovsky returned the report to Drozdovsky with the comment that he could not submit it to Denikin in its present shape. The incident was smoothed over, but Romanovsky's reputation suffered: Even then, in the fall of 1918, rumor had it that the chief of staff kept the commander in chief from knowing the whole truth. From the middle of 1919, General Wrangel waged a determined campaign against Romanovsky. As the chief of staff was considered a liberal, monarchist circles immediately labeled him a "Freemason," with all the evil political implications ascribed to Masonry in Russian rightist circles. No one has ever been able to prove that Romanovsky belonged to a Masonic organization. As regards his liberalism, Professor K. N. Sokolov (a Cadet) considered Romanovsky to be a man of inherently rightist views who "inclined to the left for reasons of necessity." [2]

Nor is there any proof that Romanovsky used his position for personal gain. Unlike Marshal Berthier, Napoleon's chief of staff, not only did Romanovsky not acquire a fortune, but he left his family completely destitute after his tragic death in Constantinople in 1920. If Romanovsky lacked the military gifts of a Berthier, he had at least remained an honest and honorable man.

Nevertheless, Romanovsky did have traits which irritated and antagonized those who did not know him well. He combined a reserved disposition with a certain abruptness of manner, and burdened as he was by an eighteen-hour working day, did not always extend enough time or courtesy to the visitors and petitioners who daily crowded his reception room. He lacked the amiable lightness of a wordly man in dealing with strangers, and could be short and abrupt when pressed for time, or simply unable to receive all the people who wished to see him. The result was that he acquired the reputation of a dry, hidebound bureaucrat.

Even Denikin's wife said that "those who accused Romanovsky of abruptness and lack of polish were probably right. Only they did not realize that when a man is torn apart . . . there is no room left for delicacy of feeling." [3]

No one else was ever present at important conferences between the commander in chief and his chief of staff, and no one, therefore, could evaluate the degree of influence exercised by Romanovsky on Denikin. Nevertheless, people intimately acquainted with those two highly reserved persons were aware of the exceptional rapport that existed between them and believed that the strategic decisions of the *Stavka* reflected Denikin's and Romanovsky's thinking in equal part.

By the fall of 1919, General Denikin had come to the firm conclusion that the only person who could replace him if the emergency arose was Romanovsky. This consideration was prompted by persistent rumors (which later proved to be well founded) that the left wing of the Socialist Revolutionary party was plotting an attempt against his life. [4]

As the legislation in force in south Russia made no provision for the succession of power, General Denikin decided that his will would take the form of an order of the day to the troops in which he designated Lieutenant General Romanovsky as his successor in case of death.

By this act [wrote Denikin in his memoirs] I was placing a heavy burden on him. But I considered him the direct heir to my endeavor and believed that the army, although it harbored some prejudiced and sometimes even antagonistic feelings against Romanovsky, would respect the last order of its commander in chief. And the recognition of the army meant everything. The order, in a sealed envelope, lay in my safe, unknown to anyone except myself and two other people: Romanovsky and my deputy chief of staff, Pliushchevsky-

Pliushchik. Romanovsky said nothing when I advised him of my decision, but a sad smile appeared on his face. As if he were thinking, Who knows which one of us will be the first to go? [5]

Anton Ivanovich remained convinced that the secret of this decision had never been broken. Yet he had to admit that some astute minds penetrated it intuitively, so that a short time later, with the issue of an order naming Generals Romanovsky and Lukomsky as "assistants to the commander in chief," political circles in south Russia became convinced that none other than Romanovsky had been chosen as Denikin's successor. From that time on, according to Denikin, the propaganda against his chief of staff assumed a particularly aggressive form. It made him the scapegoat of the frustration and anger in the White camp.

The choice of Romanovsky, after ugly rumors had already ruined his reputation among the officers, shows the extent to which General Denikin had by then lost touch with the spirit and mood of his army.

Appalled by the chaotic conditions at the rear and by the absence of people capable of restoring it to order, Denikin devoted more of his time to the problems of civilian administration. Consequently, he could not give his full attention to the all-important task of military leadership. His visits to the front became less frequent after the Volunteer and Don Cossack armies joined forces under his command in December, 1918, and from that time on, he began to lose contact with the troops. On the one hand, Denikin could no longer keep his finger on the army's pulse. On the other, the troops no longer felt any personal tie with their leader. Many units of the active army knew their commander in chief only by the coarsely printed posters which the department of White propaganda displayed in all towns, villages, and railroad stations liberated from the Bolsheviks. The men no longer felt the special stern appeal of Denikin's personality that Markov, Timanovsky, and many others who had served under him in the Iron Division knew so well, as did those whom Denikin had saved from a seemingly hopeless situation after Kornilov's death in the First Kuban Campaign. To those who had joined his army in 1919, Denikin appeared no different from all the other staff generals in the remoteness of the army rear. Thus, it was not surprising that when the military tide turned, the men who knew the commander in chief only by hearsay began to pay attention to those who spoke of replacing him with a real "combat general."

By the fall of 1919, General Denikin had made every effort to counteract the inertia of the retreating movement, and he still believed that a significant victory could turn the whole strategic situation upside down and reverse the roles of the protagonists, as had happened in May in the coal basin. Even after the White forces lost Rostov and Novocherkassk and retreated beyond the Don River, several successful counterattacks seemed to confirm the commander in chief's optimism: On January 5, 1920, the White cavalry roughed up Budenny's forces near Bataisk; in the middle of January, the Don Cossack cavalry gave them a severe beating; on February 7, General Kutepov's Volunteer corps recaptured Rostov and a Don Cossack corps took *stanitsa* Aksaiskaia. In each case impressive numbers of prisoners and quantities of ordnance and ammunition were captured from the enemy. It seemed to Denikin that everything was far from being lost when a "defeated army" was still able to deal such blows.

Yet, the General was unable to wrest the military initiative from the Reds, as the enemy was already approaching the army's deep rear near Tikhoretskaia. The White troops finally merged with the huge masses of civilians—homeless, shelterless, on foot, on horseback, and in carts, with their children and their miserable belongings. They were fleeing the bondage of Bolshevism, and their only chance of escaping was to reach the Black Sea shores, from which they hoped somehow to get to the Crimea, that last stronghold of the White movement, still being stubbornly defended by General Slaschev. A period of agony began for all those who had linked their fate with General Denikin's endeavor.

In the meantime, the Soviet supreme command established a "Caucasian front," with its Eighth, Ninth, Tenth, and Eleventh armies, and Budenny's cavalry. Placed under the command of M. N. Tukhachevsky, later a marshal, the Caucasian front extended from Rostov to Astrakhan and was directed exclusively against General Denikin. The Soviet Thirteenth and Fourteenth armies were dispatched to act in the Ukraine and the Crimea.

XXIX

ON THE DECLINE

In the memory of Denikin's contemporaries, the reversals at the front have obliterated the efforts he made at that time to modify his rigid political approach. The changes came too late to have any real impact on the course of events, yet in making them Anton Ivanovich was profoundly affected by the necessity of forgoing his own deeply felt and sincere convictions. He finally came to realize that the excesses and disorders at the rear had completely discredited his government (i.e., the Special Council) in the eyes of the population, and that a radical revision of the White movement's slogans, of its internal administration, and of its attitude toward the postrevolutionary peripheral governments, had become indispensable.

Denikin decided to try a leftist policy implemented by rightist hands. By his order of December 16, 1919, the Special Council was dissolved. The government that replaced it, however, was headed by the former chairman of the Special Council, General Lukomsky. As a concession to the conservative elements, A. V. Krivoshein, an intelligent and experienced former dignitary of the tsarist regime, was included in the government. At the beginning of January, 1920, Denikin was obliged to remove Lukomsky, who was unpopular with the Don Cossacks, as head of the government, and replace him by the Don Cossack *Ataman,* General Bogaevsky.

By that time, the Don, Kuban, and Terek Cossacks in south Russia had already formed a Supreme *Krug,* a sort of general parliament for their combined regions. Although part of the *Krug* was in favor of forming an independent Cossack government, General Denikin still hoped to tip the scales of the tired and wavering Cossack mood in his favor. On January 16 he made a forceful speech to the members of the Supreme *Krug,* pleading for their solidarity and continued participation in the struggle:

Granted that in the Kharkov-Voronezh sector we were opposed by enormous Bolshevik forces assembled from various directions, under whose pressure our front had to recede, but to our disgrace, near Rostov and Novocherkassk, though we were stronger than the enemy in numbers and equipment, it was our spirit that had been sapped by retreat, illicit gain, and the reckless propaganda which undermined the command's authority and obscured the aims of our struggle.

In this speech General Denikin brought out an interesting and important point:

What are the real forces of Bolshevism at present? I shall not venture a personal opinion, but will limit myself to quoting Trotsky's appraisal of them at the meeting of the Revolutionary Military Council of the southern front:

"Lack of supplies, disrupted communications, hunger, cold, the secret and open discontent of the masses with ourselves—all threaten with consequences which our power, already strained to the limit, will not be able to overcome. Our enemy, too, is completely exhausted, and the whole question now is which of us will be able to survive the winter. We are in no condition to fight and neither are they. For this reason we must take the offensive at all costs."

Can't you see [continued General Denikin] that despite the apparent brilliant successes of the Bolsheviks, this is the cry of despair of an overextended gambler, and that only one last great effort on our part is required to finish him off?

Denikin then set forth the program of the government he was planning to form if an agreement could be reached between the Supreme *Krug* and the commander in chief. One of the new slogans proposed by Denikin was "All land to the peasants and to the Cossack workingmen." In view of the previous history of the White movement, it was not surprising that a justified note of reproach sounded in the answering speeches of some members of the Supreme *Krug*. They welcomed the intention to allocate the land to the peasants and Cossack workingmen, but pointed out how belated were these announcements, which should have been made at the outset of the anti-Bolshevik struggle.[1]

Denikin also modified his policy with regard to recently organized states: As a temporary expedient, he was now prepared to deal on a *de facto* basis with the governments of these newly formed states. He would not, however, extend *de jure* recognition to the countries which, in his opinion, had illegally broken away from Russia.[2]

There soon occurred another deviation from the commander in chief's original policy. He decided to drop his dictatorial powers in favor of a constitutional form of government—without, however, limiting in any way his military authority. At the end of January, 1920, he removed Bogaevsky from the position of chairman of the government of south Russia, and after consulting with the leaders of the Cossack Supreme *Krug,* replaced him with N. M. Melnikov, the former chairman of the Don Cossack government. This move indicated a shift to the left. The only interesting personality to be included in Denikin's newly formed "democratic" cabinet was the former revolutionary-Populist Nikolai Chaikovsky (1850–1925). Having joined the "fight for freedom" in early youth, Chaikovsky took an active part in the Russian revolutionary movement and later emigrated abroad. He returned to his homeland in 1907. Ten years later, he openly opposed the Bolshevik take-over, and at one time, he headed an anti-Bolshevik government in Archangel. Chaikovsky maintained that only two choices were open to the Russians during the civil war: Bolshevism and the one real force that was pitted against it. "There is no third choice," he declared.[3] Chaikovsky therefore threw in his lot with Denikin, who put him in charge of propaganda. Unfortunately, by that time, people in south Russia no longer listened to White propaganda. They were only interested in leaving the sinking ship as soon as possible.

The mounting feeling of hopelessness was intensified at the beginning of February, 1920, by the news of the collapse of the Kolchak front in Siberia and of the Admiral's tragic death.

As in south Russia, bands of insurgents raged at the rear of Kolchak's retreating troops. They invaded the towns along the main Siberian rail line, installing in them local governments whose leadership, initially composed of Mensheviks and Socialist Revolutionaries, soon passed into the hands of the Bolsheviks. A government of this type, the Political Center, had been organized in Irkutsk, toward which a train with Admiral Kolchak on board was slowly making its way. The Admiral, who occupied a second-class carriage, was guarded by Czech troops. Separated from the remainder of his units, crushed by the total defeat of his army, and having officially resigned his position as Supreme Ruler in favor of Denikin on December 2, Kolchak had accepted the Allies' proposal that he leave for the Far East under their protection. The flags of France, Great Britain, the United States, Japan, and Czechoslovakia floated over Kolchak's carriage. His train was followed by a second one, loaded with the remainder of the Russian gold reserve and other valuables. When the trains approached Irkutsk, the local Political Center demanded that Admiral Kolchak be delivered to them.

"There is no reason to suppose that the Czechs, if they had been so disposed, were not strong enough to force their way out with both the Admiral and the gold," wrote Winston Churchill. "But the atmosphere was loaded with panic and intrigue. General Janin [a French general then in charge of the Czech troops] on January 14 [Gregorian calendar] opened negotiations with the local Irkutsk government. An agreement was made that the Czechs should be assisted to depart and that the gold and the person of Admiral Kolchak should be left behind."

When this decision was communicated to Kolchak, he said with a bitter smile, "So this is the meaning of the guarantee given me by Janin for an unhindered passage to the East. An international act of treachery. . . ."

The Janin-Czech action staggered the Allied representatives in the Far East, who were stationed at that time in Harbin. Janin's supercilious answer to their accusations of treachery was that he did not recognize their authority and considered himself responsible solely to the Czech government and the Inter-Allied Council in Paris, and that only the surrender of Kolchak could guarantee the passage of the Czech troops to Vladivostok.

"And he [Janin] is reported to have added, with equal insolence and truth, *'Je répète que pour Sa Majesté Nicolas II on a fait moins de cérémonie,'*" wrote Churchill of the conclusion of this shameful episode.[4]

During his incarceration, a long period of questioning, and his execution, Admiral Kolchak bore himself with courage and dignity. He was executed by a firing squad in the freezing dawn of January 25, 1920 (Julian calendar), and his body was thrown into an ice hole in the Angara River.

I learned of the death of the Supreme Ruler when we were still at Tikhoretskaia [wrote General Denikin]. I was profoundly grieved by the news of Admiral Kolchak's demise. . . . In the opinion of some officials . . . [Kolchak's official transfer of power to Denikin] obliged me to assume the appropriate title and functions. . . . I considered this point of view completely unacceptable. The military-political situation of the ruler, government, army, and territory of south Russia in January–February, called for the utmost caution. Any pretentions of an "all-Russian" scope would have appeared presumptious at that time. . . . I left the question open in order to avoid misinterpretations, and gave as my reason the lack of official communications concerning events in the east. Misinterpretations did arise, but not of the kind I had expected: I was accused of lacking respect to the memory of the slain Supreme Ruler because no official memorial services had been held for him.[5]

Reversals at the front had necessitated moving the *Stavka* from Taganrog to Tikhoretskaia, from Tikhoretskaia to Ekaterinodar, and finally, from Ekaterinodar to Novorossiisk. That city, the only port on the eastern shores of the Black Sea from which the families of officers, the sick, the wounded, and the refugees could be evacuated, had become a veritable hornet's nest. It was overrun with unattached officers. Some of them, just recovered from typhus or wounds, had lost touch with their units through no fault of their own. The majority, however, were simply waiting for an opportunity to leave the country, with the help of the British, and to remove themselves as far as possible from the approaching catastrophe. Disenchanted and angry, they openly denounced the high command. Their nervous unrest took on menacing proportions after the contents of the letter of accusation which General Wrangel had sent General Denikin, following their final break, became public property. At the end of February, 1920, the letter was widely circulated among the officers in mimeographed form.

There had been virtually no personal communication between Denikin and Wrangel since the end of December, 1919, when Denikin learned of the discussions conducted by Wrangel concerning the overthrow of the commander in chief. At that time Anton Ivanovich had decided not to publicize this matter, which could only deepen the depression of these harrowing days, but he ceased to give responsible assignments to Wrangel. This created an extremely complicated situation. Wrangel was unquestionably the most gifted and well-known of Denikin's commanding officers. Even N. I. Astrov, a prominent member of the Cadet party who had little sympathy for Wrangel, asked the commander in chief why "he provoked his antagonists by deliberately leaving idle a man who was the center of so many rumors, intrigues, and expectations." [6]

In effect, General Wrangel was at that moment the focal point and the hope of the rightist circles and of a considerable part of the officer corps. His idleness weighed heavily on him. Deprived of any outlet for his energy, he finally filed a request for his retirement from the army. Pending its approval, he took a leave of absence and left for the Crimea. The situation there was alarming. There was a great deal of unrest among the younger officers. An armed uprising, led by a Captain Orlov, broke out. Orlov's detachment, composed of adventurers, had no political program, but adopted as its byword the fight against corruption at the rear. Concurrently, Orlov announced that "according to information received by us, our young leader, General Wrangel, has arrived in the Crimea. He is the one with whom we must and will talk. The one whom all of us trust. . . ." [7] Wrangel indignantly rejected Orlov's advances and ordered him to submit to his immediate superiors.

The situation was further complicated by the fact that the military and civilian government of the Crimea had been entrusted to General Shilling. At the beginning of October, he had been in command of the troops concentrated against Petliura. The Soviet advance cut him off from Denikin's main forces, and his units began to retreat rapidly toward Odessa. That unfortunate city was on the verge of succumbing for the third time to the Bolsheviks, and when this happened, on January 25, 1920, after another catastrophic evacuation, General Shilling was blamed for the disaster. In the meantime, a corps commanded by General Slashchev, which had been separated from Shilling's troops in order to fight Makhnó's bands, had reached the approaches to the Crimean peninsula and was defending them.

Largely as a result of circumstances beyond his control, Shilling had acquired the reputation of a loser, and people had no confidence in him. A number of prominent public figures in the Crimea telegraphed the commander in chief, requesting him to replace Shilling with Wrangel. General Lukomsky, who had arrived in the Crimea from Novorossiisk for his mother's funeral, added his voice to theirs: "Only the immediate nomination of Wrangel instead of Shilling will save the situation," he telegraphed Denikin.[8] Nor was General Wrangel idle at that moment. "I was viewed as the man who was capable of fulfilling everyone's expectations," he later wrote, in his last letter to the commander in chief.[9]

It should be noted that General Shilling himself had no desire to hold on to his illusory powers. On the contrary, he reported to General Denikin that in view of "the disintegration of the home front and the violent unrest among the officers, including high-ranking ones," the transfer of his position to General Wrangel "would answer better to the requirements of the general situation." In response to all the reports and requests he had received on that subject, General Denikin stated in a telegram dated February 8 and addressed to General Shilling, "I absolutely refuse to consider the participation of General Wrangel. . . ."[10]

On the same day, the commander in chief issued orders for the retirement from active service of Generals Lukomsky, Wrangel, and Shatilov, and of two admirals of the Black Sea fleet. "It was perfectly clear," wrote General Lukomsky in his memoirs, "that the persons listed in the telegram were being retired for allegedly participating in intrigues against General Shilling and for not minding their own business in raising the issue of General Wrangel's nomination."[11]

Actually the problem went much deeper than the intrigue against General Shilling: it marked the beginning of an open contest for the leadership of what was left of the White movement.

It would have been logical to get rid of Shilling, but the commander in chief had his reasons for not making any changes at that time. He explained as follows his refusal to part with the unpopular Shilling: "I did not agree to replace Shilling not only in order to avoid giving this satisfaction to the officer *fronde,* but for another reason as well: The Caucasian front was rapidly receding toward the sea and an evacuation was imminent. Shilling's administration and general staff would be automatically canceled out by the commander in chief's arrival in the Crimea."[12]

The long-drawn-out crisis was nearing a climax. Further collaboration between the two generals had become impossible, and the Crimea was much too restricted an area to accommodate them both. The British military representative, General Holman, was therefore asked to relay to General Wrangel the commander in chief's request that he leave the territory of the Armed Forces of South Russia.

Before leaving for Constantinople, General Wrangel sent a so-called letter of accusation to the commander in chief. A few years later, when he prepared his memoirs for publication, Baron Wrangel did not include the full text of this letter. He admitted that "it was written in anger . . . was unduly harsh and in places too personal." The version in his book was thus expurgated, but the original letter, which was being circulated at the time it was written contained Wrangel's "personal" accusations in full. These accusations must be enumerated if one is to understand the impact of the letter on the minds of the officers caught in the

White Army's debacle: "Your military luck was on the rise, your fame was growing, and with it grew the ambitious dreams in your heart," wrote Wrangel. He questioned Denikin's sincerity in submitting to Kolchak and doubted that this action, which coincided with a series of Denikin's military successes, was taken voluntarily. He accused "the ambitious man, intoxicated with recent victories," of failing to extend a helping hand to the Supreme Ruler of the White movement. Wrangel bluntly stated that "the troops of Admiral Kolchak, treacherously abandoned by us, were defeated." The letter went on to describe Denikin as a man "poisoned by ambition and the taste of power, surrounded by dishonest sycophants," who was no longer preoccupied "with saving his country, but only with preserving his power."

"You saw your prestige waning and the power slipping from your hands," wrote Wrangel. "Clutching at it blindly, you started looking for subversion and insurgence all around you." [13]

It was ironic that in reality, the dream of the "ambitious" man portrayed as clutching at his slipping power was to shed its burden as soon as his conscience allowed.

Two weeks after receiving Wrangel's missive, Denikin wrote in a hitherto unpublished letter to his wife, ". . . I am sick at heart. Surrounded by strife. What strange people to fight for power! A power which has oppressed me like a heavy yoke and tied me like a slave to a cart too heavy to pull. . . . It's hard. I am waiting for this move to be completed before doing that of which I spoke to you." [14] The move mentioned here was, in fact, nearer to its realization than he suspected.

Denikin's reply to Wrangel was delivered to him personally and did not appear in print until many years later. We are quoting it in full:

DEAR SIR, PETER NIKOLAEVICH!
Your letter has come just at the right time—at the most difficult moment when all my spiritual strength must be concentrated on preventing the collapse of our front. I hope that you are satisfied.

If I still had a vestige of doubt concerning your role in the struggle for power, your letter has eliminated it completely. It does not contain a single word of truth. You know this. It brings forth monstrous accusations which you don't believe yourself. They are obviously brought forth for the same purpose for which your preceding pamphlet-reports were multiplied and circulated.

You are doing everything you can to undermine the government and bring on disintegration.

There was a time when, suffering from a grave illness, you said to Iuzefovich that this was God's punishment for your inordinate ambitiousness.

May He forgive you now for the harm you have done to the Russian cause.
February 25, 1920   A. DENIKIN [15]

By reaching the angry and disgruntled mass of officers in Novorossiisk, General Wrangel's letter became a powerful instrument of the propaganda aimed at discrediting the commander in chief and his staff. Denikin's chief of staff, General Romanovsky, was the principal target of this campaign. He was blamed for all the reverses, and it was openly said that it was high time to shoot him.

The head chaplain of the Armed Forces of South Russia, the Right Reverend Father George Shavelsky, who was on friendly terms with Romanovsky, tried his best to convince him that he should resign from the service.

I always considered him to be an honest, intelligent, diligent, dedicated officer and a kind man [wrote Father Shavelsky about Romanovsky]. . . . I realized how unfounded and unjust were the accusations directed at Romanovsky. . . . It was not easy for me to tell him of the officers' attitude toward him, but it was indispensable to do so for his own sake. . . .

"Of what, then, am I accused in the army?" asked Romanovsky sadly.

"Of everything, literally everything dear Ivan Pavlovich," I replied. "Hatred is blind and heartless."

"Of what, for example?" he insisted.

"Among other things, it was affirmed at the officers' mess that you had shipped a whole boatload of tobacco from Novorossiisk. I know that this is a lie but am repeating it to you to make you realize that the hatred and calumny directed against you are unbounded. . . ."

At these words Romanovsky, whose eyes had been fixed on me all this time, turned away and leaning against the table covered his face with his hands. I saw how much he suffered.

Shavelsky tried to impress on the General the hopelessness of fighting calumny. Romanovsky answered that being aware of the hatred against him, he had implored the commander in chief several times to retire him, but always met with refusal. "Please try to use your influence on him," he begged Shavelsky.

Romanovsky himself arranged a meeting between Shavelsky and the commander in chief at the beginning of March. At that time, General Denikin's quarters were located in a train near the cement factories adjoining the port of Novorossiisk. Having presented the case to Denikin, including the persistent rumors of a projected attempt on Romanovsky's life, Father Shavelsky entreated the General to release Romanovsky from his duties.

"You think that this is simple?" rejoined Denikin emotionally. "Replace him. . . . It's easier said than done! . . . We are like a pair of oxen hitched to the same wagon. . . . Now you expect me to pull it alone. . . . I can't! . . . Ivan Pavlovich is the only person whom I absolutely trust and from whom I have no secrets. I cannot let him go. . . ."

"If you won't let him go, would you prefer to wait for him to be killed in your train? Have at least some pity for his family!" I said firmly.

Denikin stretched himself nervously, placing his hands behind his head and closing his eyes. "Oh, how hard it is," he said with a low moan. "My spiritual forces are failing me." [16]

"In this extremely trying period I felt more alone than I ever had before," wrote Denikin later. "And in the midst of my difficult work and moral suffering, only the selfless and understanding sympathy of my friend Ivan Pavlovich Romanovsky mitigated that solitude to a certain extent." [17]

Denikin finally faced the hopelessness of the situation and decided to give up his closest friend and collaborator in order to satisfy the wishes of the officers and safeguard Romanovsky's life. "We decided together," wrote Denikin, "that we would hold firm for the short time remaining to us, and then, as soon as we moved to the Crimea, he would resign from his position." [18]

By that time, General Denikin had decided that for him too the moment had come to relinquish his post. Many months earlier, after the First Kuban Campaign, General Denikin had concluded a talk with his officers concerning the problems of the Volunteer Army with this prophetic statement: "On the day when I clearly feel that the pulse of the army no longer beats in unison with mine, I shall leave my post immediately in order to continue the struggle differently, in a way which I shall judge honest and direct.

Denikin felt that the day to carry out his promise had finally come. There was no doubt that his influence with the army had weakened. After Wrangel's departure for Constantinople, there appeared two new pretenders to Denikin's position, Generals Slashchev and Pokrovsky, each of whom was deep in the intrigue and secret negotiations for overturning him. The decisive factor in Denikin's decision, however, was a telegram he received from General Kutepov on February 28. Kutepov feared that the wave of unruly and demoralized Don Cossacks would submerge Novorossiisk and seize all the means of transportation by sea which had been prepared for the army's evacuation to the Crimea. This prompted him to telegraph the commander in chief as follows: "Events of the last few days at the front prove with sufficient clearness that we cannot count on a sustained resistance of the Cossack units. . . . The situation imperatively demands the adoption of immediate and decisive measures for preserving and saving the officer cadres of the Volunteer corps and its men."

In the same telegram, General Kutepov specified ten demands, some of which, listed here were particularly damaging to General Denikin's self-esteem. In blunt, soldierly language, Kutepov demanded that three or four transport ships under convoy of four destroyers and submarines be concentrated in Novorossiisk as soon as the retreating Volunteer corps was to reach Krymaskaia station, a short distance from the port. He stated that the purpose of this arrangement was to cover the embarkation of the entire Volunteer corps and the officers of other armies who desired to join it, and he specified that the transports should have capacity for at least ten thousand people, with the greatest possible allowance for food and armament. Kutepov further demanded that dictatorial powers be granted him as soon as his corps approached the Krymskaia-station area, so that he could control all means of water transportation as well as all public and private property located in the Krymskaia-Novorossiisk region.

A point in Kutepov's telegram which General Denikin found particularly insulting was the demand that "all branches of the *Stavka* and the general administrative offices must embark on transports at the same time as the last Volunteer unit to be embarked, but by no means earlier." [19]

Denikin had known and valued Kutepov since the very beginning of the White movement. They understood each other well, having many traits in common: the same military and civic courage, forthrightness in expressing their views, and dislike for intrigue. Besides, Denikin never doubted Kutepov's sincere devotion to him. How then was he to interpret such demands?

"This is the end!" flashed through his mind.

The state of mind that made such a communication from a Volunteer to his commander in chief psychologically possible predetermined the future course of events [wrote Denikin]. On that day I decided irrevocably to abandon my post. I could not do this immediately without creating complications at the front, which was already in critical condition. I proposed to withdraw after emptying to the dregs the bitter cup of the Novorossiisk evacuation, settling the army in the Crimea, and stabilizing the Crimean front.

My reply to the corps commander read:

"TO GENERAL KUTEPOV

"While fully understanding your worry and anxiety for the lot of the officers and Volunteers, I request that you keep in mind that their fate is no less dear to me than to you, and that though I willingly accept advice from my war comrades, I also demand that they observe the correct attitude of subordinate to superior. . . . Here are my answers:

"Evacuation of the wounded and sick is proceeding according to our means and those provided by the Allies. I hasten it as much as I can. Families are also evacuated; delays are due only to their refusals or hesitations.

"Transports are being prepared.

"The government agencies and *Stavka* will leave when I consider it necessary. No one has a right to reproach the *Stavka* in this respect. Volunteers ought to know that the commander in chief will be the last to leave, if he does not perish earlier.

. . . "All authority belongs to the commander in chief, who will delegate to the commander of the Volunteer corps such powers as he deems necessary." . . .

February 28 was one of the hardest days of my life [Denikin later recalled].

General Kutepov, who arrived at the *Stavka* a few days later, expressed regret for his action, explaining it by the nervous atmosphere which prevailed in his corps as a result of its mistrust of the government and the Cossacks. "Only my sincere desire to help you clear up the rear prompted me to send you this telegram," he said.

This conversation could no longer influence my decision.[20]

The decision to remove the troops to the Crimea had already been made. However, an orderly evacuation from Novorossiisk did not seem possible. There were not enough transports and other craft to accommodate all the ranks. Removing the horses, artillery, army trains, and the huge stockpiles that had accumulated in Novorossiisk was simply out of the question. There remained only one possible way to save the artillery and horses—ferrying them to the Crimea from Taman.

Taman, a low-lying, lake-covered peninsula of the Caucasus, is bordered on the west by Kerch Strait, which connects the Black Sea to the Sea of Azov. The strait is approximately forty kilometers long and does not exceed fifteen kilometers at its widest. Denikin chose this narrow waterway for transferring his artillery, horses, and a considerable number of troops from the Caucasus to the Crimea. He ordered the concentration of transports and other vessels in the Crimean port of Kerch, from which they could cross to the shores of Taman when the need arose.

When the time came to put this plan into effect, the commander in chief, in his order of March 7, instructed the Don Cossack army and the Volunteer corps to defend the Taman peninsula. The brunt of the operation fell to General Kutepov, whose orders were to occupy the peninsula with part of his forces and to defend its northern approaches from the Reds.

Neither Kutepov nor Sidorin carried out their assignments.

"The Bolsheviks easily achieved the crossing of the Kuban with insignificant forces," gloomily noted Denikin. "Whole regiments of Cossacks threw down their arms and went over to the Greens. There was utter confusion and turmoil. All liaison was lost between the staffs and the troops. . . . The mistrust and antagonism between the Volunteers and the Cossacks, developed by the events of recent months, now flared up in full force. The retreating wave of Cossacks, which threatened to flood the entire rear of the Volunteer corps and cut it off from Novorossiisk, provoked extreme nervousness in its ranks." [21]

All the hopes and plans of the commander in chief were ruined. The essentially simple operation he had conceived for transferring the artillery and horses to the Crimea was no longer possible. His troops had lost the will to fight and had panicked. Leadership of the army was slipping away from Denikin.

All of the General's remaining troops surged toward Novorossiisk, where catastrophe awaited them. It was essential to hold the port for a few more days, until the ships which had already left with their loads of wounded and refugees could return. Novorossiisk should not have been difficult to defend, as it was protected by steep mountains to the north and east and by naval artillery to the south. But the moral condition of the troops made armed resistance—and with it an orderly evacuation—impossible. General Milne, Great Britain's commander in chief in the east, spurred by a feeling of responsibility for the dying cause, arrived in Novorossiisk from Constantinople with Admiral Seymour's fleet. "The British were enormously helpful," wrote Denikin to his wife, who had already been evacuated to Constantinople. "The dry Milne, the choleric Admiral Seymour, the noble Holman, did everything they could, particularly the last two—splendid people!" [22]

Several French ships hurriedly sent to Novorossiisk were also of great help. But neither the British, nor the French, nor the returning Russian vessels could any longer cope with the evacuation. On March 13, General Kutepov, who had been placed in charge of the defense of Novorossiisk, reported to Denikin, "The morale of the troops and their extreme nervousness make it impossible to remain in the city any longer, and it is imperative to leave it this very night." [23]

Chaos reigned in the city. A vivid description of its final hours was written by Colonel B. A. Lagodovsky, an outstanding officer of the Volunteer Army, who in 1919 commanded the First Battery of the Horse Artillery of the Guard, attached to the Fifth Cavalry Corps:

In the midst of incredible confusion, threading our way through an infinity of stationary army trains which block everything, our cannon constantly grazing the multiple rows of carts and refugee conveyances; through people of all ages, conditions, and classes aimlessly standing and sitting on, under, and between the carts, in the midst of abandoned guns and riderless saddled and unsaddled horses and so on, we finally reach the port. The same confusion reigns there as in the city. The picture is unforgettable!

. . . I contact the commander of the port requesting instructions as to which ship to board. The answer is that there is no more room on the ships, we are to find our division and attempt to embark with it. The word "attempt" bodes no good. At long last, the division staff is located, but this does not improve matters: The battery is to board any ships that still have some available space. We are not allowed to load our cannon, materiel, horses, and army train. Everything is to be abandoned. We are to retain our firearms, and if possible, our saddles. A terrible order! . . .

. . . Now comes the darkest moment!—the carrying out of the fateful order to destroy with our own hands, calmly and in cold blood, that which we have created and assembled with such devotion: the guns, the horses. . . .

I can't bring myself to utter the words of command, but I have no choice. Orders are orders, and besides, it is quite clear without them that only by the grace of God may we succeed in placing all of our men on board. There is no longer room on the ships for all the people standing at the waterfront, let alone those who are still in town.

We begin by unsaddling the horses. Then all our belongings tumble off the pier. A final moment of delay—"Remove gunlocks!" The gunlocks fly into the water. . . . "Remove panoramic sights." "Marksmen take them with you." There is no further excuse for delay. A ghastly moment. . . .

"Roll up the first!" The faces around me are strained; I feel my own eyes prickling with tears. The first gun hits the green water, sending up a sparkling white fountain.

Quickly, quickly, to end this torture—"Roll up the second!" It, too, disappears in the water. I walk to the edge of the pier and look dully at the spot where my cannon have just disappeared, and it seems to me that I can discern them at the bottom.

After several futile attempts, Colonel Lagodovsky finally succeeded in embarking his men on a tiny vessel, the *Khrisi,* a coastal boat built for sailing on the Sea of Azov and transporting grain from Taganrog and Mariupol to the Novorossiisk grain elevators.

The dry reports of shots can be heard nearby [continues Lagodovsky's story], followed by the heavy fall of horses whose owners don't want to abandon their war comrades to the Bolsheviks. . . . We await sailing orders from the port commander. I sit on a pillar at the dock. A fire that must have been deliberately set breaks out in a huge hangar near the pier. People emerge from it carrying chocolate, rice, cans of corned beef, i.e., everything that we lacked and that is now being left to the Bolsheviks. Rifle shots can be heard in the town. There are fires all around. Beyond the town, one can see through field glasses endless columns moving toward Novorossiisk. Who are they? Ours or the Reds? There are but a few ships in the port. Far from shore, British and French warships are riding at anchor. Nearest to us is the huge and dirty French *Waldeck Rousseau.* . . . It's getting late. Sharp as the crack of a whip a cannon shot rends the air, raising multiple echoes in the mountains. The *Waldeck Rousseau* has opened fire. A British destroyer follows suit. We can't see the hits.

Late on the night of March 13, Colonel Lagadovsky and his companions left Novorossiisk, and they disembarked the next day in Theodosia.[24]

"Considering the nightmare conditions," wrote another witness of the Novorossiisk disaster, "one must admit that the commanding officers who had kept their heads retained a good grip on the combat units." [25]

What went on among the refugees who had swarmed into the city with the White Army's rearguard units defies description. All were concerned solely with their personal safety, and the wave of humanity surging to the docks constantly threatened to force the Russian and British patrols into the water.

The embarkation of troops on ships and other vessels continued the entire night of March 13. Not everyone was able to board. Many men who were separated from their units were left behind. Soviet sources affirm that "22,000 enemy soldiers and officers" were captured by the Red Army in Novorossiisk.[26]

Among those deprived of any means of transportation were several thousand Don Cossacks. Left to their own devices, they departed southward along the Black Sea shore toward the Georgian border. Approximately five thousand Don Cossacks were later evacuated from there to the Crimea.[27]

On the other hand, most of the Kuban Cossack units, together with their government, *Rada,* and recently elected *Ataman,* Bukretov, bypassed Novorossiisk and retreated across the mountains to the Black Sea shore between Tuapse and Sochi. They did not believe in the possibility of further resistance in the Crimea and wanted to break with Denikin. As a result, *Ataman* Bukretov (who had had a serious run-in with Denikin after the occupation of Ekaterinodar in 1918) through the Kuban general Morozov, concluded an agreement with the Bolsheviks for the surrender of his army. Only a small fraction of it could later be salvaged and transported to the Crimea. The Kuban general Kuchuk Ulagai, with the still-disciplined units remaining to him, left for the Crimea from Novorossiisk.

The commander in chief and General Romanovsky were the last to leave Novorossiisk. After their staff, as well as the staffs of the Don Cossack army and the Don Cossack *Ataman* had been embarked on the steamer *Tsesarevich Georgi,* they boarded the Russian destroyer *Kapitan Saken.* They spent a sleepless night on its deck, watching the last of the ships leave the port, until their destroyer alone remained in the harbor. Toward morning, they saw from the captain's bridge that a military unit had arrived and stationed itself at the dock. Denikin ordered the captain of the destroyer to draw up to the shore.

Their eyes were fixed on our destroyer with hope and prayer [related Denikin]. We took on as many people as we could and steamed out of the bay. . . . The outlines of Novorossiisk were still clearly visible. What was happening there? . . . A destroyer suddenly turned back and went off at full speed toward the docks. We heard cannon booming and the crackling of machine guns: The destroyer had joined battle with the front units of the Bolsheviks, who had already occupied the town. It was the *Pylki;* on board was General Kutepov, who upon learning that the Drozdovsky Regiment was still on shore, having been assigned to defend the port until the embarkation was completed, had gone to its rescue. After this, everything grew quiet. The contours of the city, the shoreline, and mountains became misty as they receded into the distance . . . into the past. The hard and painful past.[28]

Three days after leaving Novorossiisk, in a letter sent from the Crimea to his wife in Constantinople, through Admiral Seymour, Anton Ivanovich wrote, "I am desperately sick at heart: huge stockpiles, all the artillery, all the horses were abandoned, the army has been bled white." [29]

XXX

MORAL SOLITUDE

General Denikin's stay in the Crimea was extremely short—from March 14 to March 22. During these nine days he put into effect the decision he had reached in Novorossiisk.

But his first duty was to assure the defense of the Crimea, which necessitated an evaluation and reorganization of the troops remaining to him. For this purpose, Denikin called a council of war in Theodosia, where he had established his *Stavka*. The army had been reduced to 30,000 to 45,000 men, a hundred cannon, and about five hundred machine guns. The Volunteer units (which had been obliged to abandon their horses, artillery, and army trains in Novorossiisk) had retained only small firearms and machine guns. The Don Cossacks proved completely unarmed and, of course, horseless. The military units were immediately reclassified into three army corps—the Crimean, Volunteer, and Don Cossack—plus a composite cavalry division and a composite Kuban brigade. For the time being, the whole brunt of defending the peninsula was borne by the five-thousand-strong Crimean corps, commanded by General Slashchev.[1]

Denikin was aware of Slashchev's intrigues and underhand activities, as well as of his addiction to alcohol and narcotics, but in his memoirs, he also gave their due to his positive qualities. He pointed out that Slashchev, who had joined the Volunteer Army during the Second Kuban Campaign, "must have been originally a better person than he became under the influence of anarchic times, success, and coarse flattery," and that despite a good dose of adventurism, he unquestionably had military ability, drive, initiative, and determination.[2]

It was Slashchev's defense at that moment of the approaches to the Crimea that gave the units evacuated from Novorossiisk a chance to rest and regain their military efficiency. Slashchev's success was largely due to the grave error committed by the Red command and by a Revolutionary Military Council member, Joseph Stalin, who later claimed credit for all the victories against Denikin and shifted the blame for this particular failure onto Trotsky. Instead of bringing their main forces to bear on the Crimea, the Bolsheviks directed a mere five or six thousand men against it. These units, moreover, were obliged to fight on two fronts, as Makhnó's bands were raging at their rear.

The Red's mistake consisted in their overestimating the demoralized condition of the White troops. They never expected that after losing all their materiel and horses, the Whites would be able to recover from their defeat, break out of the Crimea into northern Taurida, defeat the Soviet cavalry there in June, and having appropriated its horses, reassemble once more a mighty cavalry force.

This phase of the struggle, however, belongs to the final part of the civil war's history, in which General Denikin no longer participated.

On March 16 he issued an order relieving I. P. Romanovsky of his duties as chief of staff. Romanovsky was replaced by General P. S. Makhrov who had held the position of deputy chief of staff (having recently replaced General Pliushchevsky-Pliushchik).

On the same day, Denikin disbanded the latest government of south Russia, presided over by Melnikov, and replaced it with what he termed in his order a "business organization," the choice of whose members he entrusted to M. V. Bernatsky. The decree came as a complete surprise to Melnikov and his colleagues. Denikin, however, had definite reasons for his abrupt behavior. Melnikov's government, which had been formed with the approval of the Supreme *Krug,* irritated and angered the Volunteers, who hated the *Krug,* blamed it for the moral disintegration of the Cossacks, and accused it of treason. Fearing foul play against the members of this government, particularly on the part of Slashchev, the commander in chief had already provided a ship for transporting them from the Crimea to Constantinople.

This unexpected decree made an extremely painful impression on the members of the government . . . [wrote Denikin in his memoirs]. I am not justifying the procedure [they learned of their dismissal from the order itself], but essentially the reorganization was dictated by obvious necessity and the personal safety of the ministers. . . . Before leaving for Constantinople . . . [the ministers] came to Theodosia to take leave of me. After a short address by N. M. Melnikov, I was accosted by N. V. Chaikovsky: "May I ask you, General, what prompted you to overturn the government?"

This way of stating the question surprised me, coming as it did after the break with the Supreme *Krug,* and especially, after the catastrophic "overturn" of the entire White Russian south.

"What overturn do you mean? I assigned you to your posts and I relieved you of your duties—that's all." [3]

The foregoing conversation was another example of the extent to which the commander in chief's advisers, whether rightist or leftist, were divorced from reality. The rightists lived in the past and in the desire to restore it; the left-wingers, despite the civil war with all its wantonness and cruelty, dwelt in a world of illusions, deeming it possible to establish in a country deprived of constitutional traditions a political regime based on the premises of legality, freedom, and limitation of the executive power by popular representation, on which the statehood of all cultured peoples is founded.

Late in the evening of March 19, Kutepov came to see Denikin on an urgent matter. He reported to the commander in chief that on that day, General Slashchev had sent a railroad engine and car for him to Sebastopol, requesting that he come immediately to Dzhankoi to discuss an extremely important problem. The problem had turned out to be a proposal to call on March 23, with Kutepov's approval, "a conference of representatives of the clergy, the army, the navy, and the civilian population," in order to demand the removal of General Denikin from his post. Kutepov had brusquely interrupted Slashchev, saying that he refused to participate in any conferences without the commander in chief's permission, that the plan proposed by Slashchev did not correspond to the wishes of the Volunteers, and that in view of the great importance attached by him to the entire conversation, he would immediately report it to General Denikin. Kutepov had then traveled by train from Dzhankoi to Theodosia, and had gone to the *Stavka* to see the commander in chief as soon as he arrived. Kutepov's report did not surprise Denikin, who already knew what Slaschev was up to, and realized that the Don Cossack general Sidorin was waging an open campaign against him. He also knew that the local bishop, Veniamin, an extreme reactionary, took an active part in these political intrigues. "Sidorin, Slashchev, Veniamin . . . essentially all this no longer mattered very much," wrote Denikin later; ". . . the time to carry out my intention had arrived. Enough!" [4]

Denikin's isolation was becoming unbearable. He was losing his friends and closest associates one by one. General Timanovsky, with whom he had shared memories of the Iron Division's glorious battles in the World War and of combat in the First and Second Kuban campaigns, was dead of typhus. Denikin had with difficulty found his coffin, covered by a torn tarpaulin, in the column of army trains retreating from Bataisk. Another victim of typhus was Colonel Bleish, commander of the Markov division, whose bravery Denikin deeply admired. He had been obliged to separate himself from Romanovsky, and was now on the verge of losing another devoted friend, General Holman, who was being recalled to London to report on the state of affairs in south Russia. In his farewell speech, delivered in Russian (which he spoke fluently) Holman said, "I leave with a feeling of the most profound respect and heartfelt friendship for your commander in chief and with an even stronger determination to remain loyal to the handful of brave and honorable people, who have for two year led the hard struggle for their homeland.[5] General Holman remained Denikin's true and loyal friend for the rest of his life.

Still remaining with Denikin were Kutepov and a considerable number of loyal Volunteers. But the majority of those who had once curried favor with the commander in chief were now ready to behave like the hirelings of a bankrupt patron.

After his report, and a short exchange of opinions with Denikin, Kutepov left. Denikin remained alone, but not for long. That same night, he summoned his new chief of staff, General Makhrov. "He [Denikin] looked worn-out, tired," related Makhrov. "He handed me for distribution an order for the election of a new commander in chief and ended our short interview by saying, 'My decision is irrevocable. I have weighed and thought out everything. I am ill physically and broken-down morally; the army has lost faith in its leader, and I—in the army.' " [6]

The order given to Makhrov was in the form of a telegram addressed to all the senior commanders—including, of course, the commanders of the Volunteer and Crimean corps (Kutepov and Slashchev)—as well as to division and brigade commanders and to senior officers of the navy, the *Stavka,* the other staffs, and so on. The telegram ordered them to convene on March 21 in Sebastopol for a Military Council "in order to elect a successor to the commander in chief of the Armed Forces of South Russia."

"I also included among the participants the pretenders to power who were known to me and were not on active duty, as well as the most active representatives of the opposition," wrote General Denikin. General Wrangel was summoned to the Military Council from Constantinople by a special telegram. [7]

At the same time as the telegrams, General Denikin dispatched a letter to the president-designate of the Military Council, General Dragomirov:

I have led the fight for three years of the Russian turmoil, giving it all my strength and carrying the brunt of power as a heavy cross imposed on me by fate.

God did not bless with success the troops I was leading. And although I have not lost faith in the vitality of the army and its historic mission, the spiritual ties between the leader and the army have been severed. I no longer have the strength to lead it.

I propose that the Military Council elect a worthy candidate, to whom I shall transmit the succession to the power and military command. [8]

General Denikin remained in Theodosia to await the decision of the Military Council. The council was in session for two days. The Volunteers firmly and unanimously insisted that General Denikin should be asked to remain in power because, as one of them (General Polzikov) expressed it, "we could not conceive of a different commander in chief." The commander of the Drozdovsky division, General Vitkovsky, stated that "the officers of his division consider it impossible for them to participate in the election and categorically refuse to do so." His statement was immediately adhered to by the leaders of the Kornilov, Markov, and Alekseev divisions and other units of the Volunteer corps. In the name of the

Don Cossacks, General Sidorin refused to "express any preference for a successor, considering their representation too restricted in numbers to correspond to the size of the military complement." General Slashchev also refused to vote in the name of his corps, giving as his reason that only three representatives of the corps were able to attend the council. The representatives of the navy were the only exception. They chose General Wrangel as their candidate.

The position of General Dragomirov, who presided at the council, was becoming difficult. On March 22, he sent General Denikin a telegram reporting what had occurred and advising him that the Military Council had found it impossible to settle the question of a successor to the commander in chief; that it appealed to him to retain the supreme command, as it feared the army's disintegration in the event of his departure; and that it considered it inadmissible to establish a precedent for electing superiors and therefore requested General Denikin, should his decision to renounce the command be inalterable, personally to designate his successor.

At the same time, a large number of people who were devoted to Denikin exerted every means in their power to convince him that he should revoke his decision. "They ravaged my soul," wrote Anton Ivanovich, "but were not able to change my decision."

He answered Dragomirov by telegram: "Morally shattered, I cannot remain in power another day. Consider Generals Sidorin's and Slashchev's refusal to lend me their advice inadmissible. I demand that the Military Council carry out its duty. Otherwise the Crimea and the army will be plunged into anarchy. . . . The number of representatives is immaterial. But if the Don Cossacks consider it necessary, allow them a number of members proportionate to their organization."

Meanwhile, the telegram dispatched to General Wrangel, in care of the Russian embassy in Constantinople, reached him on March 20. On the same day, the British high commissioner in Constantinople, Admiral de Robeck, placed at Wrangel's disposal the destroyer H.M.S. *Emperor of India,* which landed him in Sebastopol on the morning of March 22. It was clear to the participants in the conference that Wrangel's arrival meant that in principle he was willing to accept the supreme command. Having finally become convinced that General Denikin would not alter his decision, the Military Council chose Wrangel as its candidate. Dragomirov immediately telegraphed this news to Denikin, asking him at the same time to issue an order nominating Wrangel "without mentioning his election by the Military Council." [9]

Many members of the council doubted that the commander in chief would issue such an order. "Many of us . . . still had doubts as to whether or not General Denikin would confirm our choice," wrote one of the participants. "We did not know the details, but we all knew that there had been bad blood between them [Denikin and Wrangel] and that it was not Denikin who was to blame for it." [10]

Such doubts, however, proved to be unfounded. When Denikin tele-graphed Wrangel summoning him to attend the session of the Military Council, he must have known beyond the shadow of a doubt that if Wrangel came to the Crimea, he would be elected to succeed as com-mander in chief. In his military record, his popularity with the troops, and his glamorous appearance, he outshone all other possible candidates. Denikin never referred by a single word, either in his writings or in conver-sation with friends, to his thoughts and feelings during the long, unbear-able hours when the question of transferring the leadership of the White movement was being decided. The subject was too painful to discuss. But the very fact that forgoing military tradition, Denikin insisted on his successor being elected by a Military Council, testifies to the conflict that was taking place in his mind at that time; after all that had happened between them, Denikin could not personally select Wrangel, though he was prepared to confirm the unanimous decision of the Military Council.

In response to Dragomirov's telegram, Denikin issued on March 22 his last order of the day to the troops:

"Lieutenant General Baron Wrangel is appointed commander in chief of the Armed Forces of South Russia.

"My· deepest homage to all those who honorably followed me in this hard struggle. Lord grant victory to the army and save Russia." [11]

On the preceding night, a farewell dinner had been given for General Romanovsky. Denikin attended it, but looked gloomy and depressed and took little part in the conversation. An emotional speech was delivered by General Chaperon du Larré (at one time aide-de-camp to Alekseev, then liaison general for Denikin, and finally commander of the Drozdovsky cavalry regiment). In a voice charged with emotion, unable to hide his tears, Chaperon spoke about the farewell they were saying not only to Romanovsky but to General Denikin as well, the last of the immortal dynasty of the Kornilovs, Markovs, and Alekseevs, who had decided to relinquish his leadership.

On March 22, the day of Wrangel's election to the post of commander in chief, Denikin left Russia. He sailed to Constantinople on the British destroyer, H.M.S. *Emperor of India,* which had brought Wrangel back to the Crimea. He was accompanied by two faithful friends, General Romanovsky and the British representative, General Holman. He had taken leave of his staff in the afternoon, and at seven o'clock, came out of the Hotel Astoria in Theodosia to get into his car.

The entrance and corridors of the hotel were crowded with faithful followers of Denikin who watched his departure with tears in their eyes. As for the General, he moved forward mechanically—distraught, and seemingly unaware of those around him. But suddenly he came to a stop in front of an officer whom he recognized as having been a fellow prisoner in the Bykhov jail in 1917, and silently embraced him.

According to an eyewitness, the Hotel Astoria on that day resembled a house from which the body of some one dearly beloved had just been carried out. In one of its rooms, Denikin's former liaison officer lay with his face buried in a pillow, sobbing like a child.[12]

Anton Ivanovich himself left only a few short notes concerning that trying day:

> Evening of March 22. Depressing farewells with my coworkers at the *Stavka* and the officers of my military escort. Afterward went down to the officer guard company, composed mainly of old Volunteers, most of them gravely wounded in combat, with many of whom I was linked by common memories of the difficult days of the first campaigns. They are perturbed. I hear suppressed sobbing. . . . A deep emotion took hold of me also. A lump rose in my throat and would not let me speak. They keep asking, Why?
>
> "It's hard to speak of this now. Some day you will find out and understand——"
>
> Drove with General Romanovsky to the British mission, thence, together with Holman, to the dock. Honor guards and representatives of foreign missions. A brief leave-taking. We board the British destroyer. . . .
>
> When we reached the open sea, night had already fallen. Only the densely clustered lights studding the darkness still indicate the Russian shores that we are leaving. The lights grow dimmer and go out.
>
> Russia, my country. . . .[13]

As he signed his last order of the day and left Russia, General Denikin was not yet aware that General Wrangel had brought from Constantinople a note from the British government addressed to him. The note was in effect an ultimatum enjoining Denikin to "put an end to the uneven struggle." Further, the British government offered to enter into negotiations with the Soviet government in order to secure an amnesty for the members of the Volunteer Army. Should Denikin refuse this offer, however, the British declined all future responsibility and threatened to withdraw "all support and assistance" to his cause.[14]

The General learned of this note, which never reached him in the turmoil of that last day, when he was already abroad and the curtain had fallen on the Denikin period of the Russian civil war.

Shortly after four in the afternoon of March 23, a cutter brought Generals Denikin, Romanovsky, and Holman from the destroyer to the Topkhane landing in Constantinople. They were greeted on shore by a British officer and by General V. P. Agapeev (the Russian military representative to the British and French commands in Constantinople). As soon as the generals stepped off the boat, the Englishman hastily approached Holman and said something to him with a worried expression. General Holman immediately turned to Denikin: "Your Excellency, let us go directly aboard a British ship."

The British were obviously worried by something. But Denikin's wife had already been in Constantinople for nearly two weeks, residing at the Russian embassy there, and the General wanted to see his family first of all. He asked Agapeev whether his and Romanovsky's presence at the embassy would be inconvenient either because of limited space or for political reasons. Agapeev having politely answered that their presence could not possibly inconvenience him, Generals Denikin and Romanovsky took leave of Holman and set out for the embassy in an automobile provided by the British command. Agapeev followed in his own car.

Denikin knew that part of the embassy had been transformed into a refugee shelter. But he had had no idea that the huge building was literally packed with a varied assortment of people, among whom discontented and rebellious officers who had escaped from south Russia predominated. Most of these officers had never been in combat, but had belonged to various staffs and intelligence and counterintelligence units. The period spent in Constantinople by Generals Wrangel and Shatilov, who openly criticized Denikin's *Stavka,* and the circulation of Wrangel's letter of accusation to Denikin, had brought the atmosphere in the embassy refuge to the boiling point.

Under such conditions, an effective system of protection was difficult to organize. The British knew it, and General Agapeev must have known it too. General Denikin never forgave Agapeev for not warning him at the dock about the dangerous mood prevailing at the embassy.

Upon reaching Constantinople, Xenia Vasilievna had secured with difficulty two rooms and a bathroom in the embassy for herself and the eight people (mostly members of the family, along with the daughter and small son of General Kornilov) who had arrived with her.

Xenia Vasilievna was extremely upset by her husband's coming to the embassy, as she realized that Agapeev had not warned him or advised him against it. Her two rooms, with their nine inhabitants, could not accommodate the two generals, and Denikin asked the chargé d'affaires, who was present at his arrival, to allocate an extra room for them. He received a dry and evasive answer. It seemed that a room could not be found in the Russian embassy for the former commander in chief. Agapeev saved the situation by offering quarters in the military attaché's wing.

As luck would have it, the aides-de-camp of Denikin and Romanovsky had had to leave Theodosia on a different ship, and they arrived in Constantinople an hour later than the generals. In the interim, Romanovsky assumed their duties, and so he left to arrange the details of his and Denikin's quarters.

While Denikin was still talking with Agapeev, two shots resounded in the building. A moment later, Colonel B. A. Engelhardt, pale and distraught, burst into the room: "Your Excellency, General Romanovsky has been killed!"

"Denikin was sitting on a chair at a table," recounted Colonel V. S. Khitrovo, who had run into the room behind Engelhardt. "He didn't answer, but remained silent, clutching his head with both hands." [15]

"This blow finished me off," wrote Denikin. "My consciousness blurred and I lost all my strength—for the first time in my life." [16]

At that moment, General Kornilov's daughter, Natalia Lavrovna, knelt beside Romanovsky, who lay on the floor of the embassy's billiard room; she was desperately calling, "For God's sake, get a doctor quickly!" But by the time a doctor was finally brought to the billiard room, Romanovsky had died without regaining consciousness.

The murderer escaped. He was never found.

Appalled by the tragedy, General Milne, the British commander in chief and military governor of Constantinople, without consulting anyone, ordered a guard of New Zealanders commanded by British officers to enter the Russian embassy to protect Denikin. From the moment he left the Crimea, General Denikin was considered to be the guest of the British government and under its protection.

A first requiem service was held on the same evening. The coffin with Romanovsky's body was placed in a small room. Anton Ivanovich approached it and fixed his eyes on the "sad and peaceful" face of his closest friend, then withdrew with tears in his eyes to a dark corner of the room.

After the service, at General Milne's insistence, Denikin, with his family, Kornilov's children, and other members of his household, moved to a British hospital ship under the escort of British officers. The next morning, he left Constantinople and sailed for England on the dreadnought H.M.S. *Marlborough*.

Later, many people criticized Denikin for not demanding the withdrawal of the British security guard from the Russian embassy building and not protesting this breach of extraterritorial rights. "It [the guard] was called in without my or my wife's knowledge or participation," he noted in one of his unpublished papers. "We ought to have demanded its withdrawal. . . . Unfortunately, I was so shaken and broken up that the matter did not register in my consciousness at that time." [17]

Who was the slayer of General Romanovsky?

The investigation was conducted by an Englishman, Colonel Ballard, who was in charge of the international police in Constantinople. However, all efforts to discover the identity of the assassin remained fruitless, and only one thing was clear—that the assassination was political and was intended as revenge for Romanovsky's alleged responsibility in the failure of the White movement.

Many years later, in the middle 1930's, new data on this unsolved crime appeared in one of the Russian émigré papers published in Paris and in a document submitted to the military historian General N. N. Golovin, who was acting as a purchasing agent for what was then the Hoover War Library, in Stanford, California. This new information was based on the testimony of two trustworthy persons; the details of Romanovsky's murder had been confided to one of these by the assassin himself and to the other by an active member of the conspiracy. The assassin was Mstislav

Kharuzin, a disgruntled member of a secret ultrarightist monarchist organization which put the entire blame for the failure of the White movement on Romanovsky.

According to these sources, Kharuzin left Constantinople for Ankara soon after Romanovsky's murder, allegedly to establish a liaison with the Turkish nationalist movement headed by Kemal Pasha, and was killed on the way to Ankara, possibly by some of the bandits who were rife in the region at that time.[18]

The document describing General Romanovsky's assassination, which was acquired by Golovin for the Hoover War Library, was subsequently lost. However, the author was able to track down the writer of the lost document, B. S. Kutsevalov, who has reconstructed its text and given permission to quote from it.[19] This previously unpublished paper is of definite interest to students of the Russian civil-war period; among other things, it gives a true picture of the rebellious mood that prevailed at the time among a certain group of discontented former Russian officers who had escaped to Constantinople.

By accident, Mr. Kutsevalov happened to attend a macabre gathering which followed Romanovsky's funeral in Constantinople.

The meal was apparently a sort of memorial repast in honor of the deceased General [wrote Kutsevalov], but the expressions of those present were far from fitting the occasion. None of them looked upset and saddened; all were gay, joyful, pleased. No one at this "memorial" luncheon uttered a kind word in memory of the General, . . . on the contrary, . . . and when Colonel von Lampe [assigned by General Wrangel's headquarters in the Crimea to make all arrangements for the burial of General Romanovsky] related how the Greek mortician manipulated General Romanovsky's legs, because the body of the deceased would not fit in any available coffins, and there was no time to order and make a special one of the right size,—everyone burst into loud laughter and someone remarked acidly that at last, after his death, a way was found to bring the omnipotent chief of staff down to size.

Romanovsky's assassination was completely meaningless as a political action. He had already relinquished all power and could have no further influence on the course of events. His murder could only be explained as an outcome of the distorted psychology resulting from the civil strife and of a primitive urge to avenge the misdeeds attributed by false rumors to the former chief of staff.

For General Denikin this event was a profound personal drama and a cruel epilogue to his service. The death of his best friend destroyed one of the last links between Denikin and the heroic period of the anti-Bolshevik struggle, an epoch of great hopes, profound emotions, joy, and inconsolable grief.

X X X I

IN SEARCH
OF AN ANSWER

Some of the reasons which led to the defeat of the White forces have already been discussed in the preceding chapters: inadequate handling of the agrarian problem and unsatisfactory relations with the peasants, requisitions of supplies from the population which took the form of looting, lack of discipline in the army and inability to bring its senior commanders to order, the deplorable administration of the huge territory captured from the enemy, the rigoristic slogan of "A united and indivisible Russia" and the lack of understanding of the nationalist aspirations of the ethnically varied peoples on Russia's periphery.

There were other, equally important, internal and external reasons.

After his victory, Lenin admitted quite frankly that the Bolsheviks' success in the civil war was due not to their strength, but to their opponents' weakness. He was referring specifically to the Allies, who at a certain moment could have crushed the Soviet power by a concentrated effort. But their lack of confidence in each other prevented their acting in concert and they were hopelessly divided by their separate selfish motives.[1]

In relation to south Russia, the only "Allies" involved were Great Britain and France, whose governments were, as we know, swayed by several conflicting political currents. Some politicians desired the downfall of the Soviet dictatorship; others wished to establish commercial relations with it. Churchill stood for Russia's unity; Lloyd George approved of its dismemberment. France distrusted Great Britain, which returned the compliment.

Churchill spoke and wrote with indignation about the lack of vision of the Allies at that time. And Lord Curzon affirmed in August, 1919, that a coordinated Allied political approach to the Russian problem was out of the question—that, in fact, there "is no policy at all!"[2]

Another of the external reasons for the defeat was General Denikin's belief in the possibility of a military collaboration with Poland. He has been blamed for his credulity and for his badly organized intelligence system, which failed to notify him of the true intentions of Pilsudski and his entourage. This accusation would be valid if Denikin and his staff had been the only ones to be taken in by the Poles. But in like manner the representatives of the Allies had been deceived into supplying Pilsudski with arms for what they believed would be a coordinated military effort with Denikin against the Bolsheviks. Despite their widespread intelligence network, the British and French agents in Warsaw did not suspect that Pilsudski had concluded an armistice with the Soviet government behind their (and Denikin's) back, thus allowing the Reds to remove their troops from the Polish front and direct them against General Denikin.

As regards the internal conditions in Russia, the advantage was definitely on the side of the Reds. Their location at the very center of the country, with a relatively close network of railroad radiating in every direction from Moscow, placed them in a very strong strategic position. Also, while the distant provinces of Russia where the White movement began were populated by different nationalities and races, the Bolsheviks had the advantage of dealing with the homogeneous population of central Russia.

The defeat of the White Army encouraged the fairly widespread theory that in a civil war any movement stemming from the periphery is doomed to failure. Advocates of this theory cited the example of the French revolution and the struggle between Girondists and Montagnards. The latter, who were situated at the center of France, defeated the Girondists despite the fact that three-quarters of the country sided with the Girondists. However, the more recent example of the Spanish civil war appears to contradict this theory. In any case, the acute conflict which developed between Denikin and the separatist leaders on the Russian periphery cannot be considered the principal reason for his failure. Instead of being attributed to the Volunteer Movement's inception in the distant provinces, Denikin's failure can best be ascribed to his political mistakes and to some of his strategic miscalculations.

But let us return to the internal situation in Russia.

The revolution had destroyed the old foundations of life in the country. In their stead, the Bolsheviks now offered the Russian people the prospect of a tempting new life built on the ruins of the old. They promised all the land to the peasants, the factories to the workers, and self-determination to the many nationalities of the former Russian Empire.

Throughout his life, Lenin had been dominated by the single idea of revolution and the seizure of power. To achieve this purpose he had brought together a group of professional revolutionaries bound to him by total obedience and an iron discipline. He had also thought out in minute detail the slogans and propaganda to be used for achieving his purpose, considering them among the most effective instruments of political warfare.

"All political life," wrote Lenin as early as 1902, "is an endless chain made of innumerable links. The whole art of politics consists precisely in discovering and clutching in an iron grip the particular little link which has the least chance of slipping out of one's hand, which is the most important one at the given moment, and which gives its owner the best chance of controlling the entire chain." [3] Propaganda and agitation formed the "little link" of which he spoke.

By contrast, Denikin (like Kolchak) had had nothing to do with politics in his prerevolutionary career. When he came to power, he could not, as a soldier brought up in the traditions of honor and chivalry, tolerate the idea of making promises which he sincerely believed impossible to carry out. He was an intelligent, well-read, and highly educated military man, but he was inexperienced in the business of government, and having come face to face with the grandiose demagogy of Communism, reacted to this new phenomenon in a purely military way. He decided that Communism had to be crushed by the force of arms, rather than by political maneuvering. Considering himself responsible solely for this transitional phase of the war against Communism, Denikin wished to avoid the political issues of the future until Russia was ready for a Constituent Assembly, which would then choose a form of government. It was this approach to the struggle which found expression in all the nonpolitical slogans proclaimed by Denikin, such as the declaration of the principle of non-predetermination or his appeal to save the country. In comparison with Lenin's propaganda, Denikin's slogans were pale, anemic and diffuse, while his motto of "A united and indivisible Russia" definitely antagonized the nationalities which had proclaimed their independence.

The White movement did not bring forth a dynamic, creative idea capable of firing the imagination of the masses. In a period of tremendous upheavals, it lacked the revolutionary drive of a search for new political horizons. It was devoid of a sense of reality and failed to grasp the range and scope of the psychological changes that were affecting the entire country. Its basis was the negation of Bolshevism, not a positive program of reconstruction and reorganization. This negative approach and the absence of a definitely formulated policy were aces in Lenin's hand. His propaganda loudly asserted that the leaders of the "White guards" were attempting to fool the people by their nebulous program, that they were members of the Black Hundred * who had sold out to capitalism, and that their aim was to revenge themselves on the workers and peasants and restore the prerevolutionary regime.

Lenin pursued his aims relentlessly, supervising every detail of the

---

* The Black Hundred was a reactionary and anti-Semitic organization formed in Russia during the revolution of 1905–6.

struggle. Even at the rear of the enemy, he cast a wide net of agitators and agents who fomented uprisings and engaged in sabotage.

The Whites too had tried to organize uprisings in the rear of the Red Army, but these efforts were badly managed and poorly coordinated. We know already of Savinkov's secret organization, Union for the Defense of the Motherland and Freedom, and its attempt on July 6, 1918 to capture several towns in Moscow's vicinity—Iaroslavl, Rybinsk, Murom—and then to march on Moscow. We also know that this uprising failed, and that though Savinkov escaped, most of the members of his organization were exterminated by the Reds.

A year later, another important conspiracy aimed at overthrowing the Soviet regime was organized in Moscow by N. N. Schepkin, a member of the Cadet party. But his group, which included some former officers serving in the Red Army, was uncovered by the Soviet secret police, and in the middle of September, 1919, the Moscow paper *Izvestia* announced the execution of sixty-seven men, including Schepkin, as agents of General Denikin.

Denikin lacked the qualities of a dictator even in his own military sphere and failed to enforce rigid discipline on his troops when there was still time to do so.

Some of the serious students of the Russian civil-war period have expressed the opinion that among the many reasons for the defeat of the Whites, despite their educational superiority and military experience, was "the decadence and weakness of a group on which history had already passed its sentence of condemnation," and that in the Communist camp "the crude strength of a fresh ruling class," and the will to power, were "stronger than the efforts of the former privileged classes to retain their old position." [4]

This opinion seems to be a philosophical oversimplification of the actual facts. Both the Reds and the Whites knew that the civil war was a gigantic struggle for survival, that the losing side, as Stalin clearly said, would be exterminated. The fear of that fate was in itself a powerful incentive. In addition, at times both the Reds and the Whites displayed an amazing amount of courage, daring, and self-sacrifice on behalf of their cause. Nevertheless, at the crucial moment of the struggle, those who formed the backbone of Bolshevism retained faith in their leadership, which managed to keep a firm grip on all party members; whereas the backbone of the Whites the members of the officer corps—lost faith in their leaders, who had failed to enforce the same degree of ruthless discipline in the ranks of their followers and to mold them into an obedient and unified force.

After the defeat of the White movement, many military critics censured the former commander in chief for his decision to deploy all of his comparatively small army in a wide fan facing the interior of Russia, stretching out his forces to the limit, leaving no substantial reserves behind them, and failing to establish well-defended strongholds on the way of his advance.

The most severe critic was General Wrangel. On December 9, 1919, after assuming the command of the Volunteer Army, he sent the commander in chief the drastic report, already mentioned, which stressed the *Stavka*'s systematic neglect of the basic principles of warfare, and the complete disorganization of the army rear. Wrangel considered that in view of the great numerical superiority of the enemy, a simultaneous advance in several operational directions was beyond the scope of Denikin's forces. "In pursuing the conquest of wide spaces," wrote Wrangel, "we have stretched ourselves out as thin as a spider web, and in our desire to retain everything and demonstrate our strength in all places, we have proved our weakness everywhere. . . . As we moved forward, we did nothing to secure the spaces we had conquered. Not a single fortified line, not one point of resistance, had been prepared at the rear of the entire stretch between the Sea of Azov and Orel. And now there is nothing to arrest the momentum of the retreating army." [5]

These and similar reproaches attacked General Denikin's self-esteem at the most vulnerable spot, as they concerned the purely military sphere of activity to which he had devoted his life. For this reason Denikin's reply to this criticism, written several years later, is of special interest:

The strategy of external warfare is governed by its own constant and immutable laws, which were as valid in the days of Caesar, Hannibal, and Napoleon as in the recent World War. The conditions of a civil war, however, though they do not diminish the intrinsic value of the permanent laws of strategy, sometimes alter their relative meaning to such an extent that the superficial observer is unable to decide whether the law is invalid per se, or whether it is being criminally broken. . . .

Strategy does not tolerate the dispersement of forces, but requires that they be proportionate to the size of the front. Whereas we dispersed over hundreds of versts, sometimes deliberately and sometimes because we were forced to do so. . . .

We occupied enormous areas because only by pressing forward on the heels of the enemy, and not allowing him to regain his senses and reorganize, did we have a chance to overcome the resistance of his numerically superior forces. We tore away from the Soviets their most fecund provinces, depriving them of bread, huge quantities of military supplies, and inexhaustible sources of army reinforcements. Our strength lay in the uplift of victory, in maneuvering, and in the momentum of our offensive movement. Exhausted by numerous mobilizations, the North Caucasus could no longer adequately supply the army, and only the new areas and a fresh current of life-giving force could save its organism from wasting away.

We were widening the front by hundreds of versts and this made us not weaker, but stronger. . . .

From May to October, the complement of the Armed Forces of South Russia grew consistently, from 64,000 to 150,000. Such was the result of our widespread offensive. Only on this condition were we able to continue the struggle.

Otherwise we would have been stifled by the immense superiority of the enemy, who could draw on inexhaustible human resources. . . .

Theory speaks of securing the lines of defense; in practice, the civil war, with its great distances and fronts, with the exceptional importance of the psychological factor not only in the armies but in the population of provinces overrun by the war, testifies to the insurmountable difficulty and sometimes the complete inadequacy of the method of stabilized warfare. . . .

[At this point, Denikin drew attention to the fact that] the defenses constituted by the exceptional configuration and natural characteristics of the "impregnable" Crimean isthmuses proved no stronger than a spider web in the tragic autumn days of 1920 [when the army was led no longer by Denikin but by his critic Wrangel, and when the Soviet troops forced these defenses without excessive losses or efforts and occupied the Crimea].

Our liberation of immense regions should have given rise to popular enthusiasm and the uprising of all anti-Soviet elements, and not only reinforced our ranks but strengthened the morale of the White armies. The question was: Had the popular masses become sufficiently disenchanted with Bolshevism and was their will to overcome it sufficiently strong? Would the people come with us or remain, as before, inert and passive between two oncoming waves, between two camps sworn to a deadly struggle?

By the force of a whole series of complex reasons—some of them elemental and others controllable, life gave first a wavering, then a negative answer.[6]

It should be recalled at this point that all the planning of the White command was based on the overturn of the Soviet power by purely military means, i.e., by crushing the Red Army in the course of the summer and early autumn of 1919. This type of lightning campaign (which later evolved into the mechanized German *Blitzkrieg*), was based at that time on the advantages of having a strong cavalry capable of maneuvering, outflanking, surrounding, and demoralizing the enemy.

Realizing the importance of cavalry in the circumstances of a civil war, General Denikin had formed numerous mounted units which had contributed greatly to his successes. However, these units were scattered along the entire front and not gathered into a single mighty fist capable of dealing a decisive blow in the required direction, as was later done by the Bolsheviks. In the opinion of some military experts, this absence of a special cavalry army was one of the principal reasons for the defeat.

General Wrangel had developed the idea of creating such an army. In June, 1919, his chief of staff presented his plan in detail in a written report to General Romanovsky. The report stressed the dominant role played by cavalry in the preceding period of the Russian civil war, and the need to create without delay an independent cavalry army to be placed under the direct orders of the commander in chief. Such a cavalry force, not assigned to any specific front, would deal lightning blows to the enemy in any direction, according to the strategic needs of the moment. It would fulfill the role formerly played by Joachim Murat's cavalry in Napoleon's army, clearing the way for the advance of the infantry. "A mighty cavalry force, launched in the most important direction, will be capable of deciding the issue of the struggle in the shortest time with a minimum expenditure of lives," stated the report, and it pointed out that time was of essence for many reasons, including the need "to terminate the march on Moscow toward the fall."

The report proposed the formation of the cavalry army within three weeks, out of already existing Volunteer and Cossack cavalry groups— the Volunteer, Don, and Kuban cavalry corps, plus a corps composed of the First Cavalry and First Terek divisions. The report stressed that only cavalry gathered into a single massive force could lead to decisive results for the entire campaign, and that the refusal to form a cavalry army would result in the "scattering of the existing cavalry on minor objectives." The report ended with the suggestion that General Wrangel should be placed at the head of the cavalry army, as unquestionably the most outstanding cavalry leader.[7]

Wrangel's plan was placed before Denikin in Tsaritsin, immediately after the Caucasian army had captured that town, at a time when the outstanding successes of all the White armies of south Russia had given rise to a great surge of optimism and the feeling that the spirit and resistance of the Soviet troops had finally been broken.

General Wrangel referred to this episode in his memoirs as follows: "Having heard us out [Wrangel and his chief of staff] and in the act of receiving our report, General Denikin said with a grin, 'Well, of course, you want to be the first to get to Moscow.' As we took our leave, the commander in chief said that he would have the occasion to speak to us tomorrow." [8]

And on the next day General Denikin announced his Moscow Directive, which nullified Wrangel's plan. Denikin's decision not to create a special cavalry army was not, of course, influenced by personal considerations. It was due to the fear that the separation from the Caucasian army of a Kuban Cavalry corps, a cavalry division, and a Terek division, would expose the front to the danger of a breakthrough in the Tsaritsin area. Though badly mauled by Wrangel, the Soviet Tenth Army still remained the most combat-worthy of the Red Army units.

The subsequent course of events showed that a unique opportunity had been missed by the *Stavka* at that time. In the summer of 1919, when the Red cavalry was only in the process of being formed, a mighty thrust by a White cavalry army in the direction of Moscow, in cooperation with General Kutepov's infantry, could have decided the campaign in Denikin's favor. Thus, the assertion of those who considered that the White Movement was a priori inevitably doomed to failure, appears highly debatable.

Notwithstanding all the political and administrative errors and the numerical superiority of the enemy, in the summer and early fall of 1919, General Denikin still had the possibility of defeating the Red Army and overturning the Soviet government. Among those who adhered to this opinion was the historian S. P. Melgunov. A member of the People's Socialist party, he hated the Bolsheviks and was in hiding from them in an area which in the fall of 1919, was almost captured by the advance units of the Volunteer Army. "Had General Denikin taken Moscow with the most insignificant forces," wrote Melgunov, "without paying attention to the deterioration at the 'rear,' he would have won the civil war, and who knows, might have succeeded in pacifying and restoring our unfortunate country." [9]

The defeat of Denikin's army led to the expatriation of many thousands of people, including the flower of the Russian intelligentsia, who refused to live under the Communist regime; they represented every shade of Russian political orientation, from monarchists to moderate socialists. The hard school of exile helped to erase and soften many of the political prejudices and private grudges of Denikin's compatriots and brought them to a less emotional and fairer view of him. They came to realize that Denikin stood out with the simplicity and greatness of a true soldier and patriot whose chivalry and integrity could not be obscured by his all-too-human errors. Objective students of history came to realize that there was not a particle of political guile, no class or personal interest, in Denikin's makeup.

In some ways Denikin invites comparison with Robert E. Lee, who in a different period and country, also suffered defeat in a civil war and emerged from it with his honor intact and with the respect of his contemporaries and of future historians.

XXXII

ENGLAND

———◄ ►———

The Denikins journeyed slowly from Constantinople to England, with stops at Malta and Gibraltar. In the Atlantic Ocean their ship met a serious storm, to the great affright of little Marina's nurse, who alternated loud prayers with lamentations of "no one will bury me and the fish will eat me." Mrs. Denikin noted this down not without malice, as there was some rivalry between the two women for the child's affection.[1]

Denikin and his party arrived in London by train from Southampton at 2:40 P.M. on April 17. He was met at Waterloo station by a representative of the War Office and by General Holman, who had just returned to England. The Russian chargé d'affaires, E. V. Sablin, at the head of several military and diplomatic officials, also came to meet Denikin, as did a number of recently arrived prominent Russians, including P. N. Milyukov. All of them wished to pay homage to the general.

"All the Russians stood bare-headed [reported the *Weekly Dispatch* a day or two later] and tears glistened in the eyes of many of them as, with warm handshakes, they greeted the leader to whom the last three years have brought so many vicissitudes of fortune."

The General told the *Weekly Dispatch* that he would visit the British War Office almost immediately to express his gratitude for all the British people had done for his unhappy country.

Sablin handed Denikin a telegram from Paris, addressed to him in care of the Russian embassy, and signed by Prince G. E. Lvov, S. D. Sazonov, V. A. Maklakov, and B. V. Savinkov. The signators of the telegram considered it their duty to express their deep-felt respect for the General in "these days of harrowing moral suffering."

"Your name," read the telegram, "will stand among the glorious and precious names of true leaders of the Russian land."[2]

Savinkov's signature under this text came as a total surprise to Denikin. Savinkov knew, of course, that Denikin would no longer have any dealings with him after his strange behavior in the Kornilov affair; yet at this moment, he apparently wished to emphasize that his respect for Denikin's patriotism and integrity stood above any personal feelings.

From the station, the General and his party were driven in cars of the British War Office to the Cadogan Hotel, where an excellent suite had been retained for them. The General's household proved considerable, including his wife and daughter, Mrs. Denikin's grandfather (Mr. Tumsky), General Chaperon du Larré, General Kornilov's son and daughter, a Captain Grishin, little Marina's nurse, the General's orderly, and young Nadia Kolokolov (whom the Denikins had taken in after the death of her father, Denikin's predecessor as commander of the Arkhangelgorod regiment, and whom the local papers described as the Denikin's adopted daughter).

The London papers, including the Labor party's *Daily Herald,* commented in a respectful tone on the former commander in chief's arrival in England. The *Times* article included the following:

One of the noblest characters brought into prominence by the war, he [Denikin] now seeks asylum among us, asking only the right to rest from his labours in the quiet of an English home. Less than a year ago his forces stood within 200 miles of Moscow. Singlehanded, he was unable to maintain his advantage and doubtless, faults of administration and inability to cope with political problems which his training as a soldier had not fitted him to face, accelerated the disasters that overtook his troops. Nevertheless, we owe to him, and to those who, with him, strove to overthrow a hideous tyranny of which the masses in this country are only now beginning to perceive the real nature, a debt of gratitude and of respect. We can best pay it for the present by refraining from intrusion upon the quiet which he seeks—and by extending to the Russian people, for whom he fought so hard against such heavy odds, the compassion and, as occasion may offer, the help to which their unexampled sufferings and their imperishable services to the Allies have abundantly entitled them.[3]

We have no way of telling whether this article was inspired by Churchill, but it definitely reflected his ideas.

In those days, the Russian embassies and consulates, whose personnel had been assigned in 1917 by the Provisional Government, were still functioning. After the Bolshevik take-over, they had become the representatives of the leaders of the White movement. Their activity was under the control of S. D. Sazonov, once Minister of Foreign Affairs under the Tsar, who continued to fulfill this function in the governments of Kolchak and Denikin.

Sazonov was in Paris, where he received the reports and telegraphed messages of the different embassies on all matters which concerned Russian affairs. A whole series of letters regarding the first days of General Denikin's sojourn in England were therefore sent to Sazonov from London by E. V. Sablin. On April 17, 1920, Sablin reported on Denikin's arrival and reception, adding that the General's principal wish was to be left alone.[4]

On April 19, Sablin wrote to Sazonov that the former commander in chief considered himself a private person: "In his own words, he is morally shattered and physically tired, and is in need of calm and rest. He still has before his eyes the dreadful scenes of the last days of the retreat and the painful reverses. Of the British statesmen he has only visited Mr. Churchill. He has already thanked the King in his excellent telegram." The General greatly praised the British military, and said that General Holman was going to look for a place for him to live.[5]

On April 21, 1920, Sablin wrote, "General Denikin handed me yesterday for exchanging 23,000 tsarist [paper] rubles, a few hundred Kerensky bills, Austrian kronen, and Turkish liras, and a small box containing forty-nine rubles in ten-kopeck coins minted in 1916.

"That is the entire capital of the former commander in chief!"

According to Sablin, the rate of exchange for tsarist paper currency at that time was 1,800 rubles to the English pound. Thus, the bulk of Denikin's capital, consisting of tsarist paper currency, amounted to less than thirteen pounds sterling. Austrian kronen had practically no exchange value, and the Kerensky paper money even less; the silver coins were worth considerably less than their equivalent in melted silver.[6]

On the same date, Sablin also informed Sazonov that General Denikin was receiving offers from various English people to reside in their estates completely free of cost.[7]

What was General Denikin's own reaction to all this? He was horrified by the whole situation, as we can see from an entry in his unpublished papers: "They don't understand our situation—have lodged us in the expensive Hotel Cadogan. . . . We are looking for an inexpensive home in a secluded spot. Holman is helping in our search. Churchill summoned the [Russian] consul, Onu [and asked him], 'Are the Russians taking any steps? If not, I and a group of members of Parliament will arrange to provide for General Denikin.'

"Onu arrives and relates this to me. I categorically refuse!"[8]

Anton Ivanovich was distressed by the thought that because of his family he was obliged to accept "charity" (his own word) from Great Britain. But at that time he literally had nothing except the clothes on his back. At home he wore his uniform. Outdoors he wore a military raincoat without insignia and a checked cap he had accidentally acquired.

His wife had brought some table silver with her and wanted to sell it. Denikin thought that the proceeds of the sale could support his family for another two or three months in England. He realized that the cost of living there was considerably higher than in the other countries of Western Europe, and wished, therefore, to limit his stay in England to no more than three or four months, long enough to acquire the necessary information and make arrangements to move to a country where living was less expensive.

Milyukov had also discussed these questions with Denikin. To help tide him over the beginning of his stay abroad, he proposed to speak with the persons responsible for disbursements made from the funds of the former Russian government which were deposited in European banks. Denikin answered that such a move was out of the question; in his view, the funds referred to by Milyukov were state property, and being a private citizen, he had no right to accept them. He also told Milyukov that he planned to earn a living by writing historical works, but that for the time being he wished to "escape from everything and leave with his family for some remote place." [9]

Denikin saw Churchill several times. The day after his arrival in London, he went to call on him at the War Office, accompanied by General Holman. Then he had lunch with Churchill. "[There were] several ladies," wrote Denikin, "my wife, Churchill and his wife, two or three high-ranking officials of the War Office. Conversations about Russia, the struggle . . . and, of course, about the causes of the defeat." [10] It was at this luncheon that Churchill asked the question, mentioned in an earlier chapter, "General, why didn't you proclaim a monarchy?"

After the meal, Churchill sent for his nine-year-old son Randolph and introduced him to Anton Ivanovich, saying, "This is the Russian General who beat the Bolsheviks." This interested Randolph, who wanted to find out how many Bolsheviks General Denikin had personally killed. Upon hearing "not a one," he quickly lost interest in his new acquaintance.[11]

General Denikin was feeling very depressed. The attentions of the Russian colony, though sincere and kind, reminded him of the conventional expressions of sympathy traditionally extended to people who have suffered a bereavement. They oppressed him. He had no wish to see anyone or go anywhere. Sablin had some difficulty persuading the General to accept the invitation of an influential group of members of Parliament to dine with them. The details of this occasion were recorded, as usual, in one of the letters sent by Sablin to Sazonov.

The dinner in honor of General Denikin took place on April 27 in the House of Commons. The following members of the House were reported as present: Mr. Gersham Stewart, Lord Winterton, Viscount Curzon, Sir Samuel Hoare, Colonel Guinness, Sir T. Royden, Sir H. Craik, Mr. MacCallum Scott, Sir J. Hope, Colonel John Ward, Mr. Strauss. The reception was marked by great hospitality and warmth. There were two welcoming addresses, one by Gersham Stewart, who presided, and the other by Colonel Ward (Labor party member) who had been stationed for several months in Siberia with Admiral Kolchak. Colonel Ward declared that the English were quite aware that they shared with the Russians the

responsibility for the reverses undergone by the Russian national movement in the south. At the time when General Denikin's troops were vic-
toriously advancing on Moscow, the front was overflown by Bolshevik
planes scattering leaflets quoting Prime Minister Lloyd George's speech
announcing that aid to the General would be discontinued. The English,
said Colonel Ward, must remember that such speeches played a bigger
role in the defeat than Denikin's lack of ammunition or of satisfactory
organization.[12]

In a short answering speech, Denikin thanked the English for their
hospitality. He pointed out that despite the failure of the White movement, he did not consider his efforts to have been in vain. By deflecting
the forces of the Bolsheviks for two years, he had contained their westward advance, which with the disintegration of the German army, and
the unrest in Germany and the components of old Austria-Hungary,
could have overrun all Europe. By controlling the Ukraine, the North
Caucasus, and the Caspian and Black Sea basins, the White movement
isolated Rumania, Hungary, Turkey, Iran, and Afghanistan from possible
incursions by the Red Army, and gave Hungary the chance to overthrow
the Communist government of Béla Kun.

Within Russia, said Denikin, the armed resistance to Bolshevik dictatorship had been an act of patriotic duty. It rose against the dishonorable
separate peace treaty concluded by the Bolsheviks with Germany at
Brest-Litovsk. It rose in defense of human dignity, persecuted religion,
and accepted morality. In the heroic struggle of a handful of people
against the elemental destructiveness which had gripped the entire country, rested the inner meaning and achievement of the White movement.[13]

On the very first day of Denikin's arrival, the leader of the Cadet party,
P. N. Milyukov, had insistently and systematically questioned him concerning the changes that had occurred in the Crimea. What authority
remained with Denikin? he wanted to know. How much had been transferred to Wrangel? Was it the overall supreme authority or only the military one? What would Denikin do if Wrangel suddenly concluded peace
with the Bolsheviks? "Would we then recognize the Wrangel government," pursued Milyukov, "and if we decided to reject it, in the name
of whose government would we do so, if not in Denikin's?" For, declared
Milyukov in his account of this conversation, "Denikin is a symbol and
standard which cannot be lowered."

Denikin answered these somewhat Talmudic questions by repeating
what he had already said many times since the Novorossiisk catastrophe
—that he was morally shattered, did not wish to be involved in politics,
and desired to be left in peace. Concerning Wrangel, he said that he had
transferred to him the command of the south Russian troops, that after
all that happened, he could not consider himself the head of the government, and that at the present time he was simply a private person. In

conclusion, he said with great firmness, "Do not interfere with Wrangel; he may be able to achieve something. I wish to be out of politics, do not involve me."

Milyukov noted all the details of this conversation in his diary.[14]

For his part, General Denikin left in his unpublished papers the following remarks concerning this talk:

Milyukov visited me. He talked for over an hour on the subject that it is indispensable that I assume the succession of Russian authority from Kolchak and announce the fact in a suitable declaration. I refused categorically.

"But what will happen then? You realize that Kerensky will come to power." . . .

I expressed my doubts of such a possibility. "In any event, I personally, withdraw from the running."

"In that case, will you at least refrain from declaring that you refuse the succession . . . ?"

"In general, I intend to make no declarations of any kind. I did not accept the supreme authority from Kolchak and have, therefore, nothing to resign from."

After this, we corresponded two or three times and, notably, exchanged views on Poland's action at that time [its war against the Soviets]. A short time later, Milyukov changed his "tactics," adopting an attitude of condemnation toward the White movement, and I severed my relations with him.[15]

Despite the fact that he had no further personal communication with Wrangel, General Denikin was faultlessly correct in discussing him with others: "When Churchill, Briggs, Holman, Milyukov, and other Russian and British public figures questioned me as to the attitude that should be taken in relation to Wrangel, I replied, 'Wrangel is at the head of the Armed Forces of South Russia, leading the anti-Bolshevik struggle. He must therefore be given maximum assistance." [16]

With General Holman's help, the Denikins soon found comparatively inexpensive living quarters away from London, moving first to Pevensey Bay, then to Eastbourne (Sussex). They continued to exchange visits with their British friends—Generals Briggs, Holman, Poole, Knox, and Keyes, and Colonel Rawlinson (a formerly rabid anti-Russian, turned Russophile), all of whom did their best to dispel Denikin's low spirits. They were also invited to the estate of Countess Natalie Brassov, the morganatic wife of Grand Duke Michael who had been murdered by the Bolsheviks, together with his English secretary Johnson, in June, 1918, in Perm. The widow of the late Tsar's brother was mystically inclined. She consulted various fortune-tellers and assured Anton Ivanovich in all seriousness that the Grand Duke was alive but in hiding for the time being, and that he would assert his rights to the Russian throne when the right moment came.

Denikin's stay in England was quite short. He had decided to move to Belgium in the autumn, hoping that life there would be considerably cheaper. As it happened, he left England even earlier for quite unexpected reasons.

In mid-August, 1920, the *Times* printed a note which had been sent at the beginning of April by Lord Curzon to Moscow's People's Commissar for Foreign Affairs, Chicherin. The note proposed that the Soviet government put a stop to the civil war. To his great surprise, the General read in it the following statement by Lord Curzon: "I have exerted my utmost influence with General Denikin to induce him to abandon the contest, and have promised him that if he did so I would use my best efforts to make peace between his forces and yours, and assure the safety of the rank and file of his followers and the population of the Crimea. General Denikin finally decided to act upon this advice, and has left Russia, resigning his command to General Wrangel."

It is true that almost on the eve of the Novorossiisk evacuation, General Bridge, a member of the British military mission, came to offer Denikin the intercession of the British government in negotiating a truce with the Red Army. Denikin, however, had answered this suggestion with one word—Never! It is interesting to note that General Holman had refused flatly to undertake this mission. He told his immediate superior, Winston Churchill, that he would "rather join the ranks of the armies of the south [Russia] as a Volunteer private, than engage in negotiations with the Bolsheviks." [17]

The actual outcome of the British attempt in Novorossiisk was obviously in complete contradiction to Lord Curzon's statement, since Denikin had never agreed to act upon the British advice to negotiate a truce with the Red Army.

Denikin was greatly upset and offended by its deliberate juggling of facts and evident untruthfulness. He immediately sent a sharply worded refutation to the *Times,* where it appeared on August 27, 1920. After quoting Lord Curzon's text, Denikin wrote,

I am deeply indignant at this statement and affirm:
1. That Lord Curzon could have exerted no influence upon me, since I have never had any dealings with him.
2. That the only occasion on which, during my command of the army, the question of mediation arose was at Novorossiisk, when the British Military Representative, judging the situation critical and evacuation to the Crimea impossible, offered his intervention in order to bring about an armistice with the Bolsheviks. I did not accept his offer, and, although with a loss of supplies, transported the troops to the Crimea, where the struggle was immediately renewed.
3. That the note of the British Government concerning peace negotiations with the Bolsheviks was handed, as is well known, not to me, but to my successor, General Wrangel, and his negative answer was published at the time in the press.
4. That my decision to leave the post of Commander in Chief was due to complex reasons wholly unconcerned with the policy of Lord Curzon.

5. That now, as before, I consider it inevitable and absolutely necessary to fight the Bolsheviks till they are completely defeated. Otherwise not only Russia but the whole of Europe will be in ruins.

August 21　　　　　　　　　　　　　　　　　　　GENERAL DENIKIN

After this episode, the General considered it impossible to remain in England. Other factors which contributed to this decision were the British government's desire to establish normal commercial relations with Soviet Russia and the negotiations taking place on this subject in London between Lloyd George and the Soviet representative, Krasin, which Denikin expected to be followed by England's recognition of the Soviets as the legal government of Russia. As it happened, the Anglo-Soviet trade agreement would be signed only in March, 1921; but at the time, Denikin expected it to take effect at any moment, and his departure was intended as a demonstration against it.

He considered it impossible to conceal his point of view on the Anglo-Soviet negotiations. In his opinion, they opened the doors of Europe to the frightful and poisonous propaganda of the Third International, while in Russia, where the civil war was still raging, they placed an ace in Lenin's hand.

Notwithstanding his gratitude for the hospitality of the British, and despite his desire to avoid politics, the General was convinced that for many, his name was a symbol of uncompromising opposition to Communism, and he acted as his conscience dictated. Denikin's hurried departure did not affect his relations with his English friends. They understood very well the reasons which prompted his decision, and respected their outspoken friend all the more for making it.

XXXIII

DENIKIN WRITES
HIS MEMOIRS

The Denikins lived in Belgium from August, 1920 to the end of May, 1922. They settled down in a small house with a garden in the vicinity of Brussels. The companions with whom they had arrived in England had gradually gone their different ways, reducing the Denikin household to five members—husband, wife, daughter, the wife's grandfather, and the nurse. A regular routine of life was soon established. Anton Ivanovich rose at 7 A.M., opened the shutters, brought in the coal, lit fires in the rooms, and in the kitchen stove. His wife, who was the next to get up, boiled the milk and brewed the coffee for the breakfast. Other household chores followed breakfast—Anton Ivanovich swept, grandfather dusted, Xenia Vasilievna tidied the kitchen, peeled potatoes, and cooked lunch. The nurse's only duty was taking care of the baby.

The fact that her husband was obliged to do manual work did not particularly disturb Mrs. Denikin. "He needs exercise," she wrote, "for once he settles down to his writing, nothing will make him budge even for a short walk." [1]

Having begun to work consistently on his *Ocherki Russkoi Smuty* (*The Russian Turmoil*) while still in England, Anton Ivanovich had almost finished the first volume of this extensive work by the end of 1920. "I have completely withdrawn from politics and immersed myself in history," he told General Briggs in a Christmas letter in 1920. "Am finishing the first volume of *Ocherki,* which comprises the events of the Russian revolution from February 27 to August 27, 1917. To a certain extent my work helps me forget the difficulties I have experienced." [2]

Though the General led a secluded life, saw very few people, and avoided any political involvement, his demonstrative departure from

England had attracted the attention of the Belgian government. Shortly after his arrival in Brussels, he was asked to call at the Administration de la Sûreté Publique, whose director requested him, with utmost politeness, to sign a statement that he would not actively engage in politics while on Belgian territory. The General signed, but upon returning home, sent a letter to the Belgian Minister of Justice, the well-known socialist Émile Vandervelde. Denikin had come to know him well in April, 1917, when he was chief of staff and Vandervelde came to the *Stavka* in Mogilev to confer with him. The General wished to express his displeasure at the incident and wrote Vandervelde:

As you are perfectly aware of my secluded mode of life, which can in no way cause any difficulties to the Belgian government, your request came merely as an additional humiliation to a man who has been sorely tried by fate. . . .

I cannot help going back to an episode in the past when, in 1917, while occupying the post of chief of staff of the Russian armies, I received at the *Stavka* the Belgian minister Vandervelde. He was unhappy then, a man without a homeland, in short, a political émigré such as many Russians are at the present time, since Belgium was as crushed by its enemies then as Russia is today. But we did everything possible not to let Mr. Vandervelde be in the least conscious of the difficulty of his position. For we sincerely shared the distress of your country and its heroic army.

I did not expect or seek attention. But I was certain that a Russian general would not be exposed to humiliation in Belgium. I do not have in mind my role as commander in chief of the Armed Forces of South Russia—there has been too much slander and misunderstanding concerning this matter. . . . Rather, I speak of myself as the former chief of staff, as the commander in chief of Russian army fronts during the World War, and finally, as the general of an Allied army whose regiments in the first two years of the war depleted the Austro-German ranks of tens of thousands of soldiers.

I consider it necessary to tell you all this in the hope that the attitude of your government toward other Russian public figures whom fate may accidentally bring to Belgium will be somewhat different. [3]

This letter, like his departure from England, was typical of all of Denikin's subsequent behavior abroad. In his role as a political émigré, he continued to be as boldly outspoken in regard to what he considered to be the truth, as he had been throughout his preceding life. Modest by nature, but possessed of a great sense of dignity, he was fully aware of the merit of his military performance in World War I, and was proud of it, but there was nothing personal or petty in this pride. It was the pride of belonging to the Russian army, which boasted a record in the history of that war rich in high courage and sacrifice, and which had come to the rescue of its allies in many difficult situations. Denikin was incensed by the fact that all this was now forgotten, to the extent that one of the principal representatives of that wartime Russia could be exposed to such cavalier treatment by one of its former allies.

Vandervelde immediately responded with a polite, semiapologetic letter.

He referred to certain rules allegedly enforced in Belgium, reminisced about the past, and assured Denikin that it would never occur to the Belgian government, and least of all to himself, to do anything that could offend the General. Subsequently, on the few occasions when Denikin came into contact with Belgium's bureaucracy, he was treated with the greatest courtesy.

Denikin's resources were so limited that life in Belgium seemed too expensive to him, and he decided to move to Hungary, where, at the time, life was very cheap. The Hungarian ambassador immediately and courteously granted him permission to take up permanent residence in that country, and even offered to transport the general's archive by diplomatic pouch. However, he simply refused to believe that the General's reason for the move was purely one of economy. . . . The Denikins had to apply for transit visas in order to reach Budapest. "The German minister was the most polite of all," noted Anton Ivanovich. "He was interested in my attitude toward the Germans, criticized the Bolsheviks, and conceived the future as an alliance between Germany and the real Russia." [4]

The General's attitude toward Germany was sufficiently well known, and the German minister was wasting his time in hoping to detect in him a shift toward a more favorable view of Germany. Though a German transit visa was granted to the entire family, Denikin decided that he, personally, would bypass Germany and travel to Hungary by way of Paris, Geneva, and Vienna.

At that time, Hungary was passing through a difficult phase of its history. It had been subjected first to a civil war which brought internal ruin; then to the invasion of the Rumanians, who finished the looting begun by the local Communists; and finally to the Treaty of Trianon, which deprived it of its richest provinces. The chaos and humiliation of this period stimulated in the Hungarian bourgeoisie and ruling class sympathy for the Russians who had opposed the same destructive forces in their own country, and after their defeat, had sought asylum in Hungary.

This accounts for the happy and fond memories that Anton Ivanovich and his wife retained of their life in Hungary, where they remained for three years (from early June, 1922, to the middle of 1925). On the advice of the Hungarian minister in Brussels, they settled first in an inexpensive suburban hotel near the town of Sopron.

Mrs. Denikin's journal for that period reflects the family's contentment. On June 5, 1922, she wrote,

. . . Life is really much cheaper here, . . . and the people too are more pleasant. For the time being, we live out of town in a *pension* surrounded by a forest. The air and surrounding country are wonderful. It is a long time since we have taken such wonderful walks. . . . . The little town is full of refugees from the provinces taken away from Hungary.

And a month later:

I like Hungary or, rather, Sopron, for this is all I have seen of it. What a plentiful region! It is long since I have seen "the fruits of the earth" in such abundance. We are surrounded by mountains and woods. We walk far. . . . We reach some clearing with a good view of the fields, the villages, and the town below, and a large lake in the distance. The air is a delight to breathe! . . . And there are moments when peace envelops my soul, a peace more complete than I have known since before the war. . . . Many people here speak Russian. They are former prisoners of war, whom Anton Ivanovich calls his "godsons" [the General's nickname for the prisoners captured by his Iron Division]. They speak Russian well, almost without accent.[5]

And here is a note from Anton Ivanovich's unpublished papers:

As a general rule—no trace of hostility following the war. A very warm attitude toward Russians. One out of every three former combatants has been a prisoner in Russia, and despite the hardships undergone in the Bolshevik period, they came out of there with the best of memories—of the Russian people, the vastness, hospitality, and wealth of the country. . . . Because of the prisoners, Russian is widely spoken. . . . The Hungarian prisoners have brought back Russian wives. . . . I met quite a few of my "godsons." A pediatrician we once called for Marisha turned out to have been the personal physician of Archduke Joseph during the war. We remembered the episode, behind Sambor, when the Fourth Sharpshooter [Iron] Division fought against the Archduke's corps. Having stormed across the mountain pass and taken Gorny Lujek, it emerged at the Austrian's rear. . . . The doctor [who was then with the Archduke's corps] was now delighted by our encounter. I have also met officers of the excellent Thirty-eighth Division, whom fate often opposed to the Iron Division, and whom we have had occasion to defeat, but always with great difficulty and considerable bloodshed. We reminisced about the past. And in all those encounters there was never any trace of resentment. On the contrary, there was only great interest for the past which we seemed to share as allies rather than enemies. . . .

Morally, we lived a good life in Hungary.[6]

The presence of the former Russian commander in chief was bound to attract the attention of the local military and civilian authorities, who found it difficult to understand the solitary mode of life of the General, who spent most of his time working on his book. Like Prince Wolkonsky, the White Russian representative in Budapest, they saw that he behaved with dignity and great simplicity, but some of them found his aloofness unfriendly and disparaging. Sensing this, Prince Wolkonsky insistently advised the General to call on the regent of Hungary, Admiral Horthy. "But," wrote Denikin, "after a year [of living in Hungary] this seemed embarrassing, and I didn't go. Thus we spent three peaceful years, having preserved the freedom of a secluded private life." [7]

In these years the Denikins changed residence three times. After Sopron they spent several months in Budapest, then moved once more to a small provincial town, Balatonlelle, near the large and beautiful Lake Balaton.

By the end of this period, Denikin had completed his monumental, five-volume opus, *Ocherki Russkoi Smuty*. The volumes came out gradually: Volume I in October, 1921; Volume II in November, 1922; Volume III in March, 1924; Volume IV in September, 1925, and Volume V in October, 1926. Starting with the period preceding the revolution, Denikin's history, written from the viewpoint of a Russian officer, and later, of the leader of the White movement, terminated with the assassination of General Romanovsky in Constantinople.

Ocherki was an event in Russian memoir literature. Written in a forceful and expressive style, the General's work can best be described as memoirs with a wide historical background, as it gives a detailed history of Denikin's army and the entire civil-war period in the south. Concurrently, using available documents, Denikin included short histories of the anti-Bolshevik war in Siberia under Kolchak, in the north under Miller, and in the west under Iudenich.

The wide historical conception of this work, interesting and talented though it is, was criticized by some of its readers, who regretted that the author had not limited himself to frankly personal memoirs instead of deliberately keeping himself in the shade while describing the events in which he had participated.

There is a good deal of truth in this reproach. Extremely reticent by nature, Anton Ivanovich was loath to expose his personal feelings. Yet, despite the unquestionable value of his historical approach, the pages that deal with his personal feelings are more exciting and emotionally stimulating than any others in the book.

The narrative, which in places attains an almost epic calm, is extraordinarily objective—to the extent, of course, that objectivity can be practiced by the leader of one of two irreconcilable factions. Having been at the heart of the dramatic events of the past, and having reflected deeply on them, General Denikin showed himself capable of rising above self-justification. His work describes the exploits and self-sacrifice of his movement, but also its shady sides, its mistakes and failings. He fully realized that in his capacity as ruler and commander in chief, his actions were subject to the stern judgment of history, but he did not write *Ocherki* in order to show himself in a favorable light. Rather, he wished to leave behind a confession, a truthful account of his actions in a framework of events described as dispassionately as possible. The personal integrity of the author constitutes one of the indisputable qualities of his book.

Denikin's unpublished papers contain some interesting notes on the difficulties he encountered while working on *Ocherki*. The archive he had personally brought out of Russia was far from complete. He had to search for, systematize, and verify various documents, draw up maps, and so on. The trunk containing the archive of the Special Council (i.e., the former government of south Russia), brought to Constantinople during the evacuation, became available to him only in 1921. In addition to the Special Council's records, it contained the original orders of the commander in chief, his correspondence with foreign countries, and information on existing conditions in all the newly established governments on Russia's periphery. The problem of obtaining the archive of the former *Stavka* was more complicated, as Denikin did not wish to request it from his successor as commander in chief. Fortunately, the problem resolved itself; General Kusonsky, Wrangel's deputy chief of staff, placed the archive at Denikin's disposal. Later, Wrangel himself ordered all documents of the commander in chief's staff pertaining to the period of Denikin's command, to be returned to the latter for safekeeping.

Denikin also had to engage in voluminous correspondence with his former associates and subordinates in order to ascertain the details of various events. He did not request General Lukomsky's assistance in this matter because he knew that the latter was working at that time on his own memoirs which were due to appear earlier than *Ocherki*. "However," noted Denikin, "Lukomsky, who knows a great deal, said nothing in his book." In all probability, this remark referred to the struggle for power in south Russia, concerning which Lukomsky could have said a great deal if he had not preferred to remain silent.

"The former Kuban *Ataman,* Filimonov, also offered to collaborate with me . . . ," wrote Anton Ivanovich, "I did not pick up his offer, which I regret."

The general's closest and most constant collaborator was his wife. She typed his manuscripts and was, according to Anton Ivanovich, "his first reader and censor, offering remarks that were often very pertinent, particularly, as she said, from the point of view of the average reader." [8]

Many books, with differing approaches and interpretations, have been written about the Russian civil war. However, General Denikin's books can still be considered the basis and the primary source for any serious study of the south Russian aspect of this struggle. Recognizing this in principle, the Soviet publishing house Federatsia issued in 1928 a 313-page book entitled *Pokhod na Moskvu* (*The March on Moscow*), consisting of excerpts from the fourth and fifth volumes of Denikin's *Ocherki*. "We tried to extract all the most curious pages of Denikin's work" stated the preface. As it turned out, these pages in their new context became a deliberate and one-sided juggling of facts. This was nothing, however, compared to the adulteration of history that took place as soon as Stalin felt himself in control of the situation in Russia. Then the juggling of facts deteriorated into their complete perversion, and insofar as Denikin's role is concerned, Soviet historical literature is still occupied in falsifying them.

XXXIV

AMONG WRITERS

————————   ————

Immersed in the writing of *Ocherki Russkoi Smuty,* Denikin saw very few people during the first six years of his life in exile. One reason for this was his desire to complete the work as soon as possible. There was another, perhaps even more important reason. He was troubled by uncertainty—General Romanovsky's assassination might have been an indirect attack on his superior, and Anton Ivanovich was not sure of the present attitude of those who had formerly believed in him and followed his leadership, but were now gripped by disaster. As the years went by, however, he was relieved of these doubts by the quantities of respectful and sympathetic letters that he received. They came from all sides, from people of different political orientations, from those who had been rich and those who had been poor, from former companions-in-arms, from persons he had known and others he had never seen. These letters showed that with the passage of time, the general's compatriots had come to realize and value his disinterestedness and honor. They convinced Anton Ivanovich that the slander and personal rancor he had experienced had not created a permanent breach between him and his former followers, and this gradually helped to dissipate the bitterness of his feelings.

During these years, concern for the fate of his former army dominated all his other emotions. From his remote position, he followed with anguish the last act of the great tragedy in the Crimea.

The downfall of the White movement ejected over a million people from the confines of Russia. The waves of refugees flowed from several directions: from Siberia, with the remainders of Kolchak's army; from northwestern Russia, with the retreating troops of Iudenich; and in much smaller numbers, from Archangel and Murmansk in the north. But the wave of humanity leaving the Black Sea shores of south Russia was the greatest. First came the so-called Denikin evacuation, and then began the great exodus at the end of General Wrangel's Crimean epic, when on one day, November 16, 1920, 126 vessels left the Crimean ports, carrying to the shores of the Bosporus 145,673 people, nearly forty thousand of whom were the last fighters of the White Army. The former Allies placed them in Gallipoli, on the island of Lemnos, and in other areas in the vicinity of Constantinople. But this was a purely temporary measure. It was necessary to decide without delay what was to be done with the former army, which though defeated, still retained its military discipline.

At first its commander in chief, General Wrangel, harbored the illusion that he could preserve his government apparatus, and most important of all, keep his army intact in order to renew the armed struggle against Bolshevism at the first opportunity.

General Denikin saw the matter in a different light. It was clear to him that the army's fate had been decided from the moment it had left Russian territory, that none of the former Allies would continue to support it, and that any attempt to preserve abroad the political power of General Wrangel's government and the army as such, would provoke a sharp reaction in the parliamentary and governmental circles of Europe.

Denikin did consider that "the army must be preserved," but he felt different means should be employed: "If you succeed in preserving the organizational cells," he wrote in answer to a letter from Kutepov, "then the internal, unifying ties on which the Volunteer units always prided themselves will preserve them from dissipation." [1]

At that time, Denikin did not envisage the future struggle with Bolshevism as taking the form of intervention from abroad. The sailors' uprising in Kronstadt, and the peasant revolt (named, after its leader, the "Antonov movement") which engulfed a large area of central Russia, though they both ended in failure, led Denikin to believe that further internal upheavals would occur in Russia, at which time his Volunteers could gradually make their way back, to join an all-Russian anti-Communist movement.

The longer Denikin remained abroad, the more definitely he expressed his opposition to the participation of Russian political émigrés (and particularly of his war comrades) in any form of foreign adventure directed against Russia. He pointed out the danger which Japan represented to the Russian Far East; and later, when Hitler appeared on the German horizon, Denikin was one of the first to say,

Don't grasp at the phantom of intervention; don't put your faith in an anti-Bolshevik crusade, for though Communism is being crushed in Germany, the question there does not concern the extermination of Bolshevism in Russia, but centers on the "eastern program" of Hitler, whose dream is to appropriate the south of Russia for German colonization.

I consider the nations which desire Russia's partition to be her worst enemies. I believe any foreign invasion aimed at dismembering her to be a calamity. And resistance to the enemy on the part of the Russian people, the Red Army, and the émigrés—their imperative duty.[2]

These observations were made by Denikin at the end of 1933, and as events pointed more and more to the possibility of a second world war, he expressed himself on this subject with growing insistence and clarity. The opinions he set forth, however, could not be taken to indicate that he had reached a compromise in relation to the Communist government, to which he always remained irreconcilable. The apparent contradiction in this desire to uphold his country and its army, but not its government, at a time of danger was explained in detail by Denikin during a public appearance in Paris a short time before the war. His speech, which was reprinted in condensed form by most of the Russian newspapers abroad, made a deep impression on the Russian émigrés. We shall come to it in due course.

In the meantime, let us return to Denikin's life in the 1920's.

Refraining from inflicting his point of view on anyone, and voicing his opinion only when his advice was sought, General Denikin abstained from interfering in the affairs of his successor, "not wishing," he said, "even indirectly or by a single word to stand in the way of the new command." [3] But it was precisely this meticulousness which provided Denikin's ill-wishers with an excuse to turn his policy against him. A rumor was deliberately circulated that the former commander in chief was avoiding the Volunteers and was indifferent to their fate.

Thus, General Denikin remained an outside observer of what was happening to his former army, which was eventually moved from Gallipoli, Lemnos, and Chatalja to Bulgaria and Yugoslavia. In Bulgaria, the former officers and soldiers were formed into contingents to work in the mines, build roads, and the like. In Yugoslavia, King Alexander enrolled most of the former cavalry units in his army as frontier guards. A few years later began their gradual dispersal to other countries.

In the fall of 1923, to preserve the military cadres of the White forces, General Wrangel formed the Russian Armed Services Union (*Russkii Obshche Voinskii Soiuz,* or ROVS) with branches in all the countries in which there were former participants in the White struggle. Having assumed the position of chairman of the Union, Wrangel submitted himself to the authority of Grand Duke Nicholas, the former commander in chief of the Russian imperial armies. The Grand Duke was greatly respected by the rightist circles, who hoped that all the "nationally minded" elements among the Russian émigrés could be rallied around him. The fact that he resided in France placed the Paris branch of ROVS in a dominant position.

The creation of the Russian Armed Services Union, a clearly anti-Communist extraterritorial organization, immediately attracted Moscow's attention. And when Soviet agents abroad reported that General Aleksandr Pavlovich Kutepov, the former commander of the Volunteer corps, had left the Balkans for Paris in order to organize a militant branch of ROVS for sabotage work within the USSR, government circles in Moscow became very worried indeed.

General Denikin's five-volume opus, which later appeared in greatly condensed form in English and French, provided him temporarily with a semblance of material security, while peaceful life in a Hungarian province, with its lack of human contacts and cultural activity, began to pall. A letter from the faithful General Chaperon du Larré, who had married General Kronilov's daughter in Belgium and was trying to get Anton Ivanovich to return to Brussels, helped precipitate Denikin's decision to leave Hungary. The family moved in the middle of 1925, but did not remain in Belgium for long. In the spring of the following year, Denikin decided to settle permanently in France.

By that time, Paris had become the cultural center of the Russian emigration. Three of the well-known Russian novelists in exile, Bunin, Kuprin, and Shmelev, welcomed Denikin with particular warmth and friendliness, as did the poets Balmont and Tsvetaeva. They visited him often, spending long evenings in discussions of literary and historic subjects, and tried to prove their affectionate respect for him in every way. Ivan Alekseevich Bunin, later a Nobel prizewinner, presented his book *Chasha Zhizni* (*The Cup of Life*) to the General with what was for him an unusually effusive dedication: "To Anton Ivanovich Denikin, in remembrance of the most beautiful day of my life—September 25, 1919, in Odessa, when I would have unhesitatingly and gladly died for him!" [4] This inscription referred to the occasion when Denikin arrived in Odessa just after it had been liberated from the Bolsheviks, and the inhabitants (including Bunin) gave a delirious welcome to the commander in chief.

Kuprin, who liked to drink, detested Balmont, who suffered from the same weakness, partly perhaps because both of them were violent and irrepressible in their cups, but even more because of their totally incompatible natures. Whenever Kuprin dropped in on the Denikins, he cautiously inquired, "Is Balmont here by any chance?"

While Kuprin was simple and natural, Balmont was an inveterate poseur. During his recitations, he sometimes fell into a "poetic trance," alternating sweet and ingratiating whispers with thunderous pathos. Once, he even managed to scare little Marina Denikin. Reading aloud one of his poems and staring straight at the child, he suddenly raised his voice to a roar:

"Who said? Who said?!!!"

"You, yourself, said it!" tearfully shouted back little Marina, completely overcome by this playacting.[5]

Marina Tsvetaeva was the same age as the General's wife. During the civil war she had burned with hatred toward Communism and her best poems were devoted to the courageous feats of the White struggle in south Russia. The Russian émigrés were divided in their attitude toward this poet. She was a stranger to the rightists, who were intimidated by her rebellious spirit and contempt for bourgeois security, while the leftists saw in her the "bard of the White Dream." [6] For Tsvetaeva, Denikin was one of the greats, along with Kornilov, Markov, Alekseev.

She suddenly decided to go back to Russia in 1939, two years after Kuprin had returned there. Anton Ivanovich did not pass judgment on either of his friends, but he was infinitely sad. He grieved at their having taken what he considered to be a very rash decision.

Marina Tsvetaeva went to Russia to rejoin her daughter and her husband, Sergei Efron, who had gone over to the Bolsheviks. A short time later, her husband was shot and the daughter exiled to Siberia. During World War II, in a moment of total solitude and despair, Marina Tsvetaeva hung herself. Twenty years later, when a volume of her selected poems was printed posthumously in the Soviet Union, the former "bard of the White Dream" became a loved and revered poet in her native country.

As for Kuprin (whose stories and novels in the early years of this century created a sensation in Russia), ill health and sclerosis of the brain had weakened both his body and his mind in the 1930's. Kuprin's material situation became desperate. At the same time, the Soviet embassy in Paris was promising him and his wife a peaceful and secure life in a rest home for writers near Moscow.

In late spring of 1937, Kuprin came to the Denikins' apartment. The General's wife remembers vividly how he walked without a word toward Anton Ivanovich's room, seated himself on a chair next to the desk, looked at the General a long time in silence and suddenly burst out crying with the abandonment of a little child. Then the door to the room was closed, and Xenia Vasilievna could only hear Kuprin's voice, and after that, her husband's. After a while, Anton Ivanovich politely accompanied his visitor as far as the staircase. "What's happened?" asked his astonished wife. "He's going back to Russia," answered Anton Ivanovich shortly.

Soon after this, the Denikins learned from the papers that the Kuprins had left for Moscow at the end of May. In actual fact, it was the wife who took away her sick and helpless husband. He died there peacefully a year later.[7]

Anton Ivanovich gave a short description of his life in France in a letter to General A. M. Dragomirov dated May 17, 1928:

We came to France in the spring of 1926. Our life here began inauspiciously— my wife had to undergo an operation as soon as we arrived. In general, during these two years, as in the preceding ones, she has been in constant ill health. We have changed doctors, systems, and regimens, but without much success. Marina and I are in good health, praise God. We have settled down permanently in Vanves. It is not quite the hole you think it is. Vanves is a suburb of Paris, only ten minutes away by train from the Gare Montparnasse. My wife has learned to make hats, I continue to write—an occupation which, in our refugee situation, is paid less well than factory labor. I am presently at work on sketches describing life in the old army. It is absolutely necessary to devote one of these sketches to the memory of M. I. Dragomirov.[8] I would be most grateful if you could provide me with materials.

Marina is growing and studies very well. She is at the head of her class at the French school.

To be exact we spend about seven months a year in Vanves. We sublet our apartment in the summer and move to the country—south to the ocean, where life is quieter and cheaper and the air is wonderfully pure. Our village is called Cap-Breton. The poet Balmont resides there permanently, and Shmelev, in the summer, so that, as you see, the fraternity of writers is well represented.[9]

By that time, Denikin could legitimately consider himself a member of the "fraternity of writers." The year 1928 saw the publication of his book *Ofitsery* (*The Officers*), a collection of stories in which the author described the various stages through which Russian officers had been fated to pass, beginning with the army's disintegration after the revolution and continuing with the tragedy of the civil war.

The book was well received by the critics of the Russian press abroad. The newspaper *Dni* (organ of the Socialist Revolutionary party, edited in Berlin by A. F. Kerensky), which usually attacked Denikin, broke precedent by unexpectedly reprinting one of his tales, with the following foreword:

The Paris publishing house Rodnik is bringing out a moderate-sized book of fiction stories by A. Denikin, entitled *The Officers*. We are not proposing to criticize this book from an artistic point of view. But the author's name has such significance and popularity, is so bound with history, that we wish to acquaint our readers with this apparently fortuitous aspect of activity of the most prominent participant in the White movement. For this reason, we are printing today, with the publisher's permission, an excerpt from the story "Vragi" ("Enemies"), which aroused our interest by the wholeness of its conciliatory spirit and by its sustained psychological approach.[10]

Even Trotsky, on the eve of his exile from the Soviet Union, ironically noted that the vagaries of fate had taught some Russian émigré generals, such as General Denikin, how to wield a pen.

Both Kerensky and Trotsky, however, were mistaken in implying that Denikin's authorship was a casual sideline, forgetting that even before World War I, his articles and short stories had appeared regularly in military publications.

The Russian émigré newspaper *Za Svobodu,* established in Warsaw by B. V. Savinkov and later edited by Dmitri Filosofov, said in its review of Denikin's latest book, "Should future historians, strategists, and politicians fail to recognize Denikin as an outstanding military leader, the literary critics will gladly welcome him to the fold of unquestionably talented writers."

While these opinions were being voiced, Anton Ivanovich was already at work on *Staraia Armia* (*The Old Army*), a valuable and informative book which was published a year later.

XXXV

INVOLVEMENT
FROM A DISTANCE

Denikin kept an attentive eye on the life of the Russian émigrés in France. They were predominantly educated people, and Denikin noted, in a series of letters to friends, the dignity and simplicity with which they resigned themselves to menial work—in factories and mines, as Paris taxi drivers, and the like. On the other hand, he was irritated by the behavior of former Russian political figures who, entrenched in a series of separate, antagonistic circles, had apparently learned very little from the bitter lessons of the past, and instead of seeking unity, continued to quarrel and settle old political debts.

Their discord made a painful impression on Denikin. Engrossed by his writing activity, he stayed away from "émigré squabbles." He also remained aloof from the Russian Armed Services Union organized by General Wrangel, and from the entourage of Grand Duke Nicholas.

Because of his personal relationship with Kutepov, Denikin knew about the underground work going on in Russia. Kutepov confidentially discussed his activity with him, occasionally seeking his advice, and the more Denikin learned about this work, the more worried he became. And although Kutepov's activity did not actually involve Denikin, it was to play, indirectly, an important role in his life.

Denikin respected Kutepov as a straightforward and courageous man and an excellent combat officer, but he questioned his ability to cope with the tortuous problems of underground activity and political conspiracy, for which he had neither experience nor inclination. Denikin feared that the Soviet secret police would succeed in infiltrating their opponent's organization with its own agents.

What actually happened, however, surpassed his darkest premonitions.

The GPU not only succeeded in introducing its agents into ROVS and eventually placing them in key positions there, but managed to create a legend and inveigle many émigrés and even foreign intelligence agencies (British, Polish, Finnish, Baltic, Rumanian, and the French Sûreté) into believing that a secret, closely knit, and vast underground monarchist organization existed in Russia, and that its members had infiltrated important positions in Soviet government bureaus for the purpose of sabotage. The said organization was purportedly preparing a *coup d'état* and wished to secure the cooperation of foreign powers and the political representatives of the Russian émigrés, and most of all, the assistance of the Russian Armed Services Union.

This ostensibly monarchist organization, named Trust, was actually dreamed up by the GPU's top management—Dzerzhinsky, Artuzov, Pillar. They picked their agents for it with utmost care from among the representatives of Russia's prerevolutionary ruling classes. By subjecting them to a preliminary workout in the torture chambers of the GPU and threatening them with the possibility of reprisals against their families, the Soviet secret police succeeded in acquiring obedient instruments for carrying out their delicate and complex machinations abroad.

Forty years later (in the mid-1960's) detailed information about this carefully thought out provocation appeared for the first time in the Soviet press. The functions of Trust were "to intercept the channels" through which foreign intelligence agencies and White émigrés maintained communications with Russia; to transform these "into a sort of window" for keeping an eye on the plans of Soviet Russia's enemies and misinforming foreign intelligence departments; and by clever masquerading, to penetrate in depth the émigré circles, "stimulate their distrust of each other, incite mutual suspicion, instigate quarrels." But the first and foremost assignment of Trust was to neutralize the militant enthusiasm of Kutepov's organization by convincing its leaders that "terrorism and subversive activities" would interfere with the underground organization inside Russia,[1] which was, of course, totally mythical.

An underground monarchist organization did indeed exist in Moscow and Leningrad at that time. Known as the Monarchist Organization of Central Russia, or MOCR, it was not large, and presented no real danger to the Soviet regime. Having infiltrated it with its agents, the GPU arrested its most prominent members, among them A. A. Iákushev, but did this with such secrecy and skill that no one knew about it. By threats and pressure, the GPU completely subjected these people to its will. From then on, the Communists had ringside seats within the organization. However, the GPU left the nucleus of the organization unmolested, not for internal but for external reasons, in order to maintain the legend and be able to fool any "inspectors" from abroad and remain informed of their plans; and also in order to pass out false information to representatives of foreign intelligence agencies.

In the early 1920's, Trust—i.e., the GPU, which controlled it—sent Iákushev abroad, first alone and later in the company of a general of the old army, N. M. Potápov. The latter had quite openly gone over to the Soviets from the first day of the October revolution, and in the present instance, apparently agreed without any coercion to deceive his old acquaintances and colleagues in exile.

Communications between the emissaries of Trust and émigré underground organizations and foreign intelligence agencies continued for about five years, from November, 1922 to April, 1927. Iákushev and Potápov traveled abroad under assumed names, after being thoroughly prepared for their roles by the GPU's foreign department. They had been provided with plausible explanations of the circumstances which allowed them to leave Russia. Their primary assignment was to establish liaison with Kutepov's organization and with foreign intelligence agencies, and by gaining their confidence, to concentrate in the hands of the GPU all the threads of the foreign network leading into Russia.

Because of their careers in tsarist times, the two emissaries of Trust knew many of the most prominent émigrés. Potápov had attended the Academy of the General Staff at the same time as Wrangel and was able to secure a personal interview with him. Iákushev not only held discussions with Kutepov, but was received by Grand Duke Nicholas.

These interviews and discussions, however, did not prove that the people who had arrived from "over there" were completely trusted. The émigrés wanted to believe that a considerable anti-Soviet organization existed in Russia. Nevertheless, there was a great deal about Iákushev and Potápov which aroused suspicion both in Wrangel and Kutepov. The facility with which they left Russia and returned there appeared suspicious, as well as the ease with which they later managed, without the knowledge of the GPU, to smuggle in and out, across the Soviet border, some of Kutepov's agents of whose arrival they had been warned in advance. The émigrés considered that Potápov was a somewhat unprincipled opportunist. Finally, the very fact of such a protracted and safe existence of a large underground organization inside Russia was in itself suspicious.

At the beginning of 1926, Trust arranged a trip through Russia for V. V. Shulgin, the same Shulgin who, together with Guchkov, had come to the last Tsar to ask for his abdication. Shulgin was immensely impressed by the power of the "underground" organization. He was convinced that Trust's agents had protected him from the all-seeing eye of the GPU, and upon his return and at Iákushev's insistence, described his journey in a book which he entitled *Tri Stolitsy* (*The Three Capitals*) because he had traveled to Kiev, Moscow, and Leningrad.

In permitting, or rather, prompting, Shulgin to relate his experiences, the GPU had overlooked one essential fact: The book not only praised the "all-powerful Trust," but by its naïve disclosure of its unhampered activity within a police state, opened the eyes of émigré organizations and foreign intelligence agencies to the fact that they had been the victims of a colossal hoax perpetrated by the GPU.

Kutepov had not shown all his cards in dealing with Potápov and Iákushev. But in order not to arouse their suspicions, and in order to make use of Trust for his own organization's ends, Kutepov considered it necessary to give Iákushev and Potápov a modicum of what he considered to be nonessential information.

From Denikin's point of view this information was far from harmless. We find a note on this affair, which was to achieve widespread publicity later, in his unpublished papers:

Kutepov kept me informed of the overall aspects of his work. Having complete confidence in me, he was not afraid of naming names, which I stopped him from doing—as such frankness is inadmissible in this game. Though I thus limited my own knowledge in the matter, I was made increasingly uncomfortable by what Aleksandr Pavlovich [Kutepov] told me. And once I said to him frankly, "I don't believe it. It all looks like provocation to me," to which Kutepov replied, "But I am taking no risks. I tell 'them' nothing, but only listen to what 'they' are saying."

Eventually, this turned out to have been not quite true. . . . The risk had been considerable—as it involved the lives of the active agents.

. . . Two circumstances completely opened my eyes to the Bolshevik provocation: Shulgin's book *Tri Stolitsy* and the episode with General Mónkewitz.

Kutepov, who knew my housing problems, advised me to sublet Mónkewitz's apartment in Fontainebleau where he [Kutepov] and his family had spent the summer. While we corresponded on the matter, the apartment had already been let. I went to Fontainebleau and leased a different house [this was in the fall of 1926]. I soon met General Mónkewitz, who lived in the town with his daughter. Their clothing, domestic articles, and modest spending allowance, all testified to their great poverty. . . .

A few days later, General Mónkewitz's children, his daughter and the son, whom I had not met before, came to us in a highly emotional state. They showed me a note from their father, who wrote that he was committing suicide because of his financial entanglements. But in order not to burden his family with funeral expenses, he would take his life in such a way that his body would never be found.

All I felt at the time was distress and pity. The doubts came later. . . . Mónkewitz's daughter asked permission to transfer to our house her father's secret papers concerning the Kutepov organization (she knew that I was informed of this matter), as they had not yet paid the landlady for the apartment to which they had recently moved, and she could attach all their belongings. Besides, the police might be involved, in view of the suicide. I agreed. Five or six suitcases were brought to us piecemeal and dumped in the dining room. My wife took to the post office my telegram in which I advised Kutepov of what happened and asked him to arrive immediately and "pick up his belongings." But it was only two days later that Colonel Zaitsov [Kutepov's closest assistant in his conspiratorial work] arrived and removed the papers, in two or three trips. Through Zaitsov, I invited Kutepov for the second time to come for a talk with me.

The point of the matter was that wishing to protect at least the most important documents from a possible search by the French police, my wife and I had spent all of twenty-four hours sorting the papers. Besides current correspondence of little interest, the archive contained the entire correspondence with Trust. . . .

As I had looked through this, my horror had mounted at the clearness with which the Bolshevik provocation leapt to the eyes. The letters from "over there" were filled with unrestrained flattery on Kutepov's behalf: "You and only you will save Russia; among us your name alone enjoys popularity, which is growing and expanding," etc. Trust expressed itself with restraint and even haughtiness in regard to Grand Duke Nicholas Nikolaevich, and with irony concerning General Wrangel. They described how spectacularly their membership grew and Trust's activity expanded; there had allegedly been a secret meeting of several hundred members at some unspecified spot, in the course of which Kutepov had been elected as either honorary member or honorary chairman. . . . They reiterated their request for money and, above all, information.

Unfortunately, as he believed in Trust's genuine anti-Bolshevism, Kutepov periodically informed it, rather frankly and in detail, concerning the affairs of the émigrés, their organizations, and the relationship between them. Among other things, there was an urgent query from "over there" as to the meaning of General Denikin's arrival in Paris for the Markov Regiment's reunion and the celebrations connected with it. And a copy of Kutepov's answer to the effect that this had no political significance, as the Volunteers simply wished to greet their former commander in chief. Generally speaking, Trust showed a great deal of curiosity, which was, alas, very recklessly satisfied. . . . I cannot, even now, reveal everything I read in that sinister correspondence. . . . [This account is not dated, but it was undoubtedly written in the very early 1930's.]

Among other things, we discovered a fact of a purely personal nature, which testified to Kutepov's unbounded confidence in Trust, but was extremely painful for us.

At this point, Anton Ivanovich related an incident concerning his father-in-law. His wife's father, Vassili Ivanovich Chizh, had remained in Russia. He lived in the Crimea and had a modest position with the railroad. "So far, no one had molested him—an old and destitute man, or knew who he was." The Denikins conceived the idea of bringing him to France, and Anton Ivanovich asked Kutepov to find out through his organization whether this could be done and how much it would cost, specifying at the same time that only the man's age and geographical location could be mentioned, but that his name and relationship with the Denikins was on no condition to be revealed.

Imagine our distress [wrote the General] when I read in Kutepov's letter addressed to Trust, that "Denikin is asking for information regarding the cost of bringing his father-in-law from Yalta"!

There was no further news from the father-in-law until, several years later, the Denikins learned the date of his death from a relative who had managed to leave Russia. Anton Ivanovich took up with Kutepov the matter of this indiscretion.

Kutepov was embarrassed, but refused to give in. He assured me that he had "channels" and "windows" * that were not connected and did not even know each other, and that he had already severed all relations with the channel by which Shulgin had traveled.[2]

To cross the frontier to the Soviet Union and later return from it, it was necessary to use "windows" on both sides of the border. These were established by Trust on the Soviet side, and by representatives of foreign intelligence agencies on the opposite side. In Finland, the Baltic countries, and Poland, this responsibility belonged to local officers of the General Staff who had formerly served in the imperial army, were fluent in Russian, and were personally known to Kutepov. With their knowledge, Kutepov had met on their territory with emissaries of Trust. The following, related by Kutepov, was noted down by Denikin: "Meeting in Finland with Iákushev and others. They drove him [Kutepov] to the Russian border 'to have a look, if only from a distance, at his homeland.' . . . Another time, they proposed a meeting at the Russo-Polish frontier. . . ." As Denikin listened to this tale, he was appalled by Kutepov's "tragic naïveté" in the realm of conspiratorial activity; he warned him that the meetings were not being arranged at the Russian border without a reason, but were for the purpose of first taking Kutepov off his guard by sweet-sounding phrases, and then dragging him to "the other side" by force.[3]

By that time it was clear that the tentacles of the GPU had penetrated into all the underground organizations in Russia. Neither the monarchists, nor the Socialist Revolutionaries were able to escape them.

The experienced conspirator Boris Savinkov believed that he had trustworthy contacts "over there." But after being subjected to torture in Soviet prisons, these "trustworthy" persons enticed him into Russia and handed him over to the GPU. The same thing happened to the well-known British agent Sidney Reilly, to Prince Pavel Dolgorukov, and to many others.

The Bolsheviks decided to make use of Savinkov for propaganda purposes. His case marked the beginning of the stage-directed trials which later became so numerous and familiar, in which the accused unfailingly repented his political sins against Soviet authority and professed that he had at last recognized the wisdom and justice of the Communist regime. Churchill wrote that the Soviet government had succeeded in trampling to the ground Savinkov's proud soul, blackening his memory, dishonoring him in the eyes of his former friends, and branding him with the mark of Judas Iscariot.[4]

Denikin left the following unpublished notes concerning this matter: "In

* By "windows" Kutepov meant certain points along the Soviet border where his agents, at a prearranged time, could be smuggled in and out of the Soviet Union.

the Moscow tribunal, during his staged trial, Savinkov voiced some extremely harsh judgments about me and the government of south Russia; about how he lectured us and "made demands." He also related that Churchill shared in his indignation against us. . . . I had, at first, the desire to make public certain documents in refutation of his statements, but later thought better of it: Why harm a man who is doomed." [5]

At the beginning of May, 1925, Savinkov committed suicide in a Moscow prison. Such was, in any case, the official version of the Communist press.

It was difficult to expect that the secret organizations of the émigrés would escape being infiltrated by Soviet agents. One of the first to be suspected of having played that role was General Mónkewitz, who had been in charge of communications with Trust in Kutepov's organization and who disappeared, leaving a note saying that he was going to commit suicide because of financial difficulties. Mónkewitz's body was never found, and a number of people, including S. P. Melgunov, at first suspected and later became certain, that he had fled to Soviet Russia. No one, however, has ever been able either to prove or to disprove this theory.[6] The identity of the other agents was not yet known, but a few years later, under General Kutepov's successor, they were to play a decisive role in the affairs of the Russian Armed Services Union.

Kutepov, however, had his own "windows" into Russia which had never been revealed to the agents of Trust. He decided, therefore, on a drastic course of action in order to rehabilitate himself and his organization. Soon it became known in the Soviet Union and abroad that Kutepov's agents had thrown a bomb into the central club of the Communist party in Leningrad, and a while later, they threw a second bomb, into the GPU headquarters at the Lubianka in Moscow.

In April, 1928, General Wrangel died in Brussels at the age of forty-nine, and was succeeded as chairman of the Russian Armed Services Union by Kutepov. Wrangel's death was followed, in January of the following year, by that of Grand Duke Nicholas. General Lukomsky, who was in close touch with the Grand Duke, told Denikin later that Nicholas Nikolaevich "had been grievously disappointed in the mission he had undertaken." [7]

After the Grand Duke's death, General Kutepov became the sole head of the Russian émigré military organization. He knew that he was constantly shadowed by Soviet agents, but refused to have bodyguards, believing that he had no right to deplete the modest funds at his disposal by that extra expense. Nevertheless, at the insistence of the former Volunteers (who had organized the Gallipoli Association in memory of the White Army's sojourn on that peninsula after its evacuation), he consented to use the services of his former war comrades, many of whom had become taxi drivers in Paris, and they now took turns transporting him around the city and its environs during the week. He did not wish to burden them with extra work on Sundays, and this decision contributed to his tragic end.

A year later, all the world's major newspapers, except those in the Soviet Union, broadcast the news that on January 26, 1930, in broad daylight, in Paris, General Kutepov disappeared without leaving a trace. Headlines in *The New York Times* stated, "Leader of Russians in exile disappears. White organization officers in Paris believe he has been assassinated. French borders watched. Koutiepoff vanishes in daylight while on a short walk to his headquarters." [8]

No one doubted that this was the work of the Bolsheviks. The French papers were indignant; many of them demanded the severance of diplomatic relations with Moscow.

On Sunday, January 26, at 10:30 A.M. General Kutepov left his Paris apartment on rue Rousselet, after telling his wife that he was going to the church of the Gallipoli Association on rue Mademoiselle, and would be home for lunch at one o'clock. He never came back.

On the strength of the testimony of various witnesses, the French police were able to establish with exactitude all the stages of General Kutepov's kidnapping, his removal from France, and the involvement of Soviet agents in this affair. Unfortunately, the investigation was excessively long, and by the time it was ended, the French government preferred to hush up the matter rather than risk a break with the Soviet Union.

On January 28, according to one witness, two cars, a gray-green Alfa Romeo and a red Renault taxicab, were parked at the corner of rue Rousselet and rue Oudinot; three men, one of them wearing the uniform of the French police, stood next to the cars. At about 11 A.M., a man of medium height with a neatly trimmed black beard, wearing a dark overcoat and a felt hat, appeared on the street. Suddenly, one of the three men grabbed his right hand, another his left hand, and in spite of his struggles, pushed him into the gray-green car, while the policeman sprang into the seat next to the chauffeur, after which both cars took off in the direction of the Boulevard des Invalides. Upon being shown a photograph of General Kutepov, the witness identified him as the man with the black beard. A second witness also testified to seeing the struggle which took place in the gray-green automobile. Both witnesses had felt reassured by the presence of the "policeman" and concluded that a routine arrest was taking place. On the Alma bridge, where both cars were held up in traffic, a woman saw one of the passengers of the gray-green Alfa Romeo hold a handkerchief to the face of his neighbor, and a policeman jump down from the front seat and begin directing the traffic in order to let the automobile through. She asked what the trouble was with the man in the car and was told by the "policeman" that the unfortunate fellow's legs had been crushed in a traffic accident and they were giving him ether to deaden the pain. Both cars, with the "policeman" in the lead one, were later observed by various passersby on roads leading to the Normandy coast. And finally, at about four o'clock that afternoon, a pair of lovers concealed in the dunes and brush of Falaises des Vaches Noires, between Cabourg and Trouville, were fascinated by the arrival of two cars on that deserted beach. One was gray-green and the other a red taxi. The couple also noticed a motorboat cruising near the shore and a steamer standing at anchor in the distance. As soon as the automobiles arrived, the motorboat headed for the beach, but it was obliged to stop a few paces away from it. Then the two men, the "policeman," and a "woman in a beige overcoat" hoisted to their shoulders a large oblong object covered with sacking, waded into the water and laid it on the bottom of the boat, into which the two civilians also sprang. The motorboat took off at full speed toward the steamship, which raised anchor and left as soon as the occupants of the boat and their mysterious cargo had been lifted on board. The ship proved to be the *Spartak,* a Soviet vessel which had unexpectedly left Le Havre on the preceding day. The two cars, with the pseudo-policeman and the "woman in the beige overcoat," quickly drove off in the direction of Paris.

A private investigation into the Kutepov affair was conducted by Vladimir Burtsev, formerly a member of the Russian revolutionary movement, who had become an émigré during the tsarist regime, and who later lent his support to Denikin and Kolchak during the civil war. Burtsev, made famous by his exposure of Azef, head of the terrorist organization of the Socialist Revoluntionary party as *agent provocateur* of the tsarist secret police, now directed all his energy to solving the Kutepov mystery. He got in touch privately with a certain Fechner, who had just defected from the post of "resident GPU agent" in Berlin and was hiding somewhere in Germany. Fechner had been kept informed about the Kutepov affair, and gave Burtsev the names of four people who had been in charge of Kutepov's kidnapping. The most important of these were Vladimir B. Ianovich and Lev B. Helfand, two GPU agents attached to the Soviet embassy in France. Both of them disappeared from Paris immediately after the kidnapping. Subsequently, their names were constantly linked with General Kutepov's abduction, both in the Russian émigré and in the foreign-language press.[9]

While Ianovich fell victim to Stalin's purges in the 1930's, Helfand had better luck. The interesting fact is that this man (a nephew of the notorious Helfand-Parvus who was instrumental in arranging Lenin's passage to Russia through Germany in 1917) gained political asylum in the United States, promptly adopted a new name, became a prosperous businessman in New York, and in the 1960's died a natural death, although as a rule the GPU skillfully exterminated former agents who defected to the side of its ideological enemies (Walter Krivitsky slain in Washington, Ignatz Reisz slain in Lausanne, and so on).

After the Kutepov abduction, Helfand made a successful career in the Soviet foreign service, and during the period of the Hitler-Stalin pact, was Soviet chargé d'affaires in Rome. There, in July, 1940, with the help of Mussolini's son-in-law, Count Ciano, who was then the Italian Foreign

Minister, and with the assistance of the American embassy in Rome, Helfand succeeded in leaving secretly for the United States, under the pretext that he might be liquidated in Moscow.[10] Doubtless, Helfand had to repay America's hospitality by sharing some of his secret knowledge with United States intelligence agencies. But it is unlikely that it ever occurred to the latter to question him regarding his role in the Kutepov affair. In any event, Helfand died taking with him the secrets he could have divulged with regard to the Paris crime.

The first admission of the role played by the Soviet government in the Kutepov abduction appeared in the Moscow press in 1965, in *Krasnaia Gazeta*.[11] Yet, the General's ultimate fate remains a mystery to this day. Kutepov's doctor, the well-known surgeon Professor I. A. Aleksinsky, affirmed that because of severe chest wounds sustained in the war, his patient could not endure the effects of anesthesia, and therefore, the application of ether or chloroform by his captors, combined with bodily struggle and emotion, must unquestionably have led to his death.[12]

Denikin was deeply affected by the Kutepov tragedy: "A feeling of profound grief overcame me when the alarming news of Aleksandr Pavlovich's disappearance reached us. I knew in my heart that the matter was hopeless. . . . Death and physical suffering are nothing compared to the horror of moral torture of a man fallen in the clutches of the GPU. . . . If Kutepov perished, it was not at the right post or on the right job. . . . Burtsev asserts that he is already dead. And I think so too." [13]

XXXVI

SOVIET AGENTS

———————

Unknown to most people, and quite independently of Kutepov and his activity, there existed a small "intimate anti-Bolshevik organization" of which (by his own admission) Denikin himself was a member.[1]

Even later, he remained very reticent on this subject. However, his mention of S. P. Melgunov as one of the participants in certain "meetings," connects the General with the Melgunov Committee, whose activity Melgunov revealed years later (in 1955) in a series of newspaper articles entitled "Zagadki v Dele Generala Kutepova" ("The Mysteries of the Kutepov Affair").

I was in no way related to the work of the Kutepov organization in Russia [wrote Melgunov]. "My connections with Aleksandr Pavlovich [Kutepov] were limited to receiving . . . information which reached him through the diplomats of a border country, to the obligation undertaken by Kutepov of conveying across the border a certain number of copies of *Bor'ba za Rossiu* [an anti-Communist periodical published by Melgunov in Paris], and to my participation in a committee created for the specific purpose of collecting funds and apportioning them among organizations actively involved in fighting Bolshevism. This committee included Pavel O. Gukasov, whose name carried weight with industrialists, Generals A. I. Denikin and A. P. Kutepov, A. P. Markov [Milyukov's closest collaborator at the time], M. M. Fedorov, and myself.[2]

For those who contributed money toward anti-Bolshevik activity, the names of Denikin and Melgunov guaranteed the integrity of the persons entrusted with allocating the funds collected by the committee.

However, the "intimate organization" had a wider scope than that described by Melgunov. Both he and Denikin proved to have been quite competent conspirators. Whatever notes Anton Ivanovich may have kept concerning this matter were carefully destroyed by him. More or less the same thing happened to Melgunov's archive, later donated by his widow to the London School of Economics. Studies made of this archive point to the extreme caution exercised by Melgunov. Nevertheless, they hint at activity of considerable importance which came to a sudden and unexpected halt in 1930.[3]

Undoubtedly it ceased when the infiltration of all Russian émigré organizations by Soviet agents became evident, as was painfully illustrated by the Kutepov affair. "In 1930, disappointed in émigré politics, my wife and I moved to the country and became farmers," wrote Melgunov.[4] In the fall of 1930, Denikin decided to follow their example. His close relationship with Melgunov at that time prompted him to join the latter at his farm in St. Piat, near Chartres. Melgunov's extensive historical library, which he placed at Anton Ivanovich's disposal, was an added attraction. But as often happens, sharing one small kitchen became a strain for the two housewives; furthermore, Sergei Petrovich Melgunov, though an honorable and decent man, proved difficult and quite unpleasant in domestic life. In short, as soon as the Denikins found an opportunity to move elsewhere, in the spring of 1931, both ménages drew a sigh of relief, although the respect of the two men for each other remained unchanged.

After Kutepov's kidnapping, people close to General Denikin became worried for his personal safety. He knew too much. His participation in Melgunov's "intimate organization" was bound to be known to the Bolsheviks as a result of the close watch they had been keeping on Kutepov, who also was a member of the Melgunov Committee. Moreover, the very name of Denikin was a constant irritant to the Soviets. Among those who worried most about him was N. I. Astrov, to one of whose letters the former replied, "As regards safety . . . it is in doubt everywhere. God will keep me."[5] And this time Denikin's trust in Providence was justified, as only chance saved the General, who never took any precautions, from the fate that befell Kutepov and the man who succeeded him at the head of the Russian Armed Services Union.

As we have seen, General Kutepov had kept Denikin informed of that organization's activity. After his disappearance, Denikin had no further communication with ROVS.

I am in a rather delicate position in regard to the Russian Armed Services Union [he wrote to Astrov as early as April, 1930]. Generally speaking, the *mere fact of my existence* is apt to make its leaders nervous, which was particularly true of the late baron [Wrangel], and any expression of goodwill toward me on the part of the Volunteers was cause for worry. . . . In order not to create difficulties for the "authorities" and not to undermine the Union, I not only abstain from criticism, but despite my sympathy for them, have reduced to the minimum my relationship with the military organizations. To such an extent, that it is being said there that "the General is keeping away and has lost interest in us."[6]

General Kutepov's successor—General Evgenii Karlovich Miller, the former leader of the White movement in the north of Russia—had previously occupied a post as treasurer and first assistant to the chairman of the Russian Armed Services Union. He was a tactful, restrained, and careful man of conservative views. His service in the army had been spent in administrative and staff work remote from combat action and he was thus a complete stranger to most of the ROVS members, who had participated in the civil war in the south of Russia. Their somewhat skeptical attitude in relation to him further complicated the already confused situation in ROVS, which had been shaken to its foundations by the Kutepov tragedy. Miller accepted the leadership of the Union against his personal wishes, feeling that as his predecessor's senior associate, he had a duty to do so. His immediate aim was to keep the organization from breaking up. He had to act with extreme caution.

Denikin had met Miller only after coming to Paris, and their relationship was limited to occasional casual conversations and encounters at official gatherings.

One such gathering, in 1937, was organized to celebrate the twentieth anniversary of the Kornilov Regiment. It was an important event in the life of the émigrés, so many of whom had served in the White armies and revered the memory of General Kornilov. It was to be marked by two church services: vespers, followed by a requiem for those who fell in the anti-Bolshevik struggle; and a *Te Deum,* with massing of the colors and prayers for all those who had remained alive. The first was to take place on Saturday evening, September 18, in the church of the Gallipoli Association; and the second, on the morning of September 19, following the liturgy, at the St. Alexander Nevsky cathedral on rue Daru. There were also to be an anniversary meeting and a banquet at the Gallipoli Association, at which General Denikin was to be the guest of honor.

Denikin had spent the summer of 1937 in the village of Mimizan (Landes) on the Atlantic coast, where his family still remained to enjoy the warm autumn days. He had come up to Paris for a few days only—to attend the Kornilov celebration and to put the apartment in order, before returning to Mimizan and bringing his wife and daughter back to Paris.

The organizer of the Kornilov celebration was Nikolai Vladimirovich Skoblin. Having joined the Volunteer Army with the rank of captain, Skoblin took part in all its campaigns, became commander of the Kornilov division under Denikin, and was promoted to the rank of major general by Wrangel in 1920. He was a brave but ruthless man; ambition and the thirst for promotion and success predominated in him over the ideological aspects of the struggle. Skoblin's wife, Nadezhda Vasilievna Plevitskaia, was born in a peasant family. Her outstanding voice, innate artistry, and remarkable interpretation of folk songs had brought her fame, wealth, and the honorary title of Soloist to His Majesty.[7] During the civil war Plevitskaia remained in the Soviet zone, performing for the troops of the Red Army front against Denikin, where her second husband served as an officer. In the fall of 1919, they were both taken prisoner by the Kornilov division which Skoblin commanded. Plevitskaia divorced her second husband and married her captor in Gallipoli in 1921. Skoblin, who was seven years younger than his wife (he was forty-five in 1937), fell completely under her spell. Though uneducated and almost illiterate, she was extremely intelligent and a consummate actress; her talent allowed her to assume the guise of a helpless, trusting, and kindly woman, when in reality she was as hard as flint, coldly calculating, and devoid of any compassion. Her true nature only became evident, however, when the goal she and her husband were pursuing was almost within reach, and a mere hazard disclosed their role in a crime that made headlines throughout Europe.

Unlike his former fellow Volunteers, Skoblin was not unduly burdened by the effort to make a living. Most of his time was spent in traveling, allegedly as his wife's agent and accountant, to the various countries where she gave concerts. She still enjoyed great success in the early 1920's, especially in the Baltic countries, where Russian was a familiar language and the memory of her former triumphs was fresh. In 1927, she and her husband toured the United States, and at a Russian benefit in New York's Plaza Hotel, Sergei Rachmaninoff himself unexpectedly volunteered to play her accompaniment. This gesture contributed greatly to Plevitskaia's success in America. But by the end of the 1920's it became common knowledge in the Russian colony of Paris that Plevitskaia's concert engagements were becoming scarce and that the Skoblins were in financial straits. Then, suddenly, everything changed, and they were once more flush with money, though the source of this affluence was unknown. The Skoblins bought a fine two-story house at Ozoir-la-Ferrière, fifty minutes by train from the Gare de l'Est in Paris. They acquired a car, spent several days a week in a Paris hotel, and assiduously cultivated friendships in the milieux connected with the Russian Armed Services Union and the Gallipoli Association. Their unexpected and unexplained affluence appeared suspect, especially at a time when the disastrous economic depression in America and Western Europe had affected many of Skoblin's former colleagues. But human nature being what it is, the Skoblins' sweeping hospitality did much to blunt undue curiosity and silence gossiping tongues, even if the host's conversation sometimes struck his guests as strange. Skoblin hinted that Miller was totally inactive, afraid of his own shadow, and that it was time to replace the old armchair general with a young and energetic combat officer. Skoblin's not-too-subtle intriguing left little doubt as to his personal ambition to climb to the top of the Russian Armed Services Union.

Yet, strange though it may seem, General Miller, who had ample reason to question Skoblin's integrity, chose to entrust him with a very responsible post. ROVS contained a secret section, known as the Inner Line, which had two main functions. On the one hand, it kept under observation the members of the Russian Armed Services Union, as well as other émigrés, suspected of pro-Soviet sympathies. On the other hand, it selected trustworthy agents for the Outer Line, whose activity took place in Russia. In 1935, General Miller put Skoblin in charge of the Inner Line. Within a short time, however, this move elicited a disturbing reaction from the governments of some peripheral states. Finland's military intelligence informed Miller, through the representative of ROVS in Helsinki, that it suspected Skoblin of being in contact with the GPU. Rumors of Skoblin's liaison with Soviet agents also began to circulate in the Russian colony of Paris. These various accusations against Skoblin were brought before a court of honor composed of senior generals, who having found no conclusive proof of Skoblin's guilt, were obliged to rehabilitate him. Nevertheless, at the end of 1936, Miller terminated Skoblin's work with the Inner Line. The fact remains, however, that even before the information from Finland, and the various disturbing rumors, had reached Miller, he was already in possession of sufficient evidence to be convinced that Skoblin was morally and politically suspect.

Such was the complicated and somewhat confusing situation of ROVS at the outset of the Kornilov celebration, whose official host was the ranking senior officer of the Kornilov Regiment, Major General Nikolai Vladimirovich Skoblin.

The periodical *Chasovoi,* published in Brussels by former officers of the White Army, announced in September that "this noteworthy event will be described in our next issue." But the next issue, in October, was to come out with the headline, "Criminal abduction of General Miller!" [8]

The solemn anniversary meeting took place at the headquarters of the Gallipoli Association on September 19, 1937. Skoblin presided at the center of the table, flanked on his right by General Denikin and on his left by General Miller.

Denikin's feelings toward Skoblin had been negative for a long time; he neither liked nor trusted him, but being out of touch with the business of ROVS, knew less about his activities than did General Miller. Having come to Paris to honor General Kornilov's memory, Denikin had made up his mind not to let his personal antipathy for Skoblin interfere with the celebration. He was happy at the thought of meeting with many of the "First Campaigners," who, with Kornilov, Alekseev, and himself, had set out from Rostov into the cold snowy steppe on the dark night of February 9, 1918. He also looked forward to seeing General Kornilov's daughter, Natalia Lavrovna Chaperon du Larré, who now lived with her husband in Brussels.

The anniversary celebration proceeded in an atmosphere of friendship and reminiscences, occasionally interspersed with speeches. The official part of the event ended on Sunday, September 19. But some of the honored guests from out of town lingered on. The Chaperon du Larrés were to return to Belgium on the afternoon of Wednesday, September 22, and for reasons of his own, Skoblin chose to see them off personally on that day, and after this, to make a series of calls on the senior commanders whom he wished to thank for taking part in the celebration.

Skoblin had prepared the day's schedule with utmost care, taking into account not only hours, but even minutes. There were to be no mistakes or miscalculations. All of his movements (except one) were to be observed by a whole series of people, who—should the need arise—could testify to his whereabouts for the entire day. Skoblin had to establish enough alibis and confuse his tracks sufficiently to cover up the hour and a half he needed to achieve his aim, and thus avoid being suspected of participating in the crime he was contemplating.

On Wednesday, September 22, General Miller, as was his custom, left his modest apartment in Boulogne shortly after 9 A.M. and proceeded to the offices of ROVS on 29 rue du Colisée. He carried a dark-brown briefcase under his arm. Around twelve noon, he left his office, after telling one of his assistants, General P. V. Kusonsky, that he had a business appointment in town and would then come back to the office. Before leaving, however, he gave Kusonsky some unusual instructions: Should he fail to return, Kusonsky was to open the sealed envelope he handed him and read its contents.

The envelope contained the following note: "Today I have an appointment at twelve thirty with General Skoblin at the corner of rue Jasmin and rue Raffet, and he must accompany me to a meeting with a German officer, Strohman, who is a military attaché with the peripheral states, and with Mr. Werner, who is on the staff of the local embassy. They both speak Russian well. The meeting is arranged at Skoblin's initiative. This may be a trap, and I am leaving this note just in case."

Miller's signature and the date followed.[9]

General Miller never returned from this meeting. As a result of the negligence of Kusonsky, who forgot all about it, the envelope was not opened until nearly eleven at night, after General Miller's wife, alarmed by her husband's failure to come home, had succeeded in reaching the employees of ROVS at their homes and demanded that the police be notified.

Miller's note dumbfounded Kusonsky and Admiral Kedrov, General Miller's deputy at the Russian Armed Services Union. The Admiral's wife was so alarmed by the late summons to the rue du Colisée that she accompanied her husband to the office, where one of the trusted officers of the organization also joined them. The officer was dispatched to Skoblin's hotel, without, however, being informed concerning the note left by

Miller. This turned out to have been a grave mistake. When the officer arrived at the hotel it was already nearly 1 A.M., and Skoblin and Plevitskaia had gone to bed. Skoblin took the news of Miller's disappearance quite calmly; got dressed, threw his black summer coat over his arm, and departed by taxi to the rue du Colisée with the officer who had come to fetch him. He calmly mounted the stairs and entered the ROVS office, leaving the officer and Admiral Kedrov's wife in the anteroom.

In the office, he was bombarded with questions by the overwrought Kusonsky and Kedrov. As he did not suspect the existence of the telltale note, Skoblin coolly replied that he had not seen General Miller since Sunday. He paled when the note was shown to him, and momentarily lost his self-control, but quickly recovered and continued to affirm that he had not seen Miller and that at twelve thirty he and his wife were lunching at a Russian restaurant, which could be confirmed by witnesses. Admiral Kedrov thereupon demanded that Skoblin and those present go to the police together. Before leaving, Kusonsky and Kedrov lingered behind to compare notes. Skoblin made the best of this brief delay. He left the office, passed by Kedrov's wife and the officer (who still knew nothing about Miller's note), and was the first to reach the staircase. When Kusonsky and Kedrov emerged from the ROVS office, Skoblin had disappeared. There was no trace of him either on the stairs or in the street.

That night he was seen in two other places. About 4 A.M., he came to a garage at the corner of boulevard de Pressbourg and the Porte des Ternes where his sister's husband was employed.[10] The brother-in-law was not there, and Skoblin left. The garage night watchman, to whom he spoke, later told the police that Skoblin was pale and disheveled. About fifteen minutes later, in Neuilly, he woke up the wife of a former Kornilov officer, greedily gulped a glass of water, and borrowed two hundred francs, saying that he had lost his wallet and was without a cent. Skoblin left after promising to return the money on the following day, and that was the last that was ever seen of him.

General Miller's disappearance created as much of a sensation in the press as that of General Kutepov, and caused great excitement in Paris.

The French authorities ordered all railroad stations, seaports, and border points watched, and distributed descriptions of Skoblin, who was to be detained on sight. But through no fault of theirs, it was already too late when these orders were issued. Nevertheless, through the testimony of witnesses, the French investigation succeeded in reconstructing the exact sequence and chronology of the events of September 22, 1937. In their broad outlines they were a replica of what had happened to Kutepov.

The investigation established that Miller's meeting with Skoblin took place in a district of Paris where the Soviet embassy owned and rented several houses for its agents and the employees of various Soviet missions. Within a block of the corner of rue Jasmin and rue Raffet stood the building which housed the school attended by the children of the embassy employees. At that time, the school was closed for the summer vacation. From the window of a nearby house a witness, who knew both Miller and Skoblin, saw them standing at the entrance of the empty school building. Skoblin gestured with his hand, apparently inviting Miller to enter. A third man, of solid build, also stood with them, but with his back turned to the witness. This was at approximately 12:50 P.M. About ten minutes later, a gray closed Ford truck drew up in front of the Soviet school. The same Ford truck, with diplomatic license plates, arrived at Le Havre at about 4 P.M. and parked on a dock next to the Soviet merchant ship *Maria Ulianova*. The car was covered with dust, and its windshield was splattered with traces of insects from rapid driving. (On a weekday, the 203 kilometers between Paris and Le Havre could easily be covered in three hours.) A heavy-looking wooden crate, approximately six feet long and two and a half feet wide, was unloaded from the truck with the help of four Soviet sailors, and carefully carried up the ship's gangplank. A short time later, the *Maria Ulianova* raised anchor and steamed into the open sea, without giving the customary warning to the port authorities, and before completing the unloading of her cargo, which consisted of sheepskins ordered by a firm in Bordeaux.

The port inspector, who happened to be visiting the *Maria Ulianova*'s captain on a matter of business, later told the police that during their conversation, a man hurriedly entered the captain's quarters and spoke to him in Russian, after which the captain cut their talk short, saying that he had received a radiogram ordering his immediate return to Leningrad. The inspector made a mental note that such orders are usually addressed to the agent of the maritime company and not directly to the ship's captain. As he left the steamer, he noticed the Ford truck and saw the large wooden crate being taken aboard. A check of the truck's diplomatic license showed that it had been purchased by the Soviet embassy a month before Miller's disappearance.

On the evening of the following day, France's Minister of National Defense, Édouard Daladier, summoned the Soviet ambassador. In view of the existence of damaging evidence and the uproar created in the press by General Miller's abduction, he asked the ambassador to demand the *Maria Ulianova*'s immediate return to France. The Soviet ambassador, however, was able to enlist the support of some members of the French cabinet (Vincent Auriol and Marx Dormoy), who were afraid that a major political crisis with Soviet Russia might be set off at a time of particularly strained relations with Germany, and they managed to have Daladier's demand revoked. Concurrently, Auriol (later President of France, then Minister of Justice) and Dormoy (Minister of the Interior), succeeded in temporarily reducing to silence the French officials at Le Havre.

Thus, because of political considerations, the official version of the French investigation bypassed the role of the Soviet embassy in the affair, and stressed Skoblin's role as the direct perpetrator of the kid-

napping. A careful study of his schedule on the day of the crime (corroborated by the questioning of numerous witnesses) uncovered an unexplained gap of an hour and a half which coincided exactly with the
time of Miller's appointment with Skoblin. Furthermore, Skoblin's flight
pointed to his guilt.

It was discovered later that Skoblin had been a Soviet agent since the
end of the 1920's, and had also been dealing with the German Gestapo.

A search of the Skoblin house established beyond doubt that Plevitskaia
was involved in the crime, and incidentally, revealed that her green-
bound "family Bible" contained the code for the ciphered correspondence
carried on by the couple. At Plevitskaia's trial, attention was drawn to the
curious fact that Plevitskaia, who had never been intimate with Kutepov's wife, had never left her side during the first few days after the
General's disappearance. She had thus been able, under the guise of her
deep sympathy for Mrs. Kutepov, to learn all the details of the Kutepov
investigation communicated by the police.

On Wednesday, September 22, at about 2 P.M. (i.e., right after General Miller's abduction) a large group of former Volunteers gathered on
a platform of the Gare du Nord to see off the Chaperon du Larrés, who
were returning to Brussels. Plevitskaia and Skoblin arrived there separately. The latter had promised one of his fellow officers to give him a
lift to the station in his car, but had failed to do so. The officer, Captain
Grigul, annoyed and flustered, arrived by taxi a few minutes before the
departure of the train and heard Skoblin asking Chaperon, as he took
leave of him, to intercede in Brussels in connection with his application
for a Belgian visa. There was to be a banquet of former members of the
Kornilov Regiment in Brussels which Skoblin wished to attend, but the
application he had made at the Belgian consulate some time ago had not
yet been answered.

After the train left, Skoblin proposed to Captain Grigul and another
Kornilov Regiment officer, Colonel Troshin, that they come with him to
call on Generals Denikin and Miller to thank them for their participation in
the Kornilov celebration.

While they visited Denikin, Skoblin insistently tried to persuade Anton
Ivanovich to drive with him to Brussels on the following day to attend
the local banquet honoring Kornilov. "Do come with me, your Excellency" begged Skoblin, "I shall drive you in my car. If you wish, we could
leave tomorrow, Thursday." [11] Captain Grigul listened with amazement
to Skoblin and his talk about a trip to Belgium, after he had just over-
heard him asking Chaperon to assist him in obtaining a Belgian visa.

Denikin drily rejected the offer. His suspicions were aroused by this
importunate insistence. Skoblin was perfectly aware that the former
commander in chief was not well disposed toward him and had done his
best to avoid him in the last ten years. Yet, in the past three days, he had

repeatedly offered Denikin transportation in his car: First he had come to the General's apartment in Sèvres to thank him for coming to Paris and honoring the Kornilov celebration with his presence, and at that time, respectfully but very insistently, had offered to drive Anton Ivanovich personally back to his family in Mimizan. This conversation had been unexpectedly interrupted by the appearance of a Cossack devoted to Denikin, a tall, powerful fellow whom Anton Ivanovich had called in beforehand to wax the floors and put the apartment in order. Upon his arrival, Skoblin cut short his arguments and took his leave. Glancing out of his apartment window, Anton Ivanovich noticed that two other men, completely unknown to him, were sitting in Skoblin's car.[12] This first offer was followed by a second one: to drive the general, according to his preference, either to Mimizan or to Belgium, to attend the Kornilov banquet. And finally, the third offer was made, in the presence of Colonel Troshin and Captain Grigul, to drive Denikin to Brussels on the following day, September 23.

Only on September 24, after having learned the distressing news, including Skoblin's flight, from the newspapers, did the General realize how close he had been to sharing General Miller's fate. Who knows how the first visit, when Skoblin was accompanied by the two characters he left in the car, would have ended if the fortunate arrival of the floor-waxing Cossack had not upset his plans? There was no longer any doubt that Denikin had escaped being the victim of foul play on Skoblin's part. But there remained the puzzling question as to what had prompted the Soviet government to risk a diplomatic crisis in order to abduct a man who was at that time a lonely figure, far removed from any connection with émigré activists.

Denikin did not leave a single clue in his papers concerning his thoughts or guesses in this matter. He also refused to discuss the subject with the newspaper correspondents who besieged him, and reduced them to reporting that "General Denikin refuses to see anyone." But in theory, several reasons for an attempt to kidnap Denikin may be ascertained: Despite the existence of controversial opinions about him, General Denikin was greatly respected by a large part of the Russian émigré community; his voice had weight, and he remained irreconcilable to Communism. The capture of such an opponent would have suited the Soviet government very well. And the simultaneous capture of Denikin and Miller would have raised the confusion in the ranks of the anti-Bolshevik émigrés to an incredible pitch, doubling the impression that Moscow was as able to control the fate of its political enemies abroad as at home. Besides, Denikin had learned a great deal about the Russian Armed Services Union's conspiratorial activity in Kutepov's time. Information in that area could be of great value to the Soviet secret police even if it was considerably dated. Finally, there may have been an even more direct and urgent reason: Denikin, who had been wary of Skoblin for many years past, would never have countenanced his advancement to a governing position in ROVS after General Miller's disappearance. Although Denikin had no direct connection with ROVS, his opinion carried authority with its members. He presented an obstacle which could shatter the ambitious plans of Soviet agent and *provocateur* Skoblin, who was certain that his crime would never be discovered.

Before her trial, Plevitskaia spent 14½ months of preliminary confinement in the women's prison of Petite Roquette. The trial, which attracted attention throughout France, lasted from December 5, through December 14, 1938. One of the two lawyers who defended Plevitskaia was Maximilian Filonenko, the former commissar of the Provisional Government at the *Stavka* of the Supreme Commander in Mogilev—the same Filonenko who, after taking part in the Kornilov revolt in August, 1917, later confided to newspapermen, "I love and respect General Kornilov, ... but it is necessary to have him shot, and I shall bare my head before his grave." After the Bolshevik take-over, Filonenko made his way to Paris and qualified to practice law in France.

The lawyers for the plaintiff, i.e., General Miller's family, were the well-known attorney Maurice Ribet and A. N. Strelnikov, a former White army officer who like Filonenko, had been admitted to the French bar.

General Denikin was summoned to court as a witness. His interrogation was reported in detail in the Paris Russian-language paper *Poslednie Novosti,* edited by Milyukov:

General A. I. Denikin's appearance causes a sensation. Heads are raised in curiosity to look at the former commander in chief of the Armed Forces of South Russia. The general slowly crosses the courtroom and takes the witness stand. He gives his testimony in Russian, through an interpreter, in short and precise phrases. His dignified bearing, the directness and clearness of his answers, greatly impress the court.

Asked the standard question as to whether or not he is related to the defendant, General Denikin replies, "God preserved me from that!"

Concerning the abductions of General Kutepov and General Miller, the witness states that he knows "no more than anyone else."

The most significant part of Denikin's testimony followed the prosecutor's question, "Did Skoblin call on you on September 22?"

General Denikin: "Skoblin, Captain Grigul, and Colonel Troshin came to thank me for attending the Kornilov banquet. At that time General Miller had already been kidnapped."

"Did Skoblin propose that you journey in his car to Brussels for the Kornilov celebration?"

"He offered twice before to take me on a trip in his car; this was the third offer."

"Why did you refuse?"

"I have always . . . or, more exactly, since 1927, suspected him of Bolshevik sympathies."

"Were you apprehensive of him or of her?"

"I distrusted them both."

Maurice Ribet reminds the court that General A. I. Denikin was chief of staff of the Supreme Commander in 1917. . . .[13]

Plevitskaia never admitted anything, denied her guilt, and claimed to be "as pure as a dove." In the course of the trial, however, she became completely entangled in contradictory statements; the alibi prepared beforehand by herself and Skoblin proved completely worthless, and the sum total of evidence against her turned out to be so overwhelming that she was sentenced to twenty years of hard labor.

She died in prison a few years later without revealing anything.

The secret of Skoblin's disappearance was never discovered. However, several years later, during the occupation of Paris by the German army in World War II, the Gestapo searched the office of ROVS and discovered some interesting facts. It appeared that a certain Nikolai Sergeevich Tretiakov, a relative of the founder of the famous Tretiakov Gallery in Moscow, owned three apartments at 29 rue du Colisée. He rented one of them to the Alliance for Commerce and Industry, an organization composed of former businessmen who still harbored the hope of reestablishing their claim on concerns which had been confiscated from them in Russia. The second apartment was rented to ROVS, and the third, on the floor above, was occupied by Tretiakov himself. The Gestapo search uncovered listening devices on the premises of the Alliance for Commerce and Industry and ROVS. The microphones were connected with Tretiakov's apartment. The former wealthy merchant turned out to have been a Soviet agent who had served the Bolsheviks for several years. The Gestapo arrested Tretiakov and deported him to Germany, where all traces of him disappeared. But their discovery gave rise to the suspicion that when Skoblin left the ROVS office, instead of trying to reach the street, he may have run up one flight to Tretiakov's apartment and left it only when the coast was clear, to go to the other two places where he was last seen in Paris. Another curious detail is that during her trial, Plevitskaia insisted on Filonenko's asking Tretiakov for financial assistance. "He must get us money!" wrote Plevitskaia to him from prison. "Money can be obtained with Tretiakov's help!" [14]

Where did Skoblin go? Rumor had it that he had escaped to a part of war-torn Spain which was, with Soviet help, fighting against Franco, and that Soviet agents finished him off there as a former spy who was no longer useful to them, but actually dangerous as a potential blackmailer.

XXXVII

BETWEEN
TWO EVILS

Toward the beginning of the 1930's, the books written by Denikin had been sold out and no second editions were contemplated. Once again the Denikins were facing a period without any established source of income. When it came to assuring his personal welfare, the general was as helpless as a child. The thought that his family might find itself without any means of support distressed him, though he found some consolation in the fact that unlike many others, he had amassed no wealth while he was in power, arriving to it with empty pockets and leaving it in the same way.

His long and painful meditations on how to improve his finances resulted in the decision to give periodic lectures on the international situation, a subject of great interest and immediacy for Denikin and his compatriots.

These lectures enjoyed great popularity and were also published as separate brochures, which sold very well and constituted an additional source of income.[1] However, the General's public appearances were not motivated solely by material considerations. He had a great deal to say and wanted to share his convictions with his fellow Russians in exile. In his lectures he discussed certain matters of principle which were extremely important to him.

In the twenty-seven years of his life in exile, Denikin was upheld by the faith that conditions in Russia would change and that he would be able to return to his country and serve it again, if only in the most humble and modest fashion. He compared the Russian émigré dispersion throughout the world to the Jewish Diaspora: "The Hebrew world too," he was wont to say, "suffers from dissension and cannibalism, though this is seldom brought to light in the general press. . . . However, there is one area where they have no dissension and maintain an indissoluble, absolute unity—it is in the defense of their own race." And here the general sadly commented that "a similar concentration of forces with regard to the all-important, the fundamental question of defending the Russian nation, is lacking in us." [2]

In the years preceding World War II, Denikin attempted to create such a "concentration of forces" for defending the national interests of Russia. He warned the émigrés not to become enthusiastic about German National Socialism as an anti-Communist weapon. While he remained irreconcilable to the Soviet regime, Denikin did everything to combat the "defeatism" of certain émigré circles who were prepared to accept the idea of a foreign invasion of Russia if it could terminate the Communist rule.

Denikin's public lectures became a traditional annual event. They always attracted capacity audiences and were reviewed and commented on at length in the émigré press. The following excerpts from a report on Denikin's first lecture (in March, 1932), in the Paris newspaper *Poslednie Novosti,* give an idea of the public interest these addresses aroused, an interest which continued unflagging through the years.

Starting at eight in the evening, the rue Daru in front of the Salle Chopin was crowded with people trying to gain admission to General Denikin's lecture *The Russian Problem in the Far East* [*Russki Vopros na Dal'nem Vostoke*]. The public lecture of the former commander in chief of the Volunteer Army, who for twelve years had avoided taking any part in the political life of the émigrés, proved eventful by virtue of its content, which was both unexpected and significant for many of his listeners.

The article went on to list, as among those present at the lecture, the best-known and most distinguished individuals in the Russian émigré community, representing its whole political spectrum from the ultrarightists to the Socialist Revolutionaries and Mensheviks. The overwhelming majority of the audience, however, consisted of former participants in the White movement.

Most of those present rise and give the lecturer an ovation. . . . His first few words captivate the attention of his listeners. . . . General Denikin not only does not share the hope pinned by certain émigré circles on "Japanese assistance," but frankly considers it to be harmful to Russia's interests. . . . Frequently interrupted by applause, General A. I. Denikin energetically condemns false patriots: "Our participation on the side of those who want to appropriate Russian territory is inadmissible!" . . .

One of the thoughts expressed by Anton Ivanovich in this lecture merits particular attention:

Our national consciousness is deeply wounded by the examples of the past. This is why, for me personally, the word "intervention" calls forth very bitter feelings.[3]

Denikin, who had learned through personal experience that chivalry has no place in the realm of international politics, did his best to warn his listeners against placing too much trust in "new allies" and repeating the mistakes previously made by his own administration.

As the danger to Russia presented by Japan began to pale by comparison with the menace of German belligerence, Denikin shifted the emphasis of his political discourses to vigorous opposition of German National Socialism and its Fuehrer.

One of his most memorable lectures on this subject, entitled *Mirovye Sobytia i Russkii Vopros* (*World Events and the Russian Question*), took place in December, 1938. Because of its length, the lecture was delivered in two installments—on December 17 and December 25. It made a deep impression on those who attended it as well as on those who later read it in a specially printed eighty-seven-page brochure. The lecture formulated with complete clarity Denikin's views on the role that should be played by the Russian émigrés in the event of a war between Germany and the Soviet Union:

Our duty, besides anti-Bolshevik activity and propaganda, is to promote the idea of a "national" Russia and to defend Russia's interests in general. Always and everywhere, in all the countries of our dispersion. We must do this openly wherever freedom of speech and favorable political conditions exist; and secretly, wherever they don't. At worst, let us be silent but not render lip service. *We are neither for hire nor for sale.*

I would like to say—not to those who have sold themselves—they are beyond recall, but to those who, out of sincere but erroneous conviction, are planning to join Hitler's campaign against the Ukraine: If Hitler has decided to take this step, he will probably be able to manage without your help. Why then lend moral justification to an undertaking which, though it may not, in your opinion, be aimed at the annexation of Russian territory, is extremely suspect to say the least? . . . Such anti-national activity and connections are commonly justified by the explanation that this is only to get things going, and later we can reverse our arms. . . . Assertions of this type have been made openly by two publications which lay claim to be leaders of opinion among the émigrés. . . . Forgive me, but this is really too naïve. It is naïve, upon entering into a business relationship with a partner, to warn him in advance that he will be fooled, and naïve to count on his complete trustfulness. You will not reverse your arms, for *having used you as agitators, interpreters, turnkeys, perhaps even as an armed force— wedged between the pincers of its machine guns—this partner in his own time will disable and disarm you, if he doesn't make you rot in concentration camps. And for this you will have spilled not the blood of Chekists, but simply Russian blood—your own and that of your compatriots—and not for the liberation of Russia, but for its even greater enslavement.*[4] [Italics added.]

In the same two lectures, in 1938, Denikin, who considered a war with Germany to be inevitable, examined several possibilities which would, in his opinion, allow the émigrés to further the "Russian cause" should the war strike. Denikin believed that in the event of war, the Russian people would rise against the Communist regime which had enslaved it. But what action should the émigrés take, if this possibility failed to materialize? "What should we do," queried Denikin, "if the Russian people and army, threatened by war, forgo the struggle with the internal usurpers in order to join in a unified effort against the foreign enemy?"

Denikin answered this question as follows: "I cannot believe that, once armed, the Russian people would not rise against its oppressors. But if this happened, and only if this happened, we would be unable to fight the Soviet regime directly, even though our attitude toward it would remain unchanged. Under any circumstances, it would be morally impossible for us to join efforts with the army which is presently known as 'Red' until it had thrown off the Communist yoke. *But even so our activity would have to be directed, in one way or another, not for, but against the foreign invaders* [italics added].[5] Denikin's viewpoint in this case was perfectly consistent with his policy during the civil war period.

The possibility which in 1938 Denikin refused to accept became reality a few years later, and Denikin, without altering his attitude toward the Soviets, concentrated his activity against Russia's foreign enemies, the Germans. At that time, his appeal to overthrow the Soviet regime and defend Russia appeared unrealistic and strangely contradictory to many. Denikin's critics pointed out that one could not at one and the same time defend Russia and undermine its strength by overthrowing its government; just as one could not overthrow the Soviet regime without the help of outside forces. In a word, it was "either the Bolshevik noose or the foreign yoke." Anton Ivanovich's answer was, "I accept neither the noose nor the yoke!"

General Denikin was scrupulously careful of the historical documents that remained in his possession. He considered them public property, which would form part of the historical archive of the Russian state after it had been liberated from the Bolsheviks. Meanwhile, worried about the security of his archive, he wished to place it in the safekeeping of some permanent government institution abroad, which would guarantee him the right to use it for historical research, and would otherwise give access to it only to individuals armed with the General's personal authorization. In August, 1935, he signed an agreement to that effect with the Russian Historic Archive Abroad at the Ministry of Foreign Affairs of the Republic of Czechoslovakia, in Prague, and transferred the following documents to its care: the archive of the Special Council, i.e., Denikin's government in south Russia (incomplete); materials of his personal archive relating to the Russian revolution and civil war (831 documents plus photographs and posters); the archive of the deputy chief of staff of the Armed Forces of South Russia, concerning military operations (extensive but incomplete).

While Anton Ivanovich was negotiating with the Czechs, and when he had already made up his mind to transfer his documents to their care, the military historian N. N. Golovin was striving to secure the Denikin archive for the Hoover War Library, at Stanford University, in California. Golovin was then a purchasing agent for the library, and on its behalf was collecting Russian documents pertaining to the civil war. Apparently he had acquired the traits of a high-pressure salesman, for in writing to Denikin he did his best to disparage his "competitors." "There is no guarantee that the Czechs won't transmit the documents . . . to the Bolsheviks," wrote Golovin. "The Czechs did not hesitate to give up Admiral Kolchak to the Bolsheviks—they will hesitate even less with the Archives." [6]

At that time Denikin's agreement with the Czechoslovak government, prepared by experienced lawyers, seemed completely foolproof. But its validity had meaning only while Czechoslovakia retained its independence. As soon as this independence was threatened, so was the security of the entire Russian archive in Prague, and Golovin's argument thus, turned out to have been prophetic.

In the 1930's, Denikin made several lecture tours in Yugoslavia and Czechoslovakia, where he was welcomed with hospitality and respect not only by the local Russian émigrés, but also by those countries' administrative and intellectual circles. He also gave some addresses in England. Perhaps his most memorable trip was one he made to Bucharest, in 1937, at the invitation of the King of Rumania. General Denikin was a knight of the Rumanian Order of St. Michael, having received this distinction for bravery and combat achievements in 1916 and 1917, as commander of the Russian Eighth Army Corps, sent to Rumania's assistance after that country declared war on Germany. On the feast day of St. Michael, all the bearers of the Order were required to don its traditional white cape. Denikin's cape was presented to him by courtesy of the royal court. Curiously enough, it was to be worn at another ceremony several years later, during the German occupation of France, when it was made into a wedding dress for Denikin's daughter, Marina. The former commander in chief of the White Army was the object of warm hospitality and attention on the part of King Carol and of Rumanian society. The Rumanian press noted that on November 7, while the Soviet ambassador in Bucharest was celebrating the twentieth anniversary of Soviet rule, the King was entertaining General Denikin at his palace.

The Denikins spent their summer vacations in the country, in various parts of France. They stayed in Cap-Breton, in Allemont (Isère), where they passed four consecutive summers, and in Mimizan. The summer of 1938 was spent in the Savoie and that of 1939 in Monteuil-au-Vicomte (Creuse). Denikin described his first impressions of Allemont in a letter to N. I. Astrov:

Complete solitude; though guests do gather here in the summer. A good house, real country, friendly people. Living is about one and a half times cheaper than in Paris. This allows us to breathe a little easier. . . . The altitude is eight hundred meters, with mountains and snowy peaks all around, wonderful air and quantities of "grazing," which varies according to season and zone. . . . The first "gifts" have just appeared at our altitude—they are morels, which are good to eat and revive memories of the past and of the northern Russian countryside. You surely understand that in our circumstances even plain Russian dill has ceased to be an ordinary herb and become one of the remedies of nostalgia. . . .

For the first time in our lives, we had to spend Easter in solitude, without a midnight service and the mysticism of the Easter ritual, customs, and chants. . . . Only Marina, who had invited her little girl friends from the village, thoroughly enjoyed herself.[7]

The nostaliga mentioned by Anton Ivanovich pursued him wherever he went. He was so completely Russian, so uncosmopolitan, that living abroad was a trial to him, and only his constant and complete concentration on his work helped to ward off depression. He read and reflected a great deal.

The civil war in Spain interested him intensely. Not unnaturally, his sympathies were on Franco's side. Nevertheless, he was categorically opposed to the participation of former Russian Volunteers in a foreign civil war and expressed this opinion very firmly to the many White Army men who sought his advice on the subject.

Despite his former conflicts with the representatives of the French command in south Russia, General Denikin became genuinely attached to France as a country. But the politics of the French government, which like all "politics" ran contrary to his simple code of military honor, depressed him. He could not reconcile himself to the idea that all the sacrifices made by Russia in World War I had been forgotten by the French and that their desire to establish cordial relations with the Soviet Union had obliterated the memory of the former "national" Russia.

In May, 1937, a committee of prominent Russian émigrés asked the French Minister of War to send a representative to the consecration of a monument at St-Hilaire-le-Grand, on the Marne, erected to the memory of Russian soldiers fallen in France during the war of 1914–1918. These soldiers had been sent to the French front at the insistent request of the French government. The *chef de cabinet* of the Minister of War declined the invitation in a curt message: *J'ai l'honneur de vous faire connaître qu'il n'a pas été reconnu possible de donner une suite favorable à cette demande, et je vous en exprime mes regrets.*[8]

General Denikin, who attended the unveiling of the monument as an honored guest and speaker, expressed his indignation at this reply in his speech:

Today, by consecrating this memorial church, we have paid tribute to the memory of the Russian soldiers who died with honor at the French front. Those who fell here symbolize the great sacrifices undergone by Russia and the old Russian army for what was then our common cause. Our former allies must not forget that by 1917 the Russian army was holding back the onslaught of 187 enemy divisions, i.e., one half of the entire enemy forces active on all European and Asian fronts; . . . that even in 1918, when the Russian army no longer existed, the Russian legion fought here on French soil to the very end, and buried many of its brave men in the fields of Champagne. . . . It was not we who concluded the Brest-Litovsk Treaty. . . . That was done by others. . . . We have no doubt that the French army understands this, but we can't help experiencing a feeling of bitterness when this truth is being forgotten or adulterated to suit the political conditions of the times. Bitterness on behalf of "national" Russia; bitterness for those who survived and were cast on alien soil by the turmoil; bitterness for those who fell in the field.

World conscience is dormant. Our wish to those who are alive is to witness its awakening.[9]

This wartime cemetery, forgotten by Russia's former allies, was visited in May, 1960, by none other than Nikita Khrushchev and the Soviet Marshal and Minister of Defense, Rodion Malinovsky. As a very young man in World War I, Malinovsky fought with the Russian expeditionary corps in France. He and Khrushchev visited the cemetery to honor the memory of Russian soldiers fallen so far away from their native land.

In 1932, after twelve years of silence and semiseclusion, Denikin decided to take an active part in the affairs of the Russian émigré community. His attempt at unifying the conflicting elements among the émigrés was, of course, doomed to failure. But the voice of Denikin insisting that Russia's national interests were mortally threatened, and that it was inadmissible to support those who were determined to dismember the nation, nevertheless affected many people.

According to Melgunov, "A considerable portion of the émigrés adopted this stand. Denikin's authoritative voice kept many people from taking a path that clearly was historically false, as was proved by later events." Melgunov summed up his opinion of the General's role in exile as follows: "Though in the civil-war years, Anton Ivanovich's personal qualities sometimes had a tragic effect on his situation, these same qualities became of the greatest benefit to the Russian community in the trying days of its life in exile, when a great effort of will was required from all of us in order to keep up our spirit. The inflexible firmness and moral prestige of the Volunteers' former leader served as a guarantee of our irreconcilable attitude toward the coercive power which dominates our native land."[10] Melgunov might have added, And as a guarantee of our irreconcilable attitude toward the external enemies of Russia.

The outbreak of World War II came as no surprise to Denikin, but the Hitler-Stalin pact which preceded it was totally unexpected. Which will be the first one to breach the agreement? Which one will knife the other in the back? were his first thoughts when he learned of the event from the papers.

Neither was Denikin prepared for the instantaneous collapse of the French front in May, 1940. He realized at that point that having temporarily secured their position in the west, the Germans would surge eastward, convinced of their ability rapidly to defeat the Red Army, deprived of its leaders by Stalin's purges—purges to which, incidentally, the Germans themselves had contributed by forging the documents which compromised the Soviet military command.

UNDER
THE GERMANS, I

In the second half of May, 1940, when the collapse of the French army became evident, chaos and panic engulfed all of France. There began a mass exodus to the south and west of France, by those who hoped to avoid the enemy and escape from the zone of military operations.

General Denikin, who did not wish to find himself under German domination, also decided to leave Paris. He chose as a temporary refuge the village of Mimizan, on the Atlantic coast, some eighty-five kilometers north of Biarritz, where he had spent the summer of 1937 with his family.

Paris was doomed, and its inhabitants poured out of it in every direction, flooding trains and all other means of transportation and blocking the roads with vehicles. At the very end of May, the Denikins piled their belongings into a taxi owned by a former officer of the White Army, and with their daughter Marina, left the Paris suburb of Bourg-la-Reine, where they were living at the time. The journey southwest, along the crowded roads, was extremely slow. It was hot and dusty, and they suffered from hunger and thirst. All the hotels were filled to overflowing with refugees, and only once, somewhere in the Charente, a French lady having found out that this was General Denikin, invited him and his companions for dinner and a night's rest in her estate.

The department of Landes, in southwestern France, is a sandy and swampy region with miles of sand dunes stretching along its shoreline. To arrest their slow invasion of the countryside, the minister Necker, in the late 1780's, had had them planted with pine trees, which in the years that followed spread inland over a large part of the province. Today, the main industry of Landes is the extraction of resin and tar from the pine trees. It is one of the least populated parts of France, and its inhabitants are among the least literate. They live in fairly poor scattered farms, villages, and hamlets. The Denikins were to be stranded here in squalid conditions for five years. They stayed in Mimizan throughout the German occupation and left it only in June, 1945.

At the very beginning, however, they were comfortably settled in a good house lent to them by the parents of one of Marina's friends. The house stood on a dune near the shore and had a beautiful view of the ocean. But this pleasant interlude was short. As soon as the Germans reached Bordeaux, the General realized that they were bound to occupy all strategic points and habitations along the shore, as far as the Spanish border. He preferred to avoid an encounter with the Germans, and without waiting for their arrival, left the Mimizan shore and moved to a primitive barracks in the woods near Lake Mimizan. As he had foreseen, the shore house was immediately requisitioned by the German army; it was eventually destroyed during the construction of the "Atlantic Wall."

Marina Denikin remained in Mimizan until December, 1940, then returned to Paris, where she stayed with the parents of her fiancé, Jean Boudet. She was married to him in February, 1941, in the Russian Orthodox church in Bordeaux. For Anton Ivanovich and Xenia Vasilievna the day was marred by a grievous disappointment: the only bus for Bordeaux, which left Mimizan every twenty-four hours, passed them by without stopping, and they never got to their daughter's wedding.

The marriage did not turn out well, and in the summer of 1943, Marina Denikin asked for a divorce. In January, 1942, she had given birth to a son, Michael. She stayed with him at her parents' in Mimizan for one summer month in 1942, and later, she and the baby remained with them from the mid summer of 1943 to March or April of the following year. After this, she returned to Paris for good.

Stranded in the wilderness and isolated from the rest of the world, Xenia Vasilievna decided to keep a journal. Twenty-eight school notebooks contain the thoughts and impressions she recorded during this gloomy five-year period.

Mrs. Denikin's notebooks are not so much a diary in the regular sense of the word as a commentary on the military and political news which reached Mimizan through the radio and newspapers. The household's routine existence was too monotonous to merit recording day by day. The notebooks had to be well hidden, and even buried underground at times, to prevent confiscation by the Germans. For this reason, there are many gaps and omissions in the journal, which unfortunately fails to mention some of the important events in the Denikins' personal lives. Nevertheless Xenia Vasilievna's notes are interesting, because of her acute observation, her ability to relate personal impressions, conversations, and moods, and her vivid descriptions of encounters with a variety of people. Here are some excerpts from this journal:

August 5, 1940

We have settled at the edge of the village, right next to the wood but far from the sea. Our lodgings are very primitive; they are part of a long barracks built for German prisoners in the preceding war; the well and outhouse are behind the owner's chicken coop, but thank heaven, we have electricity. . . . The center of the barracks is occupied by our elderly landlords, and the other end, opposite ours, by other lodgers.

September 10, 1940

No Paris papers, no radio. Life has become very restricted. Our poor receiver was squashed during our journey, and no wonder, considering the way our car was stuffed with our belongings. I sat hunched together all the way—knees under chin, a roll of pillows behind my back, a suitcase filled with books under my feet, the cat in his basket on my knees. It's pretty bad without a radio in times like these.

One already has to stand in line for bread, which they say will soon be rationed. . . . Our remote little village is settling down to a routine of life, which trickles on quietly but with a certain wariness, for parallel to it, the invader's life is also becoming organized.

October 27, 1940

We have moved to new lodgings as our old barracks proved completely unsuitable for the winter. Here, at least, the house is of stone, although the heating is equally bad. To make up for it, we have the advantage of being on a highway and of seeing the Germans from morning till night—on foot, bicycles, motorcycles, light cars, huge trucks, and even on horseback. . . . I got a radio!

October 29, 1940

Ivanych [a shortened form of Ivanovich by which Mrs. Denikin occasionally called her husband] is banging on something in the next room and says, in answer to my question, "I am putting up a map of former France and a map of former Europe."

December 27, 1940

This is the fifth day of severe frost. Calamity . . . our potatoes, of which about ten kilos remained, are frostbitten. I don't know what the temperature is in the room, but I doubt that it is more than 2 or 3 degrees [centigrade]. I am in bed, dressed in four layers of wool, with a featherbed over me and a hot-water bottle, and my hands are too numb to write. . . . Ivanych, who has put on everything he owns, looks like an Eskimo.

March 30, 1941

Yesterday we ate our last tin of sardines, but saved the oil for today's lentils, to the great indignation of Vas'ka, the cat, who considers the licking of sardine boxes to be his special prerogative. The poor old boy has learned to eat gray, slightly sour macaroni, but not without casting reproachful glances at us. . . . Our greatest concern, however, is a shortage of trousers, of which I didn't have time to buy enough while it was still possible. My husband is wearing out his last pair, although his jackets are still holding out.

May 2, 1941

Great events are taking place in the world while we are stranded by fate in this wilderness, in the modest company of workmen, peasants, and villagers.

It is solitude *à deux*. I am often confined to my bed for weeks on end by my illness. Our friends and acquaintances, all the people who share our way of thinking, are far away. And so I have decided to write down what I see, hear, and think. Thanks to the radio we keep up with world events and can form an opinion of them. At the same time, the conditions of our present existence allow us to observe life at the very bottom of the scale, in the thick rural life, and to perceive the moods and reactions of simple people.

To these excerpts from Mrs. Denikin's journal should be added the fact that her knowledge of German, which she had spoken fluently from childhood, placed her in a unique position in Mimizan. She was practically the only person there who could communicate with the German occupation authorities without an interpreter. Soon the entire district became aware of this, and large numbers of people began to come to General Denikin's wife for help. They were grateful for her generous and disinterested aid; friendly relationships were gradually established, and soon, without quite knowing how it happened, Xenia Vasilievna became a trusted confidante of the local intellectuals—the doctor, the pharmacist, the curé. These people listened to the forbidden broadcasts from London and repeated after de Gaulle, *La flamme de la Résistance française ne doit pas s'éteindre et ne s'éteindra pas!*

They hated the Germans and refused to accept the defeat of France. Some of them hid the Jews who had accidentally drifted into these backwoods; others went a great deal further in their efforts to resist the invader.

On June 22, 1941, the day the Germans invaded Russia, their occupation forces in Paris arrested, as a precaution, a number of Russian émigrés whose loyalty appeared uncertain or suspect. The arrests started early in the morning, before the émigrés had had a chance to learn that a Russo-German war had erupted. Men and women of all ages were taken indiscriminately. In the French provinces, however, including the department of Landes, such arrests started several days earlier (without explanation) and applied to Russians under fifty years of age.[1] In Mimizan they began exactly one week before the start of Russo-German hostilities. As all newspapers were severely censored, the Germans apparently had no fear that news of the mass arrests of Russians in the provinces would be reported abroad.

On June 15, a military truck with a chauffeur, three German privates, and a noncommissioned officer stopped in front of the Denikins' house in Mimizan. The noncom asked for Mrs. Denikin's documents, glanced at her date of birth, and ordered her into the truck. While this was happening, the unsuspecting General, who had no idea of what was going on at his front door, was working away at his vegetable garden in the back.

When his wife shouted to him that the Germans had arrested her and were taking her away in a truck, the General was completely taken aback. "You're crazy," he exclaimed; "they must have come for me!" But he was wrong, and after a short delay for packing, the truck bore Mrs. Denikin away. It already contained several other people, among whom were Mrs. Denikin's niece and her husband, who lived in the vicinity of Mimizan. Neighbors brought the couple's six-year-old son to Anton Ivanovich, and the old man and the little boy remained alone together for nearly two weeks.

The arrested Russians were driven to the department capital, Mont-de-Marsan, and incarcerated in a private house, with a garden surrounded by an iron railing, which the Germans had requisitioned and transformed into a prison. The prisoners were taken to the Gestapo in the center of the town for questioning. They were not charged with any offenses but simply detained as prisoners until July 1.

During her imprisonment, Xenia Vasilievna heard occasional broadcasts on the radio in the guardroom next door. She jotted down her impressions and later incorporated them into her journal:

June 21, 1941
The radio is full of "rumors" of a German attack on the USSR, stemming mainly from Sweden. Radio Moscow is completely emasculated and doesn't even drop a hint. Its abstractness and correctness are unnatural. What are we to think? Should we grieve, rejoice, hope? We are torn asunder. Unquestionably, the USSR image is abhorrent to us, but behind the image is our homeland, our Russia, our huge, uncouth, incomprehensible, but beloved and beautiful Russia!

June 23, 1941
This cup did not pass away from Russia. The two Antichrists have joined combat. . . . Meanwhile, German bombs are tearing into Russian flesh, their accursed mechanized army is crushing Russian bodies and spilling our Russian blood. Lord, have mercy on our people, have mercy and help them!"

Mrs. Denikin also gave in her journal a detailed account of life in the Mont-de-Marsan prison:

July 6, 1941
We were decently treated and constantly assured that we were not arrested, but interned. The food wasn't bad; neither better nor worse than what we had all been eating. Nevertheless, we were held behind bars, guarded by sentries, and bedded without sheets or pillows. We were interrogated twice, mainly about our *curriculum vitae,* and very insistently, as to who was Ukrainian. As I was the interpreter, our group did not turn up any Ukrainians. What I found most interesting in this little incident of my life were my conversations with our sentries. They were all men over forty, most of them Bavarian workmen, but there were also peasants from Brandenburg and the Schwarzwald . . . about thirty people all told, who guarded us in threes, spelling each other every twenty-four hours. They were likable, good-natured people, who were not only well disposed toward us but treated us with obvious sympathy. They often shared their rations with us and gave us fruit and beer. We conversed at length and about everything. Some of them, quite belligerently inclined, assured us that

they would finish with Soviet Russia in six weeks; that the Ukraine, including the Don Basin, the Kuban, the Caucasus, and the Baku oil wells, would become a protectorate similar to Czechoslovakia, while a "national" Russian government would be established in Moscow. In short, that Bolshevism would be *ganz kaput*. . . . After the fall of Russia, the Fuehrer would make another peace offer, but as England is sure to refuse it, that wicked isle will be conquered and most of its population will perish in the process. Too bad, but the gangrene must be done away with. By winter, peace will begin to be gradually restored; there will be a new order and Germany will arrange it so that it will become impossible for anyone to start a new war.

. . . They all assured us that Russia attacked them first, disregarding all her treaties. They also unanimously expressed their disdain for Italy.

Mrs. Denikin's incarceration ended as suddenly as it had begun. Worrying about Anton Ivanovich and the six-year-old boy of the niece who had been arrested at the same time as herself, Xenia Vasilievna wrote in German to the commander of the German troops in the Biarritz sector, whose name she had obtained from the soldiers on guard at the prison. She explained in the letter that she had been detained for an unknown reason, without any definite accusation. The letter, which was sent through an officer of the prison guards, reached its destination and apparently made a considerable impression.

The German general arrived at Mont-de-Marsan personally and immediately asked for Mrs. Denikin. "What is your connection with General Denikin? Are you a relative?" was his first question.

"I am his wife."

"Then why did you not assert your identity?"

"I thought that your authorities knew whom they were arresting," she answered.

The German general ordered the immediate release of General Denikin's wife, but being the only interpreter for the group of Russian prisoners, she requested that her release be postponed until a replacement for her could be found. "I believe, General," she concluded, "that you would do the same thing in my place."

Three days later, the entire group, including Mrs. Denikin, was released from captivity.[2]

Mrs. Denikin had good reason to worry about Anton Ivanovich. In the first year of the German occupation, he had lost twenty-five kilos and aged considerably. His mental faculties were as fresh and alert as ever, but his general physical condition was gradually deteriorating. In his concern for the health of his wife, who was constantly ailing, he tried to relieve her of as many household chores as possible—tending the stove, chopping and sawing wood, and washing the dishes. In the spring, he had the additional labor of digging, sowing, weeding, and watering the vegetable garden. He suffered from bouts of angina pectoris, which had developed recently, and from inflammation of the prostate gland. He underwent the serious operation of removing the prostate a year and a half later, in Bordeaux.

His wife's arrest stunned him. Speaking no language except Russian, and completely hamstrung by the presence of a six-year-old boy left to his care, he felt helpless. The fact that he could do nothing to protect his wife was unbearable. He did not know where she had been taken and whether her arrest was accidental or due to a definite reason. He feared that the Germans might have connected her name with some French people whose activities they suspected.

The General, who was a very inefficient cook, and practically without money or provisions, now had the problem of feeding the boy as well as himself. The solution of this problem was as welcome as it was unexpected. Every morning Anton Ivanovich found, at his doorstep, a piece of lard or some eggs and always some bread and milk. Someone was taking care of the lonely old man and the little boy. The Denikins never found out who it was.

Xenia Vasilievna's arrest, her letter, and the ensuing conversation with the German general, put an end to the Denikins' anonymity. The occupation authorities suddenly became conscious of the General's presence in their midst.

The German political administration in occupied France was undoubtedly familiar with Denikin's views as a result of his public addresses in Paris before the war. That his anti-German attitude was no secret to them is proved by the fact that the brochures containing his addresses *Brest-Litovsk, Mezhdunarodnoie Polozhenie, Rossia i Emigratsia* (*The International Situation, Russia, and the Emigration*), and *Mirovye Sobytia i Russkii Vopros* (*World Events and the Russian Question*) were later placed on the German *Index of Forbidden Russian-Language Books*,[3] and removed from book warehouses, stores, and libraries.

At the same time, the Germans tried to use Denikin's name in their propaganda activity. The German *Kommandantur* in Mimizan inquired whether General Denikin would agree to receive the Commandant of Biarritz. "The times were such," said Denikin later, "that I was obliged to agree."

On the following day, a car drew up at the Denikins' house with the Commandant of Biarritz, a staff officer, and an interpreter. The presence of the latter proved unnecessary, as Xenia Vasilievna did all the interpreting. The reason for the call was allegedly a desire on the part of the visitors to "pay their respects" to the noted Russian general, but its real purpose was to invite him to leave his present squalid surroundings in the backwoods of France and move to Germany. The Commandant advised Denikin that the personal archive which he had entrusted to the Russian Historic Archive Abroad, in Prague, had been removed by the

Germans to Berlin. In addition, much valuable material from various other Russian archives previously scattered throughout Europe had now been assembled in Berlin, and General Denikin would be able to continue his historical labor there in ease and comfort. He added, with a glance at the Denikins' miserable quarters, "In Berlin, you will, of course, be placed in different and much more favorable conditions."

After listening to all these polite phrases, the General turned to his wife, saying, "Ask him if this is a proposal or an order?" The puzzled Commandant having replied that this was obviously a proposal, Denikin curtly retorted, "Then I remain here."

The German understood that any further talk was useless. He rose and saluted, but added before leaving, "Could we be of use to you here in any way?" to which Denikin answered, "Thank you, there is nothing I need." [4]

The attempt by the Germans to draw Denikin into their orbit was unsuccessful, but they continued to communicate with him regarding the Russian archive appropriated by them in Czechoslovakia. The visit was followed up by a rather crudely worded letter to Denikin from a German major in charge of the German military archive in France, dated January 28, 1942:

A collection belonging to your Excellency was discovered at the former Czech Ministry of the Interior in Prague. In order to better ensure its safety, the archive was removed to the repository for military archives. By order of the director of military archives, I request from your Excellency a confirmation [or "consent"] to this transfer [or "removal"] and a communication regarding the conditions you attach to the use of this archive.

Further, I would greatly appreciate being informed of the location of other similar Russian archives, as the director of the military archives attaches a special importance to the seizure [*Erfassung*] and preservation of these rare historical sources.

General Denikin replied to this letter in Russian on February 3, 1942:

To the Representative of the Director of Military Archives
SIR,

With reference to your letter of January 28, No. 90, I wish to state that:

In 1935, I deposited my archives for safekeeping with the Russian Historic Archive Abroad, which was then under the jurisdiction of the Ministry of Foreign Affairs of Czechoslovakia. The Ministry undertook to fulfill the following conditions:

1. My archives are subject to being transferred to the possession of Russia after the overthrow of the Communist power and the establishment there of a regime guaranteeing a lawful system, personal freedom and public initiative. The time at which the archives should be transferred to the Russian government is to be determined by myself.

2. No one can be allowed to make use of the archives without my permission. I retain the right to use these archives for research purposes.

3. My archives cannot be diverted and transmitted for temporary safekeeping to any other establishment.[5]

Denikin's collection was first seized by the Germans, after the conquest of Czechoslovakia, and transferred to the Repository of Military Archives in Berlin. But after the collapse of Germany, it fell into the hands of the Red Army, and with the "consent" of Beneš, was transported to the Soviet Union.

According to newspaper reports, a group of Soviet archivists, visiting the United States in May, 1966, confirmed that the former Prague archives are presently held at the Central Archive in Moscow.

Another consequence of Mrs. Denikin's arrest was that starting in November, 1941, the General and his wife had to appear from time to time at the *mairie* of Mimizan "to be interrogated by a representative of the German authorities." The interrogation generally consisted in verifying that they had not moved. Another, less acceptable requirement, however, was the compulsory registration of Russians. Failure to comply with it entailed severe penalties.

Since the German aim was to dismember Russia, the Nazis formed a number of "committees" representing the various nationalities of the former Russian Empire (Russian, Ukrainian, Caucasian, and so on), including some which have never existed. Each Russian émigré was required to register with the appropriate committees. In the French provinces, this registration took place either in the local *mairie* or in the German *Kommandantur,* which forwarded the information to the corresponding committees in Paris.

For Denikin, who had devoted his life to the service of " a united and indivisible Russia," this procedure was inadmissible. He flatly refused to register. And strangely enough, the Germans decided to disregard his refusal and leave the obstinate old man alone. Most likely, they realized that at a moment when they were trying to represent their war of conquest against Russia as an anti-Communist crusade, it would have been an extraordinary blunder to imprison the best-known and most genuine of all Russian anti-Communists.

"As for me, personally," wrote Denikin later, "while remaining irreconcilable with regard to Bolshevism and refusing to recognize the Soviet regime, I have always considered and still consider myself a citizen of the Russian Empire, which as we know, includes the Great Russian, Belorussian, Little Russian or Ukrainian provinces, the Caucasus, and so on. *This is why I and my family refused to register* [italics Denikin's]. Nevertheless, I firmly advised my friends and war comrades not to ask for trouble but to comply with this formality." [6]

Denikin took the Russian defeats at the outset of the war very hard, and later followed the successes of the Russians with great satisfaction and pride.

Say what you will [he wrote], no amount of contriving could diminish the significance of the fact that, after a certain time, the Red Army fought with skill and the Russian soldier, with self-sacrifice. . . .

From time immemorial the Russian was bright, talented, and wholeheartedly devoted to his homeland. From time immemorial the Russian soldier had unlimited endurance and self-sacrificing courage. These human and military qualities could not be smothered by twenty-five years of Soviet repression of thought and conscience. . . . And when it became clear to all of them that they were faced with invasion and conquest and not with liberation, that they could only expect one yoke to be substituted by another, the people postponed their reckoning with Communism to a more fitting time and rose to the defense of Russian soil as did their ancestors in the days of the Swedish, Polish, and Napoleonic invasions. . . . The ignominious Finnish campaign and the defeat of the Red Army on the Germans' way to Moscow, took place under the sign of *International Communism;* the German armies were defeated under the slogan *Defend our Homeland!* [7]

On November 15, 1944, Denikin wrote in his address to the Volunteers, veterans of the White movement,

The enemy is expelled from the confines of our country. We—and therein lies the inevitable tragedy of our situation—are not participants but only observers of the events which shook our country in the last few years. We could only observe, with profound grief, the suffering of our people, and with pride—the greatness of its achievement.

We suffered in the days of the army's defeat, although it bears the name of "Red" and not of "Russian," and we were joyous in the days of its victories. And now, while the World War is still unfinished, we hope with all our hearts for its victorious completion, which will ensure our country against impudent encroachments from abroad. [8]

But proud though he was of the achievements and exploits of his people, Denikin remained irreconcilable to the Soviet regime: *"We cannot, dare not, close our eyes to the reverse side of the Bolshevik medal, the price of achievements paid in blood and human suffering, the crushing of the individual, the whole bestial aspect of Bolshevism, for the tolerance of evil is the first step toward its acceptance* [italics Denikin's]." [9]

Anton Ivanovich expressed similar ideas in a private letter to a friend: "Personally, I welcome the popular upsurge for the defense of Russia, rejoice at her victories over the Germans, and desire their complete defeat, but I shall not cease to condemn—as long as I live—the Bolshevik system of strangulation of the Russian people." [10]

In addition to their periodic visits to the *mairie,* the Denikins were occasionally summoned to the Mimizan *Kommandantur,* particularly when it had a change of administrative personnel. Anton Ivanovich was lucky enough to avoid any further contact with the German authorities. Xenia Vasilievna went alone to the *Kommandantur,* where she explained that her husband was old and did not speak German. She was sometimes asked ticklish questions—concerning Denikin's connections and acquaintances in France and abroad, his sources of income, his current research and writing.

While she made no secret of information about the past, which may already have been known to the Germans, and told them that her husband's modest income from his books and lectures had come to an end, Xenia Vasilievna took care not to divulge the facts that would have been of real interest to them.

"In our compulsory solitude during the German occupation," wrote Anton Ivanovich later, "my wife and I translated into Russian and circulated among the Russian émigrés the more revealing statements of prominent German figures in their press and radio." [11]

They succeeded in assembling the most blatant material from the official speeches of Hitler, Goebbels, Rosenberg, and other Nazi leaders, in which the Germans openly expressed not only their complete disdain for anything Russian, but also their determination to exploit Russian territories for purely German aims. This material was occasionally, and of course, secretly, entrusted to confidential messengers, who made copies and distributed them among former White Army officers, and other émigrés as well.

Among other things, Denikin collected information on the Germans' atrocities, on their inhuman attitude toward Russian war prisoners, on the progress of the war, on Russia, on the émigrés, and also on future means of exposing all whom he regarded as traitors to the Russian cause. He also resumed work on his unfinished autobiography, which he planned to call *My Life,* and which was published after his death with the title *Put' Russkogo Ofitsera* (*The Road of a Russian Officer*). As for the General's wife, she endeavored, whenever possible, to keep up her journal.

As a precaution against a possible German search, the General's papers, his wife's journal, and all other compromising material was not kept hidden in the house, but was buried in the adjoining barn, where many papers were yellowed by dampness and a few completely disintegrated. The small radio was concealed in the oven during the day, and brought out with extreme caution in the evening so that they could hear the forbidden broadcasts from London.

It is interesting to note that in those frightening times of rampant denunciations, no one betrayed the Denikins and that the material he and his wife circulated never fell into the hands of the Gestapo.

Even in their remote province, word about the atrocities committed by the Germans against the Jews began to reach the Denikins at a fairly early date. The news aroused their profound indignation. The following entries in the journal of Mrs. Denikin, whose views on the subject were identical with those of her husband, should help dispel any remaining notion that General Denikin was anti-Semitic:

June 4, 1942

An eighth order against the Jews. . . . Can this be called a struggle, does such ostentatious and small-minded mockery befit a great nation? Here is the text of the German order. [And Xenia Vasilievna quoted the *Ordonnance concernant les mesures contre les juifs,* regarding the compulsory wearing of a star of David inscribed with the word *Juif,* and other profoundly humiliating requirements.]

July 25, 1942

S. came here. He had been to Paris. . . . Somehow he seems to have lost his usual energy and Gallic animation. In Paris, the Germans have performed mass arrests of Jews, up to eighty thousand it is said, seventeen thousand of them were locked up in the Palais des Sports for several days. Men, women and children of three years and older. They were hardly fed at all. There was not even enough water, and people lined up at the fire hydrants, where French firemen, pressed into service as guards by the Germans, gave those unfortunates to drink. Little children howled, many were ill, women were giving birth, and to top it all, excrement overflowed from the overcrowded latrines on the second floor, onto the crowded mass of people sleeping on the floor a story below. The despair was undescribable. S. recounted all this without inflections and without gestures, stopping occasionally to stare expressionlessly at the road.

"I somehow can't bring myself to realize," he said, "that such things are happening in our cultured times, in our cultured France, that all this is real and not a horrible dream."

August 10, 1942

Young A. dropped in and also told us about the horrors of Jewish arrests in Paris. In their house a Jewish woman jumped out of a fourth-floor window with her two small children, when the Germans came to arrest the family. They therefore took only the husband, who howled like an animal when he was being led past the covered bodies of his wife and children, so that the whole block heard him.

Even though this is told by trustworthy eyewitnesses, I am unable to accept the thought that this is true! . . .

May 22, 1943

The radio says that the Jews of the Warsaw ghetto, whose end was inevitable, have revolted. The Polish population has secretly provided them with arms. We are unable to visualize this ghetto and how it can be defended, but it must be quite large, as the battle has already lasted several days. The Germans fire at it with tank guns and drop bombs from airplanes. Its unfortunate, trapped inmates are truly fighting with the courage of despair, knowing that they are doomed in any case. What horror, what carnage! . . .

Considerably later, when Russian war prisoners, pressed into the *Osttruppen* by the Germans, began to appear in Mimizan clad in German uniforms, one of them related what he had seen to the Denikins:

Of all his tales [wrote Xenia Vasilievna in her journal on May 31, 1944], the one that smote me to the heart was his terrible description of the beating of Jews. When the Germans took Russian prisoners, they asked at the first questioning, "Which are the Jews?" Then these unfortunates were undressed, laid on the ground right in the camp, and beaten with sticks until each man lost consciousness. He was then revived by a pailful of water poured over him. The bloody, half-dead man began to crawl; a few kind soldiers, risking their own lives, helped him to reach shelter and dressed his wounds; but on the next day the German guards repeated the operation, and this went on until the Jew died of the beatings.

Stepan Ivanovich (who told this) said that he is twenty-eight years old and that if he lives another seventy years, he will not be able to forget the dreadful cries of these people being beaten to death.

UNDER
THE GERMANS, II

Denikin had been suffering for several years from an inflammation of the prostate gland. Finally, an operation for its removal became inevitable. It was performed on December 5, 1942, in a Bordeaux hospital. A week later, the shock of the operation provoked his first heart attack. He remained at the hospital for almost a month.* At the beginning of January, 1943, Anton Ivanovich was discharged from the hospital, and life at Mimizan resumed its normal course. Xenia Vasilievna continued to note anything unusual in her journal:

January 7, 1943
It is impossible to understand from which side the Germans expect to be attacked in our backwoods, yet they are fortifying everything they can. They have even hoisted machine guns to the top of the bell tower, obstructed some side roads with barbed wire, and placed cannon in the woods.

January 21, 1943
The London broadcaster invited us to listen to a voice from "over there." We heard a Russian voice proclaiming with theatrical inflections and pathos, "glory to our fighters, commanders, and . . . to our military leader of genius, Stalin."
Again, again. . . . Nothing has changed, nothing can change. Accursed lies, barbaric power, frightening shadow of the vampire who has sucked Russia dry. . . .
Can this shadow possibly cover all of Europe, all of the world? We know that two evils are locked in deadly combat. But if humanity is to survive, neither

* In several of his notes and letters to friends in later years, General Denikin said that his heart ailment began in 1945 in Paris. However, his wife and daughter insist that the illness developed in 1942 in Mimizan.

of them can win. They must devour each other like two apocalyptic monsters. Then a new life may rise and flourish on the ruins. *We* believe in this. But . . . Lord help my unbelief!

January 28, 1943

It is getting worse and worse for the Germans. Their Sixth Army, near Tsaritsin, is melting day by day. Kharkov is already threatened, but the Germans still hold fast at Tikhoretskaia and Maïkop.

Such familiar names come up in the communiqués—Manych, Stavropol, Kavkazskaia, the Don and Kuban *stanitsy* whose names are already written into history with our blood. Who would have thought that the fate of Russia would be decided twice in those remote parts . . . and the fate of the whole world as well.

July 15, 1943

Yesterday was the national holiday. . . . The newspapers announced that July 14 was to be observed as a holiday, but that no demonstrations or celebrations would be permitted. The London radio requested all Frenchmen to express their protest against the invader by coming out on their main street or public square at 7:45 P.M. I don't know whether the demonstration materialized in Paris and other large cities, but here the only two French patriots who spruced up and paraded for fifteen minutes around the church in the main square—were my husband and myself.

Nezhin has been taken. The Russians are moving forward along the entire front. . . . We follow the advance of the Russian front on the map. We are proud of the way the Russian soldiers are fighting, for they are *Russian* men fighting for their homeland.

There is no such thing in nature as "Soviet people" and "Soviet patriotism."

At the beginning of November, 1943, there occurred an event that was so interesting in itself and had such an impact on the Denikins' thoughts and emotions, that it deserves a special place in the General's biography.

We shall trace it first in Xenia Vasilievna's journal and later in General Denikin's own account, neither of which has hitherto appeared in print.

November 7, 1943

Well, wonders will never cease! We expected everything, but not this! The newly arrived German soldiers, who with their horses and transport have occupied the school, the Salle des Fêtes, and the village streets, turned out to be our countrymen arrived directly from Russia! They are prisoners of war pressed into service by the Germans . . . considered as "volunteers" but having no connection with the so-called Vlasov army (Russian Liberation Army).[1] Naturally, they found out from the local people that there are Russians here, and came to visit us. They arrive awkwardly, hesitantly, not quite sure of how they should talk to us. It is so absurd and strange to see these Russians in German uniform, yet we can't just ask them, How come? Do you understand that you are serving Russia's enemies? We can't . . . we simply can't!

Both they and we are caught in the same trap. We speak in generalities, with reservations, yet they understand. They tell us of the hopelessness of their situation, the horrors of life in the prisoner-of-war camps from which dozens of corpses are carted away like dogs every morning. There was only one way in which they could escape a terrible death. They also speak of the frightful life of penal servitude under the Bolsheviks. However, this last comes mostly from the older, gray-haired men, some of whom have fought in the ranks of our White Army. Whereas some of the young ones find that things aren't as bad as all that. They, of course, did not know the old life and are unable to compare. Most of the soldiers are Don and Kuban Cossacks, but some of them are also from Siberia, from Pskov, Astrakhan, and Kursk, from all over mother-Russia.

November 9, 1943

We continue to meet and talk with our compatriots. . . .

When we told them that there were Russian war prisoners in a camp nearby, they reacted in a very reserved, even embarrassed way. "Yes," sighed a young student, "we are one kind of Russian, you are another, and they are a third one."

"But there is only one Russia and there must be only one Russian people," said Anton Ivanovich.

November 11, 1943

Our countrymen continue to visit us every day. . . . They are very interested in news from the front, but few of them react openly to the news of the Soviet offensive.

After the others left, a robust and red-faced Black Sea sailor asked us, "Do you figure that someone can conquer Russia?"

"No, no one can conquer Russia," replied Anton Ivanovich, emphasizing the word "Russia."

"That's what I think," said the sailor. "So long, Dad. Maybe we will take off for Russia together from here!"

"Maybe," smiled Anton Ivanovich, "or else they may let me and not you in, or vice versa."

"Come on, they'll let everyone in. With such droves of people killed and starved out and the whole country in ruins, who will build it up? We will all come in useful. Look at my hands and your brains. Each will contribute something."

"Right," said Anton Ivanovich cheerfully, and they shook hands a second time.

The old man, who had struggled so hard for Russia and thought only of her throughout his life, and the young, almost illiterate lad, who had fled the hard life of his homeland, understood each other perfectly.

Here is General Denikin's account of the same events, from a more historical point of view:

In the course of the last war there occurred in the east a phenomenon hitherto unknown in the history of international warfare. In order to reinforce its ranks, the German command resorted to the formation of military units composed of war prisoners, as well as of civilians from occupied Russian provinces. Such a risky experiment proved feasible as a result of the Russian people's alienation from its government, whose accursed methods had perverted the most normal foundations of national consciousness.

From the first moment of their captivity, the Russians met with unbearable conditions, immeasurably worse than those suffered by the war prisoners of other countries. Without regard to distance, the Germans marched them along the roads without food or water, and if anyone dared to stop because of complete exhaustion or in order to quench his thirst from a roadside ditch, the guards finished him off with bayonet or bullet. . . . The prisoners were made to ride for two or three days at a stretch, on open train platforms, jammed together, without water, bread, or any toilet facilities. In this tightly packed mass, which stank of human excrement, the dead stood upright among the living. . . . A released French war prisoner, whose camp was near a Russian camp, once told me that when one of these trains arrived, the Russian prisoners of war were unable to move, as their bodies were literally paralyzed from stiffness. The French were ordered by the Germans to carry the Russians out on stretchers or in their arms. The living were laid on the floor of the barracks, the dead were thrown into a common pit. . . .

"It is easy to recognize the Russian prisoners by their eyes," said the Frenchman; "their eyes burn with suffering and hatred." . . .

At the Nuremberg trials a document was produced, dated February, 1942, and signed by the German Minister of Economy. It read, "Out of 3,900,000 Russian prisoners in our camps, only 1,300,000 are still fit to work. Five hundred thousand have died during the last four months of the preceding year."

The war prisoners of all other countries were helped by their respective governments and by the Red Cross. The Russians alone were left by the Soviet regime to their own fate. Without discrimination, the Soviet government held all prisoners to be "deserters" and "traitors." In absentia, they were all stripped of their military ranks. They were called "former servicemen," and were registered with the NKVD [secret police]. Their families were deprived of help and often persecuted.

These facts, known in the camps, further aggravated the moral suffering of the war prisoners, who had nowhere to turn for either moral or material assistance.

Under such conditions, when the German command offered them normal military rations and humane treatment, many agreed to don the German uniform. This was all the more tempting as they were promised that their newly formed detachments would be used for service in the rear.

Let those who dare, cast a stone at them. . . .

And then, one day a Russian battalion arrived in the little provincial French town on the shores of the Atlantic ocean where I lived during the years of German occupation. The battalion arrived quite unexpectedly both for us and for the "volunteers," who without knowing their destination, were put on the train somewhere in western Russia, and came all the way through without changing trains, and without being allowed to leave the train at the stations. The officers and men of this battalion were people of varying ages, from sixteen to sixty, and of different social backgrounds, ranging from collective-farm workers to a professor. Among them some were men without party affiliations, others were members of the *Komsomol* [Young Communist League] or the Communist party.

These people flocked to me in crowds, and when the Germans issued orders forbidding them to visit private houses, they sneaked in after dark through the back door, either alone or in small groups. This went on for several months, until the battalion was transferred to the shores of the English Channel.[2]

We discussed everything: Soviet life, Red Army procedure, the war, the tenor of life in foreign countries, and first and foremost, our visitors' own fate.

They all had one common trait, developed by their life as Soviet citizens and as prisoners of war—an instinct for camouflage. Before surrendering, all Communists and *Komsomols* buried their party and *Komsomol* cards in the trenches and registered as non-party men. Many officers, afraid of being subjected to specially harsh treatment, tore off their insignia and decorations and passed themselves off as privates. When it became known that the families of men "missing in action" continued to receive their rations, while the families of prisoners were being persecuted, many of those who became prisoners registered under different names and false addresses. When Cossacks were called upon to "volunteer," people from Stavropol and Nizhni-Novgorod, and even the Chuvashi with their broken Russian, all registered as Cossacks. . . .

As there was always the possibility of a spy in their midst, the rather delicate questions that were often put to me, were always made to sound harmless. The Soviet nationals have become adepts in that art. . . . Our conversations went somewhat like this:

"Are we pretty far from the Spanish border?"

"A hundred kilometers."

"All woodland, I take it?"

"The last third of the way has no woods."

"The border is manned by French people?"

"No, the border is very efficiently guarded by Germans."

There was only one instance of someone upsetting the deliberate neutrality of our dialogue, either through naïveté or for a definite purpose, by the following question: "Tell me, General, why don't you join the German service? After all, General Krasnov. . . ."

"Very well, here is my answer: General Denikin has always served and continues to serve only Russia. He never has and never will serve a foreign government."

I saw my questioner quickly brought to order. "That's clear enough," proclaimed a loud bass voice. No further explanations were needed.

Not a single group visited me and not a day went by, without my being asked the crucial question: "Do you think that we will ever return to Russia?"

Once, someone cheerfully interrupted, "We shall. And we will take you, General, with us!"

"Oh no, this will never happen. It is much more probable that I will take you along with myself. . . ."

Someone shouted, "He is right!" And once again there was no need for explanations.

Plainly, no one believed any longer in a German victory, and the people who crowded in front of my large map, on which the line of the front inexorably and rapidly moved westward, were clearly in the throes of conflicting emotions: the unconscious pride in their country and their army and . . . the fear of their own uncertain fate. . . .

I was visited at different times by two Communists. One of them—an officer— even tried to convince me of the Communist "truths," which he had obviously memorized from some condensed manual of party history, and boasted of the "happy life" under the Soviets. But having been caught out in this falsehood,

admitted that the happy life had not yet arrived, but that it would soon come.
. . . The other Communist, who was more modest, made a half-hearted attempt
to justify his affiliation with the party.

I put the following question to him: "Tell me how to account for the following
fact: You are aware that if the Germans find out that you are a Communist,
they will immediately have you shot. Yet, you are not afraid to admit it to me?"
Silence.

"Very well, then, I shall answer for you. You would not divulge this to your
own Soviet people, because you have been brought up for twenty-five years in
an atmosphere of denunciations, provocation, and betrayal. Whereas you know
that, despite my anti-Bolshevism, I shall not betray you to the Germans. Therein
lies the fundamental difference between your Red, and our White, psycholo-
gies." . . .

But all, all of them without exception, were desperately homesick for their
motherland, their families, and their homes. Despite all the hardships of Soviet
life, despite the penalties awaiting them, many of them were prepared to return
to Russia at the first opportunity. Their anti-German feelings were not only
vented between the four walls of our home, but aired in the street and in the
pubs, where the Russians fraternized with the French, drowned their sorrows in
wine, and openly denounced the *"Boches."* Where a tipsy Cossack who had
learned a few words of French, would point to his uniform, saying, *"Ici—
allemand!"*

Then, flinging open his tunic, he would point to his bare chest, saying,
"Ici—russe!" . . .

For me they were unfortunate Russian people trapped in an impossible
situation, and I was sincerely sorry for them. They came to me for consolation.
I could not, of course, promise them any magnanimity on the part of the
"father of the peoples," but I assured them, with complete conviction, that
any other Russian or foreign power would not condemn, but forgive them.
Provided . . . they took off that German uniform in time. . . .

They were mutually determined, when the allies drew near, to do away with
their German officers and noncoms and go over to the Anglo-American side.
Their decision was strengthened by leaflets, dropped in the area of Russian troop
concentrations by allied planes, which appealed to the Russians not to oppose
the allies, but go over to their side, and promised them immunity from any possible reprisals.

When they asked me whether or not to believe the allies, I answered in the
affirmative with complete sincerity and conviction, because I could not imagine
that things would turn out differently. . . . Most of the Russian battalions gave
themselves over to the British and Americans at the first encounter.[3]

Denikin was profoundly shaken by his meetings and talks with his countrymen from "over there." They confirmed him once more in his conviction
that nothing had changed in Soviet Russia; that the value of human life
there was still as low as at the beginning of Bolshevism; that, as before, the
regime recognized neither human rights, nor justice, nor mercy. And although he remained uncompromisingly firm in his condemnation of the
Russian émigrés who collaborated with the Germans, Denikin saw in those
German-uniformed Russian war prisoners, nothing but plain Russian people

fallen in terrible trouble, and felt for them with all his heart, though their superficial allegiance repelled him. When he learned, a few years later, that those unfortunates who had given themselves up to the Anglo-Americans were being returned by force to the Soviet Union to face torture and death, as a result of a paragraph of the Yalta agreement between Roosevelt, Churchill, and Stalin, there was no limit to his grief, indignation, and despair.

X L

JOY AND GRIEF

The detachment of Russians in German uniform was moved to the north, away from Mimizan, and all communication with them came to an end. The Denikins were again reduced to their "solitude *à deux,*" and we turn once again to Mrs. Denikin's journal, with its description of the couple's life, which now was completely centered on the successes of the allies.

February 17, 1944
   The British have shot down two large German planes over our forest.

March 27, 1944
   There is a general alarm, with the tocsin ringing, both factories blowing their sirens, and planes buzzing above.
   We have been overflown twice by hundreds of airplanes. They flew in squadrons, quite low, paying no attention to the firing of our ack-ack battery. . . . We did not even suspect that such antiaircraft precautions had been taken here . . . but no plane was hit.
   Small fighter planes were zooming around the heavy bombers. The whole population was out in the street, looking at the sky and excitedly discussing the destination and origin of the deadly birds.

March 31, 1944
   We listened to the thunder of salutes fired in Moscow in honor of the taking of Ochakov. This is the second time in history, I believe, that the Russians have captured Ochakov. A century and a half ago, in Catherine's reign, Potemkin wrested it from the Turks. Then it was to the glory of Russia. But now? "Maybe now also," replies Anton Ivanovich.

June 6, 1944
   They have landed! On the shores of the Channel. Right in the face, so to speak, of the formidable German fortifications. That is, they are still landing and parachuting down in droves. Starting at 2 A.M. I heard the sound of planes flying above us, and this lasted until morning. I rose at 6 and woke up Anton Ivanovich to tell him that something out of the ordinary was happening. We

turned on the radio and learned that the allied aircraft and fleet are destroying the coastal defenses and that parachutists are coming down in the region of Caen, in Normandy. It has begun. . . . The local people have been talking of nothing else since 7 A.M. By 8, we already knew that troops were landing on the beaches in several places. . . . If only this could succeed. . . .

July 3, 1944

Minsk is being bypassed to the north and south. The tape, which has so long been stationary on our large Russian map, is now moved forward every day.

After listening to the evening news round up, Anton Ivanovich armed himself with a hammer and is changing the location of the fastening pins.

"How well they advance and how correctly they maneuver!"

And how the old soldier's heart bleeds. . . .

August 11, 1944

Yesterday I was sick and slept badly. Anton Ivanovich woke me up later than usual and announced that the Americans had taken Chartres. "Impossible! Only yesterday they were over a hundred kilometers away!" But it was true, as the radio confirmed in every language. In a daring raid, a tank column has reached Chartres, located seventy-five kilometers from Paris. Everyone rejoices. . . .

August 15, 1944

A whole group of us stood in front of our courtyard observing the comings and goings of the Germans, more of whom are constantly arriving in our little town. Rumor has it that they are gathering here all the garrisons of nearby villages and distant bunkers. Suddenly, the evening stillness resounded with the sharp, clear sounds of a French bugle call, made familiar by the radio broadcasts from London and Algiers. We all looked silently in the direction of the approaching sounds. A truck, tightly packed with black French war prisoners, drove past us. . . . One of the blacks, at its very center, was loudly and joyfully blowing his upraised trumpet, the others were laughing, baring their white teeth, and shouting something to us. Two phlegmatic German sentries at the rear of the truck were stolidly munching apples. . . .

A few days later, the Germans abandoned Mimizan.

September 20, 1944

A hundred and fifty German prisoners of war have arrived in our neighborhood to repair a bridge. They are billeted in barracks that were formerly occupied by black French prisoners, and the latter have been entrusted with guarding them. What a quick about-face! On the very first night, the Negroes engaged in some barter, on their own initiative. They removed and put on the good shoes of the Germans and gave them in return their own worn-out and motley footgear. Until then they had had to make do with broken-down sabots, torn espadrilles, patched-up rubber boots, and self-made objects which couldn't even be called shoes.

January 22, 1945

The world press talks of nothing but Soviet victories. . . . We Russians always knew what our people were capable of. We were not surprised, but deeply moved and elated. And in the midst of our exile and of our difficult life abroad, our souls were elevated and fulfilled.

We were filled with pride, but also assailed by painful doubts.

What is victory bringing to Russia and the rest of the world? Has it been won for the greatness of Russia, . . . for the equitable and better future life of its people? And not for the fulfillment of a diabolic plan of contaminating all humanity with the savage doctrine invented by one maniac and exploited by another? Exploited in order to satisfy his unbounded vanity, his monstrous thirst for power and his inhuman nature. Can the heroism of the Russians, all their incredible sacrifices, be nothing but a tribute paid this Moloch, nothing but a part of this terrifying plan?

May 19, 1945

Rosenberg has been caught. There is someone who should be delivered to the Soviets to be judged as they please. This one deserves everything!

June 5, 1945

Here we are, back in Paris. An end has come to our five-year-long banishment, with its vegetable garden, woodland walks, and contacts with local people, who were provincial if you wish, but spontaneous and real. I pressed many a hand with tears in my eyes and the realization that I would probably never see my friends again.

. . . Our life was difficult during these five years, but I don't regret them. This fragment of my life . . . , which chance made us spend in a remote corner of France, taught me more about her true nature and soul, her qualities and defects, than our preceding fifteen years in Paris.

The five years of the German occupation, spent in a remote French province in great poverty and under the watchful eyes of the German authorities, were an important stage of General Denikin's life. He overcame the trials of that period with honor. Though his irreconcilable attitude to the Soviet regime remained unchanged, he had firmly opposed any collaboration with the foreign invaders and enemies of Russia. He had fought defeatism in the ranks of the émigrés, denounced the collaborationists in their midst, and consistently circulated his anti-German writings among his compatriots.

Despite a deteriorating heart condition and general physical exhaustion, his spiritual energy remained unabated.

After five years of war and occupation, Paris was dingier and grimier, but still beautiful. But for Denikin the return to the city was marred by grave disappointment. He was distressed to find that in the course of the war and the liberation of France, the moral and political attitudes of many of his fellow émigrés had undergone considerable changes.

When the war ended, and the details of what had been going on in Auschwitz, Dachau, and other German concentration camps finally came to the surface, the whole world was shaken with horror. The talk was all about German atrocities, but not a word was said about the persecutions and slayings perpetrated by the Communists in the heart of their own country, against their alleged political foes. Yet, Stalin's purges of the late

1930's alone had resulted in the execution or starvation in concentration camps of over nine million such "enemies."

Denikin was one of very few people who continued to condemn both evils equally, during that period of the glossing over of the Soviet excesses.

In enumerating those who had tried to curry favor with the Germans in the name of the Russian émigrés, Denikin severely criticized certain leaders of military organizations who had, on their own initiative and without consulting their membership, presented memorandums to the German command in which they indicated their readiness to "contribute to a speedy [German] victory and to the restoration of order in our homeland." [1] He particularly blamed those expressing this attitude who, by their prominence and the prestige of their names, could seriously confuse a large section of the émigré community.

Another trend, which appeared among the émigrés in the course of the war and gathered strength as it drew to an end, distressed Denikin no less than the collaborationist tendencies. This was the desire in some émigré circles to achieve a rapprochement with the Soviet regime. The Russian troops' victorious advance, the fall of Germany, combined with nostalgia for their lost country, gave rise to the hope that the resurgence of patriotism in Russia pointed to the possibility of a gradual evolution toward a more tolerant form of government, with the army proving stronger than the party and forcing it to modify its rigors. Denikin affirmed, and proved to have been right, that all such hopes were futile.

He criticized a group of prominent émigrés who had accepted an invitation to a reception at the Soviet embassy in Paris. He was indignant that the eminent historian and politician Milyukov, who had adopted a succession of different political orientations in the course of his life, had ended up by recognizing the October revolution as an organic development in the nation's history, and praised the achievements of the Bolsheviks, saying that the people had not only accepted the Soviet regime, but become reconciled to its shortcomings and appreciative of its advantages. Denikin, to whom the dictum that the end justifies the means had always been abhorrent, could not forgive Milyukov for stating, on behalf of the Soviet regime, that upon seeing the accomplished aim, one gained a better understanding of the means by which it had been attained.

But while he condemned some of the public figures among the émigrés for their policy of appeasement in regard to the Soviet regime, for what he called their "Soviet Canossa," Denikin recognized that Milyukov and many others with him, had behaved irreproachably during the German occupation. The writer Bunin had also conducted himself with great dignity in regard to the Germans, who were anxious to secure the literary collaboration of the noted Nobel prizewinner. Their attempt to utilize Bunin's name for propaganda purposes failed in much the same way as their attempt to bring Denikin to Berlin. Both men had preferred to continue their lives in semistarvation.

The final and perhaps most bitter disappointment which awaited Denikin in Paris concerned some of his friends, members of the Alliance of Volunteers, to whom he was closely bound not only by past comradeship but also by a common wholehearted devotion to the White cause. Denikin found that even here, many persons no longer shared his views. They continued to treat him with the same love and respect as before. But this love had its roots in the past, in the heroic moments of the White struggle under Denikin's leadership.

As for the present—the brilliant victories of the Red Army had so impressed them, that they fell silent if the conversation touched on the unacceptability of the Soviet regime, and even spoke in favor of the Soviets.

Denikin by that time had already arrived at certain conclusions which he continued to maintain for the two remaining years of his life. He considered that the Soviet Union's postwar policy of occupying various countries in its vicinity, and the brutal methods by which this policy was implemented, were gradually antagonizing the entire world and turning it against the USSR (i.e., against Russia). He feared that this policy of Communist imperialism, which Russia's former allies viewed with fear and distrust, could lead to an open conflict with them and reduce to nothing all that had been achieved by the patriotism and sacrifices of the Russian people. He foresaw that if another war should threaten, Russia would find itself alone against its enemies. He expected, therefore, that at least those who had fought in the White movement for the survival of their country and the protection of its territory, would know enough to draw a sharp line between the national interests of Russia and Soviet imperialism.

"Positively nothing would threaten Russia's vital interests," he said, "if her government maintained an honest and genuinely peaceful policy. Whereas Bolshevism is pushing other states to the brink of the abyss, until driven by despair, they will rise against it. When this happens, our country will really be faced with the greatest danger in its history. Then will all the enemies of the Soviets . . . and of Russia, rise up in arms. Then will encroachments upon the vital interests of Russia, her unity, and her very existence, threaten her from all sides." [2]

There certainly was no basis for the accusation, later leveled at Denikin by the pro-Communist press in Europe and America, that he deliberately tried to incite a war against Russia. On the contrary, Denikin's behavior was dictated by his overwhelming concern for Russia's safety.

The conflict of views between Denikin and his friends was one of the reasons for his decision to leave France for the United States. Another reason was the absence of outlets in the Russian press for his opinions and articles. When the war ended, the émigré newspapers and periodicals in Paris, abolished by the Germans, did not resume publication. They were replaced by a new Soviet-oriented press. In the France of 1945, Denikin was deprived of the possibility of free public expression.

There was also a third reason. General Denikin was deeply concerned by the tragic fate of the Russian war prisoners who had put on the German uniform and later voluntarily surrendered themselves to the allies. According to the Yalta agreement, the allies were committed to returning them by force to the Soviet Union. The United States was the foremost power in the Western coalition, and General Denikin was determined to appeal personally to the military leaders of the United States and to American public opinion to prevent this act of coercion from taking place.

Anton Ivanovich and Xenia Vasilievna left France on November 21, 1945, and after a short stay in England, sailed to New York on the *Queen Elizabeth* (converted to a troopship during the war), in which a cabin had been assigned to them by courtesy of the British command. They arrived in New York on December 7.

X L I

ARRIVAL IN THE

UNITED STATES

All the arrangements and formalities connected with the Denikins' arrival in the United States as permanent residents were taken care of by a former officer of the Volunteer Army,[1] who lived in Forest Hills. They stayed with him until September, 1946, when they were fortunate enough to find some modest lodgings in the suburbs despite the housing crisis.

The news of Denikin's decision to come to the United States took Americans of Russian origin by surprise. They learned about it from a communiqué of December 5, 1945, in New York's Russian-language newspaper *Novoye Russkoye Slovo,* announcing that "General Denikin has left France for the U.S. with an immigration visa." The newspaper's correspondent added that Denikin's departure provoked a great deal of comment among the Parisian Russians, and even some worry in view of the growing Communist influence in France.

On December 9, two days after Denikin's arrival in America, the same paper printed an extensive interview with him by one of its contributors: "Anton Ivanovich Denikin has hardly changed at all in the course of the last five years; he has the same firm, steely glance and formulates his meaning with the same meticulous care. Neither have his political views altered in the course of these years. The former commander in chief of the Armed Forces of South Russia has remained a patriot and an anti-Bolshevik. As always, he is with the Russian people, but against the Soviet regime. . . ."[2]

General Denikin's arrival created a stir among American Communists. A systematic witch-hunt against him began in the Communist press. He was accused of planning to organize a new crusade against the Soviet Union, branded as a warmonger, a Black Hundreder, and an enemy of the people. He was also blamed for the Jewish pogroms in the south of Russia during the civil war. Mass meetings were organized to demand that the immigration authorities immediately deport Denikin. Some Jewish publications in New York, such as the *Jewish Daily Forward* and the *Morgen Journal*, also campaigned against Denikin. They blamed him in no uncertain terms for the pogroms.

The *Morgen Journal* got so carried away in its invectives against Denikin that it lumped him together with "Petliura, Makhnó, and other White guard Black Hundreders." One cannot help imagining the amazement of the former socialist Petliura (assassinated in Paris by Samuel Schwartzbard in revenge for the Ukrainian pogroms), and especially of the half-literate peasant-anarchist Makhnó (who ended up by a fluke as a Russian émigré in Paris and was buried at the Père-Lachaise cemetery), at being included in the category of the "White guard Black Hundreders."

The *Morgen Journal* chastised not only Denikin but *Novoye Russkoye Slavo* and its correspondent, a well-known Russian journalist of Jewish extraction, who interviewed him:

This journalist to whom General Denikin had bared his soul was no stooge of Father Coughlin or Gerald K. Smith, but a representative of the Russian paper *Novoye Russkoye Slovo,* whose publisher is the Jew V. I. Shimkin, whose chief editor is the Jew M. E. Weinbaum, and the majority of whose staff is also Jewish, including several well-known Russian-Jewish socialists and Russo-Jewish authors. . . . Can it be possible that the Jewish publishers and editorial members of *Novoye Russkoye Slovo* forgot all this and gave such a rousing welcome to General Denikin only because they share in his hostility toward Soviet Russia? [3]

In his long years in exile, Denikin had become quite used to the attacks of the Communist press, and he decided, therefore, to pay no attention to the familiar harassment of the pro-Bolshevik press. He did, however, respond to the accusations of the Jewish newspapers.

I have learned that your paper has published an article containing some unfounded and insulting accusations against me [wrote Denikin to the editors of the *Morgen Journal* and the *Jewish Daily Forward*].
    I wish to state that:
    1) I have never had, and now have, no "secret" projects. I have labored all my life, and am still laboring, for the Russian cause—formerly with arms, and now with word and pen—but always quite openly.
    2) In the last twenty-five years, I have opposed pan-Germanism and later Hitlerism in a whole series of books and brochures written by me, and by means of public appearances in various countries and five European capitals. My books have been placed on the index and banned from stores and libraries by the Gestapo. I spent the five years of German occupation in the remote French countryside, under observation by the German *Kommandantur,* without ceasing, however, to disseminate anti-German appeals among my compatriots.
    The stand adopted by me at that time, as well as the injustice of accusing me of "Black Hundredism" are clear to the entire Russian émigré community. They are, unfortunately, not clear to the editors of your newspaper.

With regard to the accusation that he was to blame for pogroms, Denikin wrote,

The wave of anti-Semitism swept over south Russia long before the White armies entered the Jewish Pale. . . . The high command took measures against Jewish pogroms . . . were it not for these measures . . . the fate of the Jews in south Russia would have been incomparably more tragic.[4]

Ever since his encounter in Mimizan with the Russian war prisoners pressed into the German army, Denikin had been filled with concern for the fate which awaited them at the conclusion of the war. His personal contact with them had opened his eyes to the moral drama which each of these men was undergoing. To them was now added the huge mass of civilians, male and female, whom the Germans had brought out of Russia as forced labor. Denikin was haunted by the thought that the hundreds of thousands of expatriated Russians presently confined in the camps of Germany and Italy were being threatened with repatriation to the USSR, which the Soviet government was pursuing with sinister determination.

He could not remain silent, and decided to intercede openly with the American authorities, asking them *not* to surrender to the Soviets the Russians held captive by the English and Americans. The following are excerpts from a letter on this subject sent by General Denikin to General Eisenhower on January 31, 1946:

YOUR EXCELLENCY,
I have read in the *Times* a description of the horrible events taking place in the Dachau camp, presently operated by Americans, involving the Russian nationals sometimes designated *Vlasovtsy,* and at other times "deserters and renegades," all of whom prefer death to being surrendered to the Soviet government.
I believe that you are not familiar with the true history of these people, and would like to acquaint you with it.

At this point General Denikin gave a résumé of the facts with which we have already become familiar.

During the German occupation [he continued], I have met with and talked to hundreds of Russian soldiers and officers in the German service, among whom were people of varying ages and social backgrounds—some were non-party men; others belonged to the *Komsomol* or the Communist party. I am therefore well acquainted with the mood which prevailed among them at that time. To begin with, there were absolutely no pro-German tendencies; they even hated the Germans and having found themselves in the midst of the French population, expressed these feelings by word and gesture with such frankness and abandon that the French came to treat them with sympathy and confidence.
These people were trapped and searching for a way out.
They were continuously evolving the most fantastic schemes—such as crossing the border to Spain or negotiating the Channel in rowboats in order to reach England. . . . All were determined that—when the allies approached—they

would exterminate the German command and go over to the side of the British-American troops or the French partisan detachments.

Your Excellency must be aware that that is exactly what was done by most of the Russian battalions.

When the war ended, the press carried an announcement by the Soviet general, Golikov, in charge of prisoner-of-war repatriation, in which he promised that all was understood, forgiven, and forgotten. A large number of men believed him, presented themselves at rallying points, and were sent to the USSR. But soon after this, news began to percolate from there by various channels, describing the terrible fate which befell the former war prisoners and particularly those "who had donned the German uniform." These last were faced with torture and death. . . .

So that those unfortunates are perfectly aware of the fate awaiting them in the "Soviet paradise," and it is not surprising, therefore, that the war prisoners being assembled at Dachau prefer to meet their death there. And what a death! . . . Slashing their throats with small razor blades and undergoing indescribable suffering before dying; setting their barracks on fire and stripping off their clothes in order to perish faster in the flames . . . anything rather than face the Bolsheviks' torture chambers. . . .

I can imagine the feelings of American officers and soldiers obliged to be accessories to such cruelty. . . .

Your Excellency, I am aware of the existence of certain paragraphs of the Yalta agreement, but also of the continued (though sadly disregarded) existence of the democratic tradition of human freedom and the right of political asylum.

There also exists a code of military ethics which precludes violence even in relation to a defeated enemy. Finally, there is Christian morality with its commitment to justice and charity.

I appeal to you, your Excellency, as one soldier to another, in the hope that my plea will be heeded.

GENERAL A. DENIKIN [5]

In the absence of General Eisenhower, Denikin's letter was answered by his acting chief of staff, General Thomas T. Handy.

General Handy referred to the paragraphs of the Yalta agreement requiring the forcible repatriation to the Soviet Union of any individual who "was both a citizen of and actually within the Soviet Union on 1 September 1939 and comes within one of the following categories: 1. was captured in German uniform; 2. was a member of the Soviet Armed Forces on or after 22 June 1941 and was not subsequently discharged therefrom; 3. has been found on the basis of reasonable evidence to be a collaborator with the enemy, having voluntarily rendered aid and comfort to the enemy."

In conclusion, General Handy stated that the American army was obliged to carry out to the best of its ability the policy established by the government of the United States.

The letter was businesslike and polite though it was addressed to "Mr. Denikin," despite the fact that the latter's former rank and position were indicated in his letter to General Eisenhower. It is very doubtful indeed that General Handy had the vaguest conception of the history of the Russian civil war or the identity of the individual to whom he was replying.[6]

Several years later, George Fisher in his *Soviet Opposition to Stalin* provided an answer to the question of why no one in America had moved a finger to rescue the *Vlasovtsy,* and others in their position. He emphasized the fact that at that moment the Western nations, seething with hatred for Germany, and naïvely believing in the possibility of friendly relations with the Soviets, refused to consider the *Vlasovtsy* as anything but wartime traitors, disregarding or ignoring the unprecedented strangeness of their situation. The tragedy of these unfortunates was precisely that under such conditions, invoking the right of political asylum, or appealing to the democratic principles of the West, was doomed to certain failure.[7]

Denikin was so affected by the tragedy of these people that in 1946 he devoted an extremely interesting and informative article to the subject of "General Vlasov and His Followers." It was submitted in a slightly abbreviated translated form to several American periodicals, all of which rejected it with various excuses. The truth was that the article did not correspond to the prevailing mood of the moment. Thus, another of the General's hopes was doomed to disappointment. The American press did not, after all, provide him with a "forum" in which to express his opinions.

At the conclusion of the English version of his article on Vlasov, Denikin mentioned that there were still some Russian war prisoners resisting repatriation in Allied camps. He expressed the hope that an awakened sense of justice among civilized nations would save the survivors.

Eventually, after Denikin was already dead, the United States did open its doors to those who had not yet been handed over to Soviet authorities. However, growing friction and disharmony between Washington and Moscow may have had more to do with this gesture than a simple sense of justice.

At the beginning of 1946, Denikin gave two lectures in New York. The first one, entitled *Mirovaia Voina i Russkaia Voennaia Emigratsia* ("The World War and the Russian Military Emigration"), was not open to the general public, but nevertheless, very well attended. Tickets to the Manhattan Center, where it took place, had been offered only to former officers of the Russian army and to former participants in the civil war.[8] The second lecture, also at the Manhattan Center, was on *Puti Russkoi Emigratsii* ("The Path of the Russian Emigration"). It was open to the general public.[9]

Both of Denikin's addresses embraced the same theme: the war and the Russian emigration. But whereas the first concentrated mainly on the former military personnel among the Russian émigrés, the second examined the political fluctuations among the entire group of émigrés in Europe in the course of the past decade. Denikin also spoke of the political and ideological aims which, in his opinion, the émigrés should pursue in the postwar period.

Despite Denikin's desperate financial situation, the profit from his first lecture was donated to the Association of Russian War Invalids in France. The second lecture brought him his first earnings in this country—a few hundred dollars which gave him a temporary respite from chronic penury.

According to the local Russian papers, approximately seven hundred people attended Denikin's second lecture. Many of them undoubtedly came out of curiosity—to see and hear the man whose name was inseparably linked with the Russian civil-war period. There were people who had fought under his leadership and were still devoted to him. There were left-wing intellectuals who, despite their distinctly negative attitude toward the White movement, had learned to appreciate Denikin's personal qualities in later years—his integrity, straightforwardness, and civic courage. Reactionaries who blamed Denikin for not having embraced the monarchist cause while he was in power were also represented, as were Russian liberals whose way of thinking was very close to Denikin's own.

A "grandiose mass demonstration" was expected to take place in front of the Manhattan Center on the day of the second lecture. The Communist press appealed to all "sympathizers" to join in a protest against "the leader of pogroms recently arrived in the U.S., General Denikin, who is trying to mobilize the forces of reaction and incite a Third World War." As it turned out, however, the picket line at 8 P.M. numbered about thirty-five people. At the end of the lecture, the picketers put away their signs and peacefully disbanded.[10]

XLII

THE LAST YEAR

———◄──── ──►———

When the war ended, public opinion in the United States demanded, with increasing insistence, the speedy demobilization of the armed forces and the return of servicemen to their homes and families. American antimilitarism was compounded in this instance by the still persistent belief in the possibility of friendly coexistence with the Soviet Union.

By April, 1946, the number of men discharged from the army alone had reached almost seven million. The United States armed forces were literally melting away.[1]

Meanwhile, the Soviet government's continuous violations of the conditions agreed upon by the allies in the course of the war were becoming more blatant. The Communist parties of the countries adjoining the Soviet Union were striving to seize control of their governments, with the direct or indirect assistance of Moscow. The principal aim of the Soviets was to counteract British-American influence in the war-torn countries of Europe, and replace it with their own ascendancy. They concentrated particularly on Germany, but also on France and Italy, where the Moscow-trained leaders of local Communist parties strove to undermine the existing regimes by means of strikes, propaganda, and occasional terrorist acts.

Denikin watched with anxiety the spread of Communist influence in both Europe and Asia. He feared that American demobilization and disarmament would create conditions so encouraging to the activities of Stalin's government that the United States and Britain would be forced to resort to armed interference in place of their ineffective diplomatic protests.

The possibility of such a confrontation, which would threaten the Russian people with dire consequences, appeared almost incvitable to Denikin. It was this conviction which finally determined him to send a memorandum to the governments of the United States and Great Britain, in which he set down what he considered to be the prerequisites for protecting Russia against dismemberment and foreign oppression, should she become involved in another war.

There was a pathetic lack of realism in this decision. How could a private person, whose name in this country was either forgotten or erroneously associated with the forces of reaction and obscurantism, hope to make his voice heard by the powers that be? Yet this course of action was but another proof of Denikin's determination to serve Russia; he deemed it his duty to apprise Washington and London of the opinions held by those whom he still considered the true, non-Communist, representatives of Russia.

General Denikin's memorandum on "The Russian Question" was mailed on June 11, 1946. In analyzing the internal situation of the Soviet Union, the memorandum maintained that at the present time a third world war was not desired by the USSR's ruling circles. It pointed out, however, that world revolution remained the ultimate aim of Communism and that hence Stalin's government would persist in its efforts to "provoke internal explosions" in the rest of the world, or at the very least, undermine the morale of non-Communist countries to such an extent that they would become easy prey to Soviet influence. Denikin maintained that France and Italy, morally undermined by the war years, as well as Spain after its recent civil war, could easily succumb to the seduction of Communism. At this point, he proceeded to develop the principal theme of his memorandum:

In the event that the Western democracies are compelled to take up arms in the face of Bolshevik provocation, it is essential that the anti-Bolshevik coalition not repeat Hitler's fundamental mistake which resulted in Germany's defeat. The war must be waged not against Russia, but solely for the purpose of overthrowing Bolshevism. One must not confuse the USSR with Russia, the Soviet regime with the Russian people, the executioner with the victim. Should the war be directed against Russia, with the aim of dividing and Balkanizing her (the Ukraine, the Caucasus) or dismembering her, the Russian people would again react to such a war by rising to the defense of their motherland.

A Western invasion of this kind would follow the pattern of similar invasions in the past. Even if temporarily successful, it would not signal the end, but the beginning of endless new wars.

On the other hand, if it were made clear that the war was not directed against Russia and her sovereignty, and that the inviolability of Russia's historic borders and her vital interests would be fully respected, then a collapse of the Bolshevik structure, either through a revolt of the people or by means of a *coup d'état,* would appear completely possible.

Sober political thinking on the part of an anti-Bolshevik coalition, even one inimical to Russia, should consider the precedents of history and come to the conclusion that Russia cannot be permanently enslaved. However, even the temporary exploitation of a turmoil called forth by internal upheavals in Russia, would be a manifestation of reckless, and for some countries, suicidal policy, leading to many years of bloody strife and chaos in the world.[2]

The copies of General Denikin's covering letters accompanying this memorandum have not been preserved, but one of the letters acknowledging its receipt remains in his papers. The letter from London, dated June 24, 1946, on stationery inscribed "the Under Secretary of State, Foreign Office" acknowledges receipt of General Denikin's memorandum "The Russian Question" at Secretary of State Bevin's request, and states that its contents have been noted.[3] We do not know to whom Denikin addressed the memorandum he sent to Washington. No answer to it has been found in the General's archive or personal papers.

In June, 1946, American government circles still believed in the possibility of collaboration with the USSR. It is possible, therefore, that the subject of the memorandum had been considered too sensitive to warrant an official answer to a private person—a person, moreover, whose name had unpleasant connotations for the Soviet embassy in Washington.

Many of the premises of the memorandum later proved to have been erroneous. Used as he was to thinking along military lines, Denikin was convinced that the rapidly growing tension in international relations would inevitably culminate in a third world war. He was far from foreseeing that the conflict would drag out indefinitely and even earn the unimaginable name of "cold war," and that, despite the flaring up of numerous armed conflicts in scattered areas of our globe, it would not result in an open clash between the two principal protagonists.

His assumption that in the event of another war the Russian people would believe the promises of the United States and Great Britain was also unrealistic. The Communists had made excellent use in their propaganda of the statements of some *Vlasovtsy* whom they had chosen not to exterminate upon their return. The latter could affirm in all honesty to all and sundry that they had been betrayed by the allies, whose planes scattered leaflets promising that all Russians in German uniform would be pardoned, and who later delivered them to the Soviet authorities.

Denikin also miscalculated the possible reaction to his views in American government circles. He expected it to be sympathetic, remembering that during the Russian civil war the United States government, despite its policy of self-determination for all peoples, had been opposed to the dismemberment of Russia and in no hurry to recognize the states that had broken away. In his anxiety to preserve the unity of his country, he did not even suspect that the American approach in such matters had undergone a complete reversal. And he was, of course, unable to foresee that in a few years, United States policy would definitely favor the dismemberment of Russia and that in 1959 Congress would adopt a resolution concerning the so-called Captive Nations, making their liberation one of the aims of the nation's foreign policy. In passing this resolution, the members of the 86th Congress, most of whom knew next to nothing about Russian history, fell victim to the hoax formerly perpetrated by Nazi propaganda, and listed in all seriousness among the countries allegedly "enslaved" by Russia, such German inventions as "Kazakia," "Idel Ural," and other figments of Hitler's, Goebbels', and Rosenberg's imaginations.[4]

Denikin's life in America gradually assumed a normal routine. He saw very few people at first—some half dozen persons he had known back in Russia. His closest friend among them was Countess Sophie Panin, one of the most outstanding Russian women of the prerevolutionary period. She had acquired a nationwide reputation in Russia through her social and cultural activity and the creation of a popular cultural center, the *Narodnyi Dom*, in St. Petersburg.

When the writer Leo Tolstoy was gravely ill in 1901, Countess Panin placed her Crimean estate of Gaspra at his complete disposal. "I live here in a luxurious palace such as I have never inhabited before," wrote Tolstoy in his journal, "fountains, various watered lawns in the park, marble staircases, etc. And in addition the extraordinary beauty of the sea and mountains." [5]

Countess Panin viewed her very large fortune as a means of providing for the spiritual needs of those whose material circumstances deprived them of cultural advantages. She became a close friend of the Denikins during the civil war in south Russia, and the General later named her as one of the executors of his will. The other executor was Colonel A. A. Kolchinsky, a close relative of General Kornilov's. Denikin had written his will, dated September 29, 1942, during the German occupation, "in case of the arrest or death" of himself and his wife.

Through Countess Panin and a few other old friends, he soon enlarged his circle of Russo-American acquaintances. The aura of the Volunteer Army's legendary early campaigns which surrounded him, the rocklike firmness, integrity, and courage of the man, fascinated his new friends, as did the penetrating gaze of his eyes. There was something adamant in him that reminded those who knew him well and listened to his conversation of the famous seventeenth-century archpriest Avvacum, who had suffered martyrdom in the cause of the Old Believers. They were alike in their uncompromising faith in the righteousness of their cause, their implacability and fighting spirit.

Denikin's new acquaintances did their best to help him achieve a semblance of material security. Not being much given to discussing his personal affairs, the General admitted that he "had no economic basis" in this country. In plain language this meant that he did not have a cent to his name.

An "economic basis" could only be established by finding an outlet for Denikin's literary work. With this purpose in mind, his friends enlisted the cooperation of Nicholas Wreden, who held a responsible position in a prominent New York publishing house. Wreden had taken part in the White movement as a youth, greatly respected General Denikin, and admired him as an author. The autobiography on which Denikin was engaged at that time immediately aroused his interest. Wreden offered to translate it into English as well as to help arrange for its publication.

We are gradually becoming used to American life [wrote Anton Ivanovich in August, 1946, to one of his former officers in Paris]. "We have acquired some good friends, many of whom have remained true to Volunteer traditions. A few of them were in the First Campaign. "The warriors speak of bygone days." . . . We are presently in the country, but despite the acute housing crisis, have been fortunate enough to secure a small apartment in the vicinity of New York, starting with September. We have thus acquired a semblance of permanence.

Am writing a book in response to an offer from a substantial publishing house. Or rather, am working simultaneously on two books—one of which concerns the past, and the other the present. Both my wife and I are in ill health. I have an enlargement of the aorta dating from the memorable Paris days of hurt and disappointment.[6]

Beginning with the spring of 1946, Denikin spent entire days at the New York Public Library on Forty-second Street. With paper and pencil in hand, he sat reading at one of the large tables of the Slavonic department, interrupting his work only long enough to eat his homemade sandwich. His meticulous research concerned military events at the Russian front during World War I and was destined for use in his autobiography, which he never completed.

At the same time, he was collecting material for a book to be called *Vtoraia Mirovaia Voina, Rossia i Zarubezhie* (*The Second World War, Russia, and the Emigration*), which also remained unfinished. Passages from the rough draft of this second book, never before in print, are included in Chapters XXXVIII and XXXIX of this volume; the manuscript is at the Columbia University Russian Archive.

In 1953, six years after Denikin's death, his unfinished autobiography, *Put' Russkogo Ofitsera* (*The Road of a Russian Officer*), was brought out in Russian by the Chekhov publishing house in New York, a firm supported by the Ford Foundation, which in the short span of its existence enriched Russian literature by publishing a series of valuable memoirs. The untimely death of Nicholas Wreden cut short his efforts to bring out the book in English, and it exists only in Russian to this day. It describes Denikin's childhood, his parents, school days, choice of career, the Academy of the General Staff, army service, the Russo-Japanese War and World War I. General Denikin intended to bring his autobiography to the point at which his *Ocherki Russkoi Smuty* (*The Russian Turmoil*), written in the 1920's, would form its logical continuation. His death interrupted his narrative as he set out to describe one of the highlights of Russian military history—the Brusilov offensive of 1916, in which Denikin himself played a distinguished role at the head of the Iron Division.

The interest of Denikin's memoirs is not limited to the biographical data. Their faithful rendering of the details and atmosphere of military life in Russia between 1870 and 1916 gives us a rare insight into the events of that period and the historic drama to which they later gave rise.

Anton Ivanovich also devoted some time to revising and editing his wife's journal, in the hope that it could be published at a later date, and to the completion of the book he was writing in answer to General Golovin's *Rossiiskaia Kontr-Revolutsia v 1917–1918* (*The Russian Counterrevolution*). This unpublished manuscript, entitled *Navét na Beloie Dvizhenie* (*Slander Against the White Movement*) is of interest to all students of the civil war in Russia, as it contains the former commander in chief's replies to Golovin's criticism of his political and strategic decisions.[7] Thus, despite his illness, Denikin continued to be creative and productive to the end of his life.

His heart condition persisted, troubling him occasionally at first, and with increasing frequency as the end approached. In 1947, at the insistence of his friends, Anton Ivanovich consulted a German specialist in addition to his Russian doctor. He wrote down his medical history as a guide for Xenia Vasilievna, who was to serve once more as his interpreter. This note, penciled on a scrap of paper, remains in Mrs. Denikin's family archive:

In the past: Chronic rheumatism of the spinal column, cured in 1945. Prostate removed in 1942. Hernias. A sixty-year-old chronic head cold.

At present: Coronary occlusion and angina pectoris.

Started in summer of 1945 [earlier, according to his wife and daughter], in a mild form; became worse since 1946 in America. Attacks: a sharp pain rises in the chest 6–7 times a day. A dose of 1/200 nitroglycerin used to stop it in one minute; now it takes 4–5 minutes.

Breathing is labored—better in the day than at night. Attacks are brought on by: physical exertion, staircases, walking, strong wind, and occasionally have no cause.

General condition: heaviness in the whole body, great weakness. After three or four blocks—exhaustion and a pill.

Life was running out. As a believing Christian, Anton Ivanovich awaited the approach of the great mystery of death without fear. He was only troubled by the thought that he would not live to see the "resurrection" of Russia and the destruction of the evil which he had fought with all his strength to overcome.

Toward the middle of 1947, his suffering from angina pectoris became almost unbearable and the recurrence of attacks increasingly frequent.

Nevertheless, in order to escape the summer heat of New York, the Denikins decided to accept the invitation of a friend to spend a few months at his farm in Michigan.

There, on July 20, Anton Ivanovich suffered a massive heart attack. He was immediately removed to a nearby hospital at the University of Michigan in Ann Arbor. Feeling somewhat better after two or three days in the hospital, he asked his wife to bring him the materials for continuing work on his autobiography. He also amused himself by composing crosswords.

But his days were counted. A second heart attack brought to an end this life filled with courage and faith. Strange as it may seem, despite all the reversals of fate and the seemingly hopeless political situation, Denikin apparently believed to the very end that some kind of miracle would happen, for his last words to his wife were: "Well, I won't see the resurrection of Russia!"

Anton Ivanovich died on August 7, 1947, at seventy-four years of age. After a requiem service at the Russian Orthodox Church of the Assumption, he was buried with military honors at the Evergreen Cemetery in Detroit. The honors were rendered him in his capacity of commander in chief of one of the Allied armies in World War I.

Later, his remains were transported to St. Vladimir's cemetery in Jackson, New Jersey. His final wish, however, was to be laid to rest in Russia whenever a change in the regime would make this possible.

NOTES

Chapter I

[1] Family document, property of Mrs. Xenia Denikin, the General's widow.

[2] General Denikin writes in his *Put' Russkogo Ofitsera,* p. 21, "The deceased first wife of my father was hardly ever mentioned in the family; apparently it had not been a happy marriage." To this scanty information should be added a notation by his widow on one of the family documents in her possession: "Ivan Efimovich's first wife, Maria Osipovna, a peasant from his home village to whom he was married off at the age of twenty, belonged to the Orthodox Church. He never saw her again after he became a soldier."

General Denikin was not sure of the name of the Saratov province village in which his father was born. He thought that it was called Orekhovka.

Put' Russkogo Ofitsera is General Denikin's unfinished autobiography. It appeared in Russian in 1953, six years after his death, and was published in New York by the now defunct Chekhov Publishing House of the East European Fund, Inc. It has not been translated into English or any other language. Interrupted by Denikin's death in 1947, *Put' Russkogo Ofitsera* covers the period from his childhood up to 1916. It represents the principal source of material concerning Anton Denikin's family background and early life. The manuscript of this book is in the Columbia University Russian Archive.

[3] Denikin, *Put' Russkogo Ofitsera,* p. 23.

[4] *Ibid.,* p. 24.

[5] *Ibid.,* p. 28.

[6] *Ibid.,* p. 22.

[7] *Ibid.,* pp. 43, 45.

[8] Denikin, *Staraia Armia,* Vol. I, Paris, 1929, p. 129.

[9] *Ibid.,* p. 146.

[10] Denikin, *Put' Russkogo Ofitsera,* pp. 75–76.

[11] See, for example, Lieutenant General N. M. Tikhmenev, "Address at a Meeting in Memory of General Denikin, March 7, 1948, at the Salle Pleyel, Paris," and Colonel P. A. Jackson, "Memorandum on General Denikin," both at the Columbia University Russian Archive. Colonel Jackson, a Russian of English descent, was Denikin's fellow officer in the Second Field Artillery Brigade stationed in Biala.

[12] Denikin, *Put' Russkogo Ofitsera,* p. 91.

[13] Tikhmenev, "Address."

[14] Denikin, *Staraia Armia,* Vol. I, pp. 76–77.

[15] Denikin, *Put' Russkogo Ofitsera,* p. 102.

[16] *Ibid.,* p. 103.

[17] Tikhmenev, "Address."

[18] Denikin, *Put' Russkogo Ofitsera,* pp. 109–117.

[19] *Ibid.,* p. 142.

[20] Colonel of the General Staff A. Kolchinsky, "In Memory of General Denikin," and Tikhmenev, "Address," both at the Columbia University Russian Archive; Denikin, *Put' Russkogo Ofitsera,* pp. 180, 207.

[21] Denikin, *Put' Russkogo Ofitsera,* p. 243.

[22] *Ibid.,* p. 96.

[23] M. A. Aldanov, *Sovremenniki,* Berlin, 1928, pp. 106–107; see also Bertram D. Wolfe, *Three Who Made a Revolution,* Boston, 1955, Ch. 22.

[24] S. G. Pushkarev, *Rossia v XIX Veke (1801–1914),* New York, 1956, p. 428. Stolypin's agrarian reform is described in detail in the following: *Russian Agriculture During the War,* New Haven, 1930; G. T. Robinson, *Rural Russia under the Old Regime,* New York, 1932; S. M. Dubrovsky, *Stolypin-skaia Zemel'naia Reforma,* Moscow, 1963; George Tokmakoff, "Stolypin's Agrarian Reform: An Appraisal," *The Russian Review,* Stanford, Vol. XXX (April, 1971), pp. 124–138.

Chapter II

[1] Denikin, *Put' Russkogo Ofitsera,* New York, 1953, p. 256.

[2] *Ibid.,* p. 270.

[3] *Ibid.,* p. 246.

[4] The Soviet army commander, and later marshal, M. N. Tukhachevsky wrote, "Military instruction in the old army underwent radical reforms after the Japanese war. All this, of course, produced good results, but these became evident only toward the years 1908–1910." See his *Izbrannye Proizvedeniia,* Vol. I, Moscow, 1964, pp. 27–28.

[5] Denikin, *Ocherki Russkoi Smuty,* Vol. I, Paris, 1921, Part I, p. 21.

[6] Denikin, *Put' Russkogo Ofitsera,* p. 287.

[7] G. E. Rein, *Iz Perezhitogo,* Vol. I, Berlin, 1935, p. 138.

[8] Bogrov was hanged twelve days after he shot Stolypin. According to Professor Rein, he stated during his interrogation that the fear of setting off a pogrom prevented him from shooting at the Tsar. Bogrov, an agent of the secret police, was a Jew, the son of a well-known Kiev barrister and homeowner. The circumstances surrounding the attempt on Stolypin's life were never made clear despite the fact that a Senate investigation of high-ranking secret police officials was undertaken at the time. (Rein, *Iz Perezhitogo,* Vol. I, pp. 124–149; see also A. Mushin, *Dmitrii Bogrov i Ubiistvo Stolypina,* Paris, 1914, pp. 31, 105.)

[9] A detailed study of this subject—"Germany's Interest in the Land Reform" —appears in *Russian Agriculture During the War,* New Haven, 1930, pp. 344–350.

Chapter III

[1] Denikin, *Put' Russkogo Ofitsera,* New York, 1953, p. 308; see also General N. N. Golovin, *Iz Istorii Kampanii 1914 Goda na Russkom Fronte,* Prague, 1926, p. 63.

[2] General N. N. Golovin, *Voiennyie Usilia Rossii v Mirovoi Voine,* Vol. II, Paris, 1939, p. 131.

[3] Golovin, *Iz Istorii,* p. 59.

[4] Golovin, *Voiennyie Usilia,* Vol. II, pp. 129–130.

[5] A. de Goulevitch, *Tsarisme et Révolution,* Paris, 1931, p. 231.

[6] Denikin, *Put' Russkogo Ofitsera,* p. 331.

[7] The military Order of the Holy Martyr St. George the Victorious was established in 1769 by Catherine the Great "as a reward for exceptional military feats and an encouragement in the art of warfare." The order included four classes of decorations for officers for bravery in the performance of exceptional feats. The Sword of St. George Studded with Diamonds was a very rare decoration, given only in cases where personal prowess contributed to important general results. There were also other classes in the order, awarded to soldiers for bravery.

[8] Denikin, *Put' Russkogo Ofitsera,* pp. 338–339.

[9] The text of Brusilov's telegram to Denikin appears both in *Put' Russkogo Ofitsera* (p. 345) and in a letter from Denikin to his mother, now belonging to the General's widow. I have quoted it in full for the following reason: After the Russian revolution, Brusilov's life took a radically different path from that of Denikin. Brusilov eventually entered the service of the Soviets, and relations between the two generals were severed. This greatly influenced the memoirs Brusilov wrote in the Soviet Union, *Moi Vospominaniia* (Moscow, 1963). In many instances the disparaging remarks made in his memoirs about General Denikin do not correspond to the praise he dispensed before the revolution, such as the telegram quoted here.

[10] Denikin, *Put' Russkogo Ofitsera,* p. 351.

[11] Colonel A. M. Leliakovsky, "Zheleznyie Strelki v Boiakh," unpublished manuscript, Columbia University Russian Archive.

[12] Golovin, *Voiennyie Usilia,* Vol. II, p. 139.

[13] Concerning the Committee for Liberating Russian Jews, see George Katkov, *Russia 1917, The February Revolution,* New York, 1967, p. 56.

[14] A. N. Iakhontov, "Tiazhelye Dni" (an account of the secret sessions of the Council of Ministers from July 16 to September 2, 1915, based on the minutes kept by the author, who was an official of the Council's chancery), *Arkhiv Russkoi Revolutsii,* Vol. XVIII, Berlin, p. 37.

[15] *Ibid.,* p. 98.

[16] Denikin, *Ocherki Russkoi Smuty,* Vol. I, Paris, 1921, Part I, p. 34.

[17] Winston S. Churchill, *The World Crisis,* Vol. V, New York, 1929, p. 79.

[18] Denikin, *Ocherki,* Vol. I, Part I, pp. 29–30.

[19] General A. A. Brusilov, *Moi Vospominaniia,* Moscow, 1963, p. 186.

[20] Colonel B. N. Sergeevsky, "Zheleznye Strelki," *Novoye Russkoye Slovo,* New York (February 3, 1952).

[21] Mrs. Xenia Denikin gave me permission to quote from her husband's letters to her, unconditionally. These are included in the family papers belonging to Mrs. Denikin.

[22] Letter to his fiancée, dated April 8, 1916.

[23] *Ibid.* Letter dated April 24, 1916.

[24] *Ibid.* Letter dated May 18, 1916.

[25] Denikin, *Put' Russkogo Ofitsera,* p. 378.

[26] Winston S. Churchill, *The Unknown War: The Eastern Front,* New York, 1931, p. 359.

[27] Winston S. Churchill, *The World Crisis,* Vol. III, New York, 1927, p. 95.

[28] The Eighth Army was commanded by General Kaledin; the Eleventh, by General Sakharov; the Seventh, by General Shcherbachev; the Ninth, by General Lechitsky.

[29] A. Serapinin, "Brusilovskoie Nastuplenie," *Novoye Russkoye Slovo,* New York (June 13–14, 1966).

[30] Denikin, "Zheleznaia Divizia v Lutskom Proryve," *Russkii Invalid,* Paris, No. 20 (June 7, 1931).

[31] Colonel B. N. Sergeevsky, "General Denikin," *Pereklichka,* New York, No. 58 (August, 1956).

[32] Letter dated May 26, 1916.

[33] Golovin, *Voiennyie Usilia,* Vol. II, p. 164.

[34] Brusilov, *Moi Vospominaniia,* p. 145.

[35] *Ibid.,* p. 186.

[36] General Peter S. Makhrov, "V Beloi Armii Generala Denikina," unpublished manuscript, Notebook No. 2, pp. 109–116, Columbia University Russian Archive.

[37] Denikin, *Ocherki,* Vol. I, Part I, p. 170.

[38] Letter dated November 5, 1916.

Chapter IV

[1] Denikin quotes figures released by the Russian Union of Towns, which estimated the victims of the February revolution in Petrograd as follows: a total of 1,443 people killed or wounded, of which 869 were military, including sixty officers. (*Ocherki Russkoi Smuty,* Vol. I, Paris, 1921, Part I, p. 47.)

[2] P. N. Milyukov, *Vospominaniia,* Vol. II, New York, 1955, p. 304.

[3] "Dokumenty k 'Vospominaniam' Generala Lukomskogo," *Arkhiv Russkoi Revolutsii,* Vol. III, Berlin, p. 260.

[4] *Ibid.,* pp. 268–269.

[5] *Ibid.,* p. 269.

[6] Denikin, *Ocherki,* Vol. I, Part I, p. 69.

[7] *Ibid.,* p. 55.

[8] *Ibid.,* pp. 64–65.

[9] *Ibid.,* pp. 60–62.

[10] *Ibid.,* p. 44.

[11] Denikin, "Piat' let 1921–1926," in a collection of articles commemorating the fifth anniversary of the Alliance of Russian Émigré Students in Warsaw, Poland, May 28, 1927, Columbia University Russian Archive.

Chapter V

[1] Denikin, *Ocherki Russkoi Smuty,* Vol. I, Paris, 1921, Part I, p. 72.

[2] *Ibid.,* Chs. 7–8.

[3] *Ibid.,* pp. 34–35.

[4] *Ibid.,* pp. 37–38.

[5] S. P. Melgunov presented the same point of view rather harshly in *Martovskie Dni 1917 Goda,* Paris, 1961, Ch. 6.

[6] Colonel D. N. Tikhobrazov, "Iz Vospominanii General'nogo Shtaba Polkovnika D. N. Tikhobrazova," unpublished manuscript, Columbia University Russian Archive.

[7] Denikin, *Ocherki,* Vol. I, Part I, p. 85.

[8] *Ibid.,* Part II, p. 40.

[9] General Erich Ludendorff, *Moi Vospominaniia o Voine 1914–1918,* translated from German into Russian, Vol. II, edited by A. Svechin, Moscow, 1924, pp. 10, 35, 25, 86.

[10] *Ibid.,* p. 89.

Chapter VI

[1] Denikin, "Zametki, Dopolnenia i Raziasnenia k *Ocherkam Russkoi Smuty,*" unpublished manuscript, Columbia University Russian Archive, p. 3. The other candidate for the post of Prime Minister, M. V. Rodzianko, was President of the State Duma.

[2] Denikin, *Ocherki Russkoi Smuty,* Vol. I, Paris, 1921, Part II, p. 235.

[3] *Ibid.,* p. 143.

[4] P. N. Milyukov, *Istoriia Vtoroi Russkoi Revolutsii,* Vol. I, Sofia, 1921, Part I, p. 125.

[5] *Ibid.,* pp. 125–127.

[6] *Ocherki,* Vol. I, Part II, p. 47.

[7] General N. N. Golovin, *Rossiiskaia Kontr-Revolutsia v 1917–1918,* Vol. I, Paris, 1937, Part I, p. 72.

[8] A stenographic record of this meeting is quoted by General Denikin in his *Ocherki,* Vol. I, Part II, pp. 48–62.

[9] P. N. Milyukov, *Rossia na Perelome,* Vol. I, Paris, 1927, pp. 57–58.

[10] Denikin, *Ocherki,* Vol. I, Part II, p. 106.

[11] *Ibid.,* p. 109.

[12] *Ibid.,* pp. 113–114.

[13] *Ibid.,* Part I, pp. 10–11.

[14] The same Colonel Timanovsky who distinguished himself during the capture of Lutsk in May, 1916, and was to be commander of the Markov division during the civil war.

[15] Denikin, *Ocherki,* Vol. I, Part II, pp. 148–150.

[16] *Ibid.,* Part I, Ch. 17.

[17] *Ibid.*

[18] Winston S. Churchill, *The World Crisis,* Vol. V, New York, 1929, pp. 60–61.

[19] Vladimir D. Nabokov, "Vremennoie Pravitel'stvo," *Arkhiv Russkoi Revolutsii,* Vol. I, Berlin, p. 41.

[20] Denikin, *Ocherki,* Vol. I, Part I, p. 177.

[21] *Ibid.,* Ch. 17.

Chapter VII

[1] Denikin, *Ocherki Russkoi Smuty,* Vol. I, Paris, 1921, Part II, pp. 157–158.

[2] *Ibid.,* p. 160.

[3] A. F. Kerensky, *Russia and History's Turning Point,* New York, 1965, p. 288.

[4] Letter to his future wife, dated June 28, 1917, property of Mrs. Xenia Denikin.

[5] Denikin, *Ocherki,* Vol. I, Part I, pp. 124–125.

[6] *Ibid.,* Part II, p. 158.

[7] *Ibid.,* p. 161.

[8] *Ibid.*

[9] General M. V. Alekseev, "Iz Dnevnika Generala Alekseeva," *Russkii Istoricheskii Arkhiv,* Vol. I, Prague, 1929, pp. 21–22.

[10] The text of this telegram is quoted by General Denikin in *Ocherki,* Vol. I, Part II, pp. 166–167.

[11] Denikin describes this conference in *Ocherki,* Vol. I, Part II, Ch. 33.

[12] Colonel D. N. Tikhobrazov, "Iz Vospominanii General'nogo Shtaba Polkovnika D. M. Tikhobrazova," unpublished manuscript, Columbia University Russian Archive: "The speech, directed at Kerensky, grew more and more powerful. The latter, no longer able to face Denikin, buried his face in the crook of his elbow lying on the table, and remained in this pitiful position to the end of Denikin's speech."

In his diary, General Alekseev indicated that Lieutenant Colonels Pronin and Tikhobrazov, "two excellent officers of the General Staff," kept a word-for-word record for the minutes of the conference ("Iz Dnevnika," p. 37).

In *The Catastrophe* (New York, 1927, p. 304), Kerensky gave a different account of his conduct during Denikin's address, saying that he and M. I. Tereshchenko listened quite calmly to "the cry of the scorched soul of an officer." It must be noted that in his historical reminiscences, Kerensky was not overly faithful in his rendering of facts.

[13] Alekseev, "Iz Dnevnika," pp. 41, 48.

[14] This episode is described by both Denikin (*Ocherki,* Vol. I, Part II, p. 187) and Kerensky (*The Catastrophe,* p. 305).

[15] Denikin, *Ocherki,* Vol. I, Part II, p. 188.

[16] Boris V. Savinkov, *K Delu Kornilova,* Paris, 1919, p. 8.

Chapter VIII

[1] P. N. Milyukov, *Istoria Vtoroi Russkoi Revolutsii,* Vol. I, Sofia, 1921, Part I, p. 244. Leon Trotsky, in his *History of the Russian Revolution* (Vol. II, New York, 1936, p. 40), considered the episode with Chernov, described by Milyukov, to be nothing but an anecdote. Nevertheless, according to Trotsky, Milyukov described the essence of the events of July, 1917, with blunt precision.

[2] This episode is described by A. F. Kerensky in *Russia and History's Turning Point,* New York, 1965, pp. 316–317.

[3] General A. S. Lukomsky, *Vospominaniia,* Vol. I, Berlin, 1922, pp. 165–167; see also General M. V. Alekseev, "Iz Dnevnika Generala Alekseeva," *Russkii Istoricheskii Arkhiv,* Vol. I, Prague, 1929, pp. 34–35, and General Basil Gourko, *War and Revolution in Russia 1914–1917,* New York, 1919, pp. 390–391.

[4] Denikin, *Ocherki Russkoi Smuty,* Vol. I, Paris, 1921, Part I, p. 76.

[5] *Ibid.,* Part II, pp. 193–194; see also Milyukov, *Istoria Vtoroi,* Vol. I, Part II, p. 69.

[6] Boris V. Savinkov, "Avtobiografia," *Almanakh Vozdushnye Puti,* Vol. V, New York, 1967, pp. 311–313. This "autobiography" is in reality a résumé in which Savinkov's complex life story is compressed into two and a half pages.

[7] Denikin, *Ocherki,* Vol. I, Part II, pp. 196–198.

Chapter IX

[1] Denikin, "Zametki, Dopolnenia i Raziasnenia k *Ocherkam Russkoi Smuty*," unpublished manuscript, Columbia University Russian Archive, p. 16.

[2] Denikin, *Ocherki Russkoi Smuty*, Vol. I, Paris, 1921, Part II, p. 199.

[3] *Ibid.*, p. 200.

[4] *Ibid.*, p. 199.

[5] Boris V. Savinkov, *K Delu Kornilova*, Paris, 1919, p. 13. Kerensky describes this episode in a different way, but the essence of the matter is the same.

[6] *Ibid.*, p. 4. Savinkov somewhat exaggerated the predominance of Bolsheviks in the Petrograd Soviet; their number was at that time quite small.

[7] *Ibid.*, p. 15.

[8] A. F. Kerensky, *Russia and History's Turning Point*, New York, 1965, p. 325.

[9] P. N. Milyukov, *Rossia na Perelome*, Vol. I, Paris, 1927, p. 85.

[10] *Ibid.*

[11] P. N. Milyukov, *Istoria Vtoroi Russkoi Revolutsii*, Vol. I, Sofia, 1921, Part II, pp. 127–128.

[12] *Ibid.*, p. 129.

[13] *Ibid.*, p. 131.

[14] *Ibid.*, p. 148.

[15] *Revolutsionnoie Dvizhenie v Rossii v Avguste 1917 Goda—Razgrom Kornilovskogo Miatezha*, Moscow, 1959, Document 367.

[16] Milyukov, *Istoria Vtoroi*, Vol. I, Part II, pp. 137–138.

[17] Denikin, *Ocherki*, Vol. I, Part II, p. 208.

[18] *Ibid.*, pp. 210–211. In his unpublished manuscript "Zametki" (p. 17), General Denikin mentioned that among the officers that the *Stavka* was planning to entrust with "restoring order" in large military districts were Khagandokov for Moscow, A. M. Dragomirov for Kiev, and Baron P. N. Wrangel for Odessa.

Chapter X

[1] Denikin, *Ocherki Russkoi Smuty*, Vol. I, Paris, 1921, Part II, p. 214. The original draft of Denikin's telegram, written in his own hand, is in the Columbia University Russian Archive.

[2] *Revolutsionnoie Dvizhenie v Rossii v Avguste 1917 Goda—Razgrom Kornilovskogo Miatezha*, Moscow, 1959, Document 446.

[3] Denikin, *Ocherki*, Vol. I, Part II, p. 215.

[4] *Ibid.*, Ch. 36.

[5] *Ibid.*, Ch. 37.

[6] Colonel N. Ukraintsev, "K Delu Kornilova," *Pereklichka*, New York, No. 64 (February, 1957).

[7] *Ibid.*

[8] *Ibid.*

[9] Lieutenant Kletsando was a Czech officer attached to the staff of the southwestern front. Before Denikin's arrest, when disorders erupted in the streets of Berdichev, he was one of the officers sent to reason with the crowd. He was attacked by Russian soldiers and slightly wounded one of them. The

mob of soldiers almost tore him to pieces; he was arrested and imprisoned in the Berdichev jail with the generals.

10 From a notebook of Mrs. Denikin's describing various episodes in the Denikins' lives, in the form of a tale for their daughter Marina.

11 General Markov had been lecturing at the Academy of the General Staff, so Denikin jokingly called him "professor."

12 Denikin, *Ocherki*, Vol. I, Part II, Ch. 37.

Chapter XI

1 Denikin, *Ocherki Russkoi Smuty*, Vol. II, Paris, 1922, pp. 14–15.

2 *U.S. News & World Report* on March 13, 1967, printed an interview with Kerensky in which he was quoted as saying that he "had made a mistake in relation to the Kornilov uprising." In its résumé of the interview, New York's *Novoye Russkoye Slovo* of March 15, stated, "For the first time in fifty years, A. F. Kerensky recognized that General Kornilov's arrest had been a 'fatal mistake,' which opened the way for the Bolshevik seizure of power." On March 15, I wrote Mr. Kerensky, stating that I was engaged in writing a biography of General Denikin in which the Kornilov affair is discussed, and asking him, in view of his former statements on the subject, to confirm that the Russian newspaper had interpreted his meaning correctly. Kerensky responded two days later by telephoning me at home. The conversation lasted over half an hour. I wrote down the conversation as soon as it was over, with the help of short notes I took during its course. The gist of the conversation is faithfully rendered; the italicized passages are quoted verbatim.

Kerensky denounced the newspaper, which had "allowed itself to ascribe to me conclusions which I have never made and couldn't have made.

"If there is one thing I regret," continued Kerensky, *"it is not having ordered Kornilov to be shot. It was he, after all, who a short time before, had obtained the restoration of capital punishment at the front."*

Then Kerensky began to speak heatedly about his previous writings on the Kornilov affair. *"I gave in my latest book* [*Russia and History's Turning Point*] *indisputable data on the conspiracy and the revolt. What further discussion can there be on this subject?"*

I objected that in the Kornilov affair, he—Kerensky—was an interested party and for this reason his arguments *"could not be considered exhaustive.*

"You do not deny," I continued, "that troops were sent to Petrograd with your consent, although you were not aware that they included the Wild Division and that General Krymov was placed in command."

"Exactly! I demanded that the Wild Division not be included and that Krymov not be placed in command of the detachment. *We agreed with Kornilov through Savinkov's intermediary that the* Stavka *would send reliable units to Petrograd for the protection of the Provisional Government. But sending the Wild Division and Krymov* were in complete contradiction to my orders and an act of insubordination to the supreme authority. *He* [Kornilov] *sent them* [the Wild Division and Krymov] *in order to liquidate the Provisional Government."*

"Alexandr Fedorovich, may I ask you the following: You probably knew Lvov's reputation for creating confusion [or, that Lvov was a notorious muddler]. How could you then take the word of such an unreliable witness and take action on the basis of what he had told you?"

"Lvov may have been a notorious fool, but he was an honest man and told the truth about Kornilov. When I said that I was prepared to go with Savinkov to the *Stavka* in Mogilev, Lvov began to implore me not to do so: 'For God's sake, don't go! They will kill you there!'

"Now, regarding the formation of a new cabinet. It was out of the question! After all, it was obvious that Kornilov wanted to concentrate all the power in his hands. And what would I be left with then? He said that I would be Minister of Justice. It was absolute nonsense! He would have introduced into the cabinet all that politically illiterate riff-raff of the Zavoiko type.

"Kornilov lied! They all lied! The only honest one there was Denikin.

"It was a large conspiracy. It included many prominent civilians: Milyukov, Guchkov, Putilov, Nabokov, and many others. They were all in the know in this affair and *none of them took the trouble to tell me about it!"*

To my question concerning Savinkov's role, A. F. Kerensky gave me the following answer: *"Savinkov was of course double-crossing.* But when he realized that Kornilov's movement was an 'insurrection,' *he stood at attention before me* and asked me to put him in charge of defending Petrograd against the 'insurgents.' I granted his request."—D. L.

[3] Denikin, *Ocherki,* Vol. II, pp. 25–26.

[4] *Ibid.,* pp. 27–28.

[5] *Ibid.,* p. 40.

[6] Winston S. Churchill, "Boris Savinkov," in *Great Contemporaries,* London, 1937, pp. 125–133.

[7] Fedor A. Stepun, *Byvsheie i Nesbyvsheesia,* Vol. II, New York, 1956, p. 83.

[8] *Ibid.,* pp. 150–151.

[9] The lightweight personality of V. N. Lvov was well described by Nabokov and Milyukov.

Vladimir D. Nabokov, "Vremennoie Pravitel'stvo," *Arkhiv Russkoi Revolutsii,* Vol. I, Berlin, p. 43: "The Chief Procurator of the Holy Synod, V. N. Lvov . . . was animated by the best intentions, but [he] amazed [everybody] by his naïveté and a kind of incredibly frivolous attitude—not toward his own particular business, but toward the general state of affairs, toward the problems which reality daily brought to the Provisional Government. He always spoke with great excitement and enthusiasm, and inevitably provoked the gayest mood not only in the government milieu, but even among office personnel." (V. D. Nabokov was executive secretary of the Provisional Government during the first two months following the February revolution.)

P. N. Milyukov, *Vospominaniia,* Vol. II, New York, 1955, p. 344: "A lanky fellow with degenerate features, quick to flare up with enthusiasm or anger, amused everyone with his incongruous speeches." Milyukov relates that when Lvov found out about the secret agreements between the Allies and the imperial government, "he declared the agreements to be 'banditry' and 'crookedness' and demanded that they be immediately revoked."

When the list of new cabinet members, under Kerensky's chairmanship, was made public on July 25, it no longer contained V. N. Lvov's name. He was replaced as Procurator of the Holy Synod by A. V. Kartashev.

[10] V. N. Lvov, "Kerensky i Kornilov," *Poslednie Novosti,* Paris, No. 190 (December 2, 1920).

[11] *Ibid.;* see also P. N. Milyukov, *Istoria Vtoroi Russkoi Revolutsii,* Vol. I, Sofia, 1921, Part II, p. 186, and Denikin, *Ocherki,* Vol. II, pp. 45–46.

[12] Lieber, alias Goldman, was a Menshevik and member of the Central Committee of the Soviet of Workers' and Soldiers' Deputies and of the Jewish *Bund.* The memoirs of F. A. Stepun give a vivid description of Lieber: puny, resembling a gnome with an Assyrian beard. He and another Menshevik—Dan —loved to make speeches in the Petrograd Soviet. Those who finally got bored with their oratory quipped that the pair "lieberdaned" all day. The incongruous but honest Lieber perished a victim of Stalin's purges in 1937.

[13] Denikin, *Ocherki,* Vol. II, p. 22.

[14] Lvov, "Kerensky i Kornilov."

[15] Milyukov, *Istoria Vtoroi,* Vol. I, Part II, p. 187.

[16] Lvov, "Kerensky i Kornilov."

[17] After V. N. Lvov left the *Stavka,* General Kornilov (apparently influenced by Filonenko) changed his initial decision with regard to restructuring the government. He decided on a collective rather than a one-man dictatorship, proposing to form a Council of National Defense, with Kornilov presiding and Kerensky, Savinkov, General Alekseev, Admiral Kolchak, and M. M. Filonenko as members. Georgii Plekhanov and Prince G. E. Lvov were to be assigned ministerial posts. But so were Alad'in and Zavoiko.

[18] Denikin, *Ocherki,* Vol. II, p. 50.

[19] Record of evidence submitted by Prime Minister A. Kerensky to the bailiff of the Sixteenth District of the Petrograd regional court regarding his negotiations with V. N. Lvov and General L. G. Kornilov. *Revolutsionnoie Dvizhenie v Rossii v Avguste 1917 Goda—Razgrom Kornilovskogo Miatezha,* Moscow, 1959, Document 441.

[20] A. F. Kerensky, *Delo Kornilova,* Moscow, 1918, p. 48.

[21] *Ibid.,* pp. 104–107.

[22] *Revolutsionnoie Dvizhenie,* Document 443; A. F. Kerensky, *Russia and History's Turning Point,* New York, 1965, pp. 347–348.

[23] Milyukov, *Istoria Vtoroi,* Vol. I, Part II, pp. 212–213.

[24] Denikin, *Ocherki,* Vol. II, p. 53.

[25] *Ibid.,* p. 52.

[26] Milyukov, *Istoria Vtoroi,* Vol. I, Part II, p. 214.

[27] Leon Trotsky, *The History of the Russian Revolution,* Vol. II, New York, 1936, p. 214.

[28] The text of the appeal to railroad workers and the order to the troops of the Petrograd region is quoted by P. N. Milyukov in his *Istoria Vtoroi,* Vol. I, Part II, p. 232.

[29] *Ibid.,* pp. 216–217.

Chapter XII

[1] *Revolutsionnoie Dvizhenie v Rossii v Avguste 1917 Goda—Razgrom Kornilovskogo Miatezha,* Moscow, 1959, Document 449.

[2] Boris V. Savinkov, "Avtobiografia," *Almanakh Vozdushnye Puti,* Vol. V, New York, 1967, p. 312. On August 28, Kerensky made Savinkov the Military

Governor General of Petrograd. Three days later, on August 31, he dismissed Savinkov from this post. Concurrently, Savinkov was expelled in absentia from the Socialist Revolutionary party for having refused to testify concerning the Kornilov affair before the Central Committee of the party. "The reason I refused," wrote Savinkov, "was because the committee included Natanson, who had arrived from Germany in a sealed railway carriage."

[3] The movement of the "Kornilov troops" toward Petrograd is well described by General P. N. Krasnov, "Na Vnutrennem Fronte," *Arkhiv Russkoi Revolutsii,* Vol. I, Berlin, p. 119.

[4] Denikin, *Ocherki Russkoi Smuty,* Vol. II, Paris, 1922, p. 38.

[5] *Ibid.,* p. 31. The various speeches and telegrams are described by Denikin. In relating the conversation with Novosiltsev, Denikin unquestionably referred to Milyukov, although he designated him only as "M."

[6] "Razskaz M. M. Filonenko," *Russkoie Slovo,* Moscow, No. 207 (September 10, 1917), p. 3.

[7] Denikin, *Ocherki,* Vol. II, pp. 64–65.

[8] General A. S. Lukomsky, *Vospominaniia,* Vol. I, Berlin, 1922, p. 255.

[9] Copy of teleprinted conversation between General M. V. Alekseev and Colonel Baranovsky on September 1, 1917, Columbia University Russian Archive.

[10] Denikin, *Ocherki,* Vol. II, pp. 76–77.

[11] *Revolutsionnoie Dvizhenie,* Document 526.

[12] Boris V. Savinkov, *K Delu Kornilova,* Paris, 1919, p. 27.

[13] Colonel N. Ukraintsev, "Delo Kornilova," *Novoye Russkoye Slovo,* New York (October 28, 1956).

[14] S. P. Melgunov, "Grubyi Pamflet," *Vozrozhdenie,* Paris, Vol. VII (January–February, 1950), pp. 194–195.

Bibliography on the Kornilov Affair

Asher Harvey, "The Kornilov Affair," *The Russian Review,* Stanford, Vol. XXIX (July, 1970), pp. 286–300.

Denikin, General Anton I., *Ocherki Russkoi Smuty,* Vol. II, Paris, J. Povolozky & Cie., 1922, Ch. 1–7.

Golovin, General N. N., *Rossiiskaia Kontr-Revolutsia 1917–1918,* Vol. II, Paris (issued as a supplement to the magazine *Illustrirovannaia Rossia*), 1937, Ch. 4–5.

Kerensky, A. F., *Delo Kornilova,* Moscow, Zadruga, 1918.

———— *Prelude to Bolshevism (The Kornilov Rebellion),* London, T. F. Unwin Ltd., 1919.

———— *Izdaleka,* Paris, J. Povolozky & Cie., 1922. A collection of articles, 1920–1921.

———— *The Catastrophe,* New York, D. Appleton & Co., 1927.

———— *The Crucifixion of Liberty,* New York, John Day, 1934.

———— *Russia and History's Turning Point,* New York, Duell, Sloan & Pearce, 1965, Ch. 20–22.

Knox, Major General Sir Alfred, "Kerenski Loses His Last Chance," *With the Russian Army, 1914–1917,* Vol. I, London, Hutchinson & Co., 1921, Ch. 23.

Lukomsky, General A. S., *Vospominaniia,* Vol. I, Berlin, Otto Kirchner & Co., 1922, pp. 217–269.

Martynov, E. I., *Kornilov, Popytka Voennogo Perevorota,* Moscow, Gosvoenizdat., 1927.

Milyukov, P. N., *Istoria Vtoroi Russkoi Revolutsii,* Vol. I, Sofia, Rossiisko-Bolgarskoe Knigoizd., 1921, Part II, Ch. 6–9.

——— *Rossia na Perelome,* Vol. I, Paris, privately printed, 1927, Ch. 7.

Revolutsionnoie Dvizhenie v Rossii v Avguste 1917 Goda—Razgrom Kornilovskogo Miatezha, Moscow, izd. Akademii Nauk SSSR, 1959. A collection of documents published by the Academy of Science.

Savinkov, Boris V., *K Delu Kornilova,* Paris, Union, 1919.

Stankevich, V. B., *Vospominaniia 1914–1919 Gg.,* Berlin, Ladyschnikov, 1920.

Stepun, Fedor A., *Byvsheie i Nesbyvsheesia,* Vol. II, New York, Chekhov Publishing House, 1956, pp. 72–180.

Trotsky, Leon, *The History of the Russian Revolution,* Vol. II, New York, Simon and Schuster, 1936, Ch. 9–10.

Verkhovsky, A. I., *Na Trudnom Perevale,* Moscow, Voennoie izd. Ministerstva Oborony SSSR, 1959.

Vladimirova, Vera, *Kontr-Revolutsia v 1917 Godu (Kornilovshchina),* Moscow, Krasnaia Nov', 1924.

In addition, the following newspaper articles should be consulted:

In *Poslednie Novosti* (a Russian daily in Paris)

Guchkov, A. L., "Iz Vospominanii Guchkova" (August–September, 1936).

Denikin, General Anton I., "Ob Ispravleniiakh Istorii" (November 13 and 14, 1936).

Milyukov, P. N., "K Statiam A. I. Denikina" (November 14, 1936).

Vakar, N. P., "Zagovor Kornilova (po Vospominaniiam A. I. Putilova)" (January 20 and 24, 1937).

Sidorin, General V., "Zagovor Kornilova" (February 26, 1937).

Vakar, N. P., "General L. G. Kornilov i A. F. Kerensky (Beseda s P. N. Finisovym)" (February 27 and March 6, 1937).

Milyukov, P. N., "O Stat'e N. P. Vakara" (March 6, 1937).

In *Novoye Russkoye Slovo* (a Russian daily in New York)

Kerensky, A. F., "Delo Kornilova" (February 16, 1949).

——— "Sryv Fevralia" (February 17, February 18, and March 6, 1949).

Denikin, Xenia, "Delo Kornilova" (March 15 and 16, 1949).

Kerensky, A. F., "Delo Kornilova" (August 12, 1956).

Gurovich, Boris, "A. F. Kerensky o Dele Kornilova" (September 2, 1956).

Denikin, Xenia, "Na Staruiu Temu" (September 23, 1956).

Kerensky, A. F., "Delo Kornilova" (October 21, 1956).

Ukraintsev, Colonel N., "Delo Kornilova" (October 28, 1956).

Chapter XIII

[1] Denikin, *Ocherki Russkoi Smuty,* Vol. II, Paris, 1922, p. 98.

[2] A copy of this letter is at the Columbia University Russian Archive, in Folder No. 31 (*Vestnik Partii Narodnoi Svobody,* Petrograd, December 28,

1917). Excerpts from this letter were quoted by E. I. Martynov, *Kornilov, Popytka Voennogo Perevorota,* Moscow, 1927, pp. 166–167.

[3] Unpublished notes, family document belonging to Mrs. Xenia Denikin.

[4] General A. S. Lukomsky, *Vospominaniia,* Vol. I, Berlin, 1922, pp. 260–261.

[5] Denikin, *Ocherki,* Vol. II, p. 86.

[6] Unpublished notes, family document belonging to Mrs. Xenia Denikin.

[7] Denikin, *Ocherki,* Vol. II, p. 86.

[8] Denikin, "Zametki, Dopolnenia i Raziasnenia k *Ocherkam Russkoi Smuty,*" unpublished manuscript, Columbia University Russian Archive, p. 42.

[9] Vladimir D. Nabokov, "Vremennoie Pravitel'stvo," *Arkhiv Russkoi Revolutsii,* Vol. I, Berlin, p. 36. A leading member of the Cadet party, Nabokov was the father of the well-known writer Vladimir Nabokov.

[10] S. P. Melgunov, *Kak Bolsheviki Zakhvatili Vlast',* Paris, 1953, p. 124.

[11] Leon Trotsky, *Lenin,* New York, 1962, p. 102.

[12] Melgunov, *Kak Bolsheviki,* pp. 228–229.

[13] Denikin, *Ocherki,* Vol. II, p. 144.

[14] *Ibid.,* p. 145.

[15] *Ibid.,* pp. 146–148, for the entire account of this journey.

[16] *Ibid.,* pp. 151–155.

Chapter XIV

[1] Denikin, *Ocherki Russkoi Smuty,* Vol. II, Paris, 1922, Ch. 14.

[2] *Ibid.,* p. 199.

[3] *Ibid.,* p. 159.

[4] *Ibid.,* p. 160.

[5] *Ibid.,* pp. 133–134; see also A. F. Kerensky, *The Catastrophe,* New York, 1927, Ch. 18, and P. N. Krasnov, "Na Vnutrennem Fronte," *Arkhiv Russkoi Revolutsii,* Vol. I, Berlin, p. 163.

[6] Denikin, *Ocherki,* Vol. II, p. 191.

[7] *Ibid.,* p. 147.

[8] *Ibid.,* p. 188. The strained relations between Generals Kornilov and Alekseev have been described in the memoirs of many witnesses who knew both White Army leaders well. These include the memoirs of General Lukomsky, Prince Grigory Troubetzkoy, and General A. P. Bogaevsky, who became *Ataman* of the Don Cossacks. General Bogaevsky wrote, "Despite his age and position, he [General Alekseev], the organizer, spiritual leader, and political guide of the White movement, modestly deferred to Kornilov, his former pupil at the Academy, and after his [Kornilov's] death did the same with regard to Denikin. Kornilov was sometimes very abrupt with him and often unjust. But Mikhail Vasilievich patiently bore these undeserved offenses and only once after one such flare-up, I heard him say with infinite sadness: 'How hard it is to work in these conditions. . . .' " (*Vospominaniia Generala A. P. Bogaevskogo 1918 God. Ledianoi Pokhod,* New York, 1963, p. 38.)

[9] General A. S. Lukomsky, *Vospominaniia,* Vol. I, Berlin, 1922, p. 289.

[10] To illustrate Denikin's complaint that huge amounts of ordnance in the Don Cossacks' military depots were being sold "on the side" by Cossack committees, we quote from a letter sent at that time by General Alekseev to General M. K. Dietrichs: "The point is that there is an artillery depot in Novo-

cherkassk. . . . At the beginning of October the Chief Artillery Administration sent to this depot 10,000 rifles from Petrograd and 12,800 from Moscow. The first shipment has been stolen for sure, and as there is no news of the second one, it must have suffered the same fate." (Quoted by General N. N. Golovin, *Rossiiskaia Kontr-Revolutsia v 1917–1918,* Vol. V, Paris, 1937, pp. 48–56.)

At that time, the Chief Artillery Administration was headed by General Vladimir Andreevich Lehovich. Foreseeing the possibility of the Bolsheviks attempting to seize power, he was doing everything possible to supply General Kaledin with ammunition for fighting them.

[11] Information furnished by Mrs. Xenia Denikin.

[12] *Istoriia Grazhdanskoi Voiny SSSR,* Vol. III, Moscow, 1957, pp. 126–127.

[13] Denikin, *Ocherki,* Vol. II, pp. 205–208.

[14] *Ibid.,* p. 220.

[15] *Ibid.,* p. 217.

[16] *Ibid.,* p. 220.

[17] *Ibid.,* p. 222.

[18] Information furnished by Mrs. Xenia Denikin.

[19] Denikin, *Ocherki,* Vol. II, p. 223.

Chapter XV

[1] Denikin, *Ocherki Russkoi Smuty,* Vol. II, Paris, 1922, p. 224. Except as otherwise noted, the material in this chapter is based on Ch. 19–29 (pp. 209–325) of Vol. II of *Ocherki.*

[2] *Ibid.,* pp. 237–238.

[3] General A. S. Lukomsky, *Vospominaniia,* Vol. II, Berlin, 1922, pp. 9–11; see also General A. P. Bogaevsky, *Vospominaniia Generala A. P. Bogaevskogo 1918 God. Ledianoi Pokhod,* New York, 1963, pp. 58–59.

[4] Denikin, *Ocherki,* Vol. II, p. 230.

[5] *Ibid.,* pp. 230–231.

[6] *Ibid.,* p. 237.

[7] *Ibid.,* p. 276.

[8] *Markovtsy v Boiakh i Pokhodakh za Rossiu,* compiled by V. E. Pavlov, Vol. I, *1917–1918,* Paris, 1962, p. 183.

[9] Denikin, *Ocherki,* Vol. II, p. 266.

[10] *Ibid.,* p. 268.

[11] *Ibid.,* p. 273.

[12] J. Kamilin, *General Sergei Leonidovich Markov,* Rostov-on-Don, 1919, p. 8.

[13] Denikin, *Ocherki,* Vol. II, p. 293.

[14] *Ibid.,* pp. 294–295.

[15] *Ibid.,* p. 295.

[16] *Ibid.,* p. 303.

[17] *Ibid.,* pp. 303–304, for the text of the order signed by General M. V. Alekseev appointing General Denikin to the post of commander of the Volunteer Army.

[18] Denikin, *Ocherki,* Vol. II, p. 299.

[19] *Markovtsy v Boiakh,* Vol. I, p. 203.

[20] Denikin, *Ocherki,* Vol. II, pp. 305–306.

21 *Ibid.,* p. 300.

22 *Ibid.,* pp. 308–309.

23 *Ibid.,* p. 311.

24 *Ibid.,* p. 339.

25 *Ibid.,* p. 345.

Chapter XVI

1 A. Klevanskii, "Voennoplennye Tsentral'nykh Derzhav v Tsarskoi i Revo-lutsionnoi Rossii (1914–1918 Gg.)," in *Internatsionalisty v Boiakh za Vlast' Sovetov,* Moscow, 1965, pp. 21–65; see also Colonel A. Zaitsov, *1918 God. Ocherki po Istorii Russkoi Grazhdanskoi Voiny,* Paris, 1934, pp. 113–114.

2 Denikin, *Ocherki Russkoi Smuty,* Vol. II, Paris, 1922, p. 237.

3 Letter to General Shcherbachev quoted by Denikin in *Ocherki,* Vol. III, Berlin, 1924, p. 130.

4 *Ibid.,* p. 132.

5 Denikin, "Zametki, Dopolnenia i Raziasnenia k *Ocherkam Russkoi Smuty,*" unpublished manuscript, Columbia University Russian Archive, pp. 30, 66.

6 Quoted by General N. M. Tikhmenev in a letter to Mrs. Xenia Denikin, dated November 25, 1953, Columbia University Russian Archive.

7 Information furnished by Mrs. Xenia Denikin.

8 General P. N. Krasnov, "Vsevelikoie Voisko Donskoie," *Arkhiv Russkoi Revolutsii,* Vol. V, Berlin, p. 201.

9 Denikin, *Navety na Beloie Dvizhenie,* unpublished manuscript, Columbia University Russian Archive, p. 40; see also K. P. Kaliugin, "Donskoi Ataman P. N. Krasnov i Ego Vremia," *Donskaia Letopis',* No. 3, Belgrade, 1924, pp. 68–162.

10 Zaitsov, *1918 God. Ocherki,* p. 126, Chart 11.

11 Denikin, *Ocherki,* Vol. III, p. 116.

12 General B. Kazanovich, "Poezdka iz Dobrovolcheskoi Armii v Krasnuiu Moskvu," *Arkhiv Russkoi Revolutsii,* Vol. VII, Berlin, pp. 184–185.

13 Denikin, *Ocherki,* Vol. III, pp. 79–80.

14 Kazanovich, "Poezdka," p. 195.

15 *Internatsionalisty v Boiakh za Vlast' Sovetov,* Moscow, 1965, pp. 21–65, 117–148, 255–296. An interesting description of the role of Hungarian prisoners of war in the Russian civil war is given by Rudolf L. Tokés in his *Béla Kun and the Hungarian Soviet Republic* (New York, 1967, p. 69). In the course of World War I, 3,600,000 men, out of a total population of 21 million people, were mobilized in Hungary. Of these, 734,000 soldiers and officers were prisoners by the end of 1917. As the Hungarian troops were principally deployed on the Russian front, most of the war prisoners were located in Russia. *During the spring and summer of 1918, approximately a hundred thousand Hungarian war prisoners joined the Red Army.* Rudolf Tokés ascribes this massive Hungarian participation in the Russian civil war not only to the effect of Communist slogans and promises of material gain which attracted them to the Bolshevik side, but also to the events taking place at the Western Front. By the end of summer, the approaching defeat of the Central Powers presented a grim perspective to the Hungarians. Unlike the Poles, Czechs, Slovaks, Serbs, and Croatians, they knew that they belonged to the defeated side, with all the consequences that this implied.

Chapter XVII

[1] Denikin, *Ocherki Russkoi Smuty,* Vol. III, Berlin, 1924, pp. 156–157.

[2] *Ibid.,* p. 151.

[3] *Ibid.,* Vol. IV, Berlin, 1925, p. 84.

[4] Colonel A. Zaitsov, *1918 God. Ocherki po Istorii Russkoi Grazhdanskoi Voiny,* Paris, 1934, p. 219.

[5] General N. N. Golovin, *Rossiiskaia Kontr-Revolutsia v 1917–1918,* Vol. II, Paris, 1937, p. 26.

[6] Zaitsov, *1918 God. Ocherki,* p. 222; see also Golovin, *Rossiiskaia Kontr-Revolutsia,* Vol. II, p. 27.

[7] Denikin, *Ocherki,* Vol. III, p. 168.

[8] *Ibid.,* p. 160.

[9] *Markovtsy v Boiakh i Pokhodakh za Rossiu,* compiled by V. E. Pavlov, Vol. I, *1917–1918,* Paris, 1962, pp. 273–274.

[10] Denikin, *Ocherki,* Vol. III, p. 160.

[11] *Ibid.,* p. 199.

[12] *Ibid.,* p. 200.

[13] *Ibid.,* p. 204.

[14] *Ibid.,* Vol. IV, p. 47.

[15] *Ibid.,* Vol. III, p. 212.

[16] *Ibid.,* Vol. IV, p. 46.

[17] *Ibid.,* Vol. III, p. 211.

[18] General A. G. Shkuró, *Zapiski Belogo Partizana,* Buenos Aires, 1961, p. 134.

[19] Denikin, *Ocherki,* Vol. III, p. 187.

[20] *Ibid.,* Vol. IV, p. 113.

[21] General Peter N. Wrangel, "Zapiski," *Beloie Delo,* Vol. V, Berlin, 1928, p. 72.

Chapter XVIII

[1] Denikin *Ocherki Russkoi Smuty,* Vol. III, Berlin, 1924, pp. 96–97.

[2] The plundering of many millions of rubles in gold and silver is described in detail by G. K. Gins in *Sibir', Soiuzniki i Kolchak* (Vol. II, Peking, 1921, pp. 16–18), in the chapter entitled "Plundering by SR's." According to General Denikin, Russia's gold reserve at the time amounted to 1,118,500,000 gold rubles—651,500,000 captured by the Whites in Kazan; 147,000,000 held by the Bolsheviks; 320,000,000 held by the Allies in Paris. (*Ocherki,* Vol. IV, Berlin, 1925, p. 226.)

[3] General V. G. Boldyrev, *Direktoria, Kolchak, Interventy,* Novonikolaevsk, 1925, pp. 60–61.

[4] Colonel A. Zaitsov, *1918 God. Ocherki po Istorii Russkoi Grazhdanskoi Voiny,* Paris, 1934, p. 201.

[5] Denikin, *Ocherki,* Vol. III, p. 156.

[6] *Ibid.,* pp. 240–244.

[7] *Ibid.,* p. 84.

[8] S. P. Melgunov, *Sud'ba Imperatora Nikolaia II Posle Otrechenia,* Paris, 1951, p. 315. Melgunov (referring to the German historian Kurt Jagow, who had access to the archive of the German Ministry of Foreign Affairs) wrote

that King Christian X of Denmark, worried by disturbing news concerning the imperial family, "approached Kaiser Wilhelm with an offer to intercede in resolving the fate of the deposed monarch and his family," and that the Kaiser declined the offer.

[9] Denikin, unpublished letter to General Kornilov's daughter, Mme. Natalia Chaperon du Larré, May 30, 1939, Columbia University Russian Archive.

[10] Denikin, *Ocherki,* Vol. III, p. 271.

[11] *Ibid.,* Vol. IV, p. 90.

[12] *Ibid.,* Vol. III, pp. 262–263.

[13] *Ibid.,* Vol. IV, pp. 45–48.

[14] *Ibid.,* Vol. V, Berlin, 1926, p. 302.

[15] *Ibid.,* Vol. III, p. 133.

[16] P. N. Milyukov, *Rossia na Perelome,* Vol. II, Paris, 1927, p. 56.

[17] Denikin, *Ocherki,* Vol. III, p. 262.

[18] *Ibid.,* p. 117.

Chapter XIX

[1] Denikin, *Ocherki Russkoi Smuty,* Vol. IV, Berlin, 1925, pp. 37–38, for both the text of the letter and Denikin's comment on it.

[2] *Ibid.,* p. 36.

[3] *Ibid.,* pp. 36–37.

[4] The conference at Jassy was organized at the initiative of the French and British ambassadors—de Saint-Aulaire and Sir George Barclay. However, the American ambassador, Charles Vopicka, and the Italian ambassador, Giacinto Auritti, also took part in it.

[5] P. N. Milyukov, *Rossia na Perelome,* Vol. II, Paris, 1927, p. 85.

[6] Denikin, *Ocherki,* Vol. IV, pp. 194–195.

[7] The promises and declarations of the French consul, Hénaud, in Kiev and Odessa, went far beyond his authority and gave rise to false expectations of immediate and determined help on the part of the French. The disappointment which followed contributed considerably to the deterioration of relations between the Russian anti-Bolsheviks and the French.

[8] At the end of the World War the Polish brigade formed in Ekaterinodar, which was on its way to Poland, found itself in Odessa at the moment when Petliura's troops captured the city.

[9] *Ocherki,* Vol. V, Berlin, 1926, p. 11.

[10] General A. S. Sannikov, *Vospominaniia,* 1926, unpublished manuscript, Columbia University Russian Archive.

[11] Denikin, *Ocherki,* Vol. V, pp. 39–40.

[12] Prince E. N. Troubetzkoy, "Iz Putevykh Zametok Bezhentsa," *Arkhiv Russkoi Revolutsii,* Vol. XVIII, Berlin, p. 195.

[13] Denikin, *Ocherki,* Vol. V, p. 47.

[14] *Ibid.,* p. 48.

[15] *Istoriia Grazhdanskoi Voiny SSSR,* Vol. III, Moscow, 1957, pp. 350–351 (Lenin's letter to the Second Ukrainian Soviet Army).

[16] André Marty, *The Epic of the Black Sea Revolt,* New York, 1941.

[17] Denikin, *Ocherki,* Vol. V, pp. 52–53.

[18] *Ocherk Vzaimootnoshenii Vooruzhonnykh Sil Iuga Rossii i Predstavitelei Frantsuzskogo Komandovania,* Ekaterinodar, May, 1919, p. 24.

[19] *Istoriia Grazhdanskoi Voiny SSSR,* Vol. III, pp. 352–353.

[20] Denikin, *Ocherki,* Vol. V, p. 61.

[21] General A. S. Lukomsky, *Vospominaniia,* Vol. II, Berlin, 1922, p. 292; Denikin, *Ocherki,* Vol. V, p. 61. With regard to moving Denikin's headquarters to Sebastopol, the General wrote in his memoirs, "This idea had to be abandoned later, due exclusively to the altered conditions at the front."

[22] Denikin, *Ocherki,* Vol. V, p. 65.

[23] *Ibid.,* p. 42.

[24] *Ibid.,* p. 71.

[25] Winston S. Churchill, *The World Crisis,* Vol. V, New York, 1929, p. 262.

[26] Denikin, *Ocherki,* Vol. IV, p. 140. Some of Lloyd George's speeches concerning Britain's policy in regard to Russia shocked the British as well as the Russians, as witnessed by C. E. Bechhofer-Roberts, *In Denikin's Russia and the Caucasus 1919–1920,* London, 1921, pp. 121–122.

[27] Prince E. N. Troubetzkoy, "Iz Putevykh Zametok Bezhentsa," *Arkhiv Russkoi Revolutsii,* Vol. XVIII, Berlin, pp. 196–197.

[28] Denikin, *Ocherki,* Vol. IV, p. 158.

[29] Churchill, *The World Crisis,* Vol. V, p. 287.

[30] Denikin, *Ocherki,* Vol. IV, pp. 37, 39.

[31] *Ibid.,* p. 41.

[32] George F. Kennan, *Russia and the West under Lenin and Stalin,* Boston, 1960, p. 127.

Chapter XX

[1] General P. N. Krasnov, "Vsevelikoie Voisko Donskoie," *Arkhiv Russkoi Revolutsii,* Vol. V, Berlin, p. 230. According to General Krasnov, the Don Cossack army at that time had 1,282 officers, 31,300 soldiers, seventy-nine guns, 267 machine guns, sixty-eight planes, three armored cars, fourteen armored trains, and a body of 20,000 young recruits.

[2] Denikin, *Ocherki Russkoi Smuty,* Vol. IV, Berlin, 1925, p. 62.

[3] *Ibid.,* p. 65. These people were attending a meeting of the *zemstvos* and town councils of south Russia.

[4] *Ibid.,* pp. 66–67, from a report by K. Karasev, dated April 16, 1919.

[5] *Ibid.,* p. 71.

[6] Krasnov, "Vsevelikoie Voisko Donskoie," pp. 280–281.

[7] Denikin, *Ocherki,* Vol. IV, p. 72.

[8] *Ibid.,* pp. 78–80.

[9] For biographical details concerning Admiral Kolchak, see the record of his cross-examination in Irkutsk: "Protokol Doprosa Admirala Kolchaka Chrezvychainoi Sledstvennoi Komissiei v Irkutskev Ianvare–Fevrale 1920 Goda," *Arkhiv Russkoi Revolutsii,* Vol. X, Berlin, pp. 177–321.

[10] Denikin *Ocherki,* Vol. V, Berlin, 1926, p. 85.

Chapter XXI

[1] General Kuchuk Ulagai was a Moslem Tatar, native of the Kuban region. A gifted cavalry leader, he took part in World War I as a platoon commander in the Severski Dragoon Regiment; during this period, S. M. Budenny, the

future commander of the First Cavalry Army of the Soviet Union, was a non-commissioned officer in his platoon.

[2] Leon Trotsky, *Kak Vooruzhalas' Revolutsia,* Vol. II, Moscow, 1924, Part II, p. 26.

[3] Leon Trotsky, *Stalin,* edited and translated by Charles Malamuth, New York, 1946, pp. 273–275.

[4] Denikin, *Ocherki Russkoi Smuty,* Vol. V, Berlin, 1926, p. 84.

[5] *Ibid.,* p. 76.

[6] General Peter N. Wrangel, "Zapiski," *Beloie Delo,* Vol. V, Berlin, 1928, p. 132.

[7] Colonel B. A. Lagodovsky, *Vospominaniia,* Vol. III, *V Riadakh Leib-Gvardii Konnoi Artillerii v Grazhdanskoi Voine na Iuge Rossii,* unpublished memoirs, property of Colonel Lagodovsky.

[8] Vice Admiral Sir Francis Pridham, *Close of a Dynasty,* London, 1956.

[9] Wrangel, "Zapiski," *Beloie Delo,* Vol. V, pp. 159–160.

[10] General A. S. Lukomsky, *Vospominaniia,* Vol. II, Berlin, 1922, pp. 143–144.

[11] Denikin, *Ocherki,* Vol. V, pp. 108–109.

[12] A curious detail: Selivachev died mysteriously within a month after this episode, and his sudden death seemed to be connected with the failure of his offensive. It is quite possible that the former general, an experienced soldier, intentionally mismanaged the operation in order to help the Whites and to sabotage the Bolsheviks, who had forced him into their service.

[13] *Iz Istorii Grazhdanskoi Voiny v SSSR,* Institut Marksizma-Leninizma pri Tsentral'nom Kom. KPSS., Vol. II, Moscow, 1961, p. 383.

[14] *Direktivy Glavnogo Komandovania Krasnoi Armii (1917–1920 Gg.),* Moscow, 1969, Documents 376, 378, 380, 385; pp. 413–415, 418.

[15] *Iz Istorii Grazhdanskoi Voiny,* Vol. II, p. 390.

[16] *Ibid.,* p. 512.

[17] *Ibid.,* pp. 386–387.

[18] *Ibid.,* p. 396.

[19] *Ibid.,* pp. 437–452.

[20] *Ibid.,* p. 462.

[21] *Ibid.,* p. 548.

[22] *Ibid.,* pp. 464–465.

Chapter XXII

[1] Prince E. N. Troubetzkoy, "Iz Putevykh Zametok Bezhentsa," *Arkhiv Russkoi Revolutsii,* Vol. XVIII, Berlin, p. 201.

[2] Unpublished letter dated August 5, 1918, property of Mrs. Xenia Denikin.

[3] Information furnished by Mrs. Xenia Denikin.

[4] K. N. Sokolov, *Pravlenie Generala Denikina,* Sofia, 1921, p. 85.

[5] Unpublished letter dated July 8, 1919, property of Mrs. Xenia Denikin.

[6] George Shavelsky, *Vospominaniia,* Vol. II, New York, 1954, pp. 327, 360. Shavelsky was head chaplain of the Russian army and navy.

[7] Sokolov, *Pravlenie,* pp. 183–184.

[8] Unpublished letter dated July 11, 1919, property of Mrs. Xenia Denikin.

[9] Shavelsky, *Vospominaniia,* Vol. II, p. 360.

10 Unpublished letter dated April 29, 1919, property of Mrs. Xenia Denikin.

11 Denikin, *Ocherki Russkoi Smuty,* Vol. IV, Berlin, 1925, p. 95.

12 Shavelsky, *Vospominaniia,* Vol. II, pp. 127–128.

13 Denikin, *Ocherki,* Vol. V, Berlin, 1926, p. 87.

14 *Ibid.,* p. 88, for the contents of Denikin's letter and his comment on it.

15 G. K. Gins, *Sibir', Soiuzniki i Kolchak,* Vol. II, Peking, 1921, pp. 234–239, for the account of Allied negotiations with Kolchak.

16 Denikin, *Ocherki,* Vol. V, p. 98.

17 Sokolov, *Pravlenie,* p. 135.

18 After the end of the civil war, Captain Vladimir Vasilievich Perfiliev came to the United States where he gained a reputation as a painter, explorer, and traveler.

19 Denikin, "Zametki, Dopolnenia i Raziasnenia k *Ocherkam Russkoi Smuty,*" unpublished manuscript, Columbia University Russian Archive, p. 44.

Chapter XXIII

1 *Iz Istorii Grazhdanskoi Voiny v SSSR,* Institut Marksizma-Leninizma pri Tsentral'nom Kom. KPSS., Vol. III, Moscow, 1961, pp. 200–202.

2 General K. V. Sakharov, *Belaia Sibir',* Munich, 1923, p. 79.

3 P. N. Milyukov, *Rossia na Perelome,* Vol. II, Paris, 1927, p. 122.

4 Denikin, *Ocherki Russkoi Smuty,* Vol. V, Berlin, 1926, p. 220.

5 Colonel S. Dobrovolsky, "Bor'ba za Vozrozhdenie Rossii v Severnoi Oblasti," *Arkhiv Russkoi Revolutsii,* Vol. III, Berlin, pp. 5–146.

6 Boris Sokolov, "Padenie Severnoi Oblasti," *Arkhiv Russkoi Revolutsii,* Vol. IX, Berlin, pp. 5–90.

7 Leon Trotsky, *Stalin,* edited and translated by Charles Malamuth, New York, 1946, p. 307.

8 Denikin, *Ocherki,* Vol. IV, Berlin, 1925, p. 19.

9 *Ibid.,* pp. 17–20, for Denikin's views on Finland and his statement to the Allied governments.

10 G. K. Gins, *Sibir', Soiuzniki i Kolchak,* Vol. II, Peking, 1921, p. 237; see also Denikin, *Ocherki,* Vol. IV, p. 32.

11 Denikin, *Ocherki,* Vol. V, p. 175.

12 *Ibid.,* pp. 175–176.

13 *Ibid.,* p. 176.

14 Denikin, *Kto Spas Sovetskuiu Vlast' ot Gibeli,* Paris, 1937. The brochure is fourteen pages long.

15 Denikin, *Ocherki,* Vol. V, pp. 178–179.

16 M. N. Tukhachevsky, *Izbrannye Proizvedeniia,* Vol. I, Moscow, 1964, p. 114.

Chapter XXIV

1 *Iz Istorii Grazhdanskoi Voiny v SSSR,* Institut Marksizma-Leninizma pri Tsentral'nom Kom. KPSS., Vol. II, Moscow, 1961, pp. 518–519.

2 General Peter N. Wrangel, "Zapiski," *Beloie Delo,* Vol. V, Berlin, 1928, p. 290.

3 Denikin, *Ocherki Russkoi Smuty,* Vol. IV, Berlin, 1925, p. 94.

4 *Ibid.,* Vol. V, Berlin, 1926, pp. 146–147.

[5] *Ibid.,* p. 150.

[6] *Politicheskii Obzor Oblastei Iuga, Iuga-Vostoka Rossii i Zakavkazia* (August 1–September 1, 1919), published by the Denikin administration, Rostov-on-Don, October 10, 1919.

[7] D. S. Pasmanik, *Russkaia Revolutsia i Evreistvo,* Paris, 1923, pp. 178–179.

[8] Denikin, *Ocherki,* Vol. V, p. 149.

[9] *Ibid.*

[10] *Ibid.,* p. 150.

[11] *Ibid.,* Vol. IV, p. 224.

[12] General A. S. Lukomsky, *Vospominaniia,* Vol. II, Berlin, 1922, p. 188.

[13] Denikin, *Ocherki,* Vol. IV, p. 223.

[14] Lukomsky, *Vospominaniia,* Vol. II, p. 150.

[15] K. V. Gerasimenko, "Makhnó," *Istorik i Sovremennik,* Berlin, Vol. III (1922), p. 151.

[16] Peter Arshinov, *Istoria Makhnovskogo Dvizhenia (1918–1921),* Berlin, 1923, p. 50.

[17] *Ibid.,* p. 55.

[18] *Ibid.,* p. 134.

[19] Denikin, *Ocherki,* Vol. V, pp. 131–132.

[20] *Ibid.,* p. 134.

[21] Leon Trotsky, *Kak Vooruzhalas' Revolutsia,* Vol. II, Moscow, 1924, Part II, p. 28.

Chapter XXV

[1] Unpublished correspondence from the archive of the Russian embassy in Paris, V. A. Maklakov collection, Hoover Institution on War, Revolution, and Peace, Stanford University.

[2] Denikin, *Ocherki Russkoi Smuty,* Vol. IV, Berlin, 1925, pp. 84–86; Vol. V, Berlin, 1926, p. 169.

[3] *Ibid.,* Vol. IV, p. 184.

[4] Unpublished letter dated November 21, 1919, Columbia University Russian Archive.

[5] Unpublished document from the Michel N. Giers archive, Hoover Institution on War, Revolution, and Peace, Stanford University, File No. 44.

[6] Denikin, *Ocherki,* Vol. V, p. 171.

[7] On April 22, 1919, Lenin telegraphed the Soviet commander in chief, Vatsetis, and a member of the Revolutionary Military Council, Aralov: "Advancement into part of Galicia and Bukovina is indispensable for liaison with Soviet Hungary. . . . The Ukrainian army must unquestionably under no circumstances be distracted from its principal aims, namely the primarily important and urgent assistance to the Don Basin. Its second assignment is to establish solid railroad communications with Soviet Hungary. Advise Antonov [Ovseenko] of your instructions and measures for checking on their execution." (*Iz Istorii Grazhdanskoi Voiny v SSSR,* Institut Marksizma-Leninizma pri Tsentral'nom Kom. KPSS, Vol. II, Moscow, 1961, p. 383.)

[8] Denikin, *Ocherki,* Vol. V, p. 140.

[9] *Ibid.,* p. 257.

[10] *Ibid.,* pp. 142–143.

[11] M. P. Chubinsky, "Na Donu," *Donskaia Letopis'*, No. 3, Belgrade, 1924, p. 272.

[12] Denikin, *Ocherki,* Vol. IV, p. 218.

[13] *Ibid.,* Vol. V, p. 275.

[14] *Ibid.,* Vol. IV, p. 206.

[15] *Ibid.,* Vol. V, p. 199.

[16] K. N. Sokolov, "Kubanskoie Deistvo," *Arkhiv Russkoi Revolutsii,* Vol. XVIII, Berlin, pp. 237–253.

[17] Denikin, *Ocherki,* Vol. V, Ch. 20, 21, 22; see also General Peter N. Wrangel, "Zapiski," *Beloie Delo,* Vol. V, Berlin, 1928, pp. 214–243, and General A. P. Filimonov, "Razgrom Kubanskoi Rady," *Arkhiv Russkoi Revolutsii,* Vol. V, Berlin, pp. 322–329.

[18] Denikin, *Ocherki,* Vol. IV, pp. 91–93.

Chapter XXVI

[1] Leon Trotsky, *Stalin,* edited and translated by Charles Malamuth, New York, 1946, Ch. 9.

[2] *Istoriia Grazhdanskoi Voiny SSSR,* Vol. IV, Moscow, 1959, p. 264. In the condensed version of his memoirs published in English, General Denikin affirmed that by mid-October of 1919, his troops were deployed against the Red Army on a front of over 1,700 kilometers along the line of Zhitomir-Kiev-Chernigov-Voronezh-Tsaritsin-Astrakhan. (*The White Army,* London, 1930, p. 324.)

[3] Denikin, *Ocherki Russkoi Smuty,* Vol. V, Berlin, 1926, p. 230.

[4] *Istoriia Grazhdanskoi,* Vol. IV, p. 258.

[5] Denikin's memoirs do not indicate the size of his cavalry in mid-October, 1919. The number given by Soviet sources (48,800 cavalrymen) appears somewhat exaggerated. (*Istoriia Grazhdanskoi,* Vol. IV, p. 258.)

[6] These figures are taken from Soviet sources. (*Istoriia Grazhdanskoi,* Vol. IV, p. 258.)

[7] General A. S. Lukomsky, *Vospominaniia,* Vol. II, Berlin, 1922, p. 201.

[8] General A. G. Shkuró, *Zapiski Belogo Partizana,* Buenos Aires, 1961, p. 230.

[9] Denikin, *Ocherki,* Vol. V, pp. 261–262.

[10] M. N. Tukhachevsky, *Izbrannye Proizvedeniia,* Vol. I, Moscow, 1964, pp. 41–42.

[11] The full text of the report submitted to General Wrangel (who had assumed the command of the Volunteer Army) by the acting commander of the Fifth Cavalry Corps, General Chekotovsky is quoted by Wrangel in his "Zapiski," *Beloie Delo,* Vol. V, Berlin, 1928, pp. 254–255.

Chapter XXVII

[1] Denikin, *Ocherki Russkoi Smuty,* Vol. V, Berlin, 1926, pp. 109–110.

[2] General Peter N. Wrangel, "Zapiski," *Beloie Delo,* Vol. V, Berlin, 1928, p. 135.

[3] Denikin, "Otvet," *Illustrirovannaia Rossia,* Paris, Nos. 22, 23, and 24 (May 24, May 31, and June 7, 1930). In this article, which appeared in three installments, he gave his reactions to the memoirs of General Wrangel.

[4] *Ibid.,* No. 24 (June 7, 1930).

[5] The quoted phrases are from the so-called letter of accusation sent by Wrangel to Denikin early in 1920. See V. von Dreier, *Krestnyi Put' vo Imia Rodiny,* Berlin, 1921, pp. 82–90.

[6] The opposition to Admiral Kolchak was directed, among others, by V. S. Zavoiko, the same Zavoiko who in August, 1917, was attached to General Kornilov's headquarters in Mogilev. (Denikin, *Ocherki,* Vol. V, p. 116.)

[7] Denikin, *Ocherki,* Vol. V, p. 260.

[8] *Ibid.*

[9] Wrangel, "Zapiski," *Beloie Delo,* Vol. V, p. 260.

[10] "In order to influence General Denikin," wrote General Wrangel in his memoirs, "I sent copies of my report simultaneously to both of the commander in chief's assistants—Generals Romanovsky and Lukomsky. I also confidentially communicated the contents of the report to N. V. Savich, asking him to exert his influence on the commander in chief." (*Ibid.,* p. 261.)

[11] Denikin, *Ocherki,* Vol. V, pp. 260–261.

[12] *Ibid.,* p. 264.

[13] Wrangel, "Zapiski," *Beloie Delo,* Vol. V, p. 269.

[14] Denikin, *Ocherki,* Vol. V, pp. 263–264; see also G. N. Rakovsky, *V Stane Belykh,* Constantinople, 1920, pp. 38–43 (based on an interview of G. N. Rakovsky with General Sidorin).

[15] Denikin, *Ocherki,* Vol. V, Ch. 31.

[16] Wrangel, "Zapiski," *Beloie Delo,* Vol. V, p. 283.

[17] Denikin, "Zametki, Dopolnenia i Raziasnenia k *Ocherkam Russkoi Smuty,*" unpublished manuscript, Columbia University Russian Archive, p. 65.

Chapter XXVIII

[1] This point of view, which was quite prevalent at one time, is reflected in the article "Novorossiiskaia Evakuatsia," by A. Bittenbinder, in *Novoye Russkoye Slovo,* New York (May 31, 1969).

[2] K. N. Sokolov, *Pravlenie Generala Denikina,* Sofia, 1921, pp. 81–82.

[3] Mrs. Xenia Denikin, article devoted to the memory of General Romanovsky, *Dobrovoletz,* Paris (1937).

[4] The group of left-wing Socialist Revolutionaries who plotted an attempt on Denikin's life during his successful offensive in the summer of 1919, consisted of the same conspirators who had assassinated the German commander in the Ukraine, Field Marshal Eichhorn, in the summer of 1918. Donskoi, the Russian sailor who killed Eichhorn, was executed by the Germans, but some of his associates managed to escape from prison. They regarded General Denikin as an agent of foreign capitalism who had to be liquidated. For various reasons the plotted attempt had to be postponed several times, and by a strange coincidence, all of the conspirators eventually contracted typhus. In the meantime, Denikin's movement in south Russia was coming to an end. (I. K. Kakhovskaia, "Delo Eichgorna i Denikina," *Puti Revolutsii,* Berlin, 1923, pp. 220–260.)

[5] Denikin, *Ocherki Russkoi Smuty,* Vol. IV, Berlin, 1925, p. 82.

Chapter XXIX

[1] Denikin, *Ocherki Russkoi Smuty,* Vol. V, Berlin, 1926, pp. 299–304.

[2] *Ibid.,* p. 306.

[3] From N. V. Chaikovsky's letter to V. G. Boldyrev, quoted in the latter's book *Direktoria, Kolchak, Interventy,* Novonikolaevsk, 1925, p. 545. Although Chaikovsky joined N. M. Melnikov's government as minister without portfolio, he was in effect slated for the functions of Propaganda Minister.

[4] Winston S. Churchill, *The World Crisis,* Vol. V, New York, 1929, pp. 256–259.

[5] Denikin, *Ocherki,* Vol. V, pp. 310–311.

[6] *Ibid.,* p. 327.

[7] General Peter N. Wrangel, "Zapiski," *Beloie Delo,* Vol. V, Berlin, 1928, p. 292.

[8] Denikin, *Ocherki,* Vol. V, p. 336.

[9] Wrangel, "Zapiski," *Beloie Delo,* Vol. V, p. 299.

[10] Denikin, *Ocherki,* Vol. V, p. 336.

[11] General A. S. Lukomsky, *Vospominaniia,* Vol. II, Berlin, 1922, pp. 171–172.

[12] Denikin, *Ocherki,* Vol. V, p. 337.

[13] The entire text of Wrangel's letter to Denikin is quoted in V. von Dreier, *Krestyni Put' vo Imia Rodiny,* Berlin, 1921, pp. 82–90. For Wrangel's version, see his "Zapiski," *Beloie Delo,* Vol. V, pp. 296–300.

[14] Letter written in March, 1920, property of Mrs. Xenia Denikin.

[15] Denikin, *Ocherki,* Vol. V, p. 339. General Iuzefovich, prior to assuming command of the Fifth Cavalry Corps of the Volunteer Army, was General Wrangel's chief of staff.

[16] George Shavelsky, *Vospominaniia,* Vol. II, New York, 1954, pp. 401–408.

[17] Denikin, *Ocherki,* Vol. V, p. 324.

[18] *Ibid.,* p. 346.

[19] *Ibid.,* pp. 340–342.

[20] *Ibid.*

[21] *Ibid.,* p. 344.

[22] Letter dated March 17, 1920, property of Mrs. Xenia Denikin.

[23] Denikin, *Ocherki,* Vol. V, p. 349.

[24] Colonel B. A. Lagodovsky, *Vospominaniia,* Vol. III, *V Riadakh Leib-Gvardii Konnoi Artillerii v Grazhdanskoi Voine na Iuge Rossii,* unpublished memoirs, property of Colonel Lagodovsky, pp. 195–199. Quoted with the permission of Colonel Lagodovsky.

[25] G. N. Rakovsky, *V Stane Belykh,* Constantinople, 1920, p. 224.

[26] *Istoriia Grazhdanskoi Voiny SSSR,* Vol. IV, Moscow, 1959, p. 299.

[27] In *Ocherki* (Vol. V, p. 351), General Denikin wrote that "according to information from General Wrangel's *stavka,*" approximately twelve thousand Don and Kuban Cossacks had been transferred to the Crimea from the Caucasian coastline. This figure differs from the one given by a former officer of the Don Cossack army, Maksim Buguraev, who wrote, "Only less than five thousand Don Cossacks (including myself) and under three thousand Kuban Cossacks, were brought by General Wrangel from the Black Sea coastline to the Crimea." (*Novoye Russkoye Slovo,* New York, June 26, 1969.) The transfer took place around April 20, 1920.

[28] Denikin, *Ocherki,* Vol. V, p. 350.

[29] Unpublished letter dated March 17, 1920, property of Mrs. Xenia Denikin.

Chapter XXX

[1] In one of his unpublished manuscripts, the General stated that the entire reorganization of all troops and military staffs in the Crimea was completed at his initiative and by his orders. ("Zametki, Dopolnenia i Raziasnenia k *Ocherkam Russkoi Smuty,*" Columbia University Russian Archive, p. 57.)

[2] Denikin, *Ocherki Russkoi Smuty,* Vol. V, Berlin, 1926, p. 330.

[3] *Ibid.,* pp. 353–354; see also V. M. Krasnov (no relation to General P. N. Krasnov), "Iz Vospominanii o 1917–1920 Godakh," Vol. XI, *Arkhiv Russkoi Revolutsii,* Berlin, pp. 165–166.

[4] Denikin, *Ocherki,* Vol. V, pp. 354–356.

[5] *Ibid.,* p. 354.

[6] General P. S. Makhrov, "Novorossiiskaia Tragedia," *Russkie Novosti,* Paris, No. 116 (1947).

[7] The text of the telegram is quoted by General Wrangel in his "Zapiski," *Beloie Delo,* Vol. V, Berlin, 1928, p. 304; see also Denikin, *Ocherki,* Vol. V, pp. 356–357.

[8] Denikin, *Ocherki,* Vol. V, p. 357.

[9] For details concerning meetings of the Military Council to select a successor to General Denikin, see the following: Denikin, *Ocherki,* Vol. V, pp. 354–363; Wrangel, "Zapiski," *Beloie Delo,* Vol. V, pp. 304–306, and Vol. VI, Berlin, 1928, pp. 5–12; Makhrov, "Novorossiiskaia Tragedia."

[10] A description of the sessions of the Military Council (to select Denikin's successor) given by one of the participants, General Polzikov, is quoted by Denikin in *Ocherki,* Vol. V, pp. 358–363; see also Denikin's unpublished manuscript "Zametki," p. 58.

[11] Denikin, *Ocherki,* Vol. V, pp. 357–358; see also Wrangel, "Zapiski," *Beloie Delo,* Vol. V, pp. 304–306, and Vol. VI, pp. 5–12. P. N. Milyukov noted in his diary a conversation he had with Denikin on the day the General arrived in London, April 17, 1920. This passage in Milyukov's diary appears to be the only record of a conversation with Denikin on the painful subject of Wrangel's appointment, and of Denikin's stating that he "already had Wrangel in mind" before the Military Council reached its decision. (P. N. Milyukov, "Dnevnik," Columbia University Russian Archive. Excerpts from the manuscript were published in March, 1962, as "Dnevnik," in *Novyi Zhurnal,* New York, Vol. LXVII.)

[12] A. A. Valentinov, "Krymskaia Epopeia," *Arkhiv Russkoi Revolutsii,* Vol. V, Berlin, pp. 5–6.

[13] Denikin, *Ocherki,* Vol. V, p. 364.

[14] In his memoirs, General Wrangel quoted the full text of the British note. ("Zapiski," *Beloie Delo,* Vol. V, pp. 304–305.)

[15] At the beginning of 1920, Colonel Vladimir Sergeevich Khitrovo was "director of the bureau of the Russian Press" at the Russian embassy in Constantinople. When I wrote asking him to describe to me the assassination of General Romanovsky, he kindly did so, in a letter to me dated January 27, 1967. The testimony of witnesses concerning this moment varies considerably. For example, Mrs. Xenia Denikin later maintained (in her notes of June, 1927) that General Agapeev was no longer in the room with them when the assassination occurred and that they did not hear the shots.—D. L.

[16] Denikin, *Ocherki,* Vol. V, p. 364.

[17] Denikin, "Zametki," p. 60.

[18] Roman Gul', "Kto Ubil Generala Romanovskogo?" *Poslednie Novosti,* Paris (February 9, 1936).

[19] B. S. Kutsevalov's statement concerning the assassination of General Romanovsky was obtained as follows: In the 1920's and 1930's the military historian General N. N. Golovin was the European representative and purchasing agent of the historical archive at the Hoover War Library (later the Institution on War, Revolution, and Peace), Stanford University, Stanford, California. In 1932, General Golovin was offered for purchase a "statement" regarding General Romanovsky's assassination, written by B. S. Kutsevalov. The latter approached Golovin through N. P. Vakar, who was then a prominent contributor to the Paris newspaper *Poslednie Novosti.* Vakar was a friend of Golovin's as well as an old acquaintance of B. S. Kutsevalov's. Golovin did acquire Kutsevalov's manuscript. In the contract with the Hoover War Library, dated October 10, 1932 (Hoover Institution archive), Kutsevalov included the condition that his statement concerning Romanovsky's assassination would not be published for another ten years and also that "for a period of fifteen years a separate envelope containing the names of the persons who took part in the assassination would not be opened."

In the course of World War II, Vakar emigrated to the United States, where he became a professor of Russian culture and literature, lecturing at Harvard, Boston University, Middlebury, Wellesley, Tufts, and Ohio State. I spent several weeks at the Hoover Institution in the fall of 1967, doing research for this book, and discovered that Kutsevalov's manuscript had mysteriously vanished from the archive. Every effort of the administration to locate it proved futile. I then wrote to Vakar, who kindly sent me Kutsevalov's address. At my request, Kutsevalov reconstructed the contents of the vanished statement and gave me permission to make use of his new manuscript in this book.—D. L.

Chapter XXXI

[1] V. I. Lenin, *Lenin o Vneshnei politike Sovetskogo Gosudarstva,* Moscow, 1960, pp. 226, 228, 338, 371.

[2] Winston S. Churchill, *The World Crisis,* Vol. V, New York, 1929, p. 244.

[3] V. I. Lenin, *Chto Delat'?,* quoted in *Lenin o Propagande i Agitatsii,* Moscow, 1956, p. 12.

[4] William Henry Chamberlin, *The Russian Revolution 1917–1921,* Vol. II, New York, 1954, Ch. 41.

[5] General Peter N. Wrangel, "Zapiski," *Beloie Delo,* Vol. V, Berlin, 1928, pp. 257–261.

[6] Denikin, *Ocherki Russkoi Smuty,* Vol. V, Berlin, 1926, pp. 117–118.

[7] Report No. 0964, June 18, 1919, from General Iuzefovich, chief of staff of the Caucasian army, to General I. P. Romanovsky. Columbia University Russian Archive.

[8] Wrangel, "Zapiski," *Beloie Delo,* Vol. V, p. 160.

[9] S. P. Melgunov, "Ocherki Generala Denikina," *Na Chuzhoi Storone,* Vol. V (1924), p. 306.

Chapter XXXII

[1] Between December, 1921, and July, 1922, Mrs. Denikin kept a notebook describing various episodes of her own and her husband's life. This notebook is among the family papers belonging to Mrs. Denikin.

[2] A copy of this telegram is in the Columbia University Russian Archive.

[3] "General Denikin in London," *London Times* (April 19, 1920).

[4] The letters from Sablin are now in the Michel N. Giers archive, Hoover Institution on War, Revolution, and Peace, Stanford University, File No. 11 (reports of the Russian diplomatic representative in England, March 21–December 31, 1920). The letter of April 17, 1920, is No. 205.

[5] Letter No. 210.

[6] Letter No. 215.

[7] Letter No. 216.

[8] Denikin, "Zametki, Dopolnenia i Raziasnenia k *Ocherkam Russkoi Smuty*," unpublished manuscript, Columbia University Russian Archive, p. 66.

[9] P. N. Milyukov, "Dnevnik," Columbia University Russian Archive. Excerpts (including the one quoted here) were published, as "Dnevnik," in *Novyi Zhurnal*, New York, Vol. LXVII (March, 1962).

[10] Denikin, "Zametki," p. 66.

[11] Information furnished by Mrs. Xenia Denikin.

[12] Sablin's letter No. 233, dated April 29, 1920.

[13] A summary of General Denikin's speech is in the family papers belonging to Mrs. Xenia Denikin.

[14] Milyukov, "Dnevnik," Columbia University Russian Archive.

[15] Denikin, "Zametki," p. 67.

[16] *Ibid.*, p. 69.

[17] For the Curzon and Holman statements, Denikin, *Ocherki Russkoi Smuty*, Vol. V, Berlin, 1926, pp. 347–348; also, "Lord Curzon's Note to Chicherin of April 14, 1920," *The New Russia*, London, Vol. II (1920), p. 543.

Chapter XXXIII

[1] Notebook, among the family papers belonging to Mrs. Xenia Denikin.

[2] Unpublished letter, copy in the Columbia University Russian Archive.

[3] Unpublished letter, copy in the Columbia University Russian Archive.

[4] Denikin, "Zametki, Dopolnenia i Raziasnenia k *Ocherkam Russkoi Smuty*," unpublished manuscript, Columbia University Russian Archive, p. 71.

[5] Notebook, property of Mrs. Xenia Denikin.

[6] Denikin, "Zametki," pp. 72–78.

[7] *Ibid.*, p. 74.

[8] *Ibid.*, pp. 62–65.

Chapter XXXIV

[1] Letter to General Kutepov from Sopron, Hungary, September, 1922, Columbia University Russian Archive.

[2] Denikin, an open letter addressed to the editor of the Russian daily in Paris, *Vozrozhdenie*, published in two installments in *Nashe Slovo*, Paris, Nos. 1 and 2 (May, 1934).

³ Letter to General A. M. Dragomirov from Sopron, Hungary, July 8, 1922, Columbia University Russian Archive.

⁴ The inscribed volume belongs to Mrs. Xenia Denikin. The date specified by Bunin in the dedication appears to be incorrect, as Odessa was liberated from the Bolsheviks in August, not September, 1919.

⁵ Information furnished by Mrs. Xenia Denikin.

⁶ Mark Slonim, "Amerikanskaiia Kniga o Marine Tsvetaevoi," *Novoye Russkoye Slovo,* New York (January 29, 1967).

⁷ Information furnished by Mrs. Xenia Denikin.

⁸ M. I. Dragomirov (1830–1905) was a well-known general and the author of many works on military subjects.

⁹ Unpublished letter, copy in the Columbia University Russian Archive.

¹⁰ *Dni,* Berlin (January 22, 1928).

Chapter XXXV

¹ Lev Nikulin, *Mertvaia Zyb',* Moscow, 1965, pp. 17–19.

² Denikin, "Kutepov," unpublished manuscript, Columbia University Russian Archive.

³ *Ibid.*

⁴ Winston S. Churchill, "Boris Savinkov," in *Great Contemporaries,* London, 1937, pp. 125–133.

⁵ Denikin, "Zametki, Dopolnenia i Raziasnenia k *Ocherkam Russkoi Smuty,*" unpublished manuscript, Columbia University Russian Archive, p. 30.

⁶ S. P. Melgunov, "Legendy i Deistvitel'nost'. Materialy o Treste," *Vozrozhdenie,* Paris, Vol. XV (May–June, 1951), p. 127.

⁷ Denikin, "Kutepov."

⁸ *The New York Times* (January 29, 1930).

⁹ Geoffrey Bailey, *The Conspirators,* New York, 1960, pp. 89–117; Paul W. Blackstock, *The Secret Road to World War II, Soviet Versus Western Intelligence, 1921–1939,* Chicago, 1969, pp. 205–223. Among many articles devoted to the Kutepov affair should be mentioned Andrei Sedykh's "25 Let so Dnia Pokhishcheniia Generala A. P. Kutepova," *Novoye Russkoye Slovo,* New York (January 27, 1955).

¹⁰ Count G. Ciano, *The Ciano Diaries,* New York, 1946, p. 275.

¹¹ General N. Shimanov, "Moi Dopolnenia k Romanu (po Povodu Knigi L. V. Nikulina *Mertvaia Zyb'*)," in the Red Army paper *Krasnaia Gazeta,* Moscow (September 22, 1965).

¹² S. P. Melgunov, "Zagadki v Dele Generala Kutepova," *Novoye Russkoye Slovo,* New York (October 3–October 11, 1955).

¹³ Denikin, "Kutepov."

Chapter XXXVI

¹ Denikin, "Kutepov," unpublished manuscript, Columbia University Russian Archive, p. 10.

² S. P. Melgunov, "Zagadki v Dele Generala Kutepova," *Novoye Russkoye Slovo,* New York (October 3, 1955).

³ Paul W. Blackstock, a former United States intelligence research specialist, now professor of international studies at the University of South Carolina, made

a study of the documents from the Melgunov archive at the London School of Economics. In a chapter on "The Melgunov Operations" in his book *The Secret Road to World War II, Soviet Versus Western Intelligence, 1921–1939* (Chicago, 1969, pp. 182–192, notes on p. 55), Blackstock states that although Melgunov's activities were conducted with extremely tight security and most of his records were destroyed, several operational reports remain in his archive. These reports indicate that the scope of Melgunov's operations was broad and that his organization had its own agents in Russia. In view of the Trotsky-Stalin feud and the resulting dissension in the Communist party, Melgunov's agents felt in 1928 that it was possible to eliminate Stalin. However, according to Blackstock, "nothing is known as to what decisions were made in Paris regarding the proposal to assassinate Stalin."

[4] Melgunov, "Zagadki" (October 3, 1955).

[5] Unpublished letter dated April 22, 1930, Columbia University Russian Archive.

[6] *Ibid.*

[7] Plevitskaia's maiden name was Vinnikov. Her first husband, Plevitsky, was a dancer with the Kiev ballet; her second husband, Levitsky, was an army officer who later joined the Red Army.

[8] *Chasovoi,* Brussels, No. 196 (September 5, 1937) and No. 197 (October 5, 1937).

[9] "Pokhishchenie Generala Millera," *Illustrirovannaia Rossia,* Paris, No. 41 (October 2, 1937); Geoffrey Bailey, *The Conspirators,* New York, 1960, p. 234.

[10] Skoblin had two brothers in Paris and a sister, married to Vorobiov. They had no connection with his crime.

[11] "Zamyshlialos' Pokhishchenie Generala Denikina?" *Poslednie Novosti,* Paris (September 25, 1937).

[12] Information furnished by Mrs. Xenia Denikin and the General's daughter, Mme. Marina Chiappe.

[13] "Protsess N. V. Plevitskoi," *Poslednie Novosti,* Paris (December 10, 1938).

[14] Unpublished letter, from the archive of M. M. Filonenko, Columbia University Russian Archive.

Chapter XXXVII

[1] These brochures were *Russkii Vopros na Dal'nem Vostoke,* Paris, 1932; *Brest-Litovsk,* Paris, 1933; *Mezhdunarodnoie Polozhenie, Rossia i Emigratsia,* Paris, 1934; *Kto Spas Sovetskuiu Vlast' ot Gibeli,* Paris, 1937 (about the role of Pilsudski); and *Mirovye Sobytia i Russkii Vopros,* Paris, 1939.

[2] Denikin, *Mirovye Sobytia.*

[3] "General A. I. Denikin o Sobytiakh na Dal'nem Vostoke," *Poslednie Novosti,* Paris (March 27, 1932).

[4] Denikin, *Mirovye Sobytia,* p. 73.

[5] *Ibid.,* pp. 67–68.

[6] Unpublished letter dated November 5, 1926, Columbia University Russian Archive.

[7] Unpublished letter dated April 22, 1930, Columbia University Russian Archive.

[8] Letter dated April 27, 1937, from the "Ministère de la Défense Nationale et de la Guerre (3ᵉ Bureau Correspondance Générale No. 6689 K)" to M. M.

Fedorov, chairman of the Russian émigré committee for the construction of a monument on the Marne in memory of Russian soldiers fallen in France during World War I, Columbia University Russian Archive.

[9] Denikin, speech delivered on May 16, 1937, Columbia University Russian Archive.

[10] S. P. Melgunov, "Grazhdanskii Podvig A. I. Denikina," *Vozrozhdenie,* Paris, Vol. XXV (January–February, 1953).

Chapter XXXVIII

[1] This age was given by Mrs. Denikin, as well as by General Denikin during his interview with Andrei Sedykh, as reported in "A. I. Denikin Obiasniaet Prichiny Svoego Priezda v New York," *Novoye Russkoye Slovo,* New York (December 9, 1945).

[2] A certificate in German was issued to Mrs. X. V. Denikin by the *Feldgendarmerie* of Mont-de-Marsan, to the effect that she had been interned from June 15 to July 1, 1941, had submitted identification papers, and had been permitted to return to her residence in Mimizan.

[3] This index, *Verzeichnis der verbotenen Bücher in russischer Sprache,* a thirty-two-page booklet, was published in Paris during the German occupation.

[4] Upon his arrival in America, Denikin described this episode to Andrei Sedykh, of *Novoye Russkoye Slovo* ("A. I. Denikin Obiasniaet," December 9, 1945). Some of the details in my account are based on information furnished by Mrs. Denikin. It should be noted that because of the lack of communication during the occupation, many facts related by word of mouth became distorted or exaggerated. The tale of the German general's visit to General Denikin soon turned into a legend—the *Kommandant* of Biarritz became a German field marshal and commander in chief, named von Rundstedt or von Manstein in different versions.

[5] Columbia University Russian Archive.

[6] Denikin, *Vtoraia Mirovaia Voina, Rossia i Zarubezhie,* unpublished and unfinished manuscript, Columbia University Russian Archive, Part I, pp. 133–134.

[7] *Ibid.,* pp. 117–118.

[8] *Ibid.,* Part II, p. 55.

[9] *Ibid.,* p. 35.

[10] Unpublished letter to General N. N. Stogov, dated November 24, 1944, Columbia University Russian Archive.

[11] Denikin, *Puti Russkoi Emigratsii,* text of a lecture delivered on February 5, 1946, Columbia University Russian Archive, p. 30.

Chapter XXXIX

[1] The Vlasov movement was an attempt to carry on the anti-Soviet struggle during World War II, based on hopes of German help. Its leader was Lieutenant General Andrei A. Vlasov, a member of the Communist party and commander of a Soviet assault army which was captured by German troops in June, 1942. Most of Vlasov's followers in Germany were Soviet war prisoners, including some anti-Stalin Communists. In May, 1945, Vlasov was captured by the Red Army. He was tried and executed in Moscow in August, 1946. For details on the Vlasov movement, see Sven Steenberg, *Vlasov,* translated from the German, New York, 1970.

[2] Denikin, "General Vlasov i Vlasovtsy," unpublished manuscript, Columbia University Russian Archive, pp. 1, 13, 14–18.

[3] Denikin, *Vtoraia Mirovaia Voina, Rossiia i Zarubezhie,* unpublished and unfinished manuscript, Columbia University Russian Archive, Part I, pp. 142–147.

Chapter XL

[1] Denikin, *Puti Russkoi Emigratsii,* text of a lecture delivered on February 5, 1946, Columbia University Russian Archive, pp. 13–14.

[2] *Ibid.,* pp. 45–46.

Chapter XLI

[1] Valerian P. Avgustinóvich (name now changed to Montwit).

[2] Andrei Sedykh, "A. I. Denikin Obiasniaet Prichiny Svoego Priezda v New York," *Novoye Russkoye Slovo,* New York (December 9, 1945).

[3] The article which appeared in *Morgen Journal* was translated from Yiddish into Russian and reprinted in full on January 15, 1946, by the New York pro-Communist Russian daily *Russkii Golos* under the title "General Denikin i Novoye Russkoye Slovo."

[4] A copy of this letter is in the Columbia University Russian Archive.

[5] A copy of the Russian text of this letter is in the Columbia University Russian Archive. In view of the reference to *Vlasovtsy* at the beginning of this letter, it should be recalled that the Russian war prisoners whom General Denikin met in Mimizan were in no way connected with the Vlasov movement.

[6] Letter dated February 18, 1946, Columbia University Russian Archive.

[7] George Fisher, *Soviet Opposition to Stalin,* Cambridge, Mass., 1952.

[8] Denikin, *Mirovaia Voina i Russkaia Voennaia Emigratsia,* text of a lecture delivered on January 21, 1946, Columbia University Russian Archive.

[9] Denikin, *Puti Russkoi Emigratsii,* text of a lecture delivered on February 5, 1946, Columbia University Russian Archive.

[10] "Doklad A. I. Denikina," *Novoye Russkoye Slovo,* New York (February 7, 1946).

Chapter XLII

[1] Harry S. Truman, *Years of Decision,* Vol. I, New York, 1958, pp. 508–509.

[2] Translated from "Russkii Vopros." Denikin's Russian draft of this memorandum is in the Columbia University Russian Archive.

[3] This letter is in the Columbia University Russian Archive.

[4] Public Law 86-90, 86th Congress, S. J. Res 111, July 17, 1959; see also George F. Kennan, *On Dealing with the Communist World,* New York, 1964, pp. 11–14.

[5] Countess Alexandra Tolstoy, *Otets,* Vol. II, New York, 1953, p. 243.

[6] Unpublished letter, to General P. K. Pisarev, Columbia University Russian Archive.

[7] General Anton I. Denikin, *Navety na Beloe Dvizhenie,* unpublished manuscript, Columbia University Russian Archive. The Hoover Institution on War, Revolution, and Peace, Stanford University, also has a copy.

BIBLIOGRAPHY

NON-SOVIET SOURCES

Unpublished Materials and Archives

ARCHIVE OF RUSSIAN AND EAST EUROPEAN HISTORY
AND CULTURE, COLUMBIA UNIVERSITY

Denikin, General Anton I., "Zametki, Dopolnenia i Raziasnenia k *Ocherkam Russkoi Smuty*" (sixty-one typewritten pages corrected in ink by the General, dated May 31, 1930). Following "Zametki" and forming part of the same sequence are "Po Povodu Sostavlenia *Ocherkov*" (pp. 62–65), "England" (pp. 66–69), "Belgium, Hungary" (pp. 70–83), "Wrangel" (pp. 84–103), and "Posle Kutepova" (pp. 119–122). Pp. 104–117 are missing, but "Kutepov," a separate manuscript fourteen pages long, apparently represents the missing portion; p. 118 was either skipped or deleted by Denikin.

———— *Navety na Beloie Dvizhenie* (seventy-one typewritten pages corrected in ink by the General). An answer to General Golovin's *Rossiiskaia Kontr-Revolutsia v 1917–1918* (1937). A copy was sent by General Denikin to the Hoover War Library (January 10, 1947).

———— "General Vlasov i Vlasovtsy" (twenty typewritten pages corrected in ink by the General, 1946). Also, an abridged version translated into English as "General Vlasov and His Followers" (thirteen pages).

———— *Mirovaia Voina i Russkaia Voennaia Emigratsia* (thirty-three type-written pages). The text of a lecture delivered by General Denikin on January 21, 1946, at the Manhattan Center, New York.

———— *Puti Russkoi Emigratsii* (forty-six typewritten pages). The text of a lecture delivered by General Denikin on February 5, 1946, at the Manhattan Center, New York.

———— "Russkii Vopros" (five typewritten pages, dated June 11, 1946). Translated into English (six pages) as "The Russian Question," this paper was mailed by General Denikin as an *aide-mémoire* to the governments of the United States and Great Britain.

———— *Vtoraia Mirovaia Voina, Rossia i Zarubezhie* (1946–1947). The rough draft of an unfinished book.

A copy of the Russian text of Denikin's letter to General Eisenhower (dated January 31, 1946). A letter from General Thomas T. Handy, acting chief of staff (dated February 18, 1946), in answer to the above.

An exchange of letters in Russian between General Denikin and Professor Harold H. Fisher, chairman of the Hoover War Library, concerning the possibility of publishing the General's manuscripts (January, 1947).

Letters to General Denikin from Generals Alekseev, Kaledin, and Kornilov;

Regent Alexander (the future King of Yugoslavia); Admiral Kolchak (four handwritten pages, dated June 28, 1919).

A letter to General Romanovsky from General Iuzefovich, chief of staff of General Wrangel's Caucasian army (dated June 18, 1919, No. 0965), proposing the formation of a special cavalry army.

An exchange of correspondence between General Denikin and General Wrangel (1919).

Several letters to the General from General Kutepov, written during the 1920's.

Copies of General Denikin's letters to General Dragomirov, N. I. Astrov, and others.

Copies of General Denikin's letters to a number of his friends and acquaintances, written during the twenty-seven years that he lived as a political émigré.

An exchange of correspondence between General Denikin and Colonel Koltyshev (1945–1946).

Three consecutive wills and testaments made by General Denikin (May, 1916; January, 1922; September, 1942).

A copy of a letter from General Chaperon du Larré to General Wrangel (December, 1920).

Reminiscences of General Denikin by Colonel P. A. Jackson, Colonel A. Kolchinsky, and Lieutenant General N. M. Tikhmenev.

Birkin, V. N., "Kornilovskii Pokhod."

Denikin, Xenia, "S. N. Tretiakov."

Filonenko, Maximilian M., correspondence with N. V. Plevitskaia during the period of her detention and trial, resulting from the 1937 kidnapping in Paris of General E. K. Miller.

Lavrov, Captain M., "Pokazania ob Ubiistve Generala Romanovskogo."

Leliakovsky, Colonel A. M., "Zheleznyie Strelki v Boiakh."

Makhrov, General Peter S., "General Wrangel i B. Savinkov."

———— "V Beloi Armii Generala Denikina."

Mel'nikov, N. M., "Pochemu Belye na Iuge Ne Pobedili Krasnykh."

Milyukov, P. N., "Dnevnik." Also, personal papers.

Panin, Countess S. V., archive. Unpublished papers and documents concerning the Cadet party, the civil war in south Russia, memoirs of N. I. Astrov, and so on.

Pliushchevsky-Pliushchik, General Y. N., formerly deputy chief of staff (*general quartirmeister*) of General Denikin's *Stavka*. Documents and papers.

Sannikov, General A. S., *Vospominaniia* (1926).

Shatilov, General P. N., "Zapiski."

Tikhobrazov, Colonel D. N., "Iz Vospominanii General'nogo Shtaba Polkovnika D. N. Tikhobrazova."

Troubetzkoy, Prince Grigory N., "Iz Dnevnika Kniazia G. N. Troubetzkogo 1918 i Nachalo 1919 Goda na Iuge Rossii."

A set of documents delivered in 1928 (after the death of General Wrangel) by General A. P. Kutepov to General Denikin for safekeeping: The original text of a proclamation (handwritten by General Wrangel, dated May 20, 1920). An original letter from *Ataman* A. P. Bogaevsky to General Wrangel (July 26,

1920) concerning the possibility of landing troops in the territory of the Don Cossacks. A copy of a "highly confidential" nine-page letter from M. N. Giers to General Wrangel (February 10, 1921). Operational documents of General Wrangel's army (thirteen items, June and July, 1920). Orders issued by General Wrangel's headquarters during August and October, 1920 (eleven documents).

Minutes of a secret conference of the Soviet Military Council headed by Krylenko, held in the city of Mogilev on January 22, 1918.

Many other items related in various ways to Denikin's activities are also to be found in this archive.

THE HOOVER INSTITUTION ON WAR, REVOLUTION, AND PEACE, STANFORD UNIVERSITY

Giers, Michel N., archive. General Denikin and the Don. General Denikin's activity in south Russia from November, 1918, to April 26, 1920. Documents prepared by General Denikin's *Stavka* on the conditions and needs of his army. Correspondence between General Denikin and the British High Command in Constantinople. Reports of the Russian diplomatic representative in England (March 21–December 31, 1920).

Maklakov, V. A., collection. "Arkhiv Russkogo Posol'stva v Parizhe 1918–1923."

UNPUBLISHED MATERIALS IN PRIVATE COLLECTIONS

Property of Mrs. Xenia Denikin

Original record of military service of Major Ivan E. Denikin (father of General Anton I. Denikin).

Birth and baptismal certificates of Anton I. Denikin.

Ninety-six letters from General Denikin to his future wife (from October 15, 1915 to the end of August, 1917, when he was arrested by order of the Provisional Government in connection with the Kornilov affair).

Forty-two letters from General Denikin to his wife (written during the civil-war period).

Letters from Mrs. Denikin to General Denikin (from October, 1915, through the civil-war period and the years that followed, to 1942).

A notebook kept by Mrs. Denikin from December 13, 1921, to July 26, 1922, in which she jotted down various episodes of her own life and the life of her husband during the five preceding years.

Journal (twenty-eight notebooks) kept by Mrs. Denikin during the German occupation of France.

Property of Dimitry V. Lehovich

Kutsevalov, B. S., "Ubiistvo Generala Romanovskogo v Konstantinopole (Kratkaia Zametka)."

Correspondence with Colonel V. S. Khitrovo, Colonel D. N. Tikhobrazov, and Colonel N. P. Ukraintsev.

Notes taken by D. V. Lehovich during numerous conversations with Mrs. Xenia Denikin, the General's widow, and Mme. Marina Chiappe, his daughter.

Notes taken by D. V. Lehovich recording an interview with A. F. Kerensky concerning the Kornilov affair.

Property of Colonel B. A. Lagodovsky

Lagodovsky, Colonel B. A., *Vospominaniia,* Vol. III (1918–1920), *V Riadakh Leib-Gvardii Konnoi Artillerii v Grazhdanskoi Voine na Iuge Rossii.*

Property of Princess Marie S. Troubetzkoy

Troubetzkoy, Princess Marie S. (née Lopukhin), "Zapiski."

Selected Published Materials

ARKHIV RUSSKOI REVOLUTSII

Twenty-two volumes, published in Berlin by I. V. Gessen between 1920 and 1937, and including the following:

Blok, Alexandr, "Poslednie Dni Starogo Regima," Vol. IV.

Budberg, Baron A., "Dnevnik," Vols. XII, XIII, XIV, XV.

"Denezhnye Dokumenty Generala Alekseeva," in the section "Dokumenty," Vol. V.

Dobrovolsky, Colonel S., "Bor'ba za Vozrozhdenie Rossii v Severnoi Oblasti," Vol. III.

"Doklad Kartasheva, Kuzmina-Karavaeva i Suvorova: 'Obrazovanie Severo-Zapadnogo Pravitel'stva'," in the section "Dokumenty," Vol. I.

"Doklad Nachalnika Operatsionnogo Otdelenia Germanskogo Vostochnogo Fronta o Polozhenii del na Ukraine v Marte 1918 Goda," in the section "Dokumenty," Vol. I.

"Dokumenty k 'Vospominaniam' Generala Lukomskogo," in the section "Dokumenty," Vol. III.

"Dokumenty po Istorii Chernomorskogo Flota (v Marte–Iyune 1918 Goda)," Vol. XIV.

Filimonov, General A. P., "Razgrom Kubanskoi Rady," Vol. V.

Goldenveiser, A. A., "Iz Kievskikh Vospominanii," Vol. VI.

Iakhontov, A. N., "Tiazhelye Dni (Sekretnye Zasedania Soveta Ministrov, Iulia 16–Sentiabria 2, 1915)," Vol. XVIII.

Igrenev, G., "Ekaterinoslavskie Vospominaniia," Vol. III.

Karinsky, N., "Epizod iz Evakuatsii Novorossiiska," Vol. XII.

Kazanovich, General B., "Poezdka iz Dobrovolcheskoi Armii v Krasnuiu Moskvu," Vol. VII.

Krasnov, General P. N., "Na Vnutrennem Fronte," Vol. I.

—— "Vsevelikoie Voisko Donskoie," Vol. V.

Krasnov, V. M., "Iz Vospominanii o 1917–1920 Godakh," Vols. VIII, XI.

Kritsky, M., "Krasnaia Armia na Iuzhnom Fronte," Vol. XVIII.

Leikhtenbergsky, Gertsog G. (Duke of Leuchtenberg), "Kak Nachalas Iuzhnaia Armia," Vol. VIII.

Maiborodov, V., "S Frantsuzami," Vol. XVI.

Mogiliansky, N. M., "Tragedia Ukrainy," Vol. XI.

Nabokov, Vladimir D., "Vremennoie Pravitel'stvo," Vol. I.

"Ocherk Vzaimootnoshenia Vooruzhennykh Sil Iuga Rossii i Predstavitelei Frantsuzkogo Komandovania," in the section "Dokumenty," Vol. XVI.

"Otchet o Komandirovke iz Dobrovolcheskoi Armii v Sibir v 1918 Godu," in the section "Dokumenty," Vol. IX.

"Protokol Doprosa Admirala Kolchaka Chrezvychainoi Sledstvennoi Komissiei v Irkutske v Ianvare–Fevrale 1920 Goda," in the section "Dokumenty," Vol. X.

Rodzianko, M. V., "Gosudarstvennaia Duma i Fevral'skaia Revolutsia," Vol. VI.

——— "Krushenie Imperii," Vol. XVII.

Sinegub, A., "Zashchita Zimnego Dvortsa," Vol. IV.

Sokolov, Boris, "Padenie Severnoi Oblasti," Vol. IX.

Sokolov, K. N., "Kubanskoie Deistvo," Vol. XVIII.

Troubetzkoy, Prince E. N., "Iz Putevykh Zametok Bezhentsa," Vol. XVIII.

Valentinov, A. A., "Krymskaia Epopeia," Vol. V.

"Verkhovnoie Komandovanie v Pervye Dni Revolutsii," in the section "Dokumenty," Vol. XVI.

Voronovich, N., "Mezh Dvukh Ognei," Vol. VII.

Zavadsky, S. V., "Na Velikom Izlome," Vols. VII, XI.

OTHER PUBLISHED SOURCES

Agapeev, General V. P., "Ubiistvo Generala Romanovskogo," *Beloie Delo,* Vol. II, Berlin, Mednyi Vsadnik, 1927.

Aldanov, M. A., *Sovremenniki,* Berlin, Slovo, 1928.

——— "Ubiistvo Uritskogo," *Sovremenniki,* Berlin, Slovo, 1928.

Alekseev, General M. V., "Iz Dnevnika Generala Alekseeva," *Russkii Istoricheskii Archiv,* Vol. I, Prague, izd. Russkogo Zagranichnogo Istoricheskogo Archiva v Prage, 1929.

American Slavic and East European Review, New York. A quarterly, published by Columbia University Press.

Andolenko, General C. R., *Histoire de l'Armée Russe,* Paris, Flammarion, 1967.

Apushkin, V. A., "Russko-Iaponskaia Voina 1904–1905 Gg.," in *Russkaia Byl',* Moscow, izd. Obrazovanie, 1911.

Aronson, Gregory, *Bolshevistkaia Revolutsia i Mensheviki,* New York, Grenich Printing Corp., 1955.

——— "Iz Razmyshlenii i Dnevnikov S. M. Dubnova," *Novoye Russkoye Slovo,* New York (September 15, 1957).

Arshinov, Peter, *Istoria Makhnovskogo Dvizhenia (1918–1921),* Berlin, izd. Gruppy Russkikh Anarkhistov v Germanii, 1923.

Asher, Harvey, "The Kornilov Affair," *The Russian Review,* Stanford, Vol. XXIX (July, 1970).

Bailey, Geoffrey, *The Conspirators,* New York, Harper & Brothers, 1960.

Barmine, Alexander, *One Who Survived,* New York, G. P. Putnam's Sons, 1945.

Bechhofer-Roberts, C. E., *In Denikin's Russia and the Caucasus 1919–1920,* London, W. Collins Sons & Co., 1921.

Belaia Rossia, compiled by General C. V. Denisov, Vol. I, New York, izd. Glavnogo Pravlenia Zarubezhnogo Soyuza Russkikh Voennykh Invalidov, 1937. A 127-page collection.

Beloie Delo: Letopis Beloi Borby, edited by A. A. von Lampe, 7 vols., Berlin, Mednyi Vsadnik, 1926–1928. A collection.

Berezhansky, N., "P. Bermont v Pribaltike v 1919 Godu," *Istorik i Sovremennik,* Berlin, Vol. I (1922), pp. 5–87.

Besedovsky, G. Z., *Na Putiakh k Termidoru,* 2 vols., Paris, izd. Mishen', 1930–1931.

Blackstock, Paul W., *The Secret Road to World War II, Soviet Versus Western Intelligence, 1921–1939,* Chicago, Quadrangle Books, 1969.

Bogaevsky, General A. P., *Vospominaniia Generala A. P. Bogaevskogo 1918 God. Ledianoi Pokhod,* New York, izd. Muzeia Belogo Dvizhenia Soyuza Pervopokhodnikov, 1963.

Boiarintsev, Colonel M., "Moi Vstrechi s Generalom Denikinym," *Chasovoi,* Brussels, No. 318 (April, 1952).

Bor'ba za Rossiu, edited by S. P. Melgunov, Paris. A periodical.

Bradley, John, *Allied Intervention in Russia 1917–1920,* New York, Basic Books, 1968.

Brinkley, George A., *The Volunteer Army and Allied Intervention in South Russia 1917–1921,* Notre Dame, Indiana, University of Notre Dame Press, 1966.

Bromberg, I. A., *Zapad, Rossia i Evreistvo,* Prague, izd. Evraziitsev, 1931.

Buchanan, Sir George, *My Mission to Russia and Other Diplomatic Memories,* 2 vols., London, Cassel & Co., 1923.

Carr, E. H., *A History of Soviet Russia. The Bolshevik Revolution 1917–1923,* London, Macmillan, Vol. I, 1954; Vol. II, 1952; Vol. III, 1953.

Chamberlin, William Henry, *The Russian Revolution 1917–1921,* 2 vols., New York, Macmillan, 1954.

Chasovoi. A monthly, published first in Paris, later in Brussels.

Chebyshev, Nikolai N. His political articles published during the 1920's and 1930's in the Paris daily newspaper *Vozrozhdenie,* collected in one folder in M. M. Filonenko's archive, Columbia University Russian Archive.

Cheka. Materialy po Deiatel'nosti Chrezvychainoi Komissii, foreword by Victor Chernov, Berlin, izd. Tsentral'nogo Buro Partii Sotsialistov-Revolutsionerov, 1922. Materials about the activity of the *Cheka.*

Chernov, V., *Rozhdenie Revolutsionnoi Rossii,* Paris, privately printed, 1934.

Chubinsky, M. P., "Na Donu," *Donskaia Letopis',* No. 4, Belgrade, izd. Donskoi Istoricheskoi Komissii, 1924.

Churchill, Winston S., *The World Crisis,* 5 vols., New York, Charles Scribner's Sons, 1923–1929.

———— *The Unknown War: The Eastern Front,* New York, Charles Scribner's Sons, 1931.

———— "Boris Savinkov," in *Great Contemporaries,* London, Butterworth, 1937.

Ciano, Count G., *The Ciano Diaries,* New York, Doubleday & Co., 1946.

Davats, V. H., and Lvov, N. N., *Russkaia Armia na Chuzhbine,* Belgrade, Russkoye Izd., 1923.

Denikin, General Anton I., *Ocherki Russkoi Smuty:* Vols. I and II, Paris, J. Povolozky & Cie., 1921 and 1922; Vols. III and IV, Berlin, Slovo, 1924 and 1925; Vol. V, Berlin, Mednyi Vsadnik, 1926.

———— *The Russian Turmoil,* London, Hutchinson & Co., 1922. An abridged translation of Vol. I of *Ocherki.*

———— *The White Army,* London, Jonathan Cape, 1930. An abridged translation (in one volume) of Vols. II–V of *Ocherki.*

———— *La Décomposition de l'Armée et du Pouvoir Février–Septembre 1917,* Paris, J. Povolozky & Cie., 1922.

———— *Ofitsery,* Paris, Rodnik, 1928. Six short stories.

———— *Staraia Armia,* 2 vols., Paris, Rodnik, 1929–1931.

———— *Russkii Vopros na Dal'nem Vostoke,* Paris, Bazile, 1932. 35 pages.

———— *Brest-Litovsk,* Paris, privately printed, 1933. 52 pages.

———— *Mezhdunarodnoie Polozhenie, Rossia i Emigratsia,* Paris, 1934. 16 pages.

———— *La Situation Internationale et le Problème Russe,* Paris, Imp. d'Art, 1934. 36 pages.

———— *Kto Spas Sovetskuiu Vlast' ot Gibeli,* Paris, Maison de la Presse, 1937. 14 pages.

———— *Mirovye Sobytia i Russkii Vopros,* Paris, izd. Soiuza Dobrovoltsev, 1939.

———— *World Events and the Russian Problem,* Paris, Rapide, 1939. 47 pages.

———— *Put' Russkogo Ofitsera,* New York, Chekhov Publishing House, 1953.

Articles

———— "Istoria," *Slovo,* Paris, Nos. 10 and 11 (August 28 and September 4, 1922). An answer to *Ataman* Krasnov's article "Vsevelikoie Voisko Donskoie," *Arkhiv Russkoi Revolutsii,* Vol. V.

———— "Pis'mo 'Ottuda' i Otvet 'Tuda'," *Bor'ba za Rossiu,* Paris, No. 70 (1928).

———— "Puti Bor'by," *Bor'ba za Rossiu,* Paris, No. 72 (1928).

———— "Puti k Iedineniu," *Russkii Invalid,* Paris, No. 1 (February 22, 1930).

———— "Otvet," *Illustrirovannaia Rossia,* Paris, Nos. 22, 23, and 24 (May 24, May 31, and June 7, 1930). An answer to the version of events given by General Wrangel in his memoirs.

———— "Beloye Voinstvo," *Bor'ba za Rossiu,* Paris, Nos. 216–217 (1931).

———— "Zheleznaia Divizia v Lutskom Proryve," *Russkii Invalid,* Paris, No. 20 (June 7, 1931).

———— "Ob Ispravleniakh Istorii," *Poslednie Novosti,* Paris (November 13 and 14, 1936).

———— "V Sovetskom Raiu," *Vozrozhdenie,* Paris, Vol. VIII (1950). The last article written by Denikin.

Denikin, Xenia, "Stranitsy iz Dnevnika," *Novyi Zhurnal,* New York, Vol. XX (1948).

———— "Delo Kornilova," *Novoye Russkoye Slovo,* New York (March 15 and 16, 1949). An answer to A. F. Kerensky.

———— "Na Staruiu Temu," *Novoye Russkoye Slovo,* New York (September 23, 1956). An answer to A. F. Kerensky.

Dni, edited by A. F. Kerensky, Berlin. A Russian daily.

Dolgorukov, Prince Pavel D., *Velikaia Razrukha,* Madrid, privately printed, 1964.

Donskaia Letopis', No. 3, Belgrade, izd. Donskoi Istoricheskoi Komissii, 1924. A collection of materials concerning the recent history of the Don Cossacks.

Dreier, V. von, *Krestnyi Put' vo Imia Rodiny,* Berlin, privately printed, 1921.

Drozdovsky, General M. G., *Dnevnik,* Berlin, Otto Kirchner & Co., 1923.

Drutskoi-Sokolinski, Prince V. A., "K Istorii Voiny 1914–18 Gg.," *Rodnye Perezvony,* No. 158, Brussels, Belgium, n.d. This is a mimeographed periodical.

Dudin, L. V., "Velikii Mirazh," *Materialy k Istorii Osvoboditel'nogo Dvizhenia Narodov Rossii (1941–1945)*, London, Ontario, izd. Soiuza Bor'by za Osvobozhdenie Narodov Rossii, 1970.

Fisher, George, *Soviet Opposition to Stalin*, Cambridge, Mass., Harvard University Press, 1952.

Florinsky, Michael T., *Russia, A History and an Interpretation*, Vol. II, New York, Macmillan, 1966.

Footman, David, "Nestor Makhnó and the Russian Civil War," *History Today*, London (December, 1956), pp. 811–820.

——— *Civil War in Russia*, New York, Frederick A. Praeger, 1962.

General Kutepov, Paris, izd. Komiteta Imeni Generala Kutepova, 1934. A collection of articles in memory of General Kutepov.

Gerasimenko, K. V., "Makhnó," *Istorik i Sovremennik*, Berlin, Vol. III (1922).

Gilliard, Pierre, *Le Tragique Destin de Nicolas II et de Sa Famille*, Paris, Payot & Cie., 1921.

Gins, G. K., *Sibir', Soiuzniki i Kolchak*, 2 vols., Peking, tipografia Russkoi Dukhovnoi Missii, 1921.

——— "O Vozmozhnostiakh i o Krakhe Belogo Dvizhenia," *Novoye Russkoye Slovo*, New York (May 3, 1969).

Golos Minuvshago na Chuzhoi Storone, edited by S. P. Melgunov, Paris (1925–1928).

Golovin, General N. N., *Iz Istorii Kampanii 1914 Goda na Russkom Fronte*, Prague, izd. Plamia, 1926.

——— *Rossiiskaia Kontr-Revolutsia v 1917–1918*, 5 vols. containing 12 books, Paris, 1937. Issued as a supplement to the magazine *Illustrirovannaia Rossia*.

——— *Voiennyie Usilia Rossii v Mirovoi Voine*, 2 vols., Paris, Les Éditeurs Réunis, 1939.

Golubintsev, General, *Russkaia Vandeia*, Munich, privately printed, 1959. Sketches of the civil war on the Don, 1917–1920.

Goulevitch, A. de, *Tsarisme et Révolution*, Paris, Librairie de la Revue Française, 1931.

Gourko, General Basil, *War and Revolution in Russia 1914–1917*, New York, Macmillan, 1919.

Guchkov, A. I., "Iz Vospominanii Guchkova," *Poslednie Novosti*, Paris (August–September, 1936).

Guering, Aleksei, *Materialy k Bibliografii Russkoi Voennoi Pechati za Rubezhom*, Paris, Passé Militaire, 1968.

Gul', Roman, "Kto Ubil Generala Romanovskogo?" *Poslednie Novosti*, Paris (February 9, 1936).

Gurovich, Boris, "A. F. Kerensky o Dele Kornilova," *Novoye Russkoye Slovo*, New York (September 2, 1956).

Hodgson, John Ernest, *With Denikin's Armies*, London, L. Williams Co., 1932.

Illiin, I., "Gosudarstvennyi Smysl Beloi Armii," *Russkaia Mysl'*, Prague (1922).

Illustrirovannaia Rossia, Paris. A weekly.

Ioganson, Vladimir, *Delo Generala Lampe*, Buenos Aires, privately printed, 1961.

Istorik i Sovremennik, Berlin. A periodical, appearing at irregular intervals.

Kadesnikov, N. Z., *Kratkii Ocherk Bor'by pod Andreevskim Flagom v 1917–1922 Gg.*, New York, privately printed by the author, 1965.

Kakhovskaia, I. K., "Delo Eichgorna i Denikina," *Puti Revolutsii,* Berlin, Skify, 1923. Memoirs.

Kaliugin, K. P., "Donskoi Ataman P. N. Krasnov i Ego Vremia," *Donskaia Letopis',* No. 3, Belgrade, izd. Donskoi Istoricheskoi Komissii, 1924.

Kamilin, J., *General Sergei Leonidovich Markov (Geroi i Vozhdi Rossii),* Rostov-on-Don, Narodnaia Biblioteka, 1919.

Karpovich, M. M., "General Denikin," *Novyi Zhurnal,* New York, Vol. XVII (1947).

Kartashev, A., "Ot Russkogo k Obshchechelovecheskomu (Pamiati A. I. Denikina)," *Za Rossiu,* Édition Russe, Paris, Les Indépendants, 1948.

Katkov, George, *Russia 1917, The February Revolution,* New York, Harper & Row, 1967.

Kenez, Peter, *Civil War in South Russia, 1918,* Berkeley, University of California Press, 1971.

Kennan, George F., *Russia Leaves the War,* Princeton, N. J., Princeton University Press, 1956.

———— *The Decision to Intervene,* Princeton, N. J., Princeton University Press, 1958.

———— *Russia and the West under Lenin and Stalin,* Boston, Little, Brown and Co., 1960.

———— *American Diplomacy 1900–1950,* New York, New American Library (Mentor), 1964.

———— *On Dealing with the Communist World,* New York, Harper & Row, 1964.

Kerensky, A. F., *Delo Kornilova,* Moscow, Zadruga, 1918.

———— *Prelude to Bolshevism (The Kornilov Rebellion),* London, T. F. Unwin Ltd., 1919.

———— *Izdaleka,* Paris, J. Povolozky & Cie., 1922. A collection of articles, 1920–1921.

———— *The Catastrophe,* New York, D. Appleton & Co., 1927.

———— *The Crucifixion of Liberty,* New York, John Day, 1934.

———— "Delo Kornilova," *Novoye Russkoye Slovo,* New York (February 16, 1949).

———— "Sryv Fevralia," *Novoye Russkoye Slovo,* New York (February 17, February 18, and March 6, 1949).

———— "Delo Kornilova," *Novoye Russkoye Slovo,* New York (August 12, 1956).

———— "Delo Kornilova," *Novoye Russkoye Slovo,* New York (October 21, 1956).

———— *Russia and History's Turning Point,* New York, Duell, Sloan & Pearce, 1965.

Kiriushin, B. T., *Puti Russkoi Revolutsionnosti,* Frankfurt, Posev, 1959.

Kniga o Russkom Evreistve, New York, Soyuz Russkikh Evreev, 1960. A collection of articles, about the period from 1860 to the revolution of 1917.

Kniga o Russkom Evreistve, New York, Soyuz Russkikh Evreev, 1968. About the period 1917–1967.

Knox, Major General Sir Alfred, *With the Russian Army, 1914–1917,* 2 vols., London, Hutchinson & Co., 1921.

Kondzerovsky, General P. K., *V Stavke Verkhovnogo 1914–1917*, Paris, privately printed, 1967.

Kornilovskii Udarnyi Polk, compiled by M. A. Kritsky, Paris, privately printed, 1936. A collection of articles.

London *Times*.

Ludendorff, General Erich, *Moi Vospominaniia o Voine 1914–1918*, translated from German into Russian: Vol. I, translated by O. G. Mirovich, Krsko, Slovenia, Yugoslavia, Milan Autman & Co., 1921; Vol. II, edited by A. Svechin, Moscow, Gosizdat, 1924.

Lukomsky, General A. S., *Vospominaniia*, 2 vols., Berlin, Otto Kirchner & Co., 1922.

Makhnó, Nestor, *Makhnovshchina i Ieyo Vcherashnie Soiuzniki—Bolsheviki*, Paris, izd. Biblioteki Makhnovtsev, 1928. An answer to M. Kubanin's book about the Makhnó movement.

———— *Pod Udarami Kontr-Revolutsii*, edited by V. M. Eichenbaum (pseudonym Volin), Paris, izd. Komiteta Nestora Makhnó, 1936. About the period April–June, 1918.

———— *Ukrainskaia Revolutsia*, edited by V. M. Eichenbaum (pseudonym Volin), Paris, izd. Komiteta Nestora Makhnó, 1937. About the period July–December, 1918.

Makhrov, General P. S., "Novorossiiskaia Tragedia," *Russkie Novosti*, Paris, No. 116 (1947).

Maklakov, V. A., *Vtoraia Gosudarstvennaia Duma*, Paris, La Renaissance, 1946.

Markovtsy v Boiakh i Pokhodakh za Rossiu, Vol. I, *1917–1918*, Vol. II, *1919–1920*, compiled by V. E. Pavlov, Paris, printed by Imprimerie Beresniak, 1962–1964.

Marty, André, *The Epic of the Black Sea Revolt*, New York, Workers Library Publishers, 1941.

Melgunov, S. P., *Krasnyi Terror v Rossii, 1918–1923*, Berlin, privately printed, 1924.

———— "Ocherki Generala Denikina," *Na Chuzhoi Storone*, Berlin-Prague, Vol. V (1924), pp. 300–308. A review of the third volume of Denikin's *Ocherki*.

———— "P. N. Milyukov o Grazhdanskoi Voine i Emigratsii," *Golos Minuvshago na Chuzhoi Storone*, Paris, No. 4/XVII (1926), pp. 277–283.

———— "Antisemitism i Pogromy," *Golos Minuvshago na Chuzhoi Storone*, Paris, No. 5/XVIII (1927), pp. 231–246.

———— *Grazhdanskaia Voina v Osveshchenii P. N. Milyukova*, Paris, privately printed, 1929.

———— *Nikolai Vasilievich Chaikovsky v Gody Grazhdanskoi Voiny*, Paris, privately printed, 1929.

————*Tragedia Admirala Kolchaka*, 4 vols., Belgrade, Russkaia Tipografia, 1930–1931.

———— *Na Putiakh k Dvortsovomu Perevorotu*, Paris, Rodnik, 1931.

———— "Rossiiskaia Kontr-Revolutsia," *Znamia Rossii*, Prague, Nos. 2–3 (February and March, 1938). A review of Golovin's book.

———— *Rossiiskaia Kontr-Revolutsia*, Paris, privately printed, 1938. A pamphlet, on the methods and conclusions of General Golovin.

———— *Zolotoi Nemetskii Kliuch Bolshevikov*, Paris, privately printed, 1940.

———— "Emigratsia i Sovetskaia Vlast'," *Novyi Zhurnal,* New York, Vol XI (1945).

———— "Grubyi Pamflet," *Vozrozhdenie,* Paris, Vol. VII (January–February, 1950).

———— *Sud'ba Imperatora Nikolaia II Posle Otrechenia,* Paris, La Renaissance, 1951.

———— "Grazhdanskii Podvig A. I. Denikina," *Vozrozhdenie,* Paris, Vol. XXV (January–February, 1953).

———— *Kak Bolsheviki Zakhvatili Vlast',* Paris, La Renaissance, 1953.

———— "Zagadki v Dele Generala Kutepova," *Novoye Russkoye Slovo,* New York (October 3–October 11, 1955). A series of articles.

———— *Legenda o Separatnom Mire,* Paris, privately printed, 1957.

———— *Martovskie Dni 1917 Goda,* Paris, Les Éditeurs Réunis, 1961.

Mel'nikov, N. M., "Novorossiiskaia Katastrofa," *Rodimyi Krai,* Paris (July–August, 1961).

———— *A. M. Kaledin–Geroi Lutskogo Proryva i Donskoi Ataman,* Madrid, Rodimyi Krai, 1968.

Military Strategy. Soviet Doctrine and Concepts, edited by Marshal V. D. Sokolovsky, with an introduction by R. L. Garthoff, New York, Frederick A. Praeger, 1963.

Milyukov, P. N., *Istoria Vtoroi Russkoi Revolutsii,* 3 vols., Sofia, Rossiisko-Bolgarskoe Knigoizd., 1921–1923.

———— *Rossia na Perelome,* 2 vols., Paris, privately printed, 1927.

———— "O Stat'e N. P. Vakara," *Poslednie Novosti,* Paris (March 6, 1937).

———— *Vospominaniia,* 2 vols., New York, Chekhov Publishing House, 1955.

———— "Dnevnik," *Novyi Zhurnal,* New York, Vols. LXVI and LXVII (December, 1961, and March, 1962).

Mushin, A., *Dmitrii Bogrov i Ubiistvo Stolypina,* Paris, privately printed, 1914.

1917–1957. Nachalo Beloi Bor'by i Ieyo Osnovopolozhnik, Buenos, Aires, izd. Argentinskogo Otdela Russkogo Obshche-Voinskogo Soyuza, 1957. A collection of articles.

Na Chuzhoi Storone, Berlin-Prague. A periodical, appearing at irregular intervals.

The New Russia, London, 1920. A weekly review of Russian politics, edited by the Russian Liberation Committee. Contributors included P. N. Milyukov, V. D. Nabokov, B. V. Savinkov, and so on.

The New York Times.

Noulens, Joseph, *Mon Ambassade en Russie Soviétique 1917–1919,* 2 vols., Paris, Librairie Plon, 1933.

Novoye Russkoye Slovo, New York. A daily.

Novyi Zhurnal, New York. A quarterly.

Oberuchev, K. M., *Ofitsery v Russkoi Revolutsii,* New York, privately printed, 1918.

Obolensky, Prince V., "Krym Pri Vrangele," *Na Chuzhoi Storone,* Berlin-Prague, Vol. IX (1925), pp. 5–55.

Ocherk Vzaimootnoshenii Vooruzhonnykh Sil Iuga Rossii i Predstavitelei Frantsuzskogo Komandovania, Ekaterinodar, izd. Upravlenie Generala Kvartirmeistera Shtaba Glavnokomanduiushchego Vooruzhennymi Silami Iuga Rossii, May, 1919.

Pamiati Ivana Sergeevicha Shmeleva, edited by V. A. Maevsky, Munich, privately printed, 1956. Collected reminiscences in memory of I. S. Shmelev.

Pares, Sir Bernard, *The Fall of the Russian Monarchy,* New York, Alfred A. Knopf, 1939.

Pasmanik, D. S., *Russkaia Revolutsia i Evreistvo,* Paris, Franko-Russkaia Pechat', 1923.

Pereklichka, Voenno-Politicheskii Zhurnal, New York. A monthly.

Pipes, Richard, *The Formation of the Soviet Union (1917–1923),* Cambridge, Mass., Harvard University Press, 1957.

Poslednie Novosti, edited by P. N. Milyukov, Paris. A daily.

Pridham, Vice Admiral Sir Francis, *Close of a Dynasty,* London, Allan Wingate, 1956.

Pushkarev, S. G., *Rossia v XIX Veke (1801–1914),* New York, Chekhov Publishing House, 1956.

———— "Belaia Bor'ba," *Novoye Russkoye Slovo,* New York (March 31, 1968).

Rakovsky, G. N., *V Stane Belykh,* Constantinople, privately printed, 1920.

———— *Konets Belykh,* Prague, Volia Rossii, 1921.

Rein, G. E., *Iz Perezhitogo,* 2 vols., Berlin, Paraboli, 1935.

Riasniansky, Colonel S. N., *K 50-letiiu 1-go Kubanskogo (Ledianogo) Generala Kornilova Pokhoda,* New York, privately printed, 1967.

Robinson, G. T., *Rural Russia under the Old Regime,* New York, Longmans, Green and Co., 1932.

Rodimyi Krai. A periodical published first in Paris, later in Madrid, by the Don Cossack Association (Donskoe Voiskovoe Ob'edinenie).

Russian Agriculture During the War, Economic and Social History of the World War, Russian Series, New Haven, Yale University Press, 1930.

The Russian Review. A quarterly, published first in Hanover, N. H., later in Stanford, California, where it was sponsored by the Hoover Institution on War, Revolution, and Peace.

Russkie Novosti, Paris. A periodical.

Russkoe Slovo, Moscow, 1917. The largest daily in pre-Communist Russia.

Sakharov, General K. V., *Belaia Sibir',* Munich, privately printed, 1923.

Savinkov, Boris V. (pseudonym V. Ropshin), *Kon' Blednyi,* Nice, M. A. Tumanova, 1913.

———— *K Delu Kornilova,* Paris, Union, 1919.

———— "Avtobiografia," *Almanakh Vozdushnye Puti,* Vol. V, New York, R. N. Grynberg, 1967.

Sedykh, Andrei, "A. I. Denikin Obiasniaet Prichiny Svoego Priezda v New York," *Novoye Russkoye Slovo,* New York (December 9, 1945).

Serapinin, A., "Brusilovskoie Nastuplenie," *Novoye Russkoye Slovo,* New York (June 13 and 14, 1966).

Sergeevsky, Colonel B. N., "Zheleznye Strelki," *Novoye Russkoye Slovo,* New York (February 3, 1952).

———— "General Denikin," *Pereklichka,* New York, No. 58 (August, 1956).

———— "Moe Pervoe Znakomstvo s Generalom Denikinym," *Voennaia Byl',* Paris, No. 62 (September, 1963).

———— *Otrechenie 1917,* New York, Voennyi Vestnik, 1969.

Shavelsky, George, *Vospominaniia,* 2 vols., New York, Chekhov Publishing House, 1954.

Shchepkin, G., *General-Leitenant Anton Ivanovich Denikin,* Novocherkassk, izd. A. Vasilieva, 1919.

Shekhtman, I. B., *Pogromy Dobrovol'cheskoi Armii na Ukraine,* Berlin, Ost-jüdisches Historisches Archiv, 1932.

Shkuró, General A. G., *Zapiski Belogo Partizana,* Buenos Aires, Seiatel', 1961.

Shmelev, Ivan, "Oblik Generala Denikina," *Russkaia Mysl',* Paris (August 16, 1947).

Sidorin, General V., "Zagovor Kornilova," *Poslednie Novosti,* Paris (February 26, 1937).

Skrylov, A. I., "Legendarnyi Kazak," *Rodimyi Krai,* Paris (July–August, 1962). About the escape of General Kornilov from the prison camp.

Slashchev-Krymskii, General J. A., *Trebuiu Suda Obshchestva i Glasnosti,* Constantinople, M. Shulman, 1921.

Smolensky, M., *Trotsky,* Berlin, Russkoe Universal'noe izd., 1921.

Sokolov, K. N., *Pravlenie Generala Denikina,* Sofia, Rossiisko-Bolgarskoe Knigoizd., 1921.

Spiridovich, General A. I., *Velikaia Voina i Fevral'skaia Revolutsia 1914–1917 Gg.,* 3 vols., New York, Vseslavianskoe Izd., 1960–1962.

Stankevich, V. B., *Vospominaniia 1914–1919 Gg.,* Berlin, Ladyschnikov, 1920.

———— *Sud'ba Narodov Rossii,* Berlin, Ladyschnikov, 1921.

Steenberg, Sven, *Vlasov,* translated from the German, New York, Alfred A. Knopf, 1970.

Stepanov, N. F. (pseudonym N. Svitkov), *Masonstvo v Russkoi Emigratsii,* São Paulo, Brazil, privately printed, 1964. A listing as of January 1, 1932.

———— *Vnutrenniaia Liniia,* São Paulo, Brazil, privately printed, 1964.

Stepun, Fedor A., *Byvsheie i Nesbyvsheesia,* 2 vols., New York, Chekhov Publishing House, 1956.

Stewart, George, *The White Armies of Russia,* New York, Macmillan, 1933.

Sukhanov, N. N., *The Russian Revolution,* abridged edition in 2 vols., New York, Harper Torchbooks, Harper & Brothers, 1962.

Svechin, General M., *Zapiski Starogo Generala o Bylom,* Nice, privately printed, 1964.

Tarsaidze, Alexandre, *Four Myths,* New York, privately printed, 1969.

Tokés, Rudolf L., *Béla Kun and the Hungarian Soviet Republic,* New York, Frederick A. Praeger, 1967.

Tokmakoff, George, "Stolypin's Agrarian Reform: An Appraisal," *The Russian Review,* Stanford, Vol. XXX (April, 1971).

Trotsky, Leon, *Perspektivy Russkoi Revolutsii,* Berlin, Ladyschnikov, 1917. The conclusion to his history of the 1905–1906 revolution.

———— *The History of the Russian Revolution,* 3 vols. in one, New York, Simon and Schuster, 1936.

———— *Stalin,* edited and translated by Charles Malamuth, New York, Harper & Brothers, 1946.

———— *Histoire de la Révolution Russe,* Paris, Éditions du Seuil, 1950.

———— *Trotsky's Diary in Exile,* Cambridge, Mass., Harvard University Press, 1958.

———— *Lenin,* New York, Capricorn Books, 1962.

———— *The Basic Writings of Trotsky,* edited by Irving Howe, New York, Random House, 1963.

Tschebotarioff, Gregory P., "The Cossacks and the Revolution of 1917," *The Russian Review,* Hanover, N. H., Vol. XX (July, 1961).

Tsvetaeva, Marina, *Lebedinyi Stan,* Munich, privately printed, 1957. Poetry, 1917–1921.

Turkul, General A. V., *Drozdovtsy v Ogne,* Munich, Iav' i Byl', 1948.

Tyrkova-Williams, A., *Na Putiakh k Svobode,* New York, Chekhov Publishing House, 1952.

———— *To Chego Bol'she Ne Budet,* Paris, Vozrozhdenie, 1954.

Ukraintsev, Colonel N., "Delo Kornilova," *Novoye Russkoye Slovo,* New York (October 28, 1956). Comments by a former member of the Extraordinary Commission of Inquiry into the Kornilov Affair.

———— "K Delu Kornilova," *Pereklichka,* New York, No. 64 (February, 1957).

Ulam, Adam B., *The Bolsheviks,* New York, Macmillan, 1965.

———— *Expansion and Coexistence, The History of Soviet Foreign Policy, 1917–1967,* New York, Frederick A. Praeger, 1968.

Ulianov, N. P., *Proiskhozhdenie Ukrainskogo Separatisma,* Madrid, privately printed, 1966.

Vakar, N. P., "Zagovor Kornilova (po Vospominaniiam A. I. Putilova)," *Poslednie Novosti,* Paris (January 20 and 24, 1937).

———— "General L. G. Kornilov i A. F. Kerensky (Beseda s P. N. Finisovym)," *Poslednie Novosti,* Paris (February 27 and March 6, 1937).

Val', E. G. von, *Kavaleriiskie Obkhody Generala Kaledina 1914–1915 Gg.,* Tallin, privately printed by the author, 1933.

Valentinoff, N., *Vstrechi s Leninym,* New York, Chekhov Publishing House, 1953.

Varshavsky, Vladimir, *Nezamechennoe Pokolenie,* New York, Chekhov Publishing House, 1956.

Vasilevsky, I. (pseudonym ne bukva), *Denikin i Ego Memuary,* Berlin, Nakanune, 1924.

Vendziagol'sky, K., "Savinkov," *Novyi Zhurnal,* New York, Vols. LXVIII and LXX (1962).

Vernadsky, George, *Lenin, Red Dictator,* New Haven, Yale University Press, 1931.

Vestnik Pervopokhodnika, Los Angeles, Nos. 79–81 (1968). A bimonthly publication of the Society of General Kornilov's Veterans of the First Kuban Campaign.

Vinaver, M., *Nashe Pravitel'stvo,* Paris, privately printed, 1928.

Vishniak, Mark, "Na Rodine," *Annales Contemporaines,* Paris, Vol. II (1920), pp. 268–297.

———— *Years of Emigration 1919–1969,* Stanford, Hoover Institution Press, 1970.

Voennaia Byl', Paris. A periodical.

Voitsekhovsky, S., "Sovetskie Sverkh-Asefy. Iz Istorii Tresta," *Vozrozhdenie,* Paris, Vol. VIII (March–April, 1950).

Vozrozhdenie, edited by S. P. Melgunov, Paris. A literary and political bimonthly first appearing in the mid-1940's; it is not to be confused with the daily of the same name which was published in the years before World War II.

V Pamiat' 1-go Kubanskogo Pokhoda, edited by B. I. Kazanovich, I. K. Kirienko, and K. N. Nikolaev, Belgrade, privately printed, 1926. A collection.

Vraga, R., "Trest," *Vozrozhdenie,* Paris, Vol. VII (January–February, 1950).

The War and the Russian Government, Economic and Social History of the World War, Russian Series, New Haven, Yale University Press, 1929.

Wilson, Edmund, *To the Finland Station,* New York, Doubleday & Co., 1953.

Wolfe, Bertram D., *Three Who Made a Revolution,* Boston, Beacon Press, 1955.

Wrangel, General Peter N., "Zapiski," *Beloie Delo,* Vols. V and VI, Berlin, Mednyi Vsadnik, 1928.

XXX (pseudonym), "Legendy i Deistvitel'nost'. Materialy o Treste," *Vozrozhdenie,* Paris, Vol. XV (May–June, 1951).

Xydias, Jean, *L'Intervention Française en Russie 1918–1919,* Paris, Les Éditions de France, 1927.

Zaitsov, Colonel A., *1918 God. Ocherki po Istorii Russkoi Grazhdanskoi Voiny,* Paris, privately printed, 1934.

Za Svobodu, edited by B. Savinkov and subsequently by D. Filosofov, Warsaw. A Russian daily.

Zeman, Z. A. B., *Germany and the Revolution in Russia 1915–1918: Documents from the Archives of the German Foreign Ministry,* London, Oxford University Press, 1958.

Zenzinov, V. M., *Perezhitoe,* New York, Chekhov Publishing House, 1953.

SOVIET SOURCES

Documents

Direktivy Glavnogo Komandovania Krasnoi Armii (*1917–1920 Gg.*), *Sbornik Dokumentov,* Moscow, Voennoe izd. Ministerstva Oborony SSSR, 1969.

Grazhdanskaia Voina na Ukraine, Sbornik Dokumentov i Materialov, 3 vols. (4 books), Kiev, Naukova Dumka, 1967.

Iz Istorii Grazhdanskoi Voiny v SSSR, 3 vols., Institut Marksizma-Leninizma pri Tsentral'nom Kom. KPSS, Moscow, izd. Sovetskaia Rossia, 1961.

Listovki Petrogradskikh Bolshevikov 1917–1920, Vol. III, Leningrad, Lenizdat., 1957.

Partizanskoe Dvizhenie v Zapadnoi Sibiri (*1918–1920*), *Dokumenty i Materialy,* Novosibirsk, Novosibirskoe Knizhnoe izd., 1959.

Revolutsionnoie Dvizhenie v Rossii v Avguste 1917 Goda—Razgrom Kornilovskogo Miatezha, Moscow, izd. Akademii Nauk SSSR, 1959.

Sovetskaia Strana v Period Grazhdanskoi Voiny 1918–1920, Moscow, izd. Vsesoiuznoi Knizhnoi Palaty, 1961. A bibliographical index of published collections of documents.

Vengerskie Internatsionalisty v Oktiabr'skoi Revolutsii i Grazhdanskoi Voine v SSSR, Sbornik Dokumentov, 2 vols., Moscow, Gosizdat. Politicheskoi Literatury, 1968.

Other Published Sources

Agureev, K. V., *Razgrom Belogvardeiskikh Voisk Denikina*, Moscow, Voennoe izd. Ministerstva Oborony SSSR, 1961.

Alakhverdov, G. G.; Kuzmin, N. F.; Rybakov, M. B.; Spirin, L. M.; Shatagin, N. I., *Kratkaia Istoriia Grazhdanskoi Voiny v SSSR*, Moscow, Gosizdat. Politicheskoi Literatury, 1960.

Aleksashenko, A. P., *Krakh Denikinshchiny*, Moscow, izd. Moskovskogo Universiteta, 1966.

Antonov-Ovseenko, V., *Zapiski o Grazhdanskoi Voine*, 4 vols., Moscow, Gosvoenizdat., 1933.

Boevye Gody, Novosibirsk, Novosibirskoe Knizhnoe izd., 1959. A collection of accounts pertaining to the civil-war period in Siberia.

Bogdanov, A. V., *Moriaki-Baltiitsy v 1917 Godu*, Moscow, Voennoe izd. Ministerstva Oborony SSSR, 1955.

Boldyrev, General V. G., *Direktoria, Kolchak, Interventy*, Novonikolaevsk, Sibirski izd., 1925.

Brusilov, General A. A., *Moi Vospominaniia*, Moscow, Voennoe izd. Ministerstva Oborony SSSR, 1963.

Budenny, Marshal S. M., *Proidennyi Put'*, Moscow, Voennoe izd. Ministerstva Oborony SSSR, 1958.

Dubrovsky, S. M., *Stolypinskaia Zemel'naia Reforma*, Moscow, izd. Akademii Nauk SSSR, 1963.

Dushen'kin, V., *Ot Soldata do Marshala (o V. K. Bluchere)*, Moscow, Gosizdat. Politicheskoi Literatury, 1960.

———— *Vtoraia Konnaia*, Moscow, Voennoe izd. Ministerstva Oborony SSSR, 1968.

Dykov, I. G., *Razgrom Kontr-Revolutsionnogo Miatezha Kerenskogo-Krasnova v 1917 Godu*, Moscow, Znanie, 1960.

Egorov, A. I., *Razgrom Denikina*, Moscow, Gosvoenizdat., 1931. The author was subsequently a marshal of the Soviet Union.

Etapy Bol'shogo Puti, Moscow, Voennoe izd. Ministerstva Oborony SSSR, 1963. A compilation of recollections of the civil war.

Galkin, V. A., *Razgrom Kornilovshchiny*, Moscow, Gosudarstv. Uchebno-Pedagogicheskoe izd. Ministerstva Prosveshcheniia RSFSR, 1959.

Gil', S. K., *Shest' Let s V. I. Leninym*, Moscow, izd. Molodaia Gvardiia, 1957. Recollections of Lenin's personal chauffeur.

Gusev, S. I., *Grazhdanskaia Voina i Krasnaia Armiia*, Moscow, Voennoe izd. Ministerstva Oborony SSSR, 1958.

Iakir, I. E., *Vospominaniia o Grazhdanskoi Voine*, Moscow, Voennoe izd. Ministerstva Oborony SSSR, 1957.

Internatsionalisty v Boiakh za Vlast' Sovetov, Moscow, izd. Mysl', 1965. A collection.

Istoriia Grazhdanskoi Voiny SSSR, Moscow, Gosizdat. Politicheskoi Literatury: Vol. III (November, 1917–March, 1919), 1957; Vol. IV (March, 1919–February, 1920), 1959; Vol. V (February, 1920–October, 1922), 1960.

Istoriia Kommunisticheskoi Partii Sovetskogo Soiuza, Moscow, Gospolitizdat., 1959. A collective work.

Istoriia SSSR. Epokha Sotsializma (1917–1957), Moscow, Gosizdat. Politicheskoi Literatury, 1957. A collective work.

Istoriia Voin i Voennogo Iskusstva, Moscow, Voennoe izd. Ministerstva Oborony SSSR, 1970.

Ivanov, N. G., *Kornilovshchina i Ieyo Razgrom,* Leningrad, izd. Leningradskogo Universiteta, 1965.

Iz Istorii Bor'by Sovetskogo Naroda Protiv Inostrannoi Voennoi Interventsii i Vnutrennei Kontr-Revolutsii v 1918 Godu, Moscow, Gosizdat. Politicheskoi Literatury, 1956.

Kakurin, N. E., *Kak Srazhalas' Revolutsia,* 2 vols., Moscow, Gosizdat., 1925.

Kamenev, S. S., *Zapiski o Grazhdanskoi Voine i Voennom Stroitel'stve,* Moscow, Voennoe izd. Ministerstva Oborony SSSR, 1963. Selected articles.

Kapustin, M. I., *Soldaty Severnogo Fronta v Bor'be za Vlast' Sovetov,* Moscow, Gospolitizdat., 1957. Events of 1917.

———— *Zagovor Generalov (iz Istorii Kornilovshchiny i Ieyo Razgroma),* Moscow, izd. Mysl', 1968.

Klevanskii, A., "Voennoplennye Tsentral'nykh Derzhav v Tsarskoi i Revolutsionnoi Rossii (1914–1918 Gg.)," in *Internationalisty v Boiakh za Vlast' Sovetov,* Moscow, izd. Mysl', 1965.

Korotkov, I. S., *Razgrom Vrangelia,* Moscow, Voennoe izd. Ministerstva Oborony SSSR, 1955.

Kovtiukh, E., *Ot Kubani do Volgi i Obratno,* Moscow, Gosvoenizdat., 1926.

Krasnyi Arkhiv, Moscow. A periodical devoted to history, published in the 1920's by Gosudarstvennoie Izdatel'stvo (Gosizdat.).

Kuts, I. F., "V Ukrainskikh Stepiakh," in *Gody v Sedle (Voennye Memuary),* Moscow, Voennoe izd. Ministerstva Oborony SSSR, 1964.

Kuzmin, G. V., *Grazhdanskaia Voina i Voennaia Interventsia v SSSR,* Moscow, Voennoe izd. Ministerstva Oborony SSSR, 1958.

Lemke, Mikhail, *250 Dnei v Tsarskoi Stavke,* Peterburg, Gosizdat., 1920. About the period September 25, 1915–July 2, 1916.

Lenin, V. I., *Lenin o Propagande i Agitatsii,* Moscow, Gosizdat. Politicheskoi Literatury, 1956. A collection.

———— *Lenin o Vneshnei Politike Sovetskogo Gosudarstva,* Moscow, Gosizdat., 1960.

Makeev, P. V., *Na Denikina!,* Riga, Latviiskoe Gosudarstvennoe izd., 1960. On the role of Lettish sharpshooters in the defeat of Denikin.

Martynov, E. I., *Kornilov: Popytka Voennogo Perevorota,* Moscow, Gosvoenizdat., 1927.

Milshtein, M. A., and Slobodenko, A. K., *O Burzhuaznoi Voennoi Nauke,* Moscow, Voennoe izd. Ministerstva Oborony SSSR, 1961.

Naida, S. F., and Naumov, V. P., *Sovetskaia Istoriografiia Grazhdanskoi Voiny i Inostrannoi Voennoi Interventsii v SSSR,* Moscow, izd. Moskovskogo Universiteta, 1966.

Nikulin, Lev, *Mertvaia Zyb',* Moscow, Voennoe izd. Ministerstva Oborony SSSR, 1965.

Oktiabr' i Grazhdanskaia Voina v SSSR, Moscow, izd. Nauka, 1966. A collection of articles.

Partiia Bolshevikov v Gody Pervoi Mirovoi Voiny. Sverzhenie Monarkhii v Rossii, Moscow, Gosizdat. Politicheskoi Literatury, 1963.

Plekhanov, G. V., *Nashi Raznoglasia,* Moscow, Gosizdat. Politicheskoi Literatury, 1956.

Pokhod na Moskvu, edited by P. E. Schogolev, with foreword by L. Kitaev, Moscow, izd. Federatsia, 1928. Excerpts from Vols. IV and V of *Ocherki Russkoi Smuty.*

Polivanov, General A. A., *Iz Dnevnikov i Vospominanii po Dolzhnosti Voennogo Ministra i Ego Pomoshchnika 1907–1916 Gg.,* Moscow, Vysshii Voennyi Revolutsionnyi Sovet, 1924.

Polkovodtsy Grazhdanskoi Voiny, Moscow, izd. Molodaia Gvardia, 1960. A series of biographies.

Prochko, I. S., *Artilleriia v Boiakh za Rodinu,* Moscow, Voennoe izd. Ministerstva Oborony SSSR, 1957.

Rachkov, V. P., *Pervaia Konnaia,* Moscow, Gosizdat. Politicheskoi Literatury, 1958.

Rostunov, I. I., *General Brusilov,* Moscow, Voennoe izd. Ministerstva Oborony SSSR, 1964.

Rybakov, M. V., *Iz Istorii Grazhdanskoi Voiny na Severo-Zapade v 1919 Godu,* Moscow, Gospolitizdat., 1958.

Savost'ianov, V., and Egorov, P., *Komandarm Pervogo Ranga (I. P. Uborevich),* Moscow, Gosizdat. Politicheskoi Literatury, 1966.

Spirin, L. M., *Razgrom Armii Kolchaka,* Moscow, Gosizdat. Politicheskoi Literatury, 1957.

Suprunenko, N. I., *Ocherki Istorii Grazhdanskoi Voiny i Inostrannoi Voennoi Interventsii na Ukraine,* Moscow, izd. Nauka, 1966.

Trotsky, Leon, *Kak Vooruzhalas' Revolutsia,* 5 vols., Moscow, Vysshii Voennyi Redaktsionnyi Sovet, 1923–1925.

Tukhachevsky, M. N., *Izbrannye Proizvedeniia,* 2 vols., Moscow, Voennoe izd. Ministerstva Oborony SSSR, 1964. The author was subsequently a marshal of the Soviet Union.

Umnov, A. S., *Grazhdanskaia Voina i Srednee Krestianstvo,* Moscow, Voennoe izd. Ministerstva Oborony SSSR, 1959.

Verkhovsky, A. I., *Na Trudnom Perevale,* Moscow, Voennoe izd. Ministerstva Oborony SSSR, 1959.

Vladimirova, Vera, *Kontr-Revolutsia v 1917 Godu (Kornilovshchina),* Moscow, Krasnaia Nov', 1924.

INDEX

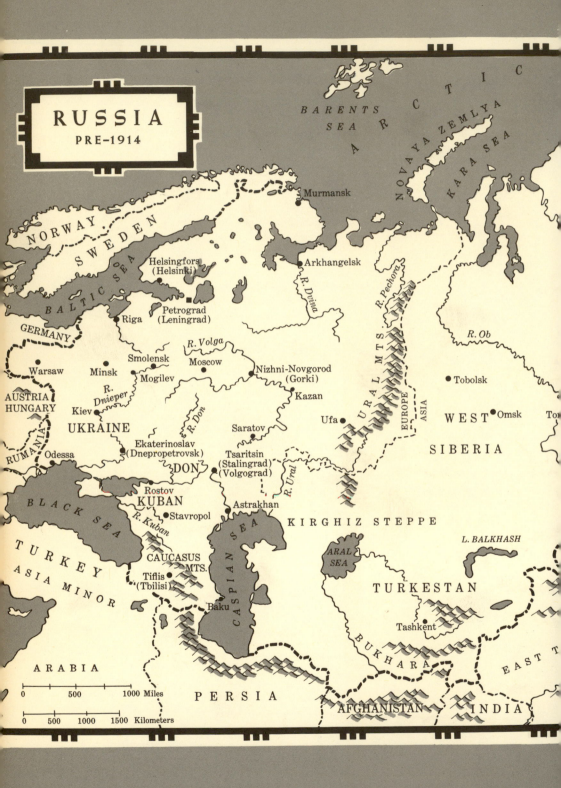

RUSSIA
PRE-1914

BARENTS SEA

ARCTIC

NOVAYA ZEMLYA

KARA SEA

Murmansk

NORWAY

SWEDEN

BALTIC SEA

Helsingfors
(Helsinki)

Arkhangelsk

R. Dvina

R. Pechora

R. Ob

GERMANY

Riga

Petrograd
(Leningrad)

URAL MTS.

Tobolsk

Warsaw

Minsk

Smolensk

R. Volga

Moscow

Nizhni-Novgorod
(Gorki)

Mogilev

AUSTRIA
HUNGARY

Kiev

R. Dnieper

UKRAINE

R. Don

Kazan

Ufa

EUROPE

ASIA

WEST

Omsk

To

SIBERIA

Saratov

RUMANIA

Odessa

Ekaterinoslav
(Dnepropetrovsk)

DON

Tsaritsin
(Stalingrad)
(Volgograd)

R. Ural

Rostov

KUBAN

BLACK SEA

R. Kuban

Stavropol

Astrakhan

KIRGHIZ STEPPE

ARAL
SEA

L. BALKHASH

CASPIAN SEA

TURKEY

CAUCASUS
MTS.

ASIA MINOR

Tiflis
(Tbilisi)

Baku

TURKESTAN

Tashkent

ARABIA

BUKHARA

EAST T

0   500   1000 Miles

PERSIA

AFGHANISTAN

INDIA

0   500   1000   1500   Kilometers